Healthcare Management

Third Edition

Healthcare Management

Third Edition

Edited by Kieran Walshe and Judith Smith

Open University Press

Open University Press
McGraw-Hill Education
8th Floor
338 Euston Road
London
NW1 3BT

email: enquiries@openup.co.uk
world wide web: www.openup.co.uk

and Two Penn Plaza, New York, NY 10121-2289, USA

First published 2006
Second edition published 2011
First published in this third edition 2016

A catalogue record of this book is available from the British Library

ISBN-13: 978-0-33-526352-3
ISBN-10: 0-33-526352-6
eISBN: 978-0-33-526353-0

Library of Congress Cataloging-in-Publication Data
CIP data applied for

Typeset by SPi Global
Printed and bound by Bell and Bain Ltd, Glasgow

Fictitious names of companies, products, people, characters and/or data that may be used herein (in case studies or in examples) are not intended to represent any real individual, company, product or event.

Praise for this book

"Walshe and Smith have assembled an invaluable introduction to healthcare management and health systems. With their fellow authors, they provide a comprehensive review of a range of issues related to the funding and provision of care, and how services are organised and managed.

Now in its third edition, Healthcare Management has been updated and revised to meet the needs of teachers and students alike."

Professor Chris Ham, Chief Executive, The King's Fund, UK

"This book covers the main areas of knowledge which managers need, and gives tools for thinking and empirical examples relevant to current challenges. Evidence based management might not always be possible, but this book gives a way for a manager to become research-informed and therefore more effective. This third edition of the book is even more relevant internationally and improved to help readers apply the ideas to their situation."

Professor John Øvretveit, Director of Research, LIME/MMC,
The Karolinska Institute, Sweden

"No-one learns to be a manager in a classroom or from a book, but books that take this disclaimer as their starting point are indispensable. Walshe and Smith (and their fellow authors) invite their audience (healthcare managers, healthcare policy makers and postgraduate students, taking courses in healthcare management) to critically combine experiential learning with academic learning and to acquire knowledge from both practice and theory. By doing so, they have found the third way between the advocates of evidence-based management and their criticasters."

Dr. Jan-Kees Helderman, Associate Professor in Public Administration,
Institute for Management Research, Radboud University,
Nijmegen, the Netherlands

Dedication Page

This book is dedicated to the National Health Service in the United Kingdom, and the many people who commit their working lives to providing healthcare to their fellow citizens, regardless of who they are or their ability to pay. A measure of any nation's values can be seen in how it looks after those in need – the old, the sick, the vulnerable and the disadvantaged. Whilst British society has changed radically during our adult lives, the deeply held sense of social solidarity, moral purpose, fairness and compassion on which the NHS is founded, endures, and is something of which our society can be very proud.

Contents

List of tables

List of figures

List of editors and contributors

Martin Bardsley is Senior Fellow in Research at the Nuffield Trust, and was previously the Trust's director of research. He is also a Senior Fellow at the Health Foundation.

Ruth Boaden is Professor of Service Operations Management at the Alliance Manchester Business School, University of Manchester and director, NIHR Collaboration for Leadership in Applied Health Research and Care for Greater Manchester.

Sophie Castle-Clarke is Fellow in Health Policy at the Nuffield Trust, London.

Naomi Chambers is Professor of Healthcare Management at the Alliance Manchester Business School, University of Manchester.

Angela Coulter is a senior research scientist in the Health Services Research Unit (HSRU) at Oxford University and a Visiting Fellow at the King's Fund, London.

Helen Crump is Fellow in Health Policy at the Nuffield Trust, London.

Natasha Curry is Senior Fellow in Health Policy at the Nuffield Trust, London.

Barrie Dowdeswell is director of research for the European Centre for Health Assets and Architecture.

Nigel Edwards is Chief Executive of the Nuffield Trust, London.

Joy Furnival holds a Health Foundation improvement science PhD scholarship at the Alliance Manchester Business School, University of Manchester.

Helen Gilburt is Fellow, Policy, the King's Fund, London.

Scott Greer is Associate Professor of Health Management and Policy at the University of Michigan School of Public Health.

Candace Imison is Director of Policy at the Nuffield Trust, London.

Stephanie Kumpunen is Fellow in Health Policy at the Nuffield Trust, London.

Ann Mahon is director of the MSc Healthcare Leadership, The Elizabeth Garrett Anderson Programme and Senior Lecturer in Health Management and Leadership at the Alliance Manchester Business School, University of Manchester.

Ruth McDonald is Professor of Health Science Research and Policy at the Alliance Manchester Business School, University of Manchester.

Chris Naylor is Senior Fellow, Policy, the King's Fund, London.

Suzanne Robinson is Associate Professor and Theme Leader for Health Systems and Health Economics in the School of Public Health, Faculty of Health Sciences, Curtin University, Perth, Australia.

Judith Smith is Professor of Health Policy and Management and Director of the Health Services Management Centre, University of Birmingham.

Paul Taylor is reader in health informatics at the Centre for Health Informatics and Multiprofessional Education, University College London.

Ruth Thorlby is Deputy Director of Policy at the Nuffield Trust, London.

Nicola Walsh is Assistant Director, Leadership Development at the King's Fund, London.

Kieran Walshe is professor of health policy and management and head of the health management group at Alliance Manchester Business School, University of Manchester.

Iestyn Williams is Reader at the Health Services Management Centre, University of Birmingham.

Gerald Wistow is Visiting Professor of Social Policy, Personal Social Services Research Unit, Department of Social Policy, London School of Economics and Political Science.

Steve Wright is executive director of the European Centre for Health Assets and Architecture.

Introduction: the current and future challenges of healthcare management

Judith Smith and Kieran Walshe

Introduction

The aim of this third edition of our textbook is to support the learning and development of practising managers in healthcare organizations and health systems, and those undertaking postgraduate study on programmes concerned with health policy, health management and related areas. Increasingly, these two groups overlap – more and more managers are undertaking a master's degree as part of their intellectual and career development, and we are firm believers in the power of the interaction between academic and experiential learning that this brings. No-one learns to be a manager in a classroom, or from a book. One learns management by doing, by experiencing the challenges and opportunities of leadership (Mintzberg, 2004). But the best and most successful managers are reflective practitioners – profoundly aware of their own behaviours, attitudes and actions, and their impact on others and on the organization, and able to analyse and review critically their own practice and set it in a wider context, framed by appropriate theories, models and concepts (Peck, 2004; Gray, 2007). The future leaders of our healthcare systems need to be able to integrate theory and practice, and to have the adaptability and flexibility that come from really understanding the nature of management and leadership.

This chapter sets the context for the book. We first describe the challenges of the political and social environment in which healthcare systems and organizations exist, and how that environment is changing. We then describe some of the particular challenges of those organizations – some of the characteristics and dynamics that make healthcare organizations so interesting and yet so difficult to lead. Finally, we then set out the structure of the rest of the book and explain how we anticipate that it might be used, both in support of formal programmes of study and by managers who want simply to develop and expand their own understanding and awareness.

Healthcare systems, politics and society

In most developed countries, the healthcare sector encompasses anything from 8 per cent to over 15 per cent of the economy, making it one of the largest industries in any state – bigger generally than education, agriculture, information technologies, tourism or telecommunications, and a crucial component of wider economic performance. In most countries, around one worker in ten is employed in the healthcare sector – as doctors, nurses, scientists, therapists, cleaners, cooks, engineers, administrators, clerks, finance controllers – and, of course, as managers. This means that almost everyone has a relative or knows someone who works in healthcare, and the healthcare workforce can be a politically powerful group with considerable influence over public opinion. Almost everyone uses health services, or has members of their family or friends who are significant healthcare users, and everyone has a view to express about their local or national healthcare system.

In many countries, the history of the healthcare system is intertwined with the development of communities and social structures. Religious groups, charities, voluntary organizations, trade unions and local municipalities have all played important roles in building the healthcare organizations and systems we have today, and people in those communities often feel connected in a visceral manner to 'their' hospitals, community clinics, ambulance service and all the other parts of the healthcare system. They raise funds to support new facilities or equipment, and volunteer to work in a wide range of roles that augment or support the employed healthcare workforce. That connection with the community also comes to the fore when anyone – especially government – suggests changing or reconfiguring healthcare provision. Proposals to close much-loved community hospitals, reorganize district hospital services or change maternity services are often professionally driven – by a laudable policy imperative to make health services more effective, safe and efficient. But when evidence of clinical effectiveness and technocratic appraisals of service options collide with popular sentiment and public opinion, what matters is usually not 'what works' but what people want.

For many local and national politicians, health policy and the healthcare system offer not only opportunities to shine in the eyes of the electorate when things are going well, but also threats to future electoral success when there are problems with healthcare funding or service provision and people look for someone to hold to account (as is explored in detail in Chapter 3 on the 'Politics of healthcare and the health policy process'). Constituents bring to politicians in their local offices concerns about healthcare services, and politicians are keenly aware of the attitudes and beliefs of the public about their local health service. While they will happily gain political benefit from the opening of a new facility or the expansion of clinical services, they will equally happily secure benefit by criticizing the plans of 'faceless bureaucrats' in the local healthcare organization for unpopular changes in healthcare services, and argue that there are too many managers and pen-pushers.

Finally, for the press, TV, radio, online and social media, both locally and nationally, the healthcare system is an endless source of news stories, debates and current affairs topics.

From patient safety to MRSA and pandemic flu, from dangerous doctors to hospital closures, from waiting lists to celebrity illnesses and possible new miracle cures, the healthcare system is news. Big healthcare stories can command pages of news coverage in national dailies and repeated presentation on TV news bulletins and websites, while at a local level it would be rare to find a newspaper that did not have some content about hospitals, clinics or other healthcare services in each issue. Healthcare organizations and their leaders can use this level of media interest to their advantage, to raise public awareness of health issues and communicate with the community, but they can also find themselves on the receiving end of intense and hostile media scrutiny when things go wrong.

In other words, healthcare organizations exist in a turbulent political and social environment, in which their actions and behaviour are highly visible and much scrutinized. Leadership and management take place in this 'goldfish bowl', where their performance and process can be just as important as their outcomes. But as if that were not enough, in every developed country the healthcare system is subject to four inexorable and challenging social trends:

- the demographic shift;
- the pace of technological innovation;
- changing user and consumer expectations; and
- financial pressures within a context of global economic recession.

The only certainty is that if it is difficult to make the sums add up for the healthcare system today, these pressures mean it will be even harder to do so tomorrow.

The demographic challenge is that because people are living longer, the numbers of elderly and very elderly people are rising fast – and those people make much greater use of the healthcare system. People may live longer but they cost more to keep alive, they are more likely to have complex, chronic health conditions, and their last few years of life tend to require significant support and thus prove more expensive. A further dimension to this demographic challenge is the rising incidence of chronic disease in the wider population of developed countries. The World Health Organization suggests that this is a direct result of risk factors such as tobacco use, physical inactivity and unhealthy diets (WHO, 2005, 2014).

The second challenge is related to the first in that it reflects an increasing ability to cure illnesses and control chronic disease and thus extend life – the pace of technological innovation. Most obviously in pharmaceuticals, but also in surgery, diagnostics, telehealth and other areas, we keep finding new ways to cure or manage disease. Sometimes that means new treatments that are more effective (and usually more expensive) than the existing ones. But it also means new therapies for diseases or problems that we simply could not treat before. Furthermore, the rise of genomic medicine means that the possibility of treatments tailored to the individual is now very much a reality, and likely to bring about significant change in the future to the ways in which disease is anticipated, prevented and treated.

This in turn connects with and feeds the third challenge – changing user and consumer expectations. People want more from the health service than their parents did. They are not content to be passive recipients of healthcare, prescribed and dispensed by providers at their convenience. Accustomed to ever-widening choice and sovereignty in decisions in other areas of life, such as banking and education – and accessible through a smartphone or other device – they expect to be consulted, informed and involved by healthcare providers in any decisions that affect their health. They are better informed, more articulate and more likely to know about – and demand – new and expensive treatments.

The first three challenges are in large measure responsible for the fourth – rising costs. Each of them contributes to the constant pressure for more healthcare funding, a pressure that, for many countries, is currently more acute as a result of the global economic recession and its aftermath. However much governments or others increase spending on healthcare, it never seems to be enough. In almost every other area of the economy, productivity is rising and costs are falling through competition and innovation. We have better, faster, cheaper computers, cars, smartphones, consumer goods, food, banking, and so on, yet in healthcare, costs are stubbornly high and continue to rise, along with demand for services. In a time of economic recession, this challenge is made more acute by real-term reductions in the resources available for healthcare in many countries, and hence a focus on setting priorities or rationing availability of services.

In short, the social, political and economic context in which healthcare organizations have to exist is often a hostile, fast-changing and pressured environment. Managers and leaders strive to balance competing, shifting and irreconcilable demands from a wide range of stakeholders – and do so while under close public scrutiny. The task of leadership in healthcare organizations – defining the mission of the organization, setting out a clear and consistent vision, guiding and incentivizing the organization towards its objectives, and ensuring safe and high-quality care – is made much more challenging by the social, economic and political context in which they work.

Healthcare organizations and healthcare management

Organizations are the product of their environment and context, and many of the distinctive characteristics and behaviours of healthcare organizations result from some of the social, political and economic factors outlined above. However, some also result from the nature of the enterprise – healthcare itself. The uniquely personal nature of health services, the special vulnerability and need for support and advocacy of patients, the complexity of the care process, and the advanced nature of the technologies used, all contribute to the special challenges of management in healthcare organizations.

Of course, we should be cautious that this does not lead us to be parochial or narrow minded in our understanding of what we do, or of what we can learn from other sectors and settings. We are all prone to exceptionalism, believing that our job, organization, profession or community is in some ways uniquely different. It can give us an excuse for why we perform less well or do not need to change in ways expected of other sectors. We may claim that our patients are sicker, facilities less modern, community disadvantaged and clinicians more difficult or disengaged. It also provides the perfect reason for not adopting new ideas from elsewhere – it would not work here, because our organization or health system is different. Healthcare systems and organizations have a strong tendency to exceptionalism, something that needs to be challenged on a regular basis. Healthcare organizations are large, complex, professionally dominated entities providing a wide range of highly tailored and personalized services to large numbers of often vulnerable users. But those characteristics are shared in various degrees by local authorities, police and emergency services, universities, schools, advertising agencies, management consultancies, travel agencies, law firms and other organizations. Healthcare is nevertheless distinctive, and three important areas of difference deserve some further consideration: the place of professions; the role of patients; and the nature of the healthcare process.

For managers entering healthcare organizations from other sectors – whether from other public services, commercial for-profit companies or the voluntary sector – one of the first striking differences they notice is the absence of clear, hierarchical structures for command and control, and the powerful nature of professional status, knowledge and control (see Chapter 3 for a more in-depth discussion). Sir Roy Griffiths, who in the 1980s led a review of the management of the National Health Service (NHS) in the UK, famously wrote in his report about walking through a hospital looking in vain for 'the person in charge' (Griffiths, 1983). But to do so would be to miss the point, which is that healthcare organizations are professional bureaucracies in which more or less all the intellectual, creative and social capital exists in the frontline workers – clinicians of all professions, but particularly doctors. Like law firms and universities, it makes no sense to try to manage these talented, highly intelligent individuals in ways that are reductionist, or which run counter to their highly professionalized self-image and culture. This does not mean that they should not be managed – just that the processes and content of management and leadership need to take account of and indeed embrace the professional culture. Things get done not through instruction or direction, but by negotiation, persuasion, peer influence and agreement. Leaders need to make skilful use of the values, language and apparatus of the profession to achieve their objectives, and learn to lead without needing to be 'in charge'.

The people who use healthcare services, whether you call them patients, users, consumers or whatever, are ordinary people, but they are not like the consumers of many other public or commercial services. First, there is a huge asymmetry of power and information in the relationship between a patient and a healthcare provider. Even the most highly educated, confident, social media-savvy patient cannot acquire the detailed knowledge, expertise and wisdom that come with clinical practice. Very few patients are prepared to go against the explicit advice of senior clinicians, and many patients seek actively to transfer responsibility for decision-making to these professionals. At some level, patients have to be able to trust that healthcare providers are competent, and take their advice on important decisions about their health. No amount of performance measurement, league tables, audit or regulation can substitute for this trust.

Second, when people become patients and use healthcare services, they are often at their most vulnerable and are much less able to act independently and assertively than would normally be the case. They may be emotionally fragile following an unwelcome diagnosis of disease, and weakened by the experience of illness or the effects of treatment. When lying flat on a wheeled trolley, nauseous and in pain, surrounded by the unfamiliar noise and clatter of an emergency department and frightened by sudden intimations of mortality, we are at our most dependent. We are not likely to feel well placed to exercise choice, or to assert our right to self-determination. We want and need to be cared for – a somewhat unfashionable and paternalistic notion that does not sit comfortably with concepts of the patient as a sovereign consumer of health services. This all means that healthcare organizations, and those who lead them, have a special responsibility to compensate for the unavoidable asymmetry of power and information in their relationships with patients, by providing mechanisms and systems to protect and advocate for patients, seek their views, understand their concerns, and make services patient centred.

Despite all the high-technology medicine, complicated equipment and advanced pharmaceuticals available today, the healthcare process itself is still organized very much as it was one hundred years ago. It is a craft model of production in which individual health professionals ply their trade, providing their distinctive contribution to any patient's treatment when called upon. This is not mass production. Healthcare organizations such as hospitals are much more like marketplaces than they are like factories, with the patients moving from stall to stall to get what they want, not being whisked smoothly along on a conveyor belt from start to finish. Fundamentally, it is an often unmanaged and undocumented process. Usually, there is no written timetable or plan showing how the patient should move through the system, and no one person acts as 'process manager', steering and coordinating the care that the patient receives and assuring quality and efficiency. This model has endured because of its flexibility. The patient care process can be adapted endlessly or tailored to the needs of individual patients, the circumstances of their disease and their response to treatment. But the complexity of modern healthcare processes, with multiple handovers of patients from one professional to another, the ever-accelerating pace of care as lengths of stay get shorter and shorter, and the risks and toxicity of many new healthcare interventions (the flip side of their much greater effectiveness) all mean that the traditional model is increasingly seen as unreliable, unsafe and prone to error and unexplained variation (Walshe and Boaden, 2005; Shekelle et al., 2013). More and more, healthcare organizations use care pathways, treatment plans, clinical guidelines and electronic records to bring some structure and explicitness to the healthcare process. Techniques for process mapping and design, commonplace in other sectors, are increasingly used not just to describe the healthcare process but in so doing to identify ways in which it can be improved (Kaplan and Porter, 2011). Like any area where custom, practice and precedent have long reigned supreme, healthcare processes are often ripe for challenge. Why does a patient need to come to hospital three times to see different people and have tests before they get a diagnosis? Can't we organize the process so that all the interactions take place in a single visit? Why are certain tasks undertaken only by doctors or nurses? Could they be done just as well by other healthcare practitioners such as pharmacists or physiotherapists? Gradually, the healthcare process is being made more explicit, exposed for discussion, debate and challenge, and standardized or routinized in ways that make the delivery of healthcare more consistent, efficient and safer.

In conclusion, there is one other important feature of healthcare organizations. Whether they are government-owned, independent not-for-profits or commercial healthcare providers, they all share to some degree a sense of social mission or purpose concerned with the public good (Drucker, 2006; Benington and Moore, 2011). The professional values and culture of healthcare are deeply embedded, and most people working in healthcare organizations have both an altruistic belief in the social value of the work they do and a set of more self-interested motivations to do with reward, recognition and advancement. Similarly, healthcare organizations – even commercial, for-profit entities – do some things that do not make sense in business terms, but that reflect their social mission, while at the same time they respond to financial incentives and behave entrepreneurially. When exposed to strong competitive pressures, not-for-profit and commercial for-profit healthcare providers behave fairly similarly, and their social mission may take second place to organizational survival and growth. The challenge, at both the individual and organizational level, is to make proper use of both sets of motivations, and not lose sight of the powerful and pervasive beneficial effects that can result from understanding and playing to the social mission.

About this third edition and how to use the book

The second edition of this book received very positive and encouraging feedback from the outset, particularly in relation to the balance between academic rigour and practical application of concepts and ideas. When given the opportunity to prepare a third edition, there were a number of key areas on which we wished to focus our attention:

- concentrating on core content relevant to healthcare management, and not trying to cover material that can be found in a general management text;
- being genuinely multinational in approach and making the content more international in outlook and application; and
- designing and presenting content in ways that support structured learning, application and further study.

We have therefore made further significant revisions for this third edition. First of all, in relation to the structure of the book and a stronger focus on healthcare (as opposed to general) management, this time we organize our material into twenty chapters within three main sections: effective healthcare management; health systems; and health services and organizations. Thus we move from macro topics such as politics, funding, resource allocation, through an examination of the issues concerned with the management of specific services such as primary, secondary, mental health and social care, to an examination of organizational concerns such as public and patient involvement, health purchasing, quality improvement and measuring and managing performance.

In addressing the need for the book to be even more international in its focus, we have again included a chapter on the internationalization of health systems and policies. All chapter authors were strongly encouraged to draw on a wider range of international material and case studies and this they have done, with many examples of research and practice from across the world.

In terms of adopting a design that supports structured learning, each chapter has a common framework that places greater emphasis on separating out core ideas and content from their application in one or more case studies. Self-test activities can be found throughout each chapter and the authors provide a more extensive listing of key internet sources for further reading and application.

All chapters have been rewritten and edited to a significant degree, reflecting both the pace of change within the world of healthcare and also our desire to ensure that the book is constantly improved in the manner that we exhort within a number of the chapters. We hope that you will appreciate the changes that we have made and find the book to be as useful and thoughtful as ever, but with an even stronger international flavour and a deeper base of evidence from research and practice.

The twenty chapters of the book that follow this introduction and overview are split into three main parts.

Part 1: Effective healthcare management

Chapter 2 examines policy, research and practice related to evidence-based management, considering how healthcare managers make decisions, reflect on their practice and learn for the future. There is an emphasis on the sources and forms of evidence available to and used by managers, and the potential for better decisions through more informed and effective use of evidence and learning. The aim of putting this chapter first is that we hope it will help to frame the way you use the rest of the book – seeking to use and apply evidence in your own decision-making.

Part 2: Health systems

Chapters 3–8 aim to set out the wider political, social and economic context in which health-care organizations exist, namely 'health systems'. These chapters provide the 'big picture', which helps to explain how health systems are shaped, and the way in which their constituent healthcare organizations behave, remembering that, as observed earlier, organizations are very much a product of their environment and context. This part covers the politics of healthcare and the health policy process (Chapter 3); financing healthcare, funding systems and healthcare costs (Chapter 4); allocating resources, and setting and managing priorities (Chapter 5); research and innovation in healthcare (Chapter 6); global health policy and governing health systems across borders (Chapter 7); and health and well-being and the wider context for healthcare management (Chapter 8).

Part 3: Healthcare services and organizations

Part 3 aims to covers the issues that are particular to the services that make up the business of healthcare itself, and the organizational concerns that preoccupy managers and leaders. In other words, it explores the different care sectors of a health system, examining the management and other issues associated with each sector, before moving on to consider more generic topics of vital interest to managers. It starts with five chapters about managing in different care sectors: primary care (Chapter 9); chronic disease and what is increasingly referred to as 'integrated care' (Chapter 10); acute care, including elective and emergency, secondary and tertiary services (Chapter 11); mental health (Chapter 12); and social care – known as disability services in some countries (Chapter 13).

We then move on to examine more generic topics that form the underlying architecture of health systems and organizations. The first of these topics is the purchasing or commissioning of healthcare (Chapter 14) – an examination of the way in which managers in a health system allocate resources to providers in a way that ensures that people's health needs are met. This is followed by a consideration of the issues associated with buildings, facilities and equipment in healthcare (Chapter 15), and an exploration of the ways in which informatics for healthcare systems are being developed and used, and the challenges and opportunities presented by their increasing capability and complexity (Chapter 16). The array of issues associated with the healthcare workforce is explored in Chapter 17, prior to a consideration of the role and experience of patients, users and the public within health systems and organizations (Chapter 18). Three final chapters explore enduring and overarching topics for healthcare managers and leaders within all healthcare systems: governance and accountability in healthcare (Chapter 19); quality improvement in healthcare, including the organizational and leadership aspects of healthcare improvement approaches (Chapter 20); and measuring and managing healthcare performance (Chapter 21).

While the content of each chapter has led its design, we asked our authors to follow a broadly consistent format in order to make the materials in the book as useful and readable as possible. You will therefore find each chapter is structured into around five or six sections, and we make judicious use of figures, tables, charts and diagrams to illustrate the content. Each chapter includes the following:

- **Learning activities** designed to help you to apply the content of the chapter and your learning to your own organizations. The exercises generally consist of a number of questions that we suggest you use as the basis either for personal reflection or for discussion with colleagues.
- **Case study examples** setting out international experience within health systems and services of the topic under consideration within the chapter.
- **Learning resources** that can be discovered online where you might seek further information. We have done our best to ensure the website links are as up to date as possible, but bear in mind that content on the internet does change rapidly and so some links could no longer be current when you read this book.
- **References** with details of books, reports, journal articles and other materials referenced in the chapter. Items such as these could be useful as additional background reading.

This book is a collective endeavour, with about thirty contributors to the twenty-one chapters it contains, many drawn from among our current and former colleagues. We are as appreciative as we hope you will be of the time, effort and skill they have invested in designing and planning chapters that will facilitate learning in their specialist areas.

It is great to get feedback on this book. We (the editors) have met people who have used previous editions of the book throughout a course and it makes our day when someone tells us that using the book to support their learning has helped them to develop as a manager and leader. Equally, we welcome comments on and ideas for improvement, and we can promise they will be used when – hopefully not too soon! – we start to think about a fourth edition of the book. Whether you use it casually for your own development or more intensively as part of a postgraduate programme of study, we would like your feedback. Please email us at kieran.walshe@manchester.ac.uk or j.a.smith.20@bham.ac.uk.

References

Benington, J. and Moore, M. (eds.) (2011) *Public Value: Theory and Practice.* Basingstoke: Palgrave Macmillan.

Drucker, P. (2006) *Managing the Nonprofit Organisation.* London: HarperCollins.

Gray, D.E. (2007) Facilitating management learning: developing critical reflection through reflective tools, *Management Learning*, 38 (5): 495–517.

Griffiths, R. (1983) *Report of the NHS Management Inquiry.* London: Department of Health and Social Security.

Kaplan, R.S. and Porter, M.E. (2011) How to solve the cost crisis in healthcare, *Harvard Business Review*, September: 46–64.

Mintzberg, H. (2004) *Managers not MBAs.* London: Prentice-Hall.

Peck, E. (2004) *Organisational Development in Healthcare: Approaches, Innovations, Achievements.* Oxford: Radcliffe Medical Press.

Shekelle, P.G., Pronovost, P.J., Wachter, R.M., McDonald, K.M., Schoelles, K., Dy, S.M. et al. (2013) The top patient safety strategies that can be encouraged for adoption now, *Annals of Internal Medicine*, 158 (5, Pt 2): 365–8.

Walshe, K. and Boaden, R. (eds.) (2005) *Patient Safety: Research into Practice.* Maidenhead: Open University Press.

World Health Organization (WHO) (2005) *Preventing Chronic Diseases: A Vital Investment.* Geneva: WHO.

World Health Organization (WHO) (2014) *Global Status Report on Noncommunicable Diseases 2014.* Geneva: WHO.

Part

1

EFFECTIVE HEALTHCARE MANAGEMENT

Evidence-based management: a critical appraisal

Kieran Walshe

Introduction

Managers and leaders in healthcare systems spend too much time doing things and too little time thinking about what they do and why they do it. Life as a manager in any organization is frequently stressful and frenetic, with disruption and interruption to tasks and activities commonplace. We have known for decades, since the pioneering work of Henry Mintzberg (1973) and Rosemary Stewart (1999), that the real nature of managerial work is far from the ordered, rational, planned world you sometimes see presented in management textbooks and management courses. But we are perhaps too accepting that it has to be like that. And I might add that some managers may like it that way. They enjoy the firefighting, crisis-solving, problem-hopping, adrenalin-generating nature of their work and may even generate some of the chaos, pressure and challenge themselves.

The purpose of this chapter is to encourage managers in healthcare organizations to think and reflect about the nature of their work and the way they choose to enact their role – and they do have a choice. Of course, managers exist within organizational cultures and contexts that shape how they behave, but every manager still has the opportunity to choose how they will go about doing their job, and what that says about them, their organization and the nature of management. In particular, this chapter makes the case for healthcare managers to be more evidence based in the way they work, and to learn some things from the way evidence is used in decision-making by clinicians in their organizations. This is not some naïve, simplistic call for management to be treated like a 'science' or for managers to adopt a blindly empirical, cook-book approach to making decisions. Management is about getting things done through other people, in organizations which are first and foremost social constructions. So often in manage-ment, *how* things are done and *who* does something matters as much or if not more than *what* is done. But that is all the more reason why we should still bring social sciences like anthropology, sociology, operations management, organizational behaviour and psychology to bear on thinking about management decisions and behaviour. And we cannot do that unless we make sure that managers have time and space to think more, and act less. The subtitle of this chapter sums up what we think is needed – a critical appraisal, in which managers bring their intelligence and skills to bear on management problems by thinking them through, considering a wide range of evidence, and using that thinking to reach the best decisions and actions they can.

This is all given much greater salience because we work in healthcare systems and organizations. These are highly knowledge-intensive organizations, in which sciences like biomedicine, nursing, clinical epidemiology, medical physics and many others play a huge part in many strategic and operational decisions. These are also among the most professionalized and pluralistic organizations (Denis et al., 2001) that exist – staffed by highly intelligent clinicians and scientists who bring a strong culture of empiricism and the primacy of empirical evidence to what they do and without the simple hierarchies that often exist in other organizations – you can't tell people what to do, but have to negotiate, persuade and influence and, in that process, evidence is often of central importance.

To succeed in such an environment as a manager, if you are not yourself a clinician or a scientist, you need to be able to engage with the evidence and debate it with them on equal terms. Should we invest in robotic surgery for prostate cancer? What would be the costs and benefits of changing the hip prosthesis we use in hip replacement surgery? Would it be a good idea to recruit and deploy physician assistants to work alongside doctors in our accident and emergency department? What changes could we make to patient toileting procedures that would reduce the risks of falls in frail, elderly inpatients? These sorts of decisions lie at the heart of the clinical business and process of healthcare and any manager who can't get to grips with the evidence and use it productively is unlikely to be seen as credible and authoritative by the clinicians and scientists in their organization. More importantly, they will be abdicating their responsibilities as a manager if they simply cede such decisions to the clinicians and scientists, saying 'you tell me what you think we should do'.

The rest of this chapter is structured into four main sections. First, we explore why managers don't make good use of evidence in their decision-making and what problems that can cause. To do this we need to engage with some ideas about the nature of management – art, craft or science – and management knowledge. But our focus is relentlessly practical and aimed at showing that better use of evidence will lead to better decision-making, and to better management and better organizational performance. In part, we do that through looking at what might be termed some 'great management disasters'. Second, we turn to setting out – and demystifying – the key concepts of evidence-based management. It is not that complicated, neither does it take much effort to bring evidence to bear in managerial decision-making, but it does require some ideas and skills that are rarely talked about or taught in management courses. Third, we apply those ideas to two case studies – real-life examples of major management decisions where the use of evidence can make a real difference. And it is important to recognize that the difference is about more than just money or resources – it is also about patients and service users and their lives. Finally, we try to draw together some conclusions, and think about how to apply these ideas to the rest of this book. Each chapter of the book is, in its own way, a synthesis of evidence on its topic – from primary care to commissioning to quality improvement. The challenge is not just to read the book but to use it to become a better manager.

Learning activity 2.1

Choose one of the four questions below and spend an hour doing searches using Google Scholar or, if you prefer, another internet source to look for evidence:

- Should we invest in robotic surgery for prostate cancer?
- What would be the costs and benefits of changing the hip prosthesis we use in hip replacement surgery?
- Would it be a good idea to recruit and deploy physician assistants to work alongside doctors in our accident and emergency department?
- What changes could we make to patient toileting procedures that would reduce the risks of falls in frail, elderly inpatients?

Focus on finding a small number of high-quality, authoritative publications (they might be guidelines from national agencies or professional organizations). Prepare some notes on the four or five key things you would want to talk to clinicians about in a meeting.

Now reflect on what went well and what did not. Did you find the evidence you were seeking (or did you need help from a librarian or information scientist)? Did you understand the evidence you found, or did you lack the skills in critical reading and appraisal? Were the key issues clear or was the evidence very ambiguous or contradictory?

Management: art, craft or science?

For almost as long as there have been managers, people have been debating the nature of what managers do and how people learn to manage. Some of this discussion is frankly a waste of time and energy – for example, many thousands of words have been written about the allegedly profound differences between management and leadership when this is truly a distinction without a difference (Carroll and Levy, 2008). Management and leadership are pretty much the same thing and most attempts to draw a boundary between them (such as the widespread argument that 'leaders are transformational but managers are transactional' or that 'leaders do the right thing, but managers do things right') are facile and simply come to grief when you look at the evidence on what managers and leaders actually do.

But there is one important issue that it is worth spending some time on, and that is the idea of whether management is a science, on the one hand, or an art or craft, on the other. By a science, we mean something that is amenable to developing generalizable ideas or theories, testing them empirically in real life, using the results to confirm, disconfirm or modify those theories, and building over time a body of knowledge that can be transferred to others and used. By an art or craft, we mean something that is essentially personal, subjective and constructed or enacted individually by each of us depending on ourselves and our context, so everything is highly contingent and experiential. These two perspectives (admittedly accentuated somewhat for comparative effect) are set out in Table 2.1. It outlines how the two schools of thought can influence your thinking about what managers do, how they learn, how they make decisions and how we seek to improve management.

Many people – myself included – would argue that the truth lies somewhere in between the two. Mintzberg has contributed a great deal to our thinking about the nature of management through his pioneering body of work on what managers do (Mintzberg, 1973), on how we learn to manage through a combination of ideas and theories and experience and practice (Mintzberg, 2004), and on the nature of management knowledge and its application (Mintzberg, 1989). He presents a view of management as a practice, or craft, in which wisdom and experience are hugely important, but where that wisdom and experience must be grounded in a foundation of knowledge both about what management consists of and how it is done, and about how managers learn and make decisions. An immediate parallel with the practice of medicine is apparent – doctors study anatomy, physiology, pharmacology and epidemiology to provide the foundation of knowledge needed for them to then learn to *be* a doctor, which entails applying that body of knowledge to the endlessly varying complexities of clinical practice and learning in clinical practice to connect the science and the craft of medicine. There has been an equally lively debate about the nature of 'evidence-based medicine' and the relationship between the science and craft perspectives on clinical practice (Greenhalgh et al., 2014).

Table 2.1 What is management?: two schools of thought

What is management?	**Science** – there are knowable facts and provable theories from which we can generalize and develop a codified body of knowledge that managers can then use in their practice.	**Art or craft** – there is little in management that is not subjective, open to contestation, dependent on prevailing social and cultural norms. Generalization is highly problematic, there are few if any right or wrong answers, and most practices are contingent and dependent on the situation.
What do managers do?	Managers plan, organize, control, communicate and coordinate. Their job is about deploying resources to maximize efficiency and effectiveness in achieving organizational goals.	Managers communicate, motivate and lead. Their job is fundamentally a social and relational one – about getting things done through other people and so about creating and sustaining organizational environments that enable those things to get done.
How do managers learn?	Managers learn empirically by applying the body of knowledge to their own situation. They first need to acquire that knowledge, and then know how to apply it analytically to different situations and problems. They also need to learn to learn.	Managers learn experientially, through the practice of management, in what might be called an apprenticeship. They learn most from their own and close colleagues' experience, and they accumulate the wisdom of their craft slowly, over time. Much of their knowledge is innate and implicit, and so very hard to codify or transfer to others.

(continued)

What knowledge do managers need?	Managers need to be able to acquire, assimilate and apply knowledge or evidence of different kinds. Often they are combining generalized knowledge (from a wider body of research and learning) with specific knowledge (about their own organization and context).	Managers need to be reflective practitioners who think about their own practices and learn from their own experiences. Mostly they are using specific knowledge about their own organization, context and experience. Often their access to and use of knowledge is intuitive, implicit and highly personal.
How do managers make decisions?	Managers should have a rational, comprehensive and explicit approach to making decisions. Options should be listed, appraised and then chosen on the basis of costs and benefits. Data and evidence should be to the fore.	Managers should have a social, relational and political approach to making decisions, in which they seek to negotiate agreement and progression among competing interests in the longer term interests of the organization, recognizing that there is no one deterministically right outcome, but many potential and indeterminate outcomes.
How do we improve the effectiveness of managers and management?	Focus on giving managers the skills, training and ideas needed to be evidence-based managers; seek to bring research and management communities closer together to do better research and see it used more effectively.	Seek to improve the apprenticeship and learning of managers through mentoring and support from the most experienced and expert practitioners; promote reflective practice through coaching and peer feedback.
Further reading	van de Ven, A.H. (2007) *Engaged Scholarship: A Guide for Organizational and Social Research*. Oxford: Oxford University Press.	Flyvbjerg, B. (2001) *Making Social Science Matter: Why Social Inquiry Fails and How it Can Succeed Again*. Cambridge: Cambridge University Press.

Anyone looking at the world of management from the outside might immediately question how 'scientific' management is for three reasons. First, popular literature on management is almost exclusively written from the standpoint of the 'craft' school of thought. Bookstores contain large numbers of books about management (presumably because they sell well, because managers read them or think they should read them), many of which are, frankly, rubbish! They offer a bewildering range of mutually contradictory advice on how to manage or lead; they tend to over-claim for particular ideas or practices; they present a ceaseless, churning search for novelty and gimmickry; and they are often written either by self-appointed management 'gurus' with their own nostrums or panaceas to sell, or by successful leaders who offer self-serving, biased and egocentric accounts of how and why they succeeded. Very little 'science' is on offer, with a few notable exceptions (Furusten, 1999).

Learning activity 2.2

Choose a widely read and popular management book from your own or from someone else's bookshelf and read it critically to answer the following four questions:

- What is the book saying? What are the key claims, messages or findings that the book asserts or the arguments that it presents?
- How well evidenced are the book's main claims? What evidence is advanced to support its arguments and where does it come from?
- What does the wider literature say? Using Google Scholar or a similar search engine search for academic literature relevant to the book's key arguments, and ask to what extent it supports or contradicts the book's main claims.
- In conclusion, how rigorous and robust do you think the book's claims, findings or arguments are, and should managers trust them?

Second, the way we teach managers to manage, and the nature of management education, seems to leave a great deal to be desired (Trank and Rynes, 2003). Business schools – and their much-vaunted MBA programmes – are perhaps an obvious target for criticism, because they are so costly and appear to be obsessed with metrics like post-MBA career trajectories and pay increases rather than with equipping managers with the knowledge and skills they need to be effective managers in their future careers (Mintzberg, 2004). Mintzberg's main criticisms of MBAs are that they are disconnected from the real world of management, teach superficially in the classroom, over-emphasize decision-making and analytic skills, and are taken by people who lack the experience of management that is required to make sense of the content and apply it to practice (Mintzberg, 2004). And Rousseau (2006) argues that teaching programmes do little to equip managers to think critically, to appraise and use evidence or to bring research to bear on their own practice.

Third, there is a chasm that divides the community of practice in management and the community of academics who research management (Rousseau, 2006). These are two quite separate communities, with very little overlap and hardly any mechanisms of linkage and exchange. It is astonishing that the research community chooses what to research, then undertakes the research and publishes the results in journals with almost no reference to the needs, interests and perspectives of the management community. The leading management research journals are simply not read by anyone apart from researchers and a cursory scan of some papers in *Academy of Management Review* or *Organization Science* explains why – they are opaquely written, abstruse, intentionally complex and rarely applicable to real-world management problems. Management research is essentially applied social science, and it should be providing the evidence that managers can then use in practice, but management research has become increasingly irrelevant to and disconnected from management practice (Tranfield and Starkey, 1998; Bennis and O'Toole, 2004; Ghosal, 2005).

So, where is the evidence that any of this matters, that we are not content simply to accept that the circumstances outlined above are inherently problematic? One way to explore this is to look for examples of common management decisions that have adverse consequences for individuals and organizations, and that seem to fly in the face of the evidence. In circumstances like this, we can probably argue three things: that there is a research–practice 'gap'; that the gap results in suboptimal decision-making; and that those decisions have real adverse consequences. Some brief examples are set out in Table 2.2.

Table 2.2 Examples of the research–practice gap and its impact

Management issue	The evidence	Common management practice	Impact
Lean thinking and the Toyota Production System (TPS)	Lean and TPS work to reduce cost and improve quality, but their implementation is a long-term, resource-hungry effort and requires a high level of consistent commitment that many organizations cannot muster.	Organizations 'do' 'lean' with hurried and superficial implementation, too little attention to the actual content and training required, and don't show long-term commitment. They then move on to something else.	Wasted resources of time, effort and money on Lean implementation, and a negative effect on staff engagement with future quality improvement initiatives.
Organizational mergers	It is hard to make mergers work in practice and they have high transitional costs; merger rationale needs to be robustly tested and challenged and alternatives to merger explored; cultural fit is crucial and often neglected.	Rush into merger without due diligence on finances, strategy, culture and overall rationale for merger. Mergers sometimes mandated and done for symbolic or political purposes. Real aims of merger not made explicit.	Merged organizations are often dysfunctional for years after merger and there are profound negative consequences for performance. Some mergers fail and result in demerger.
Adoption and implementation of information technology (IT)	IT systems have profound socio technical effects that are often poorly understood and lead to problems in implementation. User-led approaches to design and implementation and incremental rather than 'big bang' approaches are preferable.	Managers repeatedly embark on over-ambitious IT system implementations that are operational, technical and cultural failures. Design and implementation are often led by technical experts and enthusiasts; wider take-up is poor.	Huge waste of resources on IT systems that are sometimes abandoned and often yield disappointing value. Some IT system failures cause widespread operational harm to the organization.

(continued)

Table 2.2 (continued)

Management issue	The evidence	Common management practice	Impact
Pay for performance in healthcare	Pay-for-performance schemes (for hospitals, doctors, etc.) in healthcare rarely work well in the longer term. They tend to have small, short-term benefits. If one is to be adopted, target incentives on teams, keep it small, vary the scheme over time and use alongside other incentives/levers for performance.	Pay-for-performance schemes are put in place with large financial incentives and their effects are rarely properly measured or tested. They are often left in place long after they are likely to yield any positive effect. Clinicians comply reluctantly but resent the assumption that they are primarily driven by financial incentives.	Schemes may create some small and short-term benefits (e.g. adherence to clinical guidelines) but there are other ways to secure such changes. If used on a large scale they can be extremely expensive. Adverse and unintended consequences abound.

Another way to explore the consequences of the research–practice gap is to examine what some have called 'fad and fashion' in management practice. Even if we don't know what works, why, where and for whom in management, we must surely know that the repeated serial adoption and then discarding of managerial initiatives or practices must represent at best a waste of resources and at worst real harm to the organizations on which these fads or fashions are visited (Abrahamson, 1996; Gibson and Tesone, 2001). There is good evidence that this is exactly what happens, and that organizations and managers engage in a lot of copying or 'isomorphism' – doing things because other successful organizations have done them, and replicating the form of those things rather than intelligently adopting the function they represent. The result is often that the innovation does not work, and it is discarded as rapidly as it was adopted, in favour of 'the next new thing'.

One final observation on the science and craft argument is needed. Over the last twenty years, the evidence-based movement has risen to prominence in several areas, including medicine, education, social and public policy, and somewhat belatedly management too (Pfeffer and Sutton, 2006; Rousseau, 2006; Reay et al., 2009). This social movement began in the healthcare sector (Sackett and Rosenberg, 1995), and this is also where it has become most clearly institutionalized and embedded in healthcare organizations and systems, in part because the professionalized and empirically oriented paradigms dominant in healthcare organizations provided a receptive context. There is a long way to go before the evidence-based management movement achieves that kind of adoption more widely, but for managers working in healthcare organizations, the clinical analogy is actually very useful in putting the case for using evidence in management decisions. It may seem simplistic to some but I think it is completely reasonable that if we expect clinicians to use the best evidence available in choosing which drug to prescribe or what diagnostic tests to order, we should expect healthcare system leaders to use the best evidence available in choosing how to reconfigure services or what workforce models to use to determine future education and training investments. Table 2.3 sets out some key aspects of the evidence-based paradigm as it plays out in the separate worlds of clinicians and managers. It is worth noting, of course, that many healthcare system leaders are clinicians (doctors, nurses and other clinical professions), and so they bring their ways of thinking about evidence from clinical practice into the managerial domain.

Table 2.3 Comparing the evidence-based worlds of clinicians and managers

	Clinical practice	*Healthcare management*
Culture	• Highly professionalized, with a strong formal body of knowledge and control of entry to the profession resulting in coherence of knowledge, attitudes and beliefs. • High value placed on scientific knowledge and research, with many researchers who are also practitioners (and vice versa). ·	• Much less professionalized, with much less formal body of knowledge, less control of entry and greater diversity among practitioners. • Personal experience and self-generated knowledge highly valued, intensely pragmatic. • Less understanding of research, some suspicion of value and of motives of researchers. • Divide between researchers and practitioners, with little interchange between the two worlds.
Research and evidence	• Strong biomedical, empirical paradigm, with focus on experimental methods and quantitative data. • Belief in generalizability and objectivity of research findings. • Well-organized and -indexed literature, concentrated in certain journals with clear boundaries, amenable to systematic review and synthesis.	• Weak social sciences paradigm, with more use of qualitative methods and less empiricism. • Tendency to see research findings as more subjective, contingent and less generalizable. • Poorly organized and indexed research literature, spread across journals and other literature sources (including grey literature), with unclear boundaries, heterogeneous and not easy to review systematically or synthesize.
Decision-making	• Many clinical decisions taken every day, mostly by individual clinicians with few constraints on their decisions. • Decisions often homogeneous, involving the application of general body of knowledge to specific circumstances. • Long tradition of using decision support systems (handbooks, guidelines, etc.). • Results of decisions often relatively clear and some immediate feedback.	• Fewer, larger decisions taken, usually by or in groups, with many organizational constraints, often requiring negotiation or compromise. • Decisions heterogeneous, and less based on applying a general body of knowledge to specific circumstances. • No tradition of using any form of decision support. • Results of decision and causal relationship between decision and subsequent events often very hard to determine.

Source: Adapted from Walshe and Rundall (2001).

Evidence-based management: some key concepts

Having made the case for evidence-based management, there is a risk that the problems articulated earlier make it seem like a great idea in theory but very hard to implement in practice. This section seeks to set out, in practical terms, what is involved in making better use of evidence in managerial decision-making, and to emphasize that it's not particularly difficult or complex.

Pfeffer and Sutton (2006) set out five principles of evidence-based management that are a helpful starting point when thinking about what you could do differently:

1   *Face the hard facts, and build a culture in which people are encouraged to tell the truth, even if it is unpleasant.* This is really about building an empirical culture in your organization, in which everyone brings data to the table for any decision. It means refusing to go with hunches or guesses or what people hope and expect should be, instead focusing relentlessly on what's actually happening.
2   *Be committed to 'fact-based' decision-making – which means being committed to getting the best evidence and using it to guide actions.* Here, the question of what you mean by the 'best evidence' arises, which is something we tackle below when suggesting that you think about theoretical evidence (what we think should be happening and why), empirical evidence (hard data on what is actually happening) and experiential evidence (knowledge and learning from those involved about how things are working and ideas on what to do).
3   *Treat your organization as an unfinished prototype – encourage experimentation and learning by doing.* This is perhaps the most important of Pfeffer and Sutton's principles – the idea that it is essential in all organizations to experiment and try things out, but in a way that allows you to test whether those innovations have worked and learn from the experiment. Organizations often make one of two mistakes – they either roll out innovations without having tested them out or prototyped them or they run pilots or tests but don't evaluate them properly and so don't really know whether they worked or not.
4   *Look for the risks and drawbacks in what people recommend – even the best medicine has side effects.* This is really a call for you to be much more sceptical, especially when people claim large positive effects or results from innovations, as both research and experience show they often perform less well when tested out properly and rolled out more widely. We need to test out new ideas thoroughly and identify any drawbacks, problems or unintended consequences they might have.
5   *Avoid basing decisions on untested but strongly held beliefs, what you have done in the past, or on uncritical 'benchmarking' of what winners do.* Here, Pfeffer and Sutton list three of the most important biases that cloud our thinking and may lead us to make poor decisions. Doing what we think or believe is right, what has worked for us before, or what has (apparently) worked for other people or other organizations may sometimes make sense, but the more important the decision, the more we need to assemble and use evidence more systematically than that.

You may think these ideas are more about culture and attitude of mind than about the practicalities of using evidence, so let us turn to setting out and then applying a framework for using evidence, which we outline in Table 2.4. I suggest that you organize your search for and appraisal of the evidence around three main types or forms: theoretical evidence, empirical evidence and experiential evidence. As the definitions in Table 2.4 show, these three types of evidence contribute in different ways to your decision-making. Theoretical evidence is used to understand *how* and *why* an intervention or initiative is meant to work; empirical evidence is used to examine *what impact* the intervention or initiative has had when it has been used and evaluated; and experiential evidence is used to explore *what people do* in response

Table 2.4 A framework for using evidence in decision-making

Type of evidence	Description	How it contributes to knowledge	Problems if evidence not available or used
Theoretical evidence	Ideas, concepts and models used to describe the intervention, to explain how and why it works and to connect it to a wider knowledge base and framework.	Helps to understand the programme theories that lie behind the intervention, and to use theories of human or organizational behaviour to outline and explore its intended working in ways that can then be used to construct and test meaningful hypotheses and transfer learning about the intervention to other settings.	We don't understand how and why an intervention worked (or didn't) and we are therefore unable to replicate it in other organizations or to change it in ways that we know will improve its effectiveness.
Empirical evidence	Information about the actual use of the intervention and about its effectiveness and outcomes in use.	Helps to understand how the intervention plays out in practice and to establish and measure its real effects and the causality of relationships between the intervention and desired outcomes.	We don't really know whether it works or not, and we risk rolling out the intervention and using it elsewhere when, in fact, it is not very effective – or abandoning it because we think it hasn't worked, when, in fact, it has.
Experiential evidence	Information about people's experiences of the service or intervention, and the interaction between them.	Helps to understand how people (users, practitioners and other stakeholders) experience, view and respond to the intervention, and how this contributes to our understanding of the intervention and shapes its use.	We don't know enough about the 'human side' of the intervention and how it affects things such as culture, behaviour, attitudes, motivation and interpersonal relations. People's response to the intervention may reduce its effectiveness or have all kinds of unintended consequences.

Source: Adapted from Glasby et al. (2007).

to the intervention or initiative. We use these three headings in our two case studies later in the chapter. Table 2.4 also outlines what may happen if we don't use these different types of evidence – and the errors or problems it describes are pretty familiar from the examples of the research-practice gap listed in Table 2.2.

So the task is to seek to populate the framework with relevant, rigorous evidence. Doing so involves two basic steps – finding the evidence and then appraising and understanding what it means (Tranfield et al., 2003). Let us tackle each in turn.

Finding the evidence

This involves searching the relevant academic literature and other sources such as government and other official reports, guidelines, etc. Many managers will have had some experience of literature searching through their own undergraduate and postgraduate study, but may not have approached the task very systematically. This is one area where we think you should try to make use of expertise in your own organization – the librarians or information scientists in education or training centres. They can help you with the following:

- *Which databases to search.* They can advise on what database to use and why (NHS Evidence, Medline, Cinahl, HMIC, Abi-Inform/Proquest, etc.) and how to access them and retrieve the full text of relevant materials.
- *What you are looking for.* They can also help with defining search terms (the words you look for and their likely synonyms). When people search the literature unaided, they often find either far too much literature (thousands of 'hits') or nothing at all, and you are aiming to use your search to focus on the most relevant and useful literature. On any topic, you are likely to find there is more literature out there than you can possibly read, and the more tightly you define the topic, the easier it is to focus on what is relevant. For example, a search on patient falls will locate masses of material, while a search for literature on preventing falls in elderly patients in toilets and bathrooms will be much more focused.
- *How to extend your search.* They can help you with 'snowballing' (looking at the reference lists of papers that you retrieve, to see if any of the literature they have cited is useful to you) and 'citation tracing' (looking on the databases for any papers that have cited something you regard as a key or seminal paper on the topic, and deciding again whether these citing papers are useful to you).
- *What to retrieve first.* It is common practice to scan the lists of papers and reports produced by searching, and to focus on reading items that from their titles and abstracts look highly relevant; on items that are themselves literature reviews; and on items like clinical guidelines developed by national organizations.

Reading, appraising and interpreting the literature

The aim of this second step is to take a systematic approach and to document what you do. If you simply read through a pile of PDFs, by the fourth or fifth one you won't be able to remember which said what and you will often end up reading them all over again. Aim to read each paper once, and summarize its key points (methods/data sources, key findings, and your comments or observations) in a structured table which then becomes your main source of evidence. You may choose to have columns in the table for theoretical, empirical and experiential evidence to make it easier to summarize and synthesize the findings later. For each item you read, you should ask yourself two questions:

- Is this good research – can I rely on its findings? Essentially, you need to work out whether the paper is based on sound research, rigorously conducted and appropriately described in terms that would allow someone else to repeat the study and the analysis. You will find learning resources on critical appraisal at the end of this chapter.
- What does this research mean – what are the key results? This might appear simple, but often papers do not describe their results clearly, or choose to foreground particular (more positive or interesting) findings and pay less attention to other (less positive) findings. Your job is to look past the hyperbole and focus on what the key results are.

This is generally an iterative process: search the literature; retrieve the most highly relevant and important items of literature; read, appraise and synthesize them; and decide whether you need to do further searches and retrieval. The question you should ask yourself is whether you have reached 'saturation' – in other words, would more searching be likely to uncover new and relevant findings. If your evidence framework is pretty full, and the last iteration of searching and appraisal you did yielded little new, you may decide that it is okay to stop there. If not, you might do some more searching and appraisal specifically aimed at filling in any evidence gaps.

Making it happen: two examples of evidence-based management

Let us return to two of the questions we outlined at the start of this chapter – and which you may have done some searching and reading about for Learning activity 2.1. We will seek to populate the framework shown in Table 2.4, using the evidence from some rapid and fairly high-level searching using Google Scholar.

Should we invest in robotic surgery for prostate cancer?

You might be faced with a highly articulate and persuasive urological surgeon, who argues the case for spending over £1 million on acquiring a state-of-the-art Da Vinci surgical robot. These machines allow surgeons to operate via a console, performing radical prostatectomies and other procedures laparascopically (through a number of access holes or ports in the skin) rather than through a large open incision. In the USA, since 2003 the use of this equipment has taken off and about 80 per cent of prostatectomies are now done using such machines. They are expensive, and operating times are longer, but the procedure is less invasive and some claim it results in fewer complications and better removal of cancerous tissue. Others suggest that there is little or no clinical benefit and the rapid spread of this technology is a product of plugging by manufacturers, competition for patients and technological enthusiasm among surgeons.

Reading the evidence summarized in Table 2.5 would at least provide you with some difficult questions to ask the surgeon who wants to buy a Da Vinci robot – how will he or she be trained to use it, how do they know they will achieve better outcomes with it, what evidence do they offer to support their arguments? The business case for a robot ought to include this kind of evidence summary. This is a difficult decision, as it might make good commercial sense to invest in robotic surgery because of patient demand, but it might not be clinically or cost effective. A compromise might be to make any investment contingent on some proper evaluation and audit of results.

Table 2.5 Robotic surgery for prostate cancer: a summary of the evidence

Theoretical evidence – how and why?	The idea is that the robot allows for greater accuracy and control in undertaking very fine incisions and movements and also provides the surgeon with extended vision, higher magnification and 3D imagery. This is meant to lead to higher quality surgery, fewer complications, shorter lengths of stay and better clinical outcomes.
	There are some alternative theories to consider. One would be that learning new procedures or ways of operating takes time, so any switch to robotic equipment could adversely affect quality during this training or learning period and this might be quite dependent on the individual surgeon's ability and on the quality and availability of training.
	Another theory would be that other ways to improve the quality of surgery exist, such as promoting greater specialization and surgical volume, and improving clinical audit, feedback and training, and these might be as effective and more cost effective.
Empirical evidence – what impact?	Very few randomized controlled trials have compared surgical outcomes for patients allocated at random to robot or non-robot surgery, and observational studies comparing patients who have had traditional or robotic surgery are often biased because patient selection means the two groups are not really comparable. Recent systematic reviews have found that there might be some benefit to reducing two key adverse outcomes of prostatectomy (erectile dysfunction and incontinence) but this is not well evidenced. Robot surgery is quite a bit more expensive. The learning curve for adopting robotic surgery is important – outcomes may be worse at first when surgeons start to use the robot and estimates of how many procedures they need to perform in order first to become safe and then to achieve better outcomes vary widely.
Experiential evidence – how do people respond?	Surgeons are enthusiastic about the adoption of the new technology, which has been driven by the manufacturer of the Da Vinci robots, and by patient demand generated by the perceived or claimed benefits of robot surgery (see, for example, http://www.roboticoncology.com/robotic-prostate-surgery/). Health economists and researchers are generally more sceptical about the benefits and there is a lack of research evidence to support arguments either way. There is some suggestion that the availability of robotic surgery may lower the threshold for surgical intervention (rather than non-surgical treatments or watchful waiting).

(continued)

References   Allan, C. and Ilic, D. (2015) Laparoscopic versus robotic-assisted radical prostatectomy for the treatment of localised prostate cancer: a systematic review, *Urology Internationalis* (DOI: 10.1159/000435861).

Tandogdu, Z., Vale, L., Fraser, C. and Ramsay, C. (2015) A systematic review of economic evaluations of the use of robotic assisted laparoscopy in surgery compared with open or laparoscopic srgery, *Applied Health Economics and Health Policy*, 13 (5): 457–67.

Tewari, A., Sooriakumaran, P., Bloch, D.A., Seshadri-Kreaden, U., Hebert, A.E. and Wiklund, P. (2012) Positive surgical margin and perioperative complication rates of primary surgical treatments for prostate cancer: a systematic review and meta-analysis comparing retropubic, laparoscopic, and robotic prostatectomy, *European Urology*, 62 (1): 1–15.

Would it be a good idea to recruit and deploy physician assistants to work alongside medical and nursing staff in our accident and emergency department?

In recent years, there has been a growth in the number of subsidiary professional roles intended to act in support of healthcare professionals. Traditionally, much of this skill-mix substitution took place across the boundaries between doctors and nurses, with the evolution of advanced nurse practitioners, nurse consultants, and extended training for nurses in everything from intravenous (IV) administration to anaesthetics. It also happened on the boundary between nurses and care staff without a professional training, such as healthcare assistants or healthcare workers, as nurses moved towards planning and directing the delivery of care and many tasks such as washing, feeding and dressing patients moved to healthcare assistants.

Physician assistants were originally an American innovation, created after the Vietnam War to supplement scarce medical staff and used mainly in underserved rural areas or with underserved populations in primary care. Physician assistants are required to undertake two years of training and they work under the supervision of a physician. There are around 67,000 physician assistants currently practising in the USA, many of whom have a prior degree or some clinical experience. In the last decade, there has been a series of experiments with importing some trained physician assistants to the UK and of establishing a small number of training programmes. Recently, the British government announced it intends to expand physician assistant training programmes. Growing the physician assistant workforce is considered a potential solution to the shortages of doctors in general practice. What often is not clear is just how much autonomy physician assistants have, how close the supervision of their practice is or should be and what impact their introduction has on both the quality and costs of care provision.

After considering the evidence summarized in Table 2.6, you might conclude that although physician assistants seem a promising idea, we really don't know how they might be best used to supplement scarce medical staff in an A&E department. However, the research will have helped you to identify a number of key factors in any initiative, chief among them: the support and engagement of senior medical staff and senior nursing staff; clarity about the scope of practice and supervisory arrangements for physician assistants; the need for physician assistants to be able to initiate diagnostic tests (pathology and radiology) and undertake some prescribing of medications; and the importance of evaluating and reviewing their introduction.

Learning activity 2.3

Return to the notes that you made for Learning activity 2.1, on one of the four questions listed below:

- Should we invest in robotic surgery for prostate cancer?
- What would be the costs and benefits of changing the hip prosthesis we use in hip replacement surgery?
- Would it be a good idea to recruit and deploy physician assistants to work alongside doctors in our accident and emergency department?
- What changes could we make to patient toileting procedures that would reduce the risks of falls in frail, elderly inpatients?

If you tackled one of the two questions we have addressed in this section (on robotic surgery and physician assistants), compare your notes with the summaries above. Did you find the same data sources? Did you reach the same or similar conclusions? If not, what lies behind any divergence?

If you tackled one of the two questions we have not dealt with in this section (on hip prostheses and patient falls), try redoing your search and appraisal. Use the process set out in this section and the evidence framework from Table 2.4 to produce a summary of the evidence like that shown in Tables 2.5 and 2.6. Does your search produce the same sources? Do you reach the same or similar conclusions? If not, what lies behind any divergence?

Table 2.6 Physician assistants in A&E departments: a summary of the evidence

Theoretical evidence – how and why?	The idea is that physician assistants or associates (a grade of staff long present in the USA but only fairly recently introduced in the UK and Europe) have a shorter training than doctors and cost less to employ. They work under the supervision of a physician and undertake some less complex tasks, freeing medical staff for other work and meaning fewer medical staff are required.
	The theory behind this is skill substitution and job redesign – and it is commonly argued that job redesign can result in increased efficiency and effectiveness, as less expensive and less qualified staff undertake appropriately less complex functions. Nurse/doctor substitution is a long established such area, and there is a parallel literature on assistants to pharmacists, physiotherapists, radiographers, etc.
	There are some challenges to the basic theory of substitution. One is that tasks cannot be simply disaggregated (for example, because care is provided holistically or because complexity is not known in advance or predictable). Another is that less skilled staff may perform tasks more slowly, so the savings from reduced salary costs may be set off by lower productivity. A third is that the time released for doctors is partly taken up by supervising physician assistants and is not actually used productively on other work and so, as a consequence, savings are not realized.

(continued)

Empirical evidence – what impact?	Evaluations of advanced nurse practitioners and physician assistants in various settings have been conducted – particularly in primary care and A&E departments. A recent study in primary care found physician assistants were acceptable to patients, there were no differences in quality of care or decision-making, and the average cost per consultation was lower than for a GP. But it was also cautioned that there are many factors to consider in implementing the physician assistant role that could bear on effectiveness and costs. A rather older study looking at both primary care and A&E deployments of physician assistants suggested the former were rather more successful, and noted that supervision was challenging and support for the role was less likely from some doctors.
Experiential evidence – how do people respond?	It is important to consider how changes to skill mix may affect work processes and professional identities of existing staff, especially as positive support for and engagement with these changes is needed, since existing staff will supervise and often route work or tasks to those in assistant roles.
References	Drennan, V., Halter, M., Brearley, S., Carneiro, W., Gabe, J., Gage, H. et al. (2014) Investigating the contribution of physician assistants to primary care in England: a mixed-methods study, *Health Services and Delivery Research*, 2 (16).
	Parle, J. and Ennis, J. (2015) Physician associates: the challenges facing general practice, *British Journal of General Practice*, 65 (634): 224–5.
	Woodin, J., McLeod, H., McManus, R. and Jelphs, K. (2005) *The Introduction of US-trained Physician Assistants to Primary Care and Accident and Emergency Departments in Sandwell and Birmingham*. Final Report. Birmingham: HSMC, University of Birmingham [http://www.birmingham.ac.uk/Documents/college-social-sciences/social-policy/HSMC/publications/2005/Evaluation-of-US-trained-Physician-Assistants.pdf].

Conclusions

This chapter began by arguing – perhaps a little simplistically – that managers in healthcare organizations should think more and act less. We certainly assert that a more reflective and evidence-based approach to decision-making is possible, and that it lies within the power of individual managers and leaders to try to use the ideas set out in this chapter. As in our two case examples, decisions are always going to be influenced by things other than the evidence. Commercial interests and political considerations often loom large in healthcare decisions about, for example, the setting up of new services or the reconfiguration of healthcare delivery provision. But at least if the evidence has been raised and considered, the organization is fully informed as it embarks on its chosen course of action and the key decision-makers – senior managers and clinicians – know what they are doing.

The other key theme in this chapter has been experimentation and evaluation. For so many innovations, the important question is not whether they work – or, at least, where the answer to that question is simply and unhelpfully 'sometimes'. The important question is how, why and when they work best, and in what settings or contexts they work (Pawson and Tilley, 1997). For this, understanding the evidence is a precursor to thinking through how you can pilot, test and evaluate the innovation in your own organization. Pfeffer and Sutton's (2006) imperative to treat your organization like an unfinished prototype, and encourage experimentation and learning, is at the heart of the practice of evidence-based management. Understanding and using tools such as realist evaluation is not the exclusive domain of researchers – managers and practitioners need to be evaluators too.

Being an evidence-based manager is not impossible, or even very difficult, but it does require a fundamental change of culture and mind-set, the acquisition and application of some analytical skills, and a commitment to experimentation and learning. But healthcare organizations, as information-rich, highly professionalised places populated by some very intelligent and empirically driven health professionals, are a great place in which to try it out.

Learning resources

Center for Evidence-Based Management: The CEBMa is a non-profit member organization dedicated to promoting evidence-based practice in the field of management. It provides a wealth of resources, training materials and networks through its website [http://www.cebma.org/].

NHS Evidence: The National Institute for Health and Care Excellence (NICE) runs a useful website called NHS Evidence, through which it collects and makes available research evidence on a wide range of healthcare topics. NICE's own clinical guidelines and other products feature alongside those from many other organizations. It is often a very good place to start your search for evidence [https://www.evidence.nhs.uk/].

Cochrane Collaboration: The Cochrane Collaboration is an independent network of researchers, professionals, patients, carers and people interested in health. It is a not-for-profit organization with contributors from more than 120 countries working together to produce credible, accessible health information that is free from commercial sponsorship and other conflicts of interest. Its main work is focused on producing systematic reviews that summarize the best available evidence generated through research to inform decisions about health [http://uk.cochrane.org/].

Campbell Collaboration: The Campbell Collaboration is a sister organization to Cochrane. It is also an international network of researchers and other stakeholders who produce systematic reviews of the effects of social interventions in crime and justice, education, international development and social welfare [http://www.campbellcollaboration.org/].

Critical Appraisal Skills Programme: Based in Oxford in the UK, the Critical Appraisal Skills Programme has developed workshops and tools for critical appraisal covering a wide range of research. It has also developed 'finding the evidence workshops', interactive and e-learning resources [http://www.casp-uk.net/].

For a useful review of evidence-based management resources, see: Lim, A., Qing, D.C.J. and Eyring, A.R. (2014) **Netting the evidence: a review of on-line evidence-based management resources,** *Academy of Management Learning*, 13 (3): 495–503.

References

Abrahamson, E. (1996) Managerial fashion, *Academy of Management Review*, 21 (1): 254–85.

Allan, C. and Ilic, D. (2015) Laparoscopic versus robotic-assisted radical prostatectomy for the treatment of localised prostate cancer: a systematic review, *Urology Internationalis* (DOI: 10.1159/000435861).

Bennis, W.G. and O'Toole, J. (2004) How business schools lost their way, *Harvard Business Review*, 83 (5): 96–104, 154.

Carroll, B. and Levy, L. (2008) Defaulting to management: leadership defined by what it is not, *Organization*, 15 (1): 75–96.

Denis, J.L., Lamothe, L. and Langley, A. (2001) The dynamics of collective leadership and strategic change in pluralistic organizations, *Academy of Management Journal*, 44 (4): 809–37.

Drennan, V., Halter, M., Brearley, S., Carneiro, W., Gabe, J., Gage, H. et al. (2014) Investigating the contribution of physician assistants to primary care in England: a mixed-methods study, *Health Services and Delivery Research*, 2 (16).

Flyvbjerg, B. (2001) *Making Social Science Matter: Why Social Inquiry Fails and How it Can Succeed Again*. Cambridge: Cambridge University Press.

Furusten, S. (1999) *Popular Management Books: How They are Made and what They Mean for Organisations*. London: Routledge.

Ghosal, S. (2005) Bad management theories are destroying good management practices, *Academy of Management Learning and Education*, 4 (1): 75–91.

Gibson, J.E. and Tesone, D.V. (2001) Management fads: emergence, evolution, and implications for managers, *Academy of Management Perspectives*, 15 (4): 122–33.

Glasby, J., Walshe, K. and Harvey, G. (2007) Making evidence fit for purpose in decision making: a case study of the hospital discharge of older people, *Evidence and Policy*, 3 (3): 425–37.

Greenhalgh, T., Howick, J. and Maskrey, N. (2014) Evidence based medicine: a movement in crisis?, *British Medical Journal*, 348: g3725.

Lim, A., Qing, D.C.J. and Eyring, A.R. (2014) Netting the evidence: a review of on-line evidence-based management resources, *Academy of Management Learning*, 13 (3): 495–503.

Mintzberg, H. (1973) *The Nature of Managerial Work*. New York: Harper & Row.

Mintzberg, H. (1989) *Mintzberg on Management: Inside Our Strange World of Organizations*. New York: Simon & Schuster.

Mintzberg, H. (2004) *Managers, not MBAs: A Hard Look at the Soft Practice of Managing and Management Development*. San Francisco, CA: Berrett Koehler.

Parle, J. and Ennis, J. (2015) Physician associates: the challenges facing general practice, *British Journal of General Practice*, 65 (634): 224–5.

Pawson, R. and Tilley, N. (1997) *Realistic Evaluation*. London: Sage.

Pfeffer, J. and Sutton, R.I. (2006) *Hard Facts, Dangerous Half Truths and Total Nonsense: Profiting from Evidence-based Management*. Boston, MA: Harvard Business Press.

Reay, T., Whitney, B. and Kohn, M.K. (2009) What's the evidence on evidence-based management?, *Academy of Management Perspectives*, November: 5–18.

Rousseau, D.M. (2006) Is there such a thing as 'evidence based management'?, *Academy of Management Review*, 31 (2): 256–69.

Sackett, D.L. and Rosenberg, W.M. (1995) The need for evidence-based medicine, *Journal of the Royal Society of Medicine*, 88 (11): 620–4.

Stewart, R. (1999) *The Reality of Management*. Oxford: Butterworth-Heinemann.

Tandogdu, Z., Vale, L., Fraser, C. and Ramsay, C. (2015) A systematic review of economic evaluations of the use of robotic assisted laparoscopy in surgery compared with open or laparoscopic srgery, *Applied Health Economics and Health Policy*, 13 (5): 457–67.

Tewari, A., Sooriakumaran, P., Bloch, D.A., Seshadri-Kreaden, U., Hebert, A.E. and Wiklund, P. (2012) Positive surgical margin and perioperative complication rates of primary surgical treatments for prostate cancer: a systematic review and meta-analysis comparing retropubic, laparoscopic, and robotic prostatectomy, *European Urology*, 62 (1): 1–15.

Tranfield, D. and Starkey, K. (1998) The nature, social organization and promotion of management research: towards policy, *British Journal of Management*, 9: 341–53.

Tranfield, D., Denyer, D. and Smart, P. (2003) Towards a methodology for developing evidence-informed management knowledge by means of systematic review, *British Journal of Management*, 14 (3): 207–22.

Trank, C.Q. and Rynes, S.L. (2003) Who moved our cheese? Reclaiming professionalism in business education, *Academy of Management Learning and Education*, 2 (2): 189–205.

van de Ven, A.H. (2007) *Engaged Scholarship: A Guide for Organizational and Social Research*. Oxford: Oxford University Press.

Walshe, K. and Rundall, T. (2001) Evidence based management: from theory to practice in healthcare, *Milbank Quarterly*, 79 (3): 429–57.

Woodin, J., McLeod, H., McManus, R. and Jelphs, K. (2005) *The Introduction of US-trained Physician Assistants to Primary Care and Accident and Emergency Departments in Sandwell and Birmingham*. Final Report. Birmingham: HSMC, University of Birmingham [http://www.birmingham.ac.uk/Documents/college-social-sciences/social-policy/HSMC/publications/2005/Evaluation-of-US-trained-Physician-Assistants.pdf].

Part 2

HEALTH SYSTEMS

The politics of healthcare and the health policy process: implications for healthcare management

Ruth Thorlby

Introduction

'Politics' concerns the exercise of power and the resolution of conflicts over resources (Moran, 1999; Freeman, 2000; Marmor, 2013). It is most conventionally thought of in relation to the activities of governments within nation states, the process by which certain groups, parties or individuals assume the authority to raise taxes and set and enforce the rules within which the activities of modern societies take place, from law and order to defence, education and health.

In all industrialized countries, the resources expended on health are large and growing, and the scope of conflicts over these resources is broad, involving a range of interest groups, ideas and institutions, the most central of which is the state. Even in health systems where the role of the state is traditionally thought of as limited, for example in countries where the bulk of healthcare is provided and purchased privately, the state remains a powerful player in setting the rules by which healthcare providers function, doctors are licensed and so on.

The politics of healthcare or the politics of health?

The politics of 'health' is potentially a much broader field than the politics of 'healthcare' (see Box 3.1). A person's health is shaped by a multitude of factors, such as their genetic inheritance, family, communities, work, income, food, physical environment, and so on, all of which are influenced by the activities of multiple players, including government, multinational companies and institutions (see Chapter 8).

Box 3.1   The politics of health or healthcare?

Some have argued that establishing the scope of 'politics' is in itself a political act in relation to health and healthcare (Bambra et al., 2005). Critics of those who have confined the analysis of politics to healthcare rather than health argue that it runs in the face of over four decades of evidence that health is shaped much more by social, economic and cultural factors than by access to medical treatments and services. Viewed from this perspective, a fully rounded study of the politics of health in relation to the acts of government and the state would need to combine analysis of all the different interests and influences on government policy, from the conditions of employment to the food industry, transport policy and welfare policy more broadly. Bambra and colleagues argue that the exclusion of wider health from the politics of healthcare also derives from the dominance of political science by those who use behavioural, institutional and rational choice theories, particularly in the United States.

This chapter will focus on the politics of healthcare rather than on that of health. The unit of analysis is the nation state and the interaction of different groups within it. However, the politics played out at a national level pervades individual healthcare providers: the politics within a large hospital, for example, are highly complex. Politics also shapes the interactions between an individual patient and clinician behind the closed door of the consulting room, but that is beyond the scope of this chapter.

Why is an understanding of politics important for healthcare managers?

Why a chapter on the politics of healthcare and the health policy process in a textbook about healthcare management? The chapters of this book contain an array of techniques, strategies and solutions that aim to equip those managing aspects of their health systems to do their job effectively. It might be argued that healthcare management is a process of selecting the right tools and strategies to solve a problem and then implementing them effectively, thus representing an essentially technical (albeit complex) challenge.

A healthcare manager with a good grasp of the politics of healthcare may be more able to understand why the healthcare system in their country operates the way it does, what policies might be possible or not, understand the behaviour of the different political actors – from a national level through to the teams around them in their own institutions – and have a grasp of the forces that might shape the future, from medical technology to the changes in populations and the ideas they hold.

The structure of this chapter

In the following section, we provide a brief description of the scope of the resources at play in a modern healthcare state and the common challenges faced by all countries in terms of medical technology and changing societies. We then introduce the main players that influence the way those resources are distributed in most industrialized societies: on the supply side, the professional groups (doctors, hospitals, pharmaceutical companies, insurers); on the demand side, patients, patient groups, and the public as voters and payers of taxes or insurance premiums; and in the middle, in a mediating role, the state or government. The size and configuration of these players varies between countries. We then explore the main groupings of health system politics.

Next, we consider the dynamics of change and healthcare policy-making, by describing some of the theories put forward by political scientists and sociologists to explain how policy-making happens within the healthcare politics of individual countries and why some policies succeed and others fail. Finally, we look ahead to the main drivers of change facing healthcare politics in the future.

In this chapter, we attempt to take an international perspective on the politics of health. Although we draw on examples from developed, industrialized countries, it is hoped that these insights will apply to countries at different economic and social stages of development, especially as the burden of non-communicable, chronic illness is becoming more prominent in many regions of the globe (Murray, 2015) (see Chapter 10 for more on chronic illness).

Conflict over what?

Two facts dominate the landscape of healthcare politics today: first, the increasing cost and complexity of healthcare (a process which began in the last century – see Chapter 4); and second, the enduring support for the idea of universal health coverage, in particular, the role of governments to ensure access to healthcare for entitled citizens when they need it, regardless of their income, with limited or no financial barriers (Marmor et al., 2012).

Direct expenditure on healthcare

The story of the latter half of the twentieth century is one of increasingly large sums of money spent both publicly and privately on 'healthcare'. The different drivers of this increase are more fully explored in Chapter 4, but it is the striking upward trend since 1960 in the percentages of national wealth spent on healthcare (gross domestic product or GDP) in all industrialized nations that is important here (see Chapter 4 for details).

As economies have grown, these percentages have translated into huge sums in cash terms. Let us take one example from Europe – Germany. The total estimated spend on healthcare in 2013 (public and private) was $411.5 billion (or 11.3 per cent of GDP) (Deloitte, 2015). In 2011, 4.9 million people were employed in the healthcare sector (11.2 per cent of all people employed in Germany): 3.3 million people employed directly in healthcare and a further 1.4 million working in related services, such as cleaners and kitchen staff (Busse and Blumel, 2014).

The scale of activity in modern healthcare is, historically speaking, a relatively recent phenomenon. As Moran and others have described, doctors and hospitals were places to be avoided until the end of the nineteenth century, when innovations in surgery and medical technology transformed hospitals from places that were 'receptacle for the sick poor, and a dangerous source of disease', into institutions that were 'central to the practice of new scientific medicine' (Moran, 2000). Medicine and healthcare, particularly the care delivered in hospitals, have become highly valued attributes of modern societies. As Moran puts it: '[h]ealthcare facilities in modern industrial societies are great concentrations of economic resources – and because of that they are also the subject of political struggle' (1999: 1).

The reason that this political struggle is so profound in healthcare is partly because of its interaction with the other crucial legacy of the late nineteenth and first half of the twentieth century: the near-universal adoption of the idea of healthcare as a 'special' good, a service which citizens should be able to access regardless of their income, and which governments – as representatives of the collective will of societies – have responsibility to organize. By the middle of the twentieth century, most developed countries had established universal access to healthcare, funded collectively, either by general taxation or social insurance.

As the twentieth century progressed and we entered a new millennium, and the range and cost of healthcare treatments and technologies proliferated together with extended life spans, states have been confronted with the increasingly difficult challenge of deciding how much to spend on healthcare for their entitled populations. Even before the recessions in the 1990s and 2008 put public spending under pressure in many countries, governments were already confronting a systematic mismatch between the potential for growth in the cost of healthcare and the assumptions about what was reasonable to spend on healthcare versus other services (see Chapter 5).

Conflict between whom? The main players

The state

At the heart of the political struggle is the state. The sums of money spent on healthcare by modern societies are vast and central to most people's idea of 'politics' is the role of government: indeed, the financing, regulation and, in some countries, the provision of healthcare represents one of the largest activities of modern states. Even in countries where private providers and insurers have a large role (e.g. the United States), the government is still a major player in regulating the market, licensing healthcare providers and professionals and setting the rules within which competition in the market takes place.

The central role of the state in healthcare is a recent development: until the eighteenth century, states were concerned primarily with raising taxes for the purposes of defence against external enemies and law enforcement at home (Freeman, 2000). As Richard Freeman puts it, 'by 1980 almost all European states had guaranteed access to [to healthcare] almost all of their citizens. In 1880, none of them did' (2000: 14).

Stewardship

Traditional approaches to describe the role of the state in healthcare tended to diverge at this point, depending on whether a country was thought of as having a 'hierarchical' or command-and-control type of government, or a more market-based approach to financing and providing healthcare. The former implied a state that defined the rules, allocated resources and directly purchased or provided healthcare; the latter implied a state that aimed to regulate and incentivize private purchasers and providers. Since most countries exhibit a mix of approaches, an alternative way of thinking about the activities of the state is set out by Smith et al. (2012) deriving from the concept of 'stewardship' of the health system by national governments (WHO, 2000). According to this framework, governments have a responsibility in three key areas: priority setting, performance monitoring and holding to account. These dimensions of government stewardship in healthcare are set out in Table 3.1, together with examples.

The professions

If the state is considered to be one of the most important players, the countervailing force has been the organized power of the medical 'profession'. By the middle of the twentieth century, doctors as a profession were considered to be the most important players in European health systems (Freeman, 2000), enjoying both affluence and authority not only on a personal level but also collectively. Their professional organizations had negotiated both autonomy for individual clinicians to practise with a minimum level of interference and control over the market in terms of who could be called a doctor.

The power of the medical profession has been challenged in the last few decades, with the increasing pressure on health spending forcing encroachment into the clinical autonomy of doctors, with the state enforcing prices, setting fees for reimbursement and scrutinizing and often controlling the amount of medical care to be given in each individual clinical encounter, together with clinical guidelines or other evidence-based recommendations of best practice.

Role of professional organizations

Relationships between the organized medical profession and the state in many countries can typically be characterized as deeply oppositional. Often, the creation of universal healthcare

Table 3.1 Dimensions of government stewardship in healthcare

Priority setting	Performance monitoring	Accountability mechanisms
• Formulating overall goals/ vision for the nation's healthcare system • Translating goals into actions, e.g. via targets • Allocating resources between regions/populations/services • Specifying a 'basket' of healthcare entitlements • Setting quality standards for treatment • Establishing mechanisms for 'cost-effectiveness' analysis	• Systematic data collection from healthcare providers • Analysis and dissemination of data to providers and consumers • Data can include information tracking population health, healthcare safety, treatment pathways, volume of treatments or drugs given, cost of treatments of drugs, waiting times for treatment, etc.	• Ensuring markets deliver adequate choice and competition • Democratic processes that allow the public to voice their opinion on performance • Using direct incentives through payment or accreditation systems • Regulation of providers and professionals

Source: Adapted from Smith et al. (2012).

was met by hostility and resistance from doctors, who believed their autonomy to practise – and charge freely for their services – to be under threat.

In Canada, doctors in several provinces pushed back against the gradual nationalization of healthcare, culminating in an ultimately unsuccessful 23-day doctors' strike in Saskatchewan in 1962 after the province became the first to introduce a single-payer system (Marchildon and Schrijvers, 2011). In New Zealand, similar resistance was partially successful – as universal healthcare was introduced in the late 1930s, primary care doctors mobilized to preserve their autonomy and retain the right to charge their patients individually (Cumming et al., 2014). Germany, one of the first countries to introduce a form of universal healthcare in 1883, saw the medical profession unite to try to limit the power of social health insurance funds after the fact, in the early years of the twentieth century (Busse and Blumel, 2014).

Despite these episodes of profound polarization, most political scientists (e.g. Moran, Harrison and McDonald) describe the relationship between these two players as deeply intertwined and mutually dependent. This can most easily be understood by describing the origins and the development of doctors' professional groups in a few example countries.

United Kingdom

The professional organization of doctors substantially predates the emergence of the modern state. In the UK, the College of Physicians (later to become the Royal College of Physicians) was founded in 1518 (Harrison and McDonald, 2008). It was created to license practitioners of medicine, and in 1563 it laid down a set of professional requirements, including undertaking training and examinations, refraining from criticizing other members, and not working with unlicensed physicians. A second College was formed in 1540 for surgeons (later to become the Royal College of Surgeons) and apothecaries gained their Royal Charter in 1617.

Three important features are already visible from the early history of these professional groups: first, they all demonstrate the hallmarks of 'self-regulation' (i.e. retaining the right to decide who is to be called a 'doctor' or 'surgeon'); second, the source of this authority is the state (at this point the monarchy); and third, there is already evidence of a hierarchy between the professional groups. Formal state licensing did not arrive in the UK until the nineteenth century, with the creation of the General Medical Council in 1858, which maintained a register of 'registered medical practitioners', and specified the content of medical training (Harrison and McDonald, 2008).

A fourth feature of medical professional power also emerged in the nineteenth century, reflecting the lobbying or union function of representing doctors' interests. In the UK, this took the form of the Provincial Medical and Surgical Society, which become the British Medical Association (BMA) in 1855.

International experience

Most countries have physician organizations that in some shape or form perform the functions of licensing practitioners, on the one hand, and represent doctors' interests, on the other. There are considerable variations in how concentrated the power of these professional bodies is, or whether they are split along specialty lines, or regionally. Table 3.2 draws on

Freeman (2000) and the *Health Systems in Transition* series to summarize the attributes of medical organizations in five countries.

As is evident from Table 3.2, there are plenty of differences between countries in how their doctors' interests are represented. Although these differences are not trivial – indeed, they have important consequences for how policy emerges (discussed below) – it is striking that all countries have some form of body that licenses and protects doctors' interests. In other words, the drive for doctors to pursue their collective self-interest through self-regulation seems universal. There is considerable debate among political scientists and sociologists about how unique doctors are in this respect compared with other professionals. Theorists such as Freidson have argued that the most important variable of 'professionalism' is the extent to which it is dominant and a professional can gain control over their own work without interference

Table 3.2 Medical organizations in five countries

Country	Professional licensing	Union representation
France	Ordre des Médecins: national, regional and departmental. Registers physicians, oversees guidelines, and board of peers for disciplinary and ethical matters.	Multiple unions for self-employed doctors, fragmented along geographic and occupational lines. Separate Union of Hospital Physicians (Syndicat National des Praticiens Hopitaliers) for doctors employed by public hospitals. Learned societies also play a lobbying role.
Germany	Licensing, ethics, discipline and continuing education handled at regional state level by physician's chambers (Ärztekammer). Doctors are legally obliged to become members. To treat patients under statutory sickness insurance funds, doctors must also be members of the regional Association of Sickness Fund Doctors.	Hartmannbund represents doctors in independent local practice, acting as an interest group in the policy-making process, Marburger Bund represents hospital doctors with a direct trade union function, as hospital doctors are salaried employees. Many other specialist groups exist and have a lobbying role.
Italy	Doctors must be licensed both nationally by the Ministry of Health and at a provincial level by one of over 100 medical associations (Ordini dei Medici), which are semi-public and carry out disciplinary actions. National umbrella organization (FNOM) based in Rome establishes ethics code.	Doctors' interests have traditionally been represented via political parties (especially Christian Democrats) rather than medical professional organizations.

(continued)

Table 3.2 (*continued*)

Country	Professional licensing	Union representation
Sweden	National Board of Health and Welfare licenses doctors. Disciplinary measures, including withdrawal of the right to practise, are handled by a separate Medical Responsibility Board.	Swedish Medical Association (Sveriges Läkarförbund) represents the majority of doctors of all disciplines, with over 90 per cent membership rate.
UK	Doctors are licensed by the General Medical Council (GMC), which also licenses medical schools and conducts disciplinary hearings. Specialist medical qualifications are approved by the respective Royal Colleges.	The British Medical Association represents all doctors in contract and pay negotiations with government, with a membership of over two-thirds of practising doctors.

Sources: Freeman (2000), de Vries et al. (2009), Chevreul et al. (2010), Anell et al. (2012), Busse and Blumel (2014).

from outside and win the trust of governments and consumers in the process (Freidson, 1970, in Harrison and McDonald, 2008: 30).

Doctors have a unique standing with society and health systems because of their connection to science and technology and their contact with individual patients (often at crucial points in their lives) (Moran, 1999), and for several decades in the last century were able to function in most countries with minimal interference from the state. However, as the economic conditions facing developed countries changed after the oil crisis of the 1970s, governments everywhere came under pressure to contain the costs of healthcare, just as the costs and technological innovations of healthcare itself were rapidly expanding. As Moran as argued, the mutual interconnectedness of state and professions, which had always been present, meant that the politics of healthcare took a different turn and the state has grown in its capacity to 'see into' the work of the professions, both directly through surveillance of doctors as data on their activity, costs and quality of those activities has grown, and indirectly through the institutions of surveillance (Moran, 1999).

Other interest groups

While the presence of doctors' professional associations is common to all health systems, the political force of other entities, such as hospitals and insurance companies, varies according to the anatomy of the individual health system in question. In countries dominated by private providers, hospital associations have considerable lobbying power. For example, the American Hospital Association represents over 5000 hospitals in the United States, raising nearly $80 million in membership dues in 2014.

Learning activity 3.1

Identify the professional organizations in your country.

- Who disciplines doctors – is it their peers?
- Who licenses doctors?
- Are these membership organizations?
- If so, who pays for them? How many and what kinds of doctor are members?
- Do they have the power to strike?

Having identified these organizations, make an assessment of their influence on the policy and direction of the healthcare system in your country. Do you detect any change in this influence over the past decade?

All countries represent potential markets for pharmaceutical products and medical equipment and the large pharmaceutical companies in particular act as powerful interest groups at both national and regional level. Determining the scale and nature of their influencing activity varies depending on whether countries require disclosure of lobbying of policy-makers. In the United States, which requires disclosure of money spent on influencing policy-makers, $229 million was spent in 2014 by the pharmaceuticals and health products industry according to official figures (Center for Responsive Politics, 2014). In the European Union, by contrast, disclosure is voluntary: €40 million was declared by pharmaceutical companies on activities to influence decision-making in the European Union in 2012, but campaign groups believe the actual figure may be higher (Health Action International, 2012).

Users and the public

The role of patients and citizens in the politics of healthcare is complex and evolving, and is discussed in more detail in Chapter 18. Most political scientists draw a distinction between the role played by individuals as patients and their broader role as voters and payers of taxes and social or private insurance contributions that fund health services.

The relationship between individual patients and their physicians has traditionally been characterized as hierarchical, with most of the power being in the hands of the physician: patients visit a doctor because they do not know what is wrong with them, what treatment is required or for how long. This essentially 'passive' conceptualization of patients has been challenged over recent decades with the emergence of patient and user groups, often associated with specific diseases or conditions. The comparative study of these groups internationally is still in its infancy, but a recent overview of such groups in ten European countries found considerable variation in how they function and are funded. In some countries, such as the UK, Sweden and Finland, health consumer and patient groups were 'politically mature' and heavily engaged with policy-makers, while at the other end of the spectrum, as in Austria for example, organizations were primarily focused on self-help and giving assistance (Baggott and Forster, 2008).

The collective voice of citizens is most obviously exercised through democratic processes, but how directly this impacts on healthcare and health policy-making varies considerably between individual health systems. In centralized national health systems such as the English NHS, health is often a dominant issue in general election campaigns, although manifestos rarely contain much policy detail. Direct democratic influence may be stronger where health systems are devolved, as in Sweden for example, where health is administered by twenty-one county councils and health spending accounts for over 90 per cent of municipal council budgets. Council elections in Sweden are held every 4 years (Anell et al., 2012). Italy's national health service also has a devolved structure, with twenty-one different regions controlling the administration of local health services. Although these systems are professionally managed, after the role of politicians was limited by reforms in 1992–93, professional politicians still exercise considerable influence over the appointments of senior managers in local health services (Ferré et al., 2014).

A third strand of user influence has been fostered by policy-makers in the past two decades, with the evolution of reform policies that actively encourage patients to make choices and act more like consumers in other markets, as in Denmark and England (Dent and Pahor, 2015). Patients in Denmark have had a choice of hospital since 1993: while patients are satisfied with having a right to choose, evaluations suggest that in practice very few choose to travel further for their care (Vrangbaek, 2015).

Varieties/types of healthcare system – the consequences of politics?

We have set out above the range of possible political actors in healthcare systems. Although many countries face similar challenges (rising costs, populations living longer and more chronic disease) and the state plays some major role in all of them, the actual form of their healthcare systems is very different, the product of historical circumstance.

There is a literature which attempts to classify healthcare system 'types' across nations, much of it rooted in an older political science of classifying welfare states according to archetypes, such as laissez-faire liberalism (e.g. United States) or Bismarckian insurance states (e.g. Germany). Esping-Anderson (1990) built on this by grouping nations into three different welfare 'clusters'. In the liberal cluster are states with a strong work ethic and welfare systems characterized by means-testing and strict entitlement rules (e.g. the United States and Australia). A second cluster, exemplified by Germany, France and Italy, consists of conservative, corporatist welfare states, with a broader set of state-organized entitlements than the first cluster, but preserving traditional family structures through the exclusion of non-working wives from insurance coverage and under-developed childcare. The third cluster, 'social democratic', has universal entitlement at its heart, and is underpinned by equality of rights rather than equality of minimum standards (Esping-Anderson, 1990).

Moran (2000) and Wendt et al. (2009), among others, have attempted to refine these basic welfare state categories in order to better reflect the complexity of the politics of the healthcare state. Unlike simple cash transfers, delivering healthcare requires a huge organizational, professional and economic infrastructure between funder and recipient. Power struggles, and the exercise of political control also occur within this system, not just at its entry point. Wendt et al. (2009) define three different dimensions of control over healthcare systems:

- *Financing* – is it the state, private individuals or insurers, or non-governmental social organizations that obtain and provide the money for healthcare?
- *Health service provision* – is it state bodies, private firms or professionals, or non-governmental social organizations that actually deliver and own the means of delivering healthcare?
- *Regulation or governance* – is it the state, private individuals or insurers, or non-governmental social organizations that determine how the system is run, set targets and priorities, and govern relations with professionals, technology policy and contracts?

Moran also draws attention to the question of who governs 'consumption' by determining who can access healthcare and how costs are controlled. Both his classification and Wendt's suggest as reference points 'ideal types', where all three dimensions are controlled by the same element of the system (Burau and Blank, 2006). For instance, England is generally seen as a pure state system. Its National Health Service is funded almost entirely from central taxation and the state either directly controls, or owns at arm's length, the NHS trusts that provide most hospital care and other secondary care – although primary care doctors are independent contractors. Other frequently cited examples are the United States as an ideal private type and Germany as an ideal example of social insurance. However, both of these possess key elements that do not fit their supposed 'type', even more so than the English system.

To account for this reality, Wendt's typology (Wendt et al., 2009) allows for 'mixed systems', where the three dimensions of control are divided between two or all three of the private, state and social groups. This gives a potential total of twenty-seven different types of health system. Table 3.3 provides three examples of different mixes of control.

Table 3.3 Examples of countries' mix of control of their health system

	Regulation	Financing	Provision
United States	**Private/state** Market competition is relied on generally to drive quality and determine financial viability. Voluntary and state boards also accredit providers. Insurance is now federally regulated and mandated.	**Private/state** With most healthcare paid for by tax-subsidized private insurance, the USA is the archetypally privately funded system. However, the role of state funding has grown over decades, covering primarily poorer and older people.	**Private/social** Hospitals are mostly either charitable or for-profit, with the proportion of each varying by state. Primary care is provided by private clinics or not-for-profit community centres.

(continued)

Table 3.3   (*continued*)

	Regulation	Financing	Provision
New Zealand	**State** Overall strategy, targets for improvement and standards for providers are set by the government.	**State** The government pays the majority of costs from general taxation, although patients also pay some out-of-pocket charges.	**State/private** Public sector bodies provide most hospital and community care, with some private clinics. Primary care is provided through privately owned practices.
Japan	**State/private** Patients have a wide choice of provider but not of insurer, which is usually determined by employment. Insurers are regulated by central government. Providers are regulated for basic standards of safety by central government. Local government regulates other aspects.	**Social** The majority of Japanese hospitals, which dominate the health system, are run on a not-for-profit basis. However, local government and the private sector also run significant numbers.	**Mixed** The central government, municipal governments and voluntary organizations linked to different professions and corporations all provide health insurance for different groups. Patients also contribute copayments at the point of use, at up to 30 per cent of total cost.

Sources: Adapted from Rice et al. (2013), Cumming et al. (2014) and Tatara and Okamoto (2009) respectively.

In practice, most health systems in the developed world tend to have either private or state provision and to have predominantly state regulation (Wendt et al., 2009). Wendt et al. (2009) argue that this categorization is a useful way to gauge the depths of reforms, based on whether they move systems across the category boundaries. Only truly historic reforms will shift multiple dimensions, so that an ideal or mostly private-based system becomes mostly public. The 1938 creation of a national health system in New Zealand is an example of such major and profound reform (although primary care doctors opted out and remained in the private sector).

More modest or gradual reforms might be understood as a shift within one dimension. In 2006, the Netherlands introduced a system of 'managed competition', where the state stood in favour of market competition between privately owned insurers, following a long-term and incremental process of reform (Schäfer et al., 2010). However, treating this as a full shift in regulation from state to private would be an oversimplification: government bodies now had a new role regulating a complex market-based yet publicly funded health system.

Learning activity 3.2

Using the classification of state, social and private control, think about which institutions in your country's heath system exert most influence on: (1) the financing of healthcare; (2) the provision of healthcare; and (3) the regulation of healthcare.

- What recent or ongoing struggles have there been about changing who controls these elements of your country's healthcare system?
- What single change to each of the three dimensions above would you propose for your country's health system?

Health politics in action: policy-making

This section addresses the question of what drives health reforms, what factors determine whether policies succeed in some countries at certain points in time and why they fail in others.

Understanding the role of political institutions on policy-making

One perspective on understanding the role of political institutions on health policy-making and interest-group bargaining is set out by Ellen Immergut, in a study comparing Sweden, France and Switzerland (Immergut, 1992). In comparing the process of legislating for universal health insurance in the three countries, she argues that it is important to understand the design of each country's unique political systems and, in particular, the 'veto points' available – including to interest groups – for blocking or modifying proposed legislative changes.

In Sweden's parliamentary democracy, the first chamber of parliament represents an important veto point, but in practice stable parliamentary majorities underpinned by stable voting patterns means that there is no real veto point for opponents of national health insurance and the government has been able to enact strong reforms, including regulating doctors' fees and restricting the rights of doctors to practise privately. The absence of a powerful veto point shaped the behaviour of Sweden's Medical Association, which has tended to take a cooperative stance, channelled through 'participation in expert commissions and written responses to government proposals' (Immergut, 1992: 223) while minimizing the likelihood of a rival doctors' professional association breaking away, as it would have further limited access to the executive.

In France, reforms to create a universal national insurance scheme resulted in many of the features of the Swedish system, including regulation of doctors' fees, but the process took far longer because it was shaped by a different democratic reality. The power of the executive government was dependent on the support of parliamentary coalition partners, who behaved opportunistically and vetoed legislation in parliament. Doctors' professional interests could be pursued on a wider front than in Sweden, with doctors active as politicians and able to influence directly the leadership of some of the parties.

In Switzerland, the evolution of health policy was shaped by referendum politics, which represented the most important veto point, allowing direct electoral influence over the actions of the executive (referendum verdicts could often run counter to the parliamentary election results). Interest groups could call for referendum, giving minorities powerful influence over policy-making, and Immergut argues that the resulting shape of Switzerland's health system – government-subsidized health insurance but with a much more regressive distribution of coverage than in Sweden – is the product of this political system, which enabled professional doctors' groups to resist state interference.

Path dependency

One of the frameworks used by political scientists to explain why radical policy change does or does not happen is the concept of 'path dependency'. This theory, originally derived from the economic history literature, suggests that policy decisions made at a particular time shape the likelihood of subsequent decisions. As time goes by, these decisions shape the path to the future, increasing the probability of continuing on the same path and decreasing the probability of deviating from it. Radical reform is never impossible but becomes increasingly unlikely (Wilsford, 1994). The best example of this, as applied by political scientists, is the spectacular failure of the United States to deliver universal access to healthcare for its citizens, while such access was standard across many other industrialized nations in the decades of the twentieth century.

David Wilsford (1994) compared the radical reform of the NHS in the 1990s by the UK Conservative government led by Margaret Thatcher, which introduced a purchaser–provider split and the idea of 'fundholding' GPs, with the failure of the Clinton plan to reform US healthcare. Wilsford argues that the structural characteristics of the UK health system should have inclined it to remain on an incrementalist path, with little likelihood of radical reform. This is because the UK has a very hierarchical health system, characterized by non-autonomous decision agents (civil servants and government-employed health service managers) and a powerful professional body (the British Medical Association, BMA) with strong representation on NHS decision-making bodies.

Wilsford believes that the political environment provided a unique opportunity for change: in 1987, Margaret Thatcher had just won her second term in office and was popular with the electorate. She used her power to bypass the normal policy-making processes and set up a small unit in No. 10 Downing Street (the Policy Unit) that deliberately excluded the BMA and medical Royal Colleges (professional associations). The creation of a 'managerial' interest by the introduction of general management in hospitals in the mid-1980s also helped Thatcher to leverage another source of support in the NHS. The public's wariness of any change to the NHS was palliated by the reassurance that it would remain free at the point of use even if it adopted some market-derived principles. Wilsford argues that this opportunity was seized at the right moment yet was transient in nature: by 1992, Thatcher's political authority had been undermined and the reforms would not have had much traction.

Clinton attempted a similarly large 'non-incremental' reform but failed. This is partly because, as David Wilsford puts it, the American political institutions 'are not designed to accommodate large-scale reform; in fact they are designed to actively thwart it' (1994: 271).

The Canadian political scientist Carolyn Tuohy has refined the path dependency framework further, by focusing attention on the 'windows of opportunity' that open up to politicians and policy-makers and their interaction with the 'logic' of previous reforms and their impact on structures and institutions within healthcare politics (Tuohy, 1999). She argues that when the 'relatively rare conditions' opened a window of opportunity in the early 1990s for the UK Prime Minister to take action, the internal 'logic' of the NHS system both facilitated and tempered the impact of the reform. On the one hand, the hierarchical character of the NHS facilitated the top-down implementation of these apparently radical reforms, through the traditional mechanisms of guidance and directives from the centre. On the other hand, the traditionally collegial nature of relationships within the local NHS and the relatively primitive level of data on clinical outcomes and costs meant that many of the contracts between the new purchasers and providers looked very like the old 'block contracts' and agreements that they were meant to replace.

In the case of the United States, Tuohy argues that an earlier failure to use the window of opportunity in 1965 to press on with universal health coverage, led to only the most vulnerable getting health protection. The meant that momentum was lost to extend coverage to everyone in the ensuing decades, and allowed the 'logic' of a private market dominated system to play out (Tuohy, 1999: 121). But the logic of the private market delivered a twist of its own after the failure of the Clinton reforms in the 1990s. While the federal government might have failed to implement a universal plan, it pressed on with its reform of the public system, by adopting a prospective payment scheme for Medicare, which limited the amount providers could receive per case. Tuohy describes how providers shifted their costs onto private payers, which 'woke the sleeping dog of private finance' as costs escalated. This precipitated private payers to change their payment systems, releasing the entrepreneurial force of for-profit firms, which, unlike the state, were not committed to maintaining collegial relationships with professional groups, and developed a range of mechanisms to restrict the professional autonomy of clinicians.

Learning activity 3.3

Think of some change that you would like to be made to your country's healthcare system.

- What would most likely prevent it from happening?
- In which circumstances might it become possible for it to happen?

Map out a path of dependency for a previous change that has taken place in your healthcare system, using the approach suggested by Wilsford or Tuohy.

Conclusion: the future of healthcare politics

Theodore Marmor has neatly summarized the politics of healthcare as the process of 'resolving – or at least attenuating – conflicts about resources, rights and values' (2013: 407). These conflicts are likely to grow in the future, resulting in healthcare remaining as one of the most dynamic arenas in modern states for politics to play out in.

The scope for the diagnosis and treatment of diseases will increase, particularly as genomic medicine develops (see Chapter 6). These new technologies for fighting illness (chronic and acute) will result in longer life spans and longer periods in a person's life in which disease can be detected and treated. But this raises its own challenges, as research is beginning to reveal the scale of multi-morbidity, especially in older populations (Barnett et al., 2012), and expose the limitations of clinical guidelines based on single disease models (Guthrie et al., 2012). The care of frailer, older patients may enhance the need for the discretionary autonomy of clinicians, particularly generalists, but it will also require access to better non-medical social care, which has been considered beyond the scope of universal healthcare services in many countries to date (social care is discussed more fully in Chapter 13).

These trends will increase the possibilities of what clinicians are able to offer patients, but at the same time will intensify the search by governments (and all those paying for care) to understand value, monitor outcomes and set reasonable limits, especially if healthcare remains in the wider public's mind as something that should be available to all with minimal financial barriers.

In parallel, the huge growth of data collected on the incidence of disease and the use of services, coupled with better IT systems, will increase the ability of those managing healthcare to assess the volumes of medical care given and its outcome. Tuohy (1999) and Smith et al. (2012) emphasize the importance of IT in healthcare politics, the growth of information about what individual clinicians are doing and patient outcomes and experience on a massive scale. This allows, in theory, greater scrutiny of professionals. However, accountability based on such availability of data and outcomes has so far been limited – that is, there are large amounts of data but the will to use and act on it appears often to be lacking.

From the perspective of healthcare managers, an awareness of the institutions, values and interests that underlie healthcare politics is invaluable as a means of shedding light on the day-to-day tasks of managing and improving healthcare. At any one time, clinicians are making myriad decisions about resources as they treat their patients. Efforts to contain costs and improve quality will often encroach on clinical autonomy and patients will want access to treatments that will both prolong and improve the quality of life. An ability to think through the broader politics of healthcare management will help disentangle what sort of approaches might work to improve care, the level at which problems need to be solved (for example, what is in the control of local managers to change, and what will require regional and national action), and how best to work with – rather than against – the grain of society's values.

Learning activity 3.4

Take an example of a recent major new health policy introduced into your country.

- Given what you know of the politics of your country, what seems to have worked with this new policy and why?
- What seems not to have worked?
- If you were giving advice to policy-makers, what would you suggest that they do differently if they were to start again and introduce this health policy?

Learning resources

World Health Organization *Health Systems in Transition* series: A series of reports describing individual health systems; also reflects on policy developments and reform initiatives. They are updated on a regular basis and many are available in an official language other than English [http://www.euro.who.int/en/about-us/partners/observatory/publications/health-system-reviews-hits].

OECD Health Policies and Data: Offers extensive background data on health spending, policies and systems, as well as information about wider social policy such as family support, pensions and migration [http://www.oecd.org/els/health-systems/].

***The Guardian* health policy section:** This UK-based newspaper – which also publishes Australian and American online versions – has extensive analysis of health politics and policy [http://www.theguardian.com/politics/health].

***New England Journal of Medicine* politics of health reform section:** This US-based academic journal regularly publishes papers exploring single-country and international comparative health policy [http://www.nejm.org/medical-research/politics-of-health-care-reform].

***Milbank Quarterly*:** This US-based academic journal publishes many analytical and comparative studies of health policy and politics [http://www.milbank.org/the-milbank-quarterly].

References

Anell, A., Glenngård, A.H. and Merkur, M. (2012) Sweden: health system review, *Health Systems in Transition*, 14 (5): 1–159.

Baggott, R. and Forster, R. (2008) Health consumer and patients' organizations in Europe: towards a comparative analysis, *Health Expectations*, 11 (1): 85–94.

Bambra, C., Fox, D. and Scott-Samuel A (2005) Towards a politics of health, *Health Promotion International*, 20 (2): 187–93.

Barnett, K., Mercer, S., Norbury, M., Watt, G., Wyke, S. and Guthrie, B. (2012) Epidemiology of multimorbidity and implications for healthcare, research, and medical education: a cross sectional study, *Lancet*, 380: 37–43.

Burau, V. and Blank, R. (2006) Comparing health policy: an assessment of typologies of health systems, *Journal of Comparative Policy Analysis, Research and Practice*, 8 (1): 63–7.

Busse, R. and Blumel, M. (2014) Germany: health system review, *Health Systems in Transition*, 16 (2): 1–296.

Center for Responsive Politics (2014) *Health: Lobbying 2014* [http://www.opensecrets.org/industries/lobbying.php?cycle=2014&ind=H].

Chevreul, K., Durande-Zaleski, I., Bahrami, S., Hernández-Quevedo, C. and Mladovsky, P. (2010) France: health systems review, *Health Systems in Transition*, 12 (6): 1–291.

Cumming, J., McDonald, J., Barr, C., Martin, G., Gerring, Z. and Daube, J. (2014) New Zealand: health system review, *Health Systems in Transition*, 4 (2): 1–244.

de Vries, H., Sanderson, P., Janta, B., Rabinovich, L., Archontakis, F., Ismail, S. et al. (2009) *International Comparison of Ten Medical Regulatory Systems*. Technical Report. Cambridge: RAND Europe [http://www.gmc-uk.org/International_Comparison_of_Ten_Medical_Regulatory_Systems_final_report.pdf_25404378.pdf].

Deloitte (2015) *2015 Health Care Outlook: Germany* [http://www2.deloitte.com/content/dam/Deloitte/global/Documents/Life-Sciences-Health-Care/gx-lshc-2015-health-care-outlook-germany.pdf].

Dent, M. and Pahor, M. (2015) Patient involvement in Europe – a comparative framework, *Journal of Health Organization and Management*, 29 (5): 546–55.

Esping-Anderson, G. (1990) *The Three Worlds of Welfare Capitalism*. Princeton, NJ: Princeton University Press.

Ferré, F., Giulio de Belvis, A., Valerio, L., Longhi, S., Lazzari, A., Fattore, G. et al. (2014) Italy: health system review, *Health Systems in Transition*, 16 (4): 1–168.

Freeman, R. (2000) *The Politics of Health in Europe*. Manchester: Manchester University Press.

Guthrie, B., Payne, K., Alderson, P., McMurdo, M. and Mercer, S. (2012) Adapting clinical guidelines to take account of multimorbidity, *British Medical Journal*, 345: e6341.

Harrison, S. and McDonald, R. (2008) *The Politics of Healthcare in Britain*. London: Sage.

Health Action International and Corporate Europe Observatory (2012) *Divide & Conquer: A Look Behind the Scenes of the European Union (EU) Pharmaceutical Industry Lobby* [http://corporateeurope.org/sites/default/files/28_march_2012_divideconquer.pdf].

Immergut, E. (1992) *Health Politics: Interests and Institutions in Western Europe*. New York: Cambridge University Press.

Marchildon, G. and Schrijvers, K. (2011) Physician resistance and the forging of public healthcare: a comparative analysis of the doctors' strikes in Canada and Belgium in the 1960s, *Medical History*, 55 (2): 203–22.

Marmor, T. (2013) Healthcare politics and policy. The business of medicine: a course for physician leaders, *Yale Journal of Biology and Medicine*, 86 (3): 407–11.

Marmor, T., Okma, K. and Latham, S. (2012) Values, institutions and health policies: a comparative perspective, in T. Marmor and R. Klein (eds.) *Politics, Health and Health Care Selected Essays*. New Haven, CT: Yale University Press.

Moran, M. (1999) *Governing the Health Care State: A Comparative Study of the United Kingdom, the United States and Germany*. Manchester: Manchester University Press.

Moran, M. (2000) Understanding the welfare state: the case of health care, *British Journal of Politics and International Relations*, 2 (2): 135–60.

Murray, C. (2015) Global, regional, and national age–sex specific all-cause and cause-specific mortality for 240 causes of death, 1990–2013: a systematic analysis for the Global Burden of Disease Study 2013, *Lancet*, 385 (9963): 117–71.

Rice, T., Rosenau, P., Unruh, L.Y., Barnes, A.J., Saltman, R.B. and van Ginneken, E. (2013) United States of America: health system review, *Health Systems in Transition*, 15 (3): 1–431.

Schäfer, W., Kroneman, M., Boerma, W., van den Berg, M., Westert, G., Devillé, W. et al. (2010) The Netherlands: health system review, *Health Systems in Transition*, 12 (1): 1–229.

Smith, P., Anell, A., Busse, R., Crivelli, L., Healy, J., Lindahl, A. et al. (2012) Leadership and governance in seven developed health systems, *Health Policy*, 106 (1): 37–49.

Tatara, K. and Okamoto, E. (2009) Japan: health system review, *Health Systems in Transition*, 11 (5): 1–164.

Tuohy, C. (1999) *Accidental Logics: The Dynamics of Change in the Health Care Arena in the United States, Britain and Canada*. Oxford: Oxford University Press.

Vrangbaek, K. (2015) Patient involvement in Danish health care, *Journal of Health Organization and Management*, 29 (5): 611–24.

Wendt, C., Frisina, L. and Rothgang, H. (2009) Healthcare system types: a conceptual framework for comparison, *Social Policy and Administration*, 43 (1): 70–90.

Wilsford, D. (1994) Path dependency, or why history makes it difficult but not impossible to reform healthcare systems in a big way, *Journal of Public Policy*, 14 (3): 251–83.

World Health Organization (WHO) (2000) *World Health Report, Health Systems: Improving Performance*. Geneva: WHO.

Financing healthcare: funding systems and healthcare costs

Suzanne Robinson

Introduction

Healthcare funding in developed countries accounts for a significant percentage of gross domestic product (GDP) and is usually the largest single industry. The rise in new technology, ageing populations and increases in chronic disease mean the demand for healthcare continues to grow. The recent economic downturn and increasing financial pressures make public sector borrowing a less attractive policy option. In developed countries, policymakers are increasingly looking towards the structure and organization of healthcare systems – including revenue collection (the demand side) and organization of service provision (the supply side) – as a means of managing increasing pressures on health expenditure. Redesigning budget processes and allocation of funds between services has become a key element across the developed world (Vraniali, 2010). When considering healthcare funding, managers need to consider a number of elements, including those of efficiency and equity; their aim in resource allocation is to provide efficient, effective and equitable health services for their populations (see Box 4.1 for definitions).

In this chapter, we look at a number of aspects relating to healthcare funding in the developed world, including: how much is spent on health and the impact of the recent economic downturn; different methods of revenue generation; the concepts of fund-pooling and moral hazard; funding distribution methods and the impact these have on health expenditure and outcomes.

Box 4.1 Definition of terms

- **Efficiency:** 'An efficient, high-value health care system seeks to maximize the quality of care and outcomes given the resources committed, while ensuring that additional investments yield net value over time' (Davis et al., 2014: 22).
- **Equity:** '. . . providing care that does not vary in quality because of personal characteristics such as gender, ethnicity, geographic location, and socioeconomic status' (Institute of Medicine, 2001). Policy-makers are faced with making sure resources are spent efficiently and safeguarding ethical principles around access and distribution of resource.
- **Gross domestic product (GDP):** 'GDP is the standard measure of the value of final uses of goods and services produced by a country less the value of imports. GDP is the single most important indicator to capture these economic activities' (OECD, 2015).

Healthcare funding analytical framework

At its basic level, the financing and provision of healthcare represents a transaction between providers and purchasers of care. This can be in the form of a direct transaction from patient to provider (see Figure 4.1) or via a third party (e.g. insurer or purchaser) who transfers resources to providers on behalf of the patient (see Figure 4.2). While different countries have different funding systems in operation, the underlying logic is the same. The simplest transaction occurs when direct payments are made between patients and providers of healthcare services.

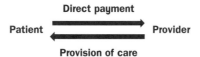

Figure 4.1 Patient–provider transaction

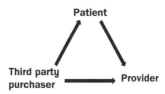

Figure 4.2 Patient–third party–provider transaction

Uncertainty surrounding ill health and the need for expensive healthcare means that most healthcare systems have a third party element – that is, a body that collects resource from individuals and makes decisions as to how to allocate that resource to providers, the third party being either public or private. This third party element offers financial protection against the risk of becoming ill and allows that risk to be shared among the protected population. Third party provision may cover part or all of a country's population, for once revenue has been collected it can then be used to reimburse either patients or providers of services. The funding system is therefore a way in which funds are collected, either via primary (patient) or secondary (third party) sources, and hence distributed to providers.

Components of healthcare funding

There are three main components to healthcare funding, as outlined in Box 4.2. Societies, usually through governments, make choices in relation to the types of revenue collection method that are used. Insurers, either public or private, make decisions around fund-pooling (including the types of individual who should be included in the pool). While individuals, governments and insurers make purchasing choices. The decisions made around each of these components can impact on a healthcare system's performance, especially in relation to efficiency and equity. Revenue collection and fund-pooling are discussed in further detail in the next section, while purchasing is the focus of Chapter 14.

Box 4.2   Components of healthcare funding

- **Revenue collection:** The way money moves around the system and is concerned with: sources of funding (e.g. individuals or employers); mechanisms of funding (e.g. direct or indirect taxes and voluntary insurance); and collection agents (e.g. central or regional government). The main mechanisms of revenue collection are through taxation, social insurance contributions, voluntary insurance premiums and out-of-pocket payments.
- **Fund-pooling:** Occurs when a population's healthcare revenues are accumulated, with financial risk being shared between the population, rather than by each individual contributor. Fund-pooling incorporates both equity and efficiency considerations: equity in so far as risk is shared among the pool or group, rather than it being assumed by individuals; and efficiency because pooling can lead to increases in population health and reductions in uncertainty around healthcare expenditure (Smith and Witter, 2004: iii).
- **Purchasing:** Can involve individual patient out-of-pocket payments or private and public insurers purchasing services on behalf of their members. Chapter 14 provides further detail on the purchasing of healthcare services.

Learning activity 4.1

Question 1: Identify the different components of health funding in your country – the Commonwealth Fund has a useful resource for this exercise: http://www.commonwealthfund.org/publications/fund-reports/2015/jan/international-profiles-2014.

Question 2: Consider the following in relation to the components identified in Question 1:

- Have these components changed over time?
- What impact are these different components having on the efficiency of the healthcare system in your country?
- What impact are these different components having on the equity of the health-care system in your country?

See Box 4.1 for definitions of efficiency and equity.

Healthcare expenditure

Health expenditure across OECD countries

Before we go on to explore the components of healthcare funding in more detail, let us consider healthcare expenditure, which is one of the most pressing policy issues for many governments across the world. Using data from the Organization for Economic Cooperation and Development (OECD, 2014), this section will focus on healthcare spending across developed countries.

All countries have a mix of mechanisms to raise funds to pay for healthcare, Denmark, Japan, Luxemburg, Sweden and the UK all having over 80 per cent healthcare expenditure incurred through public funds. Public funds include state, regional and local government bodies and social security schemes. Even in the United States, which has the largest private expenditure on healthcare (55 per cent), public healthcare expenditure still accounts for 45 per cent of total health expenditure. All countries have some form of out-of-pocket payments.

In 2011, the average total spend per capita on health across OECD countries was $3322. The USA had the highest healthcare spend per capita ($8508). The next biggest healthcare spenders are Norway and Switzerland, which although they spend less than the USA, still spend around 50 per cent more than the OECD average. Over the last forty years, there has been a rise in healthcare expenditure in all countries, although following the economic crisis in 2008 there has been a decline in the health expenditure of some countries. The highest expenditure has been in the USA, France, Germany, Belgium, Australia and Canada. Even in the UK, where increases in healthcare spending have tended to be less than in most other OECD countries, there has been an increase in healthcare expenditure. Allowing for inflation, the UK National Health Service (NHS) in 2002 cost seven times more than in 1949, with the average cost per person rising nearly six times above the 1949 level (OHE, 2004). In some OECD countries, such as China and India, we have also seen increases in spending and these are predicted to rise as their economies grow. What this demonstrates is that health spending is linked to the wider economy: as economies grow so does spending on health. The downside of this is that during an economic downturn we would expect to see a reduction in health expenditure. The next section explores the impact of the recent global economic crisis on health spending.

The global economic crisis

The global economic crisis of 2007/8 has had a major impact across the world and is considered to have been the worst financial crisis since the 1930s (United Nations, 2011). The impact was felt most keenly across a number of European countries and the USA, with all countries seeing a reduction in health spending (see Figure 4.3).

Reductions in spending were largely driven by cuts in public spending. In Ireland, spending on health fell by 7.6 per cent in 2010, compared with a growth rate of around 8.4 per cent in 2000–2009. Estonia had seen a growth rate of around 7 per cent year on year from 2000 to 2009, yet expenditure fell by around 7 per cent in 2010 (OECD, 2012). Only Japan and Israel saw increases in health expenditure in 2009–2011.

Countries achieved a reduction in health expenditure through a variety of policy initiatives, including:

- Cuts in wages or fees paid to professionals and reductions in the number of health workers (this was especially evident in Ireland).
- Cutting Ministry of Health budgets (Bulgaria, Cyprus, Czech Republic, Estonia, Finland, France, Greece, Iceland, Ireland, Italy, Portugal, Romania, Serbia, Slovenia, Spain, UK).
- Efficiency gains pursued through mergers of hospitals or ministries, or accelerating the move from inpatient hospitalization towards outpatient care and day surgery.
- Negotiation on reduced prices paid to pharmaceutical industries and an increase in the use of generic drugs.
- Investment plans have also been put on hold in a number of countries, including Estonia, Ireland, Iceland and the Czech Republic.
- Increase in out-of-pocket payments. For example, Ireland increased the share of direct payments by households for prescribed medicines and appliances, while the Czech Republic increased users' charges for hospital stays (adapted from OECD, 2012 and Thomson et al., 2014)

In the USA, spending rates have remained fairly static over recent years, although the recent health reforms introduced by the Obama government may well see a rise in public sector spending (see Commonwealth Fund website). While most OECD countries have seen reductions in public and private health spending in 2012, Chile and Mexico have seen fairly strong growth, due to their focus on moving to universal coverage and increasing access to healthcare. The slowing of spending in most countries could impact on the rise of new technology and innovations. However, the economic downturn could provide an opportunity for governments and health organizations to consider innovations around healthcare services; it can be much easier to provide a narrative for change when funding is scarce than when it is plenty (Chapter 5 provides more detailed discussion of healthcare priority setting).

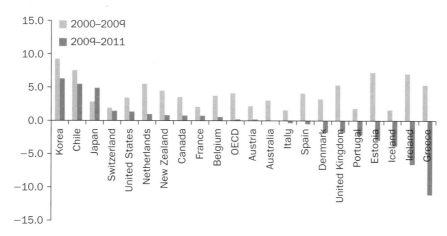

Figure 4.3 Annual average growth rate in per capita health expenditure, real terms, 2000 to 2011
Source: Adapted from OECD (2015).

While public sector health spending continues to account for a large proportion of health expenditure, the impact of the recession has led to an increase in private activity (i.e. insurance and out-of-pocket expenditure). This has been most highly prevalent in Greece and Portugal, where around one-third of health spending comes from private activity (OECD, 2015). Increases in out-of-pocket expenses could impact on access for some individuals and raise issues about equity. Reductions in payment to pharmaceutical companies through negotiation of drug prices and increases in generic drug usage could result in greater efficiency savings.

In their review of the impact of the global recession on European health systems, Thomson et al. (2014) suggest that the economic crisis demonstrated the importance of policy design of healthcare financing. For example, Greece had no 'reserves or countercyclical formulae to compensate the health insurance system for falling revenue from payroll taxes, and Ireland had no countercyclical formula to cover a huge increase in the share of the population entitled to means-tested benefits' (Thomson et al., 2014: 229). Furthermore, countries with the highest out-of-pocket expenses had significant gaps in coverage during the economic crisis and tended to have the least potential to cut public spending without having major issues on access to health services (Thomson et al., 2014).

Trends in and pressure on healthcare costs/spending

Thus while the impact of the recession continues to be felt globally, let us now turn to consider some of the major trends and pressures that will impact healthcare spending. There are two main drivers of public health expenditure: demographic and non-demographic. Demographic drivers relate to the age of the population and its evolution over time (OECD, 2013). Non-demographic drivers relate to a number of aspects, including the income of a country (as economies grow so does their health spending), rising prices and technological developments and the policy and structure of health systems. For example, hospitals are costly drivers of

Learning activity 4.2

Access health statistics data available on the OECD website [http://stats.oecd.org/index.aspx?DataSetCode=HEALTH_STAT].

Do countries that rely heavily on general government funds tend to have a higher or lower spend than those that rely heavily on social security or private insurance?

Consider the emergent trends in health expenditure for your country:

- Is healthcare expenditure in your country increasing or decreasing over time?
- What impact did the recession have on health expenditure? Consider overall spending and also the types of activity (i.e. public, private, insurance, out-of-pocket expenses).
- Do you think the reliance on public funds is set to decrease or increase in the next 5 years?
- How does this compare with other similar countries across the OECD?

care and evidence predicts that more efficient systems have a strong primary care function (see Chapter 9 for further discussion on primary care).

The last twenty years have seen a rise in consumerism as societies gain greater access to health information extending across regional and country borders, and users of healthcare systems increasingly see themselves as 'consumers'. Patients demand access to the latest technology that can assist in their care and expect to receive high-quality services that offer good access and a degree of choice (Cotis, 2005). Other factors that impact healthcare spending include the ageing population, the increase in incidence of chronic illness and rising levels of obesity. Long-term care costs will be one of the greatest pressures for developed countries, especially given the weaker productivity gains from the economy (OECD, 2013). (For a fuller discussion on the increase and impact on chronic disease, see Chapter 10.)

A further issue for healthcare funding and planning more widely is what Taleb (2007) terms 'Black Swan Events', rare events that have a high impact and are hard to predict, such as terrorist attacks, natural disasters and outbreaks of disease. Such events can and do have a significant impact on the funding and planning of healthcare. Examples include the SARS outbreak in South East Asia in 2003, the swine flu pandemic of 2009 and the 1918 flu pandemic, which killed over 50 million people. The cost and impact of such events on health systems is difficult to estimate and means that additional healthcare resources above those estimated may be needed.

What we have demonstrated so far is that there are increasing demands on health services versus an ever-decreasing resource envelope. The impact of the recession has seen reductions in health funds across many OECD countries, forcing governments to explore ways to increase the efficiency of the existing system and the components of healthcare funding are one area of focus.

Revenue generation

This section outlines the different methods of revenue generation and their associated effects on healthcare costs. All countries have a mix of funding methods, including some form of insurance as well as some form of direct payments made by citizens. Figure 4.4 highlights public and private revenue sources. Methods that fall within the public sphere (with the exception of indirect tax) use financial mechanisms to achieve a set of social objectives, such as redistributing resources across the population. In contrast, private sources such as voluntary insurance focus on an individual's needs and self-interest, rather than those of the wider population (Saltman et al., 2004). Public insurance mechanisms include general taxation and social insurance. One of the main differences in the types of insurance is that social insurance is usually a hypothecated tax – that is, funds are specifically earmarked for health.

The choice of revenue generation methods is strongly influenced by the underlying norms and values of a society. For some countries, healthcare is seen as a social and collective good, whereas for others it is perceived as a market commodity that can be bought and sold (Rice, 2001). However, even in countries that subscribe to the latter view, there are usually publicly funding mechanisms that allow for some redistribution of funds to those who are unable to pay for healthcare, often referred to as a safety net. Public insurance is one of the most widespread funding revenue generation methods providing substantial funding for health services in almost every country.

General taxation

The UK is an example of a healthcare system that is funded predominantly through general (direct) taxation, although variations exist between the four countries of England, Northern Ireland, Scotland and Wales. For example, in Scotland and Wales, all prescriptions are free,

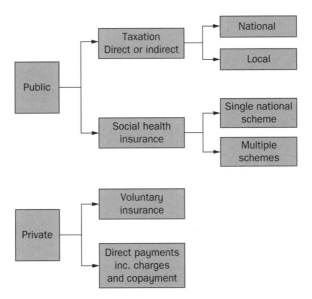

Figure 4.4 Different forms of revenue generation method.

unlike in England and Northern Ireland. In Scotland, social care for older people is funded, whereas this is not the case in the other three countries. The UK Treasury distributes funds to the four UK administrators and then to purchasers in England and to health boards in the other three countries. The majority of services across the UK healthcare system are free to users at the point of provision (for a more detailed discussion of the four countries that make up the UK, see Bevan and Mays, 2014). Other countries that primarily use a universal tax-based funding mechanism include Denmark, Finland, New Zealand, Australia, Canada and Spain.

Funding healthcare through general taxation is seen as a progressive way of raising revenue. This is because in most countries tax is proportional to income, with those on higher incomes paying more tax than those on lower incomes, thus allowing for redistribution of resources from the wealthy to the poor, from the healthy to the sick, and from those of working age to the young and old. In addition, the financing of services via general taxation is divorced from provision of services, which is important for equitable access, with resource being based on clinical need rather than ability to pay (Davis et al., 2014).

However, there is evidence to suggest that inequality of access to care is also affected by discrimination linked to age, gender, education, wealth and race (Pickett and Wilkinson, 2010). Furthermore, while tax-based models are progressive, the degree to which the whole system of funding is progressive depends on what other funding mechanisms are being utilized. For example, even though general taxation is used to fund healthcare in Portugal, the high share of out-of-pocket payments make the overall system regressive (Kronenberg and Barros, 2014), and similar concerns have influenced health policy developments in New Zealand over the past decade, where copayments for primary care have traditionally been high and attempts have been made to reduce these for people on lower incomes.

An additional advantage of tax-based revenue collection is that it is relatively efficient to administer, because the collection of funds is through the existing taxation system, and additional costs are not incurred by the health sector. The fact that government is the main payer for and purchaser of healthcare also allows general taxation to act as a mechanism to control costs, with providers not easily being able to increase revenue by raising prices or premiums, as with private and social insurance (van der Zee and Kroneman, 2007).

A major disadvantage of systems based on general taxation include the fact that health services are closely tied to the economy and wider government taxation policies. In times of economic recession, reductions in tax revenues can have major effects on the health budget. The recent global economic downturn has meant that almost all countries have had less resource to spend on public sector services and tough choices about public sector healthcare spending have had to be made. This has been particularly evident in countries such as Spain, Greece and Ireland, which have seen the largest decreases in the ratio of health spending to GDP.

Local taxation

Denmark's healthcare is predominantly funded through general taxation with central government reallocating tax income to the local regions and municipalities – this finances around 77 per cent of the regional activity with a further 20 per cent of healthcare funding being generated through local taxes (Mossialos et al., 2015). Analysis has shown that local taxes are generally less progressive than national taxes (i.e. local taxes often take a larger proportion of tax from people whose income is low), as is demonstrated by the experience of Denmark and other countries such as Finland, Sweden and Switzerland, who also have a high proportion of revenue generated by local taxation (Ping Yu et al., 2008). In the absence of a national system of redistribution, local taxation often creates regional inequity.

The decentralization of local tax funding is often seen as a major advantage over national taxation, as the clear link between revenue raised and local spending allows for potentially much greater transparency. There is also greater direct political accountability for healthcare funding and expenditure, since local politicians are likely to be closer to the electorate than their national counterparts. A further advantage is that healthcare is separated from national priorities, with this mechanism of decentralisation allowing for local needs to be more easily met.

Social insurance

Like general taxation, the system of social health insurance is redistributive and allows for universal entitlement to healthcare services and is based on need rather than ability to pay. There are large variations in the features of social health insurance systems across countries. Box 4.3 sets out some of the typical features of social health insurance systems.

Box 4.3   Typical features of social health insurance systems

- Insurance is compulsory for the majority of or the whole population.
- Insured individuals pay a regular, usually wage-based contribution, which may be flat rate or variable.
- Employers may also pay a contribution.
- There may be one or more independent 'sickness funds' or social insurers.
- Individuals may or may not be able to choose which sickness fund they join.
- Transfers are made from general taxation to cover the premiums of the unemployed, retired and other disadvantaged and vulnerable groups.
- All allow for the pooling of revenue; typically, insurance is not risk related.

Source: Adapted from McDaid (2003: 167).

Countries that operate a predominantly social health insurance system include Germany, France, Austria, Switzerland, Belgium, the Netherlands, Luxembourg and Japan. In addition, a number of Central and Eastern European countries have also adapted such models, including Hungary, Lithuania, the Czech Republic, Estonia, Latvia, Slovakia and Poland. A number of countries including the Netherlands, Germany and France have made substantial changes to their funding systems, changes that are due to ever-increasing financial pressures that have been further exacerbated by the recent economic downturn.

Under social health insurance schemes, premiums tend to be collected directly by sickness funds (e.g. Austria, France, Switzerland) or distributed from a central state-run fund (e.g. Israel, Luxembourg); Belgium uses a combination of the two. With the exception of France and Switzerland, sickness funds are private not-for-profit organizations that are governed by an elected board (visit the European Health Observatory for further details on the organization and structure of social insurance schemes).

Funding using social health insurance tends to be more transparent than tax-based methods and traditionally this meant that health services were distanced from the political arena, with concerns tending to be around contribution rates rather than political matters. However, recent economic pressures mean that governments are looking at funding mechanisms including social health insurance in an attempt to curb public spending. The majority of social health insurance systems do require some level of subsidies from general and/or local taxation. See Box 4.4 for the facts about social health insurance in Germany.

Box 4.4   Case study – social health insurance in Germany: the facts

- Germany's major source of revenue generation is through social health insurance (SHI), with around 85 per cent of the population being insured through SHI.
- SHI is mandatory for those under the opt-out threshold – which was €4462.50 per month in 2014.
- There are over 131 SHI insurers.
- High-income earners can opt out for private health insurance (PHI). Around 11 per cent of the population have PHI, including civil servants and the self-employed whose gross earnings exceed the set threshold.
- There were around 24 PHI companies in 2012.
- Copayments for ambulatory visits (GPs, specialists and dentists) were introduced in 2004, but removed in 2013.
- Copayments for some prescription drugs and hospital inpatient days remain. Out-of-pocket expenses make up around 13 per cent of total health expenditure.
- Children under 18 and those on low incomes are exempt from copayments.
- In 2012, SHI accounted for around 57 per cent of healthcare expenditure.
- Sickness funds are funded by compulsory contributions levied as a percentage of gross wages; both employer (7.3 per cent) and employee (8.2 per cent of gross earnings) make a contribution.
- Hospitals and physicians treat SHI and PHI patients.
- The Federal Joint Committee is the regulatory power that decides what services should be covered by SHI and it also sets quality measures.
- Since 1995, long-term care has been covered by a separate mandatory insurance scheme.
- In 2014, the federal government passed a bill to strengthen long-term care – the bill was implemented in early 2015.

Source: Adapted from European Observatory on Health Systems and Policies [http://www. euro.who.int/en/about-us/partners/observatory].

Learning activity 4.3

Consider the funding approaches used in Germany.

* What do you think are the main advantages and disadvantages?
* How well do you think Germany performs in terms of efficiency and equity concerns outlined in Box 4.4.

Refer to the following texts for more detailed discussion of the German system: Clarke and Bidgood (2013), Busse and Blümel (2014), Mossialos et al. (2015). Also visit http://www.euro.who.int/en/about-us/partners/observatory.

Private insurance

Private insurance can be classified into the following categories: substitutive, supplementary and complementary (Mossialos et al., 2002). Private healthcare insurance markets often develop around publicly funded systems and in many countries private insurance plays a residual role in terms of healthcare funding; for example, in countries such as the UK and Australia, private insurance provides supplementary coverage to the public system and can enable faster access to certain services such as elective hospital care (see Box 4.5).

In Germany, individuals earning higher incomes or those who are self-employed can opt out of the public health insurance system. This form of substitutive insurance undermines the redistribution effect of taxation or social insurance and leads to a regressive system of funding. Furthermore, as income is related to risk of ill health (the poorer you are, the more likely you are to fall ill), substitutive insurance means that those with the poorest health or at greatest risk are left in the public system, which reduces the overall pooling and risk-sharing mechanism in the health system, and those with the lowest income could potentially end up paying higher premiums.

Systems that rely heavily on private insurance are often criticized for their inequitable nature – that is, these systems are based on a person's ability to pay for care rather than on clinical need (Wilper et al., 2009). Around 16 per cent of Americans had no health insurance coverage in 2008, with the majority of the uninsured being on the lowest incomes (Wilper et al., 2009; Commonwealth Fund, 2010). Healthcare reforms introduced in the USA by the Obama administration in 2010 are aimed at reducing the inequities inherent in the American system. The Patient Protection and Affordable Care Act (ACA) is intended to provide affordable health insurance coverage for the majority of American citizens, improve access to primary care and reduce overall healthcare costs (Doherty, 2010).

Recent evidence suggests that an additional 7.8 million young Americans are covered because of the reform (Blumenthal, 2013; Collins et al., 2014). While insurance coverage in the USA is increasing, the Commonwealth Fund predicts that there will still be around 31 million people (one in nine of the non-elderly) uninsured in 2024. Despite recent reforms, the

US model continues to perform poorly in relation to equity and efficiency, ranking highest in OECD countries for overall level of healthcare expenditure (suggesting poor efficiency) and last for coverage (suggesting issues around equity) (Lorenzoni et al., 2014).

Private insurance systems tend to incur higher administrative costs per insured person than public health coverage systems (Litow, 2006). Countries such as the USA, which has a relatively high percentage of private insurance, have the greatest difficulty in controlling healthcare costs and tend to have the biggest healthcare spend per head of population.

Box 4.5   Case study – private insurance as supplementary insurance in Australia

In Australia, there is a mix of public and private health insurance in operation. Private insurance is a complementary and supplementary insurance to public insurance (Medicare). It offers patients access to treatment in private hospitals and covers some ancillary healthcare services. All individuals are eligible for a government rebate on private health insurance, a policy aimed at encouraging take-up and retention of private health insurance. Furthermore, those on higher incomes who do not take out private hospital insurance must pay a tax surcharge. The impacts of these incentives means that there is a sharp increase in uptake of private insurance around 30 years of age and a reduction after retirement (Mossialos et al., 2015).

Advantages
An advantage of supplementary insurance is that it can allow faster access to services for people holding private insurance, especially those systems such as Australia that have traditionally experienced significant waiting times for diagnostic tests or elective treatments. Complementary insurance has the ability to free up capacity in the public system by allowing those who can afford to pay to receive treatment in the private sector.

Disadvantages
Those opposed to supplementary insurance suggest it encourages a two-tier system that allows more rapid access to services for those who can afford to pay and thus should not be allowed on overall equity grounds.

Out-of-pocket payments

Out-of-pocket payments and charges make up a proportion of healthcare spending in all health systems. This is the main mechanism that allows for price consciousness – that is, for patients to have a true notion of the costs of service and thus be able to make judgements around the price and (possibly) value for money of care received. User charges are often introduced to curb healthcare demand. However, little evidence exists that charges actually produce efficiency savings; in fact, there is evidence to suggest they may, in fact, deter individuals from seeking appropriate and cost-effective care, especially those on low incomes (Thomson et al., 2014). Since the economic crisis of 2008, a number of countries have increased user charges, but also introduced measures to strengthen protection of the poor from user charges through a reduction in the charge, exemptions or caps (Thomson et al., 2014).

Fee-for-service payments for patient services are used in a number of countries, including New Zealand, Australia, France, Germany and the USA. There are a number of different schemes in operation across countries, such as charges to visit family doctors, and charges or copayments for treatment or services (e.g. hospital stays or dental care) (Thomson et al., 2010). There is evidence to suggest that fees can deter patients from accessing services (Thomson et al., 2010) and while patient charges are often seen as a method to curtail costs, there is the suggestion that they can actually provide incentives to increase healthcare activity (Carrin and Hanvoravongchai, 2003; Rosenthal et al., 2005; Shomaker, 2010). The argument is that they reward providers for productivity regardless of need, effectiveness or quality (Shomaker, 2010). In addition, charges for some services can deter patients from accessing services and lead to inefficiencies, with primary care patients presenting at emergency departments and the detection of disease being delayed (Eckermann, 2014).

Learning activity 4.4

Choose three of the following health systems: Australia, Italy, Germany, Sweden, the UK, USA and Netherlands. Now consider:

- The types of choice made in relation to resource revenue, i.e. the ways in which each country decides to raise funding for health.
- How efficient and equitable are these countries' revenue-raising methods?

Information about the financing of healthcare systems can be found in Mossialos et al. (2015): http://www.commonwealthfund.org/~/media/files/publications/fund-report/2015/jan/1802_mossialos_intl_profiles_2014_v7.pdf?la=en.

Fund-pooling

Fund-pooling is separated from revenue collection, as not all mechansims of revenue collection, such as out-of-pocket expenses, allow for funds to be pooled. Given the uncertainty, risk and high costs associated with health and illness, all systems have some form of healthcare insurance mechanisms. Unlike many other goods, there is a lot of uncertainty around an individual's need for healthcare. For example, it is fairly easy to predict how much individuals will spend on food, clothes and so on. However, the uncertainty around what an individual may or may not need to spend on healthcare makes it difficult for individuals to make financial provision for episodes of sickness. Insurance allows for the pooling of funds, which facilitates the pooling of financial risk across the population or defined group. Thus fund-pooling generally allows insured individuals to access healthcare in an affordable and timely manner. Insurance of any kind allows a population's revenues to be accumulated and thus any financial risk to be shared between populations. In this sense, fund-pooling can incorporate equity and efficiency considerations. A world health survey conducted by the WHO highlights that there is substancial support for pooling of funds on equity grounds (James and Savedoff, 2010).

Countries have multiple funding arrangements, including universal pooling arrangements (e.g. countries with compulsory national health insurance systems) that allow for the entire population to access healthcare services provided by the insurance fund, and smaller private funding pools that may cover subgroups of the wider population. The fragmentation of insurance and pooling arrangements across countries does raise equity concerns, especially when the risk pools are small.

While insurance allows for the pooling of funds, it does reduce the cost of treatment at the point of consumption and makes 'illness' a less undesired state. This is termed the 'moral hazard' associated with insurance (i.e. the fact of being insured leads to over-provision or accessing of services). Moral hazard can also occur on the supply side with medical staff not having to bear the full cost of the decision over supplying treatment. This is termed 'supplier-induced demand' (see Donaldson and Gerard, 2005).

There is some evidence to suggest that supplier-induced demand does take place in countries with private health insurance. For example, Savage and Wright (2003) suggest that moral hazard is apparent in the Australian private health insurance system, with evidence of an increase in the expected length of hospital stay for people who are privately insured. However, moral hazard and supplier-induced demand are problems of insurance *per se* and can be a feature of both public and private insurance systems.

Learning activity 4.5

Consider risk-pooling in your own country.

- How does this impact on equity and efficiency concerns?
- How can countries/insurers reduce moral hazard and suppler-induced demand?

Funding distribution methods

Having explored the components of health and how funds are raised, we now look at funding distribution methods. Countries vary in terms of the methods used to distribute funds around the system, with a mix of methods in operation within and across countries. The two main methods are global-based funding and activity-based funding.

Global-based funding

Global-based funding (sometimes referred to as block funding) involves placing a limit on the amount of money spent on healthcare. A fixed level of payment is agreed in advance of treatment activity occurring, with a block of money going to healthcare providers. The amount of funding is often based on historical patterns and demographic data and provided irrespective of the volume or demand for resources. Global budgets are relatively free of government intervention – that is, once the budget is allocated, providers generally exercise discretion over the types and volume of service they provide and allow local purchasers to respond flexibly to local need (Sutherland et al., 2013) (see Box 4.6).

Box 4.6 Case study – global-based funding in Canada

The most common form of funding distribution in Canada is via global funding. Canada is made up of ten provinces that regionalize healthcare services through regional health authorities, which have primary responsibility for delivering healthcare services. In the majority of provinces, governments allocate funding to local health authorities via a global budget. The amounts are generally based on historical funding patterns – inflation and politics, rather than demand or patient need (Sutherland and Repin, 2014).

A recent study of global budgets in Canada suggests the following points.

Strengths

- provide budgetary predictability and, in some cases, transparency;
- make budget capping relatively easier, which can limit growth in expenditures;
- little incentive for innovation or to improve efficiency of care;
- limited incentive for providers to over-supply.

Weaknesses

- in order to stay within budget, hospitals may restrict services – or be selective in terms of services provided;
- lack of incentive to shorten length of stay;
- lack of transparency in the allocation of funds;
- perpetuation of historical inequities or inefficiencies;
- complaints about equity in funding allocations from hospitals.

Canada is currently exploring other funding options (including activity-based funding) to help deal with equity and efficiency concerns.

Source: Adapted from Sutherland and Repin (2014) .

Few developed countries use only global-based funding and in recent years a number of countries have introduced activity-based funding.

Activity-based funding

Activity-based funding is also called episode funding, activity funding, pay for performance, payment by results, case mix, and diagnosis-related group funding. Over recent years there has been a shift towards activity-based funding – this policy direction links to a focus on efficiency savings and pays providers for activity. One of the notions behind pay for performance was to incentivize people and institutions through payment mechanisms. Activity-based funding was introduced to incentivize efficiency, quality and the opportunity to increase transparency with regard to how money is being spent in the system (O'Reilly et al., 2012; Ashish, 2013).

Critics suggest that the approach rewards volume – not quality – of service, and that there is a real possibility of hospitals developing cost-cutting strategies that could compromise the quality of services. However, recent studies suggest that activity-based funding has made no real difference to quality of care (Farrar et al., 2009). A recent study comparing waiting times found that they are less of a problem in countries that rely mainly on activity-based funding than in those that have largely fixed budgets. Results suggest a rise in activity leads to shorter waiting times and shorter lengths of stay in hospital (Farrar et al., 2007). However, in England, the reduction in waiting times may be due to the impact of other government policies (Farrar et al., 2007). Norway and Sweden have also seen efficiency savings in relation to productivity, although these have declined over time (Street et al., 2007).

While activity-based funding may help to improve efficiency, it could impact on equity and needs-based funding, focusing on productivity rather than population need. Furthermore, there is no incentive to redirect patients to other services, such as from hospital to community-based services. Just as countries have a mix of revenue generation methods, they also use a blended approach to funding distribution mechanisms. In recent years, we have seen policy-makers utilizing other incentives around value and quality and a shift in policy mantra from volume to value.

Conclusions

This chapter has explored the systems of funding used in the field of healthcare. All healthcare systems have some mix of public and private financing. While the funding sources, mechanisms and collection agents vary between countries, all countries are feeling the pressure of increasing expenditure, scarce resources and the need to provide both an efficient and equitable healthcare service. The recent economic downturn means that even greater pressures are being placed on governments that are struggling with growing financial deficits and limited public resources. This is forcing countries to look at both funding mechanisms and distribution methods in an attempt to provide efficient and equitable healthcare. There is no one best approach to revenue generation of funding distribution; each has its own strengths and weaknesses and incentives and disincentives:

> There is no healthcare system that performs systematically better in delivering cost-effective healthcare. It may thus be less the type of system that matters but rather how it is managed. (OECD, 2010)

The management and policy challenges are to deliver high-quality and safe services with an ever-decreasing resource envelope, which will require managers to focus on efficiency savings. However, this should not happen at the expense of equity. Looking forward, managers need to consider how to organize services that reflect the changing demographics of an ageing population with increased chronic health conditions. The challenges posed require a focus on resource distribution that flows to effective health services that are relevant for the changing demographic. Many countries need to rethink funding allocation and the structure of their health systems.

Learning resources

European Observatory: A partner to the World Health Organization, the European Observatory provides information on health systems and promotes an evidenced-based approach to policy-making. It provides comprehensive information on healthcare expenditure and the financing of healthcare systems in Europe [http://www.euro.who.int/en/about-us/partners/observatory].

European Union: Provides facts and figures on health across Europe with a focus on the impact of the recession [http://europa.eu/index_en.htm].

ObamaCare Facts: Provides information on the US Affordable Care Act [http://obamacarefacts.com/obamacare-facts/].

Office of Health Economics: Conducts research and analysis of health systems, with a particular focus on their efficiency and sustainability [https://www.ohe.org/].

Organization for Economic Cooperation and Development (OECD): Collates and analyses data on healthcare funding activity across OECD countries. It provides comparative analysis around expenditure and performance of health systems. It is committed to ensuring that economic and social aspects are taken into account [http://www.oecd.org].

World Health Organization (WHO): Provides analysis and reports on healthcare expenditure and performance [www.who.int/about/en].

References

Ashish, K. (2013) Time to get serious about pay for performance, *Journal of the American Medical Association*, 309 (4): 344–8.

Bevan, G. and Mays, N. (2014) *The Four Health Systems of the UK: How Do They Compare?* London: Nuffield Trust.

Blumenthal, D. (2013) *Reflecting on Health Reform: A Balanced View of the Affordable Care Act*. New York: Commonwealth Fund [http://www.commonwealthfund.org/publications/blog/2013/dec/resisting-the-rush-to-judge-the-affordable-care-act].

Busse, R. and Blümel, M. (2014) Germany: health system review, *Health Systems in Transition*, 16 (2): 1–296.

Carrin, G. and Hanvoravongchai, P. (2003) Provider payments and patient charges as policy tools for cost-containment: how successful are they in high-income countries?, *Human Resources for Health*, 1 (1): 6.

Clarke, E. and Bidgood, E. (2013) *Healthcare Systems: Germany*. London: CIVITAS.

Collins, S.R., Rasmussen, P.W. and Doty, M.M. (2014) *Gaining Ground: Americans' Health Insurance Coverage and Access to Care after the Affordable Care Act's First Open Enrollment Period*. New York: Commonwealth Fund.

Cotis, J. (2005) *Challenges of Demographics*. Paris: OECD.

Davis, K., Stremikis, K., Schoen, C. and Squires, D. (2014) *Mirror, Mirror on the Wall, 2014 Update: How the U.S. Healthcare System Compares Internationally. New York:* Commonwealth Fund [http://www.commonwealthfund.org/publications/fund-reports/2014/jun/mirror-mirror].

Doherty, R.B. (2010) The certitudes and uncertainties of healthcare reform, *Annals of Internal Medicine*, 152: 679–82.

Donaldson, C. and Gerard, K. (2005) *Economics of Healthcare Financing: The Invisible Hand.* London: Palgrave Macmillan.

Eckermann, S. (2014) Over- and under-servicing: further reasons to scrap the GP co-payment, *The Conversation*, 6 August [http://theconversation.com/over-and-under-servicing-further-reasons-to-scrap-the-gp-co-payment-30199].

Farrar, S., Sussex, J., Yi, D., Sutton, M., Chalkley, M., Scott, A. et al. (2007) *National Evaluation of Payment by Results*. Report to the Department of Health. York: Health Economics Research Unit.

Farrar, S., Yi, D., Sutton, M., Chalkley, M., Sussex, J. and Scott, A. (2009) Has payment by results affected the way that English hospitals provide care? Difference in differences analysis, *British Medical Journal*, 339: b3047.

Institute of Medicine (2001) *Crossing the Quality Chasm: A New Health System for the 21st Century*. Washington, DC: National Academic Press.

James, C. and Savedoff, W.D. (2010) *Risk Pooling and Redistribution in Healthcare: An Empirical Analysis of Attitudes Toward Solidarity*. World Health Report Background Paper #5. Geneva: WHO [http://www.who.int/healthsystems/topics/financing/healthreport/SolidarityNo5FINAL.pdf].

Kronenberg, C. and Barros, P.P. (2014) Catastrophic healthcare expenditure – drivers and protection: the Portuguese case, *Health Policy*, 115 (1): 44–51.

Litow, M.E. (2006) Medicare versus private health insurance: the cost of administration, *Health Watch Newsletter*, May (issue 52): 28–30.

Lorenzoni, L., Belloni, A. and Sassi, F. (2014) Health-care expenditure and health policy in the USA versus other high-spending OECD countries, *Lancet*, 384: 83–92.

McDaid, D. (2003) Who pays? Approaches to funding healthcare in Europe, *Consumer Policy Review*, 13 (5): 166–72.

Mossialos, E., Dixon, A., Figueras, J. and Kutzin, J. (eds.) (2002) *Funding Healthcare: Options for Europe*. Maidenhead: Open University Press.

Mossialos, E., Wenzl, M., Osborn, R. and Anderson, C. (2015) *2014: International Profiles of Health Care Systems*. New York: Commonwealth Fund [http://

www.commonwealthfund.org/~/media/files/publications/fund-report/2015/jan/1802_mossialos_intl_profiles_2014_v7.pdf?la=en].

OECD (2010) *Growing Health Spending Puts Pressure on Government Budgets According to OECD Health Data 2010*. Paris: OECD.

OECD (2012) *Health: Growth in Health Spending Grinds to a Halt* [http://www.oecd.org/health/healthgrowthinhealthspendinggrindstoahalt.htm].

OECD (2013) *What Future for Health Spending?* OECD Economics Department Policy Note #19, June.

OECD (2014) *OECD Health Data 2014: Statistics and Indicators for 30 countries*. Paris: OECD.

OECD (2015) *Gross Domestic Product (GDP) (Indicator)* [https://data.oecd.org/gdp/gross-domestic-product-gdp.htm; accessed 9 May 2015].

Office of Health Economics (OHE) (2004) *Compendium of Health Statistics 2003–2004*. London: OHE.

O'Reilly, J., Busse, R., Häkkinen, U., Or, Z., Street A. and Wiley, M. (2012) Paying for hospital care: the experience with implementing activity based funding in five European countries, *Health Economics, Policy and Law*, 7 (1): 73–101.

Pickett, K. and Wilkinson, R. (2010) *The Spirit Level: Why More Equal Societies Almost Always Do Better*. London: Penguin.

Ping Yu, C., Whynes, D.K. and Sach, T.H. (2008) Equity in healthcare financing: the case of Malaysia, *International Journal for Equity in Health*, 7: 15.

Rice, T. (2001) Individual autonomy and state involvement in healthcare, *Journal of Medical Ethics*, 27 (4): 240–4.

Rosenthal, M.B., Frank, R.G., Li, Z. and Epstein, A.M. (2005) Early experience with pay-for-performance: from concept to practice, *Journal of the American Medical Association*, 294 (14): 1788–93.

Saltman, R.B., Reinhard, B. and Figueras, J. (eds.) (2004) *Social Health Insurance Systems in Western Europe*. European Observatory on Health Systems and Policies Series. Oxford: Oxford University Press.

Savage, E. and Wright, D. (2003) Moral hazard and adverse selection in Australian private hospitals: 1989–1990, *Journal of Health Economics*, 22 (3): 331–59.

Shomaker, T.S. (2010) Commentary: healthcare payment reform and academic medicine: threat or opportunity?, *Academic Medicine*, 85 (5): 756–8.

Smith, P.C. and Witter, S.N. (2004) *Risk Pooling in Healthcare Financing: The Implications for Health System Performance*. HNP Discussion Paper. Washington, DC: World Bank Organization.

Street, A., Vitikainen, K., Bjorvatn, A. and Hvenegaard, A. (2007) *Introducing Activity-Based Financing: A Review of Experience in Australia, Denmark, Norway and Sweden*. Research Paper #30. York: Centre for Health Economics [http://www.york.ac.uk/che/pdf/rp30.pdf].

Sutherland, J. and Repin, N. (2014) *Current Hospital Funding in Canada*. Policy Brief. Vancouver: UBC Centre for Health Services and Policy Research .

Sutherland, J.M., Crump, R.T., Repin, N. and Hellsten, E. (2013) *Paying for Hospital Services: A Hard Look at the Options*. Commentary #378, April, Health Policy. Toronto: C.D. Howe Institute.

Taleb, N.N. (2007) *The Black Swan: The Impact of the Highly Improbable*. New York: Random House.

Thomson, S., Foubister, T. and Mossialos, E. (2010) Can user charges make healthcare more efficient?, *British Medical Journal*, 341: c3759.

Thomson, S., Figueras, J., Evetovits, T., Jowett, M., Mladovsky, P., Maresso, A. et al. (2014) *Economic Crisis, Health Systems and Health in Europe: Impact and Implications for Policy*. Policy Summary #12. Copenhagen: WHO Regional Office for Europe.

United Nations (2011) *The Global Social Crisis: Report on the World Social Situation 2011*. New York: UN Department of Economic and Social Affairs [http://www.un.org/esa/socdev/rwss/docs/2011/rwss2011.pdf].

van der Zee, J. and Kroneman, M.N. (2007) Bismarck or Beveridge: a beauty contest between dinosaurs, *BMC Health Services Research*, 7: 94.

Vraniali, E. (2010) *Rethinking Public Financial Management and Budgeting in Greece: Time to Reboot?* GreeSE Paper #37, Hellenic Observatory Papers on Greece and Southeast Europe, Jul. London: London School of Economics.

Wilper, A.P., Woolhandler, S., Lasser, K.E., McCormick, D., Bor, D.H. and Himmelstein, D.U. (2009) Health insurance and mortality in US adults, *American Journal of Public Health*, 199 (12): 1–7.

Allocating resources for healthcare: setting and managing priorities

Iestyn Williams

Introduction

Those allocating resources for healthcare have long had to contend with the problems posed by resource scarcity. These pressures have been heightened by the global recession of the late 2000s and subsequent constraints placed on public spending (Karanikolos et al., 2013). As governments seek to constrain rising healthcare expenditure, the invidious role of resource distribution is frequently assigned to healthcare managers. However, traditional cost-containing 'safety valves' such as waiting lists and bedside rationing are becoming increasingly outdated, and thus policy-makers and healthcare leaders across the globe are seeking other solutions (Cromwell et al., 2015). Research and practice have consistently demonstrated the limitations of any one prescription for successful priority setting, and it has become increasingly clear that the 'golden bullet' may never be found. Those involved have therefore been forced to say 'goodbye to the simple solutions' (Holm, 1998: 1000) and to rethink and rebuild strategies for managing scarce healthcare resources.

This chapter considers the implications of resource scarcity for the management function within healthcare. The discussion draws on consideration of the differences in resource allocation systems used by a range of countries, before concentrating on the main dimensions of priority setting such as ethics, evidence, process, politics and implementation and considers these from the point of view of the strategic manager and decision-maker. Finally, a series of suggestions and recommendations are proposed for managers seeking to allocate scarce healthcare resources.

Rationing and priority setting

The terms 'rationing' and 'priority setting' are often used interchangeably, although they can also be used to apply to different stages of a resource allocation process (Klein, 2010).

Common to each is the assumption that limits need to be placed on the provision of healthcare as a result of scarcity of resources (including physical resources such as transplantable organs). Whether as a result of *ad hoc* and implicit rationing, or planned and explicit priority setting, the implications are the same: some patients will be denied interventions that may be of benefit to them. In this context, *resource allocation* – the distribution of resources among competing programmes or patients – is the process by which these decisions and denials are enacted. This chapter is therefore intended to build on the preceding discussion of revenue *generation* in healthcare.

As well as economic shocks and trends, the factors driving the demand–supply gap in healthcare are commonly considered to include:

- *Changing demographics.* The reduction in size of the economically active as a percentage of the population creates cost pressures, as the overall contributions pool decreases relative to healthcare need/demand.
- *Developments in medicine.* The rate at which new, expensive healthcare interventions come to market has accelerated and this creates pressures on healthcare systems operating with fixed budgets.
- *Patient expectations.* Expectations of what public services can and should provide have changed in line with the broader 'consumerization' of Western societies. The argument goes that as patients become more expert in understanding their healthcare needs and more empowered to make demands of healthcare providers, they are prepared to tolerate fewer of the discomforts and inconveniences of previous generations (Williams et al., 2012).

These factors support the view that rationing in healthcare is inevitable and that therefore there is a need to establish fair and rigorous methods for doing this. However, the way that such resource allocation takes place varies according to setting. There are a number of reasons for this. The previous chapter outlined the range of approaches to revenue generation in healthcare. Although the link between method of funding and resource allocation is not mechanistic, certain patterns can be observed. For example, tax-funded systems create a stronger hand for government to influence distribution of resources, whereas independent payers have a more substantial role to play in systems funded through social or private insurance. Approaches to priority setting also reflect broader civic cultures and societal expectations about the role of government in relation to individuals and communities (Blank and Burau, 2008).

As with all healthcare policy decision-making, there is a tension between the role of local and national bodies in the field of priority setting. Resource allocation decisions can be made at various levels, including the national (through government departments and national organizations), local (for example, through health authorities and other purchasers) and at the level of the individual patient and clinician. Historically, governments have often sought the 'path of least resistance', preferring to devolve responsibility for unpopular decisions, for example by setting budget ceilings on provider organizations or by delegating responsibility for resource allocation to local health planning bodies.

More recently, however, a number of attempts to take a national approach to priority setting have been implemented. Sabik and Lie (2008) divide these into two categories: those focusing on *outlining principles* and those focusing on *defining practices*. The first approach involves collective discussion among specially convened panels of stakeholders and experts to identify key principles and criteria for priority setting. However, these commissions – particularly prevalent in Scandinavian countries in the 1990s – have generally been shown to have minimal impact on actual resource allocation, which remains driven largely by considerations of political and institutional expediency (Calltorp, 1999; Ham and Robert, 2003). The second approach (in countries such as the UK, Israel and New Zealand) seeks to prioritize between healthcare interventions and is characterized by decision processes dominated by experts and analysis. Although these have been shown to have more of an impact on decisions in practice, they have created tensions and difficulties for those operating at local levels (Shani et al., 2000; Ham and Robert, 2003; Birch and Gafni, 2006).

Priority setting as a management challenge

Despite these differences in national approaches, those charged with public resource allocation at local levels face a series of common challenges. These are mapped here using Mark Moore's (1995) 'strategic triangle', which depicts the strategic decision-maker as sitting at the intersection between three imperatives (Figure 5.1).

The first point of the triangle in Figure 5.1 is the 'value circle'. This relates to the substantive aims of (in this case) priority setting by which impact and performance should be measured, and underlines the normative importance of pursuing aims that will bring measurable benefit to the population served. Negotiating and articulating these aims requires ongoing deliberation with the public. The second point of the triangle relates to operational capability – that

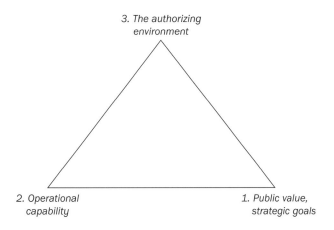

Key:
Point 1 of triangle: value circle (aims of priority setting)
Point 2 of triangle: operational capability (organizing to achieve aims)
Point 3 of triangle: authorizing environment (context within which priority setters operate)

Figure 5.1 The strategic triangle
Source: Moore (1995)

is, 'how the enterprise will have to be organized and operated to achieve the declared objectives' (Moore, 1995: 71) and the resources that can be mobilized in pursuit of these. This acknowledges that substantive aims must be practically achievable given that resources – finance, personnel, skills and technology – are limited. The third point of the triangle relates to the 'authorizing environment' within which priority setters operate. Decision-making requires the support of key external stakeholders, including government, interest groups and donors (primarily tax-paying citizens). Priority setters must be accountable upwardly and outwardly to these groups, as priority setting can only be pursued with prior authorization from government and ongoing support from the public that fund the enterprise. Priority setters must therefore use the strategies available to them to create this platform of legitimacy as well as engage internal actors such as healthcare professionals (Nedlund and Bærøe, 2014).

The challenge for priority setters is to engage the public over the fundamental aims of healthcare by which their investment and disinvestment decisions will be judged and to use the levers and resources available to ensure value is delivered. To secure legitimacy for these endeavours, they must also develop strong relationships with their authorizing environment – government, citizens and powerful opinion formers such as the medical profession and the media – so that the 'bitter pill' of priority setting is more easily swallowed.

Ethical considerations

In systems funded primarily out of public money, it is logical to assume that our priorities should be those that meet public duties and deliver demonstrable benefits in terms of the public good (Oswald, 2015). Deciding what we mean by public duty and public good requires us to engage, at least in the first instance, with questions of social values and ethics (Clark and Weale, 2012). Furthermore, in a context of resource scarcity, it is not enough for priority setters to show that their decisions bring about some benefits to the public: they must also be able to argue that more benefit could not be achieved by using resources in a different way (opportunity cost).

Although these propositions may seem uncontentious, establishing precisely what we mean by the 'public good' in healthcare priority setting remains a considerable challenge. Health economists such as Alan Williams have argued that, 'in health care, "doing good" means improving people's life expectancy and the quality of their life' (1998: 29). From this perspective, successful resource allocation will generate the greatest increase in overall population health. This maximizing principle is based on a utilitarian commitment to the greatest benefit to the greatest number of people. Health technology assessment (HTA), informed by cost-effectiveness analysis, has emerged as a key vehicle for choosing between investment options on such grounds (Sorenson and Chalkidou, 2012).

However, few if any contemporary commentators would advocate utilitarianism, or HTA, as the single driver of priority setting. The primary ethical objection stems from the need to demonstrate *distributive justice* in the allocation of public resources and therefore the belief that considerations of fairness and equity should not be entirely overridden by the health maximization principle. For example, an egalitarian perspective might hold that we should all be entitled to an equal proportion of healthcare resources regardless of our capacity to benefit, or, more commonly, that we should all be given equal opportunity to enjoy good health (Austin, 2001). From this perspective, resource distribution should be linked to levels of need, with the 'worse off' receiving greater priority than the relatively healthy.

A number of models have been developed to help identify who the 'worse off' might be and how we might weigh benefits more highly in these groups. For example, Eric Nord (2005) proposes a disease severity approach in which severe conditions are granted higher importance and Alan Williams advocates a 'fair innings' model in which resources are allocated so as to distribute the number of healthy years most equitably throughout a population (Williams, 1997). However, both of these approaches are controversial, subject to critique (see, for example, Rivlin, 2000; Rosoff, 2014), and far from being universally accepted.

The rise of individualism in attitudes to healthcare has destabilized these and other principles of collective distributive justice. For example, modern political liberalism would hold that the rights and choices of the patient-consumer outweigh considerations of equity and fairness in the allocation of scarce resources. However, this poses acute challenges for the priority setters as they seek to balance the interests of individuals against those of broader population groups.

A focus on the individual also brings into play a number of other ethical considerations. For example, commentators have argued that the 'rule of rescue' – the imperative to save the lives of individuals where these are endangered – should be a key ethical tenet of priority setting (Jonsen, 1986). Others have explored the principle of 'desert' whereby individuals are required to take responsibility for maintaining their own health and forego prioritization if they engage in personal behaviour that increases the risk of poor health (Brown, 2013). As with the collectivist principles of equity and justice, notions of choice, rescue and desert have been heavily criticized and it is to the priority setter that the unenviable task of negotiation between these competing ethical stances falls. It should not surprise us, therefore that, healthcare resource allocation often appears to reflect a confusion of ethical considerations or that there is often controversy and contestation over underlying principles (see Box 5.1).

Decision-making processes

These dilemmas reflect the absence of consensus over the desired ends of resource allocation, which, in turn, creates a powerful argument for investigation of the values of the public in order to resolve these long-standing ethical debates. Furthermore, it is frequently argued that in an explicit priority-setting process, public engagement can help to provide the informed deliberation required for the unpalatable realities of rationing to be understood and accepted (Mooney, 1998). This argument is often associated with communitarianism in its commitment to a process of citizen dialogue over the means and ends of public services. Communitarian citizen engagement requires those involved to take on the 'veil of ignorance' (Rawls, 1972), thereby shedding all considerations of personal interest when deliberating on priorities and trade-offs. Although meaningful engagement of this kind remains relatively rare and presents considerable challenges, it is increasingly accepted as essential to priority-setting decisions.

Box 5.1 Ethical standpoints and principles to consider in priority setting

- **Utilitarianism:** The injunction to bring about the maximum level of utility (for example, overall health gain).
- **Egalitarianism:** The ethical foregrounding of collective responsibility for fair distribution of resources.
- **Libertarianism:** The ethical foregrounding of individual choice and reward, whereby patients are understood as consumers with rights and choices.
- **Communitarianism:** The injunction to allocate resources according to collectively agreed citizen values.
- **Efficiency:** The concern to maximize outcomes from within a limited resource.
- **Equity:** The principle that equal people should be given equal treatment – and in some cases that those worst off should receive extra resources.
- **Desert:** The principle that individuals should be held responsible for their behaviour and that this should influence access to scarce resources.
- **Rule of rescue:** The imperative to save human life wherever possible.
- **Fair innings:** The ethical principle that resources should be distributed so as to distribute healthy years most evenly across a population.
- **Disease severity:** The ethical principle that resources should be weighted towards those in greatest need or with the most severe conditions.

Source: Williams and Robinson (2012).

Although public involvement promises to offer much to the rationing enterprise – helping to resolve disputes over substantive aims, increasing democratic accountability, and raising awareness of the difficulties faced by decision-makers – caution is required. The evidence base on deliberative methods in priority setting remains under-developed (Mitton et al., 2009). Furthermore, commentators have cautioned against the assertion that deliberative engagement can or should be viewed as a panacea for the difficulties of priority setting (Abelson et al., 2003).

Citizen engagement is invariably costly and complex and deliberative approaches (see Box 5.2) tend to be small scale and therefore do not equate to a democratic mandate for action (see Chapter 18). It is also important that the consensus seeking facilitated by deliberative engagement is not pursued at the cost of respect for diversity and recognition of genuine differences where these exist. Finally, the logic of involvement requires that decisions are genuinely open to be shaped by public preferences. This would suggest that plans need to be in place to integrate these with other decision inputs, and that engagement should be avoided when decisions are subject to strong government direction.

The communitarian commitment to procedural (as opposed to substantive) justice is behind Daniels and Sabin's framework 'Accountability for Reasonableness' (A4R) (Daniels and Sabin, 2008). They argue that social value pluralism is irreducible and therefore priority setters should set their sights on achieving decision-making processes that stakeholders will consider to be fair. This fairness, they claim, can be measured by performance against four conditions (see Box 5.3).

Box 5.2   Deliberative involvement methods

- **Citizens' juries:** 12–24 citizens deliberate over a decision over a period of several days.
- **Citizens' panels:** a similar number of citizens meet over a longer period to reach decisions.
- **Consensus conferences:** citizens meet in small groups to discuss scientific or technical issues. A second meeting assembles experts, media and the public to draw together observations and conclusions.
- **Deliberative polling:** deliberative processes are incorporated into opinion polling through follow-up discussions with respondents.

Source: Adapted from Abelson et al. (2003).

Box 5.3   The four conditions of Accountability for Reasonableness

- **Publicity:** decisions taken over the allocation of healthcare resources should be made accessible to the public.
- **Relevance:** decisions should be influenced by evidence that fair-minded people would consider relevant.
- **Appeals:** there should be mechanisms for challenge and review of decisions reached and for resolving any resulting disputes.
- **Enforcement:** there should be effective mechanisms for ensuring the other three conditions are implemented.

Through the development of a consistent approach to resource allocation decision-making, Daniels and Sabin (2008) argue that it becomes possible for a body of case law to emerge that both constrains and informs future decisions and protects decision-makers against unreasonable challenge. In this way, A4R seeks to address the legitimacy deficits of rationing as well as the challenges posed by ethical pluralism and poorly developed decision processes. Although A4R is not without its critics, it has been shown to be useful to decision-makers operating in a variety of settings (Kapiriri et al., 2009). Ultimately, however, A4R cannot entirely substitute for engagement (and public engagement in particular) on the ethical trade-offs involved in rationing, as the notion of 'relevance' remains inherently subjective and therefore contested (Friedman, 2008).

Learning activity 5.1

Processes for setting priorities for the allocation of healthcare resources can be assessed using the four conditions of A4R.

- Using media reports or other sources, identify a priority setting decision from your country such as a decision to introduce a new cancer drug or to restrict provision of an expensive surgical procedure. Using these sources, assess how the process performs in terms of: publicity, relevance, appeals and enforcement.
- Based on your analysis, identify how such decisions might be handled differently in future.

Decision analysis and deliberation

Generating evidence adds value to priority setting through its contribution to decision quality and appropriateness, for example enabling analysis of decision options, outcomes and implementation. This chapter focuses on decision-supporting evidence but there is also a need for information, such as: budget impact data; the tacit knowledge of professionals responsible for leading change and implementation; and the insights and experiences of service users implicated in proposed changes to services.

Health technology assessment (HTA)

In recent years, the pursuit of explicit priority setting has been accompanied by the development of decision support tools and methodologies. HTAs typically incorporate information relating to the efficacy, safety, ethics and costs of an intervention and help bodies making resource allocation decisions deal with the uncertainties they face. For example, this may be in determining what the benefits and risks of a new technology are and what the financial implications of coverage might be.

In many countries, HTA agencies have been set up as advisors to government, although variation exists in both their legal standing and their relationship to reimbursement and pricing (Sorenson and Chalkidou, 2012). For example, whereas adherence to guidance produced by the Institute for Quality and Economic Efficiency in Health Care (IQWiG) in Germany (see www.iqwig.de/en/home.2724.html) and the French National Authority for Health (see http://www.has-sante.fr/portail/jcms/r_1455134/en/about-has) is discretionary, much of the guidance of the UK National Institute for Health and Clinical Excellence (NICE) is legally binding on the health service in England (Stafinski et al., 2011). In New Zealand, the Pharmaceutical Management Agency (PHARMAC) has considerable authority and is empowered by government to set the conditions for funding of new medicines and also to negotiate price levels from within a fixed annual budget (see www.pharmac.health.nz/).

The inclusion of cost-effectiveness analysis (CEA) within HTAs has become increasingly routine, and prospective economic evaluation of technologies is now also a regular accompaniment to clinical trials. CEA can be defined as information on the inputs or costs and the outputs or consequences associated with alternative healthcare interventions and procedures. HTA and CEA results are increasingly reported in generic, summary outcome measures, which facilitate comparison across intervention areas (Drummond et al., 1997). Summary measures of results include: the incremental cost-effectiveness ratio (ICER), which is the ratio of additional costs to additional health effects associated with a new intervention (e.g. cost per quality-adjusted life year gained, or QALY); and the net-benefit statistic, which expresses the additional health effects in monetary units by using an estimate of the 'maximum willingness to pay' per unit of health gain, where available. These techniques are designed to inform resource allocation decisions. Typically, they enable interventions to be ranked according to their cost-effectiveness (the league table approach) or to be measured against a 'critical threshold value' (Lord et al., 2004) in order to determine cost-effectiveness. By contrast, a profile, or cost consequence, approach to reporting results sets out the impact of the intervention on resource use and costs (including specific healthcare service use and costs, and productivity losses) and health outcomes (including disease symptoms, life expectancy and quality of life) in a tabular form, without any attempt to summarize or aggregate them.

The international evidence confirms, however, that use of HTA and economic evaluation remains far more prevalent among national, guidance-producing organizations than it is among local decision-makers operating with fixed healthcare budgets (Williams and Bryan, 2015). This disjuncture reflects a number of factors, including a lack of the requisite resources and expertise within healthcare organizations. Perhaps more significant, however, is the failure of decision analytic models to capture the range of factors that influence priority setting decisions at local levels, such as budgets, service structures and arrangements, organizational practices and norms, and social and political considerations. The aims of priority setting (as we have seen) are likely to be multiple, and in order to be appropriate, decisions will need to reflect local population characteristics and trends, as well as being compatible with local systems and structures.

Programme budgeting and marginal analysis

Evidence that is more relevant to the local context of resource allocation can be generated through long-established methods such as needs assessment (Stevens and Gillam, 1998) and newer applications such as predictive modelling based on local data. Programme budgeting and marginal analysis (PBMA), an approach based on economics, offers a set of practical steps to enable decision-makers to maximize use of resources (Gibson et al., 2006) (see Box 5.4). The benefits of such processes are invariably cited by the decision-makers who adopt them. However, the costs of taking such evidence-based approaches to decision-making are considerable when measured in terms of the time, resources and expertise involved. Furthermore, the optimal division of responsibility for evidence generation and analysis – for example, between internal and external, national and local bodies – will vary from context to context. The challenge for local planning is to achieve the ideal trade-off between local specificity and appropriate economies of scale.

Box 5.4   Understanding PBMA

'Programme budgeting' enables decision-makers to analyse current expenditure and 'marginal analysis' enables comparison of the costs and outcomes of programmes (Mitton and Donaldson, 2004). The emphasis is on identification of areas where more impact could be achieved from within a finite resource to inform future allocation decisions. Typically, PBMA involves an expert panel that draws upon local knowledge and evidence, and operates according to economic principles of maximization and opportunity cost.

Deliberation

Even with full access to decision analysis and information support, decision-making processes will also incorporate elements of deliberation and this aspect of priority-setting processes remains largely non-codified and implicit. Opening up the 'black box' of deliberation is not straightforward. Priority-setting bodies at the local level usually operate according to formally adopted decision criteria. However, such frameworks can either be incidental to deliberation or else take the form of a 'litany', stifling full engagement. For example, in a case study of a priority-setting committee, Russell and Greenhalgh note the tendency to shut down discussion of complex ethical trade-offs when considering whether or not to fund new treatments. In this setting, 'predefined principles' were employed as 'rules that minimise rather than open up space for deliberation and judgement' (2009: 61).

Achieving an appropriate balance between adherence to decision rules and encouraging informed deliberation is a constant challenge to those leading priority setting at local levels. The approach adopted stands a greater chance of success (i.e. through consistency and coherence) if participants fully understand and support the model adopted and the implications for them and their contribution.

Legitimacy and external interests

Priority setting tends to be characterized by ambiguity over ends and means as well as conflict over decision outcomes. Unsurprisingly, therefore, the best laid rationing plans – from the Oregon experiment of the 1980s to the UK National Institute for Health and Clinical Exercise technology appraisal programme – have been damaged by lack of support from government, the public or key stakeholders or a combination of all of these (Jacobs et al., 1998; Sibbald et al., 2009). In the case of the US state of Oregon, the legislature sought to develop a list of core services to be funded through Medicaid but saw ongoing political revisions to the plan to the extent that the original objective of rationalizing the process of technology coverage became largely lost (Jacobs et al., 1998). More recently, analysis of priority setting in Iran found that priorities set by expert panels at the national level, without local engagement, suffered from implementation failure (Khayatzadeh-Mahani et al., 2013).

The role of government

It is not easy to determine what the role of external parties in priority setting ought to be. A key issue is the extent of delegation or devolution of responsibility away from government and the subsequent relationship between appointed bureaucrats and democratically elected representatives. The extent to which local autonomy is possible and desirable will inevitably vary according to broader political structures and the relative responsibility afforded to elected and non-elected public sector functions (Landwehr, 2015). However, the international experience suggests that governments will not hesitate to intervene where they feel the actions of subordinates threaten their own interests (Rhodes and Wanna, 2008)(see Box 5.5). For example, Yeo et al. (1999) found that the attempts of a Canadian provincial health board to adopt a principled approach to priority setting were undermined by political instability and government intrusion. This was a clear example of how the democratic authority of governments can be exercised in ways run counter to locally determined processes and priorities (Robinson et al., 2011).

Interest groups

As well as responding to government, priority setters must also contend with a plethora of sectional and cause-based interest groups. High-profile rationing decisions are invariably accompanied by media coverage and objections from patient organizations, the clinical community, industry and so on. As we have seen, the response of Daniels and Sabin (2008) is to attempt to tie such stakeholders into formalized processes so that the 'fall-out' from tough decisions can be minimized. However, this assumes that the fundamental premise of priority setting (i.e. that resources are scarce and must therefore be allocated between valid claims for investment) is commonly accepted. In practice, stakeholder contributions often reflect a rejection of the entire foundation of rationing. Therefore, while A4R can help us choose between investment options and can reduce undue influence from interest groups, it does not, in itself, rescue the overall enterprise from the threat of backlash and disengagement.

Box 5.5   Case study – Argentina

Gordon et al. (2009) describe a case study of priority setting in an acute care public hospital in Buenos Aires, Argentina, using the A4R framework as an evaluation tool. Respondents in their study consistently cited the influence of the Department of Health in shaping priorities. Government interventions were considered to be primarily 'political and personal' rather than driven by a response to perceived need (p. 188). Decision-making was also considered influenced by historical spending patterns and relationships and, in the absence of compelling evidence, the process was prey to 'union whims, prestige and uninformed biases' (p. 188). The authors noted that these unwelcome influences were made possible by transparency deficits and the absence of an appeals mechanism.

Implications for managers and leaders

It is arguable whether the local priority setter should carry the responsibility to raise awareness of resource scarcity and lead deliberations with stakeholders over its implications for healthcare services. It is difficult to see how explicit decision-making can progress until this nettle is grasped. It could be argued, for example, that raising awareness of the need for fair distribution of scarce resources and building a coalition of support for the priority setting enterprise carries greater long-term importance than does getting individual decisions 'right' according to decision criteria that few stakeholders understand or support. What is clear is that the local decision-maker needs skills that enable them to manage multiple accountabilities and a potentially hostile external environment. High-profile public engagement and a strong media and communications strategy would seem to be prerequisites of a process in which leadership, political acumen and change management expertise are also likely to be beneficial.

This terrain is rarely trodden by commentators on the topic of priority setting but much can be applied from the study and practice of leadership and management more broadly (Reeleder et al., 2006). Characterized by ever-changing political and social tensions, the challenges of rationing are 'adaptive' and therefore require skills in areas of profile and relationship management as well as decision analysis and policy implementation (Heifetz and Laurie, 2001). More controversially, it could be argued that 'pragmatism' should be added to 'principles' and 'processes' in prescriptions for effective priority setting, inasmuch as this denotes the flexibility and judgement required to assess, respond to and shape the prevailing authorizing environment in pursuit of longer term public sector goals.

Implementation

Until now, this chapter has depicted priority setting as a series of decisions and/or decision processes. In practice, formal decisions to 'cover' (i.e. fund) health interventions are a necessary – but not sufficient – element of priority setting and equal focus is required to the subsequent enactment of these decisions within healthcare delivery systems. Much of the priority-setting literature concentrates on decisions about allocating resources and fails to draw insights from disciplines such as implementation science, organizational studies and diffusion of innovation. However, such research as there is suggests some key areas of consideration for those implementing priority setting systems at local levels of healthcare.

The first of these is the need to connect priority-setting activities to actual resource allocation processes (including budget setting and finance). Where these links are weak (i.e. priority setters make recommendations that may or may not be actioned by organizations), the priority-setting enterprise runs the risk of losing 'clout' and being circumvented by other drivers and pressures (Williams and Bryan, 2007). Where ties are stronger (for example, decision-makers have a veto over entry onto a formulary list), the priority setting function is likely to be subject to greater levels of internal and external scrutiny, requiring processes that are highly robust to challenge. A second area of importance is the relationship between priority

Learning activity 5.2

Identify a priority-setting process from within your healthcare system. Try to map and appraise the relationship between your priority-setting process and the authorizing environment through the following activities.

Stage 1: Address the following questions:

- Apart from those actively involved, whose support is required for the priority-setting process to be considered legitimate?
- What other aspects of context (e.g. local events, politics and demographics) might affect support for the priority-setting process?
- What are the key media bodies that influence perceptions of healthcare locally?

Stage 2: Draw up a list of external groups and add to these: government (e.g. national or provincial) and the public. Answer the following questions of each group:

- How could this group influence the priority-setting process?
- How – if at all – does this group currently influence the priority-setting process?
- Do you actively engage this group? If so, how?
- Does this group currently have a high level of awareness of the priority-setting process?
- What is their perception of those making decisions?
- Could they be involved in the priority-setting process?
- Are they involved in the priority-setting process?
- What is the nature of the relationship between this group and other parts of the authorizing environment?
- Has this group criticized decisions in the past?
- Is this group's interests threatened by a particular decision?

Answering these questions should help you to understand the relationship between the priority-setting process and its authorizing environment.

Source: Williams (2015).

setting and other aspects of strategic planning, performance measurement, and so on. Arguably, priority setting should suffuse each of these activities. However, embedding decision-making in this way requires greater clarity over roles, responsibilities and relationships than is often evident in local healthcare systems (Robinson et al., 2011).

A third area of concern is the lack of attention paid to the implementation of priority-setting decisions, with decision-making often considered a satisfactory endpoint in itself. A wealth of literature developed in other arenas supports the claim that healthcare systems tend to be 'complex' – involving multiple interactions between groups across boundaries – and it therefore appears naïve to assume that the introduction and withdrawal of healthcare interventions can proceed in a simple, mechanistic fashion. Sophisticated implementation and improvement strategies are required if priority-setting decisions are to be fully adopted and adapted into practice.

Implementation barriers take on even greater significance when the priority-setting enterprise turns to 'disinvestment' (or 'decommissioning') of obsolete practices. This is an area on which relatively little published evidence or good practice exists. However, in the context of reduced overall budgets, substitution and disinvestment become paramount (Daniels et al., 2013). Previous studies have found that explicit priority setting tends to have an additive effect on overall spending (Sabik and Lie, 2008), suggesting that for priority setting to become an effective tool for reducing overall activity and spend, more work needs to be done.

Insights from the broader public policy literature suggest that implementation is most challenging when high levels of ambiguity and conflict surround decisions to be made (Matland, 1995; Robert et al., 2014). This may help to explain some of the difficulties priority setters face. We have seen that the ethical complexity of rationing heightens the sense of decision ambiguity (i.e. what are we trying to achieve?). Furthermore, the highly politicized context of healthcare resource allocation increases the likelihood of conflict ensuing from decisions to invest and disinvest. In these circumstances, implementation of setting decisions will be subject to the interplay of coalitions of local interest groups – including those involved in the provision and receipt of healthcare.

Addressing these barriers can therefore be understood as an attempt to *reduce* ambiguity and conflict (see Box 5.6). We have discussed the role of public engagement, and to that should be added the importance of soliciting support for the priority-setting process from clinical, governmental and other stakeholders. Explicit priority setting also implies the need for a sophisticated media and communications strategy and skills in areas of sense-making and leadership (Williams et al., 2012).

Box 5.6   Overcoming implementation barriers

Cornelissen et al. (2014) offer insights for those seeking to ensure implementation of priority setting decisions:

- Clarify scope, ownership and responsibilities for implementation of priority-setting decisions.
- Assess organizational readiness for implementation.
- Adapt implementation to context, e.g. timescales, funding streams and organizational structures.
- Ensure the resources and capacity for implementation are in place.

Learning activity 5.3

Select one of the following hypothetical decisions:

1   Decision to remove a drug from a hospital formulary.
2   Decision to implement locally national guidance on treatments for cancer.
3   Decision to cease funding for a specific surgical procedure.
4   Decision not to renew a contract with a charity providing specialist health/social care services.
5   Decision to make all treatments available according to strict considerations of cost-effectiveness.
6   Decision to close the emergency department of a local hospital.

Consider the implementation responsibilities and potential impediments to implementation and how these might be addressed:

- Has responsibility for putting the decision into practice been allocated and accepted?
- Have you assessed the readiness of your organization(s) to implement the decisions?
- Have internal and external groups been engaged in the process?
- Have sufficient implementation resources been identified?
- Has support from senior leaders and other opinion formers been obtained?
- Are mechanisms in place to feedback information following the implementation process?

Conclusion and recommendations

Explicit approaches to priority setting and rationing are increasingly advocated as an alternative (or supplement) to other cost-containment strategies. However, explicit approaches require attention to a range of factors if they are to be successful. In this chapter, we have summarized some key themes from the literature on resource allocation and priority setting in healthcare, focusing in particular on the management function. As research, policy and practice in this area have matured, there has been an increasing acceptance that a single prescription (whether ethical, analytical or structural) is unlikely to emerge as a solution for all the problems priority setters face. At this stage, therefore, we are confined to identification of some key 'ingredients' of a priority setting process that stands a reasonable chance of success (see Box 5.7).

Box 5.7   Recommendations

- Engage in debate and discussion over the ethical underpinnings and trade-offs of priority setting, including with the public and other stakeholders.
- Attend to the procedural dimensions of decision-making (e.g. using a framework such as A4R).
- Draw on appropriate evidence and analytical expertise.
- Clarify remit and roles of the priority-setting body and those involved in it.
- Understand and manage the authorizing environment.
- Ensure both leadership and management provisions are in place.

The first requirement is to explore and debate the ethical underpinnings of resource allocation: even though resolution of the tensions involved may not always be possible, this will help to make explicit the moral concerns informing decisions. Managers and decision-makers should involve the public in these discussions. Although engaging citizens is difficult and problematic, it is essential if decisions over resource allocation are to be considered legitimate. Public engagement can also help to raise awareness of the difficulties decision-makers face.

Second, there is a need to attend to the procedural dimensions of decision-making. For example, adopting process-based models (such as A4R) can improve quality, consistency and legitimacy of decisions. Priority setters should also draw on the evidence base, although decision analysis cannot be expected to replace fully debate and deliberation.

Third, there is a need to clarify the remit of decision-making bodies, the roles and responsibilities of those involved, the budgets implicated in determinations, and the link to other organizational strategies and priorities.

Finally, some management of the authorizing environment is required. Many of the above strategies can help garner legitimacy for the priority-setting enterprise. However, as rationing remains a highly politicized activity, those involved should deploy all available means to maximize public trust and stakeholder commitment, and create a coalition of support for the decision-making processes of resource allocation.

For the manager or strategic decision-maker, these ingredients can be summarized in terms of the need to align the three imperatives of the strategic triangle: maximizing value through the deployment of scarce resources in a process that reflects the authority of political overseers and bolsters public trust in the institutions of care. However, it is unlikely that this daunting challenge can be met by the management function alone. Rather, the nettle of priority setting will need to be grasped by government, interest groups and wider civic society if substantial progress is to be made. As countries wrestle with the effects of a period of global recession, effective priority setting looks set to move further into the centre ground of health policy.

Learning resources

International Society on Priorities in Health Care: The purpose of this society is to strengthen the theory and practice of priority setting in healthcare by providing a forum in which researchers, practitioners and others involved in priority setting can come together to exchange ideas and experience [www.birmingham.ac.uk/priorities2016].

Health Economic Evaluations Database (HEED): This resource provides information on studies of cost-effectiveness and other forms of economic evaluation of medicines and other treatments and medical interventions [http://onlinelibrary.wiley.com/book/10.1002/9780470510933].

Star: Socio-Technical Allocation of Resources: Star is a priority setting tool and process that helps those planning services to allocate their health resources to benefit patients in their community. Together with the London School of Economics (LSE), the Health Foundation has developed the Star approach that combines value for money analysis with stakeholder engagement, where an Excel-based tool is used alongside a facilitated stakeholder workshop [http://www.health.org.uk/learning/star].

References

Abelson, J., Forest, P., Eyles, J., Smith, P., Martin, E. and Gauvin, F. (2003) Deliberations about deliberative methods: issues in the design and evaluation of public participation processes, *Social Science and Medicine*, 57: 239–51.

Austin, S.E. (2001) *Medical Justice: A Guide to Fair Provision*. New York: Peter Lang.

Birch, S. and Gafni, A. (2006) The biggest bang for the buck or bigger bucks for the bang: the fallacy of the cost-effectiveness threshold, *Journal of Health Services Research and Policy*, 11 (1): 46–51.

Blank, R.H. and Burau, V. (2008) *Comparative Health Policy* (2nd edn.). Basingstoke: Palgrave Macmillan.

Brown, R.C.H. (2013) Moral responsibility for (un)healthy behaviour, *Journal of Medical Ethics*, 39 (11): 695–8.

Calltorp, J. (1999) Priority setting in health policy in Sweden and a comparison with Norway, *Health Policy*, 50: 1–9.

Clark, S. and Weale, A. (2012) Social values in health priority setting: a conceptual framework, *Journal of Health Organization and Management*, 26 (3): 293–316.

Cornelissen, E., Mitton, C., Davidson, A., Reid, C., Hole, R., Visockas, A. et al. (2014) Changing priority setting practice: the role of implementation in practice change, *Health Policy*, 117 (2): 266–74.

Cromwell, I., Peacock, S.J. and Mitton, C. (2015) 'Real-world' health care priority setting using explicit decision criteria: a systematic review of the literature, *BMC Health Services Research*, 15: 164.

Daniels, N. and Sabin, J. (2008) *Setting Limits Fairly: Learning to Share Resources for Health*. Oxford: Oxford University Press.

Daniels, T., Williams, I., Robinson, S. and Spence, K. (2013) Tackling disinvestment in health care services: the views of resource allocators in the English NHS, *Journal of Health Organization and Management*, 27 (6): 762–80.

Drummond, M.F.B., O'Brien, G., Stoddart, G. and Torrance, G. (1997) *Methods for the Economic Evaluation of Healthcare Programmes*. Oxford: Oxford University Press.

Friedman, A. (2008) Beyond accountability for reasonableness, *Bioethics*, 22 (2): 101–12.

Gibson, J., Mitton, C., Martin, D., Donaldson, C. and Singer, P. (2006) Ethics and economics: does programme budgeting and marginal analysis contribute to fair priority setting?, *Journal of Health Services Research and Policy*, 11 (1): 32–7.

Gordon, H., Kapiriri, L. and Martin, D.K. (2009) Priority setting in an acute care hospital in Argentina: a qualitative case study, *Acta Bioethica*, 15 (2): 184–92.

Ham, C. and Robert, G. (eds.) (2003) *Reasonable Rationing: International Experience of Priority Setting in Health Care*. Maidenhead: Open University Press.

Heifetz, R.A. and Laurie, D.L. (2001) The work of leadership, *Harvard Business Review*, December, Reprint R0111 (originally published 1997, *HBR*, January/February: 124–34).

Holm, S. (1998) Goodbye to the simple solutions: the second phase of priority setting in health care, *British Medical Journal*, 317: 1000–2.

Jacobs, L.R., Marmor, T. and Oberlander, J. (1998) *The Political Paradox of Rationing: The Case of the Oregon Health Plan*. The Innovations in American Government Program. Occasional Paper #4. Cambridge, MA: John F. Kennedy School of Government, Harvard University.

Jonsen, A.R. (1986) Bentham in a box: technology assessment and health care allocation, *Law, Medicine and Health Care*, 14 (3): 172–4.

Kapiriri, L., Norheim, O.F. and Martin, D.K. (2009) Fairness and accountability for reasonableness: do the views of priority setting decision makers differ across health systems?, *Social Science and Medicine*, 68: 766–73.

Karanikolos, M., Mladovsky, P., Cylus, J., Thomson, S., Basu, S., Stuckler, D. et al. (2013) Financial crisis, austerity, and health in Europe, *Lancet*, 381: 1323–31.

Khayatzadeh-Mahani, A., Fotaki, M. and Harvey, G. (2013) Priority setting and implementation in a centralized health system: a case study of Kerman province in Iran, *Health Policy and Planning*, 28: 480–94.

Klein, R. (2010) Rationing in the fiscal ice age, *Health Economics, Politics and Law*, 5 (4): 389–96.

Landwehr, C. (2015) Democratic meta-deliberation: towards reflective institutional design, *Political Studies*, 63 (S1): 38–54.

Lord, J., Laking, G. and Fischer, A. (2004) Health care resource allocation: is the threshold rule good enough?, *Journal of Health Services Research and Policy*, 9 (4): 237–45.

Matland, R.E. (1995) Synthesising the implementation literature: the ambiguity-conflict model of policy implementation, *Journal of Public Administration Research and Theory*, 5 (2): 145–57.

Mitton, C. and Donaldson, C. (2004) Doing health care priority setting: principles, practice and challenges, *Cost Effectiveness and Resource Allocation*, 2: 3.

Mitton, C., Smith, N., Peacock, S., Evoy, B. and Abelson, J. (2009) Public participation in health care priority setting: a scoping review, *Health Policy*, 91 (3): 219–28.

Mooney, G. (1998) 'Communitarian claims' as an ethical basis for allocating health care resources, *Social Science and Medicine*, 4 (9): 1171–80.

Moore, M. (1995) *Creating Public Value: Strategic Management in Government*. Cambridge, MA: Harvard University Press.

Nedlund, A. and Bærøe, K. (2014) Legitimate policymaking: the importance of including health-care workers in limit-setting decisions in health care, *Public Health Ethics*, 7 (2): 123–33.

Nord, E. (2005) Concerns for the worse off: fair innings versus severity, *Social Science and Medicine*, 60: 257–63.

Oswald, M. (2015) In a democracy, what should a healthcare system do? A dilemma for public policymakers, *Politics, Philosophy and Economics*, 14 (1): 23–52.

Rawls, J. (1972) *A Theory of Justice*. Oxford: Oxford University Press.

Reeleder, D., Goel, V., Singer, P.A. and Martin, D.K. (2006) Leadership and priority setting: the perspective of hospital CEOs, *Health Policy*, 79: 24–34.

Rhodes, R.A.W. and Wanna, J. (2008) Stairways to heaven: a reply to Alford, *Australian Journal of Public Administration*, 67 (3): 367–70.

Rivlin, M.M. (2000) Why the fair innings argument is not persuasive, *BMC Medical Ethics*, 1: 1.

Robert, G., Harlock, J. and Williams, I. (2014) Disentangling rhetoric and reality: an international Delphi study of factors and processes that facilitate the successful implementation of decisions to decommission healthcare services, *Implementation Science*, 9: 123.

Robinson, S., Dickinson, H., Williams, I., Freeman, T., Rumbold, B. and Spence, K. (2011) *Setting Priorities in Health: A Study of English Primary Care Trusts*. Birmingham: Nuffield Trust and the Health Services Management Centre, University of Birmingham.

Rosoff, P.M. (2014) *Rationing is Not a Four-Letter Word: Setting Limits on Healthcare*. Cambridge, MA: MIT Press.

Russell, J. and Greenhalgh, T. (2009) *Rhetoric, Evidence and Policy Making: A Case Study of Priority Setting in Primary Care*. London: University College London.

Sabik, L.M. and Lie, R.K. (2008) Priority setting in health care: lessons from the experiences of eight countries, *International Journal for Equity and Health*, 7: 4.

Shani, S., Siebzehner, M.I., Luxenburg, O. and Shemer, J. (2000) Setting priorities for the adoption of health technologies on a national level – the Israeli experience, *Health Policy*, 54 (3): 169–85.

Sibbald, S.L., Singer, P.A., Upshur, R. and Martin, D.K. (2009) Priority setting: what constitutes success? A conceptual framework for successful priority setting, *BMC Health Services Research*, 9: 43.

Sorenson, C. and Chalkidou, K. (2012) Reflections on the evolution of health technology assessment in Europe, *Health Economics, Policy and Law*, 7 (1): 24-45.

Stafinski, T., Menon, D., Phillipon, D.J. and McCabe, C. (2011) Health technology funding decision-making processes around the world: the same, yet different, *Pharmacoeconomics*, 29 (6): 475–95.

Stevens, A. and Gillam, S. (1998) Needs assessment: from theory to practice, *British Medical Journal*, 316: 1448–52.

Williams, A. (1997) Intergenerational equity: an exploration of the fair innings argument, *Health Economics*, 6 (2): 117–32.

Williams, A. (1998) Economics, QALYs and medical ethics: a health economist's perspective, in S. Dracopoulou (ed.) *Ethics and Values in Health Care Management*. London: Routledge.

Williams, A. (2015) Receptive rationing: reflections and suggestions for priority setters in health care, *Journal of Health Organization and Management*, 29 (6): 701–10.

Williams, I. and Bryan, S. (2007) Cost-effectiveness analysis and formulary decision making in England: findings from research, *Social Science and Medicine*, 65 (10): 2116–29.

Williams, I. and Bryan, S. (2015) Lonely at the top and stuck in the middle? The ongoing challenge of using cost-effectiveness information in priority setting, *International Journal of Health Policy and Management*, 4 (3): 185–7.

Williams, I. and Robinson, S. (2012) Decision making and priority setting, in J. Glasby (ed.) *Commissioning for Health and Well-Being*. Bristol: Policy Press.

Williams, I., Robinson, S. and Dickinson, H. (2012) *Rationing in Health Care: The Theory and Practice of Priority Setting*. Bristol: Policy Press.

Yeo, M., Williams, J.R. and Hooper, W. (1999) Incorporating ethics in priority setting: a case study of a rational health board in Canada, *Health Care Analysis*, 7: 177–94.

Research and innovation in healthcare

Ruth McDonald

Introduction

In this chapter, we focus on what is meant by research and innovation, as well as the challenges they pose in health settings. These are important requisites to understanding the role that research and innovation play in decision-making in healthcare. We also address why these issues are relevant more generally and for managers specifically.

Much of what we do in our working lives is based on what we might call 'common sense'. Over time we accumulate experience and, hopefully, learn from our mistakes. But should we use 'common sense' as a basis for decision-making in all aspects of healthcare? Einstein described common sense as the collection of prejudices we have acquired by the age of eighteen. Whether you agree with him or not, there is certainly an argument against relying solely on common sense as the basis for decisions about what we should do in healthcare settings.

Healthcare delivery and organization involves a lot of decision-making. Individual clinicians make decisions about how to deliver care or decisions about what is best for a specific patient. Decisions often involve groups of people (e.g. managers, nurses, doctors) coming together to make choices about operational or strategic issues. Individuals may be unsure about what the best course of action is. When decisions involve groups, sometimes there are disagreements about what is best in a particular scenario. In other cases, we may have no views or theories about, for example, a proposed new way of treating patients since we have no experience on which to judge this. In addition, human beings are often guilty of bias in making judgements and drawing inferences (Sutherland, 2013).

Using common sense may mean that we respond to surface characteristics rather than drilling down to understand what may be complex cause-and-effect relationships (Croskerry, 2002). Healthcare is a high-risk setting and leaving individuals and groups to apply common sense when trying out new treatments or ways of delivering services would be a risky strategy. It would also place huge demands on those who work in health systems. In many instances, therefore, a more systematic approach is needed.

Responding to this state of affairs, the 'evidence-based medicine' (Sackett, 1997) movement has evolved to try to make clinical practice more grounded in research evidence to achieve safer, more consistent and more effective care (Leape et al., 2002). This has resulted in a large body of research evidence being generated. In addition to this clinical research, there is a growing volume of research that can help to inform decision-making about, for example, service design, managing staff or motivating professionals. However, research evidence does not automatically get translated into practice. There are many things that can inhibit or prevent widespread adoption (Greenhalgh et al., 2004). One reason for this is that the evidence-based medicine movement has been so successful that the number of studies providing clinical evidence has grown faster than our ability to read and process them (Allen and Harkins, 2005). Another reason is that people sometimes resist change, especially if they perceive it as threatening their interests (Currie et al., 2012), and innovative practice or technologies can be costly and time consuming to implement. The existence of research evidence does not guarantee that it will be acted upon and spreading innovative practice can present a difficult challenge for managers.

Research

What is research?

Research, in simple terms, involves a systematic attempt to study a problem and to advance human knowledge. Health and medical research is concerned with deriving generalizable new knowledge or evidence that can be applied to health services. Normally researchers aim to publish their findings in journals that follow a peer-review process (peer review is discussed in more detail later in the chapter). This is different from other approaches to studying problems, such as management consultancy, where the focus is on contributing to local, often organization-specific knowledge, and findings are not published in peer-reviewed journals.

Evidence generated from research includes the development and application of new medicines and technologies as well as new ways of organizing care. The existence of research evidence is one thing, but getting that research evidence into practice can be a long and complex process.

In most countries, health research is subject to regulation that aims to provide participants with assurance that the research that they take part in is of high quality, safe and ethical. The titles of review bodies differ between countries (e.g. research ethics committees in the UK, institutional review boards in the USA, human research ethics committees in Australia). These bodies also look at study design to ensure that the results of research can be relied upon and used as evidence to inform future decisions about healthcare and treatment. This adds to the time taken to conduct research, since researchers have to complete and submit detailed applications outlining what they plan to do in their study. They have to wait until the review body convenes to discuss this and they may appear in person to answer review body members' questions. The review body may require changes to the study design and all this adds to the time taken before the research can commence.

Obtaining approval from the review body does not mean that researchers have guaranteed access to the people and organizations they plan to study. There are usually additional processes that researchers need to follow to demonstrate to organizations that they are competent professionals and that there are arrangements in place to compensate for any injury or loss that may arise as a result of the research. Again, this adds to the time spent by researchers before the research can commence.

For managers who need answers quickly and for researchers who want to start their study as soon as possible, such delays can be a source of frustration. The delays may also be puzzling for managers, since management consultants do not apply for approval to such review bodies. This is because they are not conducting research and are therefore exempt.

Who funds research?

The aim of research is 'objective', scientific investigation. Ideally, researchers should be independent of funders. Funding for research comes from many sources. There are mechanisms in place to ensure an 'arm's length' relationship between politicians and researchers, with free-standing bodies making decisions on resource allocation. In many countries, there are bodies that allocate money from the public purse for health research. The process in many countries usually involves bidders responding to a call that generates competition between groups of researchers. Managers may be involved in contributing to the call, by suggesting topics for investigation or helping to shape the format and content of the call. They might also sit on the panels that assess bids.

Independent sector bodies, such as pharmaceutical companies and producers of new technologies, typically fund research, as well as charitable organizations. Some of these may be concerned with particular diseases or patient groups. Others may be interested in improving healthcare more generally. For example, the Commonwealth Fund in the United States is a private foundation that aims 'to promote a high performing health care system that achieves better access, improved quality, and greater efficiency, particularly for society's most vulnerable, including low-income people, the uninsured, minority Americans, young children, and elderly adults' (Commonwealth Fund, n.d.). As part of this process, it supports and funds independent research on healthcare issues. Most peer-reviewed journals require authors to declare any conflict of interest and details of who funded the study. One book listed in the Learning resources at the end of this chapter (Greenhalgh, 2014) is helpful when reading a published study. It lists questions that readers should ask themselves and it highlights the importance of looking for conflicts of interest. If the funder or authors stand to benefit financially, then readers should ask whether sufficient safeguards were in place to guard against bias.

Why does research take a long time?

The requirement to tender for work and the rigours of the scientific method (which we discuss below) often means that the process from publication of the call for bids to starting the research is a lengthy one. Thus research is not always responsive to situations where decision-makers and managers need answers within a short timescale. This is not an intrinsic feature of research but instead reflects the processes that are often in operation to commission the research. At the same time, researchers follow the scientific method, which has strong assumptions about what counts as evidence and is time consuming. In the absence of other information, managers may be willing to accept what researchers would perceive as insufficiently strong evidence. This tension between practitioners facing problems today and researchers spending several years to investigate potential solutions reflects the different cultural worlds inhabited by researchers, on the one hand, and policy-makers and practitioners, on the other.

Avoiding bias in research

For non-researchers, it can be very difficult to discern what high-quality or unbiased research looks like. *How to Read a Paper* by Greenhalgh (2014) provides a good introduction to this topic, complete with a set of questions the reader should ask when trying to gauge the quality of a research paper. This section examines some of the things that managers need to be aware of when attempting to use research studies.

As outlined above, there is a potential conflict of interest related to the funding of research. For example, it is important that the commercial interests of drugs and technologies manufacturers do not influence any research studies they fund. In practice, however, evidence suggests that studies funded by pharmaceutical companies are more likely to result in findings favourable to the funder (Lexchin et al., 2003), and political interference in publicly funded research is known to occur (Shaw, 2007).

There are many reasons why bias may occur and the problem is not solely related to funder interests. Bias can happen as a result of the ways in which studies are designed and conducted. There is also the issue of publication bias. Studies that demonstrate positive effects are much more likely to be published than those which show no effect (Begg and Berlin, 1988).

Learning activity 6.1

- We know that breastfeeding confers health benefits. Do you think that it also contributes to intelligence?
- A recent study in the *Lancet* showed that babies who were breastfed in Brazil grew up to be more intelligent and earned more than their peers fed formula milk (Victora et al., 2015). A study in the *British Medical Journal* in 2006 (Der et al., 2006) found no such effect. Are you inclined to believe one of these more than the other? Why (not)?

Even when studies are published, readers do not always approach them from a neutral stance. Evidence shows that people frame findings according to their prior beliefs about what works. Did your beliefs about breastfeeding and intelligence influence your views about the papers described above? If not, you are unusual! It is important to be aware of this 'confirmation bias' (Nickerson, 1998) when interpreting published research results.

Overcoming bias? The scientific method

The scientific method is a process by which researchers have attempted to construct an accurate unbiased representation of the world. This has evolved over time and aims to minimize bias and error. Not all studies are equally protected from bias and error and there is a hierarchy of evidence in terms of study designs and their ability to reduce error and bias.

Case reports, which describe experiences related to a single patient, are useful in identifying rare events and generating hypotheses. However, they should not be used as the basis for making decisions about groups of patients. A report of an adverse event in a patient who is taking a drug might suggest that the drug is the cause of the problem. However, the cause might be one of myriad other factors. Instead, one could look at data on large groups of people to avoid relying on a single case. You could compare a group that took the drug with another group that did not. But the evidence for making cause-and-effect judgements could still be flawed, even if participants are recruited who are similar in as many respects as possible. The true reason for an adverse event might still elude us.

Research and confounding variables

The term 'confounding' factors or variables is used to describe factors or events that are not observed or measured as part of the study, but which could be causing the results observed by the researchers (see Box 6.1).

Learning activity 6.2

Research shows that, in Europe, areas that have high stork populations also have higher numbers of births, providing support for the story that storks are responsible for newborn babies. What would you conclude from this research and why?

Box 6.1   Case study – confounding and breastfeeding

Breastfeeding is promoted widely as a public health intervention, but a recent study from Brazil also found a link with IQ, educational attainment and income (Victora et al., 2015). Should we trust this result?

The researchers followed a cohort of neonates from birth for thirty years. They were careful to choose a large group to minimize the possibility that they would make erroneous conclusions based on having a small, unrepresentative sample. They ensured that the cohort included babies of all social classes. Unlike richer countries such as Sweden and Denmark, where breastfeeding is strongly related to social class, women across all the social classes in Brazil were breastfeeding their babies.

The researchers identified a range of confounding variables, including income, parental education, birthweight and household assets. They adjusted the results to reflect the impact of these, but the link between breastfeeding and offspring intelligence remained. However, the researchers did not measure the intelligence of the parents. They relied on the number of years in education of parents, but this is not the same as giving the parents an IQ test. Previous studies have shown that if you do this, the strong relationship between breastfeeding and IQ disappears (e.g. Der et al., 2006).

Hierarchy of evidence

Randomized controlled trials

Randomized controlled trials (RCTs) are towards the top of the hierarchy of evidence (see Figure 6.1) and involve carefully controlling exposure to a treatment or service and ensuring that patients in both groups are not different in relevant respects. Patients are followed prospectively (i.e. they are observed over time in 'real time' rather than data being collected retrospectively). This increases the likelihood of being able to identify and measure confounding variables compared with retrospective data collection. It also gives the researchers greater control over the context. Patients are allocated to intervention and non-intervention (control) groups on a random basis (i.e. they have an equal chance of being allocated to one or other of the two groups). RCTs are usually used to determine whether a cause-and-effect relationship exists between treatments (for example, new drugs or surgical procedures) and outcomes. Greenhalgh (2014) provides advice on how to read and critique published RCTs.

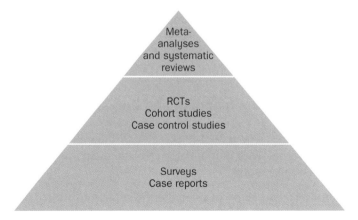

Figure 6.1 Hierarchy of evidence
Source: Adapted from Greenhalgh (2014)

Learning activity 6.3

- Since RCTs may involve withholding treatment or a particular intervention from one group of patients, this may pose ethical issues. In some circumstances, it may be fine to withhold treatment from a group of patients. Can you identify when this might be the case and when not?
- The best way to ascertain whether breastfeeding is associated with higher intelligence and income in adulthood would be to randomize neonates to receive either breastfeeding or formula milk. Are there any problems with such an approach?

Ideally, the process of allocating participants to the control and intervention groups should ensure that researchers and trial participants are 'blind' to (unaware of) the nature of treatment (e.g. placebo or active) being provided. This is not always possible. For example, in a trial comparing surgery with physiotherapy there is no 'placebo' intervention. Bringing together and analysing evidence from a number of well-designed RCTs provides many more observations to draw on than a single RCT. For this reason, systematic reviews of the evidence (systematic because their methods minimize bias) and 'meta-analyses' (statistical analyses to combine findings from a number of studies) are often placed at the top of the hierarchy of evidence.

A meta-analysis of studies examining the link between breastfeeding and cognitive development (note that this is *not* the same as intelligence) was helpful in answering an important question. A number of studies had identified a link between breastfeeding and cognitive development (e.g. Taylor and Wadsworth, 1984) but critics suggested that the apparent effect was really due to confounding factors (Jacobson and Jacobson, 1992). In particular, they were concerned that issues such as the socioeconomic status of the parents or maternal education might be what was really impacting on development. The meta-analysis of twenty different studies concluded that after controlling for confounding variables, the link between breastfeeding and development remained (Anderson et al., 1999).

Cohort and case control studies

Other study designs include cohort studies and case control studies. The former are longitudinal studies that involve following two or more groups of people to see what happens over time. The groups are selected on the basis of their exposure to something. For example, researchers investigating the link between maternal smoking during pregnancy and low birthweight followed cohorts of women and found a strong link (e.g. Horta et al., 1997). It would not have been ethical to randomize the women to smoking and non-smoking arms of an RCT.

Case control studies, like cohort studies, are usually concerned with what causes disease (unlike RCTs, which are normally concerned with treating disease). This involves matching patients with a particular condition with people who do not have that condition. Data collection involves asking participants to recollect something. For example, some recent studies looking at the link between mobile phone use and cancer have used this method. Cancer patients and people without the condition were asked to recall how often and for how long they used their phones. However, people are not always able to remember. Also, their answers may be affected by their prior beliefs about phones and cancer, and people with brain tumours may have impaired memory due to their illness. Case control studies are therefore lower down the hierarchy of evidence than RCTs and cohort studies.

Factors to consider when choosing a design

The choice of research design will depend on the research question of interest. If a new service has been provided at a number of sites and you wish to determine whether this has had an impact on outcomes and how these outcomes compare with other sites that have not adopted this approach, then you cannot use an RCT. In hospitals not adopting the approach, patients will not have been randomly assigned to intervention and control groups and you may be forced to rely on retrospective data. This does not mean not undertaking the study, but you should be aware of the potential for error and bias when conducting and interpreting the research. Furthermore, exercising careful control over the participants and factors that might influence the ability of the trial to delineate clear cause-and-effect relationships means that RCTs do not reflect 'real-world' environments. For example, if researchers want to test the relationship between a specific new drug taken by pregnant women and birth outcomes, they will need to exclude women who have various complications or health issues. If they included women with gestational diabetes, for example, then any potential adverse effects or lack of impact of the new drug might be related to the complications and not the drug. In the real world, health services deliver care to a wide range of people and do not exclude large groups in the way RCTs do. Furthermore, since RCTs often involve regular contact with trial participants, this may improve adherence to the treatment in a way that does not happen in the real world. This raises questions about how and to what extent findings translate to 'real-world' settings.

Accessing research evidence

Many studies are published every single day, so trying to make sense of and critically appraising studies can be difficult. Reviews of studies that bring together and appraise the findings of published evidence, and which come from a trusted source, can thus be very useful. The Learning resources section at the end of the chapter provides details of some of these sources.

Many initiatives to improve care are less about clinical 'products' and more about new ways of organizing care. Managers need to be able to access and interpret a range of evidence in these areas. Clinicians may not be convinced by evidence from sources other than RCTs, but as outlined above it is not always possible to conduct an RCT because of the nature of the topic. Furthermore, while RCTs try to screen out the messy 'real-world' factors, other studies conducted in a real-world context can provide more contextual information and allow a more in-depth understanding of what happened. RCTs have been described as a 'black box' approach – that is, they tell us the inputs and outputs but don't shed light on the processes inside the box. Ideally, studies should explain how and why things occurred as opposed to merely reporting outputs or outcomes. It is possible to conduct additional data collection and analysis alongside RCTs to shine a light inside the 'black box'. Furthermore, it is not just RCTs that focus on inputs and outputs, missing out the process that happens inside the 'black box'. In the case study below concerning a financial incentive initiative in the USA, for example, various studies report on the impact but they tell us little about the process. This means that if impact is not in line with expectations, we do not know whether this is because our expectations about cause and effect were flawed or because the intervention was not implemented as intended.

As outlined above, systematic reviews of the evidence aim to minimize bias. A systematic review is a critical assessment and evaluation of all research studies that concern a particular issue. It is recognized that placing reliance on one or two studies runs the risk that if those studies are flawed or limited in some way, then erroneous conclusions may be drawn. Systematic reviews highlight such flaws and limitations, but in the absence of these, it is important to be able to assess the quality of research and to be aware that research evidence can be challenged over time as new research findings are produced. The following case study provides an example of this (Box 6.2).

Box 6.2   Case study – Health Quality Incentive Demonstration (HQID), USA

The HQID initiative involved financial incentives to improve the quality of care in participating hospitals. Initial publicity suggested that the intervention had a positive impact on health and saved a vast amount of money. Much of this publicity was provided by one of the organizations involved in the initiative, which was keen to highlight the apparent success of the programme. There is no suggestion that this organization was deliberately making false claims.

Two studies reported that the intervention had achieved positive results, while another found no effect. One of these positive studies was published in a highly rated medical journal. This paper did the best job in terms of controlling for factors that might result in erroneous conclusions being drawn. However, the study only examined the impact on process measures and did not look at outcomes. It could be the case, for example, that the hospital record-keeping had improved, since payment was made for performance on process measures, but care delivery had not changed. The only study that looked at mortality found no impact.

Two years later, a well-conducted, large-scale study based on 6.7 million patients found that the intervention was not associated with a reduction in mortality. There was no impact on costs.

Source: Ryan et al. (2012).

Peer review

In order to maintain standards in published research, a system of peer review is in operation for research published in academic journals. This means that researchers submit findings for publication to a specific journal and their submission is sent out to academic subject experts who provide reviews, commenting on the submission's quality and suitability for publication. Researchers may be required to revise their submission and this may involve conducting further tests or analyses to ensure that the findings are robust. For research that is not published in academic journals, no such system may be in place. It is important to look at the source when accessing evidence and ascertain whether it has been subject to peer review. Peer review does not provide an absolute guarantee of research quality. For example, *The Lancet*, a highly regarded academic journal published a study that led to the controversy about the link between the measles-mumps-rubella (MMR) vaccine and the risk of autism (Wakefield et al., 1998). The article was later retracted. However, in general, more reliance can be placed on research that has been subject to rigorous peer review than other types of published research.

Learning activity 6.4

Make a quick list of the sorts of 'evidence' that you have accessed and/or used to help you do your job in the last week or two.

- Why did you choose these and how robust were they?
- How might you choose differently on another occasion, based on what you have read in this chapter so far?
- What factors prevent you using research evidence in your job? And what might you do about it?

Often research studies are concerned with evaluating the impact of specific innovations. The next section explains what is meant by innovation in health contexts. It also discusses some of the challenges associated with getting innovation into practice.

Innovation

Innovation in relation to healthcare has been defined as 'the intentional introduction of processes and procedures, new to the unit of adoption (team or organisation) and designed to significantly benefit the unit of adoption, staff, patients or the wider public' (Dixon-Woods et al., 2014).

There are a number of challenges in relation to innovations in healthcare. These can include a limited ability to access and interpret evidence, an unwillingness to risk trying something new, and the existence of professional hierarchies that enable people to block change (Greenhalgh et al., 2004). In addition, financial regimes that require organizations to achieve a financial balance on an annual basis make it difficult to invest 'up front' to make savings over subsequent years.

Health technology innovation

Innovation can take various forms (e.g. product, process, organizational). Health technology can be broad too, but usually we are referring to products. In many countries, efforts are being made to maximize the benefits that can be derived from limited healthcare budgets. New technologies are being developed on a continuous basis. Novelty does not always mean things get better, so it is important to evaluate these new technologies. Even if they offer benefits, they have implications for healthcare resources. Most countries have an established body that is responsible for health technology assessment (HTA). In the UK, for example, the National Institute for Health and Care Excellence (NICE) provides guidance based on assessments of health technologies that NHS commissioners are obliged to implement. There is also a National Institute for Health Research (NIHR) HTA programme. The purpose of its HTA studies is to establish the clinical and cost-effectiveness of a technology for the NHS compared with the current best alternatives (see Chapter 5 for more information). Technologies are broadly defined and include any intervention to treat, prevent or diagnose disease.

Innovative organizations and systems

Innovation is not just about products but often involves new processes. Even drugs, devices and diagnostic technologies may require many changes in processes for them to be implemented in practice. Healthcare settings involve complex contexts and managing change in these can be challenging, as the case study in Box 6.3 illustrates.

Box 6.3   Case study – surgical safety checklist, Ontario, Canada

Checklists have been used for a long time in the aviation industry. More recently, this idea has been applied in a way that is intended to significantly improve the quality in healthcare settings. A study published in 2009 found that implementation of the World Health Organization (WHO) Surgical Safety Checklist reduced the rate of surgical complications and in-hospital mortality. Many hospitals worldwide have begun using the checklist. Checklist items include:

- Has the patient confirmed his/her identity, site, procedure and consent?
- Is the surgical site marked (before induction on anaesthesia)?
- Have all team members introduced themselves by name and role?
- How much blood loss is anticipated?
- Are there are specific equipment requirements or special investigations (before start of surgical intervention)?
- Has it been confirmed that instruments, swabs and sharp counts are complete (or not applicable)?
- Have the specimens been labelled (including patient name)?
- Have any equipment problems been identified that need to be addressed, and before any member of the team leaves the operating room?

The Ontario Ministry of Health and Long-Term Care required its hospitals to incorporate safety checklists by July 2010. Many had expected that this would improve outcomes, but this was not the case. A recent study (Urbach et al., 2014) found no significant reduction in operative mortality after checklist implementation. Checklist use did not reduce surgical complications, emergency department visits, or hospital readmissions within 30 days after discharge. It is not necessarily the case, however, that the surgical checklist does not work. The study highlighted the fact that checklists are not always applied in a uniform manner. This suggests that the failure to identity improvements was due in part, at least, to the way in which the innovation was implemented.

In contrast, the use of a checklist was found to drastically reduce the rate of bloodstream infections in hospitals in Michigan, USA. However, researchers identified many factors that contributed to this success (Dixon-Woods et al., 2011). These included participating hospitals being part of a quality improvement collaborative, which involved all of the state's hospitals and created norms in relation to good practice. Additionally, the programme involved participation in a networked community, including ongoing education, support and feedback. Infection control was presented to all relevant stakeholders as a problem that could be solved by human action as opposed to requiring a technical fix. The programme also used various activities aimed at changing the culture, such as feeding back infection rates and using 'shaming' to encourage compliance.

As this case study illustrates, there is more to innovation than simply putting knowledge 'out there' and expecting it to be put into practice. Knowledge needs to be mobilized and this is discussed in the next section.

Knowledge mobilization

There is a growing recognition that the traditional view of getting research into practice, which assumes that healthcare staff are empty vessels to be filled with research knowledge, is flawed. Healthcare staff possess important knowledge about the local processes and systems that is often absent from published research findings. This change is reflected in the terminology used, which has moved away from talking about knowledge transfer towards knowledge exchange or knowledge mobilization.

In recognition of the time lag between the production of research findings and their implementation, researchers and policy-makers have begun to place more emphasis on implementation than just producing research outputs. As part of this trend, various initiatives have attempted to encourage what is sometimes called the co-creation of knowledge as part of collaboration between 'scientists' and 'practitioners' (Lockett et al., 2014; Marshall et al., 2014). Rather than seeing researchers as experts and practitioners as people who need to take the findings of research and act on them, co-creation sees both groups as having relevant knowledge and expertise. Researchers are skilled at conducting research but they have little experience of real-world practice. Practitioners understand the real-world context, so ideally these two groups need to work together to 'co-produce' knowledge that is fit for the real-world context of health organizations. This is not an easy process, since researchers and practitioners inhabit different worlds, with different views about what counts as knowledge and have different incentives. Researchers receive recognition and rewards in large part on the basis of publishing in high-status, peer-reviewed journals. The 'messy' real-world context threatens the scientific rigour of studies, and RCTs actively seek to screen out this context.

Practitioners are concerned with solving problems in the short term and are likely to accept some forms of evidence as being good enough, even though this evidence may fall short of what is required of a peer-reviewed article.

There are various barriers and facilitators in relation to knowledge mobilization. The former include lack of capacity for accessing and interpreting evidence, risk-averse culture, professional hierarchies, interests vested in the status quo, unhelpful financial regimes, a gulf between researchers and practitioners and contestable evidence. Managers need to be aware of these and, where possible, develop strategies to minimize their impact. Managers also need to be aware of things that might be helpful in getting innovative practice embedded. These include training, collaborative partnerships between researchers and practitioners, facilitative networks, knowledge brokers (see Box 6.4), research summaries tailored to specific audiences, champions, and sufficient time to make decisions.

Within the knowledge mobilization literature there has been increasing emphasis on the influence of knowledge brokers (or boundary spanners as they are sometimes called) as facilitators of innovation. These are roles that help in the sharing of knowledge and involve building relationships and promoting collective understanding among different groups. This often involves developing and creating opportunities for people from different groups (e.g. hospital doctors, nurses, primary care doctors, managers) to interact so that knowledge is passed across group boundaries. For example, doctors may have knowledge of day-to-day frontline care that would benefit managers, who are responsible for planning and organizing care. But for various reasons, this knowledge remains within the group of doctors. Bringing people together can help spread this knowledge. This needs time and space, but it may also require a process for developing the capacity of groups to work together on an ongoing basis. Ideally, the impact of the power relations that characterize many healthcare interactions should be minimized, otherwise individuals may be inhibited and may not contribute fully to the process.

Box 6.4   Processes that encourage more effective use of research in practice

Competent boundary spanners/knowledge brokers are seen as an important part of knowledge mobilization. The things they do include:

- Building sustainable relationships by communicating and listening, understanding, empathizing and resolving conflicts.
- Having appropriate personal values and characteristics (respectful, tolerant, honest, diplomatic, reliable, committed, inspiring trust).
- Managing through influence and negotiation, networking (as opposed to hierarchical command).
- Managing complexity and interdependencies by drawing on inter-organizational experience, transdisciplinary knowledge and cognitive ability.
- Managing roles, multiple accountabilities and motivations.

Source: Adapted from Williams (2002).

Sustaining innovation

Knowledge mobilization is not a 'one-off' process. Furthermore, even when changes to health services are implemented as a result of new evidence or innovation, sustaining such new practice often requires a lot of effort. The case study in Box 6.5 provides some useful lessons for those seeking to implement and sustain innovative practice.

Box 6.5 Case study – genetics service, England

In 2003, the White Paper *Our Inheritance, Our Future* announced funding for new initiatives in genetics-based care in the NHS. A series of pilots were funded introducing new models of care and these were evaluated. Each pilot set its own performance measures, as the services included were diverse. Much of the evaluation focused on processes, as there were limited outcome data. This approach was important in shedding light on what was happening and avoiding 'black box' explanations (Currie et al., 2012).

The evaluation found that boundary-spanning roles were important in establishing and maintaining new services. For example, the services which had to rely on referrals from primary care doctors (GPs) used well-known clinicians within the service to encourage GPs and other relevant stakeholders to engage. Linked to this, established relationships and social capital (which reflects the concept that social networks add value – people who know each other are more inclined to do things for each other than people who don't) were extremely important both in terms of initially setting up the pilots and maintain ongoing 'buy-in'. There was a need to be sensitive to the goals and interests of other groups (e.g. referrers and commissioners) as well as being able to provide different kinds of evidence to these different groups. Central government directives hampered the ability to work in a flexible way with networks. Linked to this, the large number and content of national targets was not helpful for these pilots. The uncertainty of funding beyond the pilot created anxieties and a focus at times on short-term issues. Professional hierarchies influenced events, with hospital consultants in a relatively powerful position. The new services presented consultant clinical geneticists with an opportunity and a threat. It offered the chance to delegate routine work to the new services. But it also risked undermining their privileged position by delegation to mainstream medicine where the new services were located. This meant being very sensitive to the need to keep the clinical geneticists on board throughout the process.

The researchers went back a few years later, and examined four services (Martin et al., 2012), to try to determine whether the innovation had been sustained. They found that the issues identified in the earlier evaluation were still relevant. By this time there was a much greater emphasis on commissioning in the context of a market. The hospital-based services were able to draw on their business support units to help align expectations of key stakeholders and service provision. The primary care-based services lacked the support of managers who could adapt and articulate their case in this way.

The service leads in the hospital were consultants, whereas the primary care services were led by a GP and a nurse respectively. The latter service had undergone fundamental changes to its ethos and service-delivery model in order to survive.

The nurse had experience in management and had good networks within the local health economy. The GP-led service did not adapt, neither did it have such active boundary spanning roles and was not re-commissioned. In all cases, sustainability of innovation was not something that was achieved in a 'one-off' manner but instead required ongoing work to maintain it.

Learning activity 6.5

- Imagine you are given the task of reviewing mental health provision in your area, with a view to deciding how services need to change to better meet the needs of the local population. What kinds and sources of evidence would you use? How would you go about drawing this evidence together? (Note that mental health is discussed in detail in Chapter 12.)
- Describe the characteristics of a knowledge broker in a health service known to you locally. Who in your organization carries out knowledge brokering? To what extent are you able to fulfil this role?
- What challenges do you face in trying to introduce innovative ways of working, which are based on robust evidence of effectiveness, in your organization? What can you do about it?

The scientific method can mean that study designs seek to screen out local contexts, yet managers have to apply findings in those complex contexts. The fact that research about service and product innovations is often not available in a format or a timeframe that meets managers' needs can also be a problem. Ensuring independence, probity and transparency adds to the time taken to commission research. Being systematic and minimizing bias are important, but this means that research takes time to review in terms of safety and ethics, to conduct, to peer review and to publish. Managers usually do not have the luxury of waiting several years until the results of a study are published. Some studies suggest that commissioning research is sometimes used as a delaying tactic by those who wish to maintain the status quo. Furthermore, my own research found that NHS staff only used research evidence when it supported what they had already decided was 'the answer' (McDonald, 2002).

The move towards an exchange-based view of knowledge production is, in theory, helpful in terms of changing practice in health settings. Human beings are not empty vessels waiting to be filled with knowledge produced outside of their organization. However, in the context of professional hierarchies and unequal power dynamics, it can be difficult to persuade some people to 'buy in' to knowledge exchange processes. Managers may be able to act as knowledge brokers and/or they may be able to work with others who carry out such roles. Having a good awareness of the barriers and facilitators outlined in this chapter should help with this process.

Conclusion

Using the findings of research and spreading innovation are activities critical to making change in healthcare and need to be carefully and skilfully managed. It is important for managers to understand the tensions and competing interests at various stages of the process. The view of research and innovation as objective and technical exercises is not always an accurate reflection of reality. The processes involved are often highly political, value-laden and can be fraught with tension. The tension between practitioners and researchers discussed in this chapter reflects two different sets of priorities and views in terms of what counts as research evidence, which has implications for managers who are involved in real-world decision-making. Collaborative approaches that seek to bridge these different worlds are welcome, but this issue is not easily resolved.

Managers need to be able to understand different types of evidence and appreciate that what counts as good evidence may be different for different groups. It may also differ according to the research context. Managers also need to be able to access, interpret and critically evaluate 'evidence'. The learning resources below should help with this process.

Learning resources

Greenhalgh, T. (2014) *How to Read a Paper: The Basics of Evidence-based Medicine* (5th edn.). Chichester: Wiley. This book provides guidance on what to look out for when reading (a) qualitative research papers, (b) systematic reviews or meta-analyses, (c) economic analyses, (d) diagnostic or screening tests and (e) drug trials. There are also sections on assessing the methodological quality of research papers and searching the research literature.

Cochrane Collaboration: The Cochrane Collaboration is a highly regarded organization that prepares, maintains and promotes the accessibility of systematic reviews of the effects of healthcare [http://www.cochrane.org/].

Campbell Collaboration: The Campbell Collaboration is also very well regarded and performs a similar function concerning the effects of interventions in social, behavioural and educational contexts [http://www.campbellcollaboration.org/].

Reviews can be accessed free of charge and these two organizations place a heavy emphasis on the hierarchy of evidence. However, this means that there is a focus on highly rated study design and quantifying impact. This is not always useful if you are interested in learning about, for example, patients' views of a particular intervention.

PubMed: PubMed is a search engine providing free access to the US National Library of Medicine database of published studies. You can use it to find abstracts (short summaries) of published papers on relevant topics to begin to locate and assess evidence. This contains many more papers than the collaborations listed above and a much broader range of studies is included [http://www.ncbi.nlm.nih.gov/pubmed].

Matthews, R. (2000) **Storks deliver babies (p = 0.008)**, *Teaching Statistics*, 22 (2): 36–8. This paper sheds light on the storks and babies issue and highlights the importance of thinking carefully about statistical relationships.

References

Allen, D. and Harkins, K. (2005) Too much guidance?, *Lancet*, 365 (9473): 1768.

Anderson, J., Johnstone, B. and Ramley, D. (1999) Breast feeding and cognitive development: a meta analysis, *American Journal of Clinical Nutrition*, 70 (4): 525–35.

Begg, C. and Berlin, J. (1988) Publication bias: a problem in interpreting medical data, *Journal of the Royal Statistical Society*, 151 (3): 419–63.

Commonwealth Fund (n.d.) *Mission Statement* [http://www.commonwealthfund.org/about-us/mission-statement].

Croskerry, P. (2002) Achieving quality in clinical decision making: cognitive strategies and detection of bias, *Academic Emergency Medicine*, 9 (11): 1184–1204.

Currie, G., Lockett, A., Finn, R., Martin, G. and Waring, J. (2012) Institutional work to maintain professional power: recreating the model of medical professionalism, *Organization Studies*, 33 (7): 937–62.

Department of Health (2003) *Our Inheritance, Our Future*, White Paper, Cm 5791. London: TSO [http://www.geneticseducation.nhs.uk/downloads/0001DH_White_paper.pdf].

Der, G., Batty, G. and Deary, I. (2006) Effect of breastfeeding on intelligence in children: prospective study, sibling pairs and meta-analysis, *British Medical Journal*, 333: 945.

Dixon-Woods, M., Baker, R., Charles, K., Dawson, J., Jerzembek, G., and Martin, G. (2014) Culture and behaviour in the English National Health Service: overview of lessons from a large multimethod study, *BMJ Quality and Safety*, 23 (2): 106–15.

Dixon-Woods, M., Bosk, C.L., Aveling, E.L., Goeschel, C.A. and Provonost, P.J. (2011) Explaining Michigan: develpoing an ex-post theory of a quality improvement programme, *Milbank Quarterly*, 89 (2): 167–205.

Greenhalgh, T. (2014) *How to Read a Paper: The Basics of Evidence-based Medicine* (5th edn.). Chichester: Wiley.

Greenhalgh, T., Howick, J. and Maskrey, N. (2014) Evidence based medicine: a movement in crisis?, *British Medical Journal*, 348: g3725.

Greenhalgh, T., Robert, G., Macfarlane, F., Bate, P. and Kyriakidou, O. (2004) Diffusion of innovations in service organizations: systematic review and recommendations, *Milbank Quarterly*, 82 (4): 581–629.

Horta, B., Victora, C., Menezes, A., Halpern, R. and Barros, F. (1997) Low birthweight, preterm births and intrauterine growth retardation in relation to maternal smoking, *Paediatric Perinatal Epidemiology*, 11 (2): 140–51.

Jacobson, S. and Jacobson, J. (1992) Breastfeeding and intelligence, *Lancet*, 339 (8798): 926.

Leape, L., Berwick, D. and Bates, D. (2002) What practice will most improve safety? Evidence-based medicine meets patient safety, *Journal of the American Medical Association*, 288 (4): 501–7.

Lexchin, J., Bero, L.A., Djulbegovic, B. and Clark, O. (2003) Pharmaceutical industry sponsorship and research outcome and quality: systematic review, *British Medical Journal*, 326 (7400): 1167.

Lockett, A., El Enany, N., Currie, G., Oborn, E., Barrett, M., Racko, G. et al. (2014) A formative evaluation of Collaboration for Leadership in Applied Health Research and Care (CLAHRC): institutional entrepreneurship for service innovation, *Health Services and Delivery Research*, 2 (31).

Marshall, M., Pagel, C., French, C., Utley, M., Allwood, D., Fulop, N. (2014) Moving improvement research closer to practice: the researcher-in-residence model, *BMJ Quality and Safety*, 23 (10): 801–5.

Martin, G., Weaver, S., Currie, G., Finn, R. and McDonald, R. (2012) Innovation sustainability in challenging healthcare contexts: embedding clinically led change in routine practice, *Health Services Management Research*, 25 (4): 190–9.

Matthews, R. (2000) Storks deliver babies (p = 0.008), *Teaching Statistics*, 22 (2): 36–8.

McDonald, R. (2002) *Using Health Economics in Health Services: Rationing Rationally?* Buckingham: Open University Press.

Nickerson, R. (1998) Confirmation bias: a ubiquitous phenomenon in many guises, *Review of General Psychology*, 2 (2): 175–202.

Ryan, A., Blustein, J. and Casalino, L. (2012) Medicare's flagship test of pay for performance did not spur more rapid quality improvement among low-performing hospitals, *Health Affairs*, 31 (4): 797-805.

Sackett, D. (1997) Evidence-based medicine, *Seminars in Perinatology*, 21 (1): 3–5.

Shaw, S. (2007) Driving out alternative ways of seeing: the significance of neo-liberal policy mechanisms for UK primary care research, *Social Theory and Health*, 5: 316–37.

Sutherland, S. (2013) *Irrationality*. Ebbw Vale: Pinter & Martin.

Taylor, B. and Wadsworth, J. (1984) Breastfeeding and child development at five years, *Developmental Medicine and Child Neurology*, 26 (1): 73–80.

Urbach, D., Govindarajan, A., Saskin, R., Wilton, A. and Baxter, N. (2014) Introduction of surgical safety checklists in Ontario, Canada, *New England Journal of Medicine*, 370: 1029–38.

Victora, C., Horta, B., de Mola, C., Quevedo, L., Pinheiro, R., Gigantes, D. et al. (2015) Association between breastfeeding and intelligence, educational attainment, and income at 30 years of age: a prospective birth cohort study from Brazil, *Lancet Global Health*, 3 (4): e199–e205.

Wakefield, A., Murch, S., Linnell, A., Casson, D., Malik, M., Berelowitz, M. et al. (1998) Ileal-lymphoid-nodular-hyperplasia, non-specific colitis and developmental disorder in children, *Lancet*, 351 (9103): 637–41.

Williams, P. (2002) The competent boundary spanner, *Public Administration*, 80, 103–24.

Global health policy: governing health systems across borders

Scott Greer

Introduction

For a long time, global health – or international health – was essentially a kind of charity: people from rich countries doing things to, or for, poor countries. It ranged from government development aid to the activities of individual charities, churches and people trying to provide services, reduce morbidity or improve capacity in poorer countries. Its impact on richer countries was often moral rather than practical (although such aid could also be distorted into a form of foreign policy or business opportunity for firms from rich countries).

Global health now has a new meaning: it refers to the health challenges and health governance structures that affect all of us, rich and poor (Table 7.1). It is growing because of growing interconnections, as diverse as medical tourism, increasing communicable disease challenges, and increasing intellectual interchange across borders (Crisp, 2010; Parker and Sommer, 2010).

Global health issues, therefore, are ones that affect multiple countries and are shaped by the presence or absence of governance mechanisms that span multiple countries. They are the focus of this chapter. We begin by addressing key global health issues, then discuss the key organizations involved in global health governance, before showing how health policy actors interact in the particularly important case of the European Union.

Table 7.1: Definitions in global health

Term	Definition
Public health	The overarching field of study and practice concerned with improving population health and creating more equal health outcomes by a variety of evidence-based means, at any territorial scale.
Global health	The study and practice of issues that directly or indirectly affect health but transcend boundaries.
International health	The study and practice of health issues of countries other than one's own, with a focus on low- and middle-income countries.
Comparative health	The study and practice of comparing different systems' and states' approaches to healthcare and public health.
Healthcare management and policy; health services research	The study and practice of the financing and delivery of healthcare services.

Source: Heavily modified from Koplan et al. (2009) and Fried et al. (2010).

Key issues in global health governance

Health systems and the social determinants of health were never fully contained by national borders, and they are now even less so. Some of the key global health issues include the following:

Professional mobility, in which doctors and nurses move from country to country in search of better or more interesting lives, with dramatic consequences for health systems, including 'brain drain' from poor countries, workforce shortages in poor countries, under-employed professionals in rich countries, and questions about the morality of international recruitment (Rutten, 2009; Glinos, 2014).

Patient mobility and medical tourism, in which patients cross borders in search of healthcare they cannot get or afford at home (Turner, 2010; Jarman and Truby, 2013; Lunt et al., 2013). One risk is that patient mobility creates 'dual systems', with one healthcare system for the foreigners that attracts the professionals. Another risk, more common in Europe, is that patient flows across borders undermine the integration and risk-pooling of existing health systems. In practice, European countries have managed these problems well.

Communicable disease control, in which diseases cross borders and therefore surveillance and response should cross borders as well (Bashford, 2006; Lakoff and Collier, 2008; Greer and Mätzke, 2012; Liverani and Coker, 2012). Some risks are that governments are poor at surveillance (monitoring populations for disease outbreaks), disguise outbreaks, refuse to share biological samples or take restrictive actions that impede trade and even aid without any justification.

Research and intellectual property (Sell, 2003). Much research is done around the world, most notably of which is when rich countries seek access to viral samples from poor countries, which they then commercialize at a price poorer countries cannot afford, but also when firms conduct trials in poorer countries (Gatter, 2014; Lemmons and Telfer, 2014). Similarly, there have been major arguments over intellectual property, especially when poorer countries seek *access to medicines* (Roffe et al., 2006; Massard, 2013). The question here is whether and how the patent protection, and high prices, enjoyed by branded pharmaceutical companies can be combined with urgent need for those drugs, particularly in the case of antiretrovirals for HIV and AIDS treatment.

Trade policy might seem boring and technical but it is intimately bound up with the future of healthcare systems. Intellectual property disputes over the availability and price of medicines are handled through the World Trade Organization (WHO) because they are covered by the TRIPS (Trade-Related Aspects of Intellectual Property Rights) agreement and a series of tobacco control measures have been challenged by tobacco companies and the states that they influence under WTO and bilateral trade law (McGrady, 2011; Jarman, 2013).

Part of the problem of trade policy is that it is built to promote free trade, reducing not just tariffs but also regulations. Part of the response has been to counteract the liberalizing push of trade policy with a Framework Convention on Tobacco Control that both provides an international standard for good tobacco control policies and gives some grounds to support tobacco control policies that are being challenged under trade and investment law (Jarman, 2014).

Complex commodity and production chains that span multiple borders have already appeared in a number of these issues. Examples include clinical trials in different countries, pharmaceuticals and devices moving across borders, data that are subject to very different rules in the United States and European Union, and research that is often dominated by rich countries which might ignore the diseases that affect poorer countries (structured, manipulable data such as clinical trials data, surveillance data or genomics are very expensive and there are understandable questions when they are collected in poor countries for the benefit of researchers and industries in rich countries). Responding to problems as diverse as neglected diseases, counterfeit and poor-quality medicines and devices and antibiotic resistance involves increasing international coordination to address clear failures of international markets and regulations.

Migrant health can be seen as a feature of global health, since migrant populations are often vulnerable, culturally distinctive and do not necessarily have good integration with healthcare systems. Migration around the world, and certainly in Europe, creates new challenges for healthcare systems and policies (Rechel et al., 2011).

Less specifically, health and healthcare systems are affected by *broader global changes*. Climate change, for example, is changing the epidemiological profile and population health of many countries while refurbishing healthcare systems to cope with increased chances of catastrophic weather will incur a serious cost. For example, malaria and other tropical diseases might become an increasing problem in rich countries. Global economic conditions lead to all sorts of health and health policy results, from worse mental health and fewer road accidents in recessions to cuts in healthcare expenditure (Karanikolos et al., 2013; Burgard and Kalousova, 2015). Offshoring jobs, pollution, tax evasion, crime and terrorism are other areas with major health and healthcare consequences and more or less imperfect global governance mechanisms. The problem is that while their health effects are clear, it is less clear that health advocates are viewed credibly in those forums. If everything is public health, then what do public health scholars and policy-makers actually know (Fox, 2003)?

Learning activity 7.1

Evaluate the effects of the above global health issues on your healthcare system.

- What are the most important global health issues for your country and why?
- For example, how might migrant health, professional mobility or trade law affect your health system?

Learning activity 7.2

Pick another country, different from your own in terms of income, health system characteristics or politics, most likely from the European Observatory's *Health Systems in Transition* series of reviews, and identify the global health policy issues that are likely to affect its health system most in the future [http://www.euro.who.int/en/about-us/partners/observatory/publications/health-system-reviews-hits].

- How does global health governance address these challenges?

These are a dramatic set of challenges, many of which cannot be addressed without global cooperation. We often look to the assemblage of institutions, actors and policies we call *global health governance* to orchestrate that cooperation and address these challenges. Governance is how decisions are made and implemented (Greer et al., 2016). Global health governance is how decisions are made and implemented in global forums and on global issues (Buse et al., 2009; Youde, 2012).

There is one key message to keep in mind here: we should expect global health governance to be undersupplied. The basic reason is that global health governance requires the solution of a series of difficult collective action problems among a wide variety of governments, and often private actors. Governments might not agree, and even if they agree they frequently have incentives to 'free ride' – reap the collective benefits but fail to pay the cost.

Consider, for example, the difficulty of forging an agreement on international professional mobility. Many regard it as a scandal that poor countries train expensive and scarce professionals who then go to work in richer countries (Taylor and Dhillon, 2013). [There are two sides to this debate: Ghana could only afford to employ a fraction of all the Ghanaian doctors practising abroad should they return and against the costs of lost professionals we can balance the benefits of their remittances to their home countries (Record and Mohiddin, 2006; Rutten, 2009).]

But any kind of binding arrangement to restrict mobility faces serious problems. More than one hundred countries would have to agree to make any binding agreement, and they would all have their own domestic politics, interests and incentives (for example, the United States constitution, by design, makes it very difficult to ratify treaties). Moreover, if the EU were to decide not to employ doctors from Africa, they would merely increase the flow of doctors to the USA, Australia and Canada. The gain to the EU or the doctors would not be clear. Finally, many countries make agreements and then fail to implement them (as the experiences of many human rights treaties attest). The Framework Convention on Tobacco Control has, on paper, been extremely well implemented by Niger. Nonetheless, it is reasonable to question just how effective Niger is at policing, for example, point of sale advertising given the difficulties that the UK or Germany faces in doing so.

In the case of communicable disease control, there is widespread agreement that there is a global interest in effective disease control and that individual governments share an interest in its effectiveness. Nobody wins from the hysteria and broken economic and social links that come with a cross-border outbreak of infectious disease. Unsurprisingly, the International Health Regulations that govern the management of major health emergencies are the most widely ratified international treaty. Their aim is to control the spread of diseases and public health risks across borders through notification and prevention. Once a country alerts the world to an outbreak, it is for WHO to declare an outbreak, or pandemic, and lead international action (Rushton, 2009; Youde, 2012). As the pandemic influenza experience of 2013 and the Ebola experience of 2014–15 showed, however, even the IHR did not prevent governments neglecting public health or taking counterproductive actions (Ebola Interim Assessment Panel, 2015).

If the basic problem is that global health governance is undersupplied because the benefits are diffuse and the costs clear and immediate, they we should expect that there will be few effective actors in global health governance, and they will be tightly grounded in power and money and reflect durable, if changing, interests. On the one hand, this means specific organizations that serve a clear function, such as the International Monetary Fund (below), which is both a bank and a guardian of fiscal stability and views health systems as frequently underperforming investments. On the other hand, it creates many opportunities for people with money: governments, and charities such as the Gates Foundation (Box 7.1), which are essentially unaccountable and can dominate debates with their resources. To a lesser extent, powerful companies in the health area, such as pharmaceutical firms, can exercise authority in the same way; they have money and clearer accountability.

While it is very popular in health policy debates to identify a problem and call for a comprehensive global solution, that call will almost uniformly fail to produce a policy outcome. Achieving effective collective action in global health issues is an extremely difficult and long-term political project that demands resources, tenacity, expertise and luck. Even the most morally justified and evidence-based call for global collective action should be expected to fail. It is no wonder that so many states and people prefer the more direct action of charity work or bottom-up action. Global health governance is frustrating, partial and ultimately not for dilettantes.

Key organizations in global health: case studies

This section discusses three of the international organizations involved in global health governance. Box 7.1 presents some more high-profile organizations (and beyond them is a whole world of international health). It is worth noting that the three big organizations here adopt a 'horizontal' approach in which strengthening or governing overall health systems and public sector organizations is presumed to be the effective way to improve health, while many of the newer, high-profile organizations, such as GAVI or UNAIDS, adopt a 'vertical' strategy of addressing individual diseases such as AIDS or specific problems such as immunizations. There is a long-standing debate in global and international health about the costs and benefits of the vertical and horizontal approaches, but the actual approaches adopted tend to be determined by the priorities of donors (Mills, 2005).

The World Health Organization

The World Health Organization (WHO) is the international agency charged with global health issues. The topics it addresses range from communicable disease control to safe water and health systems strengthening. It is old, high profile, very political and both unavoidable and frustrating in global health politics.

The WHO is not a well-run organization or a very good place to work at – something for which its leadership and staff cannot be wholly blamed (Muraskin, 1998; Chorev, 2012). Its 'glory days' were in the 1950s and 1960s when its technocratic credentials were not much questioned and it was involved in major disease eradication schemes such as the successful eradication of smallpox and the unsuccessful effort to eradicate malaria (Brown et al., 2006; Stepan, 2011). It has since had long periods of decline interspersed with moments of effectiveness, notably under Secretary-General Brundtland who steered both a controversial world health ranking and the Framework Convention on Tobacco Control (FCTC). The FCTC in particular is a major global public health treaty that helps to establish tobacco control as a legitimate policy in international law (Jarman, 2014).

The WHO's key asset is that it is the only truly global, legitimate and even somewhat representative organization working in global health and as a result it is always present in world health debates and governance for better or for worse. Its ability to influence medical practice and healthcare policy, for all its demerits, is still impressive. Even in its less effective moments, it has been involved in spreading and ratifying guidelines and expectations on a wide variety of issues, including childbirth (Wagner, 1997), tuberculosis treatment (Ogden et al., 2003), abortion and primary care (Lawn et al., 2008).

The basic problem in WHO governance is that there are two main sources of power within the organization (Chorev, 2012). One source of power is votes in the World Health Assembly, the large democratic body that elects the General-Secretary and makes policy. Poor countries have a majority in the Assembly. The other is money – the budgetary contributions that richer member states make. In the 1980s, rich countries, irritated by the policy direction of the World Health Assembly, successfully capped the WHO budget and urged the World Bank and International Monetary Fund to engage directly in health policy and systems, effectively in competition with WHO.

Over time, the funding constraint turned the WHO into a client of the wealthier countries. Its permanent budget is around one-tenth of its actual expenditure. For the rest, it functions as a very large NGO, and its policy priorities necessarily reflect those of its donors. The result is that the WHO sometimes looks like part of global health governance, but it often acts like an unwieldy NGO. Its governance is constantly under close scrutiny from governments that might not agree on basic principles: the United States government, for example, even

---

Box 7.1   Selected other players in global health policy

The Bill and Melinda **Gates Foundation**, is an enormous American charity built on the fortune of Bill Gates and Warren Buffett. It is committed to improving global health, and its combination of freedom and immense wealth make it arguably the most powerful single actor in global health.

UNICEF, the United Nations Children's Fund, is a regular actor in global health due to its focus on children's health, which involves it in issues such as vaccines. It is periodically in competition with the WHO.

UNAIDS is a specialist UN body involved in the prevention and treatment of AIDS (Piot and Marshall, 2012).

GAVI, the Global Alliance for Vaccines and Immunizations, is an international organization founded in 2000 to promote vaccination by overcoming various problems in vaccine markets such as lack of competition, fragmented procurement and sustainable prices. It is a public–private alliance with a board made up of high-profile individuals and permanent members: UNICEF, the WHO, the World Bank and the Gates Foundation.

PEPFAR, the President's Emergency Plan for AIDS Relief, is a US government initiative focused on AIDS that began in 2003 under George W. Bush. The largest commitment any country has ever made to international health work, it focuses on the provision of antiretrovirals. It was renewed in 2008 and had its objectives expanded beyond priority countries and to include tuberculosis and malaria.

The **Global Fund to Fight AIDS, Tuberculosis and Malaria** is also a public–private organization, founded in 2002, that raises money to address the three diseases in its title in partnership with governments, civil society, the private sector and people affected by the diseases. Like GAVI, it is supposed to avoid some of the problems of traditional charity or government-to-government aid with tougher performance monitoring and public–private collaboration. Its donors include over fifty governments (including PEPFAR), the Gates Foundation, and corporations such as Chevron, BHPBilliton and Coca-Cola.

The **OECD**, or the Organization for Economic Cooperation and Development, is effectively the 'rich countries' club', sharing information and developing shared guidance on good public policy. While it is often said to have a neoliberal bias, its comparative data and public policy in general, and on health in particular, are thoughtful and useful.

criticized a WHO fact sheet for using the term 'right to health' (Berman, 2014). The personality and political bases of its leader, the Secretary-General, tend to be important. It is also divided into powerful regions,[1] whose leaders are accountable to the member states that elected them rather than the central WHO in Geneva. Investigations of its politics, such as the excellent accounts of Muraskin, tend to make many of the players in global health diplomacy look rather infantile (Muraskin, 1998). Newer initiatives, such as the United States' PEPFAR, GAVI and the Global Fund all resist having any public connection with WHO – but inevitably they are all connected with it somehow. WHO might be disempowered and often dysfunctional, but it is inescapable.

The international financial institutions: the IMF and World Bank

The WHO's decline came with the increased influence of the International Monetary Fund (IMF) and World Bank in the 1980s. These two organizations (the World Bank is actually a family of organizations) are known as 'IFIs', or international financial institutions (Woods, 2006). If the WHO is hobbled by the tension between a WHA dominated by poorer states and a budget dominated by richer states, the IFIs are quite free of that problem; they are banks, and they respond to the states that own shares.

The two organizations have different missions, even if they have often worked in tandem. The World Bank's objective is development lending: supplying capital to poor and middle-income countries that could not otherwise raise it. The IMF's purpose has evolved greatly over its history, but it is effectively a lender of last resort for countries in fiscal crisis (which is why it is involved in the bailouts of Cyprus, Greece, Ireland and Portugal). Both are banks and make loans; both tend to use conditional lending in which a loan is cut into sections and disbursement made conditional on fulfilling policy objectives in what is known as 'structural adjustment lending'. In principle, they do not just help countries out of cash crises. The IFIs try to use their leverage to reform debtors so that they will grow and budget well enough to avoid future crises. The practice has been different and rather more disappointing (Greer, 2014a). Both IFIs have conflicting accountabilities and are highly political; in particular, they tend to cater to the interests of the countries with the strongest representation on their boards, and those countries often prioritize geopolitics or their own banks. This is exactly what the design of the two organizations would lead one to expect. In both, the European states are over-represented relative to their weight in the world and the USA has enough shares to veto any actions it dislikes (Babb, 2009; Bree, 2013).

Their role in global health has changed. The World Bank's focus is more diffuse, and focused on poverty. The IMF's role is most prominent when there are debt crises. In Europe, this means that the World Bank has not been very active (the European Bank for Reconstruction and Development, part of the World Bank family, does most of the lending, and that tends to be in the former Communist states). In global health, the World Bank long focused on basic needs such as oral rehydration therapy in poor countries and advocated for a market-based health system otherwise, in contradiction to the WHO's focus on universal primary healthcare and horizontal policy interventions (Lee and Goodman, 2002; Weyland, 2007). In this context, they worked to promote both the expansion of very basic health services and private provision and user fees in poor countries.

The IMF had a limited role in Europe after the powers forgave Germany's enormous debts in the 1950s until the sovereign debt crisis that started in 2010 and brought it back into Europe, overseeing effective receivership for Ireland, Portugal, Greece, Hungary, Latvia and Cyprus, and involved in the politics of rescues for fragile countries such as Spain. Europe's crisis greatly improved the IMF's international standing, which had been weakening as countries built up large enough foreign exchange reserves to avoid crises and the IMF's conditional lending, and as fiascos in Argentina and Russia undermined its claim to expertise. The IMF's deep engagement in Europe did, however, raise questions from middle-income and developing countries that noted the unprecedented size of its loans to Greece and regarded the conditionality as relatively weak compared to what poor countries experience.

The European Union's three faces

Compared with the IFIs, let alone the WHO, the European Union is an extraordinarily powerful international organization; in fact, it is so important and deeply embedded in the policies and politics of its member states that it might make more sense to regard it as a weak federation, part of the domestic politics of EU member states (see Box 7.2). Its workings are the subject of a large literature (Wallace et al., 2015), but what stands out is that unlike other international organizations it is substantially democratic (especially due to the European Parliament, but also the European Council where states make decisions), so its decisions frequently represent a shared political will. It is very powerful in that those who violate its law can suffer for it; and it has an extensive body of law (called the *acquis communautaire*) that member states must adopt and that shapes much of life. Even states outside the EU, such as Norway and Switzerland, must basically follow its regulatory and policy approaches in order to have access to its market – the world's largest. Its health policies, therefore, matter (Greer et al., 2014). It is also the world's largest actor in development aid.

Box 7.2   EU political institutions

The EU is a complex system, but there are four key institutions to keep in mind.

The **European Commission** is the executive of the European Union, responsible for proposing and implementing legislation (although most EU programmes are administered, well or badly, by member states). Its President is appointed by the member states and must be ratified by the European Parliament, which therefore exercises influence over the decision.

The **Council** can refer to two things: the *European Council*, which is the meeting of heads of state, and the ordinary *Council of Ministers*, in which relevant ministers (e.g. health or finance ministers) meet and agree budgets and legislation.

The **European Parliament** is directly elected and organized into parties; both the Parliament and the Council must approve any legislation if it is to pass.

The **Court of Justice of the European Union** is the EU's top court and guardian of the extensive EU legal system and body of law. EU law has 'direct effect', meaning that it is law even if the member states do not apply it, and 'supremacy', meaning that it trumps member state law that conflicts with it. The Court's decisions can only be overridden by changing the legislation or treaty provisions it is interpreting.

The structure of the EU and its powers are laid out in the treaties constituting the EU: the Treaty on European Union (TEU) and the Treaty on the Functioning of the European Union (TFEU). The EU's powers are enumerated there; every single EU action must be authorized by a 'treaty base'. Since the start of the financial crisis in 2008, more economic actors have played a role: notably the European Central Bank has become involved in health reform as a price for its support to countries in crisis, and the Eurogroup of Eurozone finance ministers has negotiated with crisis countries about their policies.

Source: Based on Greer et al. (2014)

For a long time, EU health policy did not seem to matter much. The treaties that constitute the EU and determine its powers made it clear that healthcare systems were outside of its competencies, and member state governments were only interested in small, benign activities such as European programmes against cancer or AIDS. Over the years, these programmes have expanded with the EU increasingly involved in promoting health and public health through research, agencies for occupational health, food safety and communicable disease control (Greer, 2012); and support for public health networks and policy development, including healthcare components of its regional development programmes. This is a logical spillover: if there is to be an agricultural policy, then there is automatically a policy affecting obesity, and it is appropriate that policy-makers take obesity into account when making agricultural policy. If there is to be trade in products, then labelling standards are required, and those have health effects. This is the first face of the EU: the modest, helpful, benign set of programmes whose effect on policies largely depends on their ability to mobilize and persuade people working in the member states, in parallel with efforts to integrate health into areas such as agricultural policy or infrastructure lending. It is the face of the EU that is clearest if one looks up Article 168 of the EU treaties, where its health actions are enabled.

EU health policy does not, however, have just one face (Greer, 2014b). The second face of EU health policy is much more important: it is the application of its extensive internal market rules to healthcare systems. These rules, elaborated by the Court of Justice of the European Union and member state courts, have had dramatic effects on healthcare systems and EU debates about health. They include:

- *Internal market law* prohibits discrimination on grounds of origin, so that a provider in one country should be allowed to serve citizens of another country on the same terms. Application of internal market law gave rise to the most obvious EU healthcare policies, as it led member states to develop an EU regulatory framework for cross-border patient mobility and, therefore, healthcare systems.

- *Professional mobility law*, which promotes the mobility of professionals across the EU and gives member states an opportunity to reform the regulation of professions, is another aspect of internal market law that affects healthcare workforces, budgets and quality (Glinos, 2012).
- *Competition law* and *state aids law* both forbid member states discriminating against companies based in other member states through regulatory measures or subsidies. Both competition and state aids law were developed through application to areas such as bailouts for airlines, and their application to healthcare has been a subject of much legal thought (Hancher and Sauter, 2012). In particular, they make it difficult for member states to discriminate in favour of publicly owned providers – it is legally suspect, for example, for English commissioning to discriminate in favour of NHS trusts.
- While *labour law* is technically a different part of EU law from the internal market, the Working Time Directive, which reduced both the total hours and the hours per day that staff could work, had big effects on staffing, quality and education in many member states.

In all of these cases, the EU – in particular its courts – has been extending its large established body of internal market law into healthcare services. The common theme is the EU fulfilling what many legal scholars call its 'constitutional' objective of the free movement of goods, services, capital and people, and undermining member state laws and policies that block such free movement. In many cases, policy-makers have been able to limit the impact of EU rules on the basic structures of finance and provision, but compliance with EU law can also be costly and produce bureaucratic distortions.

The third face of the EU is the newest, essentially dating to the sovereign debt crises that erupted in 2010 when member states socialized the debt of imprudent banks at the same time as it was discovered that Greek public accounts had no relationship to reality, triggering a long-predicted crisis in the Eurozone (Dyson, 2014). This led to Greece and three other Eurozone countries being taken into effective receivership by the European Commission, European Central Bank and IMF. But oversight of member states is not just confined to these unfortunate countries; the breadth, depth and intimacy of EU surveillance of member state health policies has been dramatically increased for all EU member states since 2010–11. Every member state's policies, including health policies, are being judged for contribution to fiscal rigour and economic growth as agreed by EU member states.

In this case, health policy is an afterthought of 'fiscal governance' structures designed to keep member states from budgetary imbalances that might endanger the Eurozone. The relationship between fiscal governance and health is complex, but the core of it is in a process called the European Semester (Zeitlin and Vanhercke, 2014; Stamati and Baeten, 2015), in which member states, including the UK, report their policies as part of an ongoing evaluation of the compatibility of the policies with a set of goals established by the European Council – above all, a structural deficit of less than 3 per cent and a debt-to-GDP ratio of less than 60 per cent. So far, the Semester's health policy recommendations, contained in Country-Specific Recommendations, have been rather vague. Examples of its suggestions include telling Austria to rationalize its organization of healthcare, suggesting better care integration in Germany and suggesting reduced lengths of stay in Czech hospitals. It is to be expected that, as the fiscal governance system establishes itself and develops new sources of information, its recommendations will become more precise. It is to be underlined that no EU member state is outside this fiscal governance system – their budgets and health policies are now scrutinized on an EU basis for their contribution to fiscal balance. Whether they will respond to the suggestions of the Semester remains to be seen; historically, EU member states tended not to comply with such suggestions, but compliance with the Semester is important for both access to EU aid and for access to EU bailouts in the event of future fiscal crises.

This third face of the EU views health policy as one more form of potential profligacy. While the contribution of health services to 'active and healthy ageing' (a goal that is necessary if pension ages are to be raised) is noted, EU fiscal governance is set up to ensure strict budgetary policies, not good health policies. Subjecting all healthcare services to scrutiny in the name of fiscal balance, it is a dramatic expansion of EU power over health whose success or failure, as a health or as an economic policy, remains to be seen.

The EU was long known as the 'common market', and its roots as a free trade zone are still apparent in its policy-making and powers. It is very good at deregulating and reregulating markets, for labour, goods, capital and services. It is more or less incapable of financing a healthcare system: its budget is about 1 per cent of EU GDP, while most health systems cost around 9 per cent of GDP. The result is that EU health policies, the second and third faces, are born of other policies and come to affect health later.

Learning activity 7.3

Why are the World Bank, IMF and European Union so much more important than the WHO in global health?

Learning activity 7.4

Pick one of the organizations identified in this chapter and visit its website. Look at its governance (i.e. rules, composition of its governing board, selection of leadership, annual report) and its budget – above all, the sources of money. What do you expect it to do well? What might be its weaknesses?

Learning activity 7.5

Imagine you are a newly appointed government minister charged with improving global health and are given a substantial budget to do it with. Which organization would you choose as a partner in determining how to spend the money, and why?

Learning activity 7.6

Imagine that you are an enormously rich person and you want to give a substantial sum of money to improve global health. Which organization would you choose as a partner in determining how to spend the money, and why? If your answer is different from your answer to Learning activity 7.5, why is that?

Conclusions

Global health governance involves the governance of big issues, from workforce migration to migrant health, and from climate change to pharmaceutical research. What it does not always involve is a great deal of governance.

The basic reason is that problems do not summon their own solutions: addressing opportunities for coordination, or even pressing needs for action, involves complex politics between many countries with different governments, priorities and commitments. Governments are tempted to lie, free ride or ignore issues, and the creation of global governance is difficult. There will never be as much global governance as the issues might demand. As a result, it is always tempting to take bottom-up action: instead of waiting for an international agreement on international recruitment, develop an ethical approach in one's own country (as the UK tried to do); instead of wait for a global accord on climate change, invest in greener technology and mitigation at home; instead of waiting for a better international political economy, take direct action by organizing charity work. The appeal of charity, and even very partial bottom-up work, is very popular and for good reason.

What is effective in global health governance? Money and power, rather than admirable objectives or evidence bases, shape global health governance. The IMF deals with money, is backed by very powerful states and wields a great deal of power over countries that lack both money and power. Within the WHO, the rich countries have successfully made their money matter more than the votes of poor country governments. It is no accident that the designers of GAVI and the Global Fund accordingly tried to create organizations that would align the interests of rich countries, big companies and powerful governments in pursuit of goals such as better functioning vaccine markets.

The European Union is in a class of its own, so integrated into the member states and such a big power on the world stage that it might be better viewed as part of a complex political system. It would be effectively impossible to leave the EU – not only would the *acquis communautaire* remain embedded in a departing country's law, but the sheer size of the EU means that countries around the world are obliged to adopt its standards and shadow its policies. Even as the EU makes a more or less intended expansion into governing healthcare services policies under the guise of reforming fiscal policy, it is still an unusually powerful, capable and open polity with many positive and negative effects on health and healthcare.

This might seem a counsel of despair – the mismatch between the scale of the issues in global health governance and the global health governance itself can be dispiriting. There are two cheerier notes to end on, however. One is that global problems often do respond to local solutions; the FCTC can promote tobacco control and help to prevent trade law undermining tobacco control measures, but ultimately regulating advertising or enabling smoking cessation must be done locally. Global problems do not always need global solutions, and frequently what look like global solutions are the accretion of local solutions around the world. Second, all politics is hard, and global politics harder, but there have been real victories – ranging from the relatively limited impact of EU internal market law on health systems to the FCTC to the relative respect given to health as a priority by the World Bank these days. As in all politics, payoffs may be rare but they happen, and ceasing entirely to engage merely leaves the field open to others. Global health is not for dilettantes.

Learning resources

European Observatory on Health Systems and Policies: A Brussels-based organization that monitors health systems as well as EU policies [http://www.euro.who.int/en/about-us/partners/observatory].

European Social Observatory: A Brussels-based think tank that does excellent research from a broadly social democratic perspective on the operation of the EU's health system governance [www.ose.be].

The Organization for Economic Cooperation and Development (OECD), discussed above, is a major source of comparative data and influential studies on health [www.oecd.org].

The **Europa** website is the vast website of the European Union. Very few things that happen in the EU go undocumented on Europa; the trick is to find the document and interpret it correctly [www.europa.eu].

Finally, all the organizations discussed here have large and comprehensive websites that are a good guide to at least their formal operations, priorities and staffing.

Note

[1] Europe, which includes Israel and the former Soviet Union; Africa; Western Pacific (running from Japan to Australia); Eastern Mediterranean (North Africa and the Middle East minus Israel), and Southeast Asia (from India to Indonesia, and including North Korea in order to prevent the diplomatic issues that would arise if North and South Korea were both in the Western Pacific region). The 'Region of the Americas' is actually the Pan-American Health Organization, which was a precursor of the WHO.

References

Babb, S. (2009) *Behind the Development Banks: Washington Politics, the Wealth of Nations, and World Poverty*. Chicago, IL: University of Chicago Press.

Bashford, A. (ed.) (2006) *Medicine at the Border: Disease, Globalization and Security, 1850 to the Present*. Basingstoke: Palgrave Macmillan.

Berman, M.L. (2014) Pursuing global health with justice, *Journal of Law and the Biosciences*, 1 (3): 348–58.

Breen, M. (2013) *The Politics of IMF Lending*. Basingstoke: Palgrave Macmillan.

Brown, T.M., Cueto, M. and Fee, E. (2006) The World Health Organization and the transition from 'international' to 'global' public health, *American Journal of Public Health*, 96 (1): 62–72.

Burgard, S.A. and Kalousova, L. (2015) The effects of the great recession: health and well-being, *Annual Review of Sociology*, 41: 181–201.

Buse, K., Hein, W. and Drager, N. (eds.) (2009) *Making Sense of Global Health Governance: A Policy Perspective*. Basingtoke: Palgrave Macmillan.

Chorev, N. (2012) *The World Health Organization between North and South*. Ithaca, NY: Cornell University Press.

Crisp, N. (2010) *Turning the World Upside Down: The Search for Global Health in the 21st Century*. London: Royal Society of Medicine Press.

Dyson, K.H.F. (2014) *States, Debt, and Power: 'Saints' and 'Sinners' in European History and Integration*. Oxford: Oxford Univesity Press.

Ebola Interim Assessment Panel (2015) *Report of the Ebola Interim Assessment Panel*. Geneva: WHO.

Fox, D.M. (2003) Population and the law: the changing scope of health policy, *Journal of Law, Medicine and Ethics*, 31: 607–14.

Fried, L.P., Bentley, M.A., Buekens, P., Burke, D.S., Frenk, J.P., Klag, M.J. et al. (2010). Global health is public health, *Lancet*, 375 (9714): 535–7.

Gatter, R. (2014) The new global framework for pandemic influenza virus- and vaccine-sharing, in I.G. Cohen (ed.) *The Globalization of Health Care: Legal and Ethical Issues*. New York: Oxford University Press.

Glinos, I. (2012) Worrying about the wrong thing: patient mobility versus mobility of health care professionals, *Journal of Health Services Research and Policy*, 17 (4): 254–6.

Glinos, I.A. (2014) Going beyond numbers: a typology of health professional mobility inside and outside the European Union, *Policy and Society*, 33 (1): 25–37.

Greer, S.L. (2012) The European Centre for Disease Prevention and Control: hub or hollow core?, *Journal of Health Politics, Policy, and Law*, 37 (6): 1001–30.

Greer, S.L. (2014a) Structural adjustment comes to Europe: lessons for the Eurozone from the conditionality debates, *Global Social Policy*, 14 (1): 51–71.

Greer, S.L. (2014b) The three faces of European Union health policy: policy, markets and austerity, *Policy and Society*, 33 (1): 13–24.

Greer, S.L. and Mätzke, M. (2012) Bacteria without borders: communicable disease politics in Europe, *Journal of Health Politics, Policy and Law*, 37 (6): 887–914.

Greer, S.L., Fahy, N., Elliott, H., Wismar, M., Jarman, H. and Palm, W. (2014) *Everything You Always Wanted to Know about European Union Health Policy but were Afraid to Ask.* Brussels: European Observatory on Health Systems and Policies.

Greer, S.L., Wismar, M. and Figueras, J.M. (2016) *Health Systems Governance.* Brussels: European Observatory on Health Systems and Policies.

Hancher, L. and Sauter, W. (2012) *EU Competition and Internal Market Law in the Health Care Sector.* Oxford: Oxford University Press.

Jarman, H. (2013) Attack on Australia: tobacco industry challenges to plain packaging, *Journal of Public Health Policy*, 34 (3): 375–87.

Jarman, H. (2014) *The Politics of Trade and Tobacco Control.* Basingstoke: Palgrave Macmillan.

Jarman, H. and Truby, K. (2013) Traveling for treatment: a comparative analysis of patient mobility debates in the European Union and United States, *Journal of Comparative Policy Analysis: Research and Practice*, 15 (1): 37–53.

Karanikolos, M., Mladovsky, P., Cylus, J., Thomson, S., Basu, S., Stuckler, D. et al. (2013) Financial crisis, austerity, and health in Europe, *Lancet*, 381 (9874): 1323–31.

Koplan, J.P., Bond, T.C., Merson, M.H., Reddy, K.S., Rodriguez, M.H., Sewankambo, N.K. et al. (2009) Towards a common definition of global health, *Lancet*, 373 (9679): 1993–5.

Lakoff, A. and Collier, S.J. (2008) *Biosecurity Interventions: Global Health and Security in Question.* New York: Columbia University Press.

Lawn, J.E., Rohde, J., Rifkin, S., Were, M., Paul, V.K. and Chopra, M. (2008) Alma-Ata 30 years on: revolutionary, relevant, and time to revitalise, *Lancet*, 372 (9642): 917–27.

Lee, K. and Goodman, H. (2002) Global policy networks: the propagation of health care financing reform since the 1980s, in K. Lee, K. Buse and S. Fustukian (eds.) *Health Policy in a Globalising World.* Cambridge: Cambridge University Press.

Lemmons, T. and Telfer, C. (2014) Clinical trials registration and results reporting and the right to health, in I.G. Cohen (ed.) *The Globalization of Health Care: Legal and Ethical Issues.* New York: Oxford University Press.

Liverani, M. and Coker, R. (2012) Protecting Europe from diseases: from the international sanitary conferences to the ECDC, *Journal of Health Politics, Policy, and Law*, 36 (1): 915–34.

Lunt, N.T., Mannion, R. and Exworthy, M. (2013) A framework for exploring the policy implications of UK medical tourism and international patient flows, *Social Policy and Administration*, 47 (1): 1–25.

Massard, E. (2013) Intellectual property enforcement in the European Union, in S.L. Greer and P. Kurzer (eds.) *European Union Public Health Policies: Regional and Global Perspectives.* Abingdon: Routledge.

McGrady, B. (2011) *Trade and Public Health: The WTO, Tobacco, Alcohol, and Diet.* Cambridge: Cambridge University Press.

Mills, A. (2005) Mass campaigns versus general health services: what have we learnt in 40 years about vertical versus horizontal approaches?, *Bulletin of the World Health Organisation*, 83 (4): 315–16.

Muraskin, W.A. (1998) *The Politics of International Health: The Children's Vaccine Initiative and the Struggle to Develop Vaccines for the Third World.* Albany, NY: SUNY Press.

Ogden, J., Walt, G. and Lush, L. (2003) The politics of 'branding' in policy transfer: the case of DOTS for tuberculosis control, *Social Science and Medicine*, 57 (1): 179–88.

Parker, R. and Sommer, M. (2010) *Routledge Handbook of Global Public Health*. Abingdon: Routledge.

Piot, P. and Marshall, R. (2012) *No Time to Lose: A Life in Pursuit of Deadly Viruses*. New York: W.W. Norton.

Rechel, B., Mladovsky, P., Devillé, W., Rijks, B., Petrova-Benedict, R. and McKee, M. (2011) *Migration and Health in the European Union*. Maidenhead: Open University Press.

Record, R. and Mohiddin, A. (2006) An economic perspective on Malawi's medical 'brain drain', *Global Health*, 2: 12.

Roffe, P., Tansey, G. and Vivas-Eugui, D. (eds.) (2006) *Negotiating Health: Intellectual Property and Access to Medicines*. London: Earthscan.

Rushton, S. (2009) Gloal governance capacities in health: WHO and infectious diseases, in A. Kay and O.D. Williams (eds.) *Global Health Governance: Crisis, Institutions and Political Economy*. Basingstoke: Palgrave Macmillan.

Rutten, M. (2009) The economic impact of medical migration: an overview of the literature, *The World Economy*, 32 (2): 291–325.

Sell, S.K. (2003) *Private Power, Public Law: The Globalization of Intellectual Property Rights*. New York: Cambridge University Press.

Stamati, F. and Baeten, R. (2015) *Healthcare Reforms and the Crisis*. Brussels: European Trade Union Institute.

Stepan, N.L. (2011) *Eradication: Ridding the World of Diseases Forever?* Ithaca, NY: Cornell University Press.

Taylor, A.L. and Dhillon, I. (2013) A global legal architcture to address the challenges of international health worker migration: a case study of nonbinding instruments in global health governance, in I.G. Cohen (ed.) *The Globalization of Health Care: Legal and Ethical Issues*. New York: Oxford University Press.

Turner, L. (2010) 'Medical tourism' and the global market in health services: U.S. patients, international hospitals, and the search for affordable health care, *International Journal of Health Services*, 40 (3): 443–67.

Wagner, M. (1997) Confessions of a dissident, in R. Davis-Floyd and C.F. Sargent (eds.) *Childbirth and Authoritative Knowledge – Cross-cultural Perspectives*. Berkeley, CA: University of California Press.

Wallace, H., Pollack, M.A. and Young, A.R. (2015) *Policy-Making in the European Union*. Oxford: Oxford University Press.

Weyland, K. (2007) *Bounded Rationality and Policy diffusion*. Princeton, NJ: Princeton University Press.

Woods, N. (2006) *The Globalizers: the IMF, the World Bank, and their Borrowers*. Ithaca, NY: Cornell University Press.

Youde, J. (2012) *Global Health Governance*. Cambridge: Polity Press.

Zeitlin, J. and Vanhercke, B. (2014) *Socializing the European Semester? Economic Governance and Social Policy Coordination in Europe*. Providence, RI: Brown University, Watson Center for International Studies.

Health and well-being: the wider context for healthcare management

Ann Mahon

Introduction

Social, economic and political contexts determine how people define and experience health and illness. They also determine the strategies that individuals, social groups and governments deem appropriate to address issues relating to them. This chapter begins by exploring lay definitions of health and how such definitions influence health and illness behaviours. Patterns of health and illness among different countries and between different groups are analysed through several learning activities. Explanations for the existence of inequalities in health are also explored. The role and relative contribution of formal systems of healthcare is thus set in a wider social context. Finally, the implications of this perspective for healthcare management are discussed. Learning activities and case studies are employed throughout the chapter to encourage the application of key concepts to management practice.

Definitions of health and illness

Health is an elusive concept and there is no single, objective definition of what it means to be a healthy person or to live in a healthy community or society. Before reading further, take a few minutes to complete the first learning activity.

The World Health Organization (WHO) defines health as both a fundamental human right as well as 'a state of complete well-being, physical, social and mental, and not merely the absence of disease or infirmity' (WHO, 1946: 100). Many empirical studies have investigated how individuals' and social groups' health beliefs and behaviours can vary according to age, gender, specific disease categories, social class and ethnicity (Greenhalgh et al., 1998; Adejoh, 2014; Pudrovska, 2015).

Learning activity 8.1   Health beliefs

Think of someone you know and who you consider to be healthy. It might be a family member, a close friend or colleague – or even a television presenter, actor or other public figure. When you think of this person, consider the following questions:

- What do they look like?
- How do they appear physically?
- How do they behave and interact with others?

Pay attention to the characteristics that you associate with being healthy in this person. What is it about their appearance, their behaviours, their attitude, their mood, what they do or do not do, what they say or do not say, that has influenced your decisions?

Finally, list all of the key words that you associate with being healthy in this person.

We will return to this activity at the end of this section. For now, continue to read the rest of the section, which explores some studies that have identified how lay people define health and illness.

In a synthesis of research into health beliefs, Hughner and Kleine (2004) identified eighteen themes that fell into four categories of how people defined health:

- Category 1: *Definitions of health*, five distinct themes. Health could be defined as the absence of disease, the ability to carry out certain functions, a state of equilibrium between mind, body and spirit, and the freedom to choose how to live life, without constraint. The final theme in this category sees health as a constraint, in that it requires, or expects, individuals to conform to certain societal demands, such as paid work. Health as a constraint is consistent with Talcott Parson's (1951) early conceptualization of the sick role.
- Category 2: *Explanations for health*, eight themes. Health was seen as being caused by, or maintained, through meditation or prayer, through a positive outlook and attitude, and through working and keeping busy. Health was also seen as being maintained through religious and supernatural explanations and through rituals. For others, individual health and the health of the family were deemed a moral responsibility and duty. Health was also explained through the maintenance of 'internal monitoring' such as regular health checks. The final theme in this category was self-blame, suggesting that if people are ill, it is often because of their own lifestyle choices.
- Category 3: *External and/or uncontrollable factors impinging on health*, three themes. Health was associated with 'health as policy' and the associated role and the function of government to determine health. Health was also associated with the way

we live our lives today – the 'modern way' of life. Finally, within this category, health was seen more fatalistically, as being a product of our genetics.

- Category 4: *The place health occupies in people's lives*, two themes. Health was seen as being influenced by how high a priority it was for people, compared with other priorities in their lives – such as coping with family responsibilities. The final theme was health being determined by the disparity between what people know about how to keep healthy and their actual behaviours.

Hughner and Kleine (2004: 397) concluded that popular worldviews about health and wellness are 'complex interweavings of information drawn from different sources including lay knowledge, folk beliefs, experiences, religious and spiritual practices and philosophy'. In addition, political beliefs and a sense of social justice can also be seen to contribute to this complex web of health beliefs.

In recent years, particularly in countries with significant indigenous populations such as New Zealand, Australia, Canada, India and the United States, there has been an increased recognition and acceptance of how indigenous peoples define health. For example, the 1999 Declaration on the Health and Survival of Indigenous Peoples proposed that indigenous peoples' concept of health is both a collective and individual inter-generational continuum:

> . . . encompassing a holistic perspective incorporating four distinct shared dimensions of life. These dimensions are the spiritual, the intellectual, physical and emotional. Linking these four fundamental dimensions, health and survival manifests itself on multiple levels where the past, present and future co-exist simultaneously. (Durie, 2003a: 510)

Factors driving the pace of change in healthcare are well documented and include economic drivers, technological advances, sociological transitions, demographic changes and a suggested reduction in levels of trust and confidence in health and public services (Mahon et al., 2009; Llewellyn et al., 2013; Centre for Workforce Intelligence, 2014). As populations become more mobile and diverse (Demireva, 2014), this may result in greater diversification of health status, health beliefs and health behaviours within and between different communities. The economic downturn, experienced in many countries, has also had a negative impact on health and well-being. Health is adversely affected as unemployment increases, work conditions become less secure and material circumstances decline, although it can take some time for the health impact to appear in official statistics at population level (OECD, 2013). How all of these changes will influence definitions and experiences of health and illness in the future provides fertile ground for further research.

Health is clearly more than the absence of disease. Beliefs about what determines our health will influence how we decide when we are ill and how we behave in this state. This has implications for the relationship between individuals and communities and the providers of care. However, health and illness are much more than the definitions, experiences and behaviours of individuals and communities. The well-being of any given society is determined by a range of factors, including housing, employment, income, work conditions and educational attainment (Marmot, 2010; OECD, 2013). This suggests, and indeed is a belief held by many public policy commentators, that health and public health have a strong connection with politics and with social justice. Martin Donohoe's reader and associated web sources provide an excellent overview of the links between social justice and public health from a US perspective, alongside some detailed analyses in particular specialist areas (Donohoe, 2013). These include in-depth explorations of the experiences of particular vulnerable groups (such as people with mental health problems, the homeless, and men and women in prison), through to the 'modern epidemics' (obesity, alcohol and suicide by firearms) and the role of corporations in 'subverting, obfuscating and repressing science in the quest for profit' (2013: xiv).

Learning activity 8.2   Influences on your health beliefs

Go back to your notes from Learning activity 8.1 and review the key words that you selected to describe the healthy person that you know. Now consider the following questions:

- What strikes you about the words you have used (or not used)?
- How do the words that you have used relate to Hughner and Kleine's (2004) four categories and associated themes?
- Do you have a preference or a bias towards some of the themes and categories?
- What factors in your life do you believe have influenced your own attitudes about what it means to be healthy and what influences your health and illness?

You might want to consider how the following have shaped your views:

- Your ethnicity
- Your family
- Your schooling and education
- Your community and neighbourhood
- Your experience of health, illness and healthcare
- The policies of your regional or national governments.

Patterns of health and illness

Complex and diverse patterns emerge when comparing indicators of health and illness among different countries. Typically, three main indicators are used to measure health and illness: life expectancy, mortality and morbidity. One important source of data that allows for global comparisons is the *World Health Statistics 2014 – Part III: Global Health Indicators* (WHO, 2014).

Learning activity 8.3   Life expectancy – comparative analysis

Access the WHO's *World Health Statistics 2014 – Part III: Global Health Indicators* (WHO, 2014). Go to Section 1 and Table 1. Select *your own country* and *five other countries* that have different patterns of life expectancy at birth and at the age of sixty.

1   Describe the life expectancy for both sexes *between* the countries you have selected. Which country has the highest life expectancy at birth and at sixty? Which country has the lowest?
2   Now describe the life expectancy for males and for females *within* and *between* the countries. What differences do you see between males and females? What patterns do you see among the six countries you have selected?
3   How do you *explain* these patterns? Develop your own hypotheses about why there are differences in life expectancy among the different countries you have selected.
4   Develop hypotheses about why life expectancy at birth and at the age of sixty is different for men and women.
5   Do your hypotheses suggest that the disparities in life expectancy between men and women are *inequities* (that are unfair and unjust) or *differences* (that are inevitable and acceptable at a societal level)?

Learning activity 8.4   Mortality rates – comparative analysis by world regions

Once again, access the WHO's *World Health Statistics 2014 – Part III: Global Health Indicators* (WHO, 2014). This time go to Section 2 and Table 2. Now look at two selected sets of indicators for cause-specific mortality and morbidity for the six WHO world regions.

The two selected indicators are:

1   Age-standardized mortality rates by cause: (i) communicable diseases, (ii) non-communicable diseases and (iii) injuries.
2   Distribution of causes of death among children < five years: (i) HIV, (ii) diarrhoea, (iii) measles and (iv) malaria.

The six world regions are:

•   African Region
•   Region of the Americas

- South-East Asian Region
- European Region
- Eastern Mediterranean Region
- Western Pacific Region.

Compare the data for each set of indicators across the six world regions. Describe the patterns that you see. What are the differences in the statistics for each set of indicators? Why do you think they exist?

Now focus on the causes of death among children < five years. If you were a government advisor in each world region, what strategies would you recommend to reduce deaths from HIV, diarrhoea, measles and malaria?

In addition to the analyses you have carried out in Learning activities 8.3 and 8.4, the *WHO World Health Statistics 2014* leads to the following conclusions:

- Health inequalities between different countries exist for all of the selected indicators of health and disease – life expectancy, mortality and morbidity.
- Although considerable advances in life expectancy have been achieved in many countries in recent decades, there are still significant inequalities in life expectancy at birth.
- Women live longer than men in most, if not all, countries in the world. In recent years, the gap in life expectancy between men and women has reduced, although the overall trend remains.
- The stage of economic, social and political development in countries is reflected in their patterns of health and illness. The populations of the poorest countries and those in political conflict typically have lower life expectancy, a greater probability of dying prematurely, and greater mortality and morbidity from infectious diseases.
- The relative burden of the three major disease categories varies considerably between different countries. The poorer developing countries continue to suffer high death rates from infectious diseases, whereas the richer countries have experienced the epidemiological transition characterized by a decline in infectious diseases and a rise in non-communicable chronic diseases such as obesity and diabetes.
- Access to basic public health amenities is vital in population health. Populations in rural regions in the poorest countries are most vulnerable to a lack of a reliable and clean supply of water.

The health inequalities evident in the *World Health Statistics 2014* are enormous and shocking. They also conceal the considerable inequalities between different socioeconomic, cultural and ethnic groups *within* countries. The existence of such inequalities in health among different groups within as well as between countries is well established (Marmot, 2010; OECD, 2013; Elgar et al., 2015).

In New Zealand, Australia, India, Canada, the USA and other countries with indigenous populations, national data conceal the poorer health status of their indigenous peoples. Indigenous peoples tend to have higher mortality and morbidity rates right across the disease spectrum and much of the excess arises from non-communicable chronic diseases (Durie, 2003a). Thus, while indigenous peoples represent a diversity of cultures, traditions and histories, they also represent the most marginalized populations in the world (United Nations, 2010). The degree of marginalization and social injustice is rather graphically illustrated by the differences in life expectancy between indigenous and non-indigenous peoples, which is a staggering twenty years in Australia, thirteen years in Guatemala and eleven years in New Zealand (United Nations, 2010). David Jones, writing about the persistence of American Indian health inequalities, draws three conclusions. First, that there is a wide range of possible aetiologies, including religion, diet and climate as well racial differences and socioeconomic explanations. Second, that this 'abundance of possible explanations' (Jones, 2013: 111) allows some observers to select particular beliefs that serve to justify political and ideological decisions. Third, explanations for the existence of inequalities are framed as choices about where we believe the responsibility for inequalities in health should be assigned and that 'these assignments have crucial implications for health policy' (2013: 111).

Culturally sensitive strategies can be applied to a range of problems experienced by indigenous communities with demonstrable improvements in health outcomes (Cunningham, 2009). The following two case studies describe strategies to address the health status of indigenous peoples in New Zealand (Box 8.1) and in India (Box 8.2).

Box 8.1   Case study – addressing the health status of indigenous peoples in New Zealand

Mason Durie identifies two broad directions for improving health services for indigenous health in New Zealand: increasing the responsiveness of conventional services and establishing dedicated indigenous programmes. In New Zealand, both these approaches are endorsed in legislation and government health policy. Section 8 of the New Zealand Public Health and Disability Act (2000) requires health services to recognize the principles of the Treaty of Waitangi, the 1840 agreement that saw sovereignty exchanged for Crown protection (Durie, 2003b). The New Zealand strategy is broad in its approach, seeking to influence macro policies, such as labour market policies and public health population approaches to health and personal health services. In this respect, it is consistent with the Maori holistic approach to health and inter-sectoral determinants of health.

Indigenous health services provide a range of healing methods, including conventional professional services and traditional healing. Durie argues that their most significant contribution is improved access to health services for indigenous peoples, enabling earlier intervention, energetic outreach, higher levels of compliance and a greater sense of community participation and ownership. Indigenous services tend to be built around indigenous philosophies, aspirations, social networks and economic realities

(Durie, 2003b). For Durie, coexistence of conventional and indigenous healthcare is not problematic:

> While there is some debate about which approach is likely to produce the best results, in practice conventional services and indigenous services can exist comfortably together. More pertinent is the type of service that is going to be most beneficial to meet a particular need. In general indigenous health services are more convincing at the level of primary health care. Higher rates of childhood immunisation, for example seem to be possible with services that are closely linked to indigenous networks, and early intervention is embraced with greater enthusiasm when offered by indigenous providers. (Durie, 2003b: 409)

The importance of partnership and collaborative working is identified as a crucial component for success:

> Conventional health services and indigenous services need, however to work together within a collaborative framework. Clinical acumen will be sharpened by cultural knowledge and community endeavours will be strengthened by access to professional expertise. It makes sense to build health networks that encourage synergies between agencies, even when philosophies differ. (Durie, 2003b: 409)

Box 8.2   Case study – addressing the health status of indigenous peoples in India

Devadasan et al. (2003) describe an initiative working with tribes in India where a health system specifically targeted at tribal people had a remarkable impact on infant and maternal mortality. Over a period of ten–fifteen years, immunization coverage increased from 2 per cent to over 75 per cent. Use of hospital services was three times the national average in a population that initially refused to go to hospital because of the fear of dead spirits circulating there. They identified the main features that characterized the success of this initiative:

- It was nested within larger development services, such as agriculture, education and housing.
- It was owned by the people. From the beginning, tribal communities participated in planning and implementing the scheme and most of the staff were from the tribal community.

The health system was developed with the worldview of the tribal community in mind. For example, initially the hospital did not have beds, as patients found it more comfortable to sleep on mats on the floor (Devadasan et al., 2003).

In Learning activities 8.3 and 8.4, you began to consider how different patterns of health and illness can be explained and implicit in the above two case studies are assumptions and beliefs about why inequalities exist. The next section of this chapter looks more closely at the relationship between where we live, how long we live for and how the quality of our lives can be explained. In other words – what factors determine health?

The determinants of health

A number of different perspectives can be employed to explain inequalities in health. Historical and cultural analyses will shed light on the history surrounding the health status of a population or a social group. For example, see Friedrich Engels on the social and economic conditions of Victorian England (Engels, 1999), Mason Durie on the experiences of Maori in New Zealand (Durie, 1994, 2003a, 2003b) and Myrna Cunningham on the indigenous concept of health and health systems (Cunningham, 2009). Different perspectives – political, sociological and biological – will yield different explanations (Jones, 2013).

Compared with many other countries, the UK has a strong tradition of producing robust data over time to describe patterns of inequalities and these data have been compiled in a number of high-profile sources over many decades. However, the evidence in relation to why these patterns exist is less robust and, of course, raises political questions about the relative roles and responsibilities of individuals, families, the community, society and the state (Baggott, 2010).

The authors of the UK Black Report describe four theoretical explanations for the relationship between health and inequality: artefact explanations, theories of natural/social selection, materialist/structuralist explanations and cultural/behavioural explanations. The authors conclude that the most significant causes are those relating to materialist/structuralist explanations, and base their recommendations for action on this perspective (Townsend and Davidson, 1982). Durie argues that explanations for current indigenous health status can be grouped into four main propositions: genetic vulnerability, socioeconomic disadvantage, resource alienation and political oppression. All four propositions can be conceptualized as a causal continuum: short-distance factors such as the impact of abnormal cellular processes at one end, and long-distance factors such as government polices at the other. Midway factors include values and lifestyles (Durie, 2003a).

Other writers (Wilkinson and Marmot, 2003; Marmot, 2010) focus upon the social determinants of health that affect populations. The role that individual health beliefs and behaviours might play, considered at the beginning of this chapter, are thus distinguished from the broader social determinants of health that are typically outside the control of individuals.

The key social factors highlighted by Wilkinson and Marmot include: health inequalities, stress, early life experiences, social exclusion, work, unemployment, social support, addiction, food and transport. Each of these factors impacts on health in different ways and with different policy implications. The research evidence for the summaries of 'what is known' and the 'policy implications' for all factors are fully sourced in the original publication, which is available on the European Public Health Alliance (EPHA) website (see the Learning resources at the end of this chapter). The nature and the extent of influence exerted by these different factors are determined by the prevailing economic and political conditions in different countries.

Economic growth and improvements in housing brought with them the epidemiological transition from infectious to chronic diseases – including heart disease, stroke and cancer. So economic growth saw a nutritional transition when diets, particularly in Western Europe, changed to the over-consumption of energy-dense fats and sugars, producing more obesity (Wilkinson and Marmot, 2003: 26). However, emerging economies, such as India, China and Brazil, are now increasingly characterized by rising obesity rates. China and India, for example, represent 15 per cent of the world's obese population and almost two-thirds of the world's obese people live in developing countries (Ng et al., 2014).

Wilkinson and Pickett detail not just the negative impact that inequalities have on health but develop the thesis that for a whole range of indicators, outcomes are worse where inequalities are greater. Where the income differences between the richest and the poorest in a society are small (as in Sweden and Japan, for example), the whole population experiences better health. Conversely, where income differences are greatest (as in the USA), then health is poorer. The existence of inequalities in itself exerts a negative social, psychological and ultimately physical effect on the population (Wilkinson and Pickett, 2009). The implications are clear – reducing income inequalities within a society improves health for the whole population – we all do better in a more equal society.

Now read the European case study in Box 8.3 that identifies five main areas of activity associated with innovative approaches to addressing inequalities.

Box 8.3   Case study – addressing health inequalities: examples of European experiences

In an analysis of policy developments on health inequalities in different European countries, Mackenbach and Bakker (2003) found that countries were in widely different phases of awareness of, and willingness to take action on, inequalities in health. Their international comparisons suggest that the UK was ahead of continental Europe in developing and implementing policies to reduce inequalities in health through comprehensive and coordinated policy. They identified factors that supported or inhibited action on inequalities, including the availability of descriptive data, the presence or absence of political will, and the role of international agencies such as the World Health Organization. Innovative approaches were identified in five main areas: policy steering mechanisms, labour market and working conditions, consumption and health-related behaviour, healthcare, and territorial approaches:

1   *Policy steering mechanisms* such as quantitative policy targets and health inequalities impact assessment. In the Netherlands, for example, quantitative policy targets were set for the reduction of inequalities in eleven intermediate outcomes, including poverty, smoking and working conditions.

2 *Labour market and working conditions* can be addressed universally or by a targeted approach. An example of a universal approach comes from France where occupational health services offer annual check-ups and preventive interventions to all employees. An example of a targeted approach is job rotation among dustmen in the Netherlands.

3 *Consumption and health-related behaviour.* Again universal and targeted approaches are identified. In the UK, women on low incomes are targeted using multi-method interventions to reduce smoking. In Finland, a universal approach is adopted by serving low-fat food products through mass catering in schools and workplaces.

4 Examples of innovative practices in *healthcare* include working with other agencies. In the UK, for example, there are community strategies led by local government agencies but integrating care across all the local public sector services.

5 *Territorial approaches* include comprehensive strategies for deprived areas such as the health action zones that were introduced in the UK (Mackenbach and Bakker, 2003).

Although there were some similarities – for example, the UK, Netherlands and Sweden have comprehensive strategies to reduce inequalities informed by national advisory committees – Mackenbach and Bakker found considerable variations in approaches which they suggest is a symptom of intuitive as opposed to rigorous evidence-based approaches to policy-making. They conclude: 'further international exchanges of experiences with development, implementation and evaluation of policies and interventions to reduce health inequalities can help to enhance learning speed' (Mackenbach and Bakker, 2003: 1409).

Navarro adopts an explicitly political stance and argues that addressing inequalities is not enough, stating: '. . . it is not *inequalities* that kill, but those who benefit from the *inequalities* that kill' (Navarro, 2013: 36). Navarro is critical of the apolitical stance adopted by organizations like the WHO. Speaking of the WHO Commission on the Social Determinants of Health he argues:

> The Commission's report goes very far in describing how inequalities are killing people. But we know the names of the killers. We know about the killing, the process by which it occurs, and the agents responsible. And we as public health workers must denounce not only the process but the forces that do the killing. The WHO will never do that. But as public health workers we can and must do so. It is not enough to define disease as the absence of health. Disease is a social and political category imposed on people within an enormously repressive social and economic capitalist system, one that forces disease and death on the world's people. (Navarro, 2013: 37)

The perspectives introduced here encourage a more critical and political perspective on the role that formal healthcare systems can have on population health. The next section in this chapter briefly considers the relative contribution of healthcare to health.

The contribution of healthcare to health status: healthcare in perspective

Until the 1970s, it was commonly assumed that the improvements in health experienced in many countries during the last century had occurred primarily as a consequence of advances in medical care. Critics from different perspectives started to challenge the relative contribution of healthcare to population health (Cochrane, 1972; Illich, 1977a, 1977b; McKeown, 1979; Kennedy, 1983). This in turn triggered a more robust assessment of the importance of healthcare to health (Bunker, 2001; Figueras and McKee, 2012). The previous section considered how the health of people, patients and populations is influenced by many factors outside of formalized systems of healthcare. The amount of money spent on healthcare is not, in itself, the major contributor to the health profile of a nation. Spending on health may reflect the relative economic affluence of a country, which in itself influences population health. It may also hide inequalities in access to timely and effective healthcare. Over-consumption of healthcare can also contribute to poor health. Although the USA spends more on healthcare per person than any other country in the world, it also performs poorly on a number of health indicators when compared with countries spending a lot less (Nolte and McKee, 2012).

Learning activity 8.5 Funding of health systems

Once more access the WHO's *World Health Statistics 2014 – Part III: Global Health Indicators* (WHO, 2014). Go to Section 7 and Table 7 and select the six countries that you selected for Learning activities 8.3 and 8.4. In addition, include the USA in your analysis.

- For each country, what is the total expenditure on health as a percentage of GDP?
- For each country, what is the proportion of expenditure on health that comes from government and private sources?
- Apart from the USA, which country spends the highest percentage of its GDP on health?
- Which country spends the lowest percentage of its GDP on health?
- Can you see any patterns between spending on healthcare and health indicators? If so, what are these patterns and how do you explain them?

Access to appropriate, acceptable and good quality healthcare is an important contributor to health and this is the case across all social and ethnic groups. Even where this is demonstrated, there is not a direct relationship between the availability of effective healthcare and health because of inequalities in access, where those in greatest need of healthcare have least access (Tudor-Hart, 1971). Furthermore, Wilkinson and Marmot suggest:

Health policy was once thought to be about little more than the provision and funding of medical care: the social determinants of health were discussed only among academics. This is now changing. While medical care can prolong survival and improve prognosis after some serious diseases, more important for the health of the population as a whole are the social and economic conditions that make people ill and in need of medical care in the first place. Nevertheless, universal access to medical care is clearly one of the social determinants of health. (Wilkinson and Marmot, 2003: 7)

Many healthcare systems across the world are making fundamental changes to the management and delivery of healthcare in attempts to reduce inequalities in both health status and access to health services and in recognition of the influence of the social determinants of health. In addition, after a period of unprecedented growth and in an era of economic downturn in many countries, there is now increasing concern about productivity, efficiency and the quality of care (KPMG, 2010).

The final two case studies in this chapter look at strategies to address health and illness at a population level, drawing on research carried out at McMaster University in Ontario (Box 8.4) and the University of Texas School of Public Health (Box 8.5).

Box 8.4 Case study – focusing on vulnerable people in a population

Findings from a series of studies of health and illness behaviour suggest that we need to rethink aspects of healthcare delivery, health education and health promotion, and the role of providers and communities. An innovative series of initiatives at McMaster in Ontario, Canada, has found that social factors are better predictors of health than clinical factors. Vulnerability is defined as being caused by the interaction between biological factors (for example, genetic predisposition), personal resources (such as resilience, cognitive and intellectual capacities) and environmental factors (such as the availability of social support). Through a series of clinical trials that have been ongoing since 1991, it has been shown that targeting vulnerable people and offering proactive and integrated care is more effective and usually less expensive than on-demand care. In this context, proactive, holistic and integrated care are both crucial to health outcomes and cost effective (Browne et al., 2012).

Box 8.5 Case study – leveraging cross-sector partnerships: lessons from Texas

Researchers at the School of Public Health, University of Texas in Brownsville found that 80 per cent of Brownsville residents were obese or overweight, one-third had diabetes (half did not previously know this) and more than two-thirds had no healthcare coverage. The School of Public Health launched a media campaign and formed a community advisory board that comprises two hundred members drawn from business, government, the community and the university. They have also launched a series of initiatives, which include:

- The Brownsville Farmers' market (making fruit and vegetables affordable).

- 'The Challenge' – an annual event to support weight loss.
- 'Master Bike and Hike Plan', which aims to provide a trail within one mile of all residences in Brownsville.

Two key collaboration tactics for engaging citizens have been identified. First, the importance of building a common fact base – the data on obesity in the community were an important factor in driving change. Second, the importance of establishing a clear governance structure with clearly articulated goals and lines of accountability between the advisory board and sub-committees (The Intersect Project, 2015).

Craig et al. offer a pragmatic and realistic view on the relative role of interventions within and outside of health systems:

> The evidence that health is determined by social, environmental and economic influences throughout a person's life is not at issue. What is lacking is secure evidence that many broad public health interventions are effective. Priority must be given to addressing this lack of evidence. In the meantime, instead of polarized positions, an appropriate balance needs to be struck between the contrasting strategies of developing health services and intervening outside the health system. (Craig et al., 2006: 1)

What does striking this 'appropriate balance' mean for healthcare management? The final section in this chapter considers the role of healthcare management in supporting this duality of task.

The role of healthcare management

Although accessible, affordable and timely healthcare is of vital importance in health outcomes, population health also depends on a wide range of social and economic determinants (Campbell, 2010; Figueras and McKee, 2012). Strategies to improve health must focus both on the effectiveness of the healthcare system as well as broader public policies. Healthcare managers can no longer work in organizational isolation and need to be externally focused to support the implementation of broad-based policies that go beyond 'healthcare'. In response, new paradigms of leadership emphasize the need for bringing together diverse networks, cross-boundary and collaborative working, innovation and entrepreneurship, along with a focus on outcomes (Brookes and Grint, 2010).

The World Health Organization (WHO, 2015) argues that a well-managed health system responds to the needs and expectations of a population in five ways:

1 It improves the health status of the population served, focusing on the needs of individuals, families and communities.
2 It defends the population against the main threats to their health.
3 It protects them from the financial impact of ill health.
4 It offers person-centred care in a fair and equitable way.
5 A well-managed system creates systems and processes that allow people to participate in decisions that affect them.

Strong public policies need to co-exist alongside strong and effective healthcare leadership and management if these ambitious aims are to be met. Six building blocks are identified as being essential in promoting and maintaining the focus on population health within health-care organizations (WHO, 2015). These are:

- leadership and governance
- health information systems
- health financing
- human resources for health
- essential medical products
- service delivery.

The next activity encourages you to think about the extent to which your organization, your healthcare system and wider public policies in your country address population health. Taking the six building blocks identified by the World Health Organization (WHO, 2015), a series of questions have been developed to encourage you to assess how well your organization and your healthcare system is prepared for supporting a broader perspective on health. It also encourages you to think about your role and responsibilities in promoting population health through your own management practice.

Learning activity 8.6   Your role, your organization and your population

The following questions encourage you to think about policies, systems and practices in place to support a broader perspective on health management. As you read other chapters in this book that explore these themes in some detail, you may wish to return to this activity.

Leadership and governance: To what extent has your government committed to high-level policy goals that focus on equity and public health that goes beyond the provision of healthcare? How far do different public services collaborate – at policy level and at the point of delivery? What is your role in fostering partnership working?

Health information systems: Do you have access to high-quality information about the health needs and community assets of the population you serve? Are you able to assess progress against targets? Can you assess access to care and the quality of ser-vices provided? What local, regional or national mechanisms are in place to provide and use information systems? How far do you use health information systems to inform your decision-making?

Health financing: How is your healthcare system financed? Is there universal cover-age of healthcare or are there financial barriers to access care and financial conse-quences of being ill? What systems are in place to ensure value for money, productivity and efficiency in the use of financial resource? In your management practice, how do you promote access, fairness and value for money?

Human resources for health: What arrangements are in place for training and recruiting staff to provide the diversity and competence needed to deliver safe and high-quality healthcare? What mechanisms are in place for your workforce to work collaboratively with patients, carers, community groups and other key stakeholders? To what extent do you engage with your staff and with patients and community groups to design, deliver and evaluate the care provided?

Essential medical products and technologies: Do you have access to affordable essential medical supplies? Are supplies distributed fairly to those in need? Are treatments effective and based on evidence or on custom?

Service delivery: How established are primary care services in your healthcare system? Who is usually the first point of contact for patients? How integrated are different parts of the healthcare system? How is the quality and safety of patient care assured?

Conclusion

We began this chapter by exploring how lay people, including yourself, define health and illness. We then looked at patterns of health and illness from a global perspective and you compared some statistics from your own country with those from others. The determinants of health and illness have been discussed with an emphasis on the social context. Finally, we introduced a series of mini case studies with the intention to illustrate the value of a wider perspective on the organization and delivery of healthcare. Ultimately, this wider perspective will improve the quality and the outcomes of care, as well as offering a more inclusive and diverse care experience for the people, patients and populations that access healthcare. The combination of effective management and leadership in healthcare organizations, the commitment and skill to work collaboratively, and coherent and strong public policies will serve to improve health outcomes for individuals, their families and their communities. Healthcare management plays a pivotal role in achieving this goal.

Learning resources

European Public Health Alliance: EPHA is a not-for-profit membership organization and describes itself as a change agent and as Europe's leading NGO advocating for better health. Its website offers extensive links and resources to a wide range of European public health initiatives across four broad areas: healthy lifestyles, healthy behaviours; quality health systems and services; health, wealth and equity; and Europe and health [www.epha.org/].

System-Linked Research Unit on Health and Social Service Utilization: The unit was launched in 1991 and is funded by the Ontario Ministry of Health and Long-Term

Care to compare the effects and costs of innovative, intersectoral, comprehensive services with the usual sectoral, fragmented approaches of serving vulnerable populations. Details on their research programme can be found online [http://fhs.mcmaster.ca/slru/unit.htm].

Public Health and Social Justice: This organization identifies national and international initiatives designed to improve public health [www.publichealthandsocialjustice.org]. It also provides access to Martin Donohoe's publications, including access to his chapters in Donohoe, M.T. (ed.) (2013) *Public Health and Social Justice: A Jossey-Bass Reader.* San Francisco, CA: Jossey-Bass.

World Health Organization: WHO is the directing and coordinating authority for health within the United Nations system. It is responsible for providing leadership on global health matters, shaping the health research agenda, setting norms and standards, articulating evidence-based policy options, providing technical support to countries, and monitoring and assessing health trends. Extensive data on a range of health topics for WHO member states are accessible on its website [http://www.who.int/].

References

Adejoh, S.O. (2014) Diabetes knowledge, health belief and diabetes management among the Igala, Nigeria, *SAGE Open*, April/June 2014: 1–8.

Baggott, R. (2010) *Public Health: Policy and Politics* (2nd edn.). Basingstoke: Palgrave Macmillan.

Brookes, S. and Grint, K. (eds.) (2010) *A New Public Leadership Challenge?* Basingstoke: Palgrave Macmillan.

Browne, G., Birch, S. and Thabane, L. (2012) *Better Care: An Analysis of Nursing and Healthcare System Outcomes.* Ottawa, Ontario:: Canadian Health Services Research Foundation and Canadian Nurses Association.

Bunker, J.P. (2001) *Medicine Matters After All: Measuring the Benefits of Primary Care, a Healthy Lifestyle and a Just Social Environment.* London: Nuffield Trust for Research and Policy Studies in Health Services.

Campbell, F. (2010) *The Social Determinants of Health and the Role of Local Government.* London: Improvement and Development Agency.

Centre for Workforce Intelligence (2014) *Horizon 2035: Health and Care Workforces Future: Progress Update.*

Cochrane, A.L. (1972) *Effectiveness and Efficiency: Random Reflections on Health Services.* London: Nuffield Provincial Hospitals Trust.

Craig, N., Wright, B., Hanlon, P. and Galbraith, S. (2006) Editorial: does health care improve health?, *Journal of Health Services Research*, 11 (1): 1–2.

Cunningham, M. (2009) Health, in *United Nations Permanent Forum on Indigenous Issues: State of the World's Indigenous Peoples.* New York: United Nations Department of

Economic and Social Affairs, Secretariat of the Permanent Forum on Indigenous Issues [http://www.un.org/esa/socdev/unpfii/documents/sowip_web.pdf].

Demireva, N. (2014) *Briefing: Immigration, Diversity and Social Cohesion*. Oxford: Migration Observatory at the University of Oxford .

Devadasan, N., Menon, S., Menon, N. and Devadasan, R. (2003) Letters: Use of health services by indigenous population can be improved, *British Medical Journal*, 327: 988.

Donohoe, M.T. (ed.) (2013) *Public Health and Social Justice: A Jossey-Bass Reader*. San Francisco, CA: Jossey-Bass.

Durie, M. (1994) *Whaiora: Maori Health Development*. Auckland: Oxford University Press.

Durie, M. (2003a) The health of indigenous peoples, *British Medical Journal*, 326 (7388): 510–11.

Durie, M. (2003b) Providing health services to indigenous peoples, *British Medical Journal*, 327 (7412): 408–9.

Elgar, F., Pfortner, T.K., Moor, I., De Clercq, B., Stevens, G.W.J.M. and Currie, C. (2015) Socio-economic inequalities in adolescent health 2002–2010: analysis of a time series analysis of 34 countries participating in the Health Behaviour in School-aged Children study, *Lancet*, 385 (9982): 2088–95.

Engels, F. (1999) *The Condition of the Working Class in England*. Oxford: Oxford University Press.

Figueras, J. and McKee, M. (eds.) (2012) *Health Systems, Health, Wealth and Societal Well-being: Assessing the Case for Investing in Health Systems*. Maidenhead: Open University Press.

Greenhalgh, T., Helman, C. and Chowdhury, A.M. (1998) Health beliefs and folk models of diabetes in British Bangladeshis: a qualitative study, *British Medical Journal*, 316 (7136): 978–83.

Hughner, R.S. and Kleine, S.S. (2004) Views of health in the lay sector: a compilation and review of how individuals think about health, *Health*, 8 (4): 395–422.

Illich, I. (1977a) *Disabling Professions*. London: Boyars.

Illich, I. (1977b) *Limits to Medicine: Medical Nemesis – the Expropriation of Health*. New York: Penguin.

Intersect Project (2015) *Leveraging Cross-sector Partnerships: Lessons from Texas* [http://pastimes.org/leveraging-cross-sector-partnerships-lessons-texas/].

Jones, D.S. (2013) The persistence of American Indian health disparities, in M.T. Donohoe (ed.) *Public Health and Social Justice: A Jossey-Bass Reader*. San Francisco, CA: Jossey-Bass.

Kennedy, I. (1983) *The Unmasking of Medicine: A Searching Look at Healthcare Today*. St. Albans: Granada.

KPMG International (2010) Case study: McMaster University, Canada, in *A Better Pill to Swallow: A Global View of what Works in Healthcare* [https://www.kpmg.com/Global/en/IssuesAndInsights/ArticlesPublications/Documents/A-Better-Pill-to-Swallow-Oct-final.pdf].

Llewellyn, S., Brookes, S. and Mahon. A. (2013) *Trust and Confidence in Government and Public Services*. New York: Routledge.

Mackenbach, J.P. and Bakker, M.J. (2003) Tackling socio-economic inequalities in health: analysis of European experiences, *Lancet*, 362 (9393): 1409–14.

Mahon, A., Walshe, K. and Chambers, N. (2009) *A Reader in Health Policy and Management.* Maidenhead: Open University Press.

Marmot, M. (2010) *Fair Society, Healthy Lives: A Strategic Review of Health Inequalities in England Post-2010.* London: The Marmot Review.

McKeown, T. (1979) *The Role of Medicine: Dream, Mirage or Nemesis?* Princeton, NJ: Princeton University Press.

Navarro, V. (2013) What we mean by social determinants of health, in M.T. Donohoe (ed.) *Public Health and Social Justice: A Jossey-Bass Reader.* San Francisco, CA: Jossey-Bass.

Ng, M., Fleming, T., Robinson, M., Thompson, B., Graetz, N., Margono, C. et al. (2014) Global, regional, and national prevalence of overweight and obesity in children and adults during 1980–2013: a systematic analysis for the Global Burden of Disease Study 2013, *Lancet,* 384 (9945): 766–81.

Nolte, E. and McKee, M.C. (2012) In amenable mortality – deaths avoidable through healthcare – progress in the US lags that of three European countries, *Health Affairs,* 31 (9): 2114–22.

OECD (2013) *How's Life? 2013: Measuring Well-being.* Paris: OECD Publishing [http://www.oecd.org/std/3013071e.pdf].

Parsons, T. (1951) *The Social System.* Glencoe, IL: Free Press.

Pudrovska, T. (2015) Gender and health control beliefs among middle-aged and older adults, *Journal of Aging Health,* 27 (2): 284–303.

Townsend, P. and Davidson, N. (eds.) (1982) *Inequalities in Health: The Black Report.* Harmondsworth: Penguin.

Tudor-Hart, J. (1971) The inverse care law, *Lancet,* 1 (7696): 405–12.

United Nations (2010) *State of the World's Indigenous Peoples.* New York: United Nations [http://www.un.org/esa/socdev/unpfii/en/sowip.html].

Wilkinson, R. and Marmot, M. (eds.) (2003) *Social Determinants of Health: The Solid Facts* (2nd edn.). Geneva: WHO.

Wilkinson, R. and Pickett, K. (2009) *The Spirit Level: Why More Equal Societies Almost Always Do Better.* London: Allen Lane.

World Health Organization (WHO) (1946) Preamble to the Constitution of the World Health Organization as adopted by the International Health Conference, New York, 19–22 June 1946; signed on 22 July 1946 by the representatives of 61 States (Official Records of the World Health Organization, 2: 100) and entered into force 7 April 1948.

World Health Organization (WHO) (2014) *World Health Statistics 2014 – Part III: Global Health Indicators.* Geneva: WHO [http://www.who.int/gho/publications/world_health_statistics/EN_WHS2014_Part3.pdf].

World Health Organization (WHO) (2015) *Key Components of a Well-functioning Health System.* Geneva: WHO [http://www.who.int/healthsystems/publications/hss_key/en/].

Part

3

HEALTHCARE SERVICES AND ORGANIZATIONS

Primary care

Judith Smith

Introduction

Primary care is widely considered to be an essential part of a country's healthcare system, the fundamental building block upon which other elements are placed. In this chapter, the nature, role and potential of primary care are explored, drawing upon the latest international research and analysis, in particular in relation to the ways in which technological, epidemiological and health system developments are influencing the scope, organization and management of this care sector. The chapter sets the scene for subsequent analysis of the organization of those services that surround and support primary care, including acute, mental health and social care.

As will be seen, primary care is extending its reach and influence within many health systems, forming ever more complex and intertwined relationships with specialist health and disability services. At the same time, this is calling into question some of the long-held tenets of primary care organization and management, such as the role of gatekeeping, the generalist primary care physician, and the local family doctor as care coordinator.

In this chapter, we examine these issues, with a particular emphasis on the implications for healthcare managers of moves towards larger primary care networks, 'medical homes', and new primary care-based funding models such as accountable care organizations. Case studies are used to illustrate and analyse the latest developments in the organization and management of primary care, drawing out common themes across nations and using these to identify the particular challenges for healthcare managers.

The nature and role of primary care

The defining moment in contemporary history of primary healthcare is generally considered to have been the declaration, at a World Health Organization conference in 1978, of what primary healthcare should provide to people in communities and nations. This declaration, known as the Alma-Ata Declaration after the name of the town in the Russian Federation where the conference took place, sets out the following statement about the nature of primary healthcare:

> Primary health care addresses the main health problems, providing preventive, curative, and rehabilitative services accordingly . . . but will include at least: promotion of proper nutrition and an adequate supply of safe water; basic sanitation; maternal and child care, including family planning; immunization against the major infectious diseases; education concerning basic health problems and the methods of preventing and controlling them; and appropriate treatment of common diseases and injuries. (WHO, 1978: Section VII)

The WHO definition of primary care is focused on primary care as a broad and central function concerned with addressing the major determinants of health. This understanding of primary care has endured across the decades, and researchers and policy-makers across the globe continue to support the assurance of strong primary care provision as the essential minimum for a country seeking to maximize the health of its population.

Vuori (1986) suggested four ways of examining primary care: as a set of activities; as a level of care; as a strategy for organizing healthcare; and as a philosophy that permeates healthcare. The idea of primary care as a level of a health system, and also a strategy or philosophy for organizing approaches to care, was taken up by Tarimo (1997) in a paper revisiting Alma-Ata. Tarimo termed the traditional WHO conception of primary care as an 'approach to health development', with 'primary' implying that this area of care is fundamental, essential and closest to people's everyday lives and experiences.

The Alma-Ata conception of primary care as an approach to health development is striking in how it differs from what is traditionally considered to be 'primary care' in many health systems, where hospitals and more technical forms of care (usually known as 'secondary care') tend to dominate people's understanding of a health system. In these countries, primary care tends to be viewed as a (typically weaker) part of the biomedical spectrum of health services provided to people who are ill, the point of 'first contact' with the health system. Thus primary care is often viewed as what Tarimo (following Vuori) termed 'a level of care', in contrast to the broader understanding of primary healthcare as an approach to overall health development.

As part of work to examine ways in which European countries might invest more effectively in health, in 2013 the European Commission established an expert group charged with exploring the current and future role of primary care within the health systems of member states. The work of this group has been published as an EU expert opinion (Expert Panel, 2014) and suggests that modern primary care might best be defined as follows:

> The provision of universally accessible, integrated, person-centred, comprehensive health and community services provided by a team of professionals accountable for addressing a large majority of personal health needs. These services are delivered in a sustained partnership with patients and informal caregivers, in the context of family and community, and play a central role in the overall coordination and continuity of people's care.

What is striking about this updated definition is its focus on primary care as provider and coordinator of a comprehensive range of services by a multidisciplinary team, and a strong emphasis on partnership with patients and their carers. Primary care is thus not only a fundamental part of ensuring sound public health (Tarimo's health development) and the first point of entry to the health system (Tarimo's level of care) but also the coordinator, referrer and advocate for people as and when they require more specialized health and social care.

The work of Barbara Starfield (1998) drew together these two main conceptions of primary care as a level in a healthcare system, and at the same time crucial to improving the health of populations. She identified four essential features of effective primary care provision, which she suggested as an organizing framework for analysis of health systems (see Box 9.1).

Box 9.1   Starfield's four Cs as an organizing framework

1   **Point of first contact** – a system of primary care gatekeeping, a single point of access to most services provided by the health system.
2   **Person-focused continuous care over time** – enrolment of patients with a single primary care practitioner or practice.
3   **Comprehensive care for all common needs** – multidisciplinary primary care and community health services that can assess, diagnose and treat common conditions.
4   **Coordination of care provided elsewhere** – role as the individual's advocate and guide through the wider health system, including the guardian of overall patient information.

Source: Adapted from Starfield (1998).

These 'four Cs' were used by Starfield to assess the effectiveness of a country's primary care system. Indeed, Starfield's research into the quality and nature of primary care in the international context suggested a link between the strength of a country's primary care system (as measured against the four Cs) and its cost-effectiveness, and the level of health outcomes achieved for the population (Starfield, 1998; Macinko et al., 2003).

More recent analyses of the relationship between primary care systems and population health (e.g. Kringos et al., 2013a, 2013b) have produced more nuanced conclusions. This work has shown that while strong primary care appears to be associated with improved population health, it is also related to higher levels of health spending, at least in the short to medium term. There does, however, seem to be a link in Kringos and colleagues' analyses between comprehensive primary care provision and slower overall growth in healthcare expenditure, making it a sound bet for countries considering how best to invest health resources over the long term in a context of financial austerity and rising demand for health services.

Learning activity 9.1

Write two to three paragraphs describing how your country's health system measures up in relation to its primary care orientation according to Starfield's 'four Cs'. In so doing, assess on a scale of 1–10 (where 1 = not at all and 10 = completely) your health system's degree of gatekeeping in primary care; extent of primary care and public health registration; provision of comprehensive primary care and community health services; and ability to provide primary care-focused coordination of care for individuals. Then consider where there is scope for improvement.

Learning activity 9.2

Make the same assessment as in Learning activity 9.1 for the health system of another country that you know to be different from that of your own nation. How do the two countries' health systems compare in respect of primary care orientation? To help you with this assessment, you might wish to use a source such as the WHO's European health system reviews [http://www.euro.who.int/en/about-us/partners/observatory/publications/health-system-reviews-hits/full-list-of-country-hits].

Managing in primary care

As primary care has increased in importance within health systems, especially given the changes in global and public health outlined in Chapters 7 and 8, so the task of managing these services has become more complex. There are three distinctive aspects of primary care development that have driven this increased complexity of the management task: the role of primary care in coordinating a wider range of services; the assumption by primary care of a wider population health function; and the embracing of technology and self-care.

Coordinating a wider range of services

Given the acknowledged importance for public health and cost containment of having a strong primary healthcare orientation to a health system, it is striking that relatively little has been written about the management (as opposed to the delivery) of primary care, especially when compared with the amount of analysis accorded to the management of hospital services. However, the management of primary care has in recent years received greater prominence in both academic and practitioner communities, as people have come to view primary care as the main locus for seeking to improve the coordination of care of the rising numbers of people living with multiple complex conditions, and hence a key priority within health system reform (e.g. Smith and Goodwin, 2006; de Maeseneer and Boeckxstaens, 2012;

Edwards et al., 2013; Kringos et al., 2013a, 2013b). For example, in 2008, the European Commission expert panel on primary care asserted:

> . . . given that many people are living much longer with multiple health problems and needing the input and advice of a range of specialist medical teams alongside the care and support of their primary care team [. . .] primary care is being expected to play a central role within larger care teams or networks, and to be a core element of what is often referred to as 'integrated care'. (Expert Panel, 2014: 20)

To bring about better integrated care within a health system, it is acknowledged that primary care itself needs to be strengthened and developed, including providing a wider range of services in community settings outside hospitals and extending access to primary care for disadvantaged communities (Hefford et al., 2005; Edwards et al., 2013; Kringos et al., 2013a, 2013b; Expert Panel, 2014). Such strengthening of primary care has seen the emergence of many new models of primary care provision, often at significant scale. These developments form a particular focus of this chapter. These developments call for more sophisticated, senior and experienced management arrangements, tailored to the specific needs and nature of primary care services, professionals and multidisciplinary relationships.

Learning activity 9.3

Analyse the strengths and weaknesses of the primary care system of the country in which you live, with particular reference to its ability to provide well-integrated services for people with complex chronic health needs. What are the particular issues requiring attention by managers and policy-makers in your country, if they are to ensure well-integrated and locally provided primary care?

Taking on a greater population health or commissioning function

A further role ascribed to primary care in some health systems, and one seen as being a lever to enable health improvement and primary care development, is that of primary care-led commissioning. This function, whereby primary care practitioners and organizations assume a role in the funding, planning and purchasing of healthcare on behalf of populations registered with local general practices, has been used most enthusiastically by state policy-makers in England and by managed care insurers in the United States, and also in more limited ways in experiments with primary care budget holding in Sweden, New Zealand, Australia and Canada. A more detailed analysis of health purchasing and commissioning is set out in Chapter 14.

Recently, a commissioning role has been given to primary care-based organizations in some countries through a capitated health service budget with responsibility for developing better integrated care for local people. A budget-holding organization of this nature typically assumes responsibility for the health outcomes of the local population, the quality of health services that people receive, and appropriate use of the budget itself (Institute for Healthcare Improvement, 2013). These bodies are known by names such as 'accountable care organizations' (Fisher et al., 2007), 'integrated care organizations' (Lewis et al., 2010), 'primary care medical homes' (Rosenthal, 2008) or 'primary care networks' (Smith et al., 2013).

Learning activity 9.4

Identify the key features of a 'primary care medical home' within the academic literature (for an example, see Rosenthal, 2008). Apply these features to the primary care service in your own region or locality and describe the actions needed to enable a fully functioning medical home approach.

Primary care embracing technology and self-care

The other factor influencing the complexity, scope and management of primary care is the increasing engagement of individuals in their own care, partly as a result of technological developments, and also through a gradual philosophical and cultural change towards regarding people as full partners in their care planning and delivery.

In addition to the internet as a frequent source of initial health advice – which is, of course, primary care in the strictest sense of the words – services are often now delivered with the support of text or email reminders (e.g. to attend screening or other appointments), mobile apps to be used for booking appointments and with supportive online resources such as for diabetic education and dietary monitoring. Some countries have been much quicker adopters of such technology-based approaches than others. Standard primary care services are increasingly being delivered in new ways, for example with phone, Skype or email consultations with family doctors or primary care nurses. Such developments are often enabled through the use of integrated electronic health records, and in some countries these are now fully accessible to – and even able to be written onto by – patients.

Technology is also being viewed as a vital ingredient of effective service integration (Ramsey and Fulop, 2008) and where the challenges of IT, data governance and cultural change across organizations are overcome, a shared electronic health record can enable very different forms of shared care. For example, primary care practices can coordinate the care of their patients in almost real time, sending electronic prescriptions to the pharmacy, requesting immediate nursing or home care support for patients, arranging for efficient care arrangements upon discharge from hospital, and keeping families and carers fully updated about plans and care.

The introduction and use of such technology in primary care – even the humble telephone for consultations – is not without its challenges however. Experience in many countries points to the difficulty in making cultural and organizational change to support such technology.

Indeed, studies of the introduction of telehealth and telecare point to the limited impact of such innovations, where the wider models of care and professional roles have not been modified and supported as part of the wider process of change (Steventon and Bardsley, 2012).

Finally, as explored in Chapter 18 ('Patient and public involvement in healthcare'), there has been significant progress in developing new approaches to shared decision-making in healthcare, and many of these are highly amenable to primary care settings and services. They do, however, require professionals to work in new ways, and provide a challenge to traditional models of care, as we explore later in this chapter when considering the use of design principles to re-imagine local primary care services.

Distinctive elements of managing primary care

As primary care has extended its scope and scale, its core functions have remained vital to the management task. These distinctive functions are most effectively captured in the organizing framework of Starfield's 'four Cs' (see Box 9.1), and are explored here in the context of the challenges facing healthcare managers.

Primary care gatekeeping

Most researchers and analysts consider primary care 'gatekeeping' crucial to the management of an effective health system, both in relation to clinical and cost-effectiveness. What gatekeeping entails is the identification of a single point of access to the health system for most of the health needs that people experience, and traditionally this has been a general practice staffed by family doctors and their teams. Within a system of primary care gatekeeping, patients cannot access hospital specialists or associated diagnostic services unless they have first consulted their family doctor. The strength of such a system is seen as being the ability of the family doctor to take a holistic view of a person's care, ensuring only appropriate referrals to more specialist services, and thus avoiding unnecessary expensive and possibly invasive tests and care in hospital settings. Gatekeeping is a function typically associated with tax-funded health systems such as those in the UK, New Zealand, Denmark, Italy and Sweden.

Critics of gatekeeping assert that it limits patients' rights and choices within a health system. Others question whether it enables sufficiently rapid and timely referral of patients for diagnostic tests where serious illness is suspected. For example, the reliance on general practitioner gatekeeping has been suggested as a reason for the relatively poor cancer outcomes in the UK, with a government taskforce being established in 2015 to consider options, including direct self-referral by patients to specialists where cancer 'red flag' symptoms are present (NHS England, 2015). Analysis of child healthcare across six European countries has similarly pointed to a reliance on generalism as a factor that may be compromising the quality and outcomes of such care (Wolfe et al., 2011), leading to the promotion of new models of integrated hospital and community paediatric care where specialists work alongside primary care colleagues within local child health teams.

In this way, countries with a tradition of gatekeeping are experimenting with the direct access to specialists enjoyed in countries such as France, Israel and the USA. This begs an important policy and management question as to whether we are reaching the limits of medical generalism. Has healthcare become just too complex for it to be reasonable to expect a single general practitioner or family physician to be able to manage the clinical and service risk of a whole population of patients? This is one issue that is driving the move towards multispecialty practice based in community settings, a trend examined later in this chapter and in Chapter 10.

Countries that have not traditionally included gatekeeping as a fundamental principle of their healthcare system have, for reasons of medical cost inflation, been experimenting with pilot projects of gatekeeping. One such experiment in the USA – *the primary care medical home* – is increasingly being seen as a way of offering patient-centred and integrated care in a manner that is affordable, of high quality and accessible to a majority of the population (Rosenthal, 2008; Davis and Stremikis, 2010). The model entails patients being enrolled with a primary care practice that holds a capitated budget for its patients, taking responsibility for referrals to specialist and other care, and coordination of the individual's care from the 'primary care home'. The primary care medical home is arguably an example of a well-functioning general practice as understood in countries such as the UK, New Zealand, Denmark, the Netherlands and Canada, albeit it does imply a strong system leadership and care coordination role for the primary care physician, which is not always a feature of day-to-day general practice in the countries cited above.

What is clear that gatekeeping in its traditional form, seeking to address all presenting symptoms and ailments, is unlikely to suffice in the ever more complex arena of healthcare. Likewise, open access to specialists will not be the answer, from both a financial and care appropriateness perspective. The combining of primary and specialist care within new 'at scale' networks and organizations represents a pragmatic and patient-focused attempt to balance these tensions. Thus the work of primary care becomes more extensive and complex, and arguably less easy to categorize or contain.

Patient registration

The registration of patients with a single practice or practitioner is viewed by public health practitioners and policy-makers as being vital in relation to both individual and population health. For individuals, it is considered to enable the development of a long-term and continuous relationship between patient and family doctor (or medical practice), meaning that the doctor and their team can have an overview of a person's medical history, firmly located within a knowledge and understanding of their broader social context, including family situation, employment status, housing provision and education. For populations, a system of registration provides managers in a health system with a register of people that sets out key health data (e.g. age, sex, any chronic ill-health problems, family situation) and thus represents the basis for carrying out population-focused health interventions such as calls for health screening, immunization campaigns, child health surveillance and health monitoring associated with specific age categories.

The importance of a system of registration has been powerfully demonstrated by the experience of New Zealand, where in 2001 the government began to explicitly develop a Primary Health Care Strategy (Minister of Health, 2001) that sought, among other things, to establish a system of patient registration, and where, just a few years later, there was evidence that levels of access to care and health promotion services had shown an improvement from their previously low base when compared with other developed countries (Cumming and Gribben, 2007).

The registered list (or a process of user enrolment) is considered fundamental to new extended models of primary care provision such as the accountable care organization, primary care medical home and multispecialty community provider. In all cases, the strength and potential of the organization is predicated on having an enrolled patient population for whom a capitated and risk-adjusted budget is allocated, and with which primary- and community-based services are provided and specialist services purchased as required. The enrolled population is also considered vital for preventive healthcare work such as immunizations, screening and chronic disease management, enabling the primary care organization to take a proactive and risk-assessed approach to the care of its patient population.

In countries where there has not been a tradition of having to be 'signed up' with a regular primary care provider, a registration or enrolment system can appear restrictive in relation to choice of practitioner. However, in countries such as France and the USA where payers or insurers have increasingly sought to use patient registration, attempts are made to ensure choice of caregiver within the primary care organization, and to move to another provider if desired. The health benefits of longitudinal care with a provider are, however, emphasized to patients as a trade-off from having free and multiple access to physicians.

Comprehensive local primary care services

The provision of comprehensive and multidisciplinary primary and community services is a goal that was set out in the Alma-Ata Declaration as being a key element in enabling effective primary healthcare. This underlines the WHO vision of primary care as being the centre of a health system and not the bottom of a pyramid of care as is often implied or asserted in management and clinical circles. Drawing on the work of Kringos et al. (2013a, 2013b), Smith et al. (2013) concluded that the core activities of primary care can be categorized as follows:

- prevention and screening
- assessment of undifferentiated symptoms
- diagnosis
- triage and onward referral
- care coordination for people with complex problems
- treatment of episodic illness
- provision of palliative care.

Saltman et al. (2006) have argued that the intermediate territory between self-care and specialist hospital care – the area typically considered as the domain of primary care – is changing as primary care assumes an increasingly significant role in planning and coordinating care provided by different services. This underlines the importance of the enrolled population referred to above and the need for primary care organizations to source skills in needs assessment, population health management, and preventive and counselling work (Thorlby, 2013).

As noted earlier, various countries are experimenting with having multispecialty group practice within community settings, and secondary care specialist medical and nursing staff integrated within what have been traditionally considered primary care teams. Some of these groups are comprehensive and seek to cover all healthcare needs in a local population, and others are segmented on care condition lines, catering for, say, older people or those living with diabetes or Parkinson's disease.

Coordination of care

The role of coordinating a person's care within the health system is perhaps the most problematic function that is ascribed to 'ideal' primary care. While care coordination is a function typically vaunted as a key element of family medicine and primary care, analysis of patient experience in many countries tends to tell a different story (Sarnak and Ryan, 2016). The reasons for this are various and contested, but seem to include the increasing complexity of individuals' health status, and in particular the rising number of people living with multiple chronic conditions (see Chapter 10 for more details). It is therefore arguably no longer reasonable to expect smaller family medicine or general practices to assume responsibility for the full range of care coordination for people with a range of complex needs requiring services from health, disability, third sector and other providers.

Primary care policy-makers and managers face a dilemma in relation to how far they focus on the concerns and priorities of individuals as opposed to those of the wider population. As with the tension between primary care gatekeeping and individual choice of practitioner, so the introduction of individual care managers for people with long-term conditions may enable greater choice of services while leading to fragmentation of overall care, unless there is careful integration of the activity of care managers within an overall local health plan (see Chapter 10 for a more detailed discussion).

Primary care organizations

One management and organizational solution to this recurring patient/population tension within primary care has been the emergence of 'primary care organizations', bodies set up to manage and develop services in order to both improve population health and enable effective and high-quality general practice provision (Ham, 1996; Smith and Goodwin, 2006; Edwards et al., 2013). Primary care organizations are a specific manifestation of the move towards more managed and extensive primary care in a number of health systems, and represent a managerial solution to the dilemma of how to draw together often diverse and autonomous general practices and other community services into a coherent local network or organization for improving health.

The scale and scope of primary care organizations varies internationally, with standalone clinics run by single-handed doctors being typical in some countries and large health centres run by multidisciplinary teams being the norm in others (Meads, 2009). This variation results from factors such as the sociopolitical context of a country (for example, a strong focus on municipality-based health centres in some Scandinavian countries and a history of polyclinics in some Eastern European nations), the method of remuneration of family doctors (for example, independent contractor status driving traditionally small practices in the UK and the Netherlands), and the degree of self-organization among groups of doctors (for example, independent practitioner associations that have morphed into care networks in California and New Zealand).

Such variation is also typical within many countries, for primary care is characterized by diversity of organizational form, on account of its local and community-focused nature. In international research carried out by the Nuffield Trust and the King's Fund (Smith et al., 2013), twenty-one different types of primary care organization were identified. Three of the broad categories used to group these models of primary care provision are employed here to illustrate some of the most commonly found 'at scale' primary care organizations that seek to fulfil Starfield's 'four Cs' while also meeting the demands of modern care coordination and extended service provision, and maximizing use of technology and self-care.

Community health organization

In some countries, including Tanzania, some New Zealand Maori and Canadian Inuit communities, local health workers or nurses form the backbone of the primary care system, acting as public health and health promotion advisers, signposting people towards medical and nursing services as and when they need them. These arrangements are typically known as community health organizations or networks and form part of the tradition of 'community-oriented primary care' (Kark, 1981).

Community health organizations, also sometimes described as polyclinics or community health centres, are often made up of multiple practices in a network and in other cases based in a single building. They seek to combine patient-centredness with a strong population-orientation and often have an ownership model that includes significant public and community involvement. Examples include the Hokianga Health Enterprise Trust in New Zealand, which is owned and run by the local community (www.hokiangahealth.org.nz); the Bromley by Bow Centre in London, UK, which links primary care with a wide range of other services including social care and welfare advice (www.bbbc.org.uk); and Community Health Centre Botermarkt in Belgium, which is a not-for-profit organization focusing on patient empowerment, social cohesion and local participation (www.wgcbotermarkt.be). A case study description of Community Health Centre Botermarkt is set out in Box 9.2.

As is demonstrated by Botermarkt, a community health organization approach to primary care delivery is defined by a strong population focus, and sees its role as being about community development alongside the provision of local health services. The model is typically found in under-served and economically deprived areas, and there is often a strong focus on one or more marginalized groups, such as refugees, homeless people or those with severe enduring mental health problems. While the governance of community health organizations usually involves a significant public dimension, many of its challenges, such as seeking to strengthen care coordination, maximize ease of access to services, and encourage proactive and preventive care are common to other forms of primary care organization.

Primary care network

General medical practice is often organized on the basis of independent self-employed doctors working in small groups (or singly), and contracting with local health authorities to provide services to a registered local population. This system operates in the UK, the Netherlands, Denmark and Canada. In other countries, doctors similarly work in independent practices but levy fees directly from patients who can in some cases seek reimbursement of fees

Box 9.2 Case study – Community Health Centre Botermarkt, Belgium

The Community Health Centre Botermarkt is a not-for-profit organization set up in 1978 in Ledeberg, a deprived area in the city of Ghent. The primary care team is composed of family physicians, nurses and other staff, including receptionists, health promoters, dieticians, social workers, ancillary staff, smoking-cessation experts and dentists. The centre takes care of 6200 patients, from over seventy different countries. All patient information is coordinated in an integrated, interdisciplinary electronic patient health record. The centre aims to deliver integrated primary care. Service delivery focuses on accessibility (no financial, geographical or cultural barriers) and quality, using a comprehensive eco-bio-psycho-socio frame of reference. The focus is on empowerment of patients and contribution to social cohesion.

Patients are registered on a population-based list. The range of services provided include: health promotion and prevention, screening, curative care, palliative and rehabilitative services (consultations and home visits), integrated home care by an interdisciplinary team, nursing services, nutrition services, social work and dental care. The centre is financed through contracts with health insurance companies that include a monthly capitation payment for every patient on the list. Since 2013, there has been an integrated, mixed, needs-based capitation funding formula for the centre that takes into account social variables, morbidity, age, sex, functional status and income of the patient. Contracts are agreed between the centre and secondary care providers, physiotherapists, psychologists, palliative services and social services, in the framework of an integrated primary care system.

In 1986, the health centre created a local care collaboration comprising primary care providers, local schools, local police, citizen organizations and organizations of ethnic-cultural minorities, and this meets every three months to undertake 'community diagnosis' and enhance inter-professional and inter-sectoral cooperation, as well as seeking to tackle the upstream causes of ill health.

Contact: www.wgcbotermarkt.be and the International Federation of Community Health Centres [www.ifchc2013.org]

from their state or private health insurance. General practitioners levy fees from patients in countries such as New Zealand, France, Australia and the USA. The practice-based system of primary care is not confined to general medical practice, but is also commonly found in community dentistry, optometry and pharmacy.

Over the past two decades, there has been a move towards a more networked and extensive approach to delivery of local primary care, with smaller practices and medical groups in many countries forming networks or federations, typically as a way of sharing responsibility for back-office functions, training and education, safety and clinical governance, after-hours care, or specialized and extended clinical services such as diabetes, maternity and child health. These networks take a range of forms, depending on their core purpose, the preference of local clinical leaders, and the history of collaboration between providers. Some networks form as a way of delivering new forms of extended primary care, such as the Tower Hamlets primary care networks in London, UK, that work collectively to manage long-term conditions and other services on a locality basis with shared incentives and outcome measures, and with demonstrated evidence of the value of such arrangements (Robson et al., 2014).

In countries such as the Netherlands, USA and New Zealand, primary care networks have evolved over twenty or thirty years, and are often now major providers of primary care services for a locality or region. One example, the Midlands Health Network in New Zealand is set out in Box 9.3.

Box 9.3   Case study – the Midlands Health Network, New Zealand

The Midlands Health Network covers the central swathe of New Zealand's North Island, and comprises ninety-one general practices and three hundred and fifty-five GPs. The network has its origins in one of the country's GP-owned independent practitioner associations (IPAs), these for-profit organizations having been formed in the late 1980s as a defensive measure by doctors wanting 'strength in numbers' when faced by market reforms of the health sector that they feared would lead to unwelcome change. Over time, the IPA evolved into a primary care network that now has as its core focus the long-term sustainability of GP-owned general practice, improvement in quality of primary care and general practice, and the development of extended services that aim to keep people out of hospital and enjoying improved outcomes.

As the range of services offered by the network has grown – both support of general practice, and the development of new services available across practices – so the organization and its management have become more complex and sophisticated. The network now comprises four arms: the Pinnacle GP Network (the original IPA); Midlands Health Network, the management arm of Pinnacle; MRHN Charitable Trust (community governance); and Primary Health Care Limited (the company that owns and runs some practices). The network uses its scale to attract, manage and deliver (or purchase) a wide range of community health services, including health promotion, chronic disease management, diagnostics, community nursing, mental and child health.

The network has weathered various local and national political storms, and credits its local ownership by clinicians and the community as being central to its having survived and thrived. Recent developments have included the network buying a small number of general practices (where continuity of service was under threat) and running local primary care services, developing a Primary Care Medical Home model based on the US approach (but adapted for the New Zealand context), and integrating community nursing services into the core general practice team. All of these changes have been enabled by stable senior leadership and management, extensive clinical engagement, an integrated electronic patient record, and significant investment in service, organizational and workforce development.

Contact: www.midlandshn.health.nz

Vertically integrated care service

A recent trend in some countries is for the care of specific conditions to be redesigned and organized across traditional primary, secondary and even tertiary care boundaries, seeking to ensure that patients are supported and treated as far as possible in their own home, workplace and community. One example of this is ParkinsonNet in the Netherlands, as set out in Box 9.4. Services such as these are closely related to the self-care movement in health, and based on a belief that the patient is the expert about their condition and care, and as such should be able to access advice, support and care that embraces this fact and seeks to enable as normal a life as possible.

These three models of primary care organization illustrate some of the ways in which managers, clinicians and policy-makers in different countries are seeking to achieve the parallel goals of improving population health, providing high-quality and tailored care for individuals, and all in a way that enables more coordinated services for individuals and their families. It is clear that for many nations, the need to 'scale up' primary care services and integrate them more effectively with other parts of the health and disability system is a core policy priority.

Box 9.4   Case study – ParkinsonNet: a vertically integrated care service in the Netherlands

The central principle behind ParkinsonNet is to work cohesively across primary and secondary care, bringing in specialist neurologist expertise when necessary, yet having the majority of care delivered at home, through the internet or by specialized allied health professionals working in primary care. ParkinsonNet is a radical new approach designed by the whole network including patients and allows people to use an interactive online tool to locate services in their area. These services are supported by hospital specialists – for example, educational updating, supervision and help with the most difficult problems – but delivered by doctors, nurses and allied health professionals in primary care wherever possible.

ParkinsonNet is a nationwide professional network of specially trained caregivers who can provide care to those with Parkinson's disease and related disorders. Each regional community currently includes twelve professional disciplines, including neurologists, Parkinson's disease nurses, physiotherapists, speech therapists, occupational therapists, dieticians, social workers, sexologists, pharmacists, psychologists and psychiatrists. Each year additional disciplines are being added and all networks will soon involve all of the nineteen disciplines involved in the care for Parkinson's disease patients. The communities of healthcare professionals are centred on community hospitals. Independent evaluations have indicated increases in the quality of care received by patients, a reduction in disease complications (including a 50 per cent reduction in hip fractures) and substantial cost savings (around 5 per cent reduction in annual expenditure on chronic Parkinson care).

Contact: www.parkinsonnet.info

Design principles for new models of primary care

Analysis of new models of primary care (e.g. Expert Panel, 2014) emphasizes the need to avoid any 'one size fits all' approach to the management and development of this sector. By its nature, primary care is local, diverse and complex, and hence is not amenable to structural or mandated solutions. In a report arising from a European summit on primary care policy, Edwards et al. (2013) set out a set of 'design principles' suggested as being potentially helpful to managers and clinicians seeking to redesign local primary care services to meet the local and specific needs of a population. The design principles, which were explored further in relation to practical international case study examples in Smith et al. (2013), are set out in Box 9.5.

Conclusion

Health systems are increasingly seeking to coordinate and manage a diverse range of providers of primary care, trying at once to develop and improve primary care services while improving the public health, and ensuring overall better integration of care and health outcomes. This poses specific management challenges, including enabling continuity and

---

Box 9.5   Design principles for primary care

Design principles – clinical care

- A senior clinician, capable of making decisions about the correct course of action, is available to patients as early in the process as possible.
- Patients can benefit from access to primary care advice and support that is underpinned by systematic use of the latest electronic communications technology.
- Patients have the minimum number of separate visits and consultations that are necessary, with access to specialist advice in appropriate locations.
- Patients are offered continuity of relationship where this is important and access at the right time when it is required.
- Care is proactive and population based where possible, especially in relation to long-term conditions.
- Care for frail people with multi-morbidity is tailored to the individual needs of patients in this group, in particular people in residential or nursing homes.
- Where possible, patients are supported to identify their own goals and manage their own condition and care.

Design principles – organization

- Primary care is delivered by a multidisciplinary team, in which full use is made of all the team members and the form of the clinical encounter is tailored to the need of the patient.

- Primary care practitioners have immediate access to common diagnostics, guided by clinical eligibility criteria.
- There is a single electronic patient record that is accessible by relevant organizations and can be read and, perhaps in future added to, by the patient.
- Primary care organizations make information about the quality and outcomes of care publicly available in real time.
- Primary care has professional and expert management, leadership and organizational support.

Source: Edwards et al. (2013) and Smith et al. (2013).

Learning activity 9.5

Using the primary care design principles, describe the primary care system for your country in 2025.

- What appear to you to be the three main actions required by policy-makers in your country to enable this primary care system to come into being?
- What will be the main challenges for primary care managers in developing and implementing the new system?

coordination of care for individuals and their carers, maximizing use of new technology, enabling appropriate degrees of self-care, and finding ways of developing a workforce for current and future community health services (see Chapter 17).

These management challenges are now finding their way into the health strategies of many countries, with primary care being seen as a key element in wider health plans. The challenge for primary healthcare managers is to be able to assure health professionals, funders and citizens of the ability of primary care organizations to fulfil the particular design principles or standards set by a particular nation (see Box 9.5).

Learning resources

Primary Health Care Research and Information Service (PHCRIS): Based at Flinders University in Adelaide, South Australia, PHCRIS offers a weekly electronic bulletin with links to newly published articles, reports and blogs on primary care from around the world. It also holds a wide range of primary care research syntheses, accessible via a tailored search filter [www.phcris.org.au].

European Forum for Primary Care: This multi-professional forum aims to improve the health of populations by promoting strong primary care and supporting primary care research. Members of the forum are sent a weekly bulletin of primary care resources and there is an annual conference [www.euprimarycare.org].

Commonwealth Fund: This New York-based research foundation aims to promote a high-performing healthcare system, particularly for the most vulnerable in society. As such, it has a strong focus on primary care, chronic disease and complex conditions, and research into new models of care for these groups. It also carries out highly respected international comparative work, including of primary care services. [www.commonwealthfund.org]

Nuffield Trust: This London-based independent health research foundation undertakes research and policy analysis, and primary care is a particular focus of its work, including study of new 'at scale' organizations. Extensive data and charts are available on their website, analysing healthcare activity and performance [www.nuffieldtrust.org.uk].

World Health Organization: WHO continues to advocate for strong primary care systems across the world and produces reports and analyses on many related topics [www.who.int/about/en]. Its regional websites and offices produce detailed analysis of comparative health data, such as the European office [http://www.euro.who.int/en/data-and-evidence].

References

Cumming, J. and Gribben, B. (2007) *Evaluation of the Primary Health Care Strategy: Practice Data Analysis 2001–2007*. Wellington: Health Services Research Centre and CBG Research.

Davis, K. and Stremikis, M. (2010) Preparing for a high-performance health care system, *Journal of the American Board of Family Medicine*, 23 (suppl.): 11–16.

de Maeseneer, J. and Boeckxstaens, P. (2012) James Mackenzie Lecture 2011: multimorbidity, goal-oriented care, and equity, *British Journal of General Practice*, 62 (600): e522–4.

Edwards, N., Smith, J.A. and Rosen, R. (2013) *The Primary Care Paradox: New Designs and Models*. London: KPMG International and the Nuffield Trust.

Expert Panel on Effective Ways of Investing in Health (EXPH) (2014) *Definition of a Frame of Reference in Relation to Primary Care with a Special Emphasis on Financing Systems and Referral Systems*. Brussels: European Commission.

Fisher, E., Staiger, D., Bynum, J. and Gottlieb, D. (2007) Creating accountable care organisations: the extended hospital medical staff, *Health Affairs*, 26 (1): w44–57.

Ham, C. (1996) Population centred and patient focused purchasing: the UK experience, *Milbank Quarterly*, 74 (2): 191–214.

Hefford, M., Crampton, P. and Macinko, J. (2005) Reducing health disparities through primary care reform: the New Zealand experiment, *Health Policy*, 72: 9–23.

Institute for Healthcare Improvement (2013) Website [http://www.ihi.org/offerings/Initiatives/TripleAim/Pages/default.aspx].

Kark, S.L. (1981) *The Practice of Community Oriented Primary Health Care*. New York: Appleton-Century-Crofts.

Kringos, D.S., Boerma, W.G.W., Bourgueil, Y., Cartier, T., Dedeu, T., Hasvold, T. et al. (2013a) The strength of primary care in Europe: an international comparative study, *British Journal of General Practice*, 63 (616): e742–50.

Kringos, D.S., Boerma, W.G.W., van der Zee, J. and Groenewegen, P.P. (2013b) Europe's strong primary care systems are linked to better population health, but also to higher health spending. *Health Affairs*, 32 (4): 686–94.

Lewis, R.Q., Rosen, R., Goodwin, N. and Dixon, J. (2010) *Where Next for Integrated Care Organisations in the English NHS?* London: Nuffield Trust and the King's Fund.

Macinko, J., Starfield, B. and Shi, L. (2003) The contribution of primary care systems to health outcomes within Organisation for Economic Co-operation and Development countries, 1970–1998, *Health Services Research*, 38 (3): 831–65.

Meads, G. (2009) The organisation of primary care in Europe: Part 1. Trends – position paper of the European Forum for Primary Care, *Quality in Primary Care*, 17 (2): 133–43.

Minister of Health (2001) *The New Zealand Primary Health Care Strategy*. Wellington: Ministry of Health [http://www.moh.govt.nz/; accessed 14 July 2011].

NHS England (2015) *NHS Launches New Bid to Beat Cancer and Save Thousands of Lives*. Press release, 11 January 2015 [http://www.england.nhs.uk/2015/01/11/beat-cancer/].

Ramsey, A. and Fulop, N. (2008) *The Evidence Base for Integrated Care*. London: King's Patient Safety and Service Quality Research Centre.

Robson, J., Hull, S., Rohini, M. and Boomla, K. (2014) Improving cardiovascular disease using managed networks in general practice: an observational study in inner London, *British Journal of General Practice*, 64 (622): e268–74.

Rosenthal, T.C. (2008) The medical home: growing evidence to support a new approach to primary care, *Journal of the American Board of Family Medicine*, 21 (5): 427–40.

Saltman, R., Rico, A. and Boerma, W. (eds.) (2006) *Primary Care in the Driver's Seat?* Maidenhead: Open University Press.

Sarnak, D. and Ryan, J. (2016) *How High Need Patients Experience the Health Care System in Nine Countries*. New York: Commonwealth Fund.

Smith, J.A. and Goodwin, N. (2006) *Towards Managed Primary Care: The Role and Experience of Primary Care Organizations*. Aldershot: Ashgate.

Smith, J.A., Holder, H., Edwards, N., Maybin, J., Parker, H., Rosen. R. et al. (2013) *Securing the Future of General Practice: New Models of Primary Care*. London: Nuffield Trust and the King's Fund.

Starfield, B. (1998) *Primary Care: Balancing Health Needs, Services and Technology*. Oxford: Oxford University Press.

Steventon, A. and Bardsley, M. (2012) *The Impact of Telehealth on Hospital Care and Mortality*. London: Nuffield Trust.

Tarimo, E. (1997) *Primary Health Care Concepts and Challenges in a Changing World: Alma-Ata Revisited*. Geneva: WHO.

Thorlby, R. (2013) *Reclaiming a Population Health Perspective*. London: Nuffield Trust.

Vuori, H. (1986) Health for all, primary health care and general practitioners, *Journal of the Royal College of General Practitioners*, 36: 398–402.

Wolfe, I., Cass, H., Thompson, M., Craft, A., Peile, E., Wiegersma, P.A. et al. (2011) Improving child health services in the UK: insights from Europe and their implications for the NHS reforms, *British Medical Journal*, 342: d1277.

World Health Organization (WHO) (1978) *Declaration of Alma-Ata*. Geneva: WHO.

Chapter 10

Chronic disease and integrated care

Nicola Walsh

Introduction

People living with chronic disease have a condition that needs to be managed – it is not cur-able. This means people with chronic diseases frequently require care and support from a range of professionals in a variety of different care settings: hospitals, primary care, clinics and at home. Too often there is duplication and gaps in information and communication, resulting in variable quality of care and high costs. The rapid rise in the number of people living with one or more chronic disease is prompting many countries to redesign their health-care services to improve patient experience and quality of care.

In this chapter, we examine the nature and prevalence of chronic disease, and the latest developments in the organization and management of healthcare services for people living with chronic illness. We conclude by identifying important issues for healthcare managers to consider when developing integrated care.

The nature of chronic disease

Chronic diseases are now the major cause of mortality and morbidity worldwide except in some African countries. In 2012, chronic diseases were responsible for 38 million of the world's 56 million deaths and more than 40 per cent of them (16 million) were premature deaths – that is, people under seventy years of age (WHO, 2014). Most of these premature deaths occurred in low- and middle-income countries. The social and economic consequences of premature mortality caused by chronic disease are felt by all countries and amount to hun-dreds of billions of dollars globally.

Table 10.1 Prevalence of diabetes among people aged 20–79 years – top ten countries in the world 2010 and 2030

Country	Rank	2010 Adults with diabetes adjusted to population	Rank	2030 Adults with diabetes adjusted to population size
Saudi Arabia	1	13.6	1	17.0
USA	2	12.3	4	14.0
Portugal	3	12.2	3	14.4
Germany	4	12.0	6	13.5
Canada	5	11.6	5	13.9
Sri Lanka	6	11.5	2	14.9
Cuba	7	11.0	6	13.5
Malaysia	8	10.9	8	13.4
Egypt	9	10.4	10	12.8
Mexico	10	10.1	9	13.3

Source: Data for 2010 taken from http://blogimages.bloggen.be/diabetescheck/attach/35622.pdf.

The term chronic disease is used to describe a range of conditions, but principally there are four major categories accounting for 82 per cent of deaths: diabetes, cardiovascular disease, cancer and chronic respiratory diseases (WHO, 2005). It should be noted that chronic diseases do appear under different names in different contexts. For example, the term 'non-communicable disease' is used to make the distinction from infectious or communicable disease. However, several chronic diseases have an infectious component such as cervical cancer and liver cancer. Long-term conditions and lifestyle-related diseases are other terms used. Table 10.1 shows the prevalence of diabetes among those aged twenty to seventy-nine years, adjusted to the national population for the years 2010 and 2030 for the top ten countries in the world.

The proportion of people living with chronic conditions rises with age, and typically older people live with more than one chronic disease. Studies in the United States show that about half of the population aged over seventy-five years has three or more chronic conditions, and that individuals aged eighty-five and older are six times more likely to have functional impairments (Anderson, 2011). The increase in the number of people with more than one chronic disease is prompting many countries to redesign their care model, as we illustrate later in this chapter.

In low- and middle-income countries, individuals develop chronic diseases at a younger age, suffer longer – often with preventable complications – and die younger than people living in high-income countries. Figure 10.1 shows the projected standardized death rates from chronic disease for individuals aged thirty to sixty-nine years in high-, middle- and low-income countries. Death rates for the younger age cohort in the UK and Canada are dwarfed by death rates in the Russian Federation, India and Nigeria.

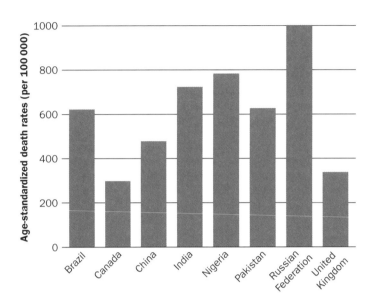

Figure 10.1 Projected standardized death rates from chronic disease for people aged 30–69 years, 2005
Source: WHO (2005)

The causes of chronic diseases

As well as ageing, many chronic diseases are linked to lifestyle factors such as smoking, lack of physical activity, unhealthy diet and high levels of alcohol consumption (WHO, 2005). These behaviours lead to four key physiological changes: raised blood pressure (hypertension), over-weight/obesity, abnormal blood lipids (hyperlipidaemia) and abnormal blood glucose (hyper-glycaemia). In terms of attributable deaths, the leading risk factor is raised blood pressure (13 per cent of global deaths), followed by tobacco use (9 per cent), raised blood glucose (6 per cent), physical inactivity (6 per cent) and overweight and obesity (5 per cent) (WHO, 2009).

Tobacco use and exposure comes in both smokeless and smoking forms. Smokeless tobacco is consumed in unburnt forms through chewing or sniffing and contains several car-cinogenic compounds. Smoking tobacco is by far the most commonly used form globally and is known to be carcinogenic. It has been estimated that there are more than 1.3 billion smok-ers worldwide with around 82 per cent residing in low- and middle-income countries (WHO, 2009). Smoking prevalence has fallen in high-income countries.

In contrast, obesity rates are rising globally. Being overweight or obese leads to adverse metabolic effects on blood pressure, cholesterol and insulin resistance, exacerbating the risk of developing certain chronic diseases such as type 2 diabetes, cardiovascular disease, hypertension, stroke and some forms of cancer. Of growing concern is the increase in child-hood obesity, indicating significant future growth in the number of people suffering from chronic disease. The highest prevalence of overweight among infants and young children are found in the upper- and middle-income bands. In the USA, for example, obesity among children under five increased from 5 per cent to 10.4 per cent between 1976/80 and 2007/8, and from 6.5 per cent to 19.6 per cent among six- to eleven-year-olds. Among adolescents aged twelve to nineteen years, obesity increased from 5 per cent to 18.1 per cent during the same period (CDC, 2015). Low-income countries have the lowest rate but the number of overweight children has risen across all country income groups (WHO, 2014).

Reducing modifiable risk factors such as physical inactivity and unhealthy diet can prevent disease and lead to rapid health gains, at both a population and individual level. In Poland, for example, death rates from heart disease have declined since 1991 by 10 per cent annually in people aged twenty to forty-four years and by 6.7 per cent in those aged forty-five to sixty-four years. Improvements in medical treatment contributed little, if at all, to the decline in death rates; other factors, such as an increase in fruit consumption, a decrease in tobacco consumption and a decrease in animal fat consumption were critical (WHO, 2005). Similarly, a large-scale community intervention in Finland in the 1970s to reduce cholesterol levels by increasing Finns' vegetable intake and lowering their consumption of dairy products led to reductions in heart disease (WHO, 2005). The need to adopt a broader population health perspective to address the causes rather than the consequences of chronic diseases is now being adopted in some other countries, including Alaska, USA and Counties Manukau in New Zealand (Alderwick et al., 2015).

The role healthcare systems have in preventing chronic disease is limited, thus more fundamental interventions are required to address the broader social and economic determinants of chronic disease. For example, globalization and urbanization create conditions in which people are exposed to new products, technologies, and marketing of unhealthy goods, and they also frequently adopt less physically active forms of employment. Critically, supportive policies at a national and local level are needed on food, transport, planning, media and trade to enable everyone, but especially those from deprived populations, to make healthier choices.

How healthcare systems are responding to rising levels of chronic disease

The structure of healthcare delivery systems varies significantly between countries and each can create barriers to effective chronic disease management. For example, in the UK, Netherlands, Denmark, Canada, Australia and New Zealand, chronic disease management is mediated by GPs, but in many other countries such as America it is directly accessed through specialists. Individuals with more than one chronic condition in America will typically therefore be under the care of multiple specialists who may not communicate with each other and may therefore duplicate investigations or inadvertently prescribe incompatible medications. By contrast, in the UK, GPs act as a central repository of medical information, coordinating the advice from different specialists, yet duplication of care and poor communication when patients transfer between different care settings is widespread (Robertson et al., 2014).

The current financing of healthcare in many countries is designed to reward increased levels of activity rather than improve health outcomes. Most funding mechanisms do not support coordinated team-based care. Healthcare costs are escalating across the world and, in many instances, this is due to an increase in the number of avoidable hospital admissions

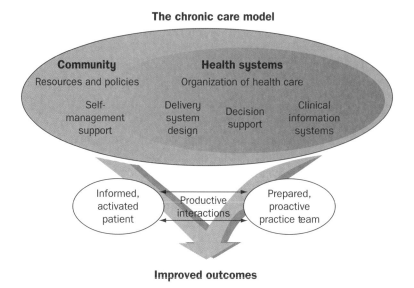

Figure 10.2 The chronic care model
Source: http//www.improvingchroniccare.org/index

among people with chronic diseases as a result of poorly coordinated care and inadequate ambulatory and primary care services.

The delivery of effective and high-quality coordinated care requires comprehensive changes that entail more than simply adding new features on to existing largely acute-focused healthcare systems. The chronic care model developed by Wagner and colleagues (1996) has been highly influential over the last two decades. It clearly sets out what elements need to change to improve the quality of care provided to people with chronic diseases, as illustrated in Figure 10.2.

The model is predicated on the idea that improved outcomes result from productive interactions between patients and their care teams. For these interactions to be productive, professional practice must be redesigned in the four areas shown in the centre of the model:

- self-management support (teaching patients and carers how to manage their condition(s));
- the care delivery system (to improve the coordination of care; in particular, greater clarity over who is part of the care delivery team and how they interact with the patient and their carers is needed);
- decision support (information and consideration given to what is the best care to be given to this patient and how can the care be delivered in a consistent manner to safeguard quality and safety of care);
- clinical information systems (capturing and using information to support the delivery of high-quality care).

These elements are designed to work together, although not necessarily in the same organization, to improve the quality and patient experience of care and overall health outcomes. Together, the four elements promote care systems that enable clinicians to proactively manage populations of patients, practise evidence-based medicine and encourage collaborative consultations between health professionals and patients. The model acknowledges that clinician–patient interactions take place in a wider context of the local healthcare system and that this will shape the way clinicians are trained and the nature of incentives available to promote the delivery of better care. The importance of the local community is also highlighted in the model. Patients living with chronic diseases spend most of their time away from formal professional caring services, so links with community groups and the use of local facilities to support greater self-management and enable individuals to adopt a healthier lifestyle are critical.

Redesigning healthcare systems to improve the management of chronic disease

There are numerous ways in which service redesign can support implementation of the chronic care model and contribute to improved patient outcomes. This section briefly describes how some countries are focusing their attention on critical areas set out in the chronic care model.

Self-management support

Self-care has been shown to enable people with chronic diseases to take control of their health, and to enhance independence and quality of life (see Chapter 18). However, people with chronic diseases will have very different motivations and capacities to self-manage their conditions, and support needs to be tailored to individuals and their circumstances. The evidence shows that there are wide gaps between what patients want and what doctors *think* patients want. When patients are fully informed about the risks and benefits of treatment options, they choose different and fewer treatments. Mulley and colleagues make a convincing case for doctors to have more and better information about what patients truly want and for patients to have more and better information about options, outcomes and evidence (Mulley et al., 2012). They argue that systematic measurement and reporting of patient preferences is essential to avoid the 'silent misdiagnosis'.

Decision support aids can help to enable shared decision-making, as can coaching patients before consultations and giving them lists of questions to ask their health professional. A variety of different professional roles have emerged over the last decade to support people living with chronic diseases and their carers to self-manage their conditions. These roles include health coaches, care navigators and expert patients (Coleman et al., 2009). They are typically focused on increasing people's ability to cope with and manage their own symptoms and to engage more effectively with their clinicians. Box 10.1 illustrates a coaching approach being adopted in Germany. This important area is covered extensively in Chapter 18 ('Patient and public involvement in healthcare').

Box 10.1 Case study – health coaching: Techniker Krankenkasse, Germany

Techniker Krankenkasse (TK), Germany's second largest statutory health insurer, introduced health coaching in 2008, initially for patients with heart failure. The programme has now expanded to include diabetes, myocardial infarction and ischaemic heart disease. At first, coaches contact patients weekly, and then on a monthly basis. They focus on behaviour change, including nutrition, exercise, alcohol consumption, smoking and adherence to medications. In 2010, TK employed fifteen coaches and had 5000 beneficiaries involved in the programme. The programme is popular with patients, with 80 per cent reporting high levels of satisfaction. Analysis of the coaching data for 1300 heart failure patients taking part in the programme found patient-reported improvement in health status irrespective of age, gender, socioeconomic status or severity of illness, and a positive correlation between number and frequency of coaching contacts and improvements in patient-reported health. Compared with patients with congestive heart failure receiving the usual care, those in the coaching programme showed significantly lower inpatient costs (KPMG International, 2010).

There are also examples of health services that have made radical shifts to place care in the hands of patients. For example, renal patients at Ryhove County Hospital in Jönköping, Sweden, receive training to use dialysis machines, read and interpret laboratory results, and document their care, and are also able to use machines and equipment while receiving dialysis. This patient-inspired model has resulted in more frequent dialysis among patients who find the process less burdensome, leading to reduced infection rates and complications. Nearly 60 per cent of peritoneal dialysis and haemodialysis patients in the clinic are now managing their own treatments in this way (Ham et al., 2012).

Health information technology

Information and communication technologies have the potential to revolutionize patients' and users' experience, transforming both how and where care is delivered. Mobile phone apps already provide lifestyle and health advice. In the UK, for example, the Met Office *Healthy Outlook* service provides recorded voice calls for people with chronic obstructive pulmonary disease when environmental conditions are forecast that would exacerbate their condition (Ham et al., 2012). Other apps can enable the capture of data on activities and vital signs and can transmit these data to healthcare professionals. Patients are increasingly going online for health information and advice, to self-diagnose and to post comments about their experience of care. Such developments can help promote greater self-management and shared decision-making, and provide direct access to peer and expert support. There are also technologies that enable hospital-based clinicians to diagnose and monitor patients in their own home or a community-based facility.

Some healthcare systems are harnessing these new information and communication technologies to transform how they provide care. Kaiser Permanente in the USA, for example, uses a comprehensive health information system – KP HealthConnect – that includes a secure patient portal, allowing patients to view portions of their record, access test results, email providers, order repeat prescriptions and arrange appointments. KP's electronic patient care record compares patient information with evidence-based guidelines (Zhou et al., 2010). This enables clinicians to identify any gaps between evidence-based recommendations and delivered care, including medicines management and any missed opportunities for timely preventative care. Data about clinical practice and patient outcomes have significant potential for enhancing service quality. Electronic health records have the capability for recording more frequent and comprehensive data about individual patients' health status such as their vital statistics, and can automatically trigger alerts when these go outside normal bounds.

Electronic records can also support self-management, and over the last five years we have seen personal access to health records become increasingly common in some countries. Patients registered with Group Health Cooperative in Seattle, for example, can access doctors by phone and email. This has enabled face-to-face consultations to be extended in length and be used primarily for patients with complex needs that cannot be met in other ways. Each appointment for such patients will last an average of thirty minutes (Reid, 2013).

Data on the utilization of services are also important, as they can be used to predict future service demand and use, in particular, levels of hospital admissions (Bardsley, 2010). If linked to information about a patient's lifestyle and attitudes to health, there is potential for sophisticated risk-stratification, allowing more anticipatory proactive care. Such data can also be used to target services and interventions at 'at-risk' groups, thereby supporting the delivery of improved outcomes and the delivery of more care in the home and community settings.

System redesign

Although many advances have been made in the treatments available to chronically ill patients, as suggested earlier these patients do not always receive optimal care. Research has shown that components of the chronic care model are slowly being implemented (Coleman et al., 2009) but too often care delivery focuses on acute problems and rapid short-term solutions, without the initiation of long-term treatment or the active involvement of chronically ill people themselves.

In many countries, a focus on integrated care is being seen as a possible route to realizing the vision set out in the chronic care model – proactive and planned care for people living with chronic disease. There are many competing definitions of the term 'integrated care' and integration and these will be examined in the next section.

Learning activity 10.1

Review the current organization of healthcare delivery in your own country giving specific consideration to whether the care and support available to people with chronic diseases is well coordinated across different care settings.

Write two or three paragraphs about each of the key areas of Wagner's chronic care model, describing how your country's health system and your local community meets or does not meet the key features of: self-management support; care delivery design; and health information technology (clinical information systems and decision support).

Use this analysis to identify areas for improvement in your country, and organize these into a brief action plan that you would propose to policy-makers in your health system.

Learning activity 10.2

Conduct the same exercise as in Learning activity 10.1 for one of the following health systems, ensuring that it is a country sufficiently different from your own: Canada, Denmark, England, Germany, Netherlands, Spain, New Zealand. Information about health systems of other countries can be found on the European Health Observatory website [http://www.euro.who.int/en/about-us/partners/observatory/publications/health-system-reviews-hits/countries] and the OECD website [http://www.oecd.org/els/health-systems/reviews-health-systems.htm].

How do the two countries compare in respect of the key areas set out in Wagner's chronic care model?

Integration and integrated care

It is helpful to distinguish between 'integrated care' and 'integration'. Integrated care is an organizing principle for care delivery with the aim of achieving improved patient care through better coordination of services and staff. Here the term is used in relation to chronic illness and multiple care needs but it is important to recognize that it is a much broader concept that applies to many other areas, such as maternity, mental and child health. The term integration is a coherent set of methods, processes and models that seek to bring about improved coordination of care. These include processes for bringing organizations and professionals together with the aim of improving patient outcomes, and funding models to support the delivery of proactive and planned care. Kodner and Spreeuwenberg have suggested that 'without integration at various levels [of health systems], all aspects of health care performance can suffer. Patients get lost, needed services fail to be delivered, or are delayed, quality and patient satisfaction decline, and the potential for cost effectiveness diminishes' (2002: 2).

Leutz (1999) has suggested that there are different degrees of integration, ranging from linkage through to coordination to bringing together services into one organization – full integration. Linkage involves organizations agreeing to collaborate to improve outcomes; coordination entails organizations putting in place defined structures and processes to overcome fragmentation; the most radical form – full integration – involves establishing new programmes in which resources are pooled and information is shared. Whatever the degree of integration, Lewis et al. (2010: 11) emphasize that the 'primary purpose of integrated care should be to improve the quality of patient care and experience and the cost effectiveness of care . . .'.

Various taxonomies of integrated care have been developed over the last decade. One of the most comprehensive is that developed by Lewis et al. (2010) and Table 10.2 builds on this analysis.

Case studies of organizations, teams and groups of professionals that have succeeded in strengthening coordination and alignment between services indicate that while there is no single model, successful approaches do share common characteristics or integrative processes (Ham and Curry, 2010). These processes – organizational, informational, clinical, functional, financial and normative – underpin a high-quality healthcare system for the management of chronic diseases in which care is coordinated and aligned between services, ensuring a less fragmented experience for patients.

As noted in the previous chapter, a distinction can be made between horizontal and vertical integration. Horizontal integration occurs when two or more organizations or services delivering care at a similar level come together. Examples include the merger of two hospitals or the merger of a health and social care organization. Vertical integration occurs when two or more organizations or services delivering care at different levels come together. Examples include the merger of a hospital with community health services and primary care with a hospital. Both horizontal and vertical integration may be real or virtual: real integration

Table 10.2 Different types of integrated care

Type	Definition	Focus	Level
Systemic integration	Coherence of rules and policies across different health and care organizations in a system of care.	Population	Macro
Organizational integration	Organizations are brought together formally by merger or virtually through coordinated provider networks and/or contracts.	Population	Macro
Functional integration	Non-clinical support such as electronic patient records and information.	Population and individual	Meso
Clinical/ professional integration	Care by professionals is integrated into a single coherent process within and/or across professional groups through the use of shared guidelines, for example.	Population, client group and individual	Meso
Service integration	Different services are integrated at an organizational level through MDTs.	Individual	Micro

entails mergers between organizations, whereas virtual integration takes the form of alliances, partnerships and networks created by a number of organizations working together. Virtual integration may occur along a continuum, ranging from formal networks with explicit governance arrangements at one extreme, to loose alliances or federations at the other. Virtual integration is often underpinned by contracts between organizations.

There is evidence to suggest that organizational integration may occur in the absence of clinical and service integration. In their review of integrated delivery systems in the USA, Burns and Pauly (2012) found that in many instances structures that were put in place to integrate different providers often failed fundamentally to alter the manner in which physicians practised medicine and collaborated with other healthcare professionals. They concluded that integrated structures rarely integrated the actual delivery of patient care. This observation has been supported by other studies. Ham and Curry (2010) suggest that alongside organizational integration, it is important to consider the extent to which care is effectively coordinated.

Care coordination depends less on organizational integration and more on the level of clinical and service integration achieved. High levels of care coordination can be achieved both within integrated organizations and between different organizations working together in networks. This brings out another important distinction – the level of care.

Learning activity 10.3

You have been asked by the hospital medical director to develop a proposal for improving local diabetic or respiratory services with local primary care doctors and community health services. First, identify the gaps and duplication in the current service model. Second, using the definitions set out in Table 10.2, consider what the key priority is for you locally.

Developing integrated care services

The case studies selected here describe the development of integrated care at three levels: macro, meso and micro. There are many difficulties associated with measuring the impact of different approaches to integration and care coordination (Coleman et al., 2009; Nolte and Pitchforth, 2014). This is in part because of a lack of common understanding of what is being referred to as integrated care, multiple aims and inconsistencies in describing different individual interventions. With these caveats in mind, this section summarizes the impact from a range of different healthcare systems. Although we distinguish between the three levels for the sake of analysis, in practice, they are often used in combination as the case studies illustrate.

Macro level integration

Some of the best examples of integration at a macro level are to be found in the USA, where there is evidence that integrated systems, which have high levels of organization, often perform better than fragmented forms of care (Ham and Curry, 2010). In the two case studies that follow (Boxes 10.2 and 10.3), provider organizations have come together with commissioning organizations.

Box 10.2   Case study – an integrated care system: Kaiser Permanente

Kaiser Permanente (KP) is a US non-profit health maintenance organization serving around 9.5 million members. It is a virtually integrated system in which health plans (commissioner), hospitals and medical groups remain distinct organizations and cooperate closely using exclusive contracts. The exclusivity of the contract means that the medical groups do not see patients from other health plans and members of the health plan generally obtain all of their care from clinicians employed by Permanente. The medical groups are allocated a capitation payment to provide care to members using KP facilities and, as such, take responsibility for the design and quality of care delivered to members as well as the management of resources. The interdependency of the three parts of the system acts as an incentive for partnership working.

KP tackles the management of people with chronic diseases by stratifying the population according to risk and adopting an approach to population management that combines an emphasis on prevention and self-management support. There has been a significant investment in information technology to support patient education programmes, as discussed earlier. Members are also able to make appointments and access their medical records online, and communicate to clinicians by email. KP also actively manages patients through the use of care pathways for common conditions such as hip replacements, and the availability of facilities and skilled clinicians to provide rehabilitation. It also makes use of general physicians and adopts case management processes for people with complex needs.

Over the past decade, KP has shifted its focus from purely treating people with co-morbidities to improving the health of the whole population they serve. They offer a range of different interventions such as smoking cessation and exercise programmes to individual members to reduce the risk of developing a disease. These interventions are combined with other secondary prevention activities to form a systematic approach to prevention and treatment. In Northern California, the rate of mortality from heart disease among KP members decreased by 26 per cent from 1995 to 2004, and members were 30 per cent less likely to die from heart disease than other Californians in 2004 (McCarthy and Mueller, 2009). KP has also established a range of community health initiatives to support the health of the population, such as improving access to green spaces and community gardens and ensuring local schools and workplaces have access to healthy food. High levels of patient satisfaction and low turnover of patients has enabled KP to invest in long-term preventative programmes and information technology.

Source: Kaiser Permanente [https://healthy.kaiserpermanente.org/static/health/en-us/pdfs/nw/459CORE_10_Commitment_to_quality_and_patient_safety.pdf; accessed 9 April 2015] and Alderwick et al. (2015).

Another example of a population-wide approach to integration is set out in Box 10.3.

Box 10.3   Case study – Veterans Health Administration: an integrated care system

The Veterans Health Administration (VA) is an example of real integration, in contrast to KP, which is virtually integrated. The VA employs physicians, owns and runs hospitals and medical offices, and manages services within a budget allocated by the federal government. As such, the VA is often linked to the NHS in the UK.

In the mid-1990s, the VA was a large hospital-centric system providing a range of services through directly managed or indirectly supported facilities. This resulted in facilities acting independently of each other, and there was frequent duplication of services. The appointment of a new leader was the trigger for a reorganization of the VA, and between 1995 and 1999 the healthcare system was re-engineered into a series of twenty-one integrated service networks serving each of the VA regions. Each network typically consists of seven to ten hospitals, twenty-five to thirty primary care clinics and four to seven nursing homes. Each has its own capitated budget, and the network managers are held to account through a set of performance measures agreed centrally. Many of these measures focus on clinical quality and financial incentives are aligned to the organizational goals. Performance of all networks is reviewed quarterly and results are widely communicated. Investment in technology enabled effective data sharing and also promoted improvements in the quality of care through the use of evidence-based guidelines, and decision-support tools (Perlin et al., 2004).

The VA also invested in a range of services outside of the hospitals facilitated by the use of telecare and telehealth technologies. This produced a 55 per cent reduction in the use of hospital beds and a measurable improvement in the quality of care (Ashton et al., 2003). The number of acute and long-term care beds fell from 92,000 to 53,000 (Kizer and Dudley, 2008). The VA's coordinated approach to chronic disease management, facilitated by data sharing and care delivery by multispeciality networks, allowed patients with two or more chronic conditions to receive coordinated care and avoid the fragmentation and overlapping of services that had existed previously. The chief executive overseeing this transformational change was a clinician and maintained a focus on improving the quality of care. The systematic introduction of quality improvement approaches across the system built internal capacity and capability of clinicians and managers working in the networks.

Over the last decade, the VA has experienced change in leadership and increases in demand – due to recent wars in Iraq and Afghanistan. Kizer and Jha (2014) identify other challenges facing the organization – insufficient funds, inadequate numbers of primary care providers, aged facilities, overly complicated and bureaucratic performance management processes – and suggest these are thwarting efforts to meet rising demand. Under new leadership, the VA is beginning to address these challenges and work with other local organizations in the communities it serves and engage with patients (and their carers) more actively.

As demonstrated by Kaiser Permanente and the VA, a system-level approach to integration requires the deployment of a number of different elements and processes. Ham and Curry(2010) identified these as:

- empowering clinicians working in primary care, to work alongside hospital generalists and specialists and share responsibility for the budget and quality of care;
- allocating population-based budgets and alignment of incentives to promote care coordination and improve health outcomes;
- investing in information technology to support the sharing of patient information and use of clinical decision-support systems;
- actively managing patients in hospital by using care pathways for common conditions and other mechanisms to support discharge processes;
- using evidence-based guidelines to manage unacceptable variations and promote best practice;
- developing effective clinical managerial partnerships to support the delivery of care coordination;
- focusing on a defined population, enabling the doctors and the wider team to develop relationships with individual patients; and
- having effective leadership at all levels in the system with a focus on quality improvement.

Meso level integration

This level of integration refers to care for particular groups of patients and populations whether they are classified by age, condition or some other characteristic. Much of the focus at this level is on older people because of the increasing number of frail older people living with co-morbidities requiring an increased level of healthcare (see Box 10.4).

Box 10.4   Case study – care of older people in Torbay, England

In Torbay, the health and social care organizations are now working closely together to deliver integrated care to the whole of the population they serve. About a decade ago, they started to redesign their health and care system for older people living locally. Five integrated health and social care teams were established across five localities, each team aligned to a group of GP practices. The interdisciplinary health and care teams keep older people in their own homes by using predictive modelling to identify patients at risk of illness and hospital admission. Teams meet regularly to review cases and to decide on actions needed. Each patient has a dedicated case manager and an active care plan. Joint decisions are made about an individual's needs and care is coordinated across organizational and professional boundaries.

The key focus of the five integrated teams is to proactively manage the care of the most vulnerable older people in their population with enhanced primary care support.

Health and social care coordinators, who are not professionally qualified, act as a single point of contact within each locality team. There is a single assessment process to remove duplication and improve patient experience. Patient held records are used and are accessible to any professional involved in the care of the patient to enable care to be more coordinated across care settings.

This horizontally integrated approach between health and social care has reduced the use of local hospital beds, lowered rates of emergency admissions for those over sixty-five years old, and delayed transfers of care. Stronger relationships between health and social care services have also been developed, which has resulted in 95 per cent of older people having 'care packages' in place within twenty-eight days (Thistlethwaite, 2011).

More recently, Torbay health and care services have introduced the concept of neighbourhood connectors, to work in every neighbourhood across Torbay. The purpose of the neighbourhood connectors is to help to combat social isolation and enable older people to engage in a wide range of activities. The connectors act as a bridge to other local services. A new community development trust bringing together voluntary organizations to tackle some of the wider issues has also been introduced – it is anticipated this will allow individuals with chronic disease to access local community assets as in Wagner's chronic care model.

For further information, see www.southdevonandtorbayccg.nhs.uk.

Many countries have sought to provide better integration of care for people and populations with certain diseases. Disease management programmes have been introduced widely in Germany (see Box 10.5); most vary in content but all have standard elements such as use of evidence-based guidelines, patient involvement and self-management, inter-sectoral care with treatment in specialized institutions, and quality assurance mechanisms.

Box 10.5   Case study – disease management programmes in Germany

Disease management programmes were introduced in Germany in 2002. Individuals with chronic diseases who are enrolled by statutory insurance funds into a disease management programme attract an additional payment from the risk equalization scheme, creating a strong incentive for insurers to recruit individuals with chronic conditions.

Patients who take part must first choose a physician who coordinates their treatment within the programme; this is usually the patient's family physician. The programme sets out how and when specialists should be involved in the patient's care, with the intention of avoiding gaps in care provision. Programmes are structured and have set disease-specific objectives, defined treatment goals and specific criteria for referral into hospital. Deviation from the programme is discouraged (Nolte and McKee, 2008).

Patient involvement is emphasized and patient education and self-management are key elements of all programmes. If a patient fails to participate, his or her registration with the programme can be cancelled by the health insurance fund. Active participation among patients and physicians is rewarded by financial incentives; for example, providers receive reimbursement for disease-specific education programmes for registered patients.

There is some evidence that such programmes can reduce unplanned admissions but few have reported on costs. Patient satisfaction measures yield favourable results. Ofman et al. (2004) noted that there are often greater improvements in the processes of care and intermediate outcomes rather than clinical outcomes with the application of such programmes. The increase in the number of people with more than one chronic disease also limits the value of such standardized programmes.

As demonstrated by the above two case studies, there are a number of methods and processes used at the meso level of integrated care. These include:

- the use of pooled budgets and shared governance arrangements across organizations;
- care delivered by a multidisciplinary team with a single point of access;
- single assessment process;
- coordinated provider networks using standardized referral procedures and shared information systems; and
- patient involvement in care management.

Micro level integration

Integration at the micro level includes the many tools and approaches adopted to improve care coordination for individual patients. Examples include the following.

Case management programmes

This is an approach often adopted for people with multiple chronic diseases. A risk stratification tool is frequently used to identify those at 'high risk' in the population. Team-based and technology-enabled approaches to care are frequently deployed with an increasing emphasis on being able to access care twenty-four hours a day, seven days a week.

Electronic patient records

Such records allow information to be shared between professionals and between patient and healthcare professionals, thereby supporting greater coordination of care services. The use of electronic health records has also been shown to increase adherence to evidence-based guidelines.

Telecare and telehealth

These are tools deployed to support self-management and the integration of services. Devices are used in patients' homes to monitor heart rate, blood pressure, body temperature, body weight and blood glucose levels, for example. Data are also accessible to clinical staff so that they can pick up early signs of exacerbation. These tools have the potential to improve the quality of care and make more effective use of resources.

In summary, developing integrated care services requires a complex range of processes and activities that need to be aligned at a number of levels.

Role of healthcare managers in developing integrated care

Healthcare managers need the skills to understand, influence and lead the local agenda in the design and delivery of integrated care. This will require them to lead and/or be involved in a number of activities, such as:

- identifying and demonstrating the core values and shared purpose that underpins the agreed approaches at a clinical and service level;
- building commitment and good relationships with partner organizations;
- engaging a range of professionals within their own organization and across other organizations;
- demonstrating good communication skills to clearly communicate the agreed new care model to a variety of different organizations and professional groups;
- nurturing effective clinical leadership; and
- supporting the development of new roles in the workforce.

Improving the coordination and alignment of care between organizations – whether by creating a single organization or a virtual network – will be made easier if the healthcare manager is working in a supportive environment. For example, are payment mechanisms designed and aligned to promote the care of the 'whole person'? Intra- and inter-organizational mechanisms to support service integration are also important, notably information technology to facilitate clinical information exchange and support consistent evidence-based clinical decision-making. These processes in turn need to be supported by the development of trusting relationships and shared values between participating organizations and professionals. It is this 'soft stuff' that is often the most difficult to achieve (Walsh, 2015). Clarity over governance arrangements and accountability will also be important as more integrated approaches to care delivery are developed (Shortell et al., 2015). Other capabilities in service improvement, change management and action research will also be beneficial (Ham and Walsh, 2013).

Conclusion

Chronic diseases are the leading cause of morbidity and mortality in OECD countries. They are also the single biggest driver of health system costs, with a substantial amount of the costs stemming from unplanned emergency and inpatient care as a result of poor care coordination between different healthcare providers and between health and social care services.

The proportion of people living with a chronic disease rises with age, with many older adults living with multiple chronic conditions. Lifestyle factors such as smoking, high alcohol consumption and obesity are major contributors to chronic disease and the growing trend in childhood obesity indicates that chronic disease will only become a bigger, more costly problem in the future. Add to this the steady growth of chronic diseases in low- and middle-income countries and it is clear that chronic disease management is the biggest global healthcare challenge, outweighing the burden of communicable disease in both low- and middle-income countries.

There is broad agreement that coordinating care across primary and specialist care and health and social care is critical to delivering high-quality, efficient care for individuals with chronic conditions, and to ensuring that patients who require care from multiple providers have a joined-up experience of care. Delivering more coordinated care requires changes in the organization of healthcare systems in many countries. These include a greater emphasis on patient self-management, a team-based approach to healthcare delivery and additional investment in informational technology to support clinical decision-making and the sharing of data between clinicians and across organizations.

In practice, there is no single model for the organization of integrated care and the management of chronic conditions because local contextual factors, and the pre-existing structure and financing of local healthcare services, will influence the redesign and implementation of any new care model.

Learning resources

Commonwealth Fund: This New York-based foundation aims to promote a high-performing healthcare system, particularly for the most vulnerable in society. As such, it has a strong focus on chronic disease and complex conditions, and research into new models of care for these groups. It also conducts highly respected international comparative work [www.commonwealthfund.org].

King's Fund: This London-based independent foundation undertakes research and policy analysis and integrated care is a particular focus of its work. A specific focus over the last five years has been on supporting the redesign of care services. Research reports and an array of supporting materials are available on the website [www.kingsfund.org].

World Health Organization: WHO website has a wealth of material on the number of people living globally with a chronic disease. It issues annual global status reports on non-communicable diseases and collates information on how different countries are preventing chronic diseases and redesigning current healthcare systems to respond to the crisis [www.who.org].

International Foundation for Integrated Care: The IFIC is a not-for-profit educational membership based network that crosses organizational and professional boundaries to bring people together to advance the science, knowledge and adoption of integrated care policy and practice. It undertakes primary research, holds conferences and publishes the latest integrated care research in its international journal [www.IFIC.org].

References

Alderwick, H., Ham, C. and Buck, D. (2015) *Population Health Systems: Going Beyond Integrated Care.* London: King's Fund [http://www.kingsfund.org.uk/publications/population-health-systems].

Anderson, G. (2011) The challenge of financing care for individuals with morbidities, in *Health Reform: Meeting the Challenges of Ageing and Multiple Morbidities.* Paris: OECD Publishing.

Ashton, C.M., Souchek, J. and Peterson, N.J. (2003) Hospital use and survival among Veterans Affairs beneficiaries, *New England Journal of Medicine*, 349, 1637–46.

Bardsley, M. (2010) *Social Care and Hospital Use.* London: Nuffield Trust.

Burns, L.R. and Pauly, M.V. (2012) Accountable care organisations may have difficulty avoiding the failures of integrated delivery networks of the 1990s, *Health Affairs*, 31 (11): 2407–16.

Centers for Disease Control (CDC) (2015) *Childhood Overweight and Obesity* .

Coleman, K., Austin, B.T., Brach, C. and Wagner, E.H. (2009) Untangling practice redesign from disease management: how do we best care for the chronically ill?, *Annual Review of Public Health*, 30: 385–408.

Ham, C. and Curry, N. (2010) *Clinical and Service Integration: The Route to Improved Outcomes.* London: King's Fund.

Ham, C. and Walsh, N. (2013) *Making Integrated Care Happen at Scale and Pace: Lessons from Experience.* London: King's Fund [http://www.kingsfund.org.uk/publications/making-integrated-care-happen-scale-and-pace].

Ham, C., Dixon, A. and Brooke, B. (2012) *Transforming the Delivery of Health and Social Care: The Case for Fundamental Change.* London: King's Fund [http://www.kingsfund.org.uk/publications/transforming-delivery-health-and-social-care].

Kizer, K. and Dudley, R. (2008) Extreme makeover: transformation of the Veterans Health Care System, *Annual Review of Public Health*, 30: 18.1–18.27.

Kizer, K. and Jha, A. (2014) Restoring trust in VA health care: perspective, *New England Journal of Medicine*, 371: 295–7.

Kodner, D.L. and Spreeuwenberg, C. (2002) Integrated care: meaning, logic, applications and implications: a discussion paper, *International Journal of Integrated Care*, 2: 1–6.

KPMG International (2010) *A Better Pill to Swallow: A Global View of what Works in Healthcare* [https://www.kpmg.com/Global/en/IssuesAndInsights/ArticlesPublications/Documents/A-Better-Pill-to-Swallow-Oct-final.pdf].

Leutz, W.N. (1999) Five laws for integrating medical and social services: lessons from the United States and the United Kingdom, *Milbank Quarterly*, 77 (1): 77–110.

Lewis, R., Rosen, R., Goodwin, N. and Dixon, J. (2010) *Where Next for Integrated Care Organisations in the English NHS?* London: Nuffield Trust.

McCarthy, D. and Mueller, K. (2009) *Kaiser Permanente: Bridging the Quality Divide with Integrated Practice, Group Accountability and Health Information Technology.* New York: Commonwealth Fund.

Mulley, A., Trimble, C. and Elwyn, G. (2012) *Patients' Preferences Matter: Stop the Silent Misdiagnosis.* London: King's Fund [http://www.kingsfund.org.uk/publications/patients-preferences-matter].

Nolte, E. and McKee, M. (eds.) (2008) *Caring for People with Chronic Conditions: A Health System Perspective.* Maidenhead: Open University Press.

Nolte, E. and Pitchforth, E. (2014) *What is the Evidence on the Economic Impacts of Integrated Care?* Copenhagen: WHO.

Ofman, J., Badamgaray, E., Henning, J.M., Knight, K., Gano, A.D., Levan, R.K. et al. (2004) Does disease management improve clinical and economic outcomes in patients with chronic diseases? A systematic review, *American Journal of Medicine*, 117 (3): 182–92.

Perlin, J.B., Kolodner, R.M. and Roswell, R.H. (2004) The Veterans Health Administration: quality, value, accountability and information as transforming strategies for patient-centered care, *American Journal of Managed Care*, 10 (11): 828–36.

Reid, R. (2013) *Re-designing Primary Care: The Group Health Journey.* Presentation at the King's Fund, September.

Robertson, R., Sonola, L., Honeyman, M., Brooke, B. and Kothari, S. (2014) *Specialists in Out-of-hospital Settings: Findings from Six Case Studies.* London: King's Fund [http://www.kingsfund.org.uk/publications/specialists-out-hospital-settings].

Shortell, S., Addicott, R., Walsh, N. and Ham, C. (2015) The NHS five year forward view: lessons from the United States in developing new care models, *British Medical Journal*, 350: h2005.

Thistlethwaite, P. (2011) *Integrating Health and Social Care in Torbay: Improving Care for Mrs Smith.* London: King's Fund [http://www.kingsfund.org.uk/publications/integrating-health-and-social-care-torbay].

Wagner, E., Austin, B.T. and Von Korff, M. (1996) Improving outcomes in chronic illness, *Managed Care Quarterly*, 4 (2): 12–25.

Walsh, N. (2015) How HR can develop systems leaders?, *HR Magazine*, 22 June, pp. 1–2.

World Health Organization (WHO) (2005) *Preventing Chronic Diseases: A Vital Investment.* Geneva: WHO [http://www.who.int/chp/chronic_disease_report/full_report.pdf].

World Health Organization (WHO) (2009) *Global Health Risks: Mortality and Burden of Disease Attributable to Selected Major Risks.* Geneva: WHO.

World Health Organization (WHO) (2014) *Global Status Report on Non-communicable Diseases,* Geneva: WHO.

Zhou, Y.Y., Kanter, M.H., Wang, J.J. and Garrido, T. (2010) Improved quality at Kaiser Permanente through e-mail between physicians and patients, *Health Affairs*, 29 (7): 1370–5.

Acute care: elective and emergency, secondary and tertiary

Helen Crump and Nigel Edwards

Introduction

Acute care comprises a complex, interrelated set of services and functions, usually characterized by being labour intensive and having high fixed costs. It is usually, but not exclusively, provided in a hospital setting, although acute hospitals may also provide services such as rehabilitation, long-term care and mental health services, including for episodes of acute mental illness. Although it is often treated as synonymous with hospital care, different definitions of acute care exist. For instance, some definitions exclude palliative care. It is therefore necessary to be cautious when distinguishing between data relating to acute or to hospital care.

In designing and providing acute services, policy-makers face different challenges, depending on how developed the health system is. For instance, in high-income countries, financial pressures stemming from growing demand, ageing populations and expensive new technologies are increasingly shaping the nature of provision. In lower income countries, a greater disease burden, poorer infrastructure, shortages of clinical staff and lower spend per capita can challenge system managers. Acute systems in low- and middle-income countries often operate on significantly lower per capita spend levels, but this has led to the development of some innovative approaches to deliver services to large populations at low cost.

In this chapter, we consider trends in the size and structure of the sector in different countries, before turning to the role of the hospital in the wider health system, drivers for change within the sector and emerging models of service delivery. Case studies highlight different models of acute provision and different approaches to addressing policy challenges.

The nature and role of acute care

Acute care is generally understood as 'time-sensitive, individually orientated diagnostic and curative actions whose primary purpose is to improve health' (Hirshon et al., 2013). The Organization for Economic Cooperation and Development (2001) describes the principal aims of acute care as follows: to manage obstetric labour; to cure illness or provide definitive treatment of injury; to perform surgery; to relieve symptoms of injury or illness (excluding palliative care); to reduce severity of illness or injury; to protect against exacerbation and/or complication of an illness or injury that could threaten life or normal functions; and to perform diagnostic and therapeutic procedures. However, beneath these descriptions lies significant complexity. The characteristics of acute care are changing over time, and acute provision varies from country to country, both in terms of what is provided, where it is performed and the type of organizations that provide it.

The late nineteenth century saw the establishment of specialist hospitals and a shift away from medical care in the community. Increased understanding of infection transmission and developments in anaesthesia meant more elective surgery could take place within a hospital setting. The dominance of the hospital continued through to the 1970s, when pharmaceutical innovation generated new cancer treatments and common conditions previously requiring long hospital stays began to be treated outside the hospital (Healy and McKee, 2002a). The increasing significance of long-term conditions, coupled with changes in the way some conditions are treated, has resulted in a growing imperative for acute care to forge closer links with other parts of the health system (see Chapter 10 on chronic disease and integrated care). This in turn is driving changes in the configuration and approach of the acute sector.

Hirshon et al. (2013: 387) view acute care as supporting 'progress towards strong health systems . . . rather than from patchwork efforts that may improve outcomes for specific conditions but not the overall functioning of the health system'. They warn that '[f]ailure to consider the time component of curative services produces fragmentation through poor coordination of care and the imprecise application of clinical interventions' (2013: 386), as services that are interdependent end up in different locations.

International trends in acute care provision

Acute care is seen in most health systems as a crucial aspect of health care, with the Organization for Economic Cooperation and Development finding that '[m]ost OECD countries guarantee a high level of coverage for acute inpatient care and medical services, as well as for laboratory tests and diagnostic imaging' (Paris et al., 2010: 21). In a study of 23 EU member states in 2012, inpatient care accounted for 31 per cent of current health expenditure on average. Expenditure on inpatient care was highest in Greece at 47 per cent and lowest in the Slovak Republic at 23 per cent, but the average rate of spending growth in Europe in inpatient care had slowed after the financial crisis of 2008, with actual decreases recorded in 2009/10 and 2010/11 (OECD, 2014).

In general, the majority of hospital beds are to be found in the acute sector. Acute beds account for on average three-quarters of all beds in OECD countries, but underlying this statistic is significant variation, with 53 per cent of beds being found in the acute sector in France in 2013, while the figure for Turkey was 97 per cent (OECD, 2013).

Across the world, acute facilities are operated by a mix of public, private for-profit and private non-profit providers. According to a report produced for the OECD (Paris et al., 2010):

> Acute hospital care is mainly provided by the public sector in all OECD countries, except Belgium, Japan, Korea and the Netherlands, where the private not-for-profit sector is the predominant provider. The private for-profit sector plays an important role in the Slovak Republic (40% of acute beds), in Mexico (35%), in Greece (28%), as well as in France and Korea (25% each).

In Japan, organizations providing 'covered' health services are not permitted to earn profits. In England, foundation trusts, which represented two-thirds of National Health Service acute provider organizations in 2015 (NHS Confederation, 2015) are publicly owned, but are allowed to generate up to 49 per cent of their revenue via private income, although increases greater than 5 per cent must be approved by a majority of a trust's governors.

The changing shape of acute care

In recent years, there have been moves, especially in high-income countries, to reduce the dominance of the acute sector in healthcare. OECD data show that between 1980 and 2013, *hospital* expenditure (including acute care, but also rehabilitative and long-term care) tended to fall as a proportion of overall healthcare spend, but there were slight increases in some cases. For instance, spending on hospitals as a proportion of total health expenditure decreased from 42.6 per cent in 1983 to 34.0 per cent in 2013 in the United States, but the lowest point was 31.5 per cent in 2003 (see Figure 11.1). Chevalier et al. (2009) attribute these decreases to 'budget control policies' for the hospital sector, faster spending growth for medications stemming from innovative drugs, the replacement of some surgical treatments by medical treatments, and the liberalization of medicines pricing in some Central and Eastern European countries.

According to the European Hospital and Healthcare Federation (2012), between 2000 and 2010, the number of acute care hospital beds per 100,000 population in Europe decreased by 17 per cent on average. The only country to buck this trend was Greece, which gained 8 per cent more beds per 100,000 over the period. The number of acute hospitals in Europe also decreased significantly over the same period.

The length of time people spend in hospital once they are admitted is also decreasing (Table 11.1). Between 2006/07 and 2012/13, the English NHS saw a reduction of 13 per cent in the number of people remaining in hospital for more than a month (Smith et al., 2014). The role of the acute hospital can therefore be seen to be shifting away from providing long periods of inpatient care towards performing specific functions as one element of a wider care pathway involving multiple providers and settings.

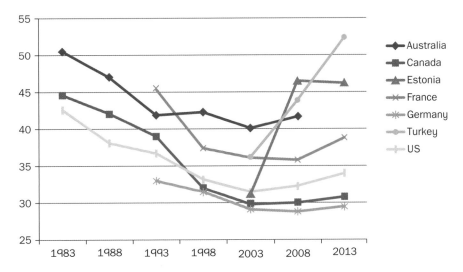

Figure 11.1 Spending on hospitals as a share of total healthcare spending
Source: Adapted from OECD health expenditure and financing data

Table 11.1 Inpatient curative care average length of stay (days)

Country	2007	2008	2009	2010	2011	2012
Australia	—	5.2	5.1	5.0	4.9	4.8
Canada	7.5	7.7	7.7	7.7	7.6	7.6
Estonia	5.9	5.7	5.6	5.5	5.5	5.6
France	5.9	5.8	5.7	5.8	5.7	5.7
Germany	8.5	8.3	8.2	8.1	7.9	7.8
Japan	19.0	18.8	18.5	18.2	17.9	17.5
Turkey	4.4	4.0	4.0	3.9	3.8	3.9
UK	6.2	6.2	6.1	5.9	5.9	5.9
USA	5.5	5.5	5.4	5.4	5.4	—

Source: Adapted from OECD health care utilization hospital aggregates.

Acute care in low- and middle-income countries

For obvious reasons, low- and middle-income countries spend less than high-income countries on acute care. For instance, in 2011, nineteen of the forty-six countries in the WHO Africa region spent less than US$44 per capita on health, which is the minimum amount recommended by the WHO (Moresky et al., 2013). In Ethiopia, lack of transportation and diagnostic equipment was viewed as a 'significant barrier to the provision of quality emergency care services' (Levine et al., 2007), while in five sub-Saharan African countries, fewer than 65 per cent of hospitals had essential basic infrastructure such as water and electricity, and fewer than half were able to provide twenty-four-hour emergency care (Hsia et al., 2012).

The differences in provision are particularly stark in acute care. Austin et al. (2014) compared access to urban acute services in seven cities across a range of high-income, upper-middle-income and lower-middle-income countries. They found a more than forty-five-fold variation in the availability of intensive care unit (ICU) beds between Boston, Massachusetts (18.8 per 100,000 population) and Kumasi, Ghana (0.4 per 100,000 population). That said, the relationship between national wealth and acute provision is not always straightforward. Although in Austin and colleagues' research, supply of hospital beds per one hundred deaths due to acute illnesses showed a strong positive correlation with national GDP per capita, the availability of ICU care itself was not correlated with GDP. In addition, some measures of supply were similar in high- and middle-income countries.

Austin et al. (2014) propose that the apparent non-linear relationship between per capita GDP and hospital beds may imply a point 'beyond which greater per capita GDP does not fuel greater supply' and that although defining 'optimal supply targets' is essential to minimizing variation, there is no consensus as to what constitutes the right amount of acute care. However, analysis of supply of hospital beds can only show part of the picture, when acute services are increasingly provided in ambulatory settings in some countries. The availability of diagnostic facilities, operating theatres and trained clinical staff are also significant drivers of cost in acute settings.

Management challenges in acute care: pressures and drivers for change

Many factors influencing how acute care is provided are outside the day-to-day control of the organizations working in the sector. Examples include how provider organizations are paid and contracted with; what laws and regulations apply to them; their cost structure; and for those in groups or under state control, what levels of devolution and delegation are in operation.

Costs, inflation and funder willingness to pay

Payment and funding systems are a key influence on acute providers (see Chapter 4). For instance, where providers are paid according to the number of cases they treat, an incentive will exist to increase throughput. By contrast, if a provider is paid to care for a group of patients over a specified period of time, the incentive will be to minimize activity. In systems where multiple health insurers are competing to attract policyholders based on the nature of their offer, payers may seek to demonstrate a competitive edge by making particular demands of providers in terms of the nature, quality and price of services offered. Equally, where a purchaser is procuring services on behalf of a population, stipulations may be put into contracts specifying how particular services should be provided (see Chapter 14). And particularly in payment-by-activity systems, services put in place by purchasers elsewhere in the system – such as admissions avoidance schemes – can act directly against the interests of the acute provider.

A side effect of technical innovation, particularly in the pharmaceutical sector, is that acute providers may contend with increasing costs stemming from the development of innovative new medicines and treatments if payment systems do not keep step with these changes. More expensive treatments, combined in higher income countries with greater numbers of older patients presenting with multiple conditions, means that the cost per patient of providing health services is increasing.

Quality, safety, regulation and transparency

The quality and safety of hospital services is coming under increased focus internationally, whether from work in response to serious failings uncovered at Mid-Staffordshire NHS Foundation Trust in England in 2009 (Francis, 2013), or from the activities of national level improvement bodies such as the Australian Commission on Safety and Quality in Health Care. As well as this 'top-down' focus on improvement, there has also been an increased emphasis on 'bottom-up' efforts to improve care, such as provider board-level action to scrutinize the quality of care hospitals are providing to patients in England (Thorlby et al., 2014) and work to improve the management and quality improvement capabilities of facility directors and administrators in Kenya (Gill and Bailey, 2010).

There has been a shift in focus from retrospective monitoring of quality and safety to an increased focus on prospective methods, such as those gauging organizations' ability to anticipate problems (Vincent et al., 2013). Across the world, hospital providers are subject to different domestic and regional legislative and regulatory requirements.

Acute providers in England must register with the Care Quality Commission, which inspects the quality and safety of the care they provide and is able to take action against poorly performing organizations. In Italy, national and regional ministries are responsible for quality and an organization called the National Commission for the Accreditation and Quality of Care evaluates accreditation models. Norwegian regional health authorities, hospitals and municipal health providers share responsibility for ensuring service quality, and although Germany has no national safety agency, an organization called the AQUA Institut develops and institutes quality assurance measures across the country. All Danish hospitals are signed up to extensive standards through the Danish Healthcare Quality Programme (Thomson et al., 2013).

In a number of countries, acute provider organizations are increasingly expected to publish information about their performance in order to help patients make decisions about their care and to incentivize hospitals to improve. For instance, in Germany, all hospitals are expected to publish results relating to a set of indicators set out by the Federal Office for Quality Assurance (Thomson et al., 2013). Some attempts have been made to try and sum up hospital performance in single indicators and ratings, such as the 'friends and family test' in the English NHS. The danger is that these can fail to capture information in ways that are useful for patients.

Markets and competition

In European Union countries, hospital providers that are deemed to be 'undertakings' (entities engaged in economic activity) must comply with EU competition legislation. Whether or not a healthcare provider is deemed to be an undertaking is determined by case law, based on the European Court's efforts to 'distinguish between government functions and the private sector'. As a consequence, the status of organizations like the English foundation trusts, which receive taxpayer funds but are also able to provide private services to patients, is unclear (Lear et al., 2010).

Some health systems have in recent years attempted to use competition and market mechanisms to drive improvement, although the evidence to support the use of these mechanisms in healthcare is mixed (see Cooper et al., 2011; Feng et al., 2015). Elective services have been the main focus for efforts to increase competition driven by patient choice in the acute sector, as it is not feasible to expect patients to make choices regarding the urgent and emergency services they use. In health systems with separate purchaser and provider functions, competition can operate either through the letting of contracts following a competitive tendering process (i.e. for-the-market competition) or by making the services of multiple providers available to patients and allowing them to choose (i.e. in-the-market competition). (For more details, see Chapter 3.)

Some countries have established organizations with a responsibility for regulating aspects of the market for healthcare. For instance, the Dutch Healthcare Authority, a regulator operating in a country where most providers are privately owned, describes itself as the market supervisor and sees its role as setting conditions and basic principles to support efficient markets and enforcing them where necessary.

Learning activity 11.1

Consider which pressures and system factors affect your local acute healthcare provider. What mechanisms might policy-makers and/or health system leaders in your area use to mitigate the effect of these pressures? Refer to any local examples you know of where health system leaders have sought to address pressures facing the local acute healthcare system.

Changes in medicine and healthcare

The way that acute services are provided, and the technology, medical science and other aspects of acute care are changing rapidly. Some of the main areas of change are explored below.

Trends in elective care

Elective care is care that does not need to be performed immediately and can therefore be scheduled in advance. Since the 1970s, the trend has been for increasing numbers of elective surgical procedures to be performed as 'day cases' or ambulatory procedures, meaning that patients return home after their operation, rather than being admitted as an inpatient. Doing so can enable providers to increase efficiency while also improving the quality of care for patients (Toftgaard and Parmentier, 2006). In the USA, there were 34.7 million ambulatory surgery visits in 2006, 14.9 million of which occurred in freestanding ambulatory centres – an increase of around 300 per cent over a ten-year period (Cullen et al., 2009).

As Jarrett and Staniszewski (2006) point out, clinically appropriate day surgery has multiple benefits for both patients and providers. Patients are able to recover at home, and the risk of contracting hospital-acquired infections or disorders is reduced. In standalone day surgery centres, there is less risk that procedures will be cancelled in order to accommodate the needs of emergency patients. Providers do not need to factor in evening and weekend nursing cover for day cases, and savings can be made on the 'hotel' element of hospital care. But attempts to increase the number of elective procedures carried out as day cases have sometimes met with opposition from medical professionals, or been hampered because payment mechanisms incentivize inpatient care.

Trends in accident and emergency and intensive care provision

There is significant variation in the way emergency departments operate from country to country. For instance, a comparison of English and Dutch patients' use of accident and emergency services (Monitor, 2014) found that almost as many patients in the Netherlands (39 per cent) were referred to accident and emergency (A&E) by their primary care doctor as the number that referred themselves (42 per cent). By contrast, only 5 per cent of English patients were referred by a GP, while 64 per cent referred themselves.

A study of differences between accident and emergency services in seven countries (McKinsey and Edwards, 2014) found differences in the staffing and performance management of emergency services, with German and Swedish emergency departments being staffed predominantly by specialists from different hospital departments rather than emergency medicine specialists, in contrast with English emergency departments. Many countries and regions (England, UK; Stockholm, Sweden; Ontario, Canada; Victoria, Australia) had implemented targets for how quickly patients must be seen in A&E departments, but these varied in their onerousness and how stringently they were enforced.

Trauma services are expensive and complex. In recent years, many health systems have moved towards systems of trauma care, rather than locating trauma units within all hospitals. The rationale for these changes has generally been that creating fewer, larger trauma centres enables trauma providers to consolidate expertise and experience, thus improving patient survival rates. For instance, the adoption of a state-wide trauma system in Victoria, Australia in 2000 has been associated with a significant reduction in risk-adjusted mortality (Cameron et al., 2008).

Significant variation also exists in ICU services, with one study finding Germany admitted six times as many patients to ICU per capita than Canada and ten times as many as the UK (Wunsch et al., 2008). The authors found only a weak correlation between ICU beds per capita and spending per capita, but a very strong correlation in all countries except the USA between critical care beds and hospital beds per capita. In the USA, resources appeared to be shifting from hospital beds to ICU beds to a much greater extent, possibly, the authors suggest, because greater use of chronic care facilities allows patients to be discharged more quickly from hospital. In countries with fewer ICU beds, patients occupying those beds tended to be sicker; there were higher numbers of patients with sepsis, and also higher hospital mortality for intensive care patients. The authors argue this makes sense because with fewer ICU beds, these would be used for the sickest patients (see Box 11.1).

Box 11.1 Case study – ICU provision in Uganda

Differences in the types of patient being treated in acute hospitals can mean that different configurations of ICU service will make sense in different countries. Firth and Ttendo's (2012) analysis of critical care provision in Mbarara, a small town in rural southwestern Uganda, shows why a plan to expand Mbarara Hospital's intensive care unit, which may appear at first glance not to be a cost-effective use of available resources, makes perfect sense when the type of patients the hospital treats is considered.

The authors show that a lack of access to early treatment means Ugandan patients often present at hospital in the late stages of disease, but many of these diseases are 'acute, isolated problems that it is possible to cure'. Moreover, the median age of patients in Mbarara's ICU is around twenty-seven years, and patients usually spend one or two days in the unit, with sepsis, post-operative care, trauma and obstetrical problems making up most cases. In comparison, the authors point out that patients in US ICUs are usually older people with multiple chronic conditions.

Source: Firth and Ttendo (2012).

Trends in specialist, tertiary and quaternary provision

Tertiary care is generally understood to mean specialist care, sometimes provided in a separate setting, by highly specialized medical professionals. The term 'quaternary care' is sometimes used to refer to the most specialized services (see Figure 11.2).

Tertiary providers can focus either on a specialist set of conditions (e.g. New York's Memorial Sloan Kettering Cancer Center) or on a patient group (e.g. children's hospital or

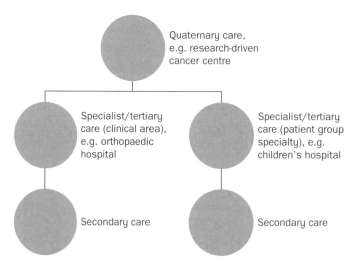

Figure 11.2 Hierarchy of services in acute care

women's hospital). The advent of innovative new treatments and the dispersal of formerly innovative treatments into mainstream healthcare means that the types of service provided by specialized and tertiary units will change over time. A good example of this is in the treatment of cancer, where drugs and treatments once used in specialist settings are made available in secondary and even community care, while newer treatments are offered in tertiary centres.

Centralization and basing services in the community

There are long-running trends in high-income countries to centralize the more specialist aspects of acute care and to decentralize those that do not require the services of a fully equipped hospital. Both trends are based on expected improvements in cost and quality and on a wish to provide more convenient services closer to patients' homes.

The case for centralizing care into higher volume units is framed in terms of improved outcomes for patients, including reduced mortality and morbidity and lower costs, or at least better use of scarce resources (Imison, 2011). The provision of specialist emergency services (e.g. trauma care) requires a level of staffing that may only be economic at a large scale, and this too has been driving centralization. The specialties and procedures where this is most common include cancer surgery, neurosurgery, abdominal surgery, trauma, neonatal care, paediatric intensive care, vascular surgery, emergency interventional cardiology, the immediate treatment of acute stroke and a number of other relatively complex activities. There is also increased centralization of obstetric care, with a number of countries increasing the minimum number of births required to qualify to operate an obstetric service.

For instance, in England, the NHS abdominal aortic aneurism screening programme follows guidance from the Vascular Society of Great Britain and Ireland which recommends that elective abdominal aortic aneurism (AAA) repair should only take place in hospitals that undertake thirty-three or more AAA procedures per year. In addition, such hospitals are required to have a 24/7 on-call rota for vascular emergencies covered by vascular surgeons and interventional radiologists, a 24/7 critical care facility that can undertake mechanical ventilation and renal support, twenty-four-hour on-site anaesthetic cover, single-sex bays or cubicles, specific X ray equipment, and various data monitoring and governance processes in place. It is clear that it would not be possible for every district hospital to comply with these requirements (see http://aaa.screening.nhs.uk/vascular-networks).

The case for the decentralization of less specialist care is also often framed in terms of efficiency and patient benefit. Current evidence (see Munton et al., 2011) suggests that moving some inpatient and day case services currently provided in hospital into other settings could benefit patients and improve cost efficiency. For instance, some services for elderly patients and those with chronic conditions could be provided in primary care (see Chapter 9). Intermediate care provided in community hospitals can lead to better outcomes for elderly people with acute illnesses, and patients appear to prefer treatment at home and early discharge from hospital into community settings is linked to better patient satisfaction and equal quality of life scores. However, there is some evidence to suggest that minor surgery performed by primary care doctors could be of a poorer quality, there is a lack of robust evidence that community-based care would be effective for a broader range of patients than the groups for whom services have been evaluated, and cost savings will not be realized until superseded acute services are decommissioned, which has not always happened. Some caution is therefore required when interpreting evidence in this area.

Seven-day working

Several studies (e.g. Bell and Redelmeier, 2001; Zare et al., 2007; Aylin et al., 2010) have found that some categories of patient have a greater risk of dying if admitted to an acute trust or having a surgical procedure at the weekend than during the week. This effect does not appear to occur in intensive care units (Wunsch et al., 2004), possibly because of the high-intensity staffing arrangements on intensive care wards. However, it is possible that increased mortality could result from other factors, such as more seriously ill patients being admitted or operated on over the weekend. The challenges of running a seven-day acute hospital illustrate some of the trade-offs managers are forced to make when attempting to provide high-quality care while remaining in budget. Aylin et al. (2010: 216) state that '[d]espite relatively consistent demand for acute care, hospitals faced with economic constraints and problems of employee satisfaction generally reduce staffing and availability of services during the weekend' (see Chapter 17).

Learning activity 11.2

Imagine you are a manager considering how a particular clinical area is to be delivered within your acute service provider. Develop a plan for how this service might ideally be delivered to suit the latest evidence about acute care, explaining:

- what needs to be done;
- why; and
- what the barriers might be.

Responses to challenges and change: tactical

As we have seen, increasing demand for healthcare and increasingly expensive interventions can drive up the cost of providing acute services. In combination with constrained public finances in countries where health services receive public funding, this means that managers of acute hospitals face greater pressure than ever to increase the efficiency of their organizations. Managers can take a variety of actions to alter how their organizations respond to such challenges.

Cost reduction and efficiency improvement

In reviewing existing evidence and interviewing staff working in English NHS hospitals that had overcome financial difficulties, Hurst and Williams (2012) concluded that improving staff productivity was 'the first place' to look for efficiencies. Approaches included reducing workforce levels to match expected activity levels, stopping the use of agency staff, managing overtime and sickness better, and exploring some skill-mix changes. The same study found mergers had a mixed impact on efficiency and although quality and efficiency were corre-lated, this could be because strong quality and efficiency performance was a consequence of sustained good management, rather than there necessarily being a direct relationship between the two.

Hurst and Williams' analysis of six NHS trusts that had turned around their financial posi-tion found that action to increase efficiency had been taken on several fronts, including staff productivity (as outlined above) and improved use of diagnostics; eliminating unnecessary tests, avoiding harm (e.g. preventing infections) and redesigning pathways to increase pro-ductivity; better use of medicines and equipment (e.g. switching to generic drugs, rational-izing ward stock levels and standardizing the procurement of medical supplies); and focusing on activity productivity by improving theatre utilization, working on waiting list manage-ment, reducing cancelled operations and missed outpatient appointments, and recovering more funds from chargeable patients. Acute providers may be able to achieve some efficien-cies via similar process improvements and service redesigns.

Reducing length of stay

Hurst and Williams also highlighted reducing bed numbers, increasing the amount of time beds are in use and closing theatres, reducing length of stay and preoperative length of stay and increasing day cases. As we have already seen, the trend internationally is towards reducing bed numbers, increasing day cases and shortening length of stay. In systems where hospitals are paid based on the number of procedures they perform, increasing the number of patients passing through the unit can increase hospital revenue. Strategies to speed up the flow of patients through hospital and reduce length of stay include organizing pathways of care through the hospital in order to facilitate timely discharge; tailoring care to particular patient groups or conditions; and using multidisciplinary and proactive care and discharge, particularly around recovery and rehabilitation.

Approaches such as seven-day access to senior decision-making, diagnostic support and proactive discharge facilitation (Sturgess, 2010), process mapping, calculating estimated dis-charge dates on admission and sharing these with patients (NHS Institute for Innovation and Improvement, 2008), have been used to reduce length of stay. For more details on reducing length of stay, see work by the Institute for Healthcare Improvement and the Health Foundation.

Another initiative has been the use of intermediate care services such as community hos-pitals and virtual wards to enable clinically stable patients to recover closer to home or in their own homes under medical supervision. The National Audit of Intermediate Care (2014) found that of 60,384 people discharged from sixty crisis response services participating in the audit, only 10 per cent required admission to hospital.

Strategic responses: emerging models of care delivery

The previous sections of this chapter have considered the challenges the acute sector faces in ensuring it remains relevant in a world where both the way care is delivered and the expectations of patients are changing. Acute providers are developing different approaches to respond to these challenges, but they cannot do so without taking into account the nature of the system they are operating in. The logic underpinning systems theory is that trying to improve the efficiency of a particular component of a system, such as a hospital, in isolation will not succeed unless the external factors that influence the behaviour of that component are also considered (Healy and McKee, 2002a, 2002b). Other forces affecting how hospitals operate include the nature and behaviour of nearby healthcare providers (competitors and/ or those offering services in a different part of the pathway); the behaviour of the consumers of a hospital's services, whether patients or purchasers; characteristics of the local population; and the ease with which the hospital can alter aspects of its fixed assets and estates. Taking these issues alongside the different drivers at play depending on the type of hospital system in use, the complexity of the relationship between an acute provider and the wider system is clear.

For instance, although treating more patients as day cases and shifting more care to primary care settings (see Chapter 9) implies that acute provision should be decreasing in influence compared with the past, it is difficult for large 'bricks and mortar' institutions like hospitals to reduce costs. In such circumstances, a logical response from an organizational perspective would be to compensate for lost income by competing more aggressively with neighbouring providers, or undertaking procedures more quickly. Neither of these actions might be in the interests of the wider health system and so system theory would advocate that policy-makers consider these risks when thinking about the likely impact of change.

Where policy-makers and purchasers have sought to reorder the balance of provision in health systems so that more services are provided off the acute campus, the main ways of achieving this have been through legislation, regulation or policy directive, or using market mechanisms. For example, market reform in the Netherlands in the 1990s that forced insurers to take on a greater share of risk encouraged insurers to reduce costs by shifting services out of hospitals into community settings (Harrison, 2004).

Integrated care

One model that has gained traction in the USA and has generated interest in the English healthcare system is that of integrating care, particularly through accountable care organizations (ACOs) (see also Chapter 10). Fisher et al. (2007) define the ACO as 'comprising local hospitals and the physicians who work within and around them'. They state that 'virtually all physicians are either directly or indirectly affiliated with a local acute care hospital, whether through their own inpatient work or through the care patterns of the patients they serve' (2007: w45). In the USA, ACOs usually comprise primary care practices, one or more hospitals, nursing homes, and sometimes home healthcare agencies and other provider organizations (see Box 11.2). Different organizational forms range from formal health systems to looser affiliations. Performance has been mixed, with some evidence that they are controlling the rate of spending but there is recognition that 'they will need a range of capabilities in order to manage cost and quality and to be able to implement what is known about the characteristics of successful integrated systems' (Shortell et al., 2014: 9).

Box 11.2 Case study – Intermountain Healthcare

Intermountain Healthcare is a health system based in Salt Lake City, Utah. It is a secular, not-for-profit provider that was set up in 1975 when the Church of Jesus Christ of Latter Day Saints donated its fifteen healthcare facilities to the community. Intermountain operates twenty-two hospitals and more than one hundred and eight-five clinics, employing 1200 primary and secondary care physicians and more than 37,000 staff in total – in this respect, it is an integrated care network that includes hospitals, providers, and a health plans division called SelectHealth. During 2015, Intermountain facilities saw more than 500,000 emergency room visits, more than 136,000 acute inpatient admissions, 39,000 inpatient surgeries and 117,000 ambulatory surgeries. Intermountain has focused on improving efficiency, including through 'eliminating tests and procedures that add only cost or risk to a patient's care – while not adding commensurate benefit in diagnosis or management of disease'. Intermountain's revenue in 2015 was $6.1 billion.

Source: www.intermountainhealthcare.org

Provider chains and networks

Research conducted by RAND Europe for the English Department of Health (2014) found evidence of an increasing international trend towards the formation of hospital groups and networks, with such organizations already present in the USA and Europe and countries such as Australia and Ireland pursuing policies that mandated their formation. The study found an expectation that the formation of these groups and networks would lead to 'greater market influence, economies of scale and scope, reduced duplication of resources, more effective training and improved efficiency in the provision of services'.

Drivers identified by RAND included regulatory actions such as the relaxation of staffing structure requirements in the USA, and also a trend towards privatization driven by capacity and economic pressures in France and Germany, where a shift towards multi-hospital groups has occurred in tandem with an increase in the proportion of providers in the private for-profit sector (Department of Health, 2014). One good example of a networked provider is German provider Agaplesion, which deploys strong lateral links between staff undertaking similar roles across its different sites in order to ensure expertise is shared across multiple locations (see Box 11.3).

Franchises and concessions

In some countries, greater use has been made of franchises and concessions. For example, in 2016, London's Moorfields Eye Hospital was operating facilities in more than twenty locations across southeast England, including within other hospital trusts. In the same year, the Mayo Clinic Health System had services in more than sixty locations across four US states.

Franchises and concessions pose different challenges. Operating a concession arrangement across broad distances can be challenging for staff, whereas franchises, where local

---

Box 11.3 Case study – Agaplesion

Agaplesion is a non-profit hospital provider headquartered in Frankfurt am Main, Germany. Established in 2002, it operates across twenty-six hospital sites, thirty-five residential and nursing care facilities, eight hundred assisted living apartments, four hospices, twenty medical care centres, eight outpatient centres and a training academy. It has 6100 acute beds and 3000 residential and nursing care beds. Agaplesion employs 19,000 staff and provides services for more than 1 million patients. In 2015, its revenues amounted to more than €1 billion in total and it takes an active role in both training staff and also furthering research projects, often in partnership with research institutes and universities in the European Union.

Agaplesion's roots are as a Christian healthcare provider, and it describes its core values as charity, esteem, responsibility, transparency, professionalism and efficiency. However, it prides itself on its modern management approach and technical knowhow. It uses an integrative management structure that links up staff working across its different locations. The approach encompasses a networked conferencing system that ensures knowledge and information is systematically exchanged and used throughout the group. As well as acute care services, the group provides some primary and public health services such as travel vaccinations, and also rehabilitation and physiotherapy.

Source: www.agaplesion.de.

---

staff are trained to provide services using the approach of the parent organization, require good-quality assurance processes.

Focused factories

There is some evidence that the 'focused factory' approach, where units focus on a particular condition or a particular category of patients, can reduce length of stay for some patients. For instance, Cook and colleagues' experiment with a focused factory model to treat cardiac surgery patients found that for the 67 per cent of patients for whom the model was appropriate, 'implementation of the model reduced resource use, length-of-stay, and cost' (2014: 746). But Bredenhoff and colleagues' (2010) comparison of four multiple case studies including focused factories was unable to establish a clear relationship between focus and efficiency. Another well-known example is that of India's Aravind Eye Care System, which uses very efficient Lean-style practices to reduce the cost of the treatment of patients with eye conditions.

The hospital at home

Hospital at home schemes enable hospitals to provide services to patients in their own homes, and have been doing so for decades. This means that although not within the hospital, the patient is still under the care of the hospital's clinical teams until the treatment period is over. Services can be offered either to patients who have been discharged from hospital earlier than under conventional schemes, or as an alternative to hospital admission.

A Cochrane Review (Shepperd and Iliffe, 2005) of evidence relating to hospital at home schemes suggested that the evidence did not support the adoption of hospital at home services 'as a cheaper substitute for in-patient care within health care systems that have well developed primary care services'. But neither did the review reveal a difference in health outcomes (although data comparability issues restricted comparison), and it found no evidence to suggest that the approach was sufficiently hazardous or expensive to warrant ending schemes for elderly medical patients, those who have had elective surgery or those with a terminal illness. Patients receiving hospital at home services expressed greater satisfaction with their care than hospital-based patients, but carers' views were more mixed. The authors suggested that for hospitals with relatively high running costs – such as city teaching hospitals – the schemes could prove more cost effective.

One of the ways that hospital at home schemes could increase hospital efficiency would be by enabling hospitals to close wards, releasing funds to be deployed elsewhere. But the review found that the low volume of patients using the scheme limited their ability to generate efficiencies.

Learning activity 11.3

Devise a list of the pros and cons of the following delivery models:

- standalone hospitals
- provider chains
- franchises
- concessions.

Conclusion

Across the world, acute providers are adapting to the challenges of cost and technological inflation, increasing demand, and heightened patient expectations by attempting to drive up efficiency and finding new approaches to providing services. Although historically the acute provider has operated as a relatively self-contained entity at the centre of the health system, this approach is increasingly unsuitable in the context of modern healthcare. As a consequence, acute providers are developing new models that enable them to broaden their reach and integrate with other parts of the health system. For this reason, it is important that policy-makers consider the acute provider as part of an overarching system, rather than as representing a complete system in itself.

Learning activity 11.4

Describe how acute care is structured in your country/area and compare this with two other international examples, focusing on: size, organizational type and range of services. How might you suggest improvements to your own health system, based on good ideas you have encountered in the other international examples?

Learning resources

African Federation for Emergency Medicine: The Federation is an international association of African national emergency medicine organizations, facilitating information exchange on topics of African and international interest, assisting collaborative research, opportunities for trainees in African emergency medicine programmes, sabbaticals and exchange opportunities, and helping solve problems regarding emergency medicine and the [delivery of emergency care in Africa [http://www.afem.info/].

British Association of Day Surgery: The Association provides information about day surgery for patients, relatives, carers and healthcare professionals [http://daysurgeryuk.net/en/home/].

Commonwealth Fund: This New York-based research foundation aims to promote a high-performing healthcare system, particularly for the most vulnerable in society, encompassing issues such as accountable care organizations, patient data and payment systems that are relevant in a hospital context [www.commonwealthfund.org].

European Observatory on Health Systems and Policies: As part of the World Health Organization, the Observatory promotes and supports evidence-based policy-making through analysis of the dynamics of health systems in Europe [http://www.euro.who.int/en/about-us/partners/observatory].

International Association for Ambulatory Surgery: This international body promotes the development and growth of high-quality ambulatory surgery by encouraging an international exchange of ideas and stimulating programmes of education, research and audit [http://www.iaas-med.com/].

World Health Organization: WHO provides a range of information about hospital services, along with a dedicated resource for healthcare managers managing hospitals [more information can be found at http://www.who.int/topics/hospitals/en/].

Wachter's World: A regularly updated blog by Bob Wachter, a leader in the 'hospitalist' movement and an academic at the University of California, San Francisco, Wachter's World explores patient safety, health policy, information technology, medical ethics, payment mechanisms and other issues from a hospital physician's perspective [http://community.the-hospitalist.org/].

References

Austin, S., Murthy, S. Wunsch, H., Adhikari, N.K., Karir, V., Rowan, K. et al. (2014) Access to urban acute care services in high- vs. middle-income countries: an analysis of seven cities, *Intensive Care Medicine*, 40 (3): 342–52.

Aylin, P., Yunus, A., Bottle, A., Majeed, A. and Bell, D. (2010) Weekend mortality for emergency admissions: a large, multicentre study, *Quality and Safety in Health Care*, 19: 213–17.

Bell, C.M. and Redelmeier, D.A. (2001) Mortality among patients admitted to hospitals on weekends as compared with weekdays, *New England Journal of Medicine*, 345: 663–8.

Bredenhoff, E., van Lent, W.A.M. and Van Harten, W.H. (2010) Exploring types of focused factories in hospital care: a multiple case study, *BMC Health Services Research*, 10 (1): 154.

Cameron, P.A., Gabbe, B.J., Cooper, D.J. (2008) A statewide system of trauma care in Victoria: effect on patient survival, *Medical Journal of Australia*, 189 (10): 536–50.

Chevalier, F., Levitan, J. and Garel, P. (2009) *Hospitals in the 27 Member States of the European Union*. Paris: Dexia.

Cook, D., Thompson, J.E., Habermann, E.B., Visscher, S.L., Dearani, J.A., Rioger, V.L. et al. (2014) From 'solution shop' model to 'focused factory' in hospital surgery: increasing care value and predictability, *Health Affairs*, 33 (5): 746–55.

Cooper, Z., Gibbons, S., Jones, S. and McGuire, A. (2011) Does hospital competition save lives? Evidence from the English NHS Patient Choice Reforms, *Economic Journal*, 121 (554): F228–60.

Cullen, K.A., Hall, M.J. and Golosinskiy, A. (2006) *Ambulatory Surgery in the United States*. National Health Statistics Reports #11, Revised. Hyattsville, MD: National Center for Health Statistics [http://www.cdc.gov/nchs/data/nhsr/nhsr011.pdf].

Department of Health (2014) *Dalton Review: Lessons from Other Sectors and International Experience* [https://www.gov.uk/government/uploads/system/uploads/attachment_data/file/385839/Dalton_Other_Sectors.pdf].

European Hospital and Healthcare Federation (2012) *Hospitals in Europe Healthcare Data 2012* [http://www.hope.be/03activities/quality_eu-hospitals/eu_country_profiles/00-hospitals_in_europe-synthesis.pdf].

Feng, Y., Pistollato, M., Charlesworth, A., Devlin, N., Propper, C. and Sussex, J. (2015) Association between market concentration of hospitals and patient health gain following hip replacement surgery, *Journal of Health Service Research and Policy*, 20 (1): 11–17.

Firth, P. and Ttendo, S. (2012) Intensive care in low income countries – a critical need, *New England Journal of Medicine*, 367 (21): 1974–6.

Fisher, E.S., Staiger, D.O., Bynum, J.P.W. and Gottlieb, D.J. (2007) Creating accountable care organizations: the extended medical hospital staff, *Health Affairs*, 26 (1): w44–57.

Francis, R. (2013) *Final Report of the Mid-Staffordshire Inquiry* [http://webarchive.nationalarchives.gov.uk/20150407084003/http://www.midstaffspublicinquiry.com/].

Gill, Z. and Bailey, P.E. (2010) Bottom up and top down: a comprehensive approach to improve care and strengthen the health system, *Journal of the Pakistan Medical Association*, 60 (11): 927–35.

Harrison, M.I. (2004) Reform outcomes and new policy trends in the Netherlands, in *Implementing Change in Health Systems: Market Reforms in the United Kingdom, Sweden and the Netherlands*. London: Sage.

Healy, J. and McKee, M. (2002a) The evolution of hospital systems, in M. McKee and J. Healy (eds.) *Hospitals in a Changing Europe.* Buckingham: Open University Press [http://www.euro.who.int/__data/assets/pdf_file/0004/98401/E74486.pdf].

Healy, J. and McKee, M. (2002b) The role and function of hospitals, in M. McKee and J. Healy (eds.) *Hospitals in a Changing Europe.* Buckingham: Open University Press [http://www.euro.who.int/__data/assets/pdf_file/0004/98401/E74486.pdf].

Hirshon, J.M., Risko, N., Calvello, E.J., Stewart de Ramirez, S., Narayan, M., Theodosis, C. et al. (2013) Health systems and services: the role of acute care, *Bulletin of the World Health Organization*, 91: 386–8.

Hsia, R.Y., Mbembati, N.A., Mcfarlane, S. and Kruk, M.E. (2012) Access to emergency and surgical care in sub-Saharan Africa: the infrastructure gap, *Health Policy and Planning*, 27: 234–44.

Hurst, J. and Williams, S. (2012) *Can NHS Hospitals Do More with Less?* London: Nuffield Trust.

Imison, C. (2011) *Reconfiguring Hospital Services.* London: King's Fund.

Jarrett, P.E.M. and Staniszewski, A. (2006) *The Development of Ambulatory Surgery and Future Challenges in Day Surgery Development and Practice.* London: International Association for Ambulatory Surgery.

Lear, J., Mossialos, E. and Karl, B. (2010) EU competition law and health policy, in E. Mossialos, G. Permanand, R. Baeten and T.K. Hervey (eds.) *Health Systems Governance in Europe.* Cambridge: Cambridge University Press.

Levine, A.C., Presser, D.Z., Rosborough, S., Ghebreyesus, T.A. and Davis, M.A. (2007) Understanding barriers to emergency care in low-income countries: view from the front line, *Prehospital and Disaster Medicine*, 22: 467–70.

McKinsey & Co. and Edwards, N. (2014) Annex 5, in *International Comparisons of Selected Service Lines in Seven Health Systems* [https://www.gov.uk/government/uploads/system/uploads/attachment_data/file/382847/Annex_5_AandE.pdf].

Monitor (2014) *Exploring International Acute Care Models.* London: Monitor [https://www.gov.uk/government/uploads/system/uploads/attachment_data/file/383021/ExploringInternationalAcutes.pdf].

Moresky, R.T., Bisanzo, M., Rubenstein, B.L., Hubbard, S.J., Cohen, H., Ouyang, H. et al. (2013) A research agenda for acute care services delivery in low- and middle-income countries, *Academic Emergency Medicine*, 2 (12): 1264–71.

Munton, T., Martin, A., Marrero, A., (2011) *Getting Out of Hospital? The Evidence for Shifting Acute Inpatient and Day Case Services from Hospitals into the Community.* London: Health Foundation.

National Audit of Intermediate Care (2014) [http://www.nhsbenchmarking.nhs.uk/CubeCore/.uploads/NAIC/NAICSummaryReport2014.pdf].

NHS Confederation (2015) *Key Statistics on the NHS* [http://www.nhsconfed.org/resources/key-statistics-on-the-nhs].

NHS England (2014) *Five Year Forward View.* Leeds: NHS England [https://www.england.nhs.uk/ourwork/futurenhs/].

NHS Institute for Improvement and Innovation (2008) *Length of Stay – Reducing Length of Stay* [http://www.institute.nhs.uk/quality_and_service_improvement_tools/quality_and_service_improvement_tools/length_of_stay.html].

OECD (2001) Acute care, in *Glossary of Statistical Terms* [https://stats.oecd.org/glossary/detail.asp?ID=4].

OECD (2013) *Health Care Resources: Hospital Beds* [http://stats.oecd.org/index.aspx?queryid=30183#].

OECD (2014) Health expenditure by function, in *Health at a Glance: Europe 2014* [http://www.oecd-ilibrary.org/docserver/download/8114211ec053.pdf?expires=1432028729&id=id&accname=guest&checksum=39643F49147E10BC6D9BEBF548F22E42].

OECD (2016) *Health Care Utilisation: Hospital Aggregates* [http://stats.oecd.org/index.aspx?queryid=30163].

Paris, V., Devaux, M. and Wei, L. (2010) *Health Systems' Institutional Characteristics: A Survey of 29 OECD Countries*, OECD Health Working Papers #50 [http://www.oecd.org/officialdocuments/publicdisplaydocumentpdf/?cote=DELSA/HEA/WD/HWP%282010%291&docLanguage=En].

Saltman, R.B., Allin, S., Mossialos, E., Wismar, M. and Kutzin, J. (2012) Assessing health reform trends in Europe, in J. Figueras and M. McKee (eds.) *Health Systems, Health, Wealth and Societal Wellbeing: Assessing the Case for Investing in Health Systems*. Maidenhead: Open University Press.

Shepperd, S. and Iliffe, S. (2005) Hospital at home versus in-patient hospital care (Review), *Cochrane Database of Systematic Reviews*, 3: CD000356. [http://onlinelibrary.wiley.com/store/10.1002/14651858.CD000356.pub2/asset/CD000356.pdf?v=1&t=ijycsqh8&s=8f1e2d0fbf81b3f29e6f18bf31a0b05cd9eaabb9].

Shortell, S., Addicott, R., Walsh, N. and Ham, C. (2014) *Accountable Care Organisations in the United States and England: Testing, Evaluating and Learning what Works*. London: King's Fund. [http://www.kingsfund.org.uk/sites/files/kf/field/field_publication_file/accountable-care-organisations-united-states-england-shortell-mar14.pdf].

Smith, P., McKeon, A., Blunt, I. and Edwards, N. (2014) *NHS Hospitals Under Pressure: Trends in Activity up to 2022*. London: Nuffield Trust [http://www.nuffieldtrust.org.uk/sites/files/nuffield/publication/ft_hospitals_analysis.pdf].

Sturgess, I. (2010) *Planning for Predictable Flows of Patients into Unscheduled Care Pathways Beyond the Emergency Department: Meeting Demand and Delivering Quality*. London: IST [http://www.nhsimas.nhs.uk/fileadmin/Files/IST/Unscheduled_Care_Pathways_meeting_demand_and_delivering_quality.pdf].

Thomson, S., Osborn, R., Squires, D. and Jun, M. (eds.) (2013) *International Profiles of Health Care Systems, 2013*. New York: Commonwealth Fund.

Thorlby, R., Smith, J., Dayan, M. and Williams, S. (2014) *The Francis Report: One Year On*. London: Nuffield Trust [http://www.nuffieldtrust.org.uk/publications/francis-inquiry-one-year-on].

Toftgaard, C. and Parmentier, G. (2006) International terminology in ambulatory surgery and its worldwide practice, in P. Lemos, P. Jarrett and B. Philip (eds.) *Day Surgery: Development and Practice*. London: IAAS.

Vincent, C., Burnett, S. and Carthey, J. (2013) *The Measurement and Monitoring of Safety*. London: Health Foundation.

Wunsch, H., Mapstone, J., Brady, T., Hanks, R. and Rowan, K. (2004) Hospital mortality associated with day and time of admission to intensive care units, *Intensive Care Medicine*, 30 (5): 895–901.

Wunsch, H. Angus, D.C., Harrison, D.A., Collange, O., Fowler, R., Hoste, E.A. et al. (2008) Variation in critical care services across North America and Western Europe, *Critical Care Medicine*, 36 (10): 2787–93.

Zare, M.M., Itani, K.M., Schifftner, T.L., Henderson, W.G. and Khuri, S.F. (2007) Mortality after nonemergent major surgery performed on Friday versus Monday through Wednesday, *Annals of Surgery*, 246 (5): 866–74.

Chapter 12

Mental health

Chris Naylor and Helen Gilburt

Introduction

Mental health is a vital component of health and well-being and is influenced by the activities of all parts of the healthcare system. As this chapter will show, an understanding of mental health is an important competency for anyone working in healthcare management, not only those managing specialist mental health services.

The prevalence of mental health problems provides one measure of the importance of mental health. The World Health Organization estimates that 13 per cent of the global burden of disease can be attributed to mental, neurological and substance abuse disorders. In high-income countries, the relative burden is higher, accounting for around one-quarter of the overall burden of disease. Depression alone is believed to affect around 400 million people worldwide. Dementia is also becoming increasingly common as the global population ages, affecting between 5 per cent and 7 per cent of all people over the age of sixty globally (Prince et al., 2013). In England, the adult psychiatric morbidity survey indicates that 23 per cent of the adult population will experience some form of mental health problem during the course of a year (McManus et al., 2009).

The importance of good mental health to individuals is clear and poor mental health can affect people's lives in multiple ways. For example, common mental health problems such as depression and anxiety have a dramatic effect on self-rated quality of life (Moussavi et al., 2007) and can significantly reduce a person's ability and motivation to manage their physical health. People with severe mental illnesses such as schizophrenia or bipolar disorder are among the most excluded groups in society, with low rates of civic and economic participation and a life expectancy fifteen to twenty years below that of the general population (Laursen et al., 2014).

The financial and economic costs of mental ill health are equally striking. High-income countries typically spend around 5 per cent of their health budgets on specialist mental health services, with some countries spending much more than this (13 per cent in England). Although significant, this investment is dwarfed by the financial impact of mental ill health on society more widely, including on the rest of the healthcare system. For example, by interacting with and exacerbating physical health problems, it is estimated that co-morbid mental health problems increase the costs of long-term conditions by at least 45 per cent per individual affected (Naylor et al., 2012). If we include the cost of lost economic output and the human costs, the overall economic impact of mental health problems in England is roughly comparable to the entire health service budget – around £105 billion in 2009/10 (Centre for Mental Health, 2010).

Mental health presents a number of challenges for healthcare management. The close interactions with physical health and with the social determinants of health make the ability to work across institutional boundaries particularly important. Additional challenges arise from the paucity of performance data in many mental health services, the contested nature of some mental health diagnoses, and the issues of stigma and discrimination, which can affect those working in mental healthcare as well as those using services. We shall argue throughout this chapter that these are challenges for the whole management community, rather than those working in any one sector.

We begin by outlining the wide range of services involved in providing mental healthcare, before identifying distinctive elements of mental health problems and services, and related challenges for managers. The chapter ends with a discussion of future directions for mental healthcare.

The nature and scope of mental health services

The World Health Organization (WHO) defines mental health as 'a state of well-being in which every individual realizes his or her own potential, can cope with the normal stresses of life, can work productively and fruitfully, and is able to make a contribution to her or his community' (WHO, 2001). Taking this positive definition, it is clear that all healthcare professionals – clinical and managerial – can do much to support the mental health of the patients and populations they serve.

The focus often, however, is on mental health problems. This umbrella term includes a highly diverse set of conditions, as illustrated in Figure 12.1. These conditions can occur throughout the life-course, from childhood to older age. About half of all mental health problems start by the mid-teenage years, and three-quarters by the mid-twenties (Kessler et al., 2007), making childhood and adolescence a critical stage for intervention. Equally, the mental health of older people is also an important focus for attention, given rising numbers of people living with dementia and evidence of substantial under-diagnosis of other mental health problems such as depression among older people (Bottino et al., 2012).

Many mental health conditions are often experienced in a chronic or relapsing pattern, and it is increasingly recognized that models of care developed for managing chronic physical disease can also be effective for supporting some of those experiencing mental health problems (Katon et al., 2004). However, it is important to recognize that this is not always the case – effective interventions are available for a number of conditions and, for many people, mental health problems are experienced as a single time-limited episode of illness, followed by complete recovery. For example, more than half of people with depression or anxiety disorders clinically recover following provision of evidence-based psychological therapies (Clark, 2011).

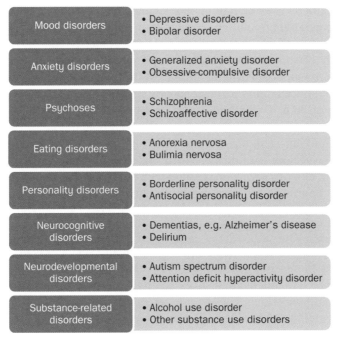

Mood disorders	• Depressive disorders • Bipolar disorder
Anxiety disorders	• Generalized anxiety disorder • Obsessive-compulsive disorder
Psychoses	• Schizophrenia • Schizoaffective disorder
Eating disorders	• Anorexia nervosa • Bulimia nervosa
Personality disorders	• Borderline personality disorder • Antisocial personality disorder
Neurocognitive disorders	• Dementias, e.g. Alzheimer's disease • Delirium
Neurodevelopmental disorders	• Autism spectrum disorder • Attention deficit hyperactivity disorder
Substance-related disorders	• Alcohol use disorder • Other substance use disorders

Figure 12.1 Examples of mental health disorders

People experiencing mental health problems are supported by a wide range of services, delivered in both institutional and community settings. In most high-income countries, the model of care for people with severe mental illnesses has shifted over the last thirty years from one centred on large psychiatric institutions to an approach that emphasizes care delivered in the community.

In countries where this 'de-institutionalization' process is well advanced, services include access to a range of staff, including psychiatrists, psychologists, community psychiatric nurses, social workers, occupational therapists, support workers and others. Many of these staff are part of multidisciplinary teams in which all members are expected to possess certain generic competencies – for example, in assessment or case management – regardless of their professional background. These community-based teams may make a referral to inpatient services when a person becomes acutely unwell, but the intention is to avoid this where possible.

Community-based service provision has expanded in many countries as the de-institutionalization process has progressed. In addition to generic services (known as community mental health teams in England), a number of other services have developed focused on supporting particular groups of people or providing a specialist aspect of care. For example, in a number of countries crisis resolution teams are used to provide more intensive support for a limited period of time to people at risk of hospital admission, with the aim of preventing deterioration of a person's condition and helping them to remain in the community. Early intervention services are used to provide rapid support to people experiencing their first episode of psychosis, as evidence suggests the duration of untreated psychosis is highly predictive of later outcomes (Marshall et al., 2005). Another widely used approach is the assertive outreach model, designed to engage people with psychosis and complex needs in treatment.

These services focus predominately on providing support and treatment for adults of a working age in the general population. A number of other forms of more specialist provision have developed focused on children and young people, older people and specific population groups. The growing focus internationally on ageing populations has resulted in the development of services to support early identification of and support for people with dementia. Another significant specialism is forensic mental health services for people in the criminal justice system. More than 70 per cent of the prison population in the UK has two or more mental health disorders (Social Exclusion Unit, 2004). A policy goal of reducing the number of people with mental illness in the criminal justice system has resulted in the emergence of liaison and diversion services in Europe, North America, Australia and New Zealand (Petrila, 2003). These seek to identify people in custody who are in need of mental health support, and divert them to the appropriate mental health facilities rather than prison. Evaluations suggest this approach is highly cost effective and can reduce re-offending by 30 per cent or more (Centre for Mental Health, Rethink and the Royal College of Psychiatrists, 2011).

In many countries, a large proportion of mental health services is provided by the statutory sector. But the increasing development of community-based care and an emphasis on supporting people to live independent lives has led to a growth in provision by voluntary and private sector organizations. The latter have also proved important in providing support for people with mental health problems in rural locations and in low-income countries where statutory mental health services may be underdeveloped.

While this array of services plays an important role for those referred to secondary care, it should be recognized that the majority of people with mental health problems (particularly those with the most common conditions such as depressive and anxiety disorders) are supported primarily or exclusively by non-specialist forms of support, most often in primary care. Around one-quarter of patients attending primary care have a mental health component to their illness (JCPMH, 2012a), including a large number of people presenting with 'medically unexplained symptoms', which often have a psychological basis. Only people with the most serious and complex mental health problems are referred on to specialist mental health services.

Mental health problems are also highly prevalent in general acute hospital settings. It has been estimated that at any given time, around 40 per cent of beds in a typical acute hospital are occupied by older people with mental health problems, mostly depression or dementia (JCPMH, 2012b). Alcohol use disorders are also prevalent in hospital settings, particularly in emergency departments. Psychiatric liaison services seek to support people in these settings by ensuring the appropriate mental health expertise is available to patients and staff in acute hospitals. Services for people with long-term conditions also support many people with mental health problems, whether recognized or not – around 30 per cent of people with long-term conditions such as diabetes or heart disease are estimated to have a co-morbid mental health problem (Naylor et al., 2012).

When thinking about mental healthcare, it is therefore important to acknowledge that this includes much more than specialist mental health services (see Table 12.1). Primary care is an indispensable part of any high-performing mental health system and hospitals providing general acute care are also *de facto* mental health providers. An important challenge for healthcare managers is ensuring that they are able to function as such.

Table 12.1 Examples of services involved in delivering mental healthcare

	Services dedicated to mental health	Other services/agencies substantially involved in the provision of mental health care
Community services	• Community mental health teams • Primary care psychology • Crisis resolution services • Early intervention services • Assertive outreach services	• General practitioners • Health visitors • Schools • Social care • Police and criminal justice • Housing agencies • Voluntary sector organizations
Hospital services	• Acute psychiatric inpatient services • Liaison psychiatry/psychological medicine in general acute hospitals	• General acute hospital inpatient services • Outpatient clinics, e.g. for people with chronic conditions • Accident and emergency services
Specialized services	• Child and adolescent mental health services • Forensic services • Eating disorder services • Dementia services • Personality disorder services • Drug and alcohol services • Psychoanalytic psychotherapy services • Other specialized community and inpatient services	

There is also an important intersection with other public services, for example housing, education and policing. The interdependency between health and social well-being is particularly important in the case of mental health, which is strongly (although not wholly) determined by social conditions and exposures. As discussed below, this has important implications in terms of the competencies and leadership styles required of healthcare managers.

Learning activity 12.1

Using global burden of disease data (available to download from the Global Health Data Exchange), list the five mental health conditions that have the greatest impact in your country, in terms of disability adjusted life years (DALYs). Using the same data source, what proportion of the total burden of disease in your country is attributable to mental and neurological disorders?

Distinctive elements of mental health problems and services

It is sometimes said that mental health is 'different'. Mental and physical health are often thought about and responded to separately, with little emphasis given to the mutual dependency between the two. Those working in specialist mental health services often report feeling that they are outside of the mainstream health community, and that health policy tends to be constructed around physical illness, with mental health featuring as an afterthought. This characterization of 'difference' is not always accurate – in many respects, mental health problems share important features with other forms of ill health and some common issues exist in terms of service delivery, management and policy. However, as described below, there are some distinctive elements that healthcare managers should be conscious of.

Contested goals and diverse understandings

The definitions of what constitutes an illness, and what the objectives of 'treatment' should be, are often highly contested in mental health. Rather than resting on objective measurements or pathology tests, mental health diagnoses are based on clusters of symptoms, including emotions, thoughts, perceptions and behaviours, which may be observed by the clinician or reported by the service user. The point at which a person is considered to have a disorder is a matter of medical convention and, in some cases; this has changed significantly over time. This in no way makes mental health problems any less 'real', but it does have several implications.

First, it has implications in terms of terminology and language. Terms such as 'patient', 'illness', 'treatment' and 'cure' may be uncontroversial in many fields of healthcare, but can be problematic in mental health, where these clash with some understandings of mental health. This is not a question of political correctness, but goes to the heart of what mental healthcare is and how managers and clinicians understand their role in relation to the people they serve.

This leads onto a second implication, which is that there are multiple perspectives regarding the purpose of mental healthcare, with tensions often arising between these different perspectives. One view is that the purpose should be to eliminate or alleviate the abnormal symptoms a person presents with. This biomedical perspective has been challenged by an alternative – or perhaps complementary – perspective, often championed by groups representing service users. This holds that the fundamental purpose of mental healthcare is to help people maintain or regain control over their lives, in whatever ways are most important to them. Models of care are being developed that give greater priority to user-defined goals, which may be social or functional in nature rather than clinical. These two perspectives are not necessarily mutually exclusive, but rather exist in parallel. Healthcare managers need to be aware of the tension between the two, which can at times be healthy and at other times problematic.

Interdependency with physical health and social circumstances

As described above, mental health and physical health are closely interrelated. In some ways, this observation may seem intuitive and unremarkable. However, the institutional architecture of health systems, and the training and education of professionals, both tend to reinforce structural and cultural barriers between mental and physical healthcare. These barriers mean that the twin pillars of health – mental and physical – are often treated as if they exist in isolation of one another.

A review of the literature suggested that around 45 per cent of people with mental health problems also have a long-term physical health problem. For example, people with cardiovascular diseases, chronic respiratory diseases, diabetes or chronic musculoskeletal disorders are around two to three times more likely to experience a mental health problem than the general population (Naylor et al., 2012). Physical health outcomes are particularly poor among people with schizophrenia and other psychoses, as shown by the fifteen–twenty year gap in life expectancy, which is largely attributable to poorer physical health (Laursen et al., 2014).

The strength of this interaction is exacerbated significantly by social deprivation – among those with multiple physical disorders living in the lowest socioeconomic groups, the prevalence of mental ill health is almost 50 per cent (Barnett et al., 2012). Some of the most intensive users of mental health services have highly complex social needs and significant instability in their lives. Social gradients do, of course, exist across many forms of illness, but are particularly steep in the case of mental health.

The shift to community-based models of care

There is an international consensus that health and social care systems need to change in order to meet the needs of ageing populations and rising rates of long-term conditions. Central to this change is a shift away from hospital-based models of care and an increased emphasis on enhanced forms of primary and community care, as discussed in Chapters 9 and 10.

A striking feature of mental healthcare is the extent to which this transformation has, in many countries, already taken place. The process of de-institutionalization over the last thirty years has led to a fundamentally different model of care in which community-based service delivery is now the norm. As discussed by Gilburt et al. (2014), this shift is in some ways analogous to the change that many in the healthcare management community now argue is required across the health system – the difference from other clinical areas being that in mental health this transformation has already occurred, as opposed to being largely an aspiration.

However, it should be recognized that this remains an unfinished journey. Many countries still lack a comprehensive system of community mental health services, and there are often important weaknesses. Notably, the role played by primary care as part of the mental health system continues to be underdeveloped.

Learning activity 12.2

Using Gilburt et al. (2014) as a guide, describe what lessons the wider health sector might learn from the history of de-institutionalization and service transformation in mental health. How relevant is this history to current attempts in other clinical areas to develop care outside hospital? Consider what the main lessons might be in terms of the following areas:

- Building a consensus that change is needed
- Designing new community-based service models
- Engaging clinical professionals and service users in processes of change
- Building a workforce suitable for the future
- Investing in change management capacity.

High levels of unmet need and under-treatment

A further distinguishing feature of mental health is the degree to which needs are not currently met. A major household survey of adults in England found that for many conditions, significantly fewer than half of those affected were currently receiving care and support from the mental health system (see Table 12.2). A review by Kohn et al. (2004) of studies conducted across twenty-two countries indicates that similar results are seen internationally, with the 'treatment gap' being particularly high in low- and middle-income countries.

Table 12.2 High levels of unmet need for mental healthcare in England

Condition	Prevalence in adult population (%)	Percentage receiving care
Post-traumatic stress disorder	3.0	28
Psychosis	0.4	80
Personality disorder	0.7	34
Attention deficit hyperactivity disorder	0.6	25
Eating disorders	1.6	23
Alcohol dependence	5.9	14
Cannabis dependence	2.5	14
Dementia	1.6 [a]	48 [b]

Source: Unless otherwise indicated, the numbers given are based on the Adult Psychiatric Morbidity Survey for England (McManus et al., 2009). [a] Prince et al. (2014); [b] Department of Health (2013).

Meeting these unmet needs will require innovative approaches from the healthcare management community, involving new roles for professionals across the system, not only mental health specialists.

Management challenges in mental health

While many of the management challenges presented by mental health are common to other areas, there are particular issues that need to be considered, some of which follow from the distinctive elements described above.

Evidence-based management

A significant limitation in mental health is the paucity of high-quality data. There is often limited measurement of outcomes, and financial and activity data are typically poorer than in other areas. The complex nature of interventions in mental health can also make it harder to assess the effectiveness of care. Finally, there is also less academic research conducted on mental health than on some other forms of care, relative to the size of the disease burden (Saxena et al., 2005). This lack of data and evidence presents a major challenge to healthcare managers involved in the design of services, operational decision-making and service evaluation.

Poor measurement of outcomes and activity has meant that there is often limited knowledge about mental health services in purchasing/commissioning organizations. Limited data have also made it more difficult to introduce forms of accountability common in other areas, such as performance targets.

However, it should not be concluded that mental health is an evidence-free zone. There are some important examples where the evidence base is strong, and where the challenge is more about putting this evidence into practice. For example, in England the Improving Access to Psychological Therapies (IAPT) programme has significantly expanded the provision of psychological therapies where the research evidence is strongest, notably cognitive-behavioural therapy. The programme has also had a major focus on systematic collection of outcomes data using standardized tools as part of routine clinical practice (Clark, 2011).

Working across sectors

Earlier in this chapter we described the extent of medical co-morbidity and social complexity among people using mental health services. What this highlights is the need for close coordination between mental healthcare, physical healthcare, and support for wider social needs. Perhaps even more than in other areas, effective management in mental health involves working across multiple sectors, including health, social care, housing, education and policing. Leaders and managers need to be skilled at building bridges between organizations, seeing the 'bigger picture' and creating a culture of collaborative working in the local health economy. They also need to enable clinical leaders to do the same, in order to strengthen relationships between practitioners working in different sectors.

Learning activity 12.3

Consider a person with poorly controlled diabetes and co-morbid depression or anxiety. Write three or four paragraphs discussing the questions listed below. In answering these questions, you may find it helpful to refer to research on integrated approaches towards physical and mental health by Naylor et al. (2016), and on the skills required for effective system leadership described in Timmins (2015).

- How might their mental health and well-being affect their diabetic outcomes, and vice versa?
- How might social conditions and circumstances exacerbate or ameliorate these problems?
- In your country, what improvements might be needed to ensure this person has their mental, physical and social needs met in a more coordinated way?
- What challenges would healthcare managers encounter in making this vision a reality?

Service user involvement and peer support

An understanding of how the experiences and perspectives of people using services can be used to inform managerial and clinical decision-making is an important competency for any healthcare manager. This has a particular significance within mental health, where there is a very real danger that the experience of using services can be a highly disempowering one. There is a rich history of service user involvement in mental health, from individuals playing an active role in developing a care plan to meet their needs (for example, through the 'care programme approach') to user-led services, through which service users act as both the recipients and providers of care.

Healthcare managers can play an important role in supporting the development and legitimacy of different forms of service user involvement. One area in which this has been particularly successful has been in the development of peer support. Peer support refers to any situation where people with personal experience of mental health problems offer each other support based on their own experience. Although many forms of peer support exist (see Box 12.1), they have in common that they place a particular emphasis on values such as empathy, trust and reciprocity. Peer support workers can promote hope and belief in the possibility of recovery, as well as improving self-esteem and ability to self-manage. Those employed as peer workers can further benefit from increased confidence and improved employment prospects (Repper and Carter, 2010). Although many forms of peer support have grown up outside of mental health services, increasingly it is being seen as an integral component of mental healthcare with professionals and peers working alongside each other towards common goals. Box 12.1 provides examples of peer support in a number of countries.

Box 12.1   Case study – examples of peer support in mental health

Peer support groups are found in many countries. Alamo is one example, set up in Peru in 1999 by an ex-mental health service user. The group consists of families, their relatives and a several voluntary psychologists. The focus of the group is on exchanging personal knowledge, views and experiences to strengthen dignity and respect for human rights. Activities provided are designed to promote mutual support, rehabilitation and social reintegration, and education for family members. Many of these projects develop organically, however support in bringing people together can facilitate the development of groups and small amounts of funding for resources and organizational development can be beneficial in the longer term (Funk et al., 2010).

A second form of peer support is that of self-help groups. These tend to be small self-organizing groups of people coming together around a particular shared need, diagnosis or self-management strategy (Faulkner, 2013). For example, the Hearing Voices network is an international network of individuals interested in, or who have experience of, hearing voices or 'auditory hallucinations'. Established in the UK in 1988 as a group in which individuals came together to talk about the experience of hearing voices, the network now comprises hundreds of similar groups across the world. The purpose of the group is to provide a safe space in which people can share their experiences and support one another, offering an opportunity for people to accept and live with their experiences in a way that helps them regain some power over their lives. Within the groups there is no assumption of illness and all explanations for voices and visions are valued. A core value of Hearing Voices groups is that they are user centred with each member playing a role in determining the direction of the group, keeping it healthy and upholding its ethos. Hearing Voices groups are not setting specific and the network includes independent community groups, voluntary sector organizations, mental health teams, inpatient units, secure mental health units and prisons. Most recently, the network has established online peer support via their website [see http://www.hearing-voices.org/].

A final approach to peer support is user-led crisis provision. While still limited in number, user-led crisis houses have emerged in a number of countries. Many of these have arisen as a response to issues around quality of care in inpatient services. The Leeds Survivor Led Crisis Service was set up by a group of mental health service users in 1999 to provide an alternative to hospital admission for people in acute mental health crisis [see http://www.lslcs.org.uk/]. The service comprises a residential 'crisis house' to which individuals can refer themselves directly for help. The approach to care is directly informed by those with personal experience of mental health problems. It includes a non-directive approach with the recognition that individuals have the resources within themselves to find their own solutions. Initially run in partnership with social services, the service became a registered charity governed and run by its users. It has since expanded to provide online information and support, specific crisis support for black and minority ethnic communities, and peer-led groups to support people in avoiding crises. The Leeds Survivor Led Crisis Service is now well embedded in the local system and provides a comprehensive service to prevent and manage mental health crises, complementing and enhancing statutory provision.

Managing risk

Competing sets of expectations are often placed on mental health professionals and managers. In addition to the primary function of supporting improved outcomes, those involved in delivering specialist mental healthcare are often also expected to play a role in management of risk, both for service users and for the general public. An unusual aspect of mental healthcare is the existence of compulsory treatment, and in most high-income countries (and an increasing number of low- and middle-income countries) there is a detailed legislative framework specifying the circumstances in which this is permissible, and the process that must be followed. An important challenge for healthcare managers is making sure the best possible balance is struck between risk management and therapeutic goals. This can sometimes involve sensitive handling and resisting calls for disproportionate and illiberal restrictions on the freedoms of people experiencing mental health problems. It is also important to be aware that by far the greatest risk posed by people experiencing mental health problems is the risk to themselves.

Stigma and discrimination

Research has repeatedly shown that both service users and mental health professionals face stigma and discrimination (Thornicroft et al., 2007). Many countries have seen improvements in public understanding of mental health over recent years, but there is still a long way to go and research indicates that many healthcare professionals themselves have highly stigmatizing attitudes (Rao et al., 2009). These attitudes affect those working in mental health as well as people using services – clinical jobs in mental health are often seen as less prestigious than equivalent roles in other specialties.

Left unchallenged, there is a danger that these attitudes and prejudices lead to 'ghettoization' of mental health, with other healthcare professionals being reluctant to take responsibility for their role in improving mental health outcomes. Managers need to be prepared to act as champions for mental health, and to promote better understanding across the system. Given the high prevalence and impact of mental ill health in primary care, general acute hospitals and elsewhere, this responsibility falls not only on the shoulders of those managing specialist mental health service, but applies to the healthcare management community generally.

Learning activity 12.4

Referring to other chapters of this book as a guide, create a table comparing management challenges in mental health with those involved in other parts of the healthcare system. In the first column, list challenges that are unique to mental health. In the second column, list challenges that are shared across many areas.

Imagine you are given the task of reviewing mental health provision in your area, with a view to deciding how services need to change to better meet the needs of the local population. Describe the steps you would take to finding out the views of mental health service users on these services and how you could then involve them in identifying the changes that are required.

Future directions for mental health

We conclude this chapter by briefly exploring some of the current trends in mental health service delivery, focusing on integration with other services, public health approaches towards mental health and the use of digital and online technologies in mental health.

Integrated care

Integrated care is an important trend across the health sector, and is seen as a key response to the profound demographic and epidemiological changes occurring globally. Often integrated care refers to integration of health and social care, or primary and secondary healthcare. One of the key arguments we have developed throughout this chapter is that integrated care also needs to involve closer coordination of mental and physical healthcare. Beyond that, there is also a need to integrate mental healthcare more effectively with other public services, including housing, education and policing.

This is an area where there has been increasing innovation in recent years, and there are numerous examples of integrated mental healthcare from a number of countries (Funk and Ivbijaro, 2008). Perhaps the greatest opportunities lie in closer working between mental health and primary care – given that this is where most people with mental health problems are supported. Collaborative care models have been shown to be effective for supporting people with depression in primary care, particularly where there are also co-morbid physical health issues (NICE, 2009). These models involve case management in primary care, a team-based approach with mechanisms to support closer working between generalists and specialists and stepped care protocols allowing escalation to more specialist support where required.

Intermountain Healthcare in the USA provides one example of an organization that has made significant investments in this kind of approach. Its mental health integration (MHI) programme involves primary care practitioners accepting an increased responsibility for providing mental healthcare, with the support of an enhanced multidisciplinary team embedded in primary care (see Box 12.2). Evaluation of the programme has highlighted a significant increase in patient satisfaction, and an estimated five-fold financial return on investment as a result of improved physical health and reduced activity in other parts of the system.

Box 12.2   Case study – a primary care-based approach to mental health: Intermountain Healthcare

Intermountain Healthcare, also referred to in the previous chapter, is a non-profit health system operating in Utah and Idaho, USA. It consists of twenty-two hospitals, a medical group with one hundred and eighty-five primary care clinics, and an affiliated health insurance company.

In the early 2000s, primary care practitioners in Intermountain identified a need for a more effective way of supporting the large number of people presenting to primary care with mental health needs, often alongside a mixture of physical illness, substance abuse problems and complex social circumstances. In response to this, Intermountain developed a mental health integration (MHI) programme, which has now been rolled out in the majority of primary care clinics.

Key elements of the model include:

- Team-based care with mental health professionals embedded in the primary care team, including input from psychiatry, psychology, psychiatric nursing and social work.
- A nurse care manager to coordinate medical, psychological and social support.
- Shared electronic medical records accessible by all team members.
- Proactive screening for mental health problems among high-risk groups in the population.
- Supported self-management of physical and mental health.
- Making use of extended community resources and peer support.
- Using disease registries and evidence-based guidelines.
- Exploiting new technologies, such as telehealth and telecare.

Under MHI, mental healthcare is delivered through a stepped care approach. An assessment algorithm is used to assign people needing support to one of three groups, depending on the level of complexity of their condition and circumstances:

- Mild complexity – managed primarily by the primary care physician with support from a case manager.
- Moderate complexity – receive collaborative care from the MHI team. Often includes people with a physical co-morbidity and those living in an isolated or chaotic social environment.
- High complexity – supported by mental health specialists, either working in primary care settings or with a referral to secondary care.

Overall, about 80 per cent of mental healthcare is delivered by non-specialists in MHI clinics.

Implementing the MHI model has been a significant change management process. The change process has involved making significant investments in training practice staff (including physicians, nurses, receptionists and others) in mental health awareness, empathic communication skills and shared decision-making. This has increased the competence and confidence of primary care practitioners in managing people with mental health problems.

A key lesson from the Intermountain MHI programme is that the implementation of new integrated service models needs to be supported by cultural change. This has required consistent messages from senior leaders within Intermountain aimed at normalizing mental health as a routine part of everyday healthcare.

Evaluations of the MHI model have found significant improvements in both physical and mental health outcomes. Specific findings reported by Reiss-Brennan et al. (2010) include:

- Per patient medical costs in the twelve months following diagnosis of depression were 48% lower in primary care clinics involved in the MHI programme.
- Patients with depression were 54 per cent less likely to attend an emergency department if their primary care clinic is part of the MHI programme.
- A significant reduction in hospital admissions for ambulatory care-sensitive conditions among people accessing mental healthcare.
- Better diabetes control among patients with diabetes and depression.

Public mental health

Earlier in this chapter we provided a definition of mental health as a state of well-being that allows individuals to flourish and lead fulfilling lives. This perspective – that mental health is something positive that can be promoted and enabled, and that the health and social care system has a role in doing so – has received increasing attention in recent years (see, for example, Herrman et al., 2005). One example of this is the growing number of employers who are now investing in creating 'mentally healthy workplaces' that promote well-being in the workforce, including through the use of best practice approaches to line management and providing access to stress management tools and advice. Examples from the Global Healthy Workplace Awards such as EDF and the pharmaceutical company GSK demonstrate the gains that can be achieved from such schemes.

Allied to this is the growing evidence base that preventative actions can be taken to reduce the incidence of mental ill health. An analysis conducted by the London School of Economics and others (Knapp et al., 2011) found that a number of interventions could deliver a significant return on investment by preventing future cases of mental ill health, including:

- schools-based interventions for improving psychological resilience, self-efficacy and interpersonal skills;
- group-based parenting programmes for parents of young children; and
- workplace-based mental health promotion programmes.

A key concept in public mental health is the use of 'asset-based' approaches that draw on the strengths and resources of individuals and the communities they live in. An asset-based approach to public mental health might involve building social capital and connectedness as a means of improving community cohesion and promoting mental health and resilience.

These examples again highlight that some of the most significant opportunities to improve mental health in the future will require joint working across sectors, with the healthcare management community potentially playing a leading role and mobilizing others to support change.

Digital mental health

Digital and online technologies hold the promise of transforming health and healthcare, and mental health is no exception to this. The growing array of online and mobile applications relating to mental health illustrates the breadth of potential uses to which these technologies can be put, including: creating less stigmatizing channels for accessing support; empowering people to manage their own mental health; reducing social isolation through the use of social media and online peer support platforms; giving people much greater access to information; and enhancing clinical management through data sharing (Hollis et al., 2015). The 'ReachOut' website provides one example of an online mental health tool that performs several of these functions (see Box 12.3).

Computer-based psychological therapy is one area that has received significant attention. Packages such as 'Beating the Blues' (a computerized form of cognitive-behavioural therapy for depression) are now widely used and recommended in clinical guidance (NICE, 2006). The Europe-wide 'Mastermind' project is exploring how these kinds of programme can be implemented at scale in nine countries and incorporated into routine clinical practice (see http://mastermind-project.eu/).

Many other aspects of digital mental health have so far been subject to less research. The speed with which these technologies evolve means they can be hard to evaluate using traditional research methodologies. Initiatives such as the MindTech Healthcare Technology Cooperative in the UK seek to address this by bringing together healthcare professionals, researchers, industry and the public to find new ways of developing, testing and adopting new technologies for mental healthcare (see http://www.mindtech.org.uk/).

Despite the gaps in the research base, the potential offered by digital technologies to improve mental health is clear. Much more evidence will be needed if this potential is to be fully realized (Hollis et al., 2015).

Box 12.3   Case study – ReachOut: online mental health support

ReachOut is Australia's leading online provider of mental health support for young people (see http://au.reachout.com/). The service was established by a national charity in direct response to a growing rate of suicide in Australia. ReachOut provides targeted information and practical tools. The website was developed in collaboration with young people and is underpinned by principles taken from cognitive-behavioural therapy and positive psychology. Content covers areas related to well-being such as managing relationships, as well as issues specific to mental health. The website contains a section on getting professional help, with links to relevant agencies and other supporting materials, including fact sheets, stories and videos. An online community forum provides an opportunity to engage with others. The forum has an explicit and reinforced set of guidelines, structured discussion threads and peer supervisors and moderators. Peer supervisors and moderators attend a series of skills and scenario-based training workshops and are supported through supervision. Moderators are trained to recognize and respond to posts that could be harmful and there are clear protocols around any posts stating an intention of harm to self or others (Webb et al., 2008).

ReachOut has since expanded to the United States and Ireland and other similar online support platforms have emerged. The scope of these sites continues to develop with several now including the delivery of structured online therapy programmes, mobile self-monitoring and in some cases the ability to interact directly with healthcare professionals (Kauer et al., 2014).

Conclusion

The World Health Organization and others have long argued that there is 'no health without mental health'. Equally, there are few illnesses or diseases that do not have a mental health component to them – if only in the sense that pain, distress and anxiety are all psychological phenomena. There has been a tendency to regard mental health as a separate and in some ways unusual specialism that sits outside the mainstream of healthcare. As a result, opportunities to improve mental and physical health outcomes in tandem have often been missed.

A key challenge for managers is to ensure that all healthcare professionals have an understanding of mental health and an appreciation of how it is relevant and manifest in their part of the system. As argued above, the mental health system includes primary care and general acute hospitals, in addition to specialist services, and healthcare managers have an important role to play in increasing skills and capacity in these parts of the system, as well as in building links with other public services.

At the same time, there are also specific management challenges relating to specialist mental health services, where significant quality issues often exist, and where stigma and discrimination remain widespread. In many countries, significant improvements have been made in mental healthcare in recent years. Despite this, however, it remains an area in which unmet needs are persistently high, and where healthcare managers can contribute much.

Learning resources

World Health Organization: WHO provides several important resources on mental health, including the *Mental Health Atlas*, which gives comparative statistics on the resources available to prevent and treat mental ill health across one hundred and eighty-four countries, and the Mental Health Gap Action Programme, supporting the scaling up of mental healthcare [http://www.who.int/mental_health/en/].

US National Institute of Mental Health: NIMH is one of the world's leading centres for research on mental health. The NIMH website provides background information on the causes, diagnosis and treatment of specific mental health problems, as well as the latest research findings [https://www.nimh.nih.gov/index.shtml].

Joint Commissioning Panel for Mental Health: A collaboration of seventeen organizations in the UK, providing evidence-based guidance on how to commission mental health services effectively [http://www.jcpmh.info/].

A global perspective on integrating mental health into primary care, with detailed case studies of integrated services from eleven countries, can be found in: Funk, M. and Ivbijaro, G. (2008) *Integrating Mental Health into Primary Care: A Global Perspective.* Geneva: WHO.

Centre for Global Mental Health: The Centre provides a range of resources relating to improving mental health in low-income countries [http://www.centreforglobalmentalhealth.org/].

Time to Change: A UK national anti-stigma and discrimination programme [http://www.time-to-change.org.uk/].

Guidance on making user involvement work in mental health is provided by Branfield, F. and Beresford, P. (2006) *Making User Involvement Work: Supporting Service User Networking and Knowledge.* York: Joseph Rowntree Foundation [http://www.jrf.org.uk/publications/making-user-involvement-work-supporting-service-user-networking-and-knowledge].

References

Barnett, K., Mercer, S.W., Norbury, M., Watt, G., Wyke, S. and Guthrie, B. (2012) Epidemiology of multimorbidity and implications for healthcare, research, and medical education: a cross-sectional study, *Lancet*, 380 (9836): 37–43.

Bottino, C.M., Barcelos-Ferreira, R. and Ribeiz, S.R. (2012) Treatment of depression in older adults, *Current Psychiatry Reports*, 14 (4): 289–97.

Branfield, F. and Beresford, P. (2006) *Making User Involvement Work: Supporting Service User Networking and Knowledge.* York: Joseph Rowntree Foundation [http://www.jrf.org.uk/publications/making-user-involvement-work-supporting-service-user-networking-and-knowledge].

Centre for Mental Health (2010) *The Economic and Social Costs of Mental Health Problems in 2009/10*. London: Centre for Mental Health.

Centre for Mental Health, Rethink and the Royal College of Psychiatrists (2011) *Diversion: The Business Case for Action*. London: Centre for Mental Health.

Clark, D.M. (2011) Implementing NICE guidelines for the psychological treatment of depression and anxiety disorders: the IAPT experience, *International Review of Psychiatry*, 23 (4): 318–27.

Department of Health (2013) *Dementia: A State of the Nation Report on Dementia Care and Support in England*. London: Department of Health [https://www.gov.uk/government/uploads/system/uploads/attachment_data/file/262139/Dementia.pdf].

Faulkner, A. (2013) *Mental Health Peer Support in England: Piecing Together the Jigsaw*. London: Mind.

Funk, M. and Ivbijaro, G. (2008) *Integrating Mental Health into Primary Care: A Global Perspective*. Geneva: WHO.

Funk, M., Drew, N., Freeman, M. and Faydi, E. (2010) *Mental Health and Development: Targeting People with Mental Health Conditions as a Vulnerable Group*. Geneva: WHO.

Gilburt, H., Peck, E. with Ashyon, B., Edwards, N. and Naylor, C. (2014) *Service Transformation: Lessons from Mental Health*. London: King's Fund [http://www.kingsfund.org.uk/sites/files/kf/field/field_publication_file/service-transformation-lessons-mental-health-4-feb-2014.pdf].

Herrman, H., Saxena, S. and Moodie, R. (2005) *Promoting Mental Health: Concepts, Emerging Evidence, Practice*. Geneva: WHO.

Hollis, C., Morriss, R., Martin, J., Amani, S., Cotton, R., Denis, M. et al. (2015) Technological innovations in mental healthcare: harnessing the digital revolution, *British Journal of Psychiatry*, 206 (4): 263–5.

Joint Commissioning Panel for Mental Health (JCPMH) (2012a) *Guidance for Commissioners of Primary Mental Health Care Services* [http://www.jcpmh.info/resource/guidance-for-commissioners-of-primary-mental-health-care-services/].

Joint Commissioning Panel for Mental Health (JCPMH) (2012b) *Guidance for Commissioners of Liaison Mental Health Services to Acute Hospitals* [http://www.jcpmh.info/good-services/liaison-mental-health-services/].

Katon, J.W., Von Korff, M., Lin, E.H.B., Simon, G., Ludman, E., Russo, J. et al. (2004) The Pathways Study: a randomised trial of collaborative care in patients with diabetes and depression, *Archives of General Psychiatry*, 61 (10): 1042–9.

Kauer, S.D., Mangan, C. and Sanci, L. (2014) Do online mental health services improve help-seeking for young people? A systematic review, *Journal of Mental Health Research*, 16 (3): e66.

Kessler, R.C., Amminger, G.P., Aguilar-Gaxiola, S., Alonso, J., Lee, S. and Üstün, T.B. (2007) Age of onset of mental disorders: a review of recent literature, *Current Opinion in Psychiatry*, 20 (4): 359–64.

Knapp, M., McDaid, D. and Parsonage, M. (eds.) (2011) *Mental Health Promotion and Mental Illness Prevention: the Economic Case*. London: LSE.

Kohn, R., Saxena, S., Levav, I. and Saraceno, B. (2004) The treatment gap in mental health care, *Bulletin of the World Health Organization*, 82 (11): 858–66.

Laursen, T.M., Nordentoft, M. and Mortensen, P.B. (2014) Excess early mortality in schizophrenia, *Annual Review of Clinical Psychology*, 10: 425–48.

Marshall, M., Lewis, S., Lockwood, A., Drake, R., Jones, P. and Croudace, T. (2005) Association between duration of untreated psychosis and outcome in cohorts of first-episode patients: a systematic review, *Archives of General Psychiatry*, 62 (9): 975–83.

McManus, S., Meltzer, H., Brugha, T., Bebbington, P. and Jenkins, R. (2009) *Adult Psychiatry Morbidity in England, 2007: Results of a Household Survey.* Leeds: NHS Information Centre.

Moussavi, S., Chatterji, S., Verdes, E., Tandon, A., Patel, V. and Ustun, B. (2007) Depression, chronic diseases, and decrements in health: results from the World Health Surveys, *Lancet*, 370 (9590): 851–8.

Naylor, C., Das, P., Ross, S., Honeyman, M., Thompson, J. and Gilburt, H (2016). *Bringing together physical and mental health. A new frontier for integrated care.* London: King's Fund. Available at: http://www.kingsfund.org.uk/publications/physical-and-mental-health

Naylor, C., Galea, A., Parsonage, M., McDaid, D., Knapp, M. and Fossey, M. (2012) *Long-term Conditions and Mental Health: The Cost of Co-morbidities.* London: King's Fund [http://www.kingsfund.org.uk/publications/long-term-conditions-and-mental-health].

NICE (2006) *Computerised Cognitive Behaviour Therapy for the Treatment of Depression and Anxiety.* Review of Technology Appraisal #51. London: NICE.

NICE (2009) *Depression in Adults with Chronic Physical Health Problems: Treatment and Management.* NICE Clinical Guideline #91. London: National Clinical Guideline Centre.

Petrila, J. (2003) An introduction to special jurisdiction courts, *International Journal of Law and Psychiatry*, 26: 3–12.

Prince, M., Bryce, R., Albanese, E., Wimo, A., Ribeiro, W. and Ferri, C.P. (2013) The global prevalence of dementia: a systematic review and metaanalysis, *Alzheimer's and Dementia*, 9 (1): 63–75.e2.

Prince, M., Knapp, M., Guerchet, M., McCrone, P., Prina, M., Comas-Herrera, A. et al. (2014) *Dementia UK: Update.* London: Alzheimer's Society.

Rao, H., Mahadevappa, H., Pillay, P., Sessay, M., Abraham, A. and Luty, J. (2009) A study of stigmatized attitudes towards people with mental health problems among health professionals, *Journal of Psychiatric and Mental Health Nursing*, 16 (3): 279–84.

Reiss-Brennan, B., Briot, P.C., Savitz, L.A., Cannon, W. and Staheli, R. (2010) Cost and quality impact of Intermountain's mental health integration program, *Journal of Healthcare Management*, 5 (2): 97–113.

Repper, J. and Carter, T. (2010) *Using Personal Experience to Support Others with Similar Difficulties: A Review of the Literature on Peer Support in Mental Health Services.* London: Together for Mental Wellbeing.

Saxena, S., Paraje, G., Sharan, P., Karam, G. and Sadana, R. (2005) The 10/90 divide in mental health research: trends over a 10-year period, *British Journal of Psychiatry*, 188 (1): 81–2.

Social Exclusion Unit (2004) *Mental Health and Social Exclusion.* London: Office of the Deputy Prime Minister.

Thornicroft, G., Rose, D., Kassam, A. and Sartorius, N. (2007) Stigma: ignorance, prejudice or discrimination?, *British Journal of Psychiatry*, 190: 192–3.

Timmins, N. (2015) *The Practice of System Leadership: Being Comfortable with Chaos.* London: The King's Fund [http://www.kingsfund.org.uk/publications/practice-system-leadership].

Webb, M., Burns, J. and Collin, P. (2008) Providing online support for young people with mental health difficulties: challenges and opportunities explored, *Early Intervention in Psychiatry*, 2: 108–13.

World Health Organization (WHO) (2001) *Strengthening Mental Health Promotion.* Fact Sheet #220. Geneva: WHO.

Chapter 13

Social care

Stephanie Kumpunen and Gerald Wistow

Introduction

Health and social services across a number of countries are increasingly expected to deliver integrated people-centred, holistic care. However, a fundamental stumbling block on the health side can be a lack of understanding of the values, purposes and organization of social care services. While 'health' and 'healthcare services' are internationally accepted terms, associated with commonly understood definitions and interventions, 'social care services' is less universally applied or recognized. For example, the term is used interchangeably with social services, social welfare, social protection, social assistance, social care, personal social services and social work (Munday, 2003).

In England, as in other countries, provision of social care services is organizationally divided between children's and adults' services, the latter comprising personal (often intimate) care and practical support for older people, adults with physical disabilities, learning disabilities, or physical or mental illnesses, as well as support for their carers (National Audit Office, 2014). Some of the core adult social care services available in England include:

- the delivery of meals where individuals are no longer able to prepare their own food;
- transport to and from a day centre where socializing and activities are undertaken among people with similar capacities for a half or full day;
- the delivery of care in an individual's home, also known as domiciliary care or home care, which enables individuals to continue living at home, where this is their preference and they are able to do so with support;
- care and accommodation in a residential home for individuals who require significant personal care and support, but whom require few daily medical interventions; and
- care, accommodation and nursing support in residential homes staffed by nurses and care workers, sometimes also called nursing homes.

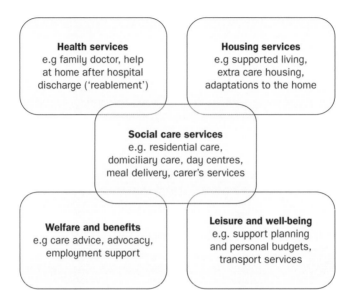

Figure 13.1 Overlap between social care services and other public services
Source: Adapted from National Audit Office (2014)

As adults often have many interrelated care needs, social care is part of a complex system of related public services and forms of support (National Audit Office, 2014). Figure 13.1 illustrates the common connections between social care services and other care and support services, namely health, housing, welfare and benefits and leisure and well-being. From a health sector perspective, Figure 13.1 highlights the importance of recognizing that social care services have to manage interdependencies with a wide range of services as well as health services. In addition, each of these services will have a range of responsibilities and goals, not all of which can be assumed to be mutually reinforcing or complementary.

Across country settings, the translations for services and their location within public care and support systems will vary. For example, the concept of 'long-term care' overlaps with large parts of the social care sector and provides a more generic synonym that is commonly used in North America and in OECD (Organization for Economic Cooperation and Development) publications to describe a blend of three services for people with a reduced degree of functional capacity (either physical or cognitive) and who are consequently dependent for an extended period of time (OECD/European Commission, 2013):

- personal care services (such as bathing, dressing, eating and using the bathroom);
- basic medical prevention (such as rehabilitation or palliative care); and
- lower level care (such as help with housework, meals and transportation).

'Long-term care' is often used in systems where health and social care are administratively integrated into single government departments, such as in Germany, the United States and parts of Canada. In these areas, long-term care is seen as services distinct from acute care that help individuals to compensate for disability and functional impairment. Their long-term nature means that services become 'enmeshed in the very fabric of people's lives', unlike with acute care where lifestyles may be only temporarily disrupted (Kane et al., 1998).

Regardless of the terminology, social care services provide care and support to some of the most vulnerable and distressed people in society. The largest group of service users across the world is older people, and approximately half of all service users are aged eighty years or more (Colombo et al., 2011). Other groups of social care service users include the disabled, both children and working-age adults. These are often the same people for whom good health services are vital to quality of life and improvements in health status.

The remainder of this chapter is divided into four sections, each accompanied by a learning activity. The first section discusses the nature and scope of social care services, so that readers can gain an understanding of the differences between health and social care services, the values inherent to social care services, and the public and private bodies that fund, plan and deliver social care services in different national settings. The second highlights distinctive elements of social care services and how historical welfare systems have shaped modern-day provision. The third highlights some of the enduring themes and challenges within social care policy. The final section focuses on perhaps the most substantial of those challenges from a health service perspective: how to ensure health and social care services are integrated to deliver person-centred, cost-effective outcomes.

Learning activity 13.1

- Create a list of the types of social care service and support available in your country, and describe the aim of each of them in two or three sentences.
- Which kinds of social care service and support might help you, as a health service manager, to achieve the goals of your organization and why?
- Which health service inputs might help a social care organization to achieve its goals?

The nature and scope of social care

Goals and values of social care services

In many countries, one of the core goals of social care services is that they should enable an individual to meet their needs and preferences holistically. For this reason, assessment and care planning is expected to take into consideration the context of how they live the whole of their lives, including their physical functionality, their pastimes and hobbies, and their social networks. In addition to these individual characteristics, assessments should also include consideration of an individual's social, economic and physical environments:

- *Social environment*: informal care and support available within the home and the community, including the support that family can provide, as well as that which can be provided by friends or local volunteer organizations or care agencies.

- *Economic environment*: the assets and income available to an individual, or in some countries, the assets and income available to a couple (such as in France) or the wider family (such as in Italy) to determine how they can contribute to the costs of care – either in full or in part.
- *Physical environment*: the structure and design of the home environment, including the presence or lack of fitted equipment to help with mobility, and proximity to services, if delivered outside of the home.

Ideally, therefore, the planning and delivery of social care will be organized around the whole person and the various environments in which they live. As a result, the goals of social care are not limited to providing care services in response to specified needs. They also aim to:

- promote an individual's sense of well-being and quality of life, rather than simply secure improved capacities for self-care or compensate for their deterioration;
- encourage and sustain feelings of independence by building on an individual's personal strengths and assets to achieve desired outcomes, such as meaningful social relationships and self-confidence to live at home for as long as possible;
- advocate on behalf of people who experience difficulties in expressing their own voice, including those who are frail, disabled or vulnerable in other ways;
- treat service users as equal partners in their care and support and empower them to take control of their lives;
- respect the dignity of service users in the way personal and intimate care is provided; and
- recognize the needs of informal carers, such as family or friends (Kane et al., 1998).

These goals of social care services and the values that underpin them are exhibited in the *functions* of social care services and stem from the *social model of care*, both of which are described below.

Functions of social care services

The functions of social care services and social workers (or care managers/coordinators) vary with the context in different countries. For example, in systems with many private providers, social work has a bigger brokerage role to help service users to choose care. Despite system-level differences, many common functions are fulfilled by social care services, as Box 13.1 demonstrates.

The differences between health and social care

Health service provision has tended to be dominated by biomedical models of health, and their focus on diagnosing and responding to primarily physical symptoms of disease and disability among individuals. Social care services, by way of contrast, are intended to focus on the whole person in the context of the physical, economic and social contexts in which they live and their relationships with others. In the traditional medical model, social care is viewed

---

Box 13.1 Functions of social care services

- **Protection** – of children, older people and disabled people and their carers who might be at risk in some way.
- **Provision of care and support** – a central role of social care in most countries, although the form it might take and who might provide this varies across regions.
- **Signposting, gatekeeping and rationing** – where care is not universally provided to all residents, local governments are responsible for determining the point at which they will step in to provide publicly funded services. When people are ineligible for publicly funded care, local governments are still responsible for signposting individuals to appropriate services.
- **Decision-making** – often in collaboration with the cared-for person about whether care and support will be provided in-kind or whether cash benefits will be offered instead.
- **Brokerage** – care and support is not always provided by the state and therefore social workers have a role in creating links between potential service users and providers. With the increase in the numbers of personal budgets, this is becoming even more pronounced.
- **Coordinating whole-person care within a mixed economy of supply** – to avoid fragmentation of services across a range of providers specializing in one aspect of direct care, local governments often play a strong role in keeping together a package of care.
- **Support for daily living at home, in the community and in residential settings** – although this occurs less often than in the past, many local governments provide direct care to service users and their carers.
- **Regulation** – in mixed economies of care, local government may have a role in overseeing and regulating providers of care services, potentially through contracting mechanisms.
- **Community development** – social care traditionally has played a role in attempting to halt social exclusion through the development of local networks and communities of carers.
- **Resource mobilization and community capacity building** – local governments often work with local community and volunteer groups to develop their roles in care provision and the development of local networks for cared-for persons as well as carers.

Source: Adapted from Dickinson and Glasby (2011).

---

as predominantly an adjunct to health services, enabling them to fulfil their goals of, for example, increasing the number of safe and timely discharges from hospital or reducing avoidable admissions, rather than as separate services with a wider range of distinct purposes.

The suggestion that social care services are merely an add-on to formal medical care has had a significant impact on the ways in which social care services are funded, planned and understood by the public. This view fails to recognize the positive externalities that have arisen from the development of the social care sector, such as the enlargement of the volunteer sector and the increase in the numbers and types of community networks available to support people and their carers. In addition, the social care model considers impairment and disability as a product of social factors, including physical, organizational and social worlds that perpetuate discrimination of people who need support to carry out daily functions (French, 1993; Oliver, 1996).

Among other significant differences between health and social care services, the former is generally considered to be a public responsibility, free at the point of use or subject to small copayments. By contrast, social care is still often means tested, subject to copayments based on levels of assets or income. This may be because most people will need to access healthcare, many at more than one point in their life. However, only one in three people will need social care, often as a result of health problems, and usually only at the end of their lives. The majority, therefore, will not need social care at all (Comas-Herrera, 2012).

The health and social care sectors also tend to have different histories, cultures and organizational frameworks. Most healthcare professionals have traditionally undertaken specialist roles based on training and formal qualifications, whereas in social care services most care is provided by unpaid carers, and where paid (formal) carers are involved they undertake more generic caring tasks learned during basic qualification or training in the role (Comas-Herrera, 2012).

Learning activity 13.2

- Construct a table to identify and compare the principal elements of the social and medical models of care in your country. Building on Learning activity 13.1, this could include contrasting, for example, aims of models, types of service users, and types of professional involved.
- Write a paragraph explaining the strengths of the social model and its relevance to health service policy development in your country.
- Write a further paragraph setting out what you think the social model could contribute to healthcare provision in your country.

Actors and activities

A wide range of actors operate at multiple levels involved in the funding, planning and delivery of social care services (Ranci and Pavolini, 2012). At the supranational level, joint governments (where they exist), such as the European Union, often have a responsibility to provide guidance to member states or regions, and collect data on the costs and types of care available.

At the national level, key actors include the politicians and civil servants responsible for social care services. Their responsibilities often include setting national eligibility criteria for publicly funded services and cash benefits (an increasingly popular alternative to in-kind services discussed on pp. 234–243). In addition, they may set the national statutory framework of needs that will be covered, services provided, resources raised, and statutory quality requirements for providers. In countries with decentralized structures, some or all of these tasks may be devolved to sub-national levels, such as regional, provincial or local levels. Therefore, local governments are often responsible for planning of services for the area they serve, based on the identification of local needs, as well as collection of their own revenue to fund care. Historically, local governments have also been the major providers of care services, but increasingly they contract out that responsibility to for-profit and not-for-profit agencies (Ranci and Pavolini, 2012).

In some countries, private and third sector actors can be heavily influential as well, yet in others equivalent actors may not exist or play a significant role. For example, in Italy and surrounding areas of high Italian migration (e.g. Switzerland), advisory services provided by trade union offices, *patronati*, are heavily relied upon to complete applications for cash benefits available at the national level (Bolzman, 2011). The location of these offices within industries ties together old age and working age benefits, a common arrangement in southern European countries with less well-established formal services.

Applying a simplified categorization of roles and responsibilities to public actors across Europe, Table 13.1 highlights the key organizations responsible for health and social care services at national, regional, provincial and local levels in England, France and Italy (Pavolini and Ranci, 2013).

Informal carers constitute another key actor in social care. In many countries, regardless of the level of access to formal services, informal carers are the main providers of care for frail, older and disabled people. The sheer number of informal carers and hours of care they provide merits detailed discussions about their contributions to the sector. Estimates of the number of informal carers vary, but it has been suggested that 70–90 per cent of all informal carers are family members (Fujisawa and Colombo, 2009) and that the most intense types of

Table 13.1 Comparison of public actors and their responsibilities in England, France and Italy

	England	France	Italy
National	**Department of Health** creates legislation and policy, funds benefits and the National Health Service. **Department for Work and Pensions** funds universal benefits.	**Caisse nationale de solidarité pour l'autonomie (CNSA)** (National Solidarity Fund for Autonomy) provides funding for benefits for 'dependent' older people.	**Istituto Nazionale della Previdenza Sociale (INPS)** (Italian National Social Security Institute) undertakes financial assessments and funds a universal needs-based benefit 'Indennità di accompagnamento' (Companionship indemnity).

(*continued*)

Table 13.1 (*continued*)

	England	France	Italy
Regional	**N/A**	**PRogramme Interdépartemental d'ACcompagnement des handicaps et de la perte d'autonomie (PRIAC)** (Disability and Loss of Autonomy Assistance Programme) puts policies in place to develop long-term care services, and predicts the needs for care homes with nursing.	**Regional authorities** create healthcare guidelines and hold a budget that is given to departments/provinces to pay for direct health and social care services and that can be applied to by local authorities for individual service user benefits.
Department/province	**N/A**	The **departmental authorities** define policies, plan and coordinate and finance a large part of the personalized allowance for autonomy (APA) benefit. **Direction Départementale de la Solidarité et de la Prévention (DDSP)** (Departmental Directorate of Solidarity and Prevention) assesses the application for APA, undertakes dependency assessments with a health and social care team, creates a care plan and agrees on the level of benefits.	**Azienda Unità Sanitaria (AUSL)** (local health authority) liaises with local authorities to deliver integrated health and social care services. AUSLs also house the national disability assessment team and commissioning team, the latter of which is responsible for regional fund-related applications.
District/local authority/municipality	**Local authorities or 'councils'** (152 across England) fund and commission and provide social care. **Clinical commissioning groups (CCGs)** fund and commission and provide healthcare via the National Health Service.	**Caisse primaire d'assurance maladie (CPAM)** (Primary Health Insurance Fund) acts as the first point of contact for the healthcare and social services systems. Frontline staff register older EU migrants if residency criteria are fulfilled, and provide information and advice if not.	**Local health authorities** assess physical need with local social care authorities and provide care. **Municipalities** assess physical need in collaboration with local AUSLs and assess finances for the regional budget and hold their own budgets to help residents with copayments.

Source: Adapted from Trigg et al. (2013).

care are usually provided by people living within the same household (Colombo et al., 2011). On average across Europe, about 6 per cent of the population aged fifty or over provides care to an older relative (Riedel and Kraus, 2011).

Attitudes towards caring roles, together with the breadth and depth of social care benefits and entitlements, shape the size of the 'workforce' of informal carers, and the influence of these factors varies between countries. In Denmark, for example, there are twice as many family carers as employees in the formal social care services sector. By comparison, in countries such as Canada, the Netherlands, New Zealand and USA, family carers are estimated to be more than ten times the size of the formal care workforce (Colombo et al., 2011).

Providing care as a family member can lead to direct and indirect costs, such as those related to lost working days and forgone career opportunities. Other costs to carers include the effects of caring on their own mental or physical health. Moreover, in some countries (e.g. France, Germany, Italy and Slovak Republic), family members may be required to contribute financially to the cost of formal care when cared-for individuals cannot meet the costs of their own care.

Many countries have started to give more explicit recognition and support to informal carers and the burdens they experience. As a result, it is increasingly common for the state to offer a range of (often small) cash and in-kind benefits and services. Cash benefits are, however, often well below the national minimum wage for experienced adult employees. For example, in Ireland in 2014/15, care allowance was valued at between €204 and €358.50 per week depending on the age of the carer and number of care recipients (Courtin et al., 2014), while an average weekly wage in the human health and social work activities sector was €666 (Central Statistics Office, 2015).

Learning activity 13.3

Compare in tabular or bullet point form the social care sector in the system where you live and/or work and that in one other country in respect of the following features:

- role and functions of national, regional and local government bodies; and
- contribution of informal care, state and independent sectors.

History and models of social care services

Until the 1990s, across Europe the rights of people needing social care and support were not well recognized; their identities were shaped as 'dependent family members' or 'social assistance recipients', and the act of caring for them was frequently constructed as a moral obligation of families and civil society, and specifically the responsibility of women rather than men (Leira and Saraceno, 2002; Pavolini and Ranci, 2013). To policy-makers and governments, the provision of care and support was mainly considered a private obligation or an individual (or community-based) activity. The state's involvement was frequently restricted to cases of particular vulnerability and risk, such as for people with a lack of family ties and living in poverty, or with a very high level of disability (Daly and Lewis, 1998; Finch, 1989). In some countries, such as the UK, many of the most disabled lived in care institutions that were run by faith or voluntary organizations or, indeed, health services (Thane, 2009).

Following the Second World War, there was a heightened awareness of the needs of disabled people, which led to the development of national charities and legislation to support the disabled, and over time local government began working with the voluntary sector (Thane, 2009). In the 1980s, societies began to worry about the implications of ageing population structures and skills shortages for the sustainability of formal and informal care. Later, in the 1990s, it became widely recognized that the increasing proportion of women in full- or part-time employment, together with growing levels of geographical mobility, were reducing the number of potential informal carers (Colombo et al., 2011). These factors drove a shift in thinking about caring responsibilities.

Yet, at the same time, pressures on social care were being further intensified by the influence of a number of other factors, including the weak status of social rights to care and support services, the historical underdevelopment of care service infrastructures and restrictions on developing more comprehensive social care systems owing to inadequate resources. This became recognized as the 'care deficit' or 'care crisis'. Overall, a tension became clear between discussions about levels of entitlements and the actual level of provision on the ground (Pavolini and Ranci, 2013).

From the 1990s, new models of care began evolving gradually from social assistance and the healthcare systems to fill in gaps in the availability of family care. For some countries, social care services are part of the private sphere, where family and friends are mainly responsible for providing unpaid care (for country examples, see the family care model in Box 13.2), while other countries consider social care services as a collective responsibility (for country examples, see the Scandinavian model in Box 13.2) (Colombo et al., 2011).

Esping-Andersen (1990) famously developed a three-fold categorization of welfare regimes to encompass all welfare states:

- liberal (e.g. USA),
- corporatist-statist (e.g. Germany), and
- social democratic (e.g. Sweden).

Anttonen and Sipilä (1996) added to this literature by analysing volumes of elderly institutional care and home help services, together with levels of children's day care and preschool services in the late 1980s. They suggested that there were two clear models of social services – the Scandinavian model and the family care model. Others included the British means-tested model and the European subsidiarity model (e.g. Germany, Netherlands and potentially also Belgium and France).

In the Scandinavian model, universal social care services are abundant and local government occupies a key role in funding and planning of care, but voluntary organizations and family child minders are also involved on the production side. For-profit commercial entities are essentially non-existent. In the family care model, there is a limited supply of formal social care services and most services are provided informally or on the grey market, and the wealthy purchase private commercial services. Companies provide services for their staff and public authorities play a modest role.

Since Anttonen and Sipilä's (1996) work, a number of researchers have contributed to discussions of welfare state regimes. For example, the Southern model has also been used to describe the family care model associated with countries such as Italy, Portugal, Spain and Greece, where the family network is important in care provision (Ferrera, 1996). Munday (2003) provides a detailed description of four common models, which are summarized in Box 13.2.

Box 13.2   Models of social care services in European welfare states

The **Scandinavian model** of public services (e.g. Sweden, Denmark, Norway and Finland) is based on the principle of universalism, meaning that regardless of the income or the age of an individual, those with levels of need or care that meet defined criteria should be eligible for care. In principle, services are offered to all residents, but most commonly service users are older people, people with disabilities and children. The system is funded by tax and social insurance contributions, which are usually classed as progressive, meaning that individuals with higher incomes contribute higher proportions to the fund. This allows individuals with lower incomes to be financially protected from the risks of contribution, but to also benefit from services. Local government often plays a strong role in planning and delivery, with limited commercial and voluntary sector involvement. This type of model is seen as being strong on service user rights compared with other models, but has come under challenge in recent years due to economic and political factors with regard to the concept of universalism.

The **family care model** (e.g. Greece, Spain, Portugal, Italy, Cyprus, Malta) tends to be based on limited state provision and an emphasis on family responsibility for care, often linked to the Catholic tradition and some use of established voluntary organizations. This model is criticized for relying on female informal carers and for service users lacking a voice.

The **means-tested model** (e.g. the UK and to some extent Ireland), also sometimes known as the safety net system, is typified by providing publicly funded support to only those unable to afford services and those with the appropriate levels of need. Access to services is limited. Individuals are often means or asset tested before they are able to access publicly funded services, which creates incentives to asset depletion and income minimization. They are usually very cash-constrained systems, and unresponsive to changes in need. There is often a limited role for the state in terms of direct service provision, with this being delivered on contract with providers from other sectors. Resources predominantly go to individuals with limited resources of their own and the greatest needs.

The **Northern European subsidiarity model** (e.g. Germany, Austria, the Netherlands and to some extent France and Belgium) provides services mainly through commercial and voluntary organizations and the state plays a major role in financing these. The family also often has a strong primary responsibility for care, although there are variations between countries.

Source: Adapted from Munday (2003).

In reality, many countries blend a variety of funding sources for social care services, making it difficult to say that, for example, universal systems are purely tax funded. Approaches to care provision have also moved on recently. Many argue, for example, that universalism was important for the dissolution of a traditional class society after the Second World War, whereas diversity and selectivism are more suited for contemporary society and universalism no longer exists due to the more widespread introduction of rationing and copayments in many systems (Anttonen et al., 2012).

Enduring themes and challenges for managers

The boundaries between health and social care

Hospital care has always been more generously funded than social care services, and coordination between the two has been challenging (Gorsky, 2013). The relationship between health and social care models is aptly captured in an English report's description of community care services as 'a poor relation: everybody's distant relative but nobody's baby' (Griffiths, 1988: iv). This picture is not dissimilar to that elsewhere: the medical model dominates health and care systems in many countries, and social care services are viewed as adjuncts to health services (as discussed on pp. 234–236).

Tensions of national policies versus local implementation

In many countries, there is a tension between national and local bodies in the funding, planning and delivery of care. National bodies often define minimum standards and criteria for determining service user eligibility for care services across the country and it is then up to local bodies and the staff within them to subjectively interpret eligibility based on their local situation, which often means weighing results of a needs assessment against the financial resources available in the local budget and the local provider market.

For service users, the operation of bureaucratic discretion combined with the localization of supply means that, in practice, service entitlements may vary across different local areas – and it is not always easy to know which types of care are available where, a situation that is further compounded where rules for copayment are set locally rather than nationally. The local variations resulting from decades of decentralized implementation of social care policies in Nordic countries has recently meant that many are trying to recentralize many aspects of care (Trydegård and Thorslund, 2010). In England, the 2014 Care Act has similarly sought to reduce local variations in eligibility criteria by introducing a single national framework in an attempt to reduce the effect of 'the postcode lottery', as it is known. As both these examples highlight, the tension between local autonomy and national standards is never far below the surface in social care even though they are frequently parts of devolved structures.

Self-directed service delivery

In the 1990s, public service provision of traditional residential and home-based social care services came in for criticism in many Western countries for being unreceptive to the voices of service users and dominated by the interests of providers rather than service users, as well as being paternalistic and bureaucratic. In response to these criticisms, many governments (e.g. Austria, England, France, Germany, Italy, the Netherlands, Sweden) began to introduce policies to personalize care services to individuals' preferences and needs, and enable self-determination through systems of direct payments and personal budgets. These forms of payment allow social care services users to receive the cash equivalent of directly provided services with which to purchase their own care or hire their own staff. The experiences of the Netherlands and England are described below.

In the Netherlands, the *persoongebonden* budget (personal budget) was piloted in 1995 and adopted in 2001, which meant that anyone needing home care could choose a personal budget, traditional in-kind services or a mix of the two. Personal budget holders were allowed to spend their budget on professional care (from any care provider, private or public) or to employ a professional or an informal caregiver (Da Roit and Le Bihan, 2010). The average budget amounted to €43,000 for those assessed for residential care and €12,000 for the others, and if the personal budget was depleted, users were required to pay privately for any additional care themselves. Between 2002 and 2010, the number of personal budget holders increased tenfold from 13,000 to 130,000, while spending increased on average by 23 per cent a year from €0.4 billion to €2.2 billion (a rate that was much faster than for those without budgets). As a result, eligibility criteria became more restrictive and only people who require nursing or residential accommodation have been able to keep their budget or apply for one (van Ginneken et al., 2012).

In England, a limited form of personal budget, or 'direct payment', was introduced from the late 1990s (Davey et al., 2007), but it was not piloted fully across all adult social care groups until 2005 (Glendinning et al., 2008) and rolled out universally in 2008. The following year, the initiative was extended to the NHS and, following the results of a pilot programme (Forder et al., 2012), is being rolled out across the country. The most recent development, from 2015, has been the introduction of a programme to pilot integrated personal budgets for both health and social care.

Marketization and choice

Since the 1970s, pressures on public finances and enthusiasm for neoliberal ideas about privatization and competition in care markets among non-state providers of care have led many governments over time to eliminate their roles as care providers and outsource care or advice services previously provided by public sector employees. Now, over 40 per cent of residential care is provided by private for-profit companies in Germany and Finland, and that figure is over 80 per cent in England. Furthermore, over 40 per cent and 60 per cent of home care is provided by private for-profit providers in Denmark and Germany respectively (Marczak and Wistow, 2015). The competition and consumer choice that is provided through the development of markets of multiple private providers, in theory, bring about greater efficiency and enhanced quality of care in providers and markets as a whole (as lower quality providers are not selected by service users and exit the market). Yet there are many who worry that choice policies can increase inequity and social exclusion, as some of the most vulnerable people making choices in care markets will not be equipped to do so independently (see, for example, Glendinning, 2008). This may be because the type or level of their needs affects their ability to express demand and exercise consumer sovereignty at the appropriate point in time, or because social care is not a field in which individuals necessarily make sufficient purchases to become experienced consumers (Wistow et al., 1996).

Striking a balance between residential and domiciliary care

The preferred setting for care for most service users is in the home. For this reason, 'de-institutionalization' has been advocated to promote the self-determination of service users (recognizing the voice and choice of service users to stay at home) and reduce costs (relative to institutional care). Yet with longer life spans and increasing incidence of dementia, the demand for residential settings that can meet high-level needs is unlikely to change significantly (Yeandle et al., 2012). Due to system structures and attitudes towards care, there is large variation in residential care around the world. For example, in OECD countries, Belgium, Australia, the Netherlands and Switzerland have the highest rates of recipients of residential care at just above 6 per cent of the population aged sixty-five years and older, while Italy, Poland and Portugal provide very limited residential care for the same populations. Israel and Switzerland have the highest rates of home care for the same populations at around 20 per cent and 14 per cent respectively, while Canada, Slovakia and Ireland provide almost no home care (Marczak and Wistow, 2015) (see Figure 13.2).

Learning activity 13.4

- Based on the analysis provided in this chapter, construct a list of the main policy challenges you think currently face the social care sector in your own country's health and social care system.
- What do you consider to be the main practice issue that needs to be addressed within the social care sector of your country? What measures would you suggest as a way of addressing this issue?
- What personal qualities and expertise would you anticipate needing to develop if you were to become an effective manager in the social care services sector in your country?

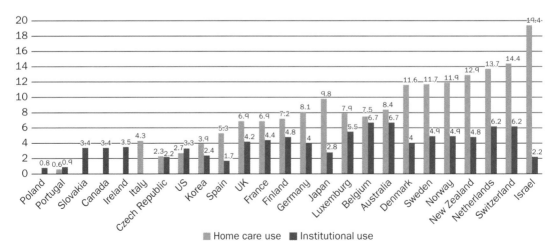

Figure 13.2 Publicly funded services for users receiving care at home versus in institutions as a percentage of population aged 65 and over in selected OECD countries, 2012 or the latest year available

Source: Adapted from Marczak and Wistow (2015), drawing on OECD Health Data Statistics

Relationships between health and social care: the English case

In this final section, we focus on the role of social care in relation to health service policy and delivery, using the example of England as a case study of approaches aimed at enabling more effective working between social care and health services.

We noted at the outset that improved integration between health and social care was increasingly becoming a priority for health managers. In England, as elsewhere, this objective has a long history, although it is shaped in particular by the establishment of the NHS as a separate, national organization responsible for local service delivery but managed from central government and accountable to ministers. By contrast, social care is the responsibility of multi-purpose, elected local government bodies, although the bulk of their funding comes from central government. A further point of difference is that while health services are intended to be comprehensive and are free at the point of access, social care services are neither. Rather, they are provided in accordance with published eligibility (rationing) criteria and following a locally administered means test, which determine financial eligibility to receive publicly funded support in whole or alongside user copayments. In recent years, copayments have increased and eligibility criteria tightened in many authorities following reductions in funding (Fernández et al., 2013).

These differences of structure, culture and accountability provide the management framework within which the philosophies and interests of the core health service and social care professions (medicine and social work) are deployed. In this sense, the English case provides a particular administrative and political context within which more universal inter-professional interests come into play. However, all relationships between health services and social care operate within some configuration of structural, financial and political systems, even where the services are located within the same apparently unified structure. In fact, England provides an example of the persistence of barriers to joint working and the dominance of health service priorities in an apparently unified structure.

National policy in England under both current and previous governments has been to support the expansion of integrated care at 'scale and pace' in order to provide improved outcomes for individuals and their families while also contributing to the financial sustainability of the NHS. The most recent national integrated care initiatives have taken two forms: establishing 'integrated care and support pioneers' in twenty-five areas deemed capable of rapid progress to share universally so that integrated care 'becomes the norm in the next five years' (National Collaboration for Integrated Care and Support, 2013); and second, a national Better Care Fund (BCF) under which the NHS and councils are required to create pooled budgets using health service funds, which can be topped up by councils if they wish.

It is still too early to assess definitively the success of either initiative (but see, for example, Erens et al., 2015; Wistow et al., 2015). The first full year of operating the BCF is 2015/16 and was designed as both an incentive for integrated planning (especially to reduce avoidable hospital admissions and lengths of stay) and also to compensate for central government cuts in council spending. Where policy for the NHS required a shift in activity from hospitals to the community, and thus in the balance of spending, macro public spending policy has protected the NHS while cutting local government expenditure. The BCF is, therefore, an attempt to square that circle by using protected NHS resources to fund jointly planned social care and other relevant local authority services. However, local authority spending is due to fall by another 20 per cent by 2019/20 and NHS spending is already under substantial pressure from increasing demand, despite small real terms growth in past and planned NHS spending (Innes and Tetlow, 2015; King's Fund, 2015). It remains to be seen whether the BCF can provide a sufficient mechanism to mitigate the fundamental incoherence between government policies for the respective roles of health and social care policies, on the one hand, and public expenditure priorities, on the other.

What is more certain, however, is that squaring this policy circle will depend on the achievement of more universally effective integration of planning and service delivery systems than currently exists. As the interim report from the early evaluation of the integration pioneers concluded, this outcome cannot be guaranteed in a fiscal environment that necessitates ever closer integration but creates incentives to protect, rather than share, resources and shift demand to other agencies (Erens et al., 2015). Moreover, while the policy imperative to integrate is urgent, a realistic timescale for implementing new models and balances of care is more long term, depending as it does on organizational redesign and change in the cultures and working practices of front line staff. Moreover, the removal of significant barriers to locally integrated service design and delivery requires the modification of national policies and systems, such as those relating to professional roles and training, payment systems, information sharing and governance, whole systems commissioning and competition between providers (Erens et al., 2015; Wistow et al., 2015).

This brief overview of integration between social care and the NHS in England illustrates some of the basic management challenges for health managers and their partners. If health service managers are to work effectively with their social care counterparts, they need to operate in resource environments that support their respective roles and in organizational environments that enable them to work with, rather than against, the grain of the operating systems in which they have to work. Local skills and competences are no less essential but will be of little consequence unless deployed in appropriately designed environments.

Learning activity 13.5

- Prepare a list of bullet points setting out the case for merging the social and healthcare sectors into a single administrative structure together with a second list summarizing the case against such an action.
- List the main drivers for health managers seeking to ensure effective working relationships between the health and social care sectors in the system where you live and/or work.
- Write a brief analysis of an integrated care initiative in your country, setting out what seems to have facilitated or inhibited its progress to date.

Conclusion

We have noted above that social care services have a set of values and principles distinct from health services. Social care services aim to provide a wide range of care and support functions to empower people to live independent lives and participate fully in communities of their choice. To secure these objectives, commissioners and providers operate within complex networks of agencies in the statutory, independent and community sectors. In some jurisdictions, social care is incorporated within health service structures. In others, the emphasis is on integrating care at the level of individuals without integrating organizational structures. As populations age and the number of people with co-morbidities grows, health services will increasingly depend on the availability of resilient care and support systems that combine the formal social care and less formal community resources needed to meet these changing patterns of disease and disability. In such circumstances, it is vital that health service managers understand both the potential contribution of social care and also possess the skills necessary to work with it more effectively.

Learning resources

Organization for Economic Cooperation and Development: The mission of the OECD is to promote policies that will improve the economic and social well-being of people around the world [www.oecd.org]. The OECD Health Division specifically examines challenges affecting long-term care (LTC) systems and services, focusing in particular on the elderly population. The webpage http://www.oecd.org/els/health-systems/long-term-care.htm provides all information on ongoing and past work on LTC.

Personal Social Services Research Unit: The PSSRU is based across three English universities: the University of Kent, the London School of Economics and the University of Manchester [www.pssru.ac.uk]. Since 1974, it has undertaken high-quality, independent research on adults' and children's health and social care, including mental health, long-term care funding, cost and outcome measurement and cost-effectiveness evaluation.

International Long-term care Policy Network: The ILPN is a network of researchers, policy-makers and other stakeholders with the aim of promoting the global exchange of evidence and knowledge on long-term care (LTC) policy [www.ilpnetwork.org]. ILPN was launched in September 2010 and is based at the London School of Economics (LSE). The ILPN is the first network of its kind to provide an interface between researchers, policy-makers and other stakeholders facilitating contributions to and sharing of evidence for shaping LTC policies and practice.

References

Anttonen, A. and Sipilä, J. (1996) European social care services: is it possible to identify models?, *Journal of European Social Policy*, 6 (2): 87–100.

Anttonen, A., Häikiö, L., Stefánsson, K. and Sipilä, J. (2012) Universalism and the challenge of diversity, in A. Anttonen, L. Häikiö and K. Stefánsson (eds.) *Welfare State, Universalism and Diversity*, Cheltenham: Edward Elgar.

Bolzman, C. (2011) Democratization of ageing: also a reality for elderly immigrants?, *European Journal of Social Work*, 15: 97–113.

Central Statistics Office (CSO) (2015) Average Weekly Earnings (Euro) by Type of Employee. Cork: CSO.

Colombo, F., Llena-Nozal, A., Mercier, J. and Tjadens, F. (2011) *Help Wanted? Providing and Paying for Long-term Care.* Paris: OECD.

Comas-Herrera, A. (2012) *Financing and organising long-term care.* Prentation to Finanziare e organizzare l'assistenza continuativa agli anziani in Europa e in Italia, 2012. Rome: LUISS Business School.

Courtin, E., Jemiai, N. and Mossialos, E. (2014) Mapping support policies for informal carers across the European Union, *Health Policy*, 118: 84–94.

Da Roit, B. and Le Bihan, B. (2010) Similar and yet so different: cash-for-care in six European countries' long-term care policies, *Milbank Quarterly*, 88: 286–309.

Daly, M. and Lewis, J. (1998) Introduction: conceptualising social care in the context of welfare state restructuring, in J. Lewis (ed.) *Gender, Social Care and Welfare State Restructuring in Europe.* Aldershot: Ashgate.

Davey, V., Snell, T., Fernández, J., Knapp, M., Tobin, R., Jolly, D. et al. (2007) *Schemes Providing Support to People Using Direct Payments: A UK Survey.* London: Personal Social Services Research Unit.

Dickinson, H. and Glasby, J. (2011) Social care, in K. Walshe and J. Smith (eds.) *Healthcare Management.* Maidenhead: Open University Press.

Erens, B., Wistow, G., Mounier-Jack, S., Douglas, N., Jones, L., Manacorda, T. et al. (2015) *Early Evaluation of the Integrated Care and Support Pioneers Programme.* London: Policy Innovation Research Unit.

Esping-Anderson, G. (1990) *The Three Worlds of Welfare Capitalism.* Cambridge: Polity.

Fernández, J.-L., Snell, T., Forder, J. and Wittenberg, R. (2013) *Implications of Setting Eligibility Criteria for Adult Social Care Services in England at Moderate Needs Level.* PSSRU Discussion Paper DP2851. London: PSSRU at LSE.

Ferrera, M. (1996) The 'Southern model' of welfare in social Europe, *Journal of European Social Policy*, 6 (1): 17–37.

Finch, J. (1989) *Family Obligations and Social Change.* Cambridge: Polity Press.

Forder, J., Jones, K., Glendinning, C., Caiels, J., Welch, E., Baxter, K. et al. (2012) *Evaluation of the Personal Health Budget Pilot Programme.* PSSRU Discussion Paper 2840–2. Canterbury: PSSRU at University of Kent.

French, S. (1993) Disability, impairment or something in between?, in J. Swain, V. Finklestein, S. French and M. Oliver (eds.) *Disabling Barriers – Enabling Environments.* London: Sage.

Fujisawa, R. and Colombo, F. (2009) *The Long-term Care Workforce: Overview and Strategies to Adapt Supply to a Growing Demand.* OECD Health Working Papers #44. Paris: OECD.

Glendinning, C. (2008) Increasing choice and control for older and disabled people: a critical review of new developments in England, *Social Policy and Administration*, 42: 451–69.

Glendinning, C., Moran, N., Rabiee, P., Challis, D., Jacobs, S., Wilberforce, M. et al. (2008) *The IBSEN Project: National Evaluation of the Individual Budgets Pilot Projects*. York: Social Policy Research Unit.

Gorsky, M. (2013) 'To regulate and confirm inequality'? A regional history of geriatric hospitals under the English National Health Service, c. 1948–c. 1975, *Ageing and Society*, 33: 598–625.

Griffiths, R. (1988) *Community Care: Agenda for Action. A Report to the Secretary of State for Social Services by Sir Roy Griffiths*. London: HMSO.

Innes, D. and Tetlow, G. (2015) *Central Cuts, Local Decision-making: Changes in Local Government Spending and Revenues in England, 2009–10 to 2014–15*. IBriefing Note #BN166. London: Institute for Fiscal Studies.

Kane, R.A., Kane, R.L. and Ladd, R.C. (1998) *The Heart of Long-term Care*. Oxford: Oxford University Press.

King's Fund (2015) *Health and Social Care Funding: The Short, Medium and Long-term Outlook*. London: King's Fund [http://www.kingsfund.org.uk/sites/files/kf/field/field_publication_file/kings-fund-spending-review-submission-sep-2015.pdf].

Leira, A. and Saraceno, C. (2002) Care: actors, relationships and contexts, in J. Lewis, B. Hobson and B. Siim (eds.) *Contested Concepts in Gender and Social Politics*. Cheltenham: Edward Elgar.

Marczak, J. and Wistow, G. (2015) Commissioning long-term care services in OECD countries, in C. Gori, J. Fernández and R. Wittenberg (eds.) *Long-term Care Reforms in OECD Countries: Successes and Failures*. Bristol: Policy Press.

Munday, B. (2003) *European Social Services: A Map of Characteristics and Trends*. Strasbourg: Council of Europe.

National Audit Office (2014) *Adult Social Care in England: Overview*. London: National Audit Office.

National Collaboration for Integrated Care and Support (2013) *Integrated Care and Support: Our Shared Commitment* [https://www.gov.uk/government/uploads/system/uploads/attachment_data/file/198748/DEFINITIVE_FINAL_VERSION_Integrated_Care_and_Support_-_Our_Shared_Commitment_2013-05-13.pdf].

OECD/European Commission (2013) *A Good Life in Old Age? Monitoring and Improving Quality in Long-term Care*. OECD Health Policy Studies. Paris: OECD.

Oliver, M. (1996) Defining impairment and disability: issues at stake, in C. Barnes and G. Mercer (eds.) *Exploring the Divide: Illness and Disability*. Leeds: Disability Press.

Pavolini, E. and Ranci, C. (2013) Reforms in long-term care policies in Europe: an introduction, in C. Ranci and E. Pavolini (eds.) *Reforms in Long-Term Care Policies in Europe*. Berlin: Springer.

Ranci, C. and Pavolini, E. (eds.) (2012) *Reforms in Long-term Care Policies in Europe: Investigating Institutional Change and Social Impacts*. New YorK: Springer Science & Business Media.

Riedel, M. and Kraus, M. (2011) *Informal Care Provision in Europe: Regulation and Profile of Providers*. ENEPRI Research Report #96, November [http://www.ancien-longtermcare .eu/sites/default/files/RR%20No%2096%20_ANCIEN_%20Regulation%20and%20Profile%20 of%20Providers%20of%20Informal%20Care.pdf].

Thane, P. (2009) *Memorandum Submitted to the House of Commons' Health Committee Inquiry: Social Care*. London: Centre for Contemporary British History.

Trigg, L., Kumpunen, S., Holder, J., Maarse, H., Gil, J. and Sole, M. (2013) *Evaluating Care Across Borders Work Package 6: Long Term Care*. Final Report.

Trydegård, G.-B. and Thorslund, M. (2010) One uniform welfare state or a multitude of welfare municipalities? The evolution of local variation in Swedish elder care, *Social Policy and Administration*, 44: 495–511.

Van Ginneken, E., Groenewegen, P.P. and McKee, M. (2012) Personal healthcare budgets: what can England learn from the Netherlands?, *British Medical Journal*, 344: e1383.

Wistow, G., Gaskins, M., Holder, H. and Smith, J. (2015) *Putting Integrated Care into Practice: The North West London Experience*. London: PSSRU/Nuffield Trust.

Wistow, G., Knapp, M.R.J., Hardy, B., Forder, J.E., Kendall, J. and Manning, R. (1996) *Social Care Markets: Progress and Prospects*. Buckingham: Open University Press.

Yeandle, S., Kröger, T. and Cass, B. (2012) Voice and choice for users and carers? Developments in patterns of care for older people in Australia, England and Finland, *Journal of European Social Policy*, 22: 432–45.

Chapter 14

Purchasing healthcare

Natasha Curry and Judith Smith

Introduction

Purchasing and contracting (sometimes also described as commissioning) are complex concepts that are hotly debated features of many modern healthcare systems. At its core, purchasing concerns the decision-making processes involved in the allocation of limited resources to providers of services in order to meet the health needs of a population. Structures and processes designed to execute purchasing vary between health systems. Furthermore, purchasing or commissioning structures do not exist in isolation and the complex array of policy mechanisms found alongside them can make assessment of the impact of purchasing problematic.

This chapter begins by exploring the theory of purchasing – how and why it has emerged, what activities are involved and the terminology that has developed. We then go on to examine the organization of purchasing functions, considering the bodies that undertake this function in different health systems, the skills required and challenges faced. The third section covers issues and challenges arising in the course of the purchasing cycle, drawing on international examples. We then consider the impact and effectiveness of healthcare purchasing, ending with the challenges presented for healthcare managers.

The theory of purchasing

The development of purchasing in healthcare

Purchasing in healthcare emerged in two phases in the late twentieth century. A central driver for changes to the way public services are delivered was a focus on containing public spending and maximizing efficiencies. The first phase in the 1970s and 1980s saw reforms intended to facilitate cost containment at a macro or national level. The second phase in the late 1980s and early 1990s focused on improving efficiency at a micro level and enabling increasing responsiveness to service users.

The development of purchasing in healthcare was part of the phenomenon known as 'new public management' (Ferlie, 1996). New public management is concerned with introducing 'greater competition into the public sector', 'setting explicit standards and measures of performance' and putting 'greater emphasis on output controls' (Hood, 1991). It essentially involves separating out the purchaser from the provider of healthcare services – often termed the 'purchaser–provider split'. Under such a regime, providers are managed via contractual mechanisms with the intention that the resulting competition between providers drives quality, efficiency and responsiveness.

In the UK, the purchaser–provider split was introduced in the early 1990s following the NHS and Community Care Act 1990 (Stationery Office, 1990). Other countries introduced similar reforms around the same time: Sweden established a purchasing function in county councils in the late 1980s (Wiley et al., 1995) while New Zealand separated its purchasing function in 1993 (Ashton, 1995). There are relatively few examples of pure 'planned' systems where there is no separate purchasing function and, instead, services are organized via a planning or allocation committee. Notable examples include Wales and Scotland, which, following devolution, moved away from a pure purchaser–provider split (in 2009 in the case of Wales and 2004 in the case of Scotland), and New Zealand where there was an abandonment of the market and return to an integrated planning and funding system in 2001 (Timmins and Ham, 2013).

Definitions of commissioning, purchasing and contracting

The evolving nature of purchasing functions has given rise to different terminology being used to describe the same concepts in different contexts or the same terms being ascribed different meanings. Definitions of the main terms are set out in Box 14.1.

Box 14.1 Definition of terms

- **Commissioning:** a set of linked activities that range from assessing the health needs of a population, defining the services required to meet those needs, contracting with providers of those services, monitoring and evaluating those services and then making decisions about which services to re- or de-commission. Commissioning has a proactive and strategic intent.
- **Purchasing:** the process of buying or funding a particular service in response to demand, need or usage. As such, purchasing is one operational activity within the more strategic process of commissioning.
- **Procurement:** the process of identifying a provider of a service. It may involve competitive tendering, competitive quotation or single tender action. It could also involve stimulating the market through awareness-raising and education.
- **Contracting:** the technical process of selecting a provider to meet the needs of the defined service specification. It involves negotiating and agreeing the terms of a contract for services and the ongoing management of that contract in terms of payment and monitoring variations.

The term 'commissioning' is specific to the English NHS and used only rarely elsewhere to denote health planning and purchasing (apart from in relation to the planning of major capital developments). Commissioning is usually used to imply a strategic and proactive intent and can also encompass wider activities such as influencing other bodies to improve or enhance the health status of the population (Øvretveit, 1995).

For the purposes of this chapter, the term strategic purchasing has been used to refer to the broadest and most strategic set of activities and contracting to refer to the narrowest and most specific. We use 'commissioning' when exploring concepts such as Øvretveit's commissioning cycle, but elsewhere focus on strategic purchasing.

The activities of strategic purchasing

Strategic purchasing (or commissioning) does not refer to a single activity but rather to a series of linked activities that have, most usefully, been described as an ongoing cycle (Øvretveit, 1995: 71–3). A number of detailed publications have analysed the practice and theory of purchasing and contracting (e.g. Øvretveit, 1995; Flynn and Wililams, 1997; Le Grand et al., 1998; Bamford, 2001; Mays et al., 2001; Smith et al., 2010, 2013). A condensed overview of the 'cycle of commissioning' (adapted from Øvretveit, 1995) is provided in Figure 14.1.

Within each stage of this simplified process is a multitude of complex tasks and activities. While the diagram suggests a series of sequential activities, reality tends to be more complicated with some elements taking place concurrently. Table 14.1 offers some more detail about the specific tasks that go to make up the main stages.

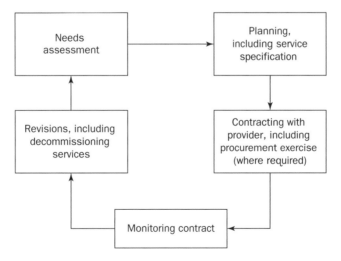

Figure 14.1 The commissioning cycle

Table 14.1 Activities within the commissioning cycle

Main stages of commissioning cycle	*Activities*
Assessing needs	• Analysis of needs of population based on epidemiological studies, census data, mortality and morbidity rates and other population data. • Quantification of need based on health records of registered population or members. • Identification of evidence-based interventions. • Patient or service user focus groups, surveys and interviews. • Professional and stakeholder views.
Planning	• Review of current provision. • Gap analysis to identify where current provision does not meet needs identified earlier. • Prioritization: difficult decisions may need to be made at this stage regarding what issues/conditions/groups are priorities. • Assessment of market capacity. • Development of specification of services required, quality standards, identification of appropriate currency and plans for monitoring and evaluation. May involve de-commissioning/disinvestment where required.
Contracting	• Educating the market: publicizing the services needed, stimulating providers. • Competitive tendering exercise – where competition is required. Where it is not, single tender action may be used. • Determination of contract currency. • Negotiations with providers on volume, quality and price. • Terms and conditions of contract. • Arrangements for variations. • Determination of routine monitoring requirements.
Monitoring	• Contract monitoring meetings. • Reconciliation of invoices. • Analysis of information provided, including activity data and/or quality monitoring data. • Reporting and investigation of trends and variances. • Agreement to/negotiations regarding variations. • Payment.
Revision	• Adjust contract volumes, prices, types in accordance with terms and conditions. • Feed trend and usage information through to longer term needs assessment and planning cycle.

Learning activity 14.1

Imagine you are the head of a health purchasing organization in your own country. You need to purchase an orthopaedic service from an acute hospital provider.

- How would you go about it?
- What information would you seek?
- How would you try to hold the provider to account?
- What challenges do you anticipate?

The organization of purchasing

The purchasing agent

The broad theory of strategic purchasing or commissioning and its components is set out above. A fundamental difference between purchasing within health systems is who the purchaser is – there may be a single or multiple payers and these payers may take an active role in shaping services, or play a more passive role where they refund providers for activity in arrears.

In tax-funded systems such as England, Sweden and New Zealand, there is a single main payer. The English NHS has established specific bodies to undertake purchasing, whereas Sweden has embedded the function within county councils. In insurance-based systems, such as the United States, the Netherlands and Germany, there are multiple payers in the form of insurance organizations or sickness funds. The body or agent that buys healthcare on behalf of individuals is referred to as a 'third party payer'; they are usually separate from the provider of services in insurance-based systems (with a few exceptions in the USA where payer and provider are integrated) (Enthoven and Tollen, 2005). Where there are multiple payers, there is potential for competition between them. This can give rise to what is known as 'cherry-picking' or 'cream-skimming' where payers (e.g. insurance companies) offer coverage only to low-risk individuals who are likely to incur relatively low costs (e.g. Friesner and Rosenman, 2012). This has been shown to occur even in highly regulated systems, such as Germany (Bauhof, 2012).

Where there is a third party payer role, there is often not a single organization in the system that undertakes this function. Even in systems with a single payer (e.g. England or New Zealand), there are multiple local commissioning bodies making decisions on behalf of population groups. An analysis of the effectiveness of different organizational models for purchasing (Smith et al., 2004) concluded that a mix of approaches is needed in each health economy according to the services involved and the context. This analysis has given rise to the idea of a 'continuum of commissioning'. This is based on the fact that, in any system, it is unlikely that a single body would be best placed to make purchasing decisions at all the different levels required – from the individual to the highly strategic, national services.

Where there is such a continuum, there are usually multiple organizations undertaking purchasing decisions at the different but overlapping levels. National commissioning typically occurs for extremely rare conditions that affect a small pool of people. At the regional level, purchasing decisions for relatively rare conditions take place, but more people are affected than those conditions addressed at the national level. Other commissioning, such as that for long-term conditions management, is usually considered to be best done at a local level. At the most micro level, in some countries an individual is assigned a budget for them to spend on the services they feel they most need. Examples of the use of personal budgets in health can be found in many countries, including the Netherlands, Germany and the USA (Health Foundation, 2011) (see Box 14.2).

Box 14.2   Case study – commissioning at the micro level: personal budgets

The Netherlands introduced personal budgets for health in 1996. They were seen as a way to offer greater control and choice to patients and service users as well as having potential to contain costs. The freedom and choice offered by budgets proved to be very popular, so much so that costs started to spiral and the scheme was closed to new entrants. In an attempt to control costs, the government tightened the eligibility criteria and have started to require budget holders to contribute more to their own costs (Health Foundation, 2011).

Skills for strategic purchasing

Purchasing has been seen largely as a managerial task in most systems with experienced managers, financial experts and lawyers leading the process. However, it has been suggested that the absence of clinical involvement in purchasing decisions means that commissioners lack power, influence and detailed knowledge about the services they are buying (see below for further discussion).

The features that a purchasing organization requires in order to be effective have been explored in depth elsewhere (see Smith et al., 2010: 8–9) and a number of these characteristics are matters of policy, such as the levels at which a budget is held. However, others – such as the skills and capabilities of staff – flow from the size and characteristics of the organization. Many purchasing organizations in tax-funded systems evolved from hierarchical and bureaucratic predecessors with little attention paid to whether the skills within the organization are appropriate or sufficiently plentiful.

Other commentators have supported this view and stressed that competencies, including negotiation, political awareness, an understanding of the needs of the population, quality management, service improvement, an awareness of evidence about effectiveness and cost-effectiveness of interventions, team working and an understanding of ethics are vital (e.g. Mays and Dixon, 1996; Jackson, 1998; Bamford, 2001; Kaufman, 2002; Velasco-Garrido et al., 2005; Smith et al., 2010; Thorlby et al., 2011). Some of these skills are commercial and are not always present in public sector bodies and governments have rarely invested in providing training and development to address this.

Contracting

Although only one part of the wider cycle of commissioning, contracting is a particularly important but complex element. Contracts fulfil a number of functions within an overall purchasing system. The contract outlines the details of the services required, the price to be paid and duration of the provision, what standards and requirements are to be met, what information is to be collected and supplied, the monitoring arrangements and the mechanisms for variation and review of the contract.

There are a number of different types of contract typically used within healthcare. The more usual types are either block contracts where the purchaser agrees a fixed sum for a broadly defined range of services, or activity-based contracts where the purchaser pays according to the number of patients treated or the volume of activity performed. There are some variations to this (see Table 14.2). In recent years, we have also witnessed growing interest in contracts that seek to integrate services, for example in the form of alliance and prime/lead provider contracts (Addicott, 2014). Some of these models, and the challenges of their implementation, are explored in more detail below.

Table 14.2 Contract types

Type of contract	Description	Use
Block	Block contracts operate like a budget for a service. The purchaser agrees to pay a sum for access to a broadly defined range of services. In these types of contract, it is usual for volume to be indicative or not to be mentioned at all.	These are used most commonly where costing and/or activity information is scarce, which means it is difficult to develop a more precise regime.
Cost and volume	Under these arrangements, numbers of patients to be treated are specified. Payment arrangements for activity above or below the specified volume are defined in the contract.	This approach can be used where reliable information is available to monitor activity and volumes are relatively high.
Cost per case	In this arrangement, a cost is set for an individual item of service or a care package.	These are used for high-cost care, which occurs relatively infrequently.
Outcomes based	Outcomes-based contracts specify the impact or results that the purchaser wishes the service to achieve. These contracts do not tend to specify numbers of patients, neither do they set out how the service should be delivered.	These can only be used where there is sufficient robust information to define and measure desired outcomes.

(continued)

Table 14.2 (*continued*)

Type of contract	Description	Use
Alliance	Where multiple providers agree to collaborate and operate under a single agreement, together taking shared responsibility for, and risks of, delivering the terms of a contract.	These are used where there is a need to integrate services that are traditionally provided by a number of providers (e.g. musculoskeletal services that are provided by primary, secondary and community providers).
Prime or lead contractor	The purchaser contracts with a single organization that is responsible for the management of the provider organizations that deliver the required service. A slight variation is the prime/lead provider contract where the principal contractor also provides services within the terms of the contract.	Similar to alliance contracts, these are used where there is a need or desire to integrate services across different providers. The risk of delivery is shifted from the commissioner to the providers.

Learning activity 14.2

Choose a country with which you are not familiar. Find out how it organizes its health-care purchasing. Consider the pros and cons of its approach, setting these out in a table of comparisons.

Use this analysis to explore ways in which the country might develop its purchasing approach further in order to meet current and anticipated health system challenges.

The challenges of purchasing

Healthcare purchasing is something that is regarded as being very difficult to do, particularly in systems where health services are tax funded:

> Purchasing health services is inherently difficult in publicly financed health systems since purchasers are continually faced with the multiple and frequently conflicting explicit and implicit expectations of politicians, central government officials, managers, clinicians, patients and the public for the health system. (Mays and Hand, 2000: 30–1)

This section explores some of these challenges, using international case study examples.

Specifying the service and defining the currency

To place a contract, it is necessary to define the product to be purchased. Indeed, the specification forms the basis of the contract and monitoring of service delivery. Designing service specifications in healthcare is one of the most challenging parts of the commissioning cycle because the product is often difficult to define (Flynn and Williams, 1997).

Traditionally, healthcare has been categorized on the basis of professional groups or service interests (e.g. general surgery, ophthalmology or physiotherapy). However, such categories do not always align with how a purchaser may wish to design a service. They may wish to focus on population groups (e.g. children or older people) or conditions (e.g. diabetes or cancer services). By taking a population or condition-based approach, there is potential for the specification to include all the required services for that group whether located in primary, community, secondary or tertiary care. Such an approach may help overcome fragmentation of services between the different sectors but it can also create new boundary issues, particularly for individuals with multiple conditions. Different approaches to overcoming fragmentation of care are emerging and are discussed below (see overcoming fragmentation).

The next step is to find a common and meaningful currency in which service activity and service interventions can be described. There are a number of options, including:

- diagnosis-related groups
- consultant or treatment episodes
- hospital stays
- outpatient attendances
- specific operations
- complex care packages
- capitation (where comprehensive care must be provided for a specified number of individuals or a wider population)
- patient pathways (where the specification describes the care for a given condition which providers must follow)
- outcomes of care measures.

The more straightforward measures tend to be focused on activity or volume. In these cases, a purchaser specifies a number of patients to be seen or procedures to be carried out, and either pays the provider a lump sum at the start of the period or pays based on the exact activity at the end of the period. While simple and measurable, such an approach has been criticized for focusing solely on how much of something is delivered rather than its quality or the outcomes it achieves. It is also often part of a system that reinforces a fragmented approach to care with different providers seeking to maximize their income.

An approach that has been gathering impetus in many countries in response to these criticisms is that of 'outcomes-based purchasing' or 'value-based commissioning'. This approach attempts to switch the focus away from volume and activity towards defining the long-term service objective. Outcomes- or value-based purchasing typically involves a group of providers being assigned a fixed budget for the care of a particular population. The purchaser specifies the outcomes required, then providers work together to deliver these. As such, incentives are theoretically aligned – all providers are working to a common goal and are exposed to the same potential risks and rewards. However, effective outcomes-based purchasing depends on high-quality, accessible and available data with which to measure outcomes. In addition, outcomes tend to be long term in nature (see Box 14.3), yet the typical healthcare purchasing cycle operates on an annual basis. This can be problematic for purchasers, particularly where financial constraints mean they are operating on tight budgets. In addition, this approach requires skilled purchasers and a long lead-in time to ensure all parties are agreed.

Box 14.3   Case study – impact of value-based purchasing: Integrated Practice Unit, Virginia Mason, Seattle, WA

The Virginia Mason Medical Centre in Seattle established a service for patients suffering from lower back pain. Patients are able to call a single number and most can be seen the same day. Physiotherapists are paired with physicians, and patients usually see both on their first visit. Those with severe problems are referred on to a pathway but most patients are treated with physiotherapy.

The service's success has been measured in terms of the outcomes achieved: patients miss fewer days of work and need fewer physiotherapy visits compared with regional averages; the use of MRI scans to evaluate low back pain has decreased by 23 per cent since the clinic's launch and costs have reduced. The clinic has also increased revenue by increasing productivity and the clinic sees over 2000 new patients a year (compared with 1400 previously) and delivers the service in the same space with the same staff.

See Porter and Lee (2013).

Making contracts effective

The contract is a means of implementing the strategies and plans of the purchaser and not an end in itself. Two of the main challenges associated with the use of healthcare contracts are information deficit and enforcement issues.

Many systems lack data collection mechanisms that are sufficiently developed to support the monitoring of activity through contracts. For instance, in the USA, many of the available data are insurance claims data and so do not always contain huge amounts of clinical detail (Walker, 2010). Effective contracts contain mechanisms such as financial incentives, penalties and the ultimate possibility of termination, which can be used to steer the provider in the direction required or to move to an alternative supplier, a feature that has been termed 'contestability' (Ham, 1996). Healthcare contracts may be commercial, legally enforceable contracts – as in the USA, New Zealand (Ashton et al., 2004), and between English NHS commissioners and foundation trusts or independent providers – or may be internal service agreements. In principle, both types are enforceable: the former with recourse to the courts if necessary and the latter through managerial action. The extent to which a real market exists will affect a purchaser's scope to enforce contract penalties. If there are no alternative suppliers in the market, the threat of termination will be hollow.

Although there is an argument that well-constructed, written and legally enforceable contracts would be beneficial for health systems (Ferlie and McGivern, 2003), there is a counter-argument that such a formal approach can carry with it obstacles. Establishing a contractual environment can carry significant transaction costs and these must be weighed against any potential benefits of the approach (Light, 1998; Light and Dixon, 2004).

Asymmetry of information

Linked to the challenge of making contracts effective is the issue of 'asymmetry of information'. This reflects the fact that in healthcare, the bulk of knowledge and expertise about services is concentrated in provider organizations, leading to an imbalance in the distribution of power in the wider system. Purchasing organizations, by comparison, are usually run and managed by non-clinical managerial staff who may lack the detailed understanding of services.

Purchasers may therefore struggle to specify services required and risk producing incomplete or flawed contractual documentation. One approach that some health systems have taken to try and overcome this asymmetry of information is to involve clinicians in purchasing activities. By embedding clinicians in the process, it is hoped that the purchaser will have greater negotiating power when faced with the provider organization (Smith and Mays, 2012) (see Box 14.4)

Box 14.4   Case study – involvement of clinicians in commissioning: the English NHS

In an attempt to strengthen commissioning, the English NHS has introduced a series of reforms since the early 1990s that aim to get GPs more involved in making purchasing decisions. The most recent of these is to have clinical commissioning groups, whereby groups of local family doctors hold a budget with which to purchase the majority of healthcare for their local enrolled population. The added value that clinicians bring to commissioning is difficult to establish. In previous forms of clinical commissioning in the English NHS (e.g. practice-based commissioning), family doctors tended to focus on small-scale re-provision of services outside hospital and were less interested in wider, more strategic approaches to commissioning (Curry et al., 2008). Such concerns are at risk of being replicated in the current iteration of NHS commissioning in England where the added value brought by family doctors is in their knowledge of their enrolled patients, while their ability to take a strategic view and systematically apply public health intelligence remain unclear (Perkins et al., 2014).

Overcoming fragmentation

New contractual mechanisms are emerging in a number of countries to support purchasers in bringing about more integrated or coordinated care for their patients. These typically take the form of alliance contracts or prime or lead contractor models, and are used to support a shift towards the outcomes-based model of purchasing described above.

In a prime contractor model, the purchaser contracts with a single organization which then oversees the delivery of a range of contracted services by subcontracting providers. The prime contractor is effectively a supply chain manager holding individual providers to account, yet the purchaser retains overall accountability for the delivery of the service. A variation on this arrangement is the prime provider contract, whereby the main organization is also a provider of the service. In both cases, the prime contractor or provider usually receives a capitated budget for the service (Addicott, 2014).

Under an alliance contract, multiple providers join together under a single contract, sharing responsibility for the potential risks and rewards (Addicott, 2014). Unlike lead or prime contractor models, all the organizations in an alliance agreement are equal partners. Because all organizations in the arrangement are bound together equally, there is an incentive for them to address inefficiencies and to implement innovations across the whole system, not just in their own organization (Addicott, 2014). New Zealand provides an example of the use of alliance contracts within healthcare (see Box 14.5).

Box 14.5   Case study – alliance contracting: Canterbury, New Zealand

In the New Zealand health system, the District Health Board (DHB) is the main purchaser for local and regional services. There has been a focus on integrated care in New Zealand since 2009 when the government invited expressions of interest from providers and purchasers to form into 'alliances' (Cumming, 2011).

One area of New Zealand, Canterbury, decided to move away from its established approach to contracting, which focused on inputs and activity, towards a form of alliance contracting for a number of services including district nursing, mental health and laboratory services (Timmins and Ham, 2013). Within the model, all providers involved in a pathway of care work together within an agreed arrangement and all providers share gains and losses. Because the success of the contract depends upon all providers, there is a strong incentive for all providers to perform. The performance of each provider in the alliance is visible to others and they can be benchmarked against each other, providing a further incentive to perform (Timmins and Ham, 2013).

An analysis of the Canterbury example suggests that it is starting to prove successful in reducing demand for hospital care and enabling more joined-up local services (Timmins and Ham, 2013).

Controlling costs: the rise of the accountable care organization

A major role of the purchaser is to ensure efficient use of resources and control costs. An extension of the models described above has begun to emerge in the USA – 'accountable care organizations' (ACOs) that formed as part of the Affordable Care Act (US Government, 2010). ACOs are groups of providers who agree to take responsibility for providing the care for a specific population over a defined period of time within a certain budget (Shortell et al., 2014).

ACOs usually take responsibility for all the care needs of a population, not just a segment or a pathway. As such, the purchaser or payer transfers risk to the provider organization. Because providers share the same overall goal, incentives throughout the system are deemed to be aligned (e.g. by reducing the number of hospital admissions and investing in proactive and preventive care to keep the population well). As such, the intention is that wasteful duplication of care or harmful care gaps are avoided and patients receive high-quality coordinated care.

The ACOs are in the early stages of development and reports on their impact to date are mixed. There are a number of different models of ACO (see Shortell et al., 2010). Public performance reports of the first phase of ACOs revealed that, out of the original thirty-two, half had resulted in losses and two had had to withdraw from the programme. The second phase, however, has delivered more promising results, with ACOs demonstrating improvements against a number of metrics, including patient experience and effectiveness (Center for Medicare and Medicaid Services, 2014). These more recent results also suggest that some ACOs are demonstrating potential to make significant savings. This potential has been noted around the world and several systems are assessing whether such an approach would deliver results in their contexts, including the NHS in England (Ahmed et al., 2015).

Learning activity 14.3

Choose one of the challenges identified above and, based on what you know about the healthcare system in your own country, consider to what extent you think the particular challenge is a problem. What are the implications for the wider system?

If you were redesigning the healthcare system in your country, what structures or processes could you put in place to mitigate the effects of this issue?

The impact of healthcare purchasing

Having considered the theory, practice and challenges of health purchasing and contracting, this section discusses the evidence on its impact and effectiveness. Every healthcare system has its own specific aims and goals, but most share the common values of efficiency, responsiveness and effectiveness. Assessing and quantifying the impact of purchasing is difficult because it is just one of a set of interdependent elements in any healthcare system.

Purchasing for efficiency

The evidence as to whether purchasing has been effective in enabling more efficient use of healthcare resources is rather mixed. The OECD states:

> . . . in systems where both financing and delivery of care is a public responsibility, efforts to distinguish the roles of healthcare payers and providers so as to allow markets to function and generate efficiencies from competition, have proved generally effective. (OECD, 2004: 17)

However, other reviews of health systems have been less positive. One particularly damning verdict came from the UK House of Commons Health Committee inquiry into commissioning in 2010:

> . . . weaknesses remain 20 years after the introduction of the purchaser–provider split. Commissioners continue to be passive, when to do their work efficiently they must insist on quality and challenge the inefficiencies of providers, particularly unevidenced variations in clinical practice. (House of Commons Health Committee, 2010: 38)

Similarly, Ashton and colleagues (2004) found no evidence of major efficiency gains in the hospital sector in New Zealand following similar market reforms of healthcare in the 1990s. In addition, a review of purchasing in the US system in 1996 concluded that: 'despite some impressive reductions in the rate of health care premium growth, it remains unclear whether these lower annual growth rates are the result of purchaser pressure or are due to exogenous factors at work in the health care market place' (Lipson and de Sa, 1996: 76).

Intended efficiency gains can be counteracted by associated transaction costs. Light and other commentators point to a range of new inefficiencies, such as 'managerialism, datamania, accountability as an end, disruptions and inefficiencies of underused losers and overused winners and an ethos of commercialism replacing ethos of service' (Light, 1997: 322). In the English NHS, commentators have largely concluded that primary care-led commissioning has not had a significant impact on secondary care and has resulted in increased transaction costs (e.g. Smith and Wilton, 1998; Mays et al., 2000; Smith et al., 2010). Often the true transaction costs within a system are not well understood but are thought to be high (Porter et al., 2013).

Purchasing for responsiveness

Purchasers, as third party payers, are acting on behalf of the population they represent, so there should be a mechanism for involving that population in decision-making through the exercise of 'voice' or 'choice' (Greener, 2008). A review of international experience identified many examples of initiatives that help patients or members of the public to influence purchasers, but it was not clear how far these mechanisms resulted in changes to the purchasers' policies or improvements in services in response to issues raised (den Exter, 2005).

There are a number of reasons why patients and the public have had apparently little impact on purchasers' decisions in some countries. Where purchasing organizations operate in systems with strong national direction, they are often constrained by nationally determined policies and hence the scope to respond to the priorities of local populations may be limited. Commissioners are often poorly understood by the public and tend to be relatively invisible compared with providers of health services, such as hospitals and family doctor services. Poor information systems may also impede the ability of purchasers to provide precise and meaningful accounts of their activities to the public on whose behalf they are acting.

Purchasing for effectiveness

Evidence for the effectiveness of healthcare purchasing in achieving the goal of improved health services in terms of quality of care or other outcomes is mixed. It is widely accepted that commissioning in the English NHS has largely failed to achieve its principal goals of shifting services out of hospital, reducing avoidable use of hospitals and developing new forms of care (Audit Commission and Healthcare Commission, 2008; House of Commons Health Committee, 2010). The Netherlands has sought to transform insurers from passive payers to active purchasers of healthcare. By introducing competition between insurers, it has sought to stimulate innovation and cost-effectiveness. However, despite these efforts, the reality has been difficult to implement and the performance of the system as a whole is largely in line with other comparable countries on a range of measures (van den Berg et al., 2011). Commentators have observed that there remains in many health systems an imbalance in power between relatively weak purchasers and more powerful providers when seeking to shape the hospital sector and reduce avoidable use of acute and emergency care (Kaplan and Babad, 2011).

Interest in improving the quality of health services through more effective purchasing has been growing across European health systems (Figueras et al., 2005). A review of international experience of outcomes-based purchasing identified a range of examples in France, Germany, Italy and the UK of quality being made a focus of healthcare contracts (Velasco-Garrido et al., 2005). Another international review of quality-based purchasing concluded that 'there is some evidence of public-sector purchasers acting as agents to improve quality, but there is almost no documentation of either formal-sector private insurers, or community-based health financing schemes promoting quality through purchasing'; and highlighted the 'large knowledge gaps concerning the results of initiatives taken' (Waters et al., 2004).

Learning activity 14.4

Consider the advantages and disadvantages of operating a purchaser–provider split within a publicly funded health system with which you are familiar, and set out a 'balance sheet' of these.

- What conclusions do you draw from this assessment?
- Would you recommend such a split of funding and provision for your own health system? If not, what would you suggest as an alternative approach to planning, funding and assuring the quality of health and health services?

Conclusion

Purchasing and contracting have been introduced into health systems against a background of high expectations about the potential of funders to exert pressure on providers to implement new and improved forms of health services that meet population health needs. A number of international studies point to the inherent difficulty in undertaking effective health purchasing and it is clear that challenges remain, particularly in assessing the impact and effectiveness of commissioning arrangements. Furthermore, difficulties in ascribing improvements in health or health services to purchasing as opposed to wider reform mechanisms compound these complexities (Le Grand et al., 1998; Figueras et al., 2005; Ham, 2008; Smith and Curry, 2011). Differences between systems and structures of health purchasing make country comparisons difficult. What is clear is that the available evidence does not point to any one approach to purchasing being superior.

Despite the caveats discussed about measuring the impact of health purchasing, there is a common message, namely that commissioners have struggled to assert their authority *vis-à-vis* providers who hold the balance of power and can exert influence through their detailed knowledge of services, control of information and the power and influence vested in their medical staff. To shift the balance of power, the purchasing role requires considerable development and investment. This will be of increasing importance as health systems grapple with ageing populations and increasing numbers of people with long-term conditions within a context of significant financial constraint.

Learning resources

Nuffield Trust: This independent health research foundation, based in London, undertakes research and policy analysis across a range of topics. It has published widely on the subject of commissioning and there are a number of reports and other resources containing detailed case studies and summaries of evidence [www.nuffieldtrust.org.uk].

Organization for Economic Cooperation and Development (OECD): This international organization aims to promote policies that will improve the economic and social well-being of people around the world. Its health arm undertakes large-scale studies into various topics, including healthcare purchasing. It is a useful source of comparable information [http://www.oecd.org/health/].

European Observatory on Health Systems and Policies: Hosted by the World Health Organization, this site contains a series of useful resources on many topics. Of particular interest is its *Health Systems in Transition* series, which provides country-by-country descriptions of different structures and systems that help to identify countries' approaches to purchasing. It also publishes some comparative data [http://www. euro.who.int/en/about-us/partners/observatory].

Policy Research Unit for Commissioning: Based in an academic institution, PRU-Comm undertakes research into commissioning on behalf of the English Department of Health. Although essentially UK-based, it produces in-depth analysis of current UK commissioning policy and consideration of the wider issues associated with healthcare purchasing and commissioning [http://www.prucomm.ac.uk/].

King's Fund: This London-based independent think-tank undertakes a wide range of research into health policy and health services management. It has published a variety of papers on commissioning in the UK [www.kingsfund.org.uk].

Health Services Management Centre, Birmingham: This department of the University of Birmingham undertakes research into health services management and policy. As part of that, it has published studies on commissioning and purchasing. It is also one of the few institutions to run dedicated courses on NHS commissioning [http://www .birmingham.ac.uk/schools/social-policy/departments/health-services-management-centre/about/index.aspx].

References

Addicott, R. (2014) *Commissioning and Contracting for Integrated Care*. London: King's Fund.

Ahmed, A., Mays, N., Ahmed, N., Bisognano, M. and Gottlieb, G. (2015) Can the accountable care organisation model facilitate integrated care in England? *Journal of Health Services Research and Policy*, 20 (4): 261–4.

Ashton, T. (1995) The purchaser–provider split in New Zealand: the story so far, *Australian Health Review*, 18 (1): 43–60.

Ashton, T., Cumming, J. and McLean, J. (2004) Contracting for health services in a public health system: the New Zealand experience, *Health Policy*, 69: 21–31.

Audit Commission and Healthcare Commission (2008) *Is the Treatment Working? Progress with the NHS System Reform Programme*. London: Audit Commission.

Bamford, T. (2001) *Commissioning and Purchasing*. London: Routledge.

Bauhof, S. (2012) Do health plans risk-select? An audit study on Germany's social health insurance, *Journal of Public Economics*, 96 (9/10): 750–9.

Center for Medicare and Medicaid Services (2014) *Medicare ACOs Continue to Succeed in Improving Care, Lowering Cost Growth*. Fact sheets [https://www.cms.gov/Newsroom/MediaReleaseDatabase/Fact-sheets/2014-Fact-sheets-items/2014-09-16.html].

Cumming, J. (2011) Integrated care in New Zealand, special 10th anniversary edition of the *International Journal of Integrated Care*, 11: e138.

Curry, N., Goodwin, N., Naylor, C. and Robertson, R. (2008) *Practice-Based Commissioning: Reinvigorate, Replace or Abandon?* London: King's Fund.

den Exter, A.P. (2005) Purchasers as the public's agent, in J. Figueras, R. Robinson and E. Jakubowski (eds.) *Purchasing to Improve Health Systems Performance*. Maidenhead: Open University Press.

Enthoven, A.C. and Tollen, L. (2005) Competition in healthcare: it takes systems to pursue quality and efficiency, *Health Affairs*, 24 (5): W5-420–33.

Ferlie, E. (1996) *The New Public Management in Action*. Oxford: Oxford University Press.

Ferlie, E. and McGivern, G. (2003) *Relationships between Health Care Organisations: A Critical Overview of the Literature and a Research Agenda*. London: National Coordinating Centre for NHS Service Delivery and Organization R&D.

Figueras, J., Robinson, R. and Jakubowski, E. (eds.) (2005) *Purchasing to Improve Health Systems Performance*. Maidenhead: Open University Press.

Flynn, R. and Williams, G. (1997) *Contracting for Health: Quasi-Markets and the National Health Service*. Oxford: Oxford University Press.

Friesner, D.L. and Rosenman, R. (2012) Do hospitals practice cream skimming?, *Health Services Management Research*, 22 (1): 39–49.

Greener, I. (2008) Choice and voice – a review, *Social Policy and Society*, 7 (2): 255–65.

Ham, C.J. (1996) Contestability: a middle path for health care, *British Medical Journal*, 312 (7023): 70–1.

Ham, C.J. (2008) *Health Care Commissioning in the International Context: Lessons from Experience and Evidence*. Birmingham: Health Services Management Centre.

Health Foundation (2011) *The Dutch Experience of Personal Health Budgets*. London: Health Foundation.

Hood, C. (1991) A public management for all seasons?, *Public Administration*, 69: 3–19.

House of Commons Health Committee (2010) *Commissioning: Fourth Report of Session 2009–10*, Volume 1. HC 268-I. London: Stationery Office.

Jackson, S. (1998) Skills required for healthy commissioning, *Health Manpower Management*, 24 (1): 40–3.

Kaplan, R.M. and Babad, Y.M. (2011) Balancing influence between actors in healthcare decision making, *BMC Health Services Research*, 11: 85.

Kaufman, G. (2002) Investigating the nursing contribution to commissioning in primary health-care, *Journal of Nursing Management*, 10: 83–94.

Le Grand, J., Mays, N. and Mulligan, J.-A. (1998) *Learning from the NHS Internal Market: A Review of the Evidence*. London: King's Fund.

Light, D.W. (1997) From managed competition to managed cooperation: theory and lessons from the British experience, *Milbank Quarterly*, 75 (3): 297–341.

Light, D.W. (1998) *Effective Commissioning: Lessons from Purchasing in American Managed Care*. London: Office of Health Economics.

Light, D.W. and Dixon, M. (2004) Making the NHS more like Kaiser Permanente, *British Medical Journal*, 328 (7442): 763–5.

Lipson, D.J. and de Sa, J.M. (1996) Impact of purchasing strategies on local health care systems, *Health Affairs*, 15 (2): 62–76.

Mays, N. and Dixon, J. (1996) *Purchaser Plurality in Healthcare: is a Consensus Emerging and is it the Right One?* London: King's Fund.

Mays, N. and Hand, K. (2000) *A Review of Options for Health and Disability Support Purchasing in New Zealand*. Treasury Working Paper #00/20. Wellington: New Zealand Treasury.

Mays, N., Mulligan, J. and Goodwin, N. (2000) The British quasi-market in health care: a balance sheet of the evidence, *Journal of Health Services Research and Policy*, 5 (1): 49–58.

Mays, N., Wyke, S., Malbon, G. and Goodwin, N. (eds.) (2001) *The Purchasing of Health Care by Primary Care Organizations*. Buckingham: Open University Press.

OECD (2004) *High Performing Health Systems*. Paris: OECD.

Øvretveit, J. (1995) *Purchasing for Health: A Multidisciplinary Introduction to the Theory and Practice of Health Purchasing*. Maidenhead: Open University Press.

Perkins, N., Coleman, A., Wright, M., Gadsby, E., McDermott, I., Persoulas, C. et al. (2014) The 'added value' GPs bring to commissioning: a qualitative study in primary care, *British Journal of General Practice*, 64 (628): e728–34.

Porter, A., Mays, N., Shaw, S.E., Rosen, R. and Smith, J. (2013) Commissioning healthcare for people with long term conditions: the persistence of relational contracting in England's NHS quasi-market, *BMC Health Services Research*, 13 (suppl. 1): S2.

Porter, M.E. and Lee, T.H. (2013) The strategy that will fix health care, *Harvard Business Review* [https://hbr.org/2013/10/the-strategy-that-will-fix-health-care].

Shortell, S., Addicott, R., Walsh, N. and Ham, C. (2014) *Accountable Care Organisations in the United States and England: Testing, Evaluating and Learning What Works*. London: King's Fund.

Shortell, S.M., Casalino, L.P. and Fisher, E.S. (2010) Achieving the vision – structural change, in F.J. Crosson and L.A. Tollen (eds.) *Partners in Health: How Physicians and Hospitals can be Accountable Together*. San Francisco, CA: Jossey-Bass.

Smith, J. and Curry, N. (2011) Commissioning, in A. Dixon and N. Mays (eds.) *Review of the Evidence of the NHS under Labour, 1997–2010*. London: King's Fund.

Smith, J. and Mays, N. (2012) GP led commissioning: time for a cool appraisal, *British Medical Journal*, 344: e980.

Smith, J., Curry, N., Mays, N. and Dixon, J. (2010) *Where Next for Commissioning in the English NHS?* London: Nuffield Trust and King's Fund.

Smith, J., Mays, N., Dixon, J., Goodwin, N., Lewis, R., McClelland, S. et al. (2004) *A Review of the Effectiveness of Primary Care-led Commissioning and its Place in the UK NHS*. London: Health Foundation.

Smith, J., Shaw, S., Porter, A., Rosen, R., Blunt, I., Davies, A. et al. (2013) *Commissioning High Quality Care for People with Long-term Conditions*. Southampton: National Institute for Health Research Service Delivery and Organization Programme [http://www.netscc.ac.uk/hsdr/files/project/SDO_FR_08-1806-264_V10.pdf].

Smith, R.D. and Wilton, P. (1998) General practice fundholding: progress to date, *British Journal of General Practice*, 48 (430): 1253–7.

Stationery Office (TSO) (1990) *National Health Service (NHS) and Community Care Act*. London: Stationery Office.

Thorlby, R., Rosen, R. and Smith, J. (2011) *GP Commissioning: Insights from Medical Groups in the United States*. London: Nuffield Trust.

Timmins, N. and Ham, C. (2013) *The Quest for Integrated Health and Social Care: A Case Study in Canterbury New Zealand*. London: King's Fund.

US Government (2010) *The Patient Protection and Affordable Care Act*, Public Law 111-148, March 23, 2010 [https://www.gpo.gov/fdsys/pkg/PLAW-111publ148/pdf/PLAW-111publ148.pdf].

van den Berg, M., Heijink, R., Zwakhals, L., Verkleij, H. and Westert, G. (2011) Healthcare performance in the Netherlands: easy access, varying quality, rising costs, *Eurohealth*, 16 (4) [http://www.lse.ac.uk/LSEHealthAndSocialCare/pdf/eurohealth/Vol16No4/vandanBerg.pdf].

Velasco-Garrido, M., Borowitz, M., Øvretveit, J. and Busse, R. (2005) Purchasing for quality of care, in J. Figueras, R. Robinson and E. Jakubowski (eds.) *Purchasing to Improve Health Systems Performance*. Maidenhead: Open University Press.

Walker, A.M. (2010) Administrative databases in clinical effectiveness research, in L.A. Olsen and M. McGinnis (eds.) *Redesigning the Clinical Effectiveness Research Paradigm: Innovation and Practice-based Approaches – Workshop Summary*. Washington, DC: National Academies Press.

Waters, H.R., Morlock, L.L. and Hatt, L. (2004) Quality-based purchasing in health care, *International Journal of Health Planning and Management*, 19: 365–81.

Wiley, M.M., Laschober, M.A. and Gelband, H. (eds.) (1995) *Hospital Financing in Seven Countries*. Washington, DC: US Office of Technology Assessment.

Capital in the healthcare system: buildings, facilities and equipment

Steve Wright and Barrie Dowdeswell

Introduction: the role of infrastructure capital in the production of healthcare services

It is now clear that the economic crisis of 2008/9 and the continuing subsequent period of austerity in public service spending are blending into the longer term economic problems of an ageing society. Europe still tends towards a hospital-centric default model of care, despite the fact that hospital-based episodic care is unlikely to be the best recourse for most chronic disease treatment – the area of growth. When seen against the current climate of austerity and changes in the nature of demand, hospital care is expensive: it predestines large areas of service delivery and can have a sedimenting impact on models of care at a time when the need for change and reform is becoming a priority. Demand and cost inflation in the health-care sector continue to rise faster than GDP growth rates, future capital and revenue investment are seen to be severely curtailed by current economic factors, and new technology is beginning to offer a range of alternative models of healthcare provision more suited to future need. All these imply significant impacts on capital asset planning and investment decisions.

By 'capital' we mean the physical infrastructure of the healthcare system – buildings and equipment, with the estate of these items being a stock concept and the investment in them being a flow, which, over time, gradually alters that stock. This capital stock acts with other factors of production, primarily human resources, to produce healthcare output. The bulk of this physical capital is in the hospital system – not all, since the same healthcare can often be delivered in numerous settings. This is not only capital and technology intensive but also paradoxically the most labour-intensive part of the healthcare production system.

One major and clear trend is towards greater system-wide integration of care. Future capital investment strategies must also recognize new limitations in the form of reduced access to financing and reduced workforce availability and affordability. There is already a notable switch in capital priorities away from major new hospital projects, which are often expensive and rigid, towards lighter renovation for reconfiguration, which is cheaper and more flexible. Building for forty-year horizons is less and less the way ahead.

This chapter highlights the health and economic factors likely to have a significant influence on UK, European and – to a certain extent – global capital asset strategies in healthcare. Many commentaries on 'healthcare capital' tend towards translating and explaining how to make the best of extant processes, guidelines and practices and can prove parochial and introspective in nature and application. However, there is a need for practitioners and managers to develop the fresh perspectives necessary for the greater freedoms and self-reliance that lie ahead, and to learn how to position the major capital assets of the healthcare system better to deliver seamless care. One word serves to describe the outlook for capital planning and financing – turbulence.

Learning activity 15.1

Reflect on the similarities and differences between healthcare as an economic activity in using physical capital stock (buildings and equipment) and human capital stock (staff competences) in generating production.

- How do other industries blend physical infrastructure, equipment and skilled and unskilled labour to generate output?
- How does your healthcare system do this?
- Building on this, how many things happen in tertiary and secondary hospital care that could take place in primary care?
- Would the results be similar, better or worse – and in what way?

The over-arching trends

The context for capital planning of major infrastructure is changing. There is now a more distinct and agreed view of *what* needs to be done, in the sense of using capital to support improvement, change and reform. This leads on to the next question: *how* it should be done. Distinct trends are emerging: a shift from centralization of guidelines and planning to greater local control and flexibility, and a move from bed-based normative planning to a more integrated and responsive system that is flow and activity based, increasingly with care (disease) pathways as the principal planning influence (a trend that is explored in more depth in Chapter 10 ('Chronic disease and integrated care').

Public sector austerity throughout Europe driven by the economic crisis has tended to focus, at least in the short term, on measures that, at minimum, stem the tide of rising costs and, at best, drive further efficiency savings – all the while somehow sustaining the quantum of service capacity and high-quality standards. Two features are often lacking in this tactical response to economic pressures: *coherence* across health-related sectors (e.g. healthcare itself but also public health, social care and housing), and finding ways and means of improving health service *productivity* (which seems to have been flat-lining for some considerable time; Bojke et al., 2013). Cuts or constraints in one part of the health system are inevitably creating unforeseen consequences in others. This has recently been manifested in the English NHS by the surge in demand, dating from the early 2000s, on hospital emergency departments and consequent blocking of hospital beds, much (though not all) of which relates to a reduced access to primary care as a result of changes to, for example, the GP contract.

A more realistic appraisal of the future shape of healthcare suggests a trend towards a more diverse yet integrated and inter-sectoral focus for care delivery (see in particular Chapters 8 and 10). Thus far, capital investment has usually remained locked within tight sectoral boundaries, and with a short horizon. But there is an important caveat when considering a new cross-cutting portfolio investment model – that of changing public opinion and expectation. Hospitals are icons in local communities and it will require a significant shift in popular culture to persuade a sceptical public to forego the apparent safety net of its local hospital in favour of investing in a more diverse range of alternative and cross-sectoral facilities – and with perhaps controversial models of ownership and funding being necessary to sustain future investment.

Other trends affecting capital planning and development include the expansion in new clinical and information technology innovations (Chapter 16) and more sophisticated health technology assessment (Chapter 5). There is likely to be a significant dilution of spending on the acute sector in favour of making good shortcomings and underinvestment in community-focused care facilities, including social care and perhaps integrated housing, as the most significant way to unlock reform based on the principles of integration. Expenditure aimed solely at the acute sector is consequently more likely to aim towards consolidation and increased concentration of specialized services in fewer but larger (regional) centres of excellence. The middle ground province of the acute district general hospital therefore looks set to feel the squeeze. While this is all fine in theory, hospitals cannot simply downsize while still offering essential services, so capital will be in demand to facilitate the change ('disinvest to invest'; Daniels et al., 2013).

In addition, there is the problem of health inequalities. As public resources continue to be squeezed, policy-makers will naturally question the contribution that major hospitals and new investment in them makes in tackling the problem: are disadvantaged communities best served in reality by complex acute hospitals? A comprehensive review of the state of capital strategy in Europe (Rechel et al., 2009a) confirmed the shortcoming (note that the report and its companion case study volume are useful as primers on health investment issues generally).

Some national authorities are picking up on these major trends (see the case study in in the next section reviewing work in Finland). In addition, the EU is attempting to prod those countries using its resources or relying on it for guidance. The EU Commission Staff Working Document, 'Investing in Health' (European Commission, 2013), encourages member states to 'follow a coherent, strategic policy approach by (amongst other aims) investing in health infrastructure that fosters a transformational change in the health system, in particular reinforcing the shift from a hospital-centred model to community based care and integrated services'. The positive endorsement of such a strategy by the Commission demonstrates a surprisingly strong leadership stance on behalf of the EU. Capital spending is prominent in this overarching policy aim, including in the health sector. The impact of the Commission's strategic view on capital investment can also be seen in the context of its European Structural Aid Investment Funds (ESIF) programme for the period 2014–20. Member states drawing on this fund are leant on heavily to abandon stand-alone major 'legacy' hospital projects (popular in previous programmes) in favour of spending that looks towards facilitating reform, with a significant shift towards primary and community care priorities. This includes those aimed at reducing health inequalities. The Commission also addresses the means by which further capital funding can be accessed over and above its own Cohesion Policy funds; this is set out in 'Europe 2020: A Strategy for Smart, Sustainable and Inclusive Growth' (European Commission, 2010). The strategy promotes a more central role for public–private partnerships as a means of transforming public services, including potentially using ESIF as a joint funding 'public' contribution.

Improving the focus of strategic capital planning

Centralism versus regionalism

The principal elements of strategic capital planning have often been embedded in centrist capital planning practice vested at national level. The picture is changing. In the English NHS, devolution of this role is signalled in the NHS England strategy document, 'Five Year Forward View' (2014), together with the 'Dalton Review' (Department of Health, 2014), where in both cases the emphasis is on partnership and local decision-making. Rather than imposing a new top-down planning process for transformation, these strongly encourage areas to develop and progress their emerging vision for the future of health and care for their populations.

Finland is a good example of new-wave thinking through its reforms that integrate health and social care, with an almost wholly devolved regional focus providing the stimulus for integrated, local population-based investment. The case study in Box 15.1 is indicative of this.

Box 15.1   Case study – Kymenlaakso region, Finland

A pilot study was established in 2012 to review strategic investment need in the Kymenlaakso region of southeast Finland. Kymenlaakso, which comprises twelve municipalities, has a predominately rural population of 180,000. Its health services are delivered through one central hospital, three peripheral hospitals and twelve health centres. The reforms will result in just two municipalities jointly accountable for a fully integrated health and social care service.

The pilot study will form the basis for integrated service and capital investment planning. The marked feature is the extent to which, from concept development stage, capital planning has formed an integral part of the whole systems development process. The following reflect headline stages at which new thinking about capital planning helped shape service planning outcomes.

Stage 1: population profiling

- Analysis demonstrated an ageing population (Table 15.1), and a shift of younger working citizens to major urban centres outside the region.
- An economic risk assessment model showed that, at a time when health costs can be expected to rise, funding availability to meet forecast need would decline in real terms.

Table 15.1 Population projection, Kymenlaakso region, 2010–40

Age groups	2010	2015	2020	2025	2030	2035	2040	Percentage change 2010 to 2040
All groups	177 802	176 190	175 070	174 276	173 476	172 405	171 068	−3.79
0–14 years	26 027	25 089	24 753	24 482	23 955	23 340	22 928	−11.90
15–64 years	114 076	106 776	101 416	97 385	94 434	92 969	92 911	−18.55
65–74 years	19 869	24 884	26 712	24 679	23 743	22 456	20 363	+2.49
75 and over	17 830	19 441	22 189	27 730	31 344	33 640	34 866	+95.55

Stage 2: future service profiling

- Demographic and epidemiological projections were used to assess the impact on the future operating cost structure of services (Figure 15.1).
- An important element was factoring in the costs of servicing capital need over a twenty-year period.

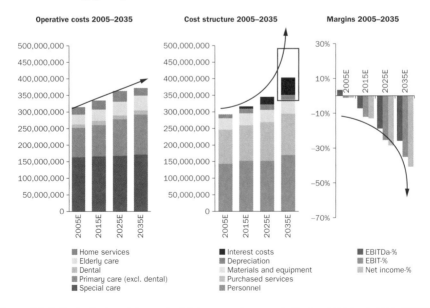

Figure 15.1 Projected cost impact of future service need, Kymenlaakso region, 2005–36

This work demonstrated that over the period 2005–35:

- The service would move from a small surplus to a significant deficit resulting from:
  - projected growth in primary care costs; and
  - a sharp increase in borrowing costs towards the end of the period caused by the conflict between reduced tax income and the need for capital renewal.
- There was a need to shift future investment priorities away from the prevalent and high cost hospital-centred model towards a lower cost community-focused and more responsive portfolio of capital facilities.
- Integrating capital planning and cost considerations at this concept development stage was regarded as a critical success factor in identifying the nature and scale of reform necessary.

Stage 3: balancing the impact of ageing with future acute service needs

- The core issue was handling effectively the health (and social) problems of an ageing population. Continuing with the same model of service for the elderly would risk the acute hospitals becoming the inappropriate default option for elderly care admissions.
- For acute interventional care, a 10 per cent increase in productivity and efficiency would be necessary to meet foreseeable operational and funding needs up to the year 2035. In this context, reconfiguring (including downsizing) the acute sector to support new models of care would be critical to success.

Stage 4: service and capital integration

This analysis formed the foundation for the reform model and capital investment implementation plan (Figure 15.2), which would necessitate:

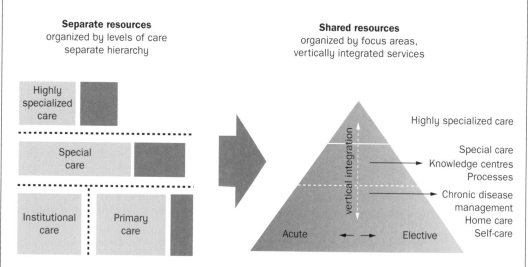

Figure 15.2 Schematic diagram of service and capital integration

- Comprehensively redesigning elderly care (including related chronic illness) services across the region with a new conceptual model for capital, a portfolio of community facilities even extending to integrated housing for the elderly.
- Reshaping acute hospital services, supported by capital redesign based on new models of integrated care pathways aimed at smoothing patient flow both within the hospital and between the hospital and its counterpart services in primary and community care.

In summary, all of the above emphasized the importance of acting rapidly in the reform of the region's healthcare service network. The key message for the capital dimension is that capital planning and investment modelling should form an integral part of the strategic planning process at every stage, including economic and functional risk assessment.

Healthcare delivery flow: developing the appropriate capacity

Hospital capital investment must necessarily relate to its primary function of supporting healthcare delivery, adapting to the trajectory of future clinical needs (McKee and Healy, 2000). Increasingly, clinical protocols are framed within care (disease) pathways, which promise tangible improvement in safety, quality and effectiveness. It might therefore seem axiomatic that they should also provide a reliable foundation on which to build capital models for the future (Panella and Vanhaecht, 2010a, 2010b). A notable feature of some of the most effective and innovative hospital projects in Europe (Rechel et al., 2009b) is the adoption of care pathways as the vocabulary for infrastructure planning: can the planned new or rebuild facility adequately deliver the processes of care?

A survey some time ago by the European Health Property Network (EuHPN) on the adoption of care pathways for capital planning purposes (Hindle et al., 2004) found that, while there was growing expectation that pathways would provide the basis for a more systemized approach to future planning and delivery, the response from capital planners when asked about their intentions to adopt care pathways for project planning purposes was disappointingly limited. Far too few had knowledge of the principles and benefits of care pathway planning. However, since the time of the survey (one of the very few to seek systematically to review the connection between service and capital models), more hospitals in practice are turning to this approach as the basis of their future capital asset planning – for example, Orbis Medical Centre in Sittard, the Netherlands, Coxa Hospital in Tampere, Finland, Helios Kliniken hospital group in Germany, and Karolinska Solna Hospital in Stockholm, Sweden.

There is a major jump from using individual patient pathways for operational planning to generic care pathways that can be aggregated and used for capital planning purposes. Nevertheless, certain key principles may inform and influence the way forward, noting that:

- clinical pathways are fundamental to clinical practice improvement;
- they are an essential input to service delivery design;

- high-quality service delivery models are an essential input to effective strategic asset planning; and
- over the next few years there will be rapid and significant growth in patients coming within the ambit of pathway-based protocols.

Those hospitals that have made the transition to this sort of planning methodology have also necessarily done so through implementation of comprehensive information and communication technology (ICT) support systems, invariably embedded as part of the core design of the facility.

In principle, the hospital can now be better thought of as a network than as a linear sequence. It is conceptually difficult to calculate the capacity of a network in healthcare – or elsewhere – particularly one faced with multiple operating units and variable types and volume of flow (Rechel et al., 2010). This also necessarily implies that hospitals need to be designed, and run, through the use of simulation modelling techniques that map the use of resources to the output of healthcare processes.

The private sector and public–private partnerships (PPPs)

There had been a marked trend in the two decades until the economic crisis towards use of PPP mechanisms to deliver public infrastructure. This now appears in many countries to have reached a pause, as discussed by Barlow et al. (2013). These authors observe that the financial markets are still to some degree in turmoil due to the credit crunch, and there is regulatory pressure on finance markets in particular to shrink bank balance sheets and reduce lending including for investment projects. There is a paradox here, in that funding costs for governments are at present exceptionally low – some governments are borrowing at *negative* interest rates – which ought to make productive investment highly attractive. However, the market rate for public debt does not tell the whole story, in that governments feel obliged to maintain austerity, almost for reputational reasons. The net result is that, if PPP markets have gummed up, governments are not investing public money either.

The requirement to modernize healthcare infrastructure will, of course, endure. How governments can induce such infrastructure, in the course of a trajectory towards large ageing-related healthcare and pension commitments (which will be of the order of several percentage points of GDP in their own right for most or all European countries), is a major challenge. The option does still remain of looking towards an increased role for the private sector, and so it is likely that many administrations will try the route again.

Public–private partnerships are often proposed as offering private sector efficiencies, accessing cheap finance or taking expenditure off government balance sheets. In fact, the last two are mostly illusions, and as an instrument PPP is largely about risk management – both reduction of risk premiums and risk transfer between parties with different degrees of risk aversion. Arguably, bundling activities across project phases (through-life management) and securing private finance, can incentivize appropriate risk management. Necessarily, this requires contract/project terms that are long enough for the private party to invest and to appropriate the returns from that investment – in the health sector, twenty years or more.

While it appears that governments are locked in to a relationship with a private sector partner for this term, in reality it is the investment duration that is the lock-in – whether done by the private sector or by the public sector.

Public–private partnerships in so-called 'economic infrastructure' sectors (transport, energy, etc.) usually involve a transfer of much of the demand or market risk. In 'social infrastructure', such as health and education, the demand risk is so heavily influenced by the government, even within social health insurance models, that the private sector is often unwilling to accept this risk. As a result of this, the risk transfer is often limited to performance of buildings and asset availability, although some models do accept demand risk.

In healthcare, there are a number of archetypal PPP models:

- *Accommodation only*. The physical buildings, and sometimes equipment. The best known is the UK Private Finance Initiative (PFI), also used in Italy, France, Spain, Portuguese 'Wave 2', and many places elsewhere. PFI is the default model for healthcare and hospital PPP, and the legal and financial templates for how to do it are much more widespread than any other type. It has succeeded, in the UK, in delivering a massive fleet of new hospitals, which would certainly otherwise have not been built. Indeed, the vast proportion of all European PPP hospitals have essentially been built via this route. The disadvantage of PFI is not, as is usually said, the excess capital cost of private financial resources (given that capital expenditure is small in a hospital's through-life cost) but rather the disconnect between the asset and the main business line, which embeds a transaction cost more or less guaranteeing inflexibility in service delivery over the decades-long lifetime of a typical hospital.
- *Twin accommodation and clinical services Special-Purpose Vehicles* (four Portuguese 'Wave 1' projects). This is effectively a PFI strapped alongside a medical services company. It has delivered substantial cost savings, almost all on the operational side.
- *Regulated privatization*, such as in Germany. For-profit hospital companies buy facilities from the non-profit sector or state organizations, but run them according to the state *Krankenhausplan* licence, which ensures that hospitals must provide full and open access to all public patients and at the common public tariff. This is also used in Finland, with the Coxa project, and elsewhere. These German chains are delivering medical care at acceptable cost and probably rather higher quality than most state hospitals (Tiemann et al., 2011). See also the comments on the new hospital in Bratislava, below.
- *Full population service structures*, with integrated hospital facilities and community medical services where the local system management has responsibility for operations and the investment in new capacity wherever it is next required (Alzira and several other Valencia region services, Spain). Politically controversial, the model outsources the full palette of healthcare activity. The operator will try to ensure that patients are dealt with in the most appropriate setting of care. Rigorous quality regulation is needed to make a system like this work for the public interest.

Payment systems can be directly linked to the PPP structure, for example performance and availability fees paid when only physical space is provided – the PFI route (National Audit Office, 2010). The major alternative is an indirect payment system – the appropriation of some proportion of the income generated by standard health sector measures, such as fee-for-service or case-mix/diagnostic-related group (the German private groups); this is the case where some demand risk is transferred to the operator. Most interesting among the indirect payment systems is population capitation, which seems to offer the best prospects for aligning short- and long-term incentives between the two sides of a capital planning and operational agreement. This is the method used in Valencia for its full-service PPP variant, and it is a key element in making the model coherent with public healthcare policy in the region.

In any event, it is worth trying to structure the PPP arrangement so that it is not purely a contractual agreement, to be characterized by an adversarial relationship between the two sides with recourse if necessary to litigation, but rather a true partnership oriented to problem-solving during the project life.

Governments around the world need to be aware of future challenges in increasing the role of PPP arrangements in healthcare infrastructure and service provision (Barlow et al., 2010). For instance, it is clear that cost control often is achievable, for the private sector partner. However, quality – for the public sector (capacity variation, performance improvements, and innovation) – is less observable, and consequently less contractible, but must not be sacrificed. One implication is that regulation and governance become *more* important in the case of PPP than for state healthcare delivery.

Furthermore, the maximization of innovation and flexibility throughout the contract period is desirable. But, as observed by Barlow et al. (2013), in order to minimize risks, both public and private organizations are often incentivized to enter into a contract that is specified in great and stifling detail. All too often there is a lack of what Luo (2002) calls 'contingency adaptability', where private and public sectors work together in partnership to resolve the inevitable changes in circumstances during the contract life.

The problematic issue within PFI of splitting control and *de facto* ownership of the capital assets (buildings and equipment) and operations, mentioned above, is leading a number of authorities tentatively to explore full-service models. A notable example is the new University Hospital in Bratislava, presently in planning. Although there are at least two university hospitals in Germany being run under full-service PPP structures, this will be one of the first outside Germany – and in a country that has not invested adequately for decades in its hospitals. Additionally, the hospital feasibility study uses a Layers model to develop the configuration (see next section).

Learning activity 15.2

Evaluate how much public sector spending constraints impact on the ability of health systems to develop their services.

- Where is this likely to push health systems with respect to the employment of private capital, and in what ways?
- Will for-profit capital have a role, or is not-for-profit better in your system?

Design and adaptability: the 'Layers' model

There is some new thinking about designing health facilities that are more responsive to the changing nature of healthcare delivery. These approaches favour a redesign and repositioning of departmental and functional elements in potentially more efficient, cost-effective and sustainable ways. The principle is to design hospitals around the multidisciplinary team concept emerging through the care pathway movement, and which undoubtedly responds well to flow modelling. One of the most promising ideas here is the 'Layers' concept. This model breaks the hospital's facilities down into a limited number of key processing modules, such as 'hot floor' (operating theatres, intensive care, imaging, etc.), 'hotel' accommodation (wards), 'utilities' (HVAC, laboratories, etc.) and 'offices' (consulting rooms, administration, and so on). The model has been developed by DuCHA and TNO in the Netherlands, and is being used in the planning and development of hospital facilities in the Netherlands and elsewhere (e.g. three Dutch hospitals: Sittard – Maaslandziekenhuis; Deventer – Deventer Ziekenhuis; and Utrecht – Mesos Medisch Centrum).

This type of representation can form the basis for scenario-testing the alignment between work processes and design configurations, and to provide the stimulus for new concepts in hospital design. The benefits of the design concept suggest that:

- The principle of 'form following process function' facilitates a clearer differentiation between the design characteristics of each element, recognizing that each will have a substantially different profile as regards building and functional cost, and rate of decay of functional effectiveness. For example, the hot floor will house technologies that have high capital (and operating) cost and generally will have a relatively short optimal life span with constant upgrading and replacement.
- It avoids the embedded dispersal of different functional systems throughout hospital buildings in a pattern that, although reflective of work practice at time of design, is likely to change considerably over the life span of the building.

Taken further, the Layers model promotes the idea that many elements of the conventional hospital can be reconfigured and relocated *outside* the hospital walls – within local and more accessible community settings (Boluijt and Hinkema, 2005).

Other critical issues in the capital investment decision

Evidence-based design

'Evidence-based design' (EBD) promotes the adoption of hospital design characteristics that have a sound evidence base in demonstrating measurable improvement in patient outcomes – for example, factors such as décor, noise, room size and type, and access to outside views. In a pioneering study, Roger Ulrich (1984) linked hospital design to better clinical outcomes, such as reduced analgesics use and lower average length of stay. The result comes about by, for example, avoiding patient falls and adverse drug events; there are also big advantages for staff welfare. Kirk Hamilton, in his EBD study series, suggests: 'Evidence-based design is . . . the conscientious, explicit, and judicious use of current best evidence from research and practice in making critical decisions, together with an informed client, about the design of each individual and unique project' (Malone et al., 2008). The EBD area has more rigorous research evidence than most others that link the hospital asset base to performance – although, clearly, more research would always be welcome (Price et al., 2009).

Where the EBD approach is conclusively becoming more topical and rising rapidly up the design agenda is as part of the armoury to combat hospital-acquired infection. In the USA, the American Institute of Architects in its 2006 'Guidelines for Design and Construction of Health Care Facilities' has called for a universal transition to single rooms. In Europe, there is a similar groundswell of opinion but with some notable differences of opinion on this issue. Many new hospital projects in mainland Europe have moved firmly in favour of a single-bed patient room configuration. Furthermore, rooms are now designed at a larger scale, for multi-functional purposes ('acuity adaptable'), as is also the case of the US studies, thus minimizing patient movement and concomitant medical errors, and reducing the risk of cross-infection. It should be noted that medical errors are a major source of litigation in the USA, which may be making the issue more urgent than in Europe; one of the EBD drivers in the USA has been reports from the Institute of Medicine there ['To Err is Human' (1999); 'Crossing the Quality Chasm' (2013)] that have acted as wake-up calls about the extent of problems – probably just as bad in Europe, but not so well identified.

Studies into current practices within existing facilities are examining cross-contamination from a range of perspectives: different room configurations for intensive care; the implied traffic and movement patterns; consequential compliance with hand washing; the division between clean and dirty spaces; cleaning regimes; and the use of statistical process control to improve cleaning efficiency. An evidence base is being developed through research and will eventually be integrated into a risk assessment and training tool kit for each discipline in a healthcare working space (see HACIRIC, work carried out by a number of British universities).

A notable outcome of the EBD line of thinking is the 'Pebble' group of hospitals, which are actually applying EBD principles, on a unit or whole-facility level. More speculatively, the reports on the 'Fable Hospital' attempt to show that the suite of EBD principles is wholly cost effective, not just 'nice to have'.

Life cycle costing

Life cycle costing (LCC) is simply a tool that offers improved insight into the full financial effects of owning and running a building. LCC is a systematized means of planning and developing the lifetime costs of projects, in which it is important to estimate and compare the costs of the investment project itself, the acquisition of property, and sustaining the capital project during its period of use. It may also include disposal of assets. In the new market-related and more competitive environment in which hospitals operate, this knowledge – prior to capital investment commitment – will become vital.

LCC is not new; and it is definitely already used in many other sectors such as manufacturing. Nevertheless, LCC in its more complete 'industrial' forms is less obvious in the healthcare sector. This may be because a number of healthcare sector-specific characteristics (e.g. the rapid and unpredictable nature of change) have not been adequately factored into the models until now. Progress is, however, being made. For example, the accelerated hospital building programme generated by the PFI in the English NHS, whatever its healthcare performance, has furthered understanding of the links between space, operational functionality and life cycle maintenance needs across long lifetimes. It is in essence a starting point for investigating how different project planning scenarios score, and is an important factor in avoiding the 'rush to certainty' phenomenon that is seen in short-term tactical investment planning.

Learning activity 15.3

Consider the ways in which current health systems are encouraged or otherwise to think long-term, that is, encompassing the life cycle. What changes should be introduced in, for example, payment systems or governance to foster operations that are sustainable in the long term?

Economies of scale and scope

The definition of what constitutes a hospital is something of a moveable feast. At the limit, a nursing home with nothing but a few beds can count, with the other end of the spectrum being large referral sites with hundreds or thousands of beds and complex equipment. One philosophy would suggest that a hospital is a facility with significant diagnostic and treatment capacity (and not just watchful waiting, i.e. it should only include facilities with 'hot floor' capacity; see above). Nevertheless, there is a lot of uncertainty concerning the appropriate scale at which a hospital should be expected to operate.

Scale issues exist in the context of both clinical performance (what is the safe volume of activity?) and economic effect (are long-term average costs of a single activity falling as volume rises?). What do we know about the scale of hospitals on either count? Amazingly, both a great deal and not very much. The literature is vast on both clinical and cost-efficiency grounds, but is not very good. In clinical terms, the process of improving outcomes in larger units is imperfectly understood; definitions of high versus low volumes vary; studies are usually of mortality and exclude morbidity; and, most important, studies usually control poorly for case-mix. When all these factors are taken into account, the volume–outcome relationships are not very strong, and more subtly are at very different levels by specialty.

For cost economies of scale, a variety of methodologies have been used (cost studies, data envelopment analysis, survival studies, etc.). The results of good international studies are surprisingly consistent: economies of scale are exhausted outside a range of two hundred to six hundred beds. That is, there is a boat-shaped cost curve, and both large and small units are more expensive to operate per unit of production than those in the sweet spot. In the UK, NHS England and the Foundation Trust regulator Monitor are aware of these findings, and of the danger that 'small' hospitals (in English terms) are being made unviable by the available tariffs – for poorly understood reasons. Note that population access will unambiguously be worsened by closing small hospitals even if there is an argument for 'larger' hospitals.

A complication is built in to some of the above statements because of the reference to 'beds' as the index of capacity. In fact, the discussion above about the Layers model indicates that the size of a hospital is its ability to do work – not that of storing patients in beds.

The hospital is a network, not a warehouse and, as said above, the capacity of a complex adaptive network is very difficult to determine. If we cannot even state the capacity of a hospital, how can we hope to determine scale efficiency? It will be a question of functional modelling, to determine where the choke points are, with the critical point that these will vary in location over time. It can also be suggested that 'economies of scope' (where it is less costly to produce services together than separately; probably centred around the emergency department) are probably more important than economies of scale.

Flexibility and adaptability

Much of the analysis in this chapter has highlighted the need to ensure adaptability of hospitals – their buildings and equipment, and their interfaces with the rest of the system – to cope with the changes that are occurring now and will surely continue, on both the demand (patient workload) and supply (medical and other technology, and cost) sides. Sometimes, flexibility can appear to designers to mean little more than architectural 'tricks' like demountable walls – but these are unlikely to suffice in the context of the varying demands falling on the hospital system over decades to come. This is not to diminish the contribution that flexible building systems can offer as part of the solution (e.g. the Martini Hospital in Groningen, the Netherlands, has been explicitly designed with standardized spaces that can be varied in fit-out to accommodate different departments as needs change; and the site allows for new buildings to be constructed in a migration while the hospital continues to function).

However, it is worth pointing out that 'adaptability' is often a dimensionless concept. How much flexibility is desirable? The answer cannot be 'as much as possible', since there is always more that could be useful. This hints at the approach that helps to make sense of the appropriate level of adaptability. An analogy can be drawn with capital markets theory, where an 'option' is an instrument that allows investors to hedge against downside or upside risk. The 'option' in this sense – to do something different in the future – offers the right, not the obligation, to a specific future action, with switches built in to the system and usable at a cost but generating a potential value. It has a price that reflects the amount of risk avoided. While some issues are likely to be incalculable ('uncertain' rather than 'risky'), the hospital designer should try to evaluate the principal risks faced, including their financial consequences, and put in place contingencies that offset those risks – but only up to the point when the assessed value of buying flexibility is greater than the cost it will bring (Carthey et al., 2009; de Neufville and Scholtes, 2011).

The carbon agenda

Finally, a demanding growth area in hospital planning, design and construction is responding to the need for reduced carbon emissions. From the emotional to the architectural value, buildings (including hospitals) occupy a key place in society as a whole. Yet, their energy performance is generally so poor that the levels of energy consumed in buildings place the sector among the most significant sources of carbon dioxide emissions in Europe. This observation by the Buildings Performance Institute Europe (BPIE) gives point to the need for substantial improvement. It further notes that while new buildings can be constructed with high-performance levels, it is the older buildings, representing the vast majority of the building stock, which are predominantly of low-energy performance and subsequently in need of renovation work. The EU has established a climate and energy 'Package' (a set of binding legislation) that commits EU countries to achievement of what is known as 20-20-20 targets. They comprise three objectives: a 20 per cent reduction in greenhouse emissions from 1990 levels, increasing the share of energy consumption from renewable sources to 20 per cent of total energy consumption, and a 20 per cent rise in energy efficiency. However, despite the analysis of building performance by BPI and EU legislation, the health sector response across Europe has been variable. In the main, there has been reliance on (within-country) building standards for energy conservation but with a weak response on renewable energy strategy. It can also be argued that hospitals should be in the forefront of reducing carbon emissions, not least in reflecting the detrimental impact that carbon pollution has on population health. In promoting a 'better way forward', the Commission has sponsored a number of initiatives designed to promote good practice, such as the so-called RES-Hospitals project. This provides a case study-based overview of best practice pilot studies from seventeen countries for investment in renewable energy, together with an extensive investment guide. Advice on the wider carbon agenda including other national pilots and mutual learning opportunities is also available through the EU portals.

Conclusion (see Box 15.2)

A notable feature of this overview of capital asset strategy is not only the complexity and rate of change but also the degree of convergence, across Europe and globally, in terms of certain recurring themes and strategies. Successful hospitals of the future will recognize both the need for change, and that change is a remorseless process. Planning must remain dynamic, and wherever possible evidence based, and keep in view key interactions within the healthcare domain, as illustrated in Figure 15.3.

Almost all health systems are moving towards models of healthcare delivery that stimulate greater efficiency and effectiveness. At the time of writing, some of the most progressive ideas are emerging in the Indian subcontinent in the shape of what some describe, unkindly but accurately, as health process factories. Notable here are two pioneering institutions: the Aravind Eye Hospitals, and a more recent development, the Narayana Hrundayala (NH) Heart Hospital, Bangalore (Bhattacharyya et al., 2008; Richman et al., 2008). An analysis of their structure and operation lies outside the scope of this chapter. Nevertheless, their performance, including building design, construction cost, and asset utilization and efficiency markedly exceed their Western counterparts.

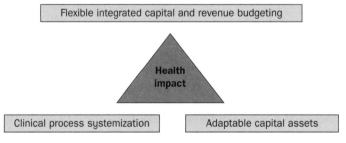

Figure 15.3 Investing for sustainable value

Box 15.2   Summary

- Although the worst of the economic crisis appears to be over, the choice of austerity in fiscal policy made by – or enforced on – governments continues, restricting their financial resources for spending, and investing, in health and healthcare. Another repercussion is that the capital markets have not settled down and banks, in particular, are shrinking their balance sheets.

- Healthcare capital planning is in transition from having been a largely centralized activity where governments issued detailed guidelines, to one where there is much more local control and flexibility.

- The shifts within capital and building planning reflect wider healthcare and societal changes related to ageing and patterns of chronic disease, technological developments, and emerging assumptions about what constitutes appropriate forms of care: the care integration agenda.

- There is a move from bed-based planning of hospitals towards a more activity and care pathway approach that emphasizes flow, and recognizes uncertainty and change for the long term across the whole life cycle. This encompasses a less static view of the healthcare capital stock, with the hospital viewed as a complex network while being merely a sub-system in the wider health and other care networks. One flow-based configuration approach ('Layers') focuses on matching functional unit types and costs of spaces more appropriately inside the hospital. Sustainability concerns are increasingly taking account of energy and carbon issues.

- One trend, currently paused, is for more outsourcing of state capital debt within healthcare capital planning and development via the use of public–private partnerships. There are different models; the previously dominant Private Finance Initiative is showing its age in favour of more complex models inclusive of clinical services (though these are more difficult to structure). Payment systems are important here in order to provide the right incentives.

- The evidence base for 'evidence-based design' continues gradually to improve, showing that micro and macro facility design issues do have a significant impact on the quality of care, and without a sacrifice in cost efficiency (Kent et al., 2009; Quan et al., 2009).

- An area that the industry does not understand well is the impact of economies of scale. For clinical issues, scale tends to be unidirectional but at very different levels by specialty. Economies of scale tend to be exhausted at a hospital size of around six hundred beds – recognizing that 'beds' are not a good index of capacity in complex flow networks. Another problematic area is the need for flexibility, where the valid approach – given that building in flexibility is costly – is to assess how much adaptability is appropriate.

Learning resources

The following web resources, reflected in this chapter, provide some useful capital-related information.

EU public–private partnership perspectives: European Commission (2010) *Europe 2020: A Strategy for Smart, Sustainable and Inclusive Growth*, Communication from the Commission. Brussels: European Commission [http://ec.europa.eu/eu2020/pdf/COMPLET%20EN%20BARROSO%20%20%20007%20-%20Europe%202020%20-%20EN%20version.pdf].

Strategic capital planning: Welsh Office Strategic Capital Investment Framework, May 2008, National Assembly for Wales [www.assemblywales.org/qg10-0011.pdf].

Structural planning, Italy [http://www.euhpn.eu/resource/stewardship-and-governance-decentralised-health-systems-italian-case-study; accessed 15 August 2010].

Integrated planning, Northern Ireland: The service vision in Northern Ireland [http://www.euhpn.eu/resource/euhpn-annualworkshop-belfastaccessed 7 June 2010].

Design and Health Canada [http://www.designandhealth.com/; accessed 18 May 2015].

Care pathways [https://www.england.nhs.uk/2015/03/02/integrated-pathways/; accessed 19 May 2015].

TNO's work, including on the **'Layers' design principles** [https://www.tno.nl/en/collaboration/expertise/earth-life-and-social-sciences/dutch-centre-for-health-assets/; accessed 18/ May 2015].

Public–private partnerships: creating effective alliances [http://www.pwc.com/ca/en/infrastructure-project-finance/public-private-partnerships.jhtml; accessed 18 May 2015].

Karolinska Solna, Stockholm [http://www.nyakarolinskasolna.se/en; accessed 18 May 2015].

Healthcare design – European Congress, Healthcare Planning and Design, Rotterdam, 2010 [http://www.tno.nl/downloads/European%20Congress%20Healthcare%20Planning%20and%20Design_DuCHA10.pdf; accessed 1 September 2010].

For **'Pebble' and other EBD issues**, see the Centre for Health Design, Texas, USA. CHD has produced a compendium of credible reference projects [http://www.healthdesign.org/; accessed 18 May 2015].

For **'Fable'**, see http://www.thehastingscenter.org/uploadedFiles/Landing_Page/SadleretalFableHospitalBusinessCase_HastingsJan11%281%29.pdf [accessed 18 May 2015].

For the new **Bratislava University Hospital**, see http://www.health.gov.sk/Clanok?studia-uskutocnitelnosti-investicii [accessed 18 May 2015].

Carbon emissions [www.res-hospitals.eu; accessed 18 May 2015; also www.lowcarbon-healthcare.eu; accessed 18 May 2015].

References

American Institute of Architects (AIA) (2006) *Guidelines for Design and Construction of Health Care Facilities.* Washington, DC: AIA.

Barlow, J., Roehrich, J. and Wright, S. (2010) De facto privatization or a renewed role for the EU? Paying for Europe's healthcare infrastructure in a recession, *Journal of the Royal Society of Medicine*, 103: 51–5.

Barlow, J., Roehrich, J. and Wright, S. (2013) Europe sees mixed results from public–private partnerships for building and managing health care facilities and services, *Health Affairs*, 32 (1): 146–54.

Bhattacharyya, O., McGahan, A., Dunn, D., Singer, P. and Abdallah, D. (2008) *Innovative Health Service Delivery Models for Low and Middle Income Countries*, Technical Partner Paper #5. Toronto: University of Toronto, Rockefeller Foundation and Results Development Institute.

Bojke, C., Castelli, A., Grasic, K. and Street, A. (2013) *NHS Productivity from 2004/5 to 2010/11*, CHE Research Paper #87. York: University of York.

Boluijt, P. and Hinkema, M.J. (eds.) (2005) *Future Hospitals: Competitive and Healing.* Utrecht: College bouw ziekenhuisvoorzieningen.

Carthey, J., Chow, V., Jung, Y.-M., and Mills, S. (2009) *Flexibility and Adaptability Report: An International Review for the NSW Context.* Sydney, NSW: Centre for Health Assets Australasia (CHAA), University of New South Wales.

Daniels, T., Williams, I., Robinson, S. and Spence, K. (2013) Tackling disinvestment in health care services, *Journal of Health Organisation and Management*, 27 (6): 762–80.

de Neufville, R. and Scholtes, S. (2011) *Flexibility in Engineering Design.* Cambridge, MA: MIT Press.

Department of Health (2014) *Examining New Options and Opportunities for Providers of NHS Care: The Dalton Review.* London: Department of Health [https://www.gov.uk/government/uploads/system/uploads/attachment_data/file/384126/Dalton_Review.pdf; accessed 6 April 2015].

European Commission (2010) *Europe 2020: A Strategy for Smart, Sustainable and Inclusive Growth*, Communication from the Commission. Brussels: European Commission [http://ec.europa.eu/eu2020/pdf/COMPLET%20EN%20BARROSO%20%20%20007%20-%20Europe%202020%20-%20EN%20version.pdf].

European Commission (2013) *Investing in Health.* Brussels: European Commission [http://ec.europa.eu/health/strategy/docs/swd_investing_in_health.pdf; accessed 25 June 2015].

Hindle, D., Dowdeswell, B. and Yasbeck, A.-M. (2004) *Report of a Survey of Clinical Pathways and Strategic Asset Planning in 17 EU Countries.* Utrecht: Netherlands Board for Hospital Facilities.

Institute of Medicine (1999) *To Err is Human: Building a Safer Healthcare System.* Washington, DC: Institute of Medicine [http://iom.nationalacademies.org/~/media/Files/Report%20Files/1999/To-Err-is-Human/To%20Err%20is%20Human%201999%20%20report%20brief.pdf; accessed 25 June 2015].

Institute of Medicine (2013) *Crossing the Quality Chasm: A New Health System for the 21st Century.* Washington, DC: Institute of Medicine [http://iom.nationalacademies.org/~/media/Files/Report%20Files/2001/Crossing-the-Quality-Chasm/Quality%20Chasm%202001%20%20report%20brief.pdf; accessed 25 June 2015].

Kent, J., Richter, L., Keller, A., Watkins, N., Bosch, S., Rasche, J. et al. (2009) *Study Guide 3: Integrating Evidence-Based Design: Practicing the Healthcare Design Process*. Concord, CA: Center for Health Design.

Luo, Y. (2002) Contract, cooperation and performance in international joint ventures, *Strategic Management Journal*, 23: 903–19.

Malone, E., Harmsen, C., Reno, K., Edelstein, E., Hamilton, D.K., Salvatore, A. et al. (2008) *Study Guide 1: An Introduction to Evidence-Based Design: Exploring Healthcare and Design*. Concord, CA: Center for Health Design.

McKee, M. and Healy, J. (2000) The role of the hospital in a changing environment, *Bulletin of the World Health Organization*, 78: 803–10.

National Audit Office (NAO) (2010) *The Performance and Management of Hospital PFI Contracts*. London: NAO [https://www.nao.org.uk/report/the-performance-and-management-of-hospital-pfi-contracts/].

NHS England (2014) *Five Year Forward View*. Leeds: NHS England [http://www.england.nhs.uk/wp-content/uploads/2014/10/5yfv-web.pdf; accessed 6 April 2015].

Panella, M. and Vanhaecht, K. (2010a) Care pathways and organizational systems: the basis for a successful connection, *International Journal of Care Pathways*, 14: 45–6.

Panella, M. and Vanhaecht, K. (2010b) Is there still need for confusion about pathways?, *International Journal of Care Pathways*, 14: 1–3.

Price, A., Sheth, A. and Adamu, Z.A. (2009) *Evidence Based Design of Built Environment Progress Report*, HaCIRIC.

Quan, X., Geboy, L., Ginsberg, R., Bosch, S., Joseph, A. and Keller, A. (2009) *Study Guide 2: Building the Evidence Base: Understanding Research In Healthcare Design*. Concord, CA: Center for Health Design.

Rechel, B., Wright, S., Barlow, J. and McKee, M. (2010) Hospital capacity planning: from measuring stocks to modelling flows, *Bulletin of the World Health Organization*, 88: 632–6.

Rechel, B., Erskine, J., Wright, S., Dowdeswell, B. and McKee, M. (eds.) (2009a) *Capital Investment for Health: Case Studies from Europe*. Copenhagen: WHO Europe [http://www.euro.who.int/__data/assets/pdf_file/0014/43322/E92798.pdf].

Rechel, B., Wright, S., Edwards, N., Dowdeswell, B. and McKee, M. (eds.) (2009b) *Investing in Hospitals of the Future*. Copenhagen: WHO Europe [http://www.euro.who.int/__data/assets/pdf_file/0009/98406/E92354.pdf].

Richman, B., Udayakumar, K., Mitchell, W. and Schulman, K. (2008) Lessons from India in organizational innovation: a tale of two heart hospitals, *Health Affairs*, 27 (5): 1260–70.

Tiemann, O., Schreyögg, J. and Busse, R. (2011) Which type of hospital has the best performance: evidence and implications from Germany, *Eurohealth*, 17 (2/3): 31–3.

Ulrich, R. (1984) A view through a window may influence recovery from surgery, *Science*, 224 (4647): 420–1.

Chapter 16

Informatics for healthcare systems

Paul Taylor

Introduction

Health informatics is the study of how information and information technology can be applied to improve the effectiveness of healthcare services. This chapter looks at the key challenges in health informatics from the perspective of a healthcare manager. We consider how information is created, stored, analysed and applied in looking after patients, in managing organizations and in medical research. Some of the different kinds of systems used in healthcare organizations are described and some of the technical challenges identified. We also address the promise of new technology and the challenges affecting its adoption.

The information cycle

The key aim in informatics is to improve our capacity to make use of data. This is partly about being better able to record and access the data relating to the patients we are treating and partly about learning from those data in order to improve the treatments and services that we offer future patients. In informatics, we often talk about the data cycle, about how data are (1) stored and retrieved, (2) analysed and interpreted and (3) used to drive improvements. We can use this data cycle to look at the use of data in the management of individual patients, the monitoring of organizations and in the biomedical sciences.

Use of data in the management of individual patients

Consider a patient who reads in her newspaper about the risks of osteoporosis in her age group and decides to visit her GP and ask his advice. The GP will need to assess the risk of osteoporosis in this patient on the basis of information about her history and exposure to key risk factors. Traditionally, this would have been a subjective assessment of the woman's risk, but now could be based on a quantitative calculation using an online calculator. The GP can then compare the risk with guidelines and, if appropriate, order a test, for example a DEXA scan to measure the patient's bone density.

Box 16.1   Case study – Choose and Book: a major health IT project in England

Choose and Book began life as a 'booked admissions' initiative. The idea of booked admissions is a simple one: patients and their doctors agree an admission date as soon as it is decided that a referral is required. This gives the patients a degree of choice about when they are treated, a greater sense of involvement in the decision and reduced uncertainty about the process. Since December 2005, all patients in England have been offered a choice of four to five hospitals or other providers once a GP decides that a referral is required. A recent parliamentary report on outpatient waiting times quoted a figure of £356 million for the cost of Choose and Book, which it described as a missed opportunity: annual savings of up to £51 million were being missed because not all hospital appointment slots are to be booked on the system and only half of all possible GP-to-first outpatient referrals are booked using it (HCCPA, 2014).

Systems such as Choose and Book, which are introduced as part of a mandated top-down process of change, are often unpopular and the resulting lack of take-up is often attributed by those at the top to be due to resistance. This barrier to change must be overcome, either through the creation of incentives or by some form of coercion. In contrast, Greenhalgh et al. argue that the relative failure of Choose and Book was because the use of it was at odds with healthcare staff's legitimate ideas about how best to deliver high-quality clinical care (Greenhalgh et al., 2014). They identified four 'foci of intelligible resistance' by healthcare staff.

First, healthcare staff resisted the policy of choice built into Choose and Book. Green-halgh et al. note: 'One of our most consistent findings when observing GP–patient con-sultations was that choice of hospital was either not offered at all or was presented to the patient as an external requirement (something the GP "had" to do), with GPs often highlighting the perceived absurdity of the situation' (2014: 215–16). Second, they resisted the practical consequences of the system's poor functionality. Choose and Book referrals took, on average, twice as long as manual referrals. Staff recounted numerous exam-ples of the technology freezing, crashing, running slowly or failing to identify a suitable appointment. A third source of resistance was the doctors' sense that the system pre-vented them from using their more personal knowledge, which deals not just with each individual patient, but also details of the services available locally, of transport services, of the expertise and interests of individual consultants, and so on. Finally, GPs were unhappy with the way in which using the system seemed to alter the roles and relation-ships in the consultation: getting involved with the detail of appointment booking seemed inappropriate and to indicate a loss of status. One GP said: 'We seem to be moving away from curing, caring and comforting to robotic automata' (2014: 217).

Choose and Book is a good example of the difficulties faced by systems that impact on the doctor–patient relationship. Many practices that made successful use of the system evolved an approach to its use whereby the GP did not access the system but delegated that task to the office staff. Both the system and the processes around it are adapted to deal with unanticipated consequences of systems implemented based on a limited understanding of the task.

Learning activity 16.1

Imagine you have been recently diagnosed with medulloblastoma, a rare brain tumour. Spend a little time thinking of questions you might have, then search online for information about the condition.

- What are the types of website you access?
- Is the information contained there helpful?
- How easy is to assess the accuracy and reliability of the information?

This scenario involves two complex computations: the risk calculation and the DEXA scan. The risk calculation involves an equation that was derived from an analysis of data on risk factors and outcomes from a large population of patients. A DEXA scan exploits the fact that the proportion of X-rays absorbed by a given tissue type is a function of the energy of X-rays. Hence, if we assume a simple mix of tissue types, a comparison of X-rays taken at two different energies allows an estimate of the proportion of bone in a given cross-section. These two applications are good examples of 'high-tech' medicine but computer systems would also be used in the booking of the appointments and the transmission of the test results. One of the key lessons of health informatics is that the computerization of simple administrative systems is often harder to achieve than the programming of apparently more sophisticated analytical tools. Yet such applications often have the potential to lead to a greater transformation in patient experience and outcomes. One high-profile and controversial project of this latter type is 'Choose and Book', as seen in Box 16.1.

Use of data in the monitoring of organizations

Organizations use data to monitor the performance of individuals and teams, to predict demand and plan capacity. Complex data sets can be analysed to identify, for example, the optimal solution to a multi-dimensional problem, an appropriate staff roster or the most effective distribution of ambulances across a city. Effective management therefore requires accurate data. It is increasingly easy to collect, analyse and disseminate data, with the result that managers sometimes describe themselves as drowning in data. What, then, are the really important data? One key distinction is between measures of process and measures of outcome such as the Hospital Standardized Mortality Ratio described in Box 16.2. Clearly, measures of outcome are of greater intrinsic interest; the clinical outcomes of a stay in hospital are the real reason for the hospital visit. A distinction is sometimes made between two classes of measures of outcome, those where the outcome is assessed by the physician, which would be the traditional approach and those where it is assessed by the patient.

Patient-reported outcome measures are being adopted in England, driven by government policy, as a way for the public to compare providers' performance. In other countries, they are used to drive improvements in the clinical care of individual patients. Measures of process have less intrinsic interest but may provide a more direct assessment of what is happening in an organization. In England, key measures of process (percentage of patients waiting for more than four hours in the A&E department, percentage of patients waiting eighteen weeks for treatment) are used to assess performance and have, at times, assumed sufficient importance for some to claim that clinical priorities are distorted in order to meet targets (Mason et al., 2012). The real challenge, often, is being sure that the measures – particularly when used to make comparisons – are a reflection of the real state of affairs and not of an arbitrary feature of the data collection process (see Box 16.2).

Box 16.2   Case study – an outcome measure: coding of palliative care deaths at Mid-Staffs

In 2000, statistician Brian Jarman and *Sunday Times* journalist Tim Kelsey persuaded the UK government to allow them to publish performance tables of NHS trusts. Jarman co-founded the Dr Foster Unit at Imperial College to analyse hospital episode statistics (HES) in order to produce a measure of the quality of care. Kelsey and others founded Dr Foster Intelligence in 2001 to publish the 'Good Hospital Guide' and provide related commercial services to NHS trusts. At the heart of both initiatives was a statistic devised by Jarman, the Hospital Standardized Mortality Ratio (HSMR):

$$\text{HSMR} = (\text{Actual Deaths/Expected Deaths}) \times 100$$

Data on actual deaths were taken from HES data and restricted to in-hospital deaths. A logistic regression model was used to calculate the risk of death for the fifty most common diagnoses, which account for over 80 per cent of admissions, based on a set of factors: sex, age, admission method (non-elective or elective), socioeconomic deprivation quintile of the area of residence of the patient, diagnosis/procedure subgroup, co-morbidities, number of previous emergency admissions, year of discharge, month of admission and source of admission and the use of the code for palliative care (Jarman et al., 1999). Using data on the mix of these factors seen by each trust, they calculated the expected death rate. If the expected death rate equalled the actual death rate, the trust had a score of one hundred. Scores tended to vary between seventy-five and one hundred and twenty. The measure proved successful in that it detected problems at one trust that became notorious: between 1997 and 2008, the HSMR of Mid-Staffordshire NHS Trust never got below one hundred and eight. In all but two years, the 95 per cent confidence interval around the HSMR was entirely above one hundred (Taylor, 2013).

The HSMR is, however, susceptible to error. Hospitals that are better at recording patients' co-morbidities will have a higher expected mortality, again making it easier to score well on the HSMR. Similar effects are found, for example, where patients are more easily discharged into a hospice, since the mortality rate used in HSMR excludes those who die immediately after discharge. The proportion of deaths coded as palliative care at Mid-Staffs rose from 0 per cent the in last quarter of 2007 to 34 per cent in the third quarter of 2008. The impact on the trust's HSMR was that it fell below one hundred for the first time since the 1990s. The Francis Report into the problems at Mid-Staffs found no evidence of a deliberate attempt to rig the results and considers other possible explanations for the change in coding practice. It is still striking that, in Jarman's phrase, the hospital seemed, in its coding practices at least, to have reinvented itself overnight as a specialist in terminal care. The timing is particularly suspicious: the changes coincided with the launch of a Healthcare Commission Inquiry into Mid-Staffs in March 2008.

Use of data in the biomedical sciences

Increasingly, medical research relies on what is called 'real world data' – that is, the secondary analysis of data that are primarily collected to support patient care. In 2003, for example, the media focus on the publication of flawed research linking autism to the MMR vaccine led to a drop in immunization rates to 82 per cent down from 92 per cent in 1995/6. An increase in measles outbreaks inevitably followed, creating an urgent need for robust evidence of the safety of MMR. In 2004, researchers from the London School of Hygiene and Tropical Medicine identified 1294 children diagnosed with autism or pervasive developmental disorder and 4469 children without such a diagnosis but drawn from the same population and matched for age, gender and GP practice (Smeeth et al., 2004). They compared the immunization records of the two groups and found no difference, providing a convincing and timely demonstration that the MMR vaccine was not causing autism. The paper appeared in the *Lancet* and its findings were widely reported in the media. The study was possible because for many years a large number of GPs had been uploading anonymized data – including diagnoses and immunizations – on all of their patients to a resource then called the General Practice Research Database, now known as the Clinical Practice Research Datalink (CPRD).

CPRD is perhaps the largest and most successful initiative in making routine patient data available for research. The MMR case-control study is just one of 1346 research papers that have been published using the huge amounts of data it contains. Other highly cited papers have looked at topics as diverse as the impact of anti-inflammatory drugs on common cancers, the epidemiology of gout, the mortality risks of severe mental illness and trends in the management of atrial fibrillation. In the past, there has tended to be a separation between the data used in research and the data collected to support routine care. We are now, however, increasingly able to take advantage of the vast amounts of data collected in GP practices and in hospitals in order to test hypotheses that, previously, would have required lengthy and complex clinical trials to investigate.

In each of the above examples there are challenges in how we improve the recording of data, how we turn data into knowledge and how we improve access to knowledge. In the next three sections, we review each of these in turn.

Improving the recording of data

A key goal for research in health informatics has been to support the development of electronic healthcare records that store information acquired by clinicians. The computerization of clinical systems means that medical data are increasingly stored digitally. This has a number of benefits that relate to the physical disadvantages of paper. However, simply replacing paper storage with some form of electronic storage isn't adequate to achieve the really important benefits that can accrue from making the data computable. For this we need to be able to extract the essential meaning from the record of each clinical encounter in a form that allows us to aggregate information across episodes, throughout populations and in different organizations. This, inevitably, requires imposing some kind of discipline on how information is recorded, constraining the clinician who previously was able to use free text to record whatever seemed relevant or important in more or less any way that allowed the efficient transfer of information between colleagues. There are two ways in which this happens: the first is to impose a structure on how data are recorded, in effect forcing the clinician to use some kind of form or template; the other is to restrict the clinician to using some set of standard terms. Work in these two fields is described in the next two sub-sections.

Standards and interoperability: technical challenges in integrating systems

A large and complex hospital will contain many – possibly hundreds – different computer systems that need to be able to exchange information if the hospital is to function efficiently. Increasingly, patients with serious conditions are cared for under collaborative arrangements, which means that the requirement for interoperability extends to systems in different hospitals and other care organizations. A precondition of this interoperability is standardization. In order for systems to work together, the implementers have to agree to define, at some level, how information is represented, so that it is mutually intelligible. The agreement and emergence of standards is a universal problem in a digital economy, and a complex one that requires a degree of cooperation between organizations that are commercial competitors.

In the healthcare IT sector, there have been multiple attempts to define standards to allow the better integration of healthcare systems. Some of these have been highly successful. DICOM, for example, is the standard for medical imaging. It defines an image format, just as jpg does, but also a messaging standard that allows different image acquisition and display devices to work together fairly seamlessly in a radiology department. HL7 defines a messaging standard for the exchange of information such as test results, as well as billing information. There are other standards that allow for the exchange of medical documents with a degree of structure (HL7 CDA, IHE XDS).

A more ambitious approach to securing interoperability has been to define a language and a set of open source tools that allow clinicians to share definitions of the kind of information required for a particular clinical application. ISO 13606 and the openEHR initiative both allow for the definition of what are known as archetypes, structured descriptions of the data fields and the data types that would be expected to be recorded as part of, for example, a blood pressure measurement (Garde et al., 2007).

Controlled clinical terminologies

There are a variety of controlled clinical terminologies in use, with different applications. The two most important ones for most readers of this book will be the International Classification of Diseases (ICD) and the Systematics Nomenclature of Medicine or SNOMED. ICD is sponsored by the World Health Organization and provides a structured list of codes, each with a succinct definition and an explicit list of inclusion and exclusion criteria for all diagnoses, grouped into a small set of broad categories known as chapters. ICD predates the world of computers and has an important history as an aid to statisticians attempting to standardize the recording of diseases, and especially of causes of death. SNOMED, in contrast, is very much the child of the computer age and was developed to provide a complete terminology covering everything that might be recorded on the computer record. It has a more flexible organization than ICD does. Terms are grouped into multiple hierarchies and although, in theory, each term is defined using an underlying logic, in practice both the meanings of the terms and the organization of the terminology are confusing. SNOMED is a vast and contentious undertaking, which, despite widespread international support, has not become a ubiquitous standard (Spackman et al., 1997).

Turning data into knowledge

This section deals with how we can analyse data to obtain new insights. A complete account would deal with every aspect of medical research, including clinical trials and epidemiological surveys. So construed, the topic is too vast to be dealt with in detail here. Instead, this section focuses on two approaches to the analysis of data that are commonly used in health informatics and are directly applicable in health service management.

Risk prediction

One obvious example of how we turn data into knowledge is when we use data to generate a rule or an equation that we can use to predict outcomes in the future. A well-known technique for this is regression, which is used to derive an equation from a set of data points for which we have values for the dependent variable (the thing we are trying to predict) and values for the independent variable (the thing we are using to do the predicting). If there are multiple 'predictor variables', the approach is called multiple regression. If the output is a binary classification (e.g. high-risk patient or not), the approach involves multiple logistic regression. The term logistic refers to the use of the logit function, a mathematical manoeuvre that allows us to adapt the world of probabilities (which lie between the bounds of zero and one) to the maths of regression (where numbers can range up and down to infinities).

One application that has received a consistent level of attention is predicting hospital admissions – specifically, looking at the readmission of patients who were admitted as emergencies (Kansagara et al., 2011). The most obvious goal of this research is to identify patients who would benefit most from 'care transition interventions' – that is, patients who could receive some additional care after discharge, which, if sufficiently well targeted and sufficiently effective, could improve their health and well-being and generate savings for the system. The aim of this kind of mathematical analysis applied to healthcare is often to devise a new test that will identify a sub-group for whom some intervention will prove cost effective. The approach is often to take a set of historical data and divide into two sets: the training set and the test set. Each set must include a set of 'input variables' and at least one 'output' or 'outcome variable'. Essentially, the task is to use the training set to explore the influence that the input variables have on the outcome in order to derive a prediction rule, and then to test the prediction rule by applying it to the input variables in the test set and seeing whether the outcome generated matches the outcome recorded in the data.

Many prediction rules have been developed, evaluated and published. It is less clear what impact they are having on patient care. The challenge, often, is to design an intervention that is cost effective for a population identified by the equation.

Statistical process control

Statistical process control (SPC) is used to distinguish 'common cause' from 'special cause' variation. The idea is to measure the variation within a sample and identify cases where the variation seems sufficiently extreme to warrant attention. To test for 'special cause variation', we must first decide what proportion of the distribution counts as extreme: how far along either extremity to set the threshold so that a data point lying beyond the threshold is said to be 'special cause variation' and therefore worthy of investigation. We generally measure variation in units known as standard deviations. In SPC, the threshold on variation is conventionally set at three standard deviations from the mean. At this threshold, 0.27 per cent of plotted data can be expected to fall in the extremities. Hence a typical plot, which might contain thirty or so points, will very rarely contain a point in the extremity, unless it is there because the data item at that point is not part of the same distribution as the other items (i.e. it reflects some 'special cause variation').

The basic analytical tool in SPC is a graphical device called the control chart. The technique is commonly used to look for fluctuations in measurements taken of a process at different points in time. The measurements are plotted, with the measured value on the y-axis and the time of measurement on the x-axis. To assess the quality of the process, we look for special cause variation. The task can be made easier by superimposing on the plot a solid line to indicate the mean and dotted lines at three standard deviations above and below the mean – these two thresholds are referred to in SPC as the upper and lower control limits.

SPC was developed in the 1920s and first used to study processes in manufacturing. It has now been applied by a variety of agencies and teams with an interest in quality to a range of problems in healthcare, including, controversially, looking for GPs or GP practices with unusually high death rates. British GP Harold Shipman was convicted of the murder of fifteen of his elderly patients but is believed to have killed many more, perhaps one hundred and sevnty five or even as many as two hundred and fifteen. It seems absolutely unbelievable that murder on such a scale could go undetected. Mohammed and colleagues argue that Shipman did stray outside SPC control limits derived from the district in which he worked. Their analysis suggests 'special cause variation' in 1993, 1995, 1996, 1997 and 1998. The difficulty in using SPC as a kind of screening test, however, is that since there are 9000 practices in England, every year forty five would be in the top 0.5 per cent of the distribution and would therefore come under investigation (Mohammed et al., 2001).

New directions

New techniques for analysing data are driven by two new related developments. The first is the potential of what is commonly referred to as 'big data'; the other is that of linked data. When we talk about 'big data', we are interested in the possibility that analysing very large data sets might enable us to find patterns or effects that would be concealed in smaller data sets. Almost inevitably these large data sets are created from data that are being used for a purpose other than that for which they were originally collected and will include items that are, in consequence, hard to interpret. The hope is that the sheer scale of the data will compensate for any problems in the accuracy or completeness of the data. Very often this kind of analysis requires a careful assessment of the nature of the problems with the data. Are there missing data and, if so, are they missing at random or is there a systematic effect at work that might prejudice any conclusions we draw? If there is an increase in, for example, adverse events, is the change due to a drop in the quality of care or an improvement in the process for recording such incidents?

The challenge of linked data is similar to that of big data. Many data sets in healthcare are of limited value because they are collected for a restricted purpose. GPs, hospitals, pharmacies, statuary authorities, all collect data about the health of the populations that they serve but each only has access to their own data and to such data as other organizations are willing to share, allowed to share and technically able to share. Where technical, legal and ethical objections to the sharing of this data can be overcome, the linking of different data sets can allow researchers to explore many new and exciting analyses, for example to unpick the relationships between exposure to risk factors early in life and disease outcomes that emerge later in life. Linked data can also help identify patients who can be targeted for interventions in primary care in order to prevent illnesses that would accrue higher costs in secondary care.

These studies almost inevitably require that the researchers have access to identifiable data that should be regarded as confidential. Some form of patient identifier must be present in the data if data from two sources are to be combined. It is possible to encrypt the identifiers in advance of releasing the data for linkage but this can mean that misspellings or transcriptions errors lead to failures to match. Often, the matching is carried out on a numerical identifier such as the patient's social security number. The coverage of such identifiers is rarely 100 per cent, so patients' names and addresses are also used, which inevitably raises concerns.

Learning activity 16.2

Search for information about the performance and quality of your local health services, for example your GP or family medical practice.

- What kind of information would you like to have access to before choosing which practice to register with?
- Is the information that is provided helpful?
- How easy is it to assess the accuracy and reliability of the information?

Improving access to knowledge

The third arc in the data cycle, after the recording and analysis of patient data, deals with how the results of the analysis can be applied to improve the delivery of healthcare. Improved access to information can be used to drive improvements in clinical outcome through improved clinical decision-making, improved management decision-making and better health behaviour.

Improving clinical decision-making

Much early research in health informatics dealt with what might now be called decision support systems, tools designed to overcome the inevitable shortcomings of a human information processor. The rationale for such systems was the assumption that a major problem in healthcare was that clinicians did not – and could not – retain all the knowledge that was needed to deliver the best possible care.

Ely and colleagues carried out a study on the information requirements of family doctors (Ely et al., 2000). The researchers waited in the corridor during consultations and then, in between consultations, spoke briefly to the doctors to identify the questions that had arisen. The researchers were not interested in the kinds of question that can be answered by looking at the record, but rather in questions about medical knowledge: 'what is the name of this kind of rash?', 'what is the right dose for this drug?' The doctors generated 1101 questions during the study, an average of 0.32 questions per patient. Of these, seven hundred and two (64 per cent) were not pursued. Doctors said that they might at a later date seek answers to one hundred and twenty-three of these questions. For a further one hundred and forty eight they said that on reflection they were confident that they knew enough to take the right decision, which leaves four hundred and thirty-one questions that were never going to be answered.

One of the most revealing findings of the study was that the mean time spent pursuing an answer was one hundred and eighteen seconds and the median time was sixty seconds. Unless the answer can be found in less than two minutes, the question will simply never be pursued. In order to be effective, decision support systems need to be able to provide clinicians with information in real time, or near real time. One way of doing this is to ensure that the systems are integrated into the systems that support the rest of clinical work. Decision support systems have been shown to be effective where evidence-based clinical guidelines have been computerized and incorporated into, for example, the systems that clinicians use to record patient histories, make referrals or order tests.

Improving management decision-making

Most business organizations, including healthcare providers, rely on complex computer systems for the storage and analysis of data. Simple relational database management systems, commonplace since the 1970s, have evolved. Data warehouse systems, central repositories of data integrated from different sources, are now used to allow a form of enterprise-level analysis known as business intelligence. This term, in use since the 1990s, is associated with technologies such as data marts (a subset of a data warehouse system focused on a single functional area), online analytical processing (OLAP) and the use of scorecards and dashboards to visualize performance metrics. Recent years have seen dramatic changes in the market for health IT products in the United States, through the Affordable Care Act (ACA) and the Health Information Technology for Economic and Clinical Health Act, a component of the 2009 economic stimulus package. The result is that data and analytical tools are now expected to play a role in the transformation of American healthcare into a more efficient, value-driven system, one in which incentives are more in line with patient health (Davidson, 2015).

The question of how best to visualize complex information is increasingly urgent as the functionality of information systems advances, enabling more users to interact with data and explore them in an open-ended way. In many industries, managers have for years had access to near real-time reports tailored to their needs; healthcare, in contrast, has typically relied on centralized production of reports which are (a) historical and (b) standardized for all recipients. A typical interface for a contemporary business intelligence system would include an interactive 'dashboard' providing customizable graphical displays of key metrics, historical trends and reference benchmarks. These will become standard in healthcare too. The health informatics literature includes some studies demonstrating that patients and clinicians make better decisions when data are provided to them in a clear and easily interpreted visual language. The impact on management decision-making is of less interest to researchers but likely to be equally important: clear and unambiguous visual displays will improve the speed and reliability of decision-making (Koopman et al., 2011).

Improving health behaviour

Improving access to knowledge can be empowering not just for clinicians and managers but also for patients and the public. Patients are empowered through access to information about their conditions – to enable them to better participate in decision-making – through access to their own records, patient forums and support groups and by access to data about the quality of process and outcomes in the different healthcare organizations they have access to. Governments around the world are looking at patients as informed consumers whose informed choices can be used as a tool to drive improvements in service providers who compete in a market. There is limited evidence to support the idea that patients either access meaningful information about the quality of services or that they value being offered this kind of choice.

Increasingly in health informatics, the goal is to improve a patient's health not by improving the clinician's performance or the efficiency of the health service but by intervening directly in the patient's own life. In fact, it may not be appropriate to talk of a 'patient' at all because these kinds of informatics initiative are increasingly aimed at improving population health. The hope is that applications delivered via smartphones or tablets can have a significant effect on health behaviour. There are now a great many apps aimed at, for example, supporting smoking cessation, improving diet and encouraging exercise. The most obvious target for these applications, from the point of view of the health service, is to improve patient self-management of long-term conditions, a set of conditions that account for a huge and growing proportion of health service spending. Box 16.3 gives some details of a telehealth experiment aimed at patients with long term conditions. The potential market for such applications is huge and the hype around them has been considerable. The evidence of benefit is more limited.

Box 16.3   Case study – Whole System Demonstrator

The Whole System Demonstrator was one of the largest attempts to assess the efficacy of telehealth in improving the health of patients with long-term conditions. In total, one hundred and seventy-nine GP practices across Kent, Cornwall and Newham were randomly assigned to intervention or control groups (Steventon et al., 2012). A variety of telehealth devices and monitoring systems were used but all participants whose practices were in the intervention group were asked to take readings using the supplied equipment, at a frequency determined by their individual history, and upload the data to centres staffed by specialist nurses and community matrons, who could then consult predefined protocols and respond as appropriate.

The study used a trusted third party, an NHS agency, to link different sources of data about health outcomes and the use of health services. Patient identifiable data were obtained and the identifying information used to identify records for an individual across primary and secondary care. Once the data were linked, the records were anonymized and only then released to the researchers. In this way, the researchers were able to quantify the impact of telehealth on subsequent healthcare, including acute care and A&E admissions.

Comparing data from the four quarters that followed the start of the trial, it is clear that more healthcare resources were being consumed in the control group than in the intervention group. At first sight, this would suggest that telehealth is having an impact. The interpretation is, however complicated by a comparison with the pre-trial period, which seems to suggest that the impact of telehealth was to increase use in the control group rather than to reduce it in the intervention group. It is possible that being in the control group (i.e. being consented for admission into a trial and then not receiving any additional care) led some participants to monitor their health more carefully and, as a result, to access conventional care more frequently. Whatever the explanation, it is clear that the evidence is inconclusive and that the impact of the intervention is small enough to be obscured by complex effects.

Learning activity 16.3

Think about the way data flow in order to support a clinical service. Reflect on an experience of your own. Identify the actors, the systems that they interact with and the data that flow between the systems. One powerful way to represent this is in a dataflow diagram. Central to such a diagram is the different processing steps by which data are transformed, with data outputs from one process providing the inputs to the next. In such a diagram, you need not only identify the processes and the data flows that connect them but also the actors that initiate the process and receive the final outputs, and any data stores where data are recorded.

Future challenges in health informatics

Twenty years ago, the key strategic goal of research in health informatics was the creation of an integrated cradle-to-grave record that would pool all the information from a patient's GP, his or her hospital records and data from any other health provider. Although much good was done and there have been successful standards to facilitate the interoperability of healthcare record systems, progress towards this goal has been slow. The more rapid change has been the personalization of information systems with the rise in smartphones, smart watches and other personal health monitors. Although the applications that generate and store the data are in some sense personal to the individual, a lot of the excitement generated comes from the potential of the aggregation and linking of these data. These two new developments, personal health records and linked data, are the two dominant themes in contemporary health informatics.

Personal health records

Traditionally, research in health informatics has focused on the systems used by clinicians to record data about their patients. Increasingly, however, patients and members of the public have access to systems for recording information relevant to their health. This is in part due to the growing market for consumer products such as fitbits and exercise bands and in part due to the increasing viability of patient self-testing in the monitoring of long-term conditions such as diabetes and hypertension.

There is also a trend towards personal health records. In many countries, there is a multiplicity of health providers and patients may contract with a variety of organizations; in such an environment, it can make sense for the patient to contract with an appropriate service provider to host an integrated record that is controlled by the patient: a personal health record. The primary market for such services is the USA and the rationale is weaker in a setting such as the UK where most healthcare is provided by the NHS. Nevertheless, patients increasingly expect access to their records and that the records should have features of personal health records, allowing them to upload data about their health, for example.

Linked data

One of the challenges facing informatics is the rising public concern about the manner in which patient records are shared. Patient consent has to be obtained before anyone outside the team immediately responsible for the patient's care can access their record. The clinician has a duty of confidentiality and the patient has a right to privacy. However, it has long been established practice in medical research that data from which all identifying information has been removed can be shared more widely – for example, with medical researchers. In recent years, the commercial value of such information has tempted some providers to exploit the data that they hold as a source of revenue, while others have made information available in a spirit of transparency or to support the public interest.

For US$50, you can obtain the 'Comprehensive Hospital Abstract Reporting System: Hospital Inpatient Dataset: Clinical Data', which provides anonymized data on all hospitalizations in Washington State. In 2011, there were 648,384. A researcher interested in privacy issues matched this anonymized hospital data with data from eighty-one news stories published in Washington State in 2011 and containing the word 'hospitalization' (Sweeney, 2013). It proved a simple task to identify the hospital records of thirty-five individuals. These people appeared anonymously in the hospital data but were named in the news reports. The hospitalizations were mostly a consequence of motor vehicle accidents and in most the hospital record contained few details beyond those found in the newspaper report. In ten cases, however, there were references in the hospital data to potentially sensitive information such as venereal diseases, drug dependency, alcohol use or payment issues.

The important point here is that where we used to think in terms of two simple categories – confidential identifiable data and less confidential anonymized data – the ease with which data can now be linked means that many anonymized data are at least potentially re-identifiable. Such data are often referred to as 'pseudonymized'. Pseudonymized data are, inevitably, a less well understood category, it can be shared but many providers will expect researchers to obtain consent, if possible. The 2012 Health and Social Care Act introduced a requirement for GPs in England to share anonymized coded data on all their patients with a government agency that would, in turn – and for a fee – share the data with health service managers, researchers and also with commercial organizations. Under the legislation, neither patients nor GPSs were given the right to opt out but patients did have the right to object and the Secretary of State announced that anyone who objected would be allowed to opt out. This created a requirement for patients to be informed of the initiative, which in turn led to a bungled exercise in patient engagement and an organized campaign of opt-outs which grew to the point that the scheme was suspended (Hagger-Johnson et al., 2014). If the potential benefits of linked data are to be achieved, researchers and clinicians will have to become much better at persuading patients and the public of the importance of their research and of the safeguards that can be put in place to prevent inappropriate use.

Learning activity 16.4

Think about what you need to measure to model the performance of a clinical service with which you are familiar.

- What are the key performance indicators for the service?
- What are the outputs on which data are collected?
- How easy would it be to collect data that would be needed to measure the outcomes that the patients or the professionals working in the service would be most concerned about?
- Are there measures of process that would be as valuable as measures of outcome?
- What would be suitable benchmarks or comparators?
- How might the performance indicators be affected by case-mix, population, selection or other potential biases?

Learning resources

American Medical Informatics Association: The AMIA is the largest and most prestigious professional body in health informatics. It runs a major journal and conference and a number of campaigns, including major initiatives in education. The website also hosts a blog as well as carrying information about health informatics meetings and events [https://www.amia.org/].

digitalhealth.net: A UK-focused website with news and comment on issues in health informatics. It carries advertising and the job adverts are a good way to look at the range of roles that health informatics specialists fufil. The site also hosts a network for chief information officers to exchange ideas [http://www.digitalhealth.net/index.cfm].

Health Informatics Forum: This forum is an international online community that claims to have over 8000 members from around the world. The website also hosts a Massive Open Online Course (MOOC) in health informatics, which provides a great way to get a grounding in the discipline. The MOOC consists of twenty health informatics courses delivered through narrated lectures and online discussions [http://www.health-informaticsforum.com/].

e-Learning for Healthcare: A training resource funded by the UK Department of Health that provides online learning materials aimed at health professionals wanting to find out more about health informatics [http://www.e-lfh.org.uk/programmes/health-informatics/].

Journal of Medical Internet Research: JMIR is one the more successful open-access journals. It focuses on applications of health informatics that support the consumers of healthcare rather than those aimed more at the practitioners of healthcare. This field is sometimes called consumer health informatics, ehealth or mhealth [http://www.jmir.org/].

References

Davidson, A.J. (2015) Creating value: unifying silos into public health business intelligence, *eGEMs*, 2 (4): 1172.

Ely, J.W., Osheroff, J.A., Ebell, M.H., Bergus, G.R., Levy, B.T., Chambliss, M.L. et al. (2000) Analysis of questions asked by family physicians regarding patient care, *Western Journal of Medicine*, 172: 315–19.

Garde, S., Knaup, P., Hovenga, E. and Herd, S. (2007) Towards semantic interoperability for electronic health records: domain knowledge governance for openEHR archetypes, *Methods of Information in Medicine*, 46 (3): 332–43.

Greenhalgh, T., Stones, R. and Swinglehurst, D. (2014) Choose and book: a sociological analysis of 'resistance' to an expert system, *Social Science and Medicine*, 104: 210–19.

Hagger-Johnson, G.E., Harron, K., Goldstein, H., Parslow, R., Dattani, N., Borja, M.C. et al. (2014) Making a hash of data: what risks to privacy does the NHS's care.data scheme pose?, *British Medical Journal*, 348: g2264.

HCCPA (2014) *NHS Waiting Times for Elective Care in England* (No. 55). London: House of Commons Committee of Public Accounts.

Jarman, B., Gault, S., Alves, B., Hider, A., Dolan, S., Cook, A. et al. (1999) Explaining differences in English hospital death rates using routinely collected data, *British Medical Journal*, 318 (7197): 1515–20.

Kansagara, D., Englander, H., Salanitro, A., Kagen, D., Theobald, C., Freeman, M. et al. (2011) Risk prediction models for hospital readmission: a systematic review, *Journal of the American Medical Association*, 306 (15): 1688–98.

Koopman, R.J., Kochendorfer, K.M., Moore, J.L., Mehr, D.R., Wakefield, D.S., Yadamsuren, B. et al. (2011) A diabetes dashboard and physician efficiency and accuracy in accessing data needed for high-quality diabetes care, *Annals of Family Medicine*, 9 (5): 398–405.

Mason, S., Weber, E.J., Coster, J., Freeman, J. and Locker, T. (2012) Time patients spend in the emergency department: England's 4-hour rule – a case of hitting the target but missing the point?, *Annals of Emergency Medicine*, 59: 341–9.

Mohammed, M.A., Cheng, K., Rouse, A. and Marshall, T. (2001) Bristol, Shipman, and clinical governance: Shewhart's forgotten lessons, *Lancet*, 357: 463–7.

Smeeth, L., Cook, C., Fombonne, E., Heavey, L., Rodrigues, L.C., Smith, P.G. et al. (2004) MMR vaccination and pervasive developmental disorders: a case-control study, *Lancet*, 364: 963–9.

Spackman, K.A., Campbell, K.E. and Côté, R.A. (1997) SNOMED RT: a reference terminology for health care, *Proceedings AMIA Annual Fall Symposium*, 1997: 640–4.

Steventon, A., Bardsley, M., Billings, J., Dixon, J., Doll, H., Hirani, S. et al. (2012) Effect of telehealth on use of secondary care and mortality: findings from the Whole System Demonstrator cluster randomised trial, *British Medical Journal*, 344: e3874.

Sweeney, L. (2013) *Matching Known Patients to Health Records in Washington State Data* (SSRN Scholarly Paper #ID 2289850). Rochester, NY: Social Science Research Network.

Taylor, P. (2013) Standardized mortality ratios, *International Journal of Epidemiology*, 42: 1882–90.

The healthcare workforce

Candace Imison and Sophie Castle-Clarke

Introduction

> *Health workers are the core of health systems: without health workers there*
> *is no health care.* (WHO, 2015)

Healthcare is highly labour intensive. The capacity to deliver high-quality healthcare depends on having a workforce of the right size, with the right skills, in the right place, at the right time. Human resources are the most important of the health system's inputs (WHO, 2000). The workforce accounts for a significant proportion of all healthcare spend. In developed countries, the healthcare sector is one of the largest sources of employment. For example, in the European Union, healthcare accounts for around 17 million jobs (or 8 per cent of all employment) (European Commission, 2012).

Yet many countries face healthcare workforce shortages. The workforce is also inequitably distributed across and between countries. Finally, there are important issues around the skills, motivation and performance of the workforce. The changing nature of healthcare alongside growing pressures on healthcare budgets demands new skills, new ways of working and new approaches to managing the healthcare workforce. Sustainable health systems require sustainable ways of working.

This chapter explores how we can develop a healthcare workforce that addresses these challenges. We begin with an exploration of the characteristics of the healthcare workforce. There are important ways in which the healthcare workforce differs from the workforce in other sectors. We then explore in some depth the challenges facing the healthcare workforce and how the workforce needs to adapt to meet these challenges. We then turn to the means by which we can adapt the workforce. This includes workforce planning, workforce regulation, education and training, and workforce modernization. Finally, we look at strategic workforce management and the means by which we can motivate and improve the performance of the healthcare workforce.

Size and characteristics of international healthcare workforce

It is estimated that there are well over 60 million healthcare workers across the globe (WHO, 2006), a figure that is growing rapidly. For example, in the European Union, the number of jobs in the healthcare sector increased by 21 per cent between 2000 and 2010, and even after the economic crisis the healthcare sector has continued to grow, albeit more slowly (European Commission, 2012).

Health workers are 'all people engaged in actions whose primary intent is to enhance health' (WHO, 2006). This includes doctors, nurses and midwives, but also allied health professionals such as therapists and healthcare scientists, public health professionals, community health workers, pharmacists, managers, administrators and all other support workers whose main function relates to healthcare, health promotion or disease prevention.

Health professionals can be salaried or self-employed. In a number of countries, general practitioners and some consultant specialists are self-employed with private practices or are contracted to provide services by insurers, commissioners or other healthcare providers.

Figure 17.1 shows the breakdown of the healthcare workforce for the NHS in England. Over 50 per cent are clinically professionally qualified, with a further quarter providing support to clinical staff.

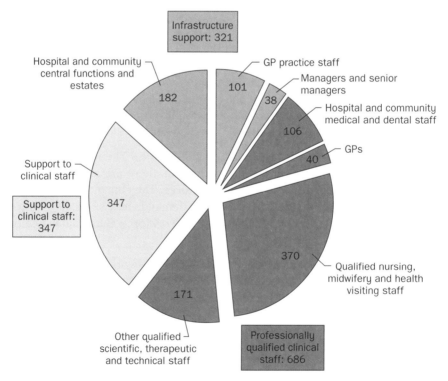

Figure 17.1 Breakdown of the NHS workforce (number of staff, 000s)
Source: Health Education England (2014)

Figures for the European Union show that more than 55 per cent of people employed in the health and social care sector hold at least a post-secondary degree, whereas the average for all sectors is below 33 per cent (European Commission, 2012). As well as being highly educated, the healthcare workforce comprises a high proportion of women. In many countries, women make up over 75 per cent of the healthcare workforce, compared with an estimated 42 per cent of the global general working population (WHO, 2008). In the EU-27 countries, women make up more than 78 per cent of the health and social care workforce and of the 4.2 million new jobs created in the sector between 2000 and 2009, 3.4 million were occupied by women (European Commission, 2010). Although skill levels are relatively high and working conditions are often demanding (for instance, night and shift work), wage levels in the health and social services sectors tend to be lower than in other sectors of the economy, which some have linked to the high percentage of women in the workforce (European Commission, 2010).

Access to healthcare professionals varies significantly between countries, with a marked association between economic wealth and overall density of skilled healthcare professionals (see Figure 17.2).

Future workforce challenges

The world's population is rising. By 2035, an additional 1.9 billion people are expected to be seeking healthcare. In addition, the world's population is ageing. Between now and 2030, every country will experience population ageing. Over the past six decades, the share of people aged sixty years and older rose from 8 per cent to 10 per cent. In the next four decades, this group is expected to rise to 22 per cent of the total population – a jump from 800 million to 2 billion people (Bloom et al., 2015). Older people have greater health and long-term care needs than younger people, and are more likely to make greater demands on health and social care systems.

The ageing population carries with it a growing burden of chronic health problems. It is estimated that chronic conditions now account for over half the global disease burden (WHO, 2004) and the chronic disease burden is even higher in developed countries. The shifting

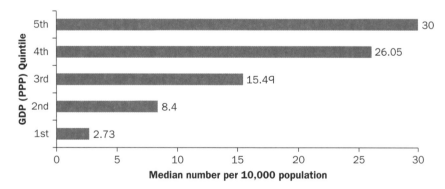

Figure 17.2 Median number of skilled health professionals per 10,000 population, countries (n = 118) grouped by quintiles of GDP (adjusted for purchasing power parity) per capita
Source: WHO (2014)

balance between acute and chronic health problems is placing new demands on the health-care workforce. As a consequence, nearly all countries have skill imbalances, which threaten the quality of care and have the potential to cause inefficiencies. In some countries, the skill mix depends too much on doctors and specialists and in most, population-based public health is neglected (Chen et al., 2004). There is also a need to ensure that the workforce develops some core competences around quality improvement, the use of information and communication technology and working collaboratively with patients and other professional staff (WHO, 2005). New medical and information technologies will also profoundly change the workforce: they will change the nature of the work, where it can be done and who does it. Technology puts power in the hands of patients and means more care can take place outside the hospital setting (Imison and Bohmer, 2013).

While the demand for the healthcare workforce is growing and changing, there are challenges to workforce supply. The workforce is also ageing, particularly in developed countries, where a significant proportion of the workforce will retire in the next ten years. In 2009, about 30 per cent of all doctors in the EU were over fifty-five years of age and by 2020 more than 60,000 doctors or 3.2 per cent of all European doctors are expected to retire annually (European Commission, 2012). In addition, as the proportion of younger people in the population is expected to fall over the next twenty years, there will be increasing competition for the best students from other sectors – which may compound challenges to train and recruit healthcare workers (OECD, 2008).

Increasing turnover is an issue of growing importance in the UK and across the EU. Preliminary findings from one of the largest nursing workforce studies ever conducted in Europe and the USA (Nurse Forecasting in Europe – RN4Cast) shows rising problems of nurse burn-out and dissatisfaction due to working conditions (European Commission, 2010).

In 2006, the World Health Organization estimated that there was a global shortage of 2.4 million midwives, nurses and physicians, largely in undeveloped countries (WHO, 2006). By 2035, the WHO estimates that there will be a deficit of 12.9 million skilled healthcare professionals, across developed and undeveloped countries (WHO, 2014). The European Commission (2012) has estimated that there will be a deficit of around 1 million healthcare workers by 2020, rising to 2 million if long-term care and ancillary professions are taken into account. If no action is taken, the consequence will be a 15 per cent shortfall in care delivery across the EU.

Workforce planning

Health workforce planning aims to achieve a proper balance between the supply and demand of health professionals in both the short and longer term. Workforce planning is particularly important in the health sector, given the time and cost of training healthcare professionals. A key objective of many countries' health workforce planning activity is to guide decisions about student numbers for the education and training programmes for doctors, nurses and other healthcare professionals.

Most countries exercise some form of control over their student intake (particularly medicine). This is motivated by a variety of factors but most notably as a means to contain

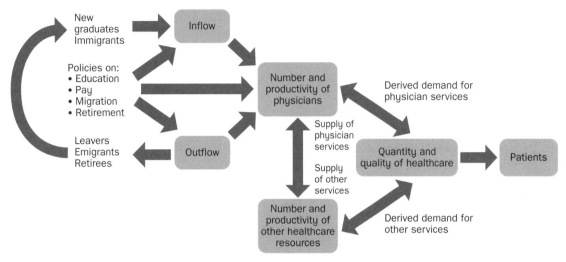

Figure 17.3: Aligning workforce supply with demand
Source: Adapted from Simoens and Hurst (2006)

costs. The way in which control is exercised varies between countries. Some, like the UK and Australia, control the number of state-funded university places. In the United States, there are no restrictions on the number of university places but the number of residency places (for postgraduate training) funded by Medicare are capped (OECD, 2008).

Workforce planners attempt to model the future demand for health workers and the future supply. The stock flow model shown in Figure 17.3, in which the stock (current number of staff) is modified by estimates and projections of future inflows and outflows to produce an estimate of actual or desired future stock, can be helpful in supporting decisions on allocation of funds for training, but it is very important to recognize the high degree of uncertainty about many predictions.

The types of factor that stockflow models tend to take into account are summarised in Box 17.1.

Box 17.1 Assessing the future supply and demand of healthcare workers

The current and future supply of health workers is affected by the 'inflows' in each occupation and the 'outflows' (exits), as well as the activity rates of the 'stock' of health workers (working hours).

- *Inflows* – include graduates from medical and nursing education, foreign-trained health professionals who immigrate and people returning to work in the health sector after a temporary exit.

- *Outflows* – include people who either leave the health sector to work in other sectors or leave the workforce altogether, health professionals who emigrate and those who retire.
- *The stock* of health workers can be measured in headcounts or full-time equivalents (FTE). FTE is a better measure as it adjusts for working hours and part-time work.

The demand for health workers

Many factors affect the current and future demand for health services and therefore for health workers. The main drivers are:

1   *Demography* – the size and structure of the population, including factors such as the changing birth and death rates.
2   *Morbidity* (or epidemiology) – the changing pattern of disease, such as changes in disease prevalence.
3   *Health service utilization* (or healthcare needs in approaches that use a broader approach to measuring demand) – for example, taking account of different utilization rates by different population groups.
4   *Different health service delivery models* (which may influence workforce requirements in primary care, hospitals and long-term care).
5   *Economic growth and related growth in health spending* (which will influence the ability to pay for health services from public or private sources).

Source: Ono et al. (2013).

While future demographic changes are fairly well understood, all the other drivers of future demand involve a high degree of uncertainty and they are also all interrelated. Given the complexities, the workforce planning process is a balancing act that requires the ability to respond flexibly and adjust to changes in the relative effect of different supply and demand factors over time. It should be less about long-term predictive precision and more about developing an adaptive and flexible process (Imison et al., 2009).

A review of twenty six workforce planning models across the OECD (Ono et al., 2013) identified the following issues in the current approaches (see Table 17.1).

- Models have failed to take account of current imbalances in the healthcare workforce.
- There have been few attempts to link health workforce projections with health expenditure projections, yet health expenditure ultimately determines the size of the healthcare workforce and different expenditure projections have a significant impact on future workforce demand.
- Some models have focused on healthcare needs rather than utilization, which requires normative judgements and is highly uncertain. Many models are uni-professional

and miss the opportunities for a degree of 'horizontal' or 'vertical' substitution. However, agreeing assumptions about the potential for this is complex and may not be widely accepted.

- Most models make arbitrary assumptions about changes in productivity, with little evidence to base this on.

Table 17.1 Modelling the future GP workforce – a comparison of two countries

Model	Netherlands	United Kingdom
Overall approach	Uses empirical data, past trends and expert opinion to assess how each factor will influence supply and demand in the future	Uses empirical data with expert opinion to develop a range of supply and demand scenarios for the future
Supply factors		
Stocks	• Current numbers (WTE + FTE)	• Current numbers (WTE + FTE)
Inflows	• Graduation rates • Completion of specialist and GP training • Immigration	• Medical school intake (assumed constant) + dropout rate (assumed constant) • Specialist and GP training – intake, dropout and length
Outflows	% leaving by age/sex – five, ten, fifteen, twenty years	• Retirement projections + early leaver projections
Demand factors		
	• Population projections • Epidemiology • Over-/under-use by particular population groups • Estimates of unmet need/demand • Opportunities for workforce substitution (vertical and horizontal)	Used experts to create four scenarios based on four factors: • Population size • Level of need (health) • Level of service • Productivity Scenarios: 1 Compression of morbidity in higher resource environment 2 Compression of morbidity in lower resource environment 3 Expansion of morbidity in higher resource environment 4 Expansion of morbidity in lower resource environment Also tested scenarios against future funding levels

Source: Based on Ono et al. (2013).

Learning activity 17.1

- How is workforce planning undertaken for the GP workforce in your country and which factors are taken into account in the planning model?
- How does this differ from workforce planning for nurses in your country?
- If you were advising your government on how the GP workforce planning model could be improved, what recommendations would you make? You might want to compare the method used in your country with that of other countries, and see if the approach could be strengthened by applying techniques of other models.

Education and training

Every year, across the globe, at least 1 million doctors, nurses and public health professionals are trained in over 3000 different higher educational institutions at a cost of over US$100 billion a year (Frenk et al., 2011). The length and costs of training vary considerably between professional groups and between countries.

Doctors

The most common pathway for training a doctor is an undergraduate degree of four to six years, followed by one or two years of basic training and then five years (or more) of specialist training in a healthcare setting. Thus training a fully qualified specialist doctor can take ten to fifteen years. Most countries have shorter training periods for general practitioners/family physicians. Here the specialist component is around two to three years, though there are moves in some countries (including England) to extend the length of training. In recent years, doctors have increasingly followed ever more specialist and subspecialist routes in their training. A 2011 survey found that in the USA, doctors can pursue up to eighty different specialist routes with a further one hundred and twenty sub-specialties. It also found the number of specialties varies between countries. For example, in the UK, there are around sixty specialties with approximately fourty sub-specialties (General Medical Council, 2011).

Not all doctors complete their specialist training, but most countries give licences to practise as a doctor after core training. Doctors who have not completed specialist training often work in supporting roles to specialists. In the UK, they are frequently known as associate specialists.

Nurses

Nurses have traditionally been trained to two levels. The first, higher level, is more academic and in most countries results in a degree-level qualification. The training is increasingly offered through higher education institutions and generally takes three or four years. The second, lower level, offers a practical route into nursing that does not require higher level qualifications and is generally undertaken 'on the job' and through schools of nursing attached to hospitals. The length of this training varies across the globe and can be anything between one and three years.

There has been a general trend towards the cessation of the second level training and a move towards nursing becoming an all-graduate profession (Robinson and Griffiths, 2007). Despite this, it is still much cheaper to train a nurse than a doctor. In the UK, it costs £70,000 to train a qualified nurse (Health Education England, 2014).

Allied health professionals

Allied health professionals (AHPs) make up a diverse group of professionals, including paramedics, physiotherapists, occupational therapists and radiographers among others. In the UK, any practising AHP must be registered with the Health and Care Professions Council (HCPC) (Dorning and Bardsley, 2014). Given the diverse range of roles and necessary skills, education and training requirements vary significantly across the different professions.

There are also significant variations in training requirements within professions. For example, in the UK, there are a number of training options for paramedics. Trainees must complete an HCPC-approved programme that can take the form of a diploma, a foundation degree, a BSc honours degree or an Institute of Healthcare Development paramedic award – the latter can be delivered by an employer. Similarly, in the USA and Canada, paramedic training courses and requirements tend to vary considerably by state or province.

Physician associates

Physician associates (or assistants) originated in the USA and have since been employed in a number of countries, including the UK, Canada, Australia and the Netherlands. A physician associate performs various medical tasks under the supervision of a doctor, including taking medical histories, performing examinations, diagnosing illnesses, analysing test results and developing management plans. In the USA, physician associates also prescribe medications, although they do not have that authority to do so in the UK. The UK definition of a physician associate is as follows: 'A new healthcare professional who, while not a doctor, works to the medical model, with the attitudes, skills and knowledge base to deliver holistic care and treatment within the general medical and/or general practice team under defined levels of supervision' (Department of Health, 2006a). In the UK, physician associate training lasts two years and an undergraduate degree is usually required to be eligible for the training.

Quality and content of current training programmes

There is a general dissatisfaction with the quality of professional education. As the Lancet Commission on the education of health professionals pointed out: 'a slow-burning crisis is emerging in the mismatch of professional competencies to patient and population priorities because of fragmentary, out-dated, and static curricula producing ill-equipped graduates from underfinanced institutions' (Frenk et al., 2010: 7). The Commission drew attention to the tribalism of professionals and the tendency for different professional groups to act in isolation or even in competition with one another.

The Commission made ten recommendations for reform to education of which six relate to the content of training (see Box 17.2).

Box 17.2 Recommendations of the Lancet Commission on the content of training

1 Adoption of competency-based curricula that are responsive to rapidly changing needs rather than being dominated by static coursework.
2 Promotion of inter-professional and trans-professional education that breaks down professional silos while enhancing collaborative and non-hierarchical relationships in effective teams.
3 Exploitation of the power of IT for learning through development of evidence, capacity for data collection and analysis, simulation and testing, distance learning, collaborative connectivity, and management of the increase in knowledge.
4 Adaptation locally but harnessing of resources globally in a way that confers capacity to flexibly address local challenges while using global knowledge, experience, and shared resources, including faculty, curriculum, didactic materials and students linked internationally through exchange programmes.
5 Strengthening of educational resources, since faculty, syllabuses, didactic materials and infrastructure are necessary instruments to achieve competencies.
6 Promote a new professionalism that uses competencies as the objective criteria for the classification of health professionals, transforming present conventional silos.

Source: Frenk et al. (2010).

---

e-Learning including simulation learning

As the Lancet Commission has identified, there are many opportunities to strengthen and extend the reach of education programmes through the use of information and other technologies. As well as a wide and growing variety of e-learning programmes (see Box 17.3), there is increasing use of simulation-based approaches where the clinical environment is recreated through physical and/or computer-based simulation aides. For example, many training centres use computer programs that recreate key clinical signs in a 'virtual patient' and simulate the patient response to the clinical decisions made by the student – often providing feedback to the student if they have taken the wrong course of action.

Box. 17.3 e-Learning in practice: advanced radiotherapy programme

Radiotherap-e is a web-based e-learning resource produced by a number of professional bodies associated with the training of radiologists in the UK.

The curriculum includes a variety of modules, each of which consists of several e-learning sessions for existing clinical oncologists, physicists, radiographers and dosimetrists, as well as trainees in clinical oncology that will be treating cancer patients with radiotherapy. The modules include videos of practical techniques, interactive techniques allowing students to identify and highlight key aspects of CT images, drawing tools for students to produce 3D images based on written descriptions, as well as multiple-choice and free text questions.

The emphasis is on sharing the lessons learned through practical experience, and stimulating critical thinking and discussion among those implementing the technique.

For more information, see: http://www.e-lfh.org.uk/programmes/advanced-radiotherapy.

Healthcare workforce regulation

Professional regulation can be defined as: '[T]he set of systems and activities intended to ensure that healthcare practitioners have the necessary knowledge, skills, attitudes and behaviours to provide healthcare safely' (Department of Health, 2006b). The main purpose of the regulators of the healthcare workforce is to protect the public.

Regulators achieve this by setting professional standards, producing a register of everyone who meets these standards and (in some cases) ensuring all those on the register remain fit to practise. Professional regulation becomes statutory when there is a ban on particular activities unless your name appears on the register (Department of Health, 2006b). The type of healthcare worker who is regulated varies from country to country. Predominantly, but not exclusively, healthcare professionals such as doctors and nurses are regulated. However, there is a growing trend to regulate healthcare workers below the level of the traditional professionals, including healthcare assistants and care support wrkers. There is also a growing interest in the regulation of managers that work in healthcare.

Regulatory action can produce barriers to the creation of a flexible and adaptable workforce. For example, in the UK, physician associates, who are trained to undertake many of the routine tasks currently undertaken by doctors, are not recognized as a clinical professional group. As a consequence, they cannot prescribe, unlike their counterparts in the USA, where they are recognized. This significantly limits their capacity to substitute for doctors in what they do. By way of contrast, while all nurses in the UK can be authorized to prescribe, in the USA the capacity for nurse practitioners to prescribe varies between states (Dower et al., 2013).

The regulation of healthcare professionals needs to reflect the increasing mobility of healthcare professionals. It also needs to recognize that technological advances such as telehealth mean that care can be provided across country borders (Barry, 2012). For example, in 2005 European legislation (Directive 2005/36/EC, amended by 2013/55/EU) dictated that certain professional qualifications obtained in EU member states must be recognized by all member states. For large parts of the healthcare workforce, this means that where equivalent qualifications have been gained in Europe, country borders do not act as a barrier to practise. The European Union working time directive has also restricted the number of hours doctors can work per week across Europe. However, despite these changes, there continue to be significant differences in the way in which healthcare workers are regulated across countries, even within Europe.

Each country has its own approach to the regulation of doctors. Some have national bodies, while others license doctors at a more local level – which can result in inconsistent training and licensing standards within a country. In some countries, the organization acting as regulator may also act as the representative body for doctors. To devolve regulatory functions to representative bodies can create a conflict of interest between the doctors they represent and the public they are there to protect. In the UK, the Medical Royal Colleges undertake some regulatory functions, helping to set educational and professional standards, but the registration and licensing of doctors is undertaken by an independent statutory body, the General Medical Council.

Another variation between countries is for how long, and on what basis, doctors are licensed. A process of recertification exists in a number of countries, including the UK and USA (in contrast to Germany and Greece, for example) (de Vries et al., 2009). Licensed doctors in the UK are usually required to revalidate every five years, and are expected to have an annual appraisal to ensure they are fit to practise in their chosen field (de Vries et al., 2009). In the UK, there is also a formal 'fitness to practise' procedure, whereby the General Medical Council brings a case against a doctor if allegations of impaired fitness to practise have been reported. A panel, appointed by open competition and consisting of medical and non-medical individuals, make the decision on whether the doctor is fit to practise.

There is considerable variation in the regulation of nursing across the world. As noted above, there are also differences within countries – exemplified by the USA, where regulation takes place at the state level. In recent years, the regulatory process for nurses has turned its attention to addressing continued competence to practise (Hudspeth, 2008). As of 1 January 2015, all nurses certified by the American Nurses Credentialing Center in the USA are required to renew their certification every five years. Certification can be renewed through various professional development activities, including: continuing education; presentations, publications or research; and professional service.

In the UK, all nurses and midwives will be required to engage in revalidation in order to demonstrate their ability to practise safely and effectively. A number of proposals have been put forward for the revalidation process and include practising a minimum number of hours, undertaking continuous professional development and obtaining feedback about practice, among other things. Proposals were scheduled to be finalized in October 2015.

Health management has typically been viewed as a generic function without formal regulation – particularly given that in many countries management is undertaken by clinicians (Smith and Chambers, 2011). However, there is a growing interest in regulating managers, largely driven by poorly performing healthcare organizations. Some countries have developed strong professional associations that codify management and organizational ethics, accredit development programmes, and operate self-regulation for managers (Smith and Chambers, 2011).

In the UK, the 2013 Francis Inquiry (an investigation prompted by serious failings at the Mid-Staffordshire NHS Foundation Trust) recommended a proper degree of accountability for senior managers as well as the development of a shared professional culture between doctors and non-clinical managers – but stopped short of regulation. This sparked a significant debate about whether healthcare managers should be regulated, and if so how.

The key issues included the fact that managerial skills are not easy to test; a concern that regulation would replace senior corporate governance; and worries regulation would stifle recruitment (Morgan, 2013).

Despite these concerns, in November 2014 the Care Quality Commission introduced the 'Fit and proper persons test' for registered health service managers. The regulation states that providers must not appoint a person to an executive director-level post (including associate directors) or to a non-executive director post unless they are of good character; have the necessary qualifications, skills and experience; are able to perform the work that they are employed for after reasonable adjustments are made; and can supply information regarding their history.

The country with the most formalized approach to the regulation of managers is France (see Box 17.4).

Box 17.4   EHESP Civil Servant Training Programmes, France

In France, anyone wishing to be a hospital director or assistant hospital director must undertake the Health Institution Management Program delivered by the École Nationale des Hautes Études en Santé Publique. There is a formal examination to gain entry to the programme, in common with other areas of French public administration within 'grandes écoles'. Individuals must also have either two years' management experience in a public hospital or four years' experience as a public hospital employee.

There are three aspects to the training, including a cultural element (acquiring new knowledge, e.g. public health, medical, legal), a human element (development of inter-personnel management skills) and a technical element (developing skills to manage human, financial, logistical, economic and technical resources).

The training consists of a twenty-seven month course – including three months of on-the-job specialization. Candidates are assessed throughout the course and need to have satisfactorily completed all parts to be certified.

For more information, see: http://www.ehesp.fr/en/programs/civil-service-executive-degree-programs/health-care-institution-management-program/.

Learning activity 17.2

- What are the major difficulties in regulating healthcare managers?
- Where healthcare managers are regulated, how have these difficulties been overcome? You may want to consider the approaches taken by France and the UK.

Workforce modernization

Medical advances, the changing health needs of the population and growing pressure on healthcare budgets are challenging current professional roles and demarcations. As such, there is a growing need to modernize the healthcare workforce. The different approaches to workforce modernization have been framed in a number of ways (Sibbald et al., 2004; Dubois and Singh, 2009) but essentially all taxonomies involve changing the work, the worker or both (Bohmer and Imison, 2013) (see Figure 17.4).

The drive for efficiency and the prospect of significant shortages in the professional workforce has resulted in considerable interest in the opportunities for 'old work' to transition to a new or alternative worker. A good example would be a physician's assistant taking on work from a general practitioner or family physician. Recent research has shown physician assistants can deliver elements of primary care with equivalent outcomes but at lower cost (Drennan et al., 2014). However, it is thought that physician assistants in the UK could be more valuable to patients and the service if they were able to prescribe (Ostler et al., 2012). As noted above, they are barred from doing this in England, as they are not recognized as a separate professional group and so have to work under the supervision of a doctor. This underlines the importance of the professional regulatory framework in facilitating or blocking new ways of working.

The re-distribution of work may also involve a degree of skills enhancement and thus avoid hand-offs between professionals and support more patient-centred care. Examples of this include care workers acquiring a mix of health and social care skills or community nurses acquiring some occupational therapy skills.

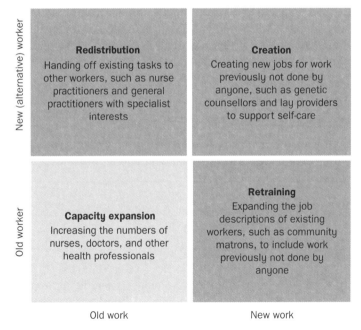

Figure 17.4 Options for workforce redesign

The changing profile of the patient population, particularly the growing numbers of older, frail individuals and those with multiple co-morbidities, also requires 'old workers' to take on new work, such as the new competencies outlined by WHO (2005). Examples include nurses taking on case management or care coordination roles, and proactively managing the care of high-risk populations (see Box 17.5). Finally, 'new workers' are taking on 'new work'. A good example of this is the growing number of 'health coaches' providing lay support to help people adopt healthy behaviours and better manage their chronic conditions.

All of the above strategies have the potential to make the workforce more efficient and effective. However, the evidence suggests that workforce redesign initiatives may not always achieve their stated aims.

The experience of developing new roles over the last twenty years has provided valuable evidence regarding their impact. While the evidence about the opportunities to delegate tasks in a way that does not compromise safety or quality is generally positive, the evidence on costs and sustainability is less positive (Bohmer and Imison, 2013).

- Cheaper staff may not be cheaper overall, for the following reasons:
  - Senior clinicians, although more expensive by the hour, tend to work more quickly, order fewer tests and use fewer bed days, admissions and procedures.
  - If new roles are added without decommissioning old roles, the new role may end up supplementing rather than substituting.
  - Dividing the work among more (cheaper) workers increases team coordination costs.
  - New types of worker (particularly support workers) often have poorly defined roles, especially in relation to the roles of others. It will limit the capacity to free up senior staff time if there is no consistency and clarity over the tasks that they can undertake.

- It can be hard to sustain new roles. Roles are often developed without consideration of a longer term career structure or the need for national recognition to support the portability of skills. This can undermine the long-term sustainability of a role.

Box 17.5   Case study – care coordinators: Trinity Mother Frances Health System, Tyler, Texas, USA

Texas has employed care coordinators in order to meet the challenges posed by shifting from a fee-for-service model to risk-sharing models that reward efficiency (i.e. reducing unnecessary utilization while optimizing revenue and quality) (Mullins et al., 2012).

The care coordinators have been used for:

- Pre-visit planning (including confirming visits, scheduling preventive services and ordering labs): This has resulted in fewer no-shows, high visit volume, improved staff satisfaction, increased adherence and revenue and improved outcomes.

- Care gap management (e.g. following up with patients who are overdue for services): This has resulted in increased adherence and revenue and improved outcomes.
- Transitions of care contacts (following up with patients upon discharge): This has resulted in decreased re-admissions (Mullins et al., 2012).

The care coordinator roles have been carried out by two licensed vocational nurses. The nurses were chosen based on their clinical ability to order tests, make referrals and use the organization's system as well as have clinical discussions with patients, if needed (Mullins et al., 2012).

Mullins et al. (2012) evaluated the approach and found that the use of care coordinators is a 'promising model for practices of all sizes'.

Learning activity 17.3

What are the benefits of employing care coordinators?
What might the drawbacks be of employing care coordinators?
What would you need to consider before employing care coordinators?

Strategic workforce management

While new roles and new ways of working may help bridge some of the future workforce and skills gaps, it will be just as important to engage and retain the current workforce – after all, the majority of tomorrow's workforce is already working today. The seminal work of Borrill, West and others (Borrill et al., 2001) has shown the link between good human resources practices, staff engagement and patient safety (see Figure 17.5).

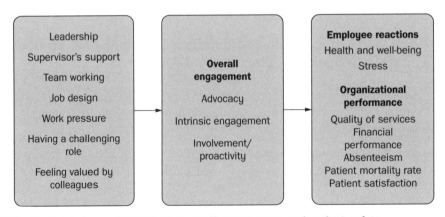

Figure 17.5 The link between HR strategies, staff engagement and patient safety

The characteristics of an engaged workforce include motivation, satisfaction, commitment, finding meaning at work and pride in, as well as advocacy for, the organization. Engaged workers are prepared to 'go the extra mile' and will exert discretionary effort. Not surprisingly, there is good evidence to show that the more positive experiences of healthcare staff, the better the outcomes for their organization (West and Dawson, 2012). West and Dawson outline key strategies to improve staff engagement, which include:

- Work environment – where staff feel valued, respected and supported.
- A culture of learning and improvement.
- Supportive line management – giving regular positive feedback.
- Effective team working – where staff have shared objectives, clear roles and responsibilities, and opportunities to reflect on their performance.
- Well-structured appraisals – based on clear objectives, and outcomes that support a member of staff to do their job better, for example through a personal development plan.
- Good job design – meaningful, clear tasks with opportunities to be involved in appropriate decision-making.

Bodenheimer and Sinsky (2014) argue that the 'triple aim' (Berwick et al., 2008) of enhancing patient experience, improving population health and reducing costs should now be a 'quadruple aim', adding the goal of improving the life of healthcare staff.

Pay and non-pay rewards

Healthcare professionals can either be salaried or self-employed. Self-employed professionals (e.g. GPs) can have their own private practice or be contracted to provide services by insurers, commissioners or other healthcare providers. Self-employed professionals may receive payment through fee-for-service (the practice of charging for each patient encounter or service provided), capitation (receiving payment based on how many patients are registered with their service) or a combination of the two. Evidence shows that physicians are more likely to make less resource-intense decisions under capitation than fee-for-service (Gosden et al., 2000; Shen et al., 2004). There is increasing evidence that mixed incentive schemes are most effective at driving up physician productivity while containing cost overall (Mohammed, 2004).

Some countries regulate payment for staff (a practice known as 'labour market regulation' and 'centralized wage setting' in the field of political economy). For example, in the UK national pay scales known as 'Agenda for Change' determine the salary of most NHS staff (other than doctors, dentists and senior managers who have separate nationally negotiated pay scales). This practice can have negative consequences. A study of acute hospitals in England assessed the relationship between quality (measured by the death rate within thirty days of emergency admission for acute myocardial infarction – or heart attack) and the pay regulation of nurses ((Hall et al., 2008; Propper and van Reenen, 2010). It found that in areas where labour markets are strong (i.e. there are higher wages available outside the hospital compared with inside), hospital quality declined. The study found that part of the reason for this decline in quality was that hospitals in strong labour markets had to rely disproportionately on temporary agency staff – and that wage centralization in other sectors does not have the same negative consequences (Hall et al., 2008).

There have also been attempts to build incentives for quality and productivity into payment systems. A good example of this is the Quality and Outcomes Framework (QOF) in the UK, which determines the additional income of GP surgeries as opposed to individual GPs (see pay-for-performance case study in Box 17.6). The QOF has resulted in a number of positive outcomes ranging from improved quality of care to strengthened team working. However, in addition to the unintended consequences outlined in the case study, there are concerns QOF has had a negative impact on the continuity of care offered to patients, possibly because a focus on meeting rapid-access targets means practices make any doctor available to patients (Campbell et al., 2009) Also, 'patient centredness' is considered to have been negatively affected due to 'protocol-driven care' and an emphasis on 'box-ticking' (Gillam et al., 2012).

Some argue that too little attention is paid to non-financial incentives. In 2009, a McKinsey survey of 1047 executives, managers and employees around the world found that respondents rated three non-financial incentives – praise from immediate managers, leadership attention (e.g. one-on-one conversations) and a chance to lead projects or task forces – as no less or even more effective motivators than the three highest rated financial incentives: cash bonuses, increased base pay, and stock or stock options (Dewhurst et al., 2009). Other research has shown that job enrichment, employee recognition, pay equity and managerial skill affect employee job satisfaction, although income is a moderating factor in how well non-financial incentives work at the individual level (Appelbaum and Kamal, 2000). Research in the health sector has identified very similar factors, including increased autonomy (Smith, 2002), feedback, recognition, training and professional development (Mathauer and Imhoff, 2006; Peterson and Luthans, 2006).

Box 17.6   Pay for performance: the Quality and Outcomes Framework in English primary care

The Quality and Outcomes Framework (QOF) was introduced to general practice in England in 2004. The QOF is the voluntary annual reward and incentive programme detailing GP practice achievement results. Although participation is voluntary, participation rates are generally very high.

The QOF awards surgeries achievement points for:

- managing some of the most common chronic diseases, e.g. asthma, diabetes;
- implementing preventative measures, e.g. regular blood pressure checks;
- the extra services offered, e.g. child healthcare and maternity services;
- the quality and productivity of the service, including the avoidance of emergency admissions to hospital;
- compliance with the minimum time a GP should spend with each patient at each appointment (http://www.hscic.gov.uk/qof).

A large systematic review has been undertaken on the impact of QOF. The study found that the QOF was associated with an increased rate of quality of care improvement in the first year, which returned to pre-QOF rates of improvement in subsequent years (Gillam et al., 2012). This finding is in line with that of an interrupted time-series analysis on the care of patients with asthma, diabetes and coronary heart disease (Campbell et al., 2009). The systematic review also found the QOF has narrowed differences in performance in deprived areas compared with areas that are not deprived; it has strengthened team working and promoted a diversity of new roles; and has led to modest reductions in mortality and hospital admissions in some areas. In addition, there is some evidence that the QOF may have diminished the workload of GPs and enabled them to focus on more complex care.

However, the review also found that administration costs are substantial and the QOF can be seen to have reduced clinical autonomy and to threaten professionalism in various ways (Gillam et al., 2012).

The Health and Social Care Information Centre publishes statistics on QOF performance. For more information, see: http://www.hscic.gov.uk/catalogue/PUB15751.

Learning activity 17.4

- What pay models are currently used in your country for doctors?
- How does the model in your country compare to the Quality and Outcomes Framework in England?
- What are the advantages and drawbacks of the Quality and Outcomes Framework?

Conclusion

The capacity to deliver high-quality health care depends on having a workforce of the right size, with the right skills, in the right place, at the right time. This chapter has explored how we might achieve this.

None of what we have described is easy. Workforce planning is particularly challenging given the complexity of factors at play and the length of professional training, particularly for doctors. Workforce planning therefore needs to be less about long-term predictive precision and more about developing an adaptive and flexible process. Key to this is the flexibility you build into your workforce. You need capacity to grow and develop staff currently in post, rather than relying on a training pipeline to bring about change. This requires a flexible education system, that supports lifelong learning, and it also requires a flexible regulatory system that can support and license new roles and new ways of working. Finally, we must never forget that staff are our most precious resource. They require support and nurturing, they are part of our 'quadruple aim' – enhancing patient experience, improving population health, reducing costs and improving the life of healthcare staff.

Learning resources

World Health Organization (2010) *Models and Tools for Health Workforce Planning and Projections*. Geneva: WHO [http://whqlibdoc.who.int/publications/2010/9789241599016_eng.pdf]. This report takes stock of available methods and tools for health workforce planning and projections and describes processes and resources needed to undertake these exercises.

Health Regulation Worldwide: This website provides a global searchable online database of health regulators and professional bodies. You can search by country to identify regulators and professional bodies for a wide range of health professions [www.healthregulation.org].

European Commission – Health Workforce: This website provides information and resources about the healthcare workforce at the EU level. It includes the action plan for the EU health workforce, European Core Health Indicators, EU legislative frameworks for professional health qualifications and ongoing European projects [www.ec.europa.eu/health/workforce].

World Health Organization – Health Workforce: Two websites provide health workforce statistics, as well as information on education and training, governance and planning and migration and retention. They also provide links to additional learning resources www.who.int/topics/health_workforce and www.who.int/hrh].

Health Systems and Policy Monitor: This website provides up-to-date information on health systems, as well as policy reform for most EU countries as well as Canada, Israel and the United States [www.hspm.org].

References

Appelbaum, S.H. and Kamal, R. (2000) An analysis of the utilization and effectiveness of non-financial incentives in small business, *Journal of Management Development*, 19: 733–63.

Barry, J. (2012) Now is the right time to re-evaluate how we educate and regulate health care professionals, *International Nursing Review*, 59: 147–8.

Berwick, D.M., Nolan, T.W. and Whittington, J. (2008) The triple aim: care, health, and cost, *Health Affairs*, 27: 759–69.

Bloom, D.E., Chatterji, S., Kowal, P., Lloyd-Sherlock, P., McKee, M., Rechel, B. et al. (2015) Macroeconomic implications of population ageing and selected policy responses, *Lancet*, 385: 649–57.

Bodenheimer, T. and Sinsky, C. (2014) From triple to quadruple aim: care of the patient requires care of the provider, *Annals of Family Medicine*, 12: 573–6.

Bohmer, R.M.J. and Imison, C. (2013) Lessons from England's health care workforce redesign: no quick fixes, *Health Affairs*, 32: 2025–31.

Borrill, C., Carletta, J., Carter, A., Dawson, J., Garrod, S., Rees, A. et al. (2001) *The Effectiveness of Health Care Teams in the National Health Service* [http://homepages.inf.ed.ac.uk/jeanc/DOH-final-report.pdf].

Campbell, S.M., Reeves, D., Kontopantelis, E., Sibbald, B. and Roland, M. (2009) Effects of pay for performance on the quality of primary care in England, *New England Journal of Medicine*, 361: 368–78.

Chen, L., Evans, T., Anand, S., Boufford, J.I., Brown, H., Chowdhury, M. et al. (2004) Human resources for health: overcoming the crisis, *Lancet*, 364: 1984–90.

de Vries, H., Sanderson, P., Janta, B., Rabinovich, L., Archontakis, F., Ismail, S. et al. (2009) *International Comparison of Ten Medical Regulatory Systems*. Cambridge: Rand Corporation.

Department of Health (2006a) *The Competence and Curriculum Framework for the Physician Assistant*. London: Department of Health.

Department of Health (2006b) *The Regulation of the Non-medical Healthcare Professions: A Review by the Department of Health*. London: Department of Health.

Dewhurst, M., Guthridge, M. and Mohr, E. (2009) Motivating people: getting beyond money, *McKinsey Quarterly*, 1: 12–15.

Dorning, H. and Bardsley, M. (2014) *Focus On: Allied Health Professionals. Can We Measure Quality of Care?* London: Health Foundation and Nuffield Trust.

Dower, C., Moore, J. and Langelier, M. (2013) It is time to restructure health professions scope-of-practice regulations to remove barriers to care, *Health Affairs*, 32: 1971–6.

Drennan, V., Halter, M., Brearley, S., Carneiro, W., Gabe, J., Gage, H. et al. (2014) Investigating the contribution of physician assistants to primary care in England: a mixed-methods study, *Health Services and Delivery Research*, 2 (16).

Dubois, C.-A. and Singh, D. (2009) From staff-mix to skill-mix and beyond: towards a systemic approach to health workforce management, *Human Resources for Health*, 7: 87.

European Commission (2010) *Second Biennial Report on Social Services of General Interest*, Commission Staff Working Document. Brussels: European Commission.

European Commission (2012) *Action Plan for the EU Health Workforce*, Commission Staff Working Document. Strasbourg: European Commission [http://ec.europa.eu/health/workforce/docs/staff_working_doc_healthcare_workforce_en.pdf].

Frenk, J., Chen, L., Bhutta, Z.A., Cohen, J., Crisp, N., Evans, T. et al. (2010) Health professionals for a new century: transforming education to strengthen health systems in an interdependent world, *Lancet*, 376: 1923–58.

Frenk, J., Chen, L., Bhutta, Z.A., Cohen, J., Crisp, N., Evans, T. et al. (2011) , *Revista Peruana de Medicina Experimental y Salud Pública*, 28: 337–41.

General Medical Council (GMC) (2011) *Specialties, Sub-specialties and Progression through Training: The International Perspective*. London: GMC.

Gillam, S.J., Siriwardena, A.N. and Steel, N. (2012) Pay-for-performance in the United Kingdom: impact of the Quality and Outcomes Framework – a systematic review, *Annals of Family Medicine*, 10: 461–8.

Gosden, T., Forland, F., Kristiansen, I., Sutton, M., Leese, B., Giuffrida, A. et al. (2000) Capitation, salary, fee-for-service and mixed systems of payment: effects on the behaviour of primary care physicians, *Cochrane Database of Systematic Reviews*, 3: CD002215.

Hall, E., Propper, C. and Van Reenen, J. (2008) *Can Pay Regulation Kill? Panel Data Evidence on the Effect of Labor Markets on Hospital Performance.* London: Centre for Economic Performance.

Health Education England (2013) *New Education and Training Measures to Improve Patient Care* [https://www.hee.nhs.uk/hee-your-area/north-west/news-events/news/new-education-training-measures-improve-patient-care].

Health Education England (2014) *Health Education England: Workforce Planning* [http://hee.nhs.uk/work-programmes/workforce-planning/].

Hudspeth, R. (2008) Complex healthcare regulation: managing the continued challenge of competence, *Nursing Administration Quarterly*, 32: 74–5.

Imison, C. and Bohmer, R. (2013) *NHS and Social Care Workforce: Meeting Our Needs Now and in the Future?* London: King's Fund.

Imison, C., Buchan, J. and Xavier, S. (2009) *NHS Workforce Planning: Limitations and Possibilities*. London: King's Fund.

Mathauer, I. and Imhoff, I. (2006) Health worker motivation in Africa: the role of non-financial incentives and human resource management tools, *Human Resources for Health*, 4: 24.

Mohammed, R. (ed.) (2004) *Incentives and Healthcare: Theory and Practice*. OPI-ESRC Seminar Series on Health Sector Productivity.

Morgan, B. (2013) Why regulation is wrong for the NHS, *Health Service Journal*, 123: 16–17.

Mullins, A., Mooney, J. and Fowler, R. (2012) The benefits of using care coordinators in primary care: a case study, *Family Practice Management*, 20: 18–21.

OECD (2008) *The Looming Crisis in the Healthcare Workforce: How can OECD Countries Respond?* Paris: OECD Publishing.

Ono, T., Lafortune, G. and Schoenstein, M. (2013) Health workforce planning in OECD countries: a review of 26 projection models from 18 countries, *OECD Health Working Papers*, #62.

Ostler, J., Vassilas, C. and Parle, J. (2012) Physician assistants: friends or foes to doctors?, *BMJ Careers* [http://careers.bmj.com/careers/advice/view-article.html?id=20008022].

Peterson, S.J. and Luthans, F. (2006) The impact of financial and nonfinancial incentives on business-unit outcomes over time, *Journal of Applied Psychology*, 91: 156–65.

Propper, C. and van Reenen, J. (2010) Can pay regulation kill? Panel data evidence on the effect of labor markets on hospital performance, *Journal of Political Economy*, 118: 222–73.

Robinson, S. and Griffiths, P. (2007) *Nursing Education and Regulation: International Profiles and Perspectives*. London: Nursing Research Unit, King's College London.

Shen, J., Andersen, R., Brook, R., Kominski, G., Albert, P.S. and Wenger, N. (2004) The effects of payment method on clinical decision-making: physician responses to clinical scenarios, *Medical Care*, 42 (3): 297–302.

Sibbald, B., Shen, J. and McBride, A. (2004) Changing the skill-mix of the health care workforce, *Journal of Health Services Research and Policy*, 9 (suppl. 1): 28–38.

Simoens, S. and Hurst, J. (2006) The supply of physician services in OECD countries, *OECD Health Working Papers*, #21: 11.

Smith, J. and Chambers, N. (2011) The regulation and development of NHS managers: a discussion paper, in *Mid-Staffs Public Inquiry: Seminar on the Training and Development of Senior NHS Leaders*, Leeds, UK .

Smith, P.C. (2002) Performance management in British health care: will it deliver?, *Health Affairs (Millwood)*, 21 (3): 103–15.

West, M. and Dawson, J. (2012) *Employee Engagement and NHS Performance*. London: King's Fund.

World Health Organization (WHO) (2000) *The World Health Report 2000 – Health Systems: Improving Performance*. Geneva: WHO [http://www.who.int/whr/2000/en/whr00_en.pdf].

World Health Organization (WHO) (2004) *The World Health Report 2004 – Changing History*. Geneva: WHO [http://www.who.int/whr/2004/en/report04_en.pdf].

World Health Organization (WHO) (2005) *Preparing a Health Care Workforce for the 21st Century: The Challenge of Chronic Conditions*. Geneva: WHO.

World Health Organization (WHO) (2006) *The World Health Report 2006 – Working Together for Health*. Geneva: WHO [http://www.who.int/whr/2006/en/].

World Health Organization (WHO) (2008) *Spotlight on Statistics: A Fact File on Health Workforce Statistics* [http://www.who.int/hrh/statistics/spotlight2/en/; accessed 27 March 2015].

World Health Organization (WHO) (2014) *A Universal Truth: No Health Without a Workforce*. Geneva: WHO.

World Health Organization (WHO) (2015) *Health Workforce 2030: A Global Strategy on Human Resources for Health*. Geneva: WHO.

Patient and public involvement in healthcare

Angela Coulter

Introduction

It can seem a little strange to talk about encouraging patient involvement in healthcare. After all, by definition healthcare involves patients. The very act of turning up at a primary care centre or hospital clinic seeking medical advice is indicative of a certain level of involvement. But the fact that the patient's role needs to be underscored, and some would argue re-defined, suggests we have a problem. The nature of that problem and ways in which it is being tackled are the subject of this chapter.

Patient and public involvement, or engagement – the terms are often used interchangeably – has been on the policy agenda in many countries for at least the last ten years. This is often interpreted as ensuring that healthcare is responsive to the needs and wishes of those who use it – in other words, paying greater attention to patients' experiences and ensuring healthcare is delivered with humanity and dignity. This is clearly very important, but involvement implies something more active than simply being responded to. People who use healthcare don't only want medical treatment. They also want information, education and support for self-care. They want to understand the causes of their illness and what they themselves can do to prevent exacerbations or recurrences. They want to be told about treatment options and to be involved in decisions about their care. They may also want to play an active part in shaping local services, ensuring their views are represented in policy decisions and quality improvement efforts. In this chapter, we will consider how these expectations can be met and what the outcomes are likely to be, drawing on international experience of initiatives designed to foster patient involvement.

Definitions

First, a word about terminology. It is easy to stumble into a semantic minefield when talking about patients. The term 'patient' is controversial in some quarters, mainly because of its implied association with two other nouns: 'patience' and 'suffering'. In fact, the *Shorter Oxford Dictionary* states that the old meaning of patient, 'a person who suffers patiently', is now obsolete and they prefer the more neutral definition of 'a person receiving or registered to receive medical treatment'.

One problem with the word 'patient' is that it implies use of medical services only, not the many other services or community support that may impact on people's health. Attempts to deal with this problem by referring to 'service users' rather than patients has the merit of breadth, but it is somewhat clumsy, implying a relationship with inanimate objects. Also 'user' carries unfortunate connotations of drug misuse. Various alternatives have been proposed – 'client', 'consumer', 'customer', 'person' – each of these terms has its proponents and detractors but all are problematic. Sadly, we don't have a better term to describe people who make use of both health and social care services.

'Involvement' is another word that can cause controversy. Some people like this word best, while others prefer 'participation', 'engagement' or 'co-production'. These terms can mean different things to different people, ranging from mere consultation to equal, reciprocal relationships, democratic control and everything in between. Numerous academic theses have devoted many pages to debating the meanings and relative merits of these terms, but this is a sideshow. The pragmatic solution is to use the term that best fits the particular context and avoid getting drawn into fruitless semantic debates.

Purpose and scope of involvement

Patient and public involvement is now rising to the top of the health policy agenda in many countries. The reasons for this are ethical, political and economic: ethical, due to the focus on human rights and commitment to self-determination and individual autonomy (WHO, 1978); political, because of great public interest in healthcare quality, accessibility and affordability (Institute of Medicine, 2001); and economic, because of a growing belief that promoting engagement with health issues and encouraging greater self-reliance may be the best way to ensure the financial sustainability of health systems (Wanless, 2002). The need to tackle health problems upstream becomes even more imperative at a time of global recession when public health is deteriorating due to economic austerity compounded by funding restrictions on health and care services (Karanikolos et al., 2013). The required shift in focus from concentrating on illness and treatment to emphasizing health and wellness cannot be achieved without popular support, so active patient and public involvement is key to the success of health reforms.

All citizens have a legitimate interest in the availability and quality of healthcare and in its organization, financing and management. This leads to demands for transparency about the performance of healthcare facilities, including responsiveness to patients' concerns. Most politicians also want to persuade their electorates that they can manage health economies efficiently, securing maximum value for the resources expended. This depends on managing the balance between demand and supply, ensuring that people get the care they need and want, based on a good understanding of the concerns and priorities of local people. Recognizing and strengthening individuals' and communities' contribution to their own health and well-being is critical to achieving the right balance.

As patients, families, carers or citizens, we can all make a difference to our health and that of our communities. There are many ways in which we can do so (see Box 18.1).

Box 18.1   People's contribution to their own and their community's health

- Understanding the causes of disease and the factors that influence health
- Diagnosing and self-treating minor conditions
- Knowing when to seek advice and professional help
- Choosing appropriate health providers
- Selecting appropriate treatments
- Monitoring symptoms and treatment effects
- Being aware of safety issues and preventing errors
- Coping with the effects of chronic illness and managing care
- Adopting healthy behaviours to prevent occurrence or recurrence of disease
- Ensuring that healthcare resources are used appropriately and efficiently
- Participating in clinical and health services research
- Articulating views in debates about healthcare priorities
- Helping to plan, govern, evaluate and improve health services
- Working collectively to tackle the causes of ill health.

Source: Coulter (2011).

Acknowledging the capabilities of ordinary people and what they can contribute to healthcare and public health is the essence of two important ideas: social capital and co-production:

- *Social capital* is a way of describing the community norms, networks and interactions – in other words, the sense of belonging – that facilitate collective action (Putnam, 2000). It is seen as the essential underpinning for economic development and for fostering inclusion and social cohesion, as well as being the key to tackling health inequalities.
- There is a belief, and some evidence to back it up, that *co-production* – delivering services in an equal and reciprocal relationship between professionals, patients, their families and communities – will lead to more responsive services and better health outcomes (Boyle and Harris, 2009).

It is important to be clear about what you are trying to achieve when initiating any change, and the same goes for efforts to involve patients and members of the public. The case for encouraging patient and public involvement is often implicit rather than specified, with most of the effort focused on mechanisms rather than objectives. This is not helpful. Unless goals are clarified and outcomes articulated, you are left with no means of measuring progress. Goals are likely to differ according to whether the focus is on improving healthcare or on wider public health and resource allocation (see Chapter 4). For example, the concern might be to improve the quality of healthcare or to promote health and reduce health inequalities.

Learning activity 18.1

Can you think of any health policy goals that might benefit from patient and public involvement? Select a specific policy goal from within your own health system to write about.
- What benefits would involvement bring?
- How would you persuade people to get involved?
- Are there any risks or downsides of involving patients and public in trying to achieve your goal?
- What indicators would you use to monitor progress?

Below we consider some examples of how patient and public involvement might help to transform the quality and sustainability of health systems. We begin by looking at how their collective power can be harnessed to improve health systems and then turn to individuals' contributions to their own care and how this can improve health outcomes.

A brief history of patient power

Patient and public involvement in healthcare is not a new idea. People have come together to look after the health of themselves, their families and communities since the dawn of civilization. Indeed, the professional takeover of responsibility for health and medical care is a relatively recent phenomenon.

Early theories about the origins of disease can be traced back to before the birth of Hippocrates in 460 BC, but healthcare remained largely a family responsibility up until the nineteenth century. Before then almost anyone could claim specialist medical knowledge and assorted healers and quacks sold 'cures' to anyone desperate enough to purchase them. The eighteenth century saw the development of the first effective medical interventions, but the full flowering of the medical profession didn't occur until the mid-nineteenth century. This was the time when those who considered themselves orthodox practitioners took control, determining what was legitimate in terms of medical knowledge and what was not and establishing the medical institutions and regulatory bodies that provided the buttresses for power of the medical profession, firmly distinguishing it from lay efforts.

First stirrings of a backlash against this professional power grab were seen in the work of twentieth-century authors like Erving Goffman (1961), Ivan Illich (1974), Thomas McKeown (1976) and the Boston Women's Health Collective (1998). Their writings pointed to risks inherent in ceding too much control to doctors and helped to fuel interest in alternative medicine and self-help. This period (the mid-twentieth century) also saw the development of the first campaigning patient groups. Roy Porter traces the origins of these groups to what he terms 'the 1960s' populist counter-culture backlash against scientific and technological arrogance' (Porter, 2003: 167–8). Others have linked it to the growing interest in human rights following the 1948 Universal Declaration of Human Rights and encouraged by the civil rights movement in the United States, which had sparked a broader questioning of establishment values.

Early health campaigns focused on issues such as freeing up hospital visiting hours to allow parents to be with their sick children, challenging medical control of childbirth and improving access to contraception. The 1980s saw rapid growth in the number of patient organizations. These ranged from very small groups focused on local communities or rare diseases to large, professionally run national or international organizations with substantial budgets. The majority of these groups were voluntary organizations or charities. While these had a reasonably good track record of influencing public policy, they tended to represent sectional interests only, for example those with specific diseases and could not speak for whole populations. To fill this gap, public funds were made available in a number of countries to establish statutory patient groups. These were introduced in Australia, Germany, the Netherlands and the UK, among other places, often linked to specific local areas or provider organizations to represent the broad range of service users.

Despite the proliferation of groups, the patient lobby struggled with the challenge of how to exert influence in the face of strong professional dominance. Early efforts to redress the balance focused on promoting patients' rights. Driven by ethical, political and economic concerns, patients' rights legislation and charters committed governments and healthcare providers to ensure that patients were treated humanely, respecting their dignity, privacy and right to self-determination (WHO, 1994).

These basic rights were clearly important and the patients' charters were one way to get them more widely understood and protected, but some critics called for more fundamental changes in the way healthcare was delivered. Writing in 1984, medical ethicist Jay Katz pointed to the problem of one-sided communications where patients were expected to relinquish their autonomy, trust the doctor and comply with doctor's orders, playing little part in decisions about their care. And in 1988 Arthur Kleinman argued that medicine was at risk of forgetting its central purpose, being so bound up with disease processes that the emotional impact of illness on patients was being ignored.

This paved the way for a chorus of commentators who criticized medical science for its obsession with understanding and manipulating the biological system while paying only cursory attention to the personal and social aspects. The complex infrastructures that have become necessary to organize and deliver an array of technical solutions to people's health needs, were felt to have obscured the things that are most valued by its users, namely people's well-being and sense of control and the personal relationships that are at the heart of healthcare.

Learning activity 18.2

Do you agree or disagree with the proposition that an excessive focus on disease processes has had an adverse impact on people's experience of healthcare? Review the arguments on both sides of the debate and state your personal point of view. Give examples to support your case.

Harnessing patient power to improve the quality of care

Patient experience is considered an important factor in the quality of care, alongside safety and clinical effectiveness, so attempts have been made to incentivize healthcare providers to focus on improving this. Two distinct approaches have been used to mobilize patient power in support of healthcare improvement:

- *Voice*: patients are encouraged to describe their experiences or express their views (compliments and complaints) through direct feedback in surveys, free text comments or via advocates, in the hope that this will encourage providers to improve standards. The results are often made available on publicly accessible websites to draw attention to variations in standards.
- *Choice*: patients are provided with information about the performance of healthcare facilities, enabling them to choose from a range of competing providers. The hope is that a proportion of patients will vote with their feet, moving to 'the best' healthcare providers, thus sending to signal to others that their standards need to improve.

Many health systems use a combination of these approaches, often simultaneously. As with all quality initiatives, securing improvements by these means can be challenging.

Gathering and using feedback

The most successful commercial companies know that maintaining a single-minded focus on the end user is the only way to guarantee success. The same ought to be true in healthcare, but this insight is often crowded out by a multitude of competing priorities, including guidelines, policies, procedures and reporting requirements that are very far from person centred. Giving due priority to patients' experience is important, both for its own sake and because it can make a real difference to health outcomes (Price et al., 2014). One of the best ways to maintain this focus is to measure it.

Patient experience surveys have become ubiquitous in developed countries. For example, England introduced annual surveys of hospital inpatients in 2002, followed a few years later by surveys of general practice patients. All NHS organizations now conduct a variety of experience surveys on a regular basis, covering topics such as access and waiting times, provision of information, communications with professionals, quality of the physical environment, involvement in decisions, support for self-care, coordination of care and so on. Similar surveys are carried out on a regular basis in many other countries, including most of Europe, Australia, Canada, Hong Kong, Japan, South Korea, Mexico, New Zealand and the USA (Garratt et al., 2008).

Some organizations supplement their patient surveys with a variety of other ways to gain feedback on their performance from patients (e.g. organizing focus groups or in-depth interviews) and by encouraging informal feedback, including comments, complaints and suggestions. The knowledge gained is useful for identifying problems that might otherwise have gone unnoticed, but this is worthless unless there is an intention to act on it.

It is now clear from experience in various countries, especially the USA where it has been studied most extensively, that systematic patient feedback is a necessary and important component of a quality improvement strategy but on its own is not sufficient to galvanize improvements (Coulter et al., 2014). Staff do not always see the relevance of patient surveys and critical reports can provoke defensive reactions. Clinical staff may need help to work out what they can do to change things and how this might benefit their patients. Sustainable change requires effective leadership and a systematic approach to continuous quality improvement.

Box 18.2   Case study – a strategic approach to patient engagement, New South Wales, Australia

In 2011, the New South Wales Clinical Excellence Commission developed a "patient based care challenge" for district healthcare services overseen by a patient advisory committee (Luxford and Newell, 2015). The aim was to strengthen patient involvement in health service governance and strategic decision-making.

Districts were encouraged to select a small number of improvement strategies and monitor their effects. They implemented a variety of initiatives, including starting each board meeting with a patient story, encouraging board members and senior staff to walk the wards, involving patients, families and carers in governance committees, persuading staff to view patients, families and carers as core members of the healthcare team, and empowering patients and families to escalate care themselves when their condition was deteriorating.

For further information, see: http://www.cec.health.nsw.gov.au/.

The New South Wales experience (Box 18.2) and that of similar programmes in other countries suggests that the following components are essential for success:

- Commitment of senior leadership
- Having clear goals and effective communication of these
- Securing active involvement of patients, families and carers
- Support to transform care by capitalizing on every opportunity to engage patients
- Using patient feedback to drive change
- Focusing on the work environment and culture

- Building staff capacity through education and training
- Creating a learning organization, including learning from patients
- Embedding accountability for patients' experience in staff job descriptions and performance reviews.

Encouraging people to vote with their feet

Empowering patients to act like discerning consumers in a healthcare market has intuitive appeal as a quality improvement strategy. The idea is that people should make use of comparative information about the performance of different healthcare providers, allowing them to select the best. In theory, this should give provider organizations a strong incentive to drive up quality standards, especially if funding flows match the choices that patients make.

Some countries have always offered a great deal of choice, allowing patients to shop around for their healthcare without restriction. In others, there have been limitations on patient choice, for example the requirement to have a referral from a GP in order to see a specialist. There are trade-offs to be made between choice and cost control, since allowing complete freedom of choice is likely to be more expensive. The idea of choice is popular with the public and more compatible with modern ideas about autonomy and self-determination, so there is pressure to reduce the restrictions and allow patients to vote with their feet. There are risks, however, in removing the gatekeeping function of primary care. Those countries with primary care gatekeepers and less patient choice tend to have better control over costs, although the impact on health and patient-related outcomes has not been well studied, so whether this also contributes to better care is debatable (Velasco Garrido et al., 2011).

Awareness of variations in quality standards is a prerequisite for encouraging people to choose between competing providers. Websites have been established in many countries making various types of performance data available for public use, but it seems that patients are often unaware of them or reluctant to use them, preferring more informal information sources such as information from friends (Ketelaar et al., 2011). The same goes for GPs, whose referral decisions tend to be more influenced by who they know than what they know (Rosen et al., 2007).

This may change as people become more familiar with using TripAdvisor-style websites to inform their choice of healthcare provider. These are now springing up all over the place. For example, Consumer Reports in the USA, better known for its comparisons of household goods like washing machines, now produces guides to choosing your doctor (see http://static3.consumerreportscdn.org/content/dam/cro/news_articles/health/PDFs/Doctor-Ratings-California-2014.pdf). Medical travel is becoming more common, so there are websites to help people find doctors and clinics across national borders; for example, Caremondo produces a guide to finding medical facilities in the German-speaking countries (see https://caremondo.com/en/c/about-caremondo/).

Of course, some people may not have a feasible choice, especially those living in remote parts of a country and some may not be able or willing to travel. In the meantime, better ways are needed to ensure that patients can access relevant information about the quality of care at the point when they have to make decisions.

Learning activity 18.3

Describe some real-life examples from your own country of the use of 'voice' and 'choice' to improve the quality of healthcare.

- How effective have they been?
- What could be done to make them more effective?

Involvement in governance and accountability

Strategies to promote participatory democracy in healthcare, enabling local people to hold decision-makers to account and to shape policy more directly, have become prevalent. Patient and public involvement is seen as important on both sides of the purchaser–provider split. Purchasers (or payers) are supposed to listen to and consult with those people for whom they fund health services, and providers (including managers of healthcare facilities) are expected to involve patients in monitoring and improving the performance of their organization. Decision-making about healthcare organization is highly centralized in some countries, including England where there has been much concern about a democratic deficit. Where systems are more decentralized, such as the Scandinavian countries, control by local politicians brings decision-making closer to ordinary people, at least in theory. In Sweden, for example, the county councils and municipalities have considerable freedom to determine the organization of services within a national framework that guarantees good access for all citizens. However, recent mergers between county councils point to difficulties in managing complex and highly technical services for relatively small populations (Anell et al., 2012).

There are several reasons why encouraging public involvement in policy-making (i.e. participatory democracy) is considered important in healthcare (Weale, 2006) (Box 18.3).

Box 18.3   Why public involvement is important for health policy decisions

- Members of the public can contribute additional perspectives to complement those of professionals.
- Citizens have a right to consider the impact of resource allocation decisions on the wider public health.
- Service plans should take account of people's competing priorities, not just the views of service users.
- Public participation is a necessary counter-weight to producer interests
- An open and transparent decision-making process enhances the legitimacy of policy decisions.
- It is especially important to elicit the views of different groups when decisions involve complex moral issues.

Opportunities to sit on hospital committees or to get involved in the governance of healthcare facilities have grown rapidly in the last ten years or so, and public consultation is often a legal requirement. Implementing these types of participatory democracy is not straightforward however. Many people welcome the opportunity to get involved, at least hypothetically, but the proportion who volunteer to sit on committees or attend public meetings when invited to do so often shrinks to a tiny, unrepresentative minority.

Public accountability requires organizations to provide clear information and give explanations for their decisions (see Chapter 5). Local people or their representatives can use the information to interrogate those responsible and require answers, invoking sanctions if they are dissatisfied with any aspect of conduct or performance. This type of involvement attracts people who are comfortable with formal bureaucratic methods of working and have the skills to get their views across. Meanwhile, new ways of reaching people through digital democracy may offer a better way to engage more representative groups. Healthcare is a popular campaigning issue for social networking sites and in California the Institute for Advanced Technology and Public Policy has developed an online platform featuring a searchable database of state legislative committee hearings, allowing the user to search videos of legislative committees by keyword, topic, speaker or date, transcribing these to inform and empower local people.

Engaging the public

One of the important aspects for which public organizations should be held to account is the extent to which they have engaged with members of their local communities. Effective engagement requires them to have adequate capacity in three areas:

- *Insight*: careful analysis of evidence on the needs and experiences of local people.
- *Communications*: clear communication plans and effective feedback loops.
- *Outreach*: good understanding of the priorities and concerns of local groups.

Purchasers of healthcare need these skills and capabilities in order to reflect local needs and concerns in their commissioning plans. Reliance on formal committees and public meetings is unlikely to be sufficient and more imaginative efforts will be required to secure input from a broad cross-section of the population. The most ambitious organizations adopt a range of strategies to engage with patients and local people, including outreach visits to community groups, shopping malls, housing estates and places of worship, online consultations and feedback mechanisms.

Various techniques can be used to secure active public engagement in determining healthcare priorities, including citizens' panels, citizens' juries and deliberative forums. These work best when people are invited to tackle specific local issues, when they are given sufficient information about options, time for careful deliberation and when there is a real commitment to listening to people's views and taking them into account prior to making decisions. The success of such groups relies on expert facilitation skills.

> **Learning activity 18.4**
>
> Describe an example of participatory democracy in healthcare from within your own country.
>
> - Did it succeed in obtaining a representative range of views?
> - How well did it adhere to the principles of accountability for reasonableness? (see Chapter 5)
> - What were the challenges faced? How were they tackled and with what result?

Promoting health

Many healthcare organizations list improving health and reducing inequalities among their goals. Recognizing and strengthening people's contribution to their health (assets), instead of focusing on their problems alone (deficits), has been proposed as a challenge to traditional ways of thinking and acting in healthcare and in wider public health. An asset-based approach can lead to very different assumptions and ways of working (Hopkins and Rippon, 2015). For example, rather than focusing on health deficiencies and needs, you might start by thinking about how to promote well-being, including mapping the strengths and potential contributions of local people and how they could be empowered to take more control of their lives.

The asset-based approach is an example of co-production. Much of the evidence on asset-based community development is descriptive rather than rigorously evaluative. There are various model projects from which we can learn a great deal, but there is no hard evidence pointing to the superior efficacy of one approach over another. Nevertheless, it is clear that any strategy to tackle health inequalities must look beyond the health service. People with the greatest health needs require more than just medical care to transform their lives (Marmot et al., 2012).

Local problems require locally developed solutions. Working with local communities to identify what might help them to improve their health can be very effective. Sometimes, as in the case of Botermarkt Community Health Centre in Belgium (see Chapter 9, Box 9.2), using local knowledge to identify the source of the problems and taking collective action on health issues can help build social capital, leading to wider social benefits. Parents were concerned that lack of green spaces and playgrounds led to lack of physical exercise and obesity among their children, so staff of the health centre worked with local volunteers to construct a playground and organize holiday activities. An evaluation of the project found that it succeeded in increasing physical fitness and led to improved interactions between the Flemish and Turkish communities. An unanticipated added bonus came when police reported a drop in street crime during the school holidays, solving another of the community's problems.

Learning activity 18.5

Design an asset-based approach to tackle health problems faced by a specific disadvantaged group in your community. Show how it differs from traditional approaches.

Ensuring appropriate care

There are often many different ways to treat a particular health problem, each of which may lead to a different set of outcomes. Indeed, it is quite unusual for there to be a simple choice between undergoing a medical intervention or not. Decisions that can affect people's quality of life in important ways should not be left to clinicians alone; patients ought to be involved in these decisions too. Indeed, informed consent regulations and legal precedents increasingly require their involvement.

Shared decision-making is a process in which clinicians and patients work together to select tests, treatments and other care management strategies based on clinical evidence and the patient's informed goals, values and preferences. The clinician is responsible for providing reliable, balanced, evidence-based information outlining treatment options, outcomes and uncertainties, together with decision support counselling to clarify options and patients' values. For their part, the patient must be willing to think about the options, discuss their preferences, and work with the doctor, nurse or other clinician to decide on the most appropriate intervention for their individual needs.

Providing this type of information verbally in a busy clinic can be challenging, so patient decision aids have been developed to summarize the key facts. These take a variety of forms, from simple one-page sheets to sophisticated web-based tools. Most include evidence-based information about different treatments and outcome probabilities, plus values-clarification exercises to help people weigh up the pros and cons of the options. More than one hundred randomized trials have shown that this process leads to better understanding of treatment options, more accurate risk perceptions, greater participation in decision-making, greater comfort with decisions, no increase in anxiety, and fewer patients electing for major surgery (Stacey et al., 2014).

Despite this convincing evidence of benefit, shared decision-making has yet to become the norm in clinical practice (Coulter et al., 2015b). The problem seems to lie in an outdated medical culture that resists attempts to transfer decision-making power to patients, together with a misalignment of incentives, making it slow to percolate into the mainstream (Mulley et al., 2012). Clinical guidelines and financial incentives (e.g. the UK's Quality Outcomes Framework for rewarding GPs) tend to assume that clinicians make all the decisions themselves, without involving patients. The belief that there is insufficient time to provide information and discuss options with patients is another very important barrier, although this may be more problematic in perception than in reality.

Box 18.4   Case study – a system-wide implementation of shared decision-making: Group Health, Seattle, USA

Group Health, a consumer-governed health system that integrates care and coverage for more than 660,000 patients in Washington state, wanted to encourage their patients to participate in a shared decision-making process, in particular those considering treatment for a range of surgical conditions: hip and knee osteoarthritis, abnormal uterine bleeding, uterine fibroids, lumbar herniated disk, lumbar spinal stenosis, chronic stable angina, benign prostatic hyperplasia, early stage prostate cancer and early stage breast cancer.

They mapped patient pathways in their organization to identify the key decision points, making relevant decision aids available to patients when they reached these points. They succeeded in distributing 27,000 decision aids over a three-year period (King and Moulton, 2013). The programme was specially designed to fit in with local routines.

Patients were delighted with the decision aids, with almost everyone agreeing that they helped them understand their condition and treatment choices, helped clarify their values, and prepared them for discussions with their clinician about the best option for them.

An evaluation focusing on the decisions about hip and knee surgery found that the introduction of decision aids was associated with 26 per cent fewer hip replacements, 38 per cent fewer knee replacements, and 12–21 per cent lower costs over six months (Arterburn et al., 2012).

Several factors were important for success in this project, notably strong support from senior leaders, having a system for distributing decision aids prior to consultations, providing timely feedback to teams about how well they were doing, engaging staff in the design of the project and finding ways to tackle problems as they arose (Hsu et al., 2013).

For further information, see: http://www.informedmedicaldecisions.org/2015/03/26/creating-a-group-health-culture-where-shared-decision-making-is-the-norm/.

Experience shows that it is possible to embed patient information and decision support into patient pathways with good results (Box 18.4), but achieving this requires rethinking existing procedures and attitudes to how decisions should be made. Time is needed to embed the changes and staff need training, supervision and support, including administrative support, to ensure the system is sustainable. Dealing with these issues is important because shared decision-making may be the best way to tackle problems of over-diagnosis and overtreatment leading to unnecessary expenditure and waste (Malhotra et al., 2015).

Learning activity 18.6

Think about a healthcare organization you know well.

- To what extent do you think patients are actively involved in decisions about their care?
- What are the barriers and facilitators to embedding shared decision-making in mainstream practice?
- What could managers do to encourage its implementation?

Supporting self-care

Self-care is the most prevalent form of healthcare, yet its importance is often unappreciated. Most people look after their own and their families' health most of the time. Professionals who assume that patients lack competence in these areas risk undermining their efforts. Patients may indeed lack knowledge and confidence, but it is incumbent on providers to foster their self-reliance, not belittle it. Because it is so prevalent, small shifts in self-care in either direction could make a major impact on reducing the demand for professional care. Strengthening people's capacity to look after themselves and their families has the potential to generate significant cost savings.

This is especially true in the case of people with long-term conditions. Health professionals often talk about how they are responsible for managing long-term conditions, but in fact their role is minor compared with that of their patients. There are 8760 hours in a year, out of which most people with long-term conditions spend only three hours on average (one consultation per month) in direct contact with a clinician, in other words 0.03 per cent of their time. The rest of the time they have to manage by themselves. Strengthening their ability to do so can reap huge rewards (deBronkart, 2015).

The chronic care model (see Chapter 10) stresses the need to transform healthcare for people with long-term health conditions from a system that is largely reactive, responding when a person is sick, to one that is much more proactive, focused on supporting patients ability to self-manage their health (Wagner, 1998). The model advocates an active role for patients, who are encouraged to become both more knowledgeable about the factors affecting their condition (including strategies for preventing exacerbations or ameliorating symptoms) and more actively involved in decisions about their care (see Chapter 10). At the heart of the model is an informed and activated patient supported by a well-prepared primary care team working together proactively to determine priorities, establish goals, create action plans and review progress.

Personalized care planning aims to ensure that individuals' values and concerns shape the way long-term conditions are managed. Instead of focusing on a standard set of disease management processes determined by health professionals, this approach encourages patients to select treatment goals and determine their specific support needs. Patients may express their personal goals in ways that are very different from those of clinicians or managers (Coalition for Collaborative Care, 2015). According to National Voices, a coalition of about one hundred and forty health and care charities in England, what patients want is to be able to work with staff who understand them and their family situation to plan their care in an enabling and empowering manner (http://www.england.nhs.uk/wp-content/uploads/2013/05/nv-narrative-cc.pdf).

The care planning conversation aims to help individuals clarify their goals, solve any problems, and ensure that clinical tests and treatments are organized to fit into the pattern of their daily lives avoiding unnecessary disruption. Knowledge and skills gaps are addressed, emotional problems are discussed and educational interventions offered if required. The resulting decisions will normally be recorded in a care plan, but this is of little value if the patient has not been involved in drawing it up. Personalized care planning is, or should be, the fulcrum of a patient-centred integrated care system.

This form of self-management support involves a shift from reactive care (waiting for people to consult with symptoms) to a proactive approach in which patients are invited to attend specially scheduled consultations. Options considered are very likely to include community and peer support, in addition to those provided by statutory services. There is evidence that this can lead to better outcomes in terms of physical health, emotional well-being and improved confidence and skills for self-management (Coulter et al., 2015a).

The model has profound implications for the organization and management of primary care, requiring integrated record systems, tailored appointments, multidisciplinary team-working, and detailed knowledge of community services. Probably the greatest challenge is changing people's expectations, both patients and clinicians. Patients may be reluctant to take on an active role because they think clinicians expect them to behave passively. Clinicians may have low expectations of patients and may not see self-management support as a legitimate part of their job description. Managing this disconnect is crucial for achieving beneficial service change.

Learning activity 18.7

Describe briefly the primary care system in your country.

- Are personalized care planning and self-management support seen as part of the everyday responsibilities of primary care practitioners?
- Thinking about the chronic care model, what changes are needed to improve the management of long-term conditions in primary care?
- How would you set about making those changes, if you had the power to do so?

Future of involvement

Patient and public involvement seems set to become an ever more important feature of the healthcare landscape, but the way we think about it is likely to evolve because of two interlinked developments: the wider accessibility of digital technologies and the re-growth of self-help and peer support.

The internet is changing the way we engage with our health and medical care. We already have instant access to a vast range of digital information on symptoms and diseases, but its interactive capabilities could totally transform patient and public involvement. All the examples of involvement discussed in this chapter can be enhanced by the use of digital technologies. Indeed, there are plenty of examples where this is already happening (see Box 18.5).

Box 18.5   Technologies for self-help

- Patients' reports on their healthcare experiences and outcomes can now be gathered electronically and analysed much more quickly, enabling timely information to inform clinical care and quality improvement efforts. Patients can hold their own records, choose who to share them with, access relevant information about their care, monitor their symptoms, and communicate directly with clinicians (see, for example, www.patientsknowbest.com).
- Patient decision aids can be integrated into patient-accessible electronic medical records so they are readily available at key decision points, making it much easier for patients and clinicians to review the information together as part of a shared decision-making process (see, for example, www.healthwise.org).
- Care planning and self-management can be greatly assisted by the use of apps that enable patients to record their goals and action plans and monitor their condition, sharing these with clinicians involved in their care (see, for example, www.truecolours.nhs.uk).
- Social media, video boxes and websites are being used to obtain and publicize the views of local people on healthcare priorities in their local area. They are also helping to show how co-production can transform people's health (see, for example, http://www.newhamccg.nhs.uk/GetInvolved/get-involved.htm).
- Meanwhile, some innovative patient leaders are forging ahead, developing their own ingenious solutions to health problems and sharing their experiences in online communities (see, for example, http://participatorymedicine.org/ and http://www.patientslikeme.com/).

The democratization of health knowledge has helped to boost the potential of peer support. Groups of people with common diagnoses are getting together face to face, over the phone or online to share their experiences and knowledge and support each other (Nesta and National Voices, 2015). Sometimes established by professional or voluntary organizations or statutory services, and sometimes genuine grassroots developments, these groups have the potential to improve their members' experience, psychosocial outcomes, health behaviours, health outcomes and service use.

Patient leaders – some might call them professional patients – are becoming increasingly visible, particularly on social media, and they are often invited onto public platforms to speak alongside professionals – it is becoming *de rigueur* to hear a patient story at health conferences. Many of these people are highly articulate speakers and writers with interesting and sometimes worrying stories to tell that can act as a catalyst, prompting health professionals to rethink traditional ways of providing care. Their influence is growing and will continue to do so.

Conclusion

What does all this mean for healthcare managers and policy-makers? They will certainly have to get to grips with people's expectations of involvement and embrace it. The drive for greater public engagement is becoming a global movement – it will not go away (WHO, 2015).

Patients, families and communities have been described as the greatest untapped resource in healthcare (Kemper and Mettler, 2002). Recognizing their capacity as assets and co-producers of health, not simply resource users, could do much to transform the quality and sustainability of health systems. What is needed is a shift away from the reactive, disease-focused, fragmented model of care that we've all come to expect, towards one that is more proactive, holistic and preventative, in which people are encouraged to play a central role in managing their own care.

People need to be treated as partners in care, not just as passive recipients. Once the lay contribution to healthcare is fully recognized, then the attitudinal and organizational changes required to improve the system become more obvious. Instead of doing things *to* patients, there needs to be a subtle shift towards working in partnership *with* them. A paternalistic and dependency-creating medical culture, where clinicians assume they know best, will be seen for what it is – anachronistic and out of sync with the way people expect to be dealt with in other aspects of their lives.

Learning resources

Person-Centred Care Resource Centre: This is the resource centre of the British charity the Health Foundation. It includes a wealth of information about patient and public involvement, including case studies, analyses and how-to-do-it guides. Their particular focus is people's engagement in their own care [http://personcentredcare. health.org.uk/].

Involve: Another London-based organization, Involve, is expert in public participation across all sectors, not just healthcare. It works with a large number of partner organizations and its website includes a wide range of useful materials [http://www.involve. org.uk/].

International Alliance of Patients' Organizations: The IAPO is an umbrella group for patients' organizations around the world. It represents two hundred and forty-one member organizations in sixty-six countries, building cross-sector alliances and speaking about patients' perspectives at numerous forums, including the World Health Organization and the United Nations [http://iapo.org.uk/].

Patient-Centered Outcomes Research Institute: Based in Washington DC, PCORI aims to ensure that patients and the public have the information they can use to make decisions that reflect their desired health outcomes. It does this by producing and promoting high-integrity, evidence-based research information guided by patients, caregivers and the broader healthcare community [http://www.pcori.org/].

References

Anell, A., Glenngard, A.H. and Merkur, S. (2012) Sweden: health system review, *Health Systems in Transition*, 14 (5): 1–159.

Arterburn, D., Wellman, R., Westbrook, E., Rutter, C., Ross, T., McCulloch, D. et al. (2012) Introducing decision aids at Group Health was linked to sharply lower hip and knee surgery rates and costs, *Health Affairs*, 31: 2094–104.

Boston Women's Health Book Collective (1998) *Our Bodies, Ourselves*. New York: Simon & Schuster.

Boyle, D. and Harris, M. (2009) *The Challenge of Co-production*. London: Nesta.

Coalition for Collaborative Care (2015) *Personalised Care and Support Planning Handbook*. Leeds: NHS England.

Coulter, A. (2011) *Engaging Patients in Healthcare*. Maidenhead: Open University Press

Coulter, A., Entwistle, V.A., Eccles, A., Ryan, S., Shepperd, S. and Perera, R. (2015a) Personalised care planning for adults with chronic or long-term health conditions, *Cochrane Database of Systematic Reviews*, 3: CD010523.

Coulter, A., Harter, M., Moumjid-Ferdjaoui, N., Perestelo-Perez, L. and van der Weijden, T. (2015b) European experience with shared decision-making, *International Journal of Person Centred Medicine*, 5: 9–14.

Coulter, A., Locock, L., Ziebland, S. and Calabrese, J. (2014) Collecting data on patient experience is not enough: they must be used to improve care, *British Medical Journal*, 348: g2225.

deBronkart, D. (2015) From patient centred to people powered: autonomy on the rise, *British Medical Journal*, 350: h148.

Garratt, A.M., Solheim, E. and Danielsen, K. (2008) *National and Cross-national Surveys of Patient Experiences: A Structured Review*. Oslo: Norwegian Knowledge Centre for the Health Services.

Goffman, E. (1961) *Asylums: Essays on the Social Situation of Mental Patients and Other Inmates*. New York: Anchor Books.

Hopkins, T. and Rippon, S. (2015) *Heads, Hands and Heart: Asset-based Approaches in Health Care*. London: Health Foundation.

Hsu, C., Liss, D.T., Westbrook, E.O. and Arterburn, D. (2013) Incorporating patient decision aids into standard clinical practice in an integrated delivery system, *Medical Decision Making*, 33: 85–97.

Illich, I. (1974) *Medical Nemesis*. London: Calder & Boyars.

Institute of Medicine (2001) *Crossing the Quality Chasm: A New Health System for the 21st Century*. Washington, DC: National Academy Press.

Karanikolos, M., Rechel, B., Stuckler, D. and McKee, M. (2013) Financial crisis, austerity, and health in Europe – authors' reply, *Lancet*, 382 (9890): 392.

Katz, J. (1984) *The Silent World of Doctor and Patient*. New York: Free Press.

Kemper, D.W. and Mettler, M. (2002) *Information Therapy: Prescribed Information as a Reimbursable Medical Service*. Boise, ID: Healthwise, Inc.

Ketelaar, N.A., Faber, M.J., Flottorp, S., Rygh, L.H., Deane, K.H. and Eccles, M.P. (2011) Public release of performance data in changing the behaviour of healthcare consumers, professionals or organisations, *Cochrane Database of Systematic Reviews*, 11: CD004538.

King, J. and Moulton, B. (2013) Group Health's participation in a shared decision-making demonstration yielded lessons, such as role of culture change, *Health Affairs*, 32: 294–302.

Kleinman, A. (1988) *The Illness Narratives: Suffering, Healing and the Human Condition*. New York: Basic Books.

Luxford, K. and Newell, S. (2015) New South Wales mounts 'patient based care' challenge, *British Medical Journal*, 350: g7582.

Malhotra, A., Maughan, D., Ansell, J., Lehman, R., Henderson, A., Gray, M. et al. (2015) Choosing wisely in the UK: the Academy of Medical Royal Colleges' initiative to reduce the harms of too much medicine, *British Medical Journal*, 350: h2308.

Marmot, M., Allen, J., Bell, R., Bloomer, E., Goldblatt, P. et al. (2012) WHO European review of social determinants of health and the health divide, *Lancet*, 380 (9846): 1011–29.

McKeown, T. (1976) *The Role of Medicine: Dream, Mirage or Nemesis?* London: Nuffield Provincial Hospitals Trust.

Mulley, A.G., Trimble, C. and Elwyn, G. (2012) Patients' preferences matter: stop the silent misdiagnosis, *British Medical Journal*, 345: e6572.

Nesta and National Voices (2015) *Peer Support: What is it and Does it Work?* London: National Voices.

Porter, R. (2003) *Blood and Guts: A Short History of Medicine*. London: Penguin Books.

Price, R.A., Elliott, M.N., Zaslavsky, A.M., Hays, R.D., Lehrman, W.G., Rybowski, L. et al. (2014) Examining the role of patient experience surveys in measuring health care quality, *Medical Care Research and Review*, 71: 522–54.

Putnam, R.D. (2000) *Bowling Alone: The Collapse and Revival of American Community*. New York: Simon & Schuster.

Rosen, R., Florin, D. and Hutt, R. (2007) *An Anatomy of GP Referral Decisions*. London: King's Fund.

Stacey, D., Legare, F., Col, N.F., Bennett, C.L., Barry, M.J., Eden, K.B. et al. (2014) Decision aids for people facing health treatment or screening decisions, *Cochrane Database of Systematic Reviews*, 1: CD001431.

Velasco Garrido, M., Zentner, A. and Busse, R. (2011) The effects of gatekeeping: a systematic review of the literature, *Scandinavian Journal of Primary Health Care*, 29 (1): 28–38.

Wagner, E.H. (1998) Chronic disease management: what will it take to improve care for chronic illness?, *Effective Clinical Practice*, 1: 2–4.

Wanless, D. (2002) *Securing our Future Health: Taking a Long-term View*. London: HM Treasury.

Weale, A. (2006) What is so good about citizens' involvement in healthcare?, in E. Andersson, J. Tritter and R. Wilson (eds.) *Healthy Democracy: The Future of Involvement in hHealth and Social Care*. London: Involve and National Centre for Involvement.

World Health Organization (WHO) (1978) *Declaration of Alma-Ata*. Geneva: WHO.

World Health Organization (WHO) (1994) *A Declaration on the Promotion of Patients' Rights in Europe: European Consultation on the Rights of Patients*. Copenhagen: WHO Europe.

World Health Organization (WHO) (2015) *WHO Global Strategy on People-centred and Integrated Health Services: Interim Report*. Geneva: WHO.

Chapter 19

Governance and accountability in healthcare

Naomi Chambers

Introduction

This chapter begins by outlining the complexity of challenges in healthcare systems and thus the importance of governance and of effective mechanisms of accountability. Evolving paradigms in healthcare leadership as a result of changing demands in healthcare delivery and broader societal influences are presented. Readers are offered access to an example of a current healthcare leadership model. At the apex of organization governance is the board, which sets goals and objectives, monitors progress, determines organization culture and addresses evidence of variations in performance. Theories and practices in healthcare board governance are discussed and two case studies in contrasting jurisdictions are described. Two learning resources that can be used to assess the effectiveness of a healthcare board are included here. There follows an analysis of theories of different external oversight, accountability and performance regimes in healthcare, and the extent to which varying accountability mechanisms result in different outcomes. The chapter concludes by outlining five healthcare governance categories that have the capacity to incorporate effective arrangements for control of healthcare organizations.

While the notion of accountability – of giving an account and of being held to account, by some body and in some way – is immediately graspable, the concept of governance is more slippery. A number of different elucidations of the term governance exist, all of which revolve around the notion of control using different mechanisms. Within a political science paradigm, Pierre and Peters (2000) argue that at a state level, governance revolves around the capacity of government to make and implement policy – in other words, to guide society. This is increasingly viewed as a 'steering' rather than a 'rowing' function (Osborne and Gaebler, 1993). Choices about what and how to steer are available. An OECD review proposed six levers in modernizing governance at state level, comprising open government, performance management, accountability and control, restructuring, marketization and new forms of employment (OECD, 2005). Therborn (1978) had earlier identified a number of modes of control that can be associated with these levers: ideology, contracts, competition, financial incentives or penalties, and negotiated order.

Within healthcare, Smith et al. (2012) argue that the main components of system governance are priority setting, performance monitoring and accountability arrangements. Davies and colleagues (2005) examine markets, hierarchies and networks as the main contrasting forms of governance, relating these to different incentives and hence to different outcomes. Newman (2005) notes that each mode of governance has its own form of leader: for example, an administrative leader in a bureaucracy, a competitive leader in a market, and a putatively transformational one in a network.

Mirroring the intent of system level governance, at the institution level, governance is concerned with setting direction for an organization and about exercising control. This is evidenced both by the architecture of governance (organization structures and so on) and by the enactment of governance, including the exercise of leadership.

There are challenges peculiar to complex healthcare systems (especially reconciling quality and safety with financial and efficiency pressures, both individualizing and standardizing the healthcare offer and managing the politics including the power of the professions).

Challenges for governance in healthcare

There is a raft of enduring governance challenges facing all healthcare systems, which have been well rehearsed by a number of authors, including WHO (2008), Blank and Burau (2013) and elsewhere in this book, in particular in the chapters on financing healthcare and global health policy. These challenges, some of which can also in places be framed as opportunities, have much in common with those in other public sector or social welfare programmes (education, housing, and so on) but it can be argued that there is a greater number and a greater complexity of strands coming together in health which makes the successful endeavour here seemingly intractable. Eight strands are identified here (see Box 19.1) that have to be handled by leaders contemporaneously. These are the sometimes conflicting and critical problems identified by Grint (2010) and which need 'clumsy' rather than elegant solutions.

Box 19.1 Eight governance challenges and opportunities in healthcare

- **Financial pressures:** need for comprehensive controls.
- **Changing demographics:** need to move to health systems focused on needs of older people living with multiple long-term conditions.
- **Quality and safety of care:** need for good systems, implementation and staff engagement.

- **National and local politics:** need for leadership astuteness over competing forces.
- **Consumer demands:** need for prioritization tools and patient engagement and centredness.
- **Power of the professions:** need for negotiation and influencing skills rather than command-and-control approaches.
- **Complexity of the health system:** need for inter-organizational governance and collaborative leadership.
- **Technological advances:** need for investments and savings to be made in equipment, services and e-health systems to achieve sustainability.

Since the global economic downturn in 2008, and given the rate of technological advances in healthcare, top of the list of challenges has to be the affordability of care. Sometime before the banking crisis, fiscal stress was identified as one of five policy drivers by the OECD in its review of common pressures faced by governments (OECD, 2005). Comprehensive controls and prioritization tools are therefore essential. Second, changing demographics with sharp rises in numbers in the over sixty-fives and in the over eighty-fives age groups also helps to pile on the pressure. In some countries, which have experienced low birth rates over many years, the age distribution is increasingly skewed to the older end, which means more burden on the shrinking working-age population to create the wealth and to care for their elders. Third is the question of quality and safety in patient care. This demands accurate data, excellent systems of tracking and monitoring and sophisticated influencing abilities over highly qualified professionals. Even in countries such as the UK, which boasts a national health service stretching back to 1948 and an elaborate professional regulation infrastructure, inquiries into failures of care, which first started in the 1960s, continue today, without, apparently, the basic lessons being learnt and applied. These governance failures are replicated worldwide (Walshe and Shortell, 2004). Fourth is the confounding factor of politics in healthcare, which nationally drives successive top-down reorganizations and restructurings (Klein, 1998), and which locally 'interferes with' evidence-based reconfigurations of services. Political astuteness in manoeuvring around this is called for. Fifth is increasing consumer demands and steadily increasing dissatisfaction with services (Ham, 2009), requiring a response that is both economic, for example through the construction and implementation of technical prioritization tools, and socioemotional, for example through ensuring the design and delivery of services that are 'patient-centred'. Sixth is the power of the professionals, particularly doctors, who deliver the services and who can sabotage attempts to make changes if they make no sense to them (Goodwin, 2006). The only realistic way forward is through co-ownership, management by influence and distributed forms of leadership. Although it increases complexity, there is a growing acknowledgement that health services are managed more effectively in health systems that cross institutional boundaries than within single organizations (Pratt et al., 1999), which requires consideration of multi-form and multi-level governance and collaborative forms of leadership. Finally, technological advances are a financial challenge, as mentioned earlier, but also a significant opportunity requiring courageous system leadership: the Human Genome Project, for example, will enable the personalizing of diagnostics and treatments for a range of conditions to the individual in ways that were recently unimaginable; and implementation of e-health strategies enables disruptive innovation in the way in which services and associated information systems are designed and delivered (Moxham et al., 2012).

It should be emphasized that there are enduring themes in stakeholder power in all types of health system (for example, whether social health insurance operated or tax funded, privately provided or government run). These include the place of doctors and other clinicians in organizations run as professional bureaucracies (Mintzberg, 1981) that have had to evolve to meet the needs of the era of New Public Management and its aftermath. The roles of other actors are also germane: the complementary or conflicting roles of politicians, civil servants, professional managers and 'lay' people in health governance contribute to a crowded scene.

The changing and distinctive features of healthcare leadership

The health sector is thus a tricky beast. If governance is about setting direction and exercising control, leadership is the human enactment of this process of steering and controlling organizations and the individuals within them. Competing theories of leadership are the subject of intense academic scrutiny and a voluminous literature (see, for example, Bass and Bass, 2008; Storey et al., 2010; Northouse, 2013). One of the characteristics of this literature is the extent to which evidence relating to each of the theories is contested and 'old' paradigms are rejected in favour of 'new' ones. This translates for managers into frames of reference around leadership that are constantly changing. A current leadership model that was first introduced into the NHS in England in 2014 is described below. It is informed by perceived desirable personal qualities and leadership styles that result in high-quality and compassionate care, engaged, motivated and productive staff, patient satisfaction and successful organizations. These desired leadership styles have come to the fore in England following the high-profile failures of care at Mid-Staffordshire NHS Trust, and the subsequent public inquiry and report (Francis, 2013).

Learning activity 19.1   The Healthcare Leadership Model (2013) in England

This model is intended to help to develop leaders in healthcare at all levels and in all settings. There are nine dimensions with five levels of performance against each (insufficient, essential, proficient, strong and exemplary) and a low/high performance rating of each depending on job role. It is free to complete online (following registration) as a personal assessment tool and generates an individual personal report on strengths and areas for development.

The nine dimensions are:

- Inspiring shared purpose
- Leading with care

- Evaluating information
- Connecting our service
- Sharing the vision
- Engaging the team
- Holding to account
- Developing capability
- Influencing for results.

Exercise: Complete the free online assessment tool and access the report that the tool generates personally for you.

- What are your strengths?
- What are your development needs as a healthcare leader?
- How do these results relate to the importance of particular leadership dimensions in your current job role?
- What actions are you going to take to be a better leader?
- Who will you share this with?

See http://www.leadershipacademy.nhs.uk/resources/healthcare-leadership-model/.

Healthcare system leadership

A recent body of theory gaining momentum in the public sector is predicated on the notion that the study of leadership based on the individual may be outmoded. Why? First, within organizations, there is a growing need for *distributed* leadership – exercised by the many rather than by a few – to tackle challenges, manage change and drive improvement in today's speeded-up times, and in acknowledgement that solo heroic leadership may have had its day (Badaracco, 2001). Second, with the growth of system management and network governance, there is a push for inter-organizational collaboration, or leadership that is *shared* across organizations (Brookes and Grint, 2010). Collective leadership, a combination of distributed and shared approaches, is argued by these authors to be the foundation of New Public Leadership (NPL). This builds on some of the concepts of New Public Management (NPM), such as continuous improvement and performance management with a shift in emphasis away from measuring targets to incorporate the idea of public value from Moore's work (Moore, 1995), and the notion of collaborative advantage, as well as the complex process and practice of leadership in the public sphere (Brookes, 2010). Discussions around public leadership are not confined to the Anglo-Saxon world: although somewhat dependent on the western academic literature, countries as diverse as China and Bulgaria are investigating these concepts (Pittinsky and Zhu, 2005).

How do notions of public leadership apply in the healthcare sector? The concept of networks, collaborations, partnerships and integrated care organizations commissioning, purchasing and delivering health services now abounds. These 'chains of care' extend across health service institutions (e.g. hospitals and primary healthcare), across professions (e.g. clinical networks) and across sectors (e.g. joint commissioning units for health and social care). Different forms of chains of care can be found in government-operated health systems such as the UK, in countries with social health insurance such as the Netherlands, and in pro-market outliers such as the United States. Operating in such systems, Goodwin (2006) has proposed four main interconnected variables from his research that resonate strongly with the public leadership discourse. These include the quality of the leadership team as perceived by others (this would be an example of distributed leadership), the history and current strength of inter-organisational relations, the development of alliances and the extent of power sharing across organizations (these last three being examples of shared leadership).

Given the increasing prominence in later iterations of theories of new public management that are given to networked governance and to performance management of programmes rather than institutions (see, for example, Pollitt, 1999), this emerging public leadership discourse has a distinctive attraction, although empirical evidence to underpin the theory remains sparse (Brookes, 2010).

A situational approach to leadership

The cultural context for healthcare leadership in many countries has thus shifted from traditional bureaucracy (leaders were administrators or hospital secretaries) to managerialism (leaders were chief executives in a unified system) to a quasi-marketized system (leaders are chief executives of either purchasing or competing providing healthcare organizations). Furthermore, if we apply the theory that leadership is situational, it follows that different styles and characteristics are appropriate in different parts of healthcare systems (for example, in primary care, mental health, hospital care, planning and provision) and in different countries. Taking primary care, the current scale and scope of which is outlined in Chapter 9 of this book, Chambers and Colin-Thome have argued that, because of the context, doctors who thrive in primary care in general are likely to be people who prefer working in networks rather than hierarchies, show clinical and managerial entrepreneurial spirit, are tolerant of ambiguity and uncertainty, are inherently optimistic, are personally resilient and can see both the 'big picture' and be concerned with detail (Chambers and Colin-Thome, 2009). It would not be difficult, by extension, to argue that hospital work may suit leaders with different preferences, since the 'command' element is likely to be relatively strong and system and strategic leadership, except in the top echelons, less in demand.

The unique feature of healthcare leadership is the role of clinicians in management and leadership. There is growing evidence of an association between involvement in the management of clinicians, from the board to the frontline, and improvements in organization performance (Bohmer, 2012; Chambers et al., 2013). Doctors have considerable 'soft' power. The social construction of leadership (Grint, 2005) can be seen in how the medical elite is formed and sustained. This elite draws on sources of reward, position, referent and expert power (see French and Raven, 1959) and, through the medium of the consultation, continuously re-enact this power and reinforce followership in patients and junior colleagues and other professions ancillary to medicine. But for clinicians, particularly doctors, the transition from clinical practice to a managerial role can be difficult. They can experience a profound clash between their professional and managerial identities, and have to find ways of reconciling conflicting loyalties and ideologies, such as around the needs of individual patients versus population groups and what change can be implemented on the basis of evidence versus *real-politik* (Walshe and Chambers, 2010).

The role of leaders is to some extent prescribed by the organization governance arrangements that are in place. These change over time. Since the Second World War, the Netherlands, which operates a compulsory social health insurance-funded system, has had three reorganizations, and is currently operating in a quasi-marketized system in which there is competition among purchasers as well as providers. In England, by contrast, which has endured reorganization more than most countries, at least six major reorganizations have affected governance since 1948 (in 1972, 1984, 1990, 2001, 2006 and 2012). Attention will therefore now turn to a consideration of healthcare governance and in particular the part played by organization governance.

Board governance in healthcare

The term 'governance' has only relatively recently gained currency as a distinct entity within the study of the management of organizations. The development of the debate around governance can be largely traced to incidents relating to the high-profile organization failures of the early 1990s (Maxwell, Polly Peck, Barings Bank), the US corporate scandals (Enron, WorldCom) a few years later and which have continued on into this century with Equity Life, Parmalat and the banking failures that heralded the global economic recession of 2008/9. The problem is international (Kakabadse and Kakabadse, 2008; Charan et al., 2014). The responses to these events have provided much of the impetus for clarifying concepts of 'good' governance and have also framed the discussions around the management of corporate risk.

At an institution level, the Cadbury Report describes corporate governance as a system by which an organization is directed and controlled (Cadbury, 1992). This is amplified by a subsequent OECD definition of corporate governance as '. . .the structure through which the objectives of the company are set, and the means of attaining those objectives and monitoring performance are determined' (OECD, 2004: 11). The Langlands review of governance for public services in the UK outlines the following as the function of governance: '. . . to ensure that an organisation or partnership fulfils its overall purpose, achieves its intended outcomes for citizens and service users, and operates in an effective, efficient and ethical manner' (Independent Commission for Good Governance in Public Services, 2004: 7).

At the apex of corporate governance is the board. There are various board structures and models in use in health services. There are non-executive boards, executive boards, two-tier boards and unitary boards. And there are models for different health service purposes: for insurers, commissioners, providers and partnerships (cross public sector and public/private). Board membership is achieved through different processes of nomination, appointment and election, and can be paid or unpaid. Many authors argue that board composition does and should vary according to circumstances. As well as national, geographical, cultural, market, sectoral and service differences, the following are often mentioned as key variables: organization life cycle (start-up, mature, decline), stability compared with transformation or crisis, and degree of professionalization of the workforce. Institutional boards vary widely according to political input (Eurohealth, 2013). While public ownership is predominant in the European hospital sector, there have been changes in recent years in hospital governance and in the level of autonomy that management and supervisory boards can exercise (see Box 19.2 for a case study on changes in hospital governance in France). England, France and Italy, for example, have all taken different approaches to implementing hospital governance changes over the past couple of decades (see Chambers et al., 2016).

Box 19.2   Case study – the impact of changes in French hospital board governance from a unitary to a two-tier model

France's healthcare system is a social insurance model, contributions to which are made by working individuals, most of whom also choose to purchase top-up voluntary private health insurance to reduce co-payments. The hospital sector contains public and private providers. Private sector hospitals (non-profit and for-profit) account for about 35 per cent of general bed capacity.

A reform in 2004/5 introduced a diagnosis-related group (DRG) payment system (*tarification à l'activité*) for all acute medical and surgical procedures in public hospitals in place of the previous block budgets. The main aim of this was to harmonize the rules on pricing under a single-fixed price model for both public and private providers. Second, under the New Public Management movement, as of 2010, the healthcare code requires public hospitals to substitute the unitary system of the board of directors with the dual system comprised of the supervisory and the management boards under the reform 'Hôpital, Santé, Patients, Territoires', or HSPT.

The two boards are mutually exclusive, with doctors in leadership positions falling into one of two categories: those who, as senior executives, are responsible for formulating and executing hospital strategy, and those who, as non-executives, participate in monitoring and advise hospital managers. The reforms were driven by the need to save costs and rationalize public sector decisions through the involvement of key actors in management. It has been challenging to implement as expected: key stakeholders seem to have had different definitions and interpretations of quality indicators and their measurement.

Source: Adapted from Chambers et al. (2016).

Board structures

Taking the case of England in more detail, since 1990 local boards in the English NHS have been derived in structure from the Anglo-Saxon private sector unitary board model that predominates in UK and US business (Ferlie et al., 1996; Garratt, 1997). The unitary board typically comprises a chair, chief executive, executive directors and a majority of appointed independent (or non-executive) directors. All members of the board bear collective responsibility for the performance of the enterprise. First established in 2004, NHS Foundation Trusts, by way of contrast, are independent public benefit corporations modelled on cooperative and mutual traditions, which by 2015 totalled one hundred and fifty-two and encompassed more than two-thirds of acute hospital and specialist mental care providers in England (Monitor, 2015). Foundation Trusts have two boards – a board of governors (of up to about fifty people) made up of individuals elected from the local community membership, and a board of directors (around eleven people) made up of a chair and non-executive directors appointed by the governors, and a chief executive and executive directors, appointed by the chair and approved by the governors. This whole structure resembles the Anglo-Saxon unitary board model we have seen adopted by the English NHS but nested within a two-tier European or Senate model, commonly found in the Netherlands, France and Germany.

The Senate model comprises a lower tier operational board that deals with management and strategic issues and an upper-tier supervisory board that ratifies certain decisions taken by the operational board, sets the direction and represents the different interests in the company, particularly those of shareholders and employees (Johnson et al., 2005). This model can be seen, for example, in public hospitals in the Belgian system, which have a four-part governance structure comprising a constituent authority, hospital board, executive committee and medical council (Eeckloo et al., 2004).

In a variant of the English NHS structures, and an example of a wholly non-executive board, New Zealand has twenty-one district health boards tasked with strategic oversight of local health services, but in this case all eleven people on the board are non-executive directors: seven are elected at the time of local government elections and four are appointed by the Ministry of Health; the chief executive is appointed by and accountable to the board but is not a board member (www.moh.govt.nz/districthealthboards). This mirrors the governance arrangements typically found in the voluntary sector where there are boards of trustees, and employed staff such as administrators or directors are invited only 'in attendance' to boards.

From the US perspective, Pointer outlines four types of board commonly found within US healthcare. Parent boards govern freestanding, independently owned institutions; subsidiary boards are local boards of large enterprises; advisory boards provide steer and guidance without a formal corporate governance role; and affiliate organization boards serve their members' interests.

Within the four countries of the UK, with the advent of devolution, there have been deepening policy differences (for example, in the role of the market) and an increasing divergence in the structures for managing health services. The Welsh board model is stakeholder based with up to twenty five members on each board, resembling the English NHS pre-1990. Scotland has an integrated health model and a unified board structure with strong local authority representation and is experimenting with democratic elections onto boards.

Purpose of boards

What are boards for? There is a common view that boards are there to set strategy and goals, to set the organization norms of behaviour, and to monitor the performance of the organisation against those goals. Beyond that, much of the territory is deeply contested. Boards were developed as a result of the growing commercial complexity of business and the gradual separation of ownership from control. Boards represented the interests of absent owners or shareholders (the principals), and management became the agents of the board (Pointer, 1999). The earliest theory about boards was thus agency theory based on the notion that the shareholders' and managers' interests are likely to be different and that the behaviours of both sets of actors are characterized by self-interested opportunism (Berle and Means, 1932). Other theories developed later and are summarized in detail in a recent literature review (Chambers et al., 2013). These include managerial hegemony (according to which the managers rather than the owners make the key decisions), stewardship theory (in which managers and owners share a common agenda and interests), resource dependency theory (in which the main role of the board is to maximize benefits of external dependencies), and stakeholder theory (according to which board members represent the different interests of members and communities with a stake in the organization).

Models of board behaviour can be related to the (sometimes unconscious) orientation of individual board members towards these different theories. Agency theory is connected to a challenging and defensive set of behaviours in the boardroom. Stewardship theory puts a premium on a high trust and collaborative style of working, with the potential disadvantage of low challenge and groupthink. In a stakeholder model, board members tend to be most engaged when articulating the interests of 'their' constituency or special interests. A resource dependency model, with members appointed for their external connections and political and social capital, can result in a 'trophy' board with inadequate grip on the business. With managerial hegemony, the board is disempowered by a chief executive and management team who control the agenda and predetermine the outcome of meetings – with the board reduced to 'rubber-stamping'. None of these models is of itself, in all circumstances, right or wrong, but dysfunctional boards can occur, whatever their composition and structure, when there is a conflict between members about what the fundamental *raison d'être* of the board really is or where there is a disjuncture between the prevailing context, circumstances and challenges and the characteristics, disposition and activities of that board.

Related to this are theories about the sources and use of board power, including the power of the chief executive (Herman, 1981), the discretionary effort and skill exercised by non-executive board members (Pettigrew and McNulty, 1995) and the increased role of the board in periods of crisis or transition (Lorsch and MacIver, 1989), which can be followed by 'coasting' according to stress/inertia theory (Jas and Skelcher, 2005). These ideas suggest that board members have enormous discretion, whatever the governance arrangements, about how they deploy their power and skill for the benefit of the organization and for the benefit of patients.

The above brief summary suggests that simplistic theories of how boards *should* work are unlikely to fit all circumstances. In particular, a binary view is inadequate for the task, such as proposing that either agency or stewardship is preferable for institution governance, in the same way as neither principal agent governance nor network governance theories adequately sum up the way forward for good state governance. Utilizing a realist approach (Pawson, 2006), the likely organization performance outcomes

Table 19.1 A realist framework for healthcare boards

Theory	Contextual assumptions	Mechanism	Intended outcome
Agency	Low trust, high challenge and low appetite for risk	Control through intense internal and external and regulatory performance monitoring	Minimization of risk and good patient safety record
Stewardship	High trust, less challenge and greater appetite for risk	Board support for management in a collective leadership endeavour	Service improvement and excellence in performance
Resource dependency	Importance of social capital of the organization; collaboration seen as more productive than competition	Institution boundary spanning and close dialogue with other healthcare providers	Improved external reputation and relationships
Stakeholder	Importance of representation; risk is shared by many	Collaboration and consensus building	Sustainable organization with high levels of staff engagement and good long-term prospects

Source: Adapted from Chambers et al. (2013: 24).

from particular board theories-in-use and mechanisms deployed in different contexts are posited in Table 19.1.

Board practices

How do boards operate in practice? An understanding of the inner workings of boards is helped by considering separately three elements: composition (board structure), focus (what the board does) and dynamics (the behavioural dimension). In addition, there are some important distinguishing characteristics of boards in the public, non-profit and healthcare sectors (Chambers et al., 2013). Social performance (public value) as well as financial performance is a core purpose. The main mission of a healthcare organization is to serve patients. Mid-Staffordshire NHS Foundation Trust hospital in the UK is an example of an organization that lost sight of this purpose (for details, see Box 19.3). Non-profit board members tend to invest more of their time and are more predisposed to 'managerial work' than their for-profit counterparts. Public boards may suffer from 'institutional isomorphism'. This is, in general, a pressure to conform to prevailing social norms and, in this case, refers to the practice of copying governance structures, rituals and procedures from the private sector without regard for their fitness for purpose for the public sector. Accountabilities on public boards may be blurred as a result of the influence of political patronage and the subversion of formal authority. Finally, as has been signalled earlier in this chapter, healthcare governance of individual organizations is increasingly embedded within a complex superordinate and subordinate governance network, which stretches across organizations that are interdependent in a healthcare system (Chambers et al., 2013).

Choosing the appropriate mechanisms (whether it be around board composition, board focus or board behaviours) to achieve the desired outcomes appears to be important according to the particular situation. For stable organizations, increased monitoring and a strengthened rein on a powerful chief executive officer (CEO) if he or she has been in position for some time may be indicated (in accordance with agency theory), in contrast to a focus on boundary spanning and on the external environment (in accordance with resource dependency theory) in circumstances of turbulence, threat and reputation issues. A framework for understanding how healthcare boards specifically may choose to operate depending on circumstances is outlined in Table 19.1.

Box 19.3 Case study – example of a failing board: Mid-Staffordshire NHS Foundation Trust – England

As discussed in Chapter 16, the Mid-Staffordshire NHS Trust scandal was about poor care and a high mortality rate and first came to light in 2007. Press reports suggested that substandard care led to the unnecessary deaths of up to 1200 patients between 2005 and 2008. An investigation, followed by two inquiries, found significant evidence of neglect of patients. Compensation was paid to families and a number of healthcare professionals have subsequently been struck off from their professional registers.

Robert Francis QC, who chaired the second public inquiry, made clear the culpability of the trust board in his letter to the Secretary of State for Health:

. . . the story . . . told is first and foremost of appalling suffering of many patients. This was primarily caused by a serious failure on the part of a provider Trust Board. It did not listen sufficiently to its patients and staff or ensure the correction of deficiencies brought to the Trust's attention. Above all, it failed to tackle an insidious negative culture involving a tolerance of poor standards and a disengagement from managerial and leadership responsibilities. (Francis, 2013)

A number of reports published following the Francis Inquiry offer advice for boards. These all emphasize the need for boards to focus on hearing the patient voice, gaining assurance on patient safety and clinical quality of services using accurate and timely data, ensuring board-level involvement of clinicians in decision-making, and improving and learning from staff engagement. *The Healthy NHS Board 2013: Principles for Good Governance* (NHS Leadership Academy, 2013), which was also published following the Francis Report (2010), sets out some guiding principles, including the collective role of the board and effective governance in relation to the wider health and social care system, activities and approaches that are most likely to improve board effectiveness in governing well, and the contribution expected of individual board members.

Learning activity 19.2   Board observation exercise to assess board effectiveness

Ask to attend a board meeting of your local hospital or other healthcare provider, commissioner or insurer and if possible obtain the board papers (agenda, minutes, other documents) in advance. Some board meetings are held in public and therefore permission to attend is not required. Note the focus of discussion, decisions and the behaviours at the board meeting. Locate your observations in the framework for understanding the work of boards in Table 19.1. What are the strengths and weaknesses of this board? What do your findings indicate about the characteristics of this board, this organization and its leadership?

Approaches to accountability: structures, processes and impacts

We have already touched on the different forms of governance and oversight regime in our reference to the debate about hierarchies, markets and networks under the influence of New Public Management theories in the public sector in general and also in the healthcare sector (Davies et al., 2005). Mechanisms of accountability are now discussed in terms of theory and in practice.

Governments introducing quasi-markets in healthcare in a hollowed-out state still wish to avoid uncontrolled 'market forces which could adversely affect these politically sensitive services. A solution is to construct accountability arrangements that keep a degree of state control over increasingly independent health-care providers' (Sheaff et al., 2015). A framework to understand healthcare purchasing or commissioning has been developed that supplements the markets–hierarchy–networks trichotomy of governance structures with a more nuanced, specific account (Sheaff et al., 2015). This framework also has utility more generally in a scrutiny of healthcare governance in practice.

International overviews indicate that healthcare commissioners and purchasers generally use one or more of six modes of power. First, managerial performance is associated with the normative cycle of assessing health needs, developing a service specification, procurement and the monitoring of performance. Second, negotiated order involves managing conflicts through relational contracting and making use of social capital already accumulated in relationships between key stakeholders. Third, discursive control, which can include soft coercion, rests on the use of prevailing ideologies about either what is considered 'important' or 'right' (for example, driving down waiting times for care) or what is considered to be evidence-based using a clinical scientific paradigm. Fourth is the use of financial incentives and penalties, which draw on the influence of resource dependencies on the behaviour of healthcare providers. Fifth is the use of or the threat of provider competition, which, when prices are fixed, arguably, improves the quality of hospital care infarction). Sixth is juridical governance, which concerns the use of contracts and the legal system for enforcement (Sheaff et al., 2015: 8–13).

The findings from case study research in three countries (England, Germany, Italy) found that the first three of these modes were widely reported to be in use but that managerial performance of providers was more effective in Germany because they had more complete contracts (deterring less off-contract work) and because of the right of insurers to inspect medical records to check whether treatments were necessary and had been correctly invoiced. Negotiated order in the case of England included micro-commissioning and often protracted discussions over detail to achieve agreed outcomes between purchaser and provider. Discursive control was the third medium of power widely cited and with significant impact: in England this was particularly associated with national policy diktats and local loyalties to local healthcare organizations. By contrast, juridical governance – the holding to account through the use of the contract mechanism – was used only exceptionally in all three countries (Sheaff et al., 2015: 88–9). Neither the use of provider competition nor the use of financial incentives, although frequently referenced by case study informants, was reported to be particularly effective in controlling or holding providers to account.

As well as being *held* to account, accountability includes the enactment – that is, the process of *giving* an account. The age-old practice of storytelling is one of the most effective tools leaders can use. Aristotle, in 350 BC, was one of the first known leaders to advocate the use of a good story. Leaders do need to pick their stories carefully and match them to the situation though (Denning, 2007). A recent approach to narrative, and one with particular relevance to the public sector, is that developed by Marshall Ganz from Harvard Business School. Ganz proposes three components for the delivery of a compelling account: the personal story that defines core values, the story of the audience's experiences and the story of achievements, or the gap between current realities and future desired state (Ganz, 2008). Based on the prominence given to performance management, negotiated order and discursive control, healthcare providers would do well to acknowledge these realities in the framing of their accounts.

Actions have consequences. Accountability also includes the possibility of the imposition of sanctions if a standard is not met. Synthesizing from an extensive literature review which identified 60 governance attributes, Greer and colleagues (2015) posit five health system governance categories of which the first is accountability. As the authors state: 'Accountability has a number of virtues that make it popular, perhaps foundational, in discussions of good governance. Without it, all kinds of incompetence, shirking, bloat and malversation are possible' (2015). Good accountability includes the appropriate use of discretion to minimize bureaucratic rigidity. Effective accountability also means clarity about who is accountable to whom and mechanisms that are workable, avoiding the trap of entanglement in a web of accountability (Tuohy, 2003).

Learning activity 19.3

Answer the following questions to find out how far your organization meets the tests of the Good Governance Standard for Public Services (adapted from the Independent Commission on Good Governance in Public Services, 2004).

1: Good governance means focusing on the organization's purpose and on outcomes for citizens and service users.

- What is this organization for?
- What is being done to improve services?
- Can I easily find out about the organization's funding and how it spends its money?

2: Good governance means performing effectively in clearly defined functions and roles.

- Who is in charge of the organization?
- How are they elected or appointed?
- At the top of the organization, who is responsible for what?

3: Good governance means promoting values for the whole organization and demonstrating the values of good governance through behaviour.

- According to the organization, what values guide its work?
- What standards of behaviour should I expect from the organization?
- Do the senior people put into practice the 'Nolan' principles for people in public life (selflessness, integrity, objectivity, accountability, openness, honesty and leadership) (Nolan, 1994)?

4: Good governance means taking informed transparent decisions and managing risk.

- Who is responsible for what kinds of decision?
- Can I easily find out what decisions have been taken and the reasons for them?
- Does the organization publish a clear annual statement on the effectiveness of its risk management system?

5: Good governance means developing the capacity and capability of the governing body to be effective.

- How does the organization encourage people to get involved in running it?
- What support does it provide for people to get involved?
- How does the organization make sure that all those running it are doing a good job?

6: Good governance means engaging stakeholders and making accountability real.

- Are there opportunities for me and other people to make our views known?
- How can I go about asking the people in charge about their plans and decisions?
- Can I easily find out how to complain and who to contact with suggestions for changes?

Conclusion

This concluding section summarizes the extent to which desirable healthcare governance mechanisms are in place to deliver the required outcomes for healthcare in the future. As we have alluded to earlier, Greer and colleagues (2015) have identified five governance categories as follows:

1 *Accountability*: giving an account and being held to account; the process of informing, explaining, being mandated and sanctioned.
2 *Transparency*: openness to the public and to informed actors who are thus able to exercise scrutiny.
3 *Policy capability*: the ability to turn ideas into workable policies that are integrated with broader organization concerns.
4 *Participation*: the ability to exert influence and access to decision-making by stakeholders, for reasons of legitimacy and justice and also effectiveness.
5 *Integrity*: clear and predictable procedures and allocations of responsibilities.

How far can we discern the governance attributes of accountability, transparency, participation, integrity and capability in the practices of healthcare governance? Attention to patient safety, improving clinical quality of care and delivering efficiencies indicate at least the architecture of accountability, transparency and integrity. The lack of attention to care integration and to community care indicates some weakness in the governance attribute of capability (if that can be translated to mean strategic understanding and implementation of different future models of care) and participation (if that is taken to mean patient-centredness of care).

Hospitals and other healthcare providers offer healthcare on a day-to-day basis as well as delivering policy objectives. They face crises and experience serendipity. They may operate in either a context of intense competition or a monopoly. We have argued earlier that there is no one simple model of how their boards *should* operate but there are clues about what works in different circumstances and there are consequences in terms of outcomes in their choice of *modus operandi*. The embeddedness of healthcare governance across networks and the coming of community-based models of care does suggest that a stakeholder model of governance, with an effort to build long-term collaborations and consensus and improve patient experience and staff engagement is needed. This does not negate the need for performance monitoring, accounting to the public and to regulatory agencies or the need, through a stewardship board mentality, to build trust, and encourage and drive innovation and renewal. The evidence is, however, growing that there are consequences, some of which are unforeseen, in espousing a particular governance approach and that a combination of mechanisms and governance attributes is called for.

Healthcare governance is stronger at the institutional level and may be less fit for purpose as we move to more out-of-hospital care and to programme rather than institution accountability. Differing and changing organizational, strategic and cultural contexts call for sophistication in leadership repertoires.

Learning activity 19.4

Analyse the strengths and weaknesses in external oversight of healthcare in your country using Greer and colleagues' (2015) five health system governance categories as a framework and in relation to the challenges that your country faces. What areas do you consider require different or strengthened governance and why?

Learning resources

Monitor: As the regulator of NHS foundation trusts in England, Monitor publishes a range of reports and assessment tools for NHS foundation trust boards to use in assessing and improving board governance [https://www.gov.uk/government/collections/nhs-foundation-trusts-documents-and-guidance#governance].

Good Governance Guide: A set of resources on governance in the international context, including the application of governance principles to government itself [http://www.goodgovernance.org.au/about-good-governance/what-is-good-governance/].

UK Corporate Governance Code: Includes guidance and reports on board effectiveness and related areas produced by the Financial Reporting Council [https://www.frc.org.uk/Our-Work/Codes-Standards/Corporate-governance/UK-Corporate-Governance-Code.aspx].

References

Badaracco, J. (2001) We don't need another hero, *Harvard Business Review*, September, pp. 111–16.

Bass, B. and Bass, R. (2008) *Bass and Stogdill's Handbook of Leadership*. New York: Simon & Schuster.

Berle, A.A. and Means, G.C. (1932) *The Modern Corporation and Private Property*. New Brunswick, NJ: Transaction Publishers.

Blank, R. and Burau, V. (2013) *Comparative Health Policy*. Basingstoke: Palgrave Macmillan.

Bohmer, R. (2012) *The Instrumental Value of Medical Leadership*. London: King's Fund.

Brookes, S. (2010) Reform, realisation and restoration: public leadership and innovation in government, in S. Brookes and K. Grint (eds.) *A New Public Leadership Challenge?* Basingstoke: Palgrave Macmillan.

Brookes, S. and Grint, K. (2010) *The New Public Leadership Challenge*. Basingstoke: Palgrave Macmillan.

Cadbury, A. (1992) *Report of the Committee on the Financial Aspects of Corporate Governance*. London: Gee.

Chambers, N. and Colin-Thome, D. (2009) Doctors managing in primary care: an international focus, *Journal of Management and Marketing in Healthcare*, 2 (1): 28–43.

Chambers, N., Harvey, G., Mannion, R., Bond, J. and Marshall, J. (2013) Towards a framework for enhancing the performance of NHS boards: a synthesis of the evidence about board governance, board effectiveness and board development, *Health Services and Delivery Research*, 1 (6).

Chambers, N., Joachim, M. and Mannion, R. (2016) Governance of public hospitals, in S. Greer, M. Wismar and J. Figueras (eds.) *Strengthening Health System Governance: Better Policies, Stronger Performance*. Maidenhead: Open University Press.

Charan, R., Carey, D. and Useem, M. (2014) *Boards that Lead: When to Take Charge, When to Partner, and When to Stay Out of the Way*. Boston, MA: Harvard Business Review Press.

Davies, C., Anand, P., Artigas, L., Holloway, J., McConway, K., Newman, J. et al. (2005) *Links between Governance, Incentives and Outcomes: A Review of the Literature*. London: National Coordinating Centre for NHS Service Delivery and Organisation R&D.

Denning, S. (2007) *The Secret Language of Leadership: How Leaders Inspire Action through Narrative*. New York: Wiley.

Eeckloo, K., Van Herck, G., Van Hulle, C. and Vleugels, A. (2004) From corporate governance to hospital governance: authority, transparency and accountability of Belgian non-profit hospitals boards and management, *Health Policy*, 68: 1–15.

Eurohealth (2013) Governing public hospitals, *Eurohealth*, 19 (1).

Ferlie, E., Ashburner, L., Fitzgerald, L. and Pettigrew, A. (1996) *The New Public Management in Action*. Oxford: Oxford University Press.

Francis, R. (2010) *Independent Inquiry into Care Provided by Mid-Staffordshire NHS Foundation Trust*. London: Stationery Office.

Francis, R. (2013) Letter to the Secretary of State, in *Report of the Mid-Staffordshire NHS Foundation Trust Public Inquiry*. London: Stationery Office.

French, J. and Raven, B. (1959) The bases of social power, in D. Cartwright and A. Zander (eds.) *Group Dynamics*. New York: Harper & Row.

Ganz, M. (2008) *What is Public Narrative?* Working paper, Harvard Kennedy School [http://www.hks.harvard.edu/about/faculty-staff-directory/marshall-ganz].

Garratt, B. (1997) *The Fish Rots from the Head*. London: HarperCollins.

Goodwin, N. (2006) *Leadership in Health Care: A European Perspective*. London: Routledge.

Greer, S., Wismar, M. and Figueras, J. (eds.) (2015) *Strengthening Health System Governance: Better Policies, Stronger Performance*. Maidenhead: Open University Press.

Grint, K. (2005) *Leadership: The Heterarchy Principle*. Basingstoke: Palgrave Macmillan.

Grint, K. (2010) *Wicked Problems and Clumsy Solutions: The Role of Leadership in the New Public Leadership Challenge*. Basingstoke: Palgrave Macmillan.

Ham, C. (2009) *Health Policy in Britain*. Basingstoke: Palgrave Macmillan.

Herman, E.S. (1981) *Corporate Control, Corporate Power*. Cambridge: Cambridge University Press Cambridge.

Independent Commission on Good Governance in Public Services (2004) *The Good Governance Standard for Public Services* (The Langlands Review). London: OPM and CIPFA.

Jas, P. and Skelcher, C. (2005) Performance decline and turnaround in public organizations: a theoretical and empirical analysis, *British Journal of Management*, 16 (3): 195–210.

Johnson, G., Scholes, K. and Whittington, R. (2005) *Exploring Corporate Strategy*. Harlow: Pearson Education.

Kakabadse, A. and Kakabadse, N. (2008) *Leading the Board: The Six Disciplines of World-class Chairmen*. Basingstoke: Palgrave Macmillan.

Klein, R. (1998) Why Britain is reorganizing its National Health Service – yet again, *Health Affairs*, 17 (4): 111–25.

Lorsch, J.W. and MacIver, E. (1989) *Pawns or Potentates: The Reality of America's Corporate Boards*. Boston, MA: Harvard Business School Press.

Mintzberg, H. (1981) Organization design: fashion or fit?, *Harvard Business Review*, 59 (1): 108–16.

Monitor (2015) Website [https://www.gov.uk/government/organisations/monitor/about].

Moore, M. (1995) *Creating Public Value: Strategic Management in Government*. Cambridge, MA: Harvard University Press.

Moxham, C., Chambers, N., Girling, J., Garg, S., Jelfs, E. and Bremner, J. (2012) Perspectives on the enablers of e-health adoption: an international interview study of leading practitioners, *Health Services Management Research*, 25: 129–37.

Newman, J. (2005) Enter the transformational leader: network governance and the micro-politics of modernization, *Sociology*, 39 (4): 735–53.

NHS Leadership Academy (2013) *The Healthy NHS Board 2013: Principles for Good Governance* [http://www.leadershipacademy.nhs.uk/wp-content/uploads/2013/06/NHSLeadership-HealthyNHSBoard-2013.pdf].

Nolan, Lord (1994) *Nolan Committee Report on Standards in Public Life* (The Nolan Report). London: HMSO.

Northouse, P.G. (2013) *Leadership: Theory and Practice* (6th edn.). Thousand Oaks, CA: Sage.

OECD (2004) *OECD Principles of Corporate Governance*. Paris: OECD [http://www.oecd.org/corporate/ca/corporategovernanceprinciples/31557724.pdf].

OECD (2005) *Modernising Government: The Way Forward*. Paris: OECD.

Osborne, D. and Gaebler, T. (1993) *Reinventing Government: How the Entrepreneurial Spirit is Transforming the Public Sector*. Reading, MA: Addison-Wesley.

Pawson, R. (2006) *Evidence-based Policy: A Realist Perspective*. London: Sage.

Pettigrew, A. and McNulty, T. (1995) Power and influence in and around the boardroom, *Human Relations*, 48 (8): 845–73.

Pierre, J. and Peters, B.G. (2000) *Governance, Politics and the State*. Basingstoke: Macmillan.

Pittinsky, T.L. and Zhu, C. (2005) Contemporary public leadership in China: a research review and consideration, *Leadership Quarterly*, 16 (6): 921–39.

Pointer, D. (1999) *Board Work: Governing Health Care Organizations*. San Francisco, CA: Jossey-Bass

Pollitt, C. (1999) *Performance or Compliance?* Oxford: Oxford University Press.

Pratt, J., Gordon, P. and Plamping, D. (1999) *Working Whole Systems: Putting Theory into Practice in Organizations*. London: King's Fund.

Sheaff, R., Charles, N., Mahon, A., Chambers, N., Morando, V., Byng, R. et al. (2015) NHS commissioning practice and health system governance: a mixed-methods realistic evaluation, *Health Services and Delivery Research*, 3 (10).

Smith, P.C., Anell, A., Busse, R., Crivelli, L., Healy, J., Lindahl, A.K. et al. (2012) Leadership and governance in seven developed health systems, *Health Policy*, 106 (1): 37–49.

Storey, J., Holti, R., Winchester, N., Green, R., Salaman, G. and Bate, P. (2010) *The Intended and Unintended Outcomes of New Governance Arrangements within the NHS*. London: National Institute for Health Research.

Therborn, G. (1978) *What Does the Ruling Class Do When it Rules?* London: Verso.

Tuohy, C.J. (2003) Agency, contract and governance: shifting shapes of accountability in the health care arena, *Journal of Health Politics Policy and Law*, 28 (2/3): 195–215.

Walshe, K. and Chambers, N. (2010) Healthcare reform and leadership, in S. Brookes and K. Grint (eds.) *The New Public Leadership Challenge*. Basingstoke: Palgrave Macmillan.

Walshe, K. and Shortell, S.M. (2004) When things go wrong: how health care organizations deal with major failures, *Health Affairs*, 23 (3): 103–11.

World Health Organization (WHO) (2008) *The World Health Report 2008 – Primary Health Care: Now More than Ever*. Geneva: WHO [http://www.who.int/whr/2008/en/].

Chapter 20

Quality improvement in healthcare

Ruth Boaden and Joy Furnival

Introduction

Quality is a term widely used not only within healthcare but throughout society, with numerous references to the quality of care, commissioning, access to care, quality and payment systems and the regulation of quality of care and service user expectations of quality in this book alone. However, the study and development of quality are often hampered by a lack of clarity of definition.

In healthcare, there has been an ongoing debate about quality so that 'quality has become a "battleground" on which professions compete for ownership and definition of quality' (Øvretveit, 1997: 221). The medical profession has traditionally 'owned' quality and used its own professional approaches to assuring and regulating it. The rise of quality improvement as something that involves more than the clinical professions therefore led to 'the quality movement being equated with a change in power or a bid for power by managers' (Øvretveit, 1997: 221) and a developing multidisciplinary perspective (Swinglehurst et al., 2015).

One pioneer of healthcare quality was Donabedian (1966), whose research was an important foundation for other developments, although some would argue that healthcare quality has been an issue since Nightingale's time (Stiles and Mick, 1994). Definitions of quality in healthcare abound (Reeves and Bednar, 1994) and a suite of healthcare-related definitions and 'dimensions of quality' have developed (see Table 20.1). The term 'service improvement' is also used in place of 'quality improvement' – possibly because of the contested nature of the term 'quality' but also because of the wide range of approaches that may be used to change or improve services.

There is no doubt that there is an increased focus on quality in all sectors, but particularly in healthcare. Many academic fields have contributed to the study of quality, including services marketing, organization studies, human resource management and organizational behaviour. However, the wide variety of approaches that may be used to improve quality

Table 20.1 Definitions of healthcare quality

Donabedian (1987)	Maxwell (1984)	Langley et al. (1996/2009)	Institute of Medicine (2001)	Department of Health (2008)
• Manner of practitioner–patient interaction • Patient's own contribution to care • Care setting amenities • Facility in access to care • Social distribution of access • Social distribution of health improvements attributable to care	• Access to services • Relevance to need • Effectiveness • Equity • Social acceptability • Efficiency and economy	• Performance • Features • Time • Reliability • Durability • Uniformity • Consistency • Serviceability • Aesthetics • Personal interaction • Flexibility • Harmlessness • Perceived quality • Usability	• Safety • Effectiveness • Patient centredness • Timeliness • Efficiency • Equity	• Patient safety • Patient experience • Care effectiveness

may not be mutually exclusive, although there is little guidance on which approaches may be appropriate in differing circumstances. There are helpful review publications that synthesize the various approaches, how and where they may be used and the supporting evidence (Boaden et al., 2008; Powell et al., 2009; Fereday, 2015).

This chapter focuses on aspects of what is often termed 'quality' because of the distinct history and underpinning systematic approaches that characterize the area of quality improvement. It considers the development of quality improvement by reflecting on those who established and defined the field, in terms of scope to service organizations and healthcare, before outlining the underlying principles of the approaches to improvement and associated tools. The chapter concludes with the challenges of service and quality improvement.

The development of quality improvement

This section describes the development of the quality improvement 'movement' in general, with reference throughout to where the approaches have been applied to healthcare.

The gurus

There are several key figures who have contributed to the development of quality improvement, often referred to as quality 'gurus' (Dale, 2003):

- *Shewhart* pioneered the concept of 'quality' outside healthcare through his work on statistical process control (SPC) (Shewhart, 1931). Most of the other quality gurus' approaches were based on Shewhart's methods.

- *Deming* developed a fourteen-point approach (Deming, 1984) for improving quality and changing organizational culture. He was also responsible for developing the concept of the Plan–Do–Check–Action (PDCA) cycle.
- *Juran* focused on the managerial aspects of implementing quality (Juran, 1951) through quality planning, quality control and quality improvement. His approach can be summarized as: 'Quality, through a reduction in statistical variation, improves productivity and competitive position' (Nielsen et al., 2004), and he maintained that providing customer satisfaction must be the chief operating goal.
- *Crosby* developed a philosophy summarized as 'higher quality reduces costs and raises profit', and defined quality as 'conformance to requirements' (Crosby, 1979). He is best known for the concepts of 'do it right first time' and 'zero defects' and believed that management had to set the tone for quality.
- *Feigenbaum* defined quality as a way of managing (rather than a series of technical projects) and the responsibility of everyone (Feigenbaum, 1961). He developed the categorization of quality costs into appraisal, prevention and failure, and emphasized that management and leadership are essential for quality improvement.

Total quality management

A commonly used term for an overall organizational approach to quality improvement is 'total quality management' (TQM), whose common themes may be summarized as follows (Berwick et al., 1992; Hackman and Wageman, 1995):

- Organizational success depends on meeting customer needs, including internal customers.
- Quality is an effect caused by the processes within the organization, which are complex but understandable.
- Most human beings engaged in work are intrinsically motivated to try hard and do well.
- Simple statistical methods linked with careful data collection can yield powerful insights into the causes of problems within processes.

Just as the term 'quality' has a variety of meanings, there is a confusion of terminology in this area, with not only TQM used but also 'continuous quality improvement' (CQI) (McLaughlin and Simpson, 1999) and 'total quality improvement' (TQI) (Iles and Sutherland, 2001), improvement science (Health Foundation, 2011a), 'quality management' (Berwick et al., 1990/2002) and 'kaizen' (Imai, 1986), although such terms appear to be interchangeable in practice.

Widening the scope of quality improvement

Initially, most of the emphasis on quality improvement was in manufacturing. The field of 'service quality' developed (Groonroos, 1984; Berry et al., 1985) during the 1980s with the widespread use of the SERVQUAL questionnaire (Parasuraman et al., 1988), as well as promotion of the concept of the 'moment of truth' and an emphasis on service recovery.

However, a tension between 'hard' (systems) approaches and 'soft' (people/culture) issues (Wilkinson, 1992) developed, partly in response to the apparent 'failure' of quality improvement (whichever term was used) to achieve sustained improvements in organizational performance. Criticism of the quality improvement literature came from those who described it as 'an evangelical line that excludes traditions and empirical data that fail to confirm its faith' (Kerfoot and Knights, 1995); a view that could be justified because of much of the prescriptive research labelled as 'quality' (Wilkinson and Willmott, 1995). However, this led to research that offers additional perspectives on quality (Hackman and Wageman, 1995; Webb, 1995) and whose findings are perhaps more applicable to the complex world of healthcare and in particular focus on individuals, their motivation, behaviour and interaction and the way in which this affects quality.

Achievements in quality improvement are the subject of national 'awards' such as the Deming Application Prize (Japan) (Deming Prize Committee, 2014), which led to the development of the Malcolm Baldrige National Quality Award (USA) (National Institute of Standards and Technology, 2013–14) and the European Foundation for Quality Management Award/ Excellence Model (Europe) (EFQM, 2014), with associated national and sector-specific derivatives. Quality can also be assessed by organizations themselves (self-assessment), with all these models attempting to integrate the 'hard' and 'soft' factors, and the term 'quality' gradually being replaced by 'excellence'.

Approaches to improvement in healthcare

Some approaches to quality improvement have been developed specifically within healthcare. These include clinical governance, clinical guidelines and pathways, the Institute for Healthcare Improvement (IHI) approach (IHI-QI), and a range of approaches focused on patient safety, although these are not always exclusively clinical (Walshe and Boaden, 2006).

Clinical governance

Clinical governance can be defined as the 'action, the system or the manner of governing clinical affairs' (Lugon and Secker-Walker, 1999). It was developed as an overall approach as part of policy on quality in the NHS in England (Scally and Donaldson, 1998) and spread quickly to other healthcare systems around the world. It led to the establishment of formal audit programmes, increased focus on clinical effectiveness and risk management among other things. It can be viewed as an overall quality improvement process, but one that focuses specifically on clinical issues while still highlighting the importance of organizational culture, individual behaviour and interaction, and may itself use a range of techniques for improvement.

Clinical pathways

Clinical guidelines/pathways are structured, multidisciplinary plans of care designed to standardize and support the implementation of clinical guidelines and protocols, providing guidance about each stage of the management of a patient with a particular condition, including details of both process and outcome. They aim to improve continuity and coordination of care and enable more effective resource planning, and provide comparative data on aspects of care quality. Clinical pathways are associated with reduced in-hospital complications and improved documentation without negatively impacting on length of stay and hospital costs (Rotter et al., 2010).

IHI-QI

The Institute for Healthcare Improvement was established in 1991 and has grown from a 'collection of grant-supported programs to a self-sustaining organization with worldwide influence' (Institute for Healthcare Improvement, 2015a). Its vision is to 'improve health and health care worldwide' (Institute for Healthcare Improvement, 2015b). The approach is informed by the work of Shewhart, Juran and Deming (Scoville and Little, 2014). The key elements of its approach are the 'Model for Improvement' (Langley et al., 2009), which asks three main questions: What are we trying to accomplish? What changes can we make that will result in improvement? And how will we know that the changes are improvements? It typically uses a collaborative approach (Institute for Healthcare Improvement, 2003a).

Patient safety

Patient safety is an emerging area of study and practice that has developed at least in part from quality improvement (Walshe and Boaden, 2006) but also from studies and reports from the USA (Harvard Medical Practice Study, 1990; Institute of Medicine and Committee on Quality Health Care in America, 2001), which demonstrated the scale and extent of the issues and led to the area being taken seriously.

Like quality, the study of patient safety draws on a range of disciplines, including psychology, sociology, clinical epidemiology and informatics. Preventing things going wrong is as important as being able to analyse them when they do, although less attention is usually given to prevention than analysis, perhaps because it often raises challenging and complex issues that cannot be easily addressed.

Many of the key issues raised in the study of patient safety (Walshe and Boaden, 2006) are also applicable to quality improvement:

- Is patient safety considered from the perspective of an individual – doctor, nurse, manager, and so on – or is it an organizational concern?
- To what extent are errors the result of individual failures, or a system property within which the individual works?
- To what extent can healthcare organizations learn from or adopt the safety practices of other industries?
- The involvement of patients in improving safety cannot be underestimated and needs continual reinforcement.

Learning activity 20.1

Given the influences on the development of the quality movement from its origins in manufacturing, what risks and opportunities does this pose for application in health-care? And what might this mean for quality improvement where you work?

Quality improvement fundamentals

There are some fundamental issues that underpin quality improvement, whatever the approach used (Table 20.2), although the emphasis on them varies.

A process view

All quality improvement approaches described in this chapter are based on the process view of organizations (Slack et al., 2004). Process management is defined as entailing three practices: mapping processes, improving processes and adhering to systems of improved processes (Benner and Tushman, 2003). It is argued that taking a process view is one of the key charac-teristics of organizations that are successful in improvement, along with adopting evidence-based practice, learning collaboratively and being ready and able to change (Plsek, 1999).

The process view has also been the basis for the development of systems thinking (Check-land, 1981), and involves the exploration of 'the properties which exist once the parts [of the system] have been combined into a whole' (Iles and Sutherland, 2001), and can be viewed as a combination of processes. Systems thinking has also been proposed as a means of under-standing medical systems (Nolan, 1998), based on the following principles:

- A system needs a purpose to aid people in managing interdependencies.
- The structure of a system determines its performance.
- Changes in system structure have the potential for generating unintended consequences.
- The structure of a system dictates the benefits for people working in the system.
- The size and scope of a system influence the potential for improvement.
- The need for cooperation is a logical extension of interdependencies within systems.
- Systems must be managed.
- System improvements must be led.

The process view examines and improves the interaction between elements of the orga-nization, including the individuals who work within them. It can also be seen in the clinical emphasis on pathways, the use of clinical guidelines and process mapping that can lead to clinical and resource utilization improvements (Trebble et al., 2010). The process view empha-sizes that all employees should focus on process flow and variation reduction to deliver high quality for customers.

Flow

Managing the flow of patients through a healthcare process draws on approaches widely used in manufacturing (Brideau, 2004). Understanding and evaluating flow requires more detailed understanding of demand and capacity than has often been the case in healthcare organizations (Horton, 2004), and to study and improve flow, the whole healthcare system alignment and goals must be considered, especially those between healthcare organizations and clinicians (Zimmerman, 2004). A focus on flow is a key element of the theory of constraints (TOC) and Lean approaches (Table 20.2).

Variation

Variation within a process is inherent and it is argued that understanding and analysing the variation are key to successful improvement (Snee, 1990). This is especially true in healthcare (Haraden and Resar, 2004) and is seen to be the result of clinical (patient) flow and professional variability (Institute for Healthcare Improvement, 2003b). Patient variability is 'random' and cannot be eliminated or reduced but must be managed, whereas non-random variability should be eliminated. It is argued that 'it is variation . . . that causes most of the flow problems in our hospital systems' (Institute for Healthcare Improvement, 2003b). The reduction of variation is a key element of the statistical process control (SPC) method and Six Sigma (Table 20.2).

The role of the 'customer'

Approaches to quality improvement developed from the private sector require the identification of the customer, who may be internal or external to the organization, and subsequently their needs. The purpose of the process has to be clear before improvement can take place, but the role of the customer varies depending on the approach used (Boaden et al., 2008).

- In Six Sigma, the factors 'critical to quality' as far as the customer is concerned are used to define the measures used to determine the 'defects' to be reduced.
- In Lean, the customer's conception of value (which might be thought of as the ratio of benefits to costs) defines which elements of processes are useful (value adding), the rest being waste (steps or components the customer would not wish to pay for).
- Six Sigma and Lean are predicated on the principle that the system should seek to provide more quality or benefit to the customer and/or at lower cost; the theory of constraints (TOC) does not automatically assume this is the way to maximize the goal of the organization.
- IHI-QI has less emphasis on the customer as a key driver of improvement, although the first question in the Model for Improvement ('What are we trying to accomplish?') can include customer requirements.

The issue of professionalism and the increasing role of the patient do, however, have an impact. It is questionable whether the 'customer' can be defined as the patient, but it is clear that patient involvement in quality improvement has been limited (Walley and Gowland, 2004), with a lack of attention to the presence of the patient in processes (Shortell et al., 1995) and lack of consumer power (Zbabada et al., 1998). The patient may be seen as the primary customer, but the patient does not pay directly for services where they are publicly funded – other customers may include the patient's family, and society in general, as well as commissioners. 'Depending on the perspective, the definition of value will hence differ. However, because the main mission of healthcare is to treat and cure patients . . . it is argued that the patient should define what creates value in healthcare' (Kollberg et al., 2006). The role of the customer is crucial in the Lean approach in defining 'value'.

The role of people

The increasing importance of people (generally staff of the organization or system where improvement is taking place) in improvement has already been described as part of the development of quality improvement. Many of the approaches to quality improvement are not explicit about the role of people and assume that people will automatically be motivated to improve quality. The collaborative approach emphasizes the role of individuals in improvement, and the involvement of people is explicit in Lean (see Table 20.2).

Approaches to quality improvement

There are a number of different approaches that can be used, all taking customer-focused process views with varying levels of focus on flow and variation and involvement of people. Despite the similarities, advocates describe significant differences between approaches mostly related to varying emphasis on the important of flow and variation and argue that one particular approach is better than another. This has led to a confusing array of approaches with different terminology that appear to include different tools despite their underlying similarity. A number of the main approaches are outlined in Table 20.2, along with references to where they have been used in healthcare.

Learning activity 20.2

There are many quality improvement approaches available, but which ones do you think would be most useful in improving quality in your area of work? Discuss with your team or a group of people within your organization or network which approaches they have used and why.

Tools to support quality improvement

Many tools claimed to be useful for quality improvement can be used as part of various approaches: a summary and basic description of commonly used tools is provided in Table 20.3 (developed from Dale, 2003). Detailed examples of specific improvement tools and how to apply them can be found in a range of sources, including Bicheno and Holweg (2008) and Brassard et al. (2002).

Table 20.2 Quality improvement approaches

Approach	Description	Key reference	Healthcare example	Origin
Business Process Redesign (or Business Process Re-engineering)	The fundamental rethinking and radical redesign of business processes to achieve dramatic performance improvements (Hammer and Champy, 1993: 35)	Hammer and Champy (1993)	Leicester Royal Infirmary (McNulty and Ferlie, 2002)	Private sector
Institute for Healthcare Improvement – Quality Improvement (IHI-QI)	Based extensively on PDSA (see below) and built on the Model for Improvement. IHI-QI draws a fundamental distinction between the system to be improved and the techniques and methods used to improve it	Institute for Healthcare Improvement (2003a, 2003b)	IHI (Kenney, 2008; Hulscher et al., 2009)	Automotive and electronics adapted for healthcare via API Associates
Lean	Focus on elimination of waste through identification of customer value and respect for people and society	Womack and Jones (1996)	Virginia Mason Medical Center (Kaplan and Rona, 2004)	Automotive
Plan–Do–Check–Act (PDCA)	An iterative four-step management method used for the control and continuous improvement of processes and products. It is also known as the Deming or Shewhart circle/cycle/ wheel, or plan–do–study–act (PDSA)	The Improvement Guide (Langley et al., 1996/2009)	Taylor et al. (2013)	Various
Six Sigma	The term 'six sigma' refers to a process that has at least six standard deviations (6σ) between the process mean and the nearest specification limit	The Six Sigma Handbook (Pyzdek and Keller, 2003)	Sehwail and DeYong (2003). However, 'six sigma has not been widely applied to patient care' (Revere et al., 2004)	Electronics manufacturing

(continued)

Table 20.2 (continued)

Approach	Description	Key reference	Healthcare example	Origin
Statistical process control (SPC)	Identification of the difference between 'natural' variation in processes – termed 'common cause' – and that which could be controlled – 'special cause' variation. Processes that exhibit only common cause variation are said to be in statistical control	Shewhart (1931)	Benneyan et al. (2003), Marshall et al. (2004)	Telecommuni-cations
Theory of constraints (TOC)	Every system has at least one constraint – anything that limits the system from achieving higher performance. The existence of constraints represents opportunities for improvement – they are not viewed as negative	Goldratt and Cox (1984)	NHS Trust (Lubitsh et al., 2004)	Manufacturing

Table 20.3 Quality improvement tools

Tool	Description	Source (if identifiable)
Benchmarking	Learning from the experience of others by comparing products or processes – within or across organizations or functional processes	Rank Xerox (Camp, 1989)
Brainstorming	Used with a variety of tools to generate ideas in groups	Described in Osborn (1953)
Checklists	Lists of key features of a process, equipment, etc. to be checked	Commonly used in a variety of situations (WHO, 2014)
Collaboratives	A collaborative is a short-term learning system that brings together teams to seek improvement in a focused area	Developed within IHI as an approach for spreading change (Institute for Healthcare Improvement, 2003a)
Departmental purpose analysis (DPA)	Tool used to facilitate internal customer relationships	Originated at IBM in 1984

(continued)

Tool	Description	Source (if identifiable)
Design of Experiments (DOE)	A series of techniques that identify and control parameters that have a potential impact on performance, aiming to make the performance of the system immune to variation	Dates back to agricultural research in the 1920s, developed by Taguchi (1986)
Driver diagrams (variant of an 'Ishikawa' diagram, also known as a fishbone diagram)	An analysis tool used to summarize theories as to what issues or faults cause the problem that is being solved, to allow the 'drivers' to be identified	Dates back to the 1920s as one of the original quality control tools. Used extensively by Ishikawa in Japan (Ishikawa and Lu, 1985) and by Deming (1984)
Failure Mode and Effects Analysis (FMEA) or Failure Mode Effect and Criticality Analysis (FMECA)	A planning tool used to 'build quality in' to a product or service, for either design or process. Looks at the ways in which the product or service might fail, and then modifies the design or process to avoid or minimize them	Developed in 1962 in the aerospace and defence industries (Joint Commission on Accreditation of Healthcare Organizations, 2005)
Flowcharts	A diagrammatic representation of the steps in a process, often using standard symbols	Developed from industrial engineering methods but no one identifiable source. Used in many industries
Mistake-proofing (Poke Yoke)	Technique used to prevent errors turning into defects in the final product – based on the assumption that mistakes will occur, however 'careful' individuals are, unless preventative measures are put in place	Developed by Shingo (1986)
Patient Safety Walkarounds ('Gemba' walks)	Used extensively within IHI-QI and Lean approaches to promote learning from the workplace and listening to staff and, in the case of healthcare, patients	Developed as part of the Toyota Production System (Womack and Shook, 2011). Patient Safety Walkarounds adapted from automotive approaches
Policy Deployment (also known as Strategy Deployment and hoshin kanri)	Used to communicate policy, goals and objectives through the hierarchy of the organization, focusing on the key activities for success	Developed in Japan in the early 1960s and adopted in the USA from the early 1980s (Dale, 2003)
Quality costing	Tools used to identify the costs of quality, often using the prevention – appraisal – failure (PAF) categorization	PAF developed by Feigenbaum (1961). Cost of (non) conformance developed by Crosby (1979)

(continued)

Table 20.3 *(continued)*

Tool	Description	Source *(if identifiable)*
Quality Function Deployment (QFD)	Tool to incorporate knowledge about needs of customers into all stages of the design and manufacture/delivery process. Closely related to FMEA and DOE	Developed in Japan at Kobe shipyard
Visual Workplace and Housekeeping	Focused on cleanliness, etc. in the environment and the concept of maintaining standards to ensure that defects are visible to allow identification and rectification	Based on what the Japanese refer to as the 5S: • *seiri* – organization • *seiton* – neatness • *seiso* – cleaning • *seiketsu* – standardization • *shitsuke* – discipline

Healthcare improvement examples

Here we describe the application of two different quality improvement approaches within healthcare: IHI-QI and Lean used in the NHS in Scotland (Box 20.1) and in the Virginia Mason Medical Center in the USA (Box 20.2) respectively (for further information, see Scoville and Little, 2014).

Box 20.1 Case study – IHI-QI in NHS Scotland

Background and impact

NHS Scotland is the publicly funded healthcare system in Scotland – where health and social care spending has been devolved from the United Kingdom. In 2004, a patient safety improvement programme was established, using the IHI-QI approach (see Table 20.2). It developed and tested practical ways to improve hospital safety and demonstrated what could be achieved through an organization-wide approach to patient safety (Health Foundation, 2011b). Ninewells Hospital took part and was particularly successful in reducing harm (Griffin and Resar, 2009) by more than 60 per cent through reducing adverse drug events and improving medication reconciliation (Haraden and Leitch, 2011). This led to the development of the Scottish Patient Safety Programme (Haraden and Leitch, 2011; Institute for Healthcare Improvement, 2015c), which aimed to reduced hospital standardized mortality ratios (HSMR) by 15 per cent within five years (Rooney and Leitch, 2010), together with other aims. This was the first country-wide national strategic and systematic approach to improving patient safety anywhere in the world.

Patient safety was indicated as a priority in each organization through board meetings, patient safety 'walkarounds' (see Table 20.3) and communications activities across the organizations. Typical results for a pressure ulcer reduction project in NHS Tayside indicated that ulcer prevalence reduced from 21 per cent to 7 per cent, and ulcer incidence reduced from 6.6 to 2.4 per cent between 2007 and 2013 (Mackie et al., 2014).

Improvement at scale

A national infrastructure was established including the development of an improvement faculty to provide training on improvement skills for teams, together with leadership development, learning forums and Scottish Patient Safety Fellows (O'Connor and Fearfull, 2015). While the programme was originally focused on safety within acute hospital settings, it has spread into mental health, maternity and primary care settings due to staff demand, although it has been more difficult to develop and adapt the approach outside of acute hospitals. The IHI-QI approach has been criticized for being too limited to a focus on patient safety and rigid in its application, when it could also be used to solve other critical problems such as financial reductions and waiting times.

Despite the critics, Scotland launched its National Quality Strategy for Healthcare in 2010 (Scottish Government, 2010), which was refreshed in 2015 (Scottish Government, 2015). By 2014, the aims of the Scottish Patient Safety Programme were achieved with a greater than 50 per cent reduction in mortality (Healthcare Improvement Scotland, 2014) and more than three hundred days without infections. NHS Scotland continues to use the IHI-QI approach across the country and is a significant example of large-scale change across the world.

Box 20.2   Case study – Lean at Virginia Mason Medical Center (VMMC)

Background

In 1998, VMMC, a three hundred-bed not-for-profit hospital and integrated care system with approximately four hundred and fifty physicians, made a financial loss for the first time in its history, which continued in 1999 (Blackmore et al., 2011). Following the appointment of a new CEO, the leadership team and external management consultants (previously from Boeing) worked together to develop a new strategy to ensure the highest level of safety, improved care delivery and the elimination of waste: the Virginia Mason Production System (VMPS) (Bohmer and Ferlins, 2005). This focused on delivering patient satisfaction and productivity, through a zero defect approach (Kaplan and Patterson, 2008) and required staff to constantly seek ways to deliver the highest quality and safest patient care on an ongoing basis. This was based on the Lean approach (see below).

Note: Case study continues below.

Lean Healthcare

The Lean approach has been developed in healthcare through the implementation of the Toyota Production System (Kaplan and Rona, 2004). There are numerous reports of the application of Lean in healthcare (see, for example, Boaden et al., 2008) but there is 'relatively little evidence of the complete Lean philosophy being applied in the public sector' (Radnor et al., 2006; Andersen et al., 2014). Lean appears to be applied in the public sector without a full understanding of the underlying principles, so that it is considered to be a set of tools rather than a fundamental shift in culture (Radnor and Boaden, 2008). Critics suggest Lean is a 'management fad' and question the appropriateness of whole-scale adoption of 'production line' Lean within professionally dominated healthcare (Waring and Bishop, 2010; McCann et al., 2015)

Box 20.2   Case study – Lean at Virginia Mason Medical Center (VMMC) (continued)

The Virginia Mason Production System (VMPS)

Staff visited Toyota in Japan to study the problem-solving approaches used in the Toyota Production System and developed the VMPS, which included agreed definitions of quality, summarized as 'better, faster and more affordable' (Blackmore et al., 2011), to ensure there was clear agreement on goals and what high quality looked like. The measures of quality could be applied across different clinical and operational silos (Pham et al., 2007).

Rapid Process Improvement Workshops (RPIWs) were used; staff were excused from their day role to work in a problem-solving team, redesigning and standardizing processes, to eliminate error and ensure flow. VMMC also introduced the idea of patient safety alerts (Furman, 2005; Furman and Caplan, 2007), based on the concept of 'jidoka': 'error-proofing' or spotting errors before they occur, often using the tool of 'poke yoke' (see Table 20.3). Alerts were flagged immediately to managers' and senior clinicians' offices to trigger a response at the site of the alert to ensure it was resolved and learned from.

The Physician Compact

The VMMC leadership worked closely with the staff within the organization to make explicit the agreements between staff and the organization, particularly doctors, about what was expected from them in terms of improvement and in return what they could expect form the organization. This 'compact' for implementing VPMS was not without challenges and some staff left the organization, but overall it helped to reduce misalignment between staff and the organization (Bohmer and Ferlins, 2005; Kenney, 2010).

Impact

Results from over ten years of operation include 91 per cent patient satisfaction and 95 per cent same-day appointments (Blackmore et al., 2011). Pham et al. (2007) describe numerous cost savings achieved through pathway redesign – for example, saving of $750,000 annually through the substitution of stress echocardiograms for nuclear perfusion imaging. The Leapfrog Group ranked VMMC in the top 1 per cent of hospitals in the USA (and also designated VMMC as 'Hospital of the Decade') (Kenney, 2015).

Many organizations are trying to emulate the success of VMMC, often on a larger scale, for example Saskatchewan province in Canada (Willis et al., 2014) and the NHS in the North East of England (Erskine et al., 2009; Hunter et al., 2014, 2015). These examples have been able to demonstrate significant success, although external reorganization, political context, union challenges and scepticism have challenged the commitment to the approach.

Does quality improvement 'work'?

There have been a range of reviews of quality improvement research; all challenged by the same issues, which makes it difficult to decide what approaches 'work'. Most of the papers are descriptive case studies based on a single site, rather than analytical reviews of the application of improvement approaches. Methodologically, many papers are relatively small-scale before and after studies, making it difficult to determine whether any reported changes are directly attributable to the quality improvement intervention or not.

There is debate about the relevance (or otherwise) of randomized controlled trial methods to investigate the effectiveness of quality improvement approaches. Some argue that quality improvement is a complex social intervention, for which methods designed to 'control out' the influence of context on the implementation of the intervention are not relevant. Trials may not be sensitive to the things that influence the success of change: the 'array of influences: leadership, changing environments, details of implementation, organisational history, and much more' (Berwick, 2008: 1183).

There are few large-scale, rigorously conducted trials that provide conclusive evidence to support the assertion that implementing quality improvement programmes and methods leads to improved processes and outcomes of care (Perneger, 2006). Very few studies contain any analysis of the economic implications (Øvretveit, 2009) or the impact of quality improvement on cost. However, many authors argue for more than one method to be used (Grol et al., 2008).

The aim is not to find out 'whether it works', as the answer to that question is almost always 'yes, sometimes'. The purpose is to establish when, how and why the intervention works, to unpick the complex relationship between context, content, application and outcomes. (Walshe, 2007: 58)

There is little independent evaluative research on the Scottish IHI-QI programmes or the Lean approach at VMMC and it remains possible that the improvements seen may have occurred in these organizations through the impact of leadership intent and clarity of priorities, without the need for the explicit use of the improvement approach. Furthermore, the impact of the political context and wider system change may have modified the results. The multi-methods study in England that evaluated the North East Transformation System (NETS) concluded that it was:

> . . . a bold and ambitious initiative which succeeded in bringing about real and lasting change in some parts of the North East [of England]. However, it was unable to fully realise its vision and purpose partly because of the widespread reorganisation of the NHS by the new . . . government. (Hunter et al., 2014)

One attempt to distil common challenges in quality improvement through a review of case studies of healthcare organizations provides a useful overview of the organizing challenges (Bate et al., 2008) (see Table 20.4).

Learning activity 20.4

- In your organization and network, how are you planning to evaluate your improvement activity?
- What challenges do you face and how can they be overcome?
- What is your role in that?

Table 20.4 Core challenges to organizing for quality

Challenge	Lack of this can lead to . . .
Structural – organizing, planning and coordinating quality efforts	Fragmentation and lack of synergy between different parts of the organization doing quality improvement
Political – addressing and dealing with the politics of change surrounding any quality improvement effort	Disillusionment and inertia because quality improvement is not happening on the ground, and certain groups or individuals are resisting change
Cultural – giving quality a shared, collective meaning within the organization	Evaporation because the change has not been properly anchored in everyday thinking and routines
Educational – creating a learning process that supports improvement	Amnesia and frustration as lessons are forgotten or fail to accumulate, and improvement capabilities fail to keep abreast of growing aspirations
Emotional – engaging and motivating people by linking quality improvement efforts to inner sentiments and beliefs	Loss of interest and fade-out as the change effort runs out of momentum due to a failure to engage frontline staff
Physical and technological – the designing of physical systems and infrastructure that supports quality efforts	Exhaustion as people try to make change happen informally, without systematic routines for necessary everyday activities

Source: Bate et al. (2008).

Conclusion

Many believe that 'in matters of quality improvement, healthcare can indeed learn from industry – and perhaps, equally important, industry can also learn from healthcare. The fundamental principles of quality improvement apply to both' (Berwick et al., 1990–2002: xiv). However, given the variety of perspectives on quality improvement, especially those from an organization/process perspective and those developed by professionals, there are challenges for all:

- Quality improvement needs to be demystified: 'much of it is common sense, accessible to all and not the preserve of a few. The tendency for each new quality improvement theory to generate its own jargon and esoteric knowledge must be resisted' (Locock, 2003: 56).
- Healthcare professionals need to recognize their role and responsibility to the wider system: 'the need to balance clinical autonomy with transparent accountability, support the systematisation of clinical work' (Degeling et al., 2003: 649).
- Managers need to recognize the limits of their authority in improvement: 'there was no evidence that managers alone could produce . . . clinical buy-in' (Dopson and Fitzgerald, 2005).

In the continually changing world of healthcare, quality is always going to be important and the differing perspectives and multidisciplinary approaches must be taken into account.

Learning resources

British Medical Journal (BMJ) Quality and Safety: *BMJ Quality & Safety* is an international peer-reviewed journal focused on the quality and safety of healthcare and improvement science [http://qualitysafety.bmj.com/].

Institute for Healthcare Improvement: The IHI website includes resources about improvement science and healthcare case studies [www.ihi.org].

Health Foundation: The Health Foundation's website includes many healthcare improvement resources linked in particular to patient safety and patient experience [http://www.health.org.uk/].

Lean Enterprise Institute: The global Lean network website includes improvement case studies, resources and blogs for healthcare and non-healthcare sectors [http://www.planet-lean.com/].

NHS Quality Improvement Scotland: A website detailing improvement tools and programmes being used across Scotland [http://www.qihub.scot.nhs.uk/default.aspx].

Virginia Mason Institute: Provides case study information regarding Lean in healthcare [http://www.virginiamasoninstitute.org/].

References

Andersen, H., Røvik, K.A. and Ingebrigtsen, T. (2014) Lean thinking in hospitals: is there a cure for the absence of evidence? A systematic review of reviews, *BMJ Open*, 4 (1): e003873.

Bate, P., Mendel, P. and Robert, G. (2008) *Organising for Quality: The Improvement Journeys of Leading Hospitals in Europe and the United States*. Oxford: Radcliffe Publishing.

Benner, M.J. and Tushman, M.L. (2003) Exploitation, exploration and process management: the productivity dilemma revisited, *Academy of Management Review*, 26: 238–56.

Benneyan, J.C., Lloyd, R.C. and Plsek, P. (2003) Statistical process control as a tool for research and healthcare improvement, *Quality and Safety in Health Care*, 12: 458–64.

Berry, L.L., Zeithaml, V.A. and Parasuraman, A. (1985) Quality counts in services too, *Business Horizons*, 28: 44–52.

Berwick, D.M. (2008) The science of improvement, *Journal of the American Medical Association*, 299: 1182–4.

Berwick, D., Endhoven, A. and Bunker, J.P. (1992) Quality management in the NHS: the doctor's role – I and II, *British Medical Journal*, 304: 235–9, 304–8.

Berwick, D., Godfrey, A.B. and Roessner, J. (1990/2002) *Curing Health Care*. San Francisco, CA: Jossey-Bass.

Bicheno, J. and Holweg, M. (2008) *The Lean Toolbox: The Essential Guide to Lean Transformation*. Buckingham: Picsie Books.

Blackmore, C.C., Mecklenburg, R.S. and Kaplan, G.S. (2011) At Virginia Mason, collaboration among providers, employers, and health plans to transform care cut costs and improved quality, *Health Affairs*, 30: 1680–7.

Boaden, R., Harvey, G., Moxham, C. and Proudlove, N. (2008) *Quality Improvement: Theory and Practice in Healthcare*. Warwick: NHS Institute for Innovation and Improvement.

Bohmer, R. and Ferlins, E.M. (2005) Virginia Mason Medical Center, *Harvard Business School*, 3: 1–28.

Brassard, M., Finn, L., Ginn, D. and Ritter, D. (2002) *The Six Sigma Memory Jogger*. Salem, NH: GOAL/QPC.

Brideau, L.P. (2004) Flow: why does it matter?, *Frontiers of Health Services Management*, 20: 47–50.

Camp, R.B. (1989) *Benchmarking: The Search for Industry Best Practice that Leads to Superior Performance*. Milwaukee, WI: ASQC Quality Press.

Checkland, P. (1981) *Systems Thinking, Systems Practice*. New York: Wiley.

Crosby, P.B. (1979) *Quality is Free*. New York: McGraw-Hill.

Dale, B.G. (ed.) (2003) *Managing Quality*. Oxford: Blackwell.

Degeling, P., Maxwell, S., Kennedy, J. and Coyle, B. (2003) Medicine, management and modernisation: a 'danse macabre'?, *British Medical Journal*, 326: 649–52.

Deming Prize Committee (2014) *The Application Guide for The Deming Prize*. Japan: Union of Japanese Scientists and Engineers.

Deming, W.E. (1984) *Out of the Crisis*. Cambridge, MA: MIT Press.

Department of Health (2008) *High Quality Care for All – NHS Next Stage Review Final Report*. London: Stationery Office.

Donabedian, A. (1966) Evaluating the quality of medical care, *Milbank Memorial Fund Quarterly*, 44: 166–206.

Donabedian, A. (1987) Commentary on some studies of the quality of care, *Health Care Financing Review*, Annual Supplement, 75–86.

Dopson, S. and Fitzgerald, L. (eds.) (2005) *Knowledge to Action?* Oxford: Oxford University Press.

Erskine, J., Hunter, D.J., Hicks, C., McGovern, T., Scott, E., Lugsden, E. et al. (2009) New development: first steps towards an evaluation of the North East Transformation System, *Public Money and Management*, 29: 273–6.

European Foundation for Quality Management (EFQM) (2014) *The European Foundation for Quality Management (EFQM) Excellence Model*. Europe: EFQM.

Feigenbaum, A. (1961) *Total Quality Control*. New York: McGraw-Hill.

Fereday, S. (2015) *A Guide to Quality Improvement Methods*. London: Healthcare Quality Improvement Partnership.

Furman, C. (2005) Implementing a patient safety alert system, *Nursing Economics*, 23: 42–5.

Furman, C. and Caplan, R. (2007) Applying the Toyota Production System: using a patient safety alert system to reduce error, *Journal of Quality and Patient Safety*, 33: 376–86.

Goldratt, E.M. and Cox, J. (1984) *The Goal*. Farnham: Ashgate.

Griffin, F.A. and Resar, R.K. (2009) *IHI Global Trigger Tool for Measuring Adverse Events*, Innovation Series White Paper. Boston, MA: Institute for Healthcare Improvement.

Grol, R., Berwick, D. and Wensing, M. (2008) On the trail of quality and safety in health care, *British Medical Journal*, 336: 74–6.

Groonroos, C. (1984) *Strategic Management and Marketing in the Service Sector*. London: Chartwell-Bratt.

Hackman, J.R. and Wageman, R. (1995) Total quality management: empirical, conceptual and practical issues, *Administrative Science Quarterly*, 40: 309–42.

Hammer, M. and Champy, J. (1993) *Reengineering the Corporation: A Manifesto for Business Revolution*. London: Nicolas Brealey.

Haraden, C. and Leitch, J. (2011) Scotland's successful national approach to improving patient safety in acute care, *Health Affairs*, 30: 755–63.

Haraden, C. and Resar, R. (2004) Patient flow in hospitals: understanding and controlling it better, *Frontiers of Health Services Management*, 20: 3–15.

Harvard Medical Practice Study (1990) *Patients, Doctors and Lawyers: Medical Injury, Malpractice Litigation and Patient Compensation in New York*. Boston, MA: Harvard College.

Health Foundation (2011a) *Improvement Science*. London: Health Foundation.

Health Foundation (2011b) *Learning Report: Safer Patients Initiative*. London: Health Foundation.

Healthcare Improvement Scotland (2014) *Highlights of the Scottish Patient Safety Programme National Conference – Driving Improvements in Patient Safety*. Edinburgh: Healthcare Improvement Scotland.

Horton, S. (2004) Increasing capacity while improving the bottom line, *Frontiers of Health Services Management*, 20: 17–23.

Hulscher, M., Schouten, L.M.T. and Grol, R. (2009) *Collaboratives*. London: Health Foundation.

Hunter, D., Erskine, J., Hicks, C., McGovern, T., Small, A., Lugsden, E. et al. (2014) A mixed-methods evaluation of transformational change in NHS North East, *Health Services and Delivery Research*, 2: 47.

Hunter, D.J., Erskine, J., Small, A., McGovern, T., Hicks, C., Whitty, P. et al. (2015) Doing transformational change in the English NHS in the context of 'big bang' redisorganisation, *Journal of Health Organization and Management*, 29: 10–24.

Iles, V. and Sutherland, K. (2001) *Organisational Change: A Review for Health Care Managers, Professionals and Researchers*. London: National Coordinating Centre for NHS Service Delivery and Organization.

Imai, M. (1986) *Kaizen: The Key to Japan's Competitive Success*. New York: McGraw-Hill.

Institute for Healthcare Improvement (2003a) *The Breakthrough Series: IHI's Collaborative Model for Achieving Breakthrough Improvement*, IHI Innovation Series White Paper. Boston, MA: Institute for Healthcare Improvement.

Institute for Healthcare Improvement (2003b) *Optimizing Patient Flow: Moving Patients Smoothly through Acute Care Settings*. Boston, MA: Institute for Healthcare Improvement.

Institute for Healthcare Improvement (2015a) *About Us – History*. Boston, MA: Institute for Healthcare Improvement.

Institute for Healthcare Improvement (2015b) *About Us – Vision, Mission and Values*. Boston, MA: Institute for Healthcare Improvement.

Institute for Healthcare Improvement (2015c) *Scottish Patient Safety Programme*. Boston, MA: Institute for Healthcare Improvement.

Institute of Medicine and Committee on Quality Health Care in America (2001) *Crossing the Quality Chasm*. Washington, DC: Institute of Medicine.

Ishikawa, K. and Lu, D.J. (1985) *What is Total Quality Control?: The Japanese Way*. Englewood Cliffs, NJ: Prentice-Hall.

Joint Commission on Accreditation of Healthcare Organisations (JCAHO) (2005) *Failure Mode Effect and Criticality Analysis*. Oak Brook, IL: JCAHO.

Juran, J. (ed.) (1951) *The Quality Control Handbook*. New York: McGraw-Hill.

Kaplan, G.S. and Patterson, S.H. (2008) Seeking perfection in healthcare, *Healthcare Executive*, 23 (3): 16–21.

Kaplan, G.S. and Rona, J.M. (2004) Seeking zero defects: applying the Toyota production system to health care, in *16th National Forum on Quality Improvement in Healthcare*. Orlando, FL.

Kenney, C. (2008) *The Best Practice: How the New Quality Movement is Transforming Medicine*. New York: Public Affairs.

Kenney, C. (2010) *Transforming Health Care: Virginia Mason Medical Center's Pursuit of the Perfect Patient Experience*. New York: Productivity Press.

Kenney, C. (2015) *Virginia Mason Blog – About This Blog*. Seattle, WA: Virginia Mason Medical Centre.

Kerfoot, D. and Knights, D. (1995) Empowering the 'quality worker'? The seduction and contradiction of the total quality phenomenon, in A. Wilkinson and H. Willmott (eds.) *Making Quality Critical*. London: Routledge.

Kollberg, B., Dahlgaard, J.J. and Brehmer, P. (2006) Measuring lean initiatives in health care services: issues and findings, *International Journal of Productivity and Performance Management*, 56: 7–24.

Langley, G.J., Moen, R.D., Nolan, K.M., Nolan, T.W., Norman, C.L. and Provost, L.P. (1996/2009) *The Improvement Guide: A Practical Approach to Enhancing Organizational Performance*. San Francisco, CA: Jossey-Bass.

Langley, G.J., Moen, R.D., Nolan, K.M., Nolan, T.W., Norman, C.L. and Provost, L.P. (2009) *The Improvement Guide: A Practical Approach to Enhancing Organizational Performance* (2nd edn.). San Francisco, CA: Jossey-Bass.

Locock, L. (2003) Healthcare redesign: meaning, origins and application, *Quality and Safety in Health Care*, 12: 53–8.

Lubitsh, G., Doyle, C. and Valentine, J. (2004) The impact of theory of constraints (TOC) in an NHS Trust, *Journal of Management Development*, 24 (2): 116–31.

Lugon, M. and Secker-Walker, J. (eds.) (1999) *Clinical Governance: Making it Happen*. London: Royal Society of Medicine Press.

Mackie, S., Baldie, D., McKenna, E. and O'Connor, P. (2014) Using quality improvement science to reduce the risk of pressure ulcer occurrence – a case study in NHS Tayside, *Clinical Risk*, 20 (6): 134–43.

Marshall, T., Mohammed, M.A. and Rouse, A. (2004) A randomized controlled trial of league tables and control charts as aids to health service decision-making, *International Journal of Quality Health Care*, 16: 309–15.

Maxwell, R.J. (1984) Quality assessment in health, *British Medical Journal*, 288: 1470–2.

McCann, L., Hassard, J.S., Granter, E. and Hyde, P.J. (2015) Casting the lean spell: the promotion, dilution and erosion of lean management in the NHS, *Human Relations*, 68: 1557–77.

McLaughlin, C.P. and Simpson, K.N. (1999) Does TQM/CQI work in healthcare?, in C.P. McLaughlin and A.D. Kaluzny (eds.) *Continuous Quality Improvement in Health Care: Theory, Implementation and Applications*. Gaithersburg, MD: Aspen.

McNulty, T. and Ferlie, E. (2002) *Reengineering Health Care: The Complexities of Organisational Transformation*. Oxford: Oxford University Press.

National Institute of Standards and Technology (2013–14) *Baldridge Excellence Framework*. Gaithersburg, MD: National Institute of Standards and Technology (NIST).

Nielsen, D.M., Merry, M.D., Schyve, P.M. and Bisognano, M. (2004) Can the gurus' concepts cure healthcare?, *Quality Progress*, 37: 25–6.

Nolan, T.W. (1998) Understanding medical systems, *Annals of Internal Medicine*, 128: 293–8.

O'Connor, P. and Fearfull, A. (2015) Evaluation of the Scottish Patient Safety Fellowship programme 2008–2013, *Clinical Risk*, 21 (2/3): 22–30.

Osborn, A.F. (1953) *Applied Imagination*. New York: Charles Scribner's Sons.

Øvretveit, J. (1997) A comparison of hospital quality programmes: lessons for other services, *International Journal of Service Industry Management*, 8: 220–35.

Øvretveit, J. (2009) *Does Improving Quality Save Money?* London: Health Foundation.

Parasuraman, A., Zeithaml, V.A. and Berry, L.L. (1988) SERVQUAL: a multiple item scale for measuring consumer perceptions of service quality, *Journal of Retailing*, 64: 14–40.

Perneger, T. (2006) Ten reasons to conduct a randomized study in quality improvement, *International Journal for Quality in Health Care*, 18: 395–6.

Pham, H.H., Ginsburg, P.B., McKenzie, K. and Milstein, A. (2007) Redesigning care delivery in response to a high-performance network: the Virginia Mason Medical Center, *Health Affairs*, 26: w532–44.

Plsek, P. (1999) Quality improvement methods in clinical medicine, *Pediatrics*, 103: 203–14.

Powell, A.E., Rushmer, R.K. and Davies, H.T.O. (2009) *A Systematic Narrative Review of Quality Improvement Models in Health Care*. Dundee: Social Dimensions of Health Institute at The Universities of Dundee and St Andrews.

Pyzdek, T. and Keller, P.A. (2003) *The Six Sigma Handbook: A Complete Guide for Green Belts, Black Belts, and Managers at All Levels*. New York: McGraw-Hill.

Radnor, Z. and Boaden, R. (2008) Editorial: lean in public services: panacea or paradox?, *Public Money and Management*, 28: 3–7.

Radnor, Z., Walley, P., Stephens, A. and Bucci, G. (2006) *Evaluation of the Lean Approach to Business Management and its Use in the Public Sector*. Edinburgh: Scottish Executive, Office of Chief Researcher.

Reeves, C.A. and Bednar, D.A. (1994) Defining quality: alternatives and implications, *Academy of Management Review*, 19: 419–56.

Rooney, K.D. and Leitch, J. (2010) Quality and safety in NHS Scotland, *British Journal of Diabetes and Vascular Disease*, 10: 98–100.

Rotter, T., Kinsman, L., James, E., Machotta, A., Gothe, H., Willis, J. et al. (2010) Clinical pathways: effects on professional practice, patient outcomes, length of stay and hospital costs, *Cochrane Database of Systematic Reviews*, 3: CD006632.

Scally, G. and Donaldson, L.J. (1998) Clinical governance and the drive for quality improvement in the new NHS in England, *British Medical Journal*, 317: 61–5.

Scottish Government (2010) *The Healthcare Quality Strategy for NHS Scotland*. Edinburgh: Scottish Government.

Scottish Government (2015) *Our NHS Scotland: Scotland's Approach to Quality Healthcare Improvement*. Edinburgh: Scottish Government.

Scoville, R. and Little, K. (2014) *Comparing Lean and Quality Improvement*, Institute for Healthcare Improvement White Paper. Cambridge, MA: Institute for Healthcare Improvement.

Sehwail, L. and DeYong, C. (2003) Six Sigma in health care, *International Journal of Leadership in Health Services*, 16 (4): 1–5.

Shewhart, W.A. (1931) *Economic Control of Quality of Manufactured Product*. New York: Van Nostrand.

Shingo, S. (1986) *Zero Quality Control: Source Inspection and the Poka-Yoke System*. Cambridge, MA: Productivity Press.

Shortell, S., Levin, D., O'Brien, J. and Hughes, E. (1995) Assessing the evidence on CQI: is the glass half empty or half full?, *Journal of the Foundation of the American College of Healthcare Executives*, 40: 4–24.

Slack, N., Chambers, S. and Johnston, R. (2004) *Operations Management*. Harlow: FT/Prentice-Hall.

Snee, R.D. (1990) Statistical thinking and its contribution to total quality, *American Statistician*, 44: 116–21.

Stiles, R.A. and Mick, S.S. (1994) Classifying quality initiatives: a conceptual paradigm for literature review and policy analysis, *Hospital and Health Services Administration*, 39 (3): 309–26.

Swinglehurst, D., Emmerich, N., Maybin, J., Park, S. and Quilligan, S. (2015) Confronting the quality paradox: towards new characterisations of 'quality' in contemporary healthcare, *BMC Health Services Research*, 15: 240.

Taguchi, G. (1986) *Introduction to Quality Engineering*. New York: Aisan Productivity Organization.

Taylor, M.J., McNicholas, C., Nicolay, C.R., Darzi, A., Bell, D. and Reed, J.E. (2013) Systematic review of the application of the plan–do–study–act method to improve quality in healthcare, *BMJ Quality and Safety*, 23: 290–8.

Trebble, T.M., Hansi, N., Hydes, T., Smith, M.A. and Baker, M. (2010) Process mapping the patient journey: an introduction, *British Medical Journal*, 341: c4078.

Walley, P. and Gowland, B. (2004) Completing the circle: from PD to PDSA, *International Journal of Healthcare Quality Assurance*, 17: 349–58.

Walshe, K. (2007) Understanding what works – and why – in quality improvement: the need for theory-driven evaluation, *International Journal for Quality in Health Care*, 19: 57–9.

Walshe, K. and Boaden, R. (eds.) (2006) *Patient Safety: Research into Practice*. Maidenhead: Open University Press.

Waring, J.J. and Bishop, S. (2010) Lean healthcare: rhetoric, ritual and resistance, *Social Science and Medicine*, 71: 1332–40.

Webb, J. (1995) Quality management and the management of quality, in A. Wilkinson and H. Willmott (eds.) *Making Quality Critical*. London: Routledge.

Wilkinson, A. (1992) The other side of quality: soft issues and the human resource dimensions, *Total Quality Management*, 3: 323–9.

Wilkinson, A. and Willmott, H. (eds.) (1995) *Making Quality Critical*. London: Routledge.

Willis, C.D., Best, A., Riley, B., Herbert, C.P., Millar, J. and Howland, D. (2014) Systems thinking for transformational change in health, *Evidence and Policy: A Journal of Research, Debate and Practice*, 10: 113–26.

Womack, J. and Jones, D. (1996) *Lean Thinking: Banish Waste and Create Wealth in Your Corporation*. New York: Simon & Schuster.

Womack, J.P. and Shook, J. (2011) *Gemba Walks*. Cambridge, MA: Lean Enterprises Institute.

World Health Organization (WHO) (2014) *Patient Safety Checklists*. Geneva: WHO.

Zbabada, C., Rivers, P.A. and Munchus, G. (1998) Obstacles to the application of TQM in healthcare organisations, *Total Quality Management*, 9: 57–67.

Zimmerman, R.S. (2004) Hospital capacity, productivity and patient safety – it all flows together, *Frontiers of Health Services Management*, 20: 33–8.

Chapter 21

Measuring and managing healthcare performance

Martin Bardsley

Introduction

Performance measurement has found a place at all levels of healthcare management across both public and private sectors. It usually takes the form of explicit frameworks for describing and measuring good/bad performance that are used to prompt change and improvement in the delivery health systems, and/or act as a means to offer wider accountability to taxpayers or purchasers. For the health services, we can see that at one end of the spectrum a Minister in Parliament may be called to account for performance on waiting times in accident and emergency departments. At the other end, hospital nursing staff may routinely monitor and publish (post on the wall) how often patients on that ward get pressure sores and use that as a spur to improving care.

Although in very different environments, both these examples rely on the structured collection and use of quantitative indicators reported in a pre-agreed format. They also share an aim of seeking to improve the way care is delivered, albeit through very different mechanisms. Such examples of performance measurement can be seen as one of the ways of exploiting the explosion in the volume of information collected in order to inform decision-making. For health services managers, these performance measures can be used to inform judgements about those most basic questions about the relative success or scope for improvement in a service. Over the past two decades, there has been a marked growth in the use of structured quantitative performance management – and in many countries this growth has also been accompanied by the creation of executive agencies whose role is to oversee the performance of public healthcare systems.

In reality, these systems use simple measurements as indicators of broader aspects of performance. The underlying idea of what constitutes good performance – and how we know it has been achieved – can appear beguilingly simple, yet the detail of how you measure it is often not so straightforward.

The capacity to make use of performance measurement systems has grown since the 1980s, largely driven by the greater accessibility of computerized information systems supporting the operational delivery of care. For many years, information for performance management had to be collected as a specific exercise, an end in itself designed for reporting upwards and typically through a series of standardized returns (Black, 1982). However, these are increasingly replaced by approaches whereby information for performance management relies on extracting data from operational systems rather than mandating a bespoke collection.

The computerization of information also enabled the creation of large data warehouses that opened up new forms of comparative analysis and the ability to compare areas of care providers has become a staple tool in assessing performance. In addition, operation information systems, growing initially from administrative systems, began to build data sets that capture summary information about individual patients and episodes of care. In many countries, individual hospital records are merged in regional and national databases that allow comparisons between hospitals. In the UK, these hospital-based systems continue to grow up to the present day and are now accompanied by a network of more or less standardized data collection from primary care (Pagliari et al., 2007).

Over the past few years, there has been renewed interest and controversy over how these person-level data sets can be exploited for planning, managing and research on the delivery of health services. This is part of a wider interest in using the ever-expanding volume of person-level information that exists in all walks of life. The science of how to use big data is increasingly becoming part of both academic platforms (see, for example, National Institute for Health Research, n.d.; Research Councils UK, n.d.) and health (Palmer, 2015) and has become part of a wider debate about transparency (see Prime Minister's Office, n.d.; White House, n.d.) that emphasizes the role of information as a means to increase public accountability and openness in government.

Who uses performance measures?

Performance measures have been developed at different levels and for different purposes. Table 21.1 summarizes some of the difference ways that performance assessment systems are used in healthcare settings. These are now discussed in more detail below.

Governments

It has become common for governments to articulate their policies in terms of a series of quantitative aspirations or targets (Pollitt, 2006; Smith et al., 2009). Although the word target itself flickers in and out of fashion, even governments that claim not to use targets still use a series of metrics and judgements that effectively behave in the same way. Such 'targets' are attractive as a simple way to capture a future policy goal. Moreover, such a statement of intent appears to offer something that is clear to the public and measurable – something that can in future be used to assess performance of that government.

Achievements or failures against such targets can be promoted through systems of rewards for achieving success and sanctions for failure. In contrast to the 'harder' targets there may also be sets of performance indicators. These usually have less weight applied to individual, specific indicators and the consequences of a breach are less draconian. In

Table 21.1 Different users of performance measurement

Users	*Examples*
Governments	Setting national health policy targets to drive change and promote accountability
Regulators	Oversight of specific elements within the care systems. Assessing adherence to pre-agreed standards or expectations of care. Accreditation systems or surveillance to identify potentially poor practice meriting further investigation. Often include some form of public reporting
Commissioners of Purchasers of Care	Using local frameworks for health outcomes to assess performance across health providers supporting given populations
Providers – managers	Regular monitoring of the quality or efficiency of services
Clinicians	Assessing team performance against agreed standards as in audit process
Patients and public	Judging the quality of care provided by local health systems – and influencing political decisions Patients may also use performance assessment information to influence their choice of care providers

practice, performance indicator sets are said to be a way of posing a question rather than providing a judgement. The interpretation of indicators is more tolerant than that of targets and in the best cases there can be a useful exploration of what underpins apparently poor performance in a specific indicator.

Although national hospital ratings in England (Box 21.1) faced considerable criticisms, there is evidence to suggest that they were successful in achieving some very specific aims – for example, around reductions in waiting times (Bevan and Hood, 2006; Propper et al., 2008). Although the earliest health service performance indicators tended to be financial – variants of keeping expenditure under control – current systems extend much further to look at the quality of care and the results delivered at individual patient and population level.

Box 21.1   Case study – star ratings of hospital performance in England

Although national health targets have existed in some form in the UK for a long time, they increased in prominence with the development of a national Performance Assessment Framework (PAF) introduced in 1999. From 2000, the Labour government relied heavily on centrally driven performance management of the health services and across the public sector. The PAF was envisaged as a single system for monitoring progress against a set of centrally determined objectives (Care Quality Commission, 2015). In practice, this meant identifying sets of indicators grouped according to six areas of care: health improvement, fair access, effective delivery of appropriate healthcare, efficiency, patient/carer experience, and health outcomes of NHS care. The indicators measured performance at the level of individual providers/commissioners and allowed comparisons between them. Its purpose was two-fold: to assist in the improvement of services, and to assess performance across areas and providers.

The assessments against indicators were originally undertaken by the Department of Health but later passed on to an independent national regulator: the Commission for Health Improvement (CHI). The composition of the ratings in terms of the indicators and the way they were scored was still subject to some degree of control from the Department of Health. Between 2001 and 2012, the NHS star ratings were one of the most important tools used by the government to incentivize change (discussed later). The way the ratings were calculated underwent a gradual evolution while under the care of CHI and its successor the Healthcare Commission. For example, the ratings extended beyond simple quantitative indicators to include findings from inspections, and assessments by other regulatory bodies as well as an element of self-declaration. From the time of the Healthcare Commission and its predecessor the Care Quality Commission (CQC), there was also recognition of some of the limitations of simple indicators and so they began to be used as a way of assessing risk to prioritize inspection – more than simple descriptions of performance itself. Although provider ratings were scrapped during the early years of the CQC, in 2013 the Secretary of State instigated a review by the Nuffield Trust – which in turn led to their reappearance. They have made a recent comeback and are now developed as a result of an inspection process (NHS Benchmarking Network, n.d.).

System managers

Below the level of national government, local health systems may have their own systems of performance measurements aimed at improving the services within an area. Performance measurement frameworks can also exist for purchasers or commissioners of services where the key concerns are around addressing the needs of a given population and the delivery of services that are effective and efficient. Very often these local systems will be a product of national performance measurement frameworks – though they can be more detailed and reflect some degree of local direction in the frameworks and indicators used. So a national target to reduce waiting times of admission is translated into a series of local measures about improving waiting times.

Many of the earliest applications of performance indicators relied on comparative measures, raising questions about how well your organization performed relative to others. The logic often applied was that of, 'if one organization can succeed on a particular indicator, "why can't we"', and so the measurement process generates a series of questions – and hints at where some of the answers may be found. This type of comparative analysis has a huge appeal – but as we shall see later, also generates some problems. Fairly early on, more sophisticated approaches evolved that compared performance not just to the national average but to specifically selected peer groups of comparator organizations. At their most advanced, these led to the development of benchmarking groups. For example, an NHS Benchmarking Network was established, which 'exists to identify and share good practice across the Health and Social Care sector' (NHS Institute for Innovation and Improvement, 2008).

The use of indicators is also commonplace in the management of individual providers across the organization or for individual departments within the organization. These usually extended beyond the requirements for reporting-up to include more detailed metrics based on local priorities and locally sourced information. In the best cases, the indicator sets and monitoring mechanisms are based on agreement between clinicians and managers about what are the important aspects of the service. One common approach is to agree a 'balanced scorecard' (NHS Institute for Innovation and Improvement, 2008), which summarizes performance across some key domains covering financial performance, the implementation of key processes, the experience of patients or service users, and indicators on sustaining change. Box 21.2 gives an example of a balanced scorecard used by one large hospital in England.

Box 21.2   Case study – performance indicators used by one large English teaching hospital

The example below is an edited list of indicators used by one large teaching hospital in the UK to report performance at board level. There are a range of indicators covering different aspects of the organization, clinical outcomes, financial stability, staff well-being, and so on, in a typical 'balanced scorecard' approach. For each indicator there are also explicit statements about the expected standards to be achieved. As is common in such lists, there are also some 'place-holders' for indicators where the measurement is not yet routine. Note this was taken from 2014 – many of the N/A values are now mainstream.

Strategic aim	Indicator	Standard
Deliver the best clinical outcomes	MRSA 0	0
	MSSA	Five or fewer per month
	Clostridium difficile	Six or fewer per month
	Serious untoward incidents	N/A
	Number of patient falls per 10,000 bed nights	N/A
	Number of pressure ulcers per 10,000 bed nights	N/A
	Number of never events	0
	Number of days since last never event	N/A
	% patients receiving harm free care	90
	Average LOS per elective spell	0.7
	Average LOS per non-elective spell	7
	Average LOS (excluding day cases)	3.2
	Summary Hospital-level Mortality Indicator	N/A
	Hospital Standardized Mortality Ratio	N/A
	% staff who would recommend STH to a relative for treatment	TBC
	CQC risk rating	N/A
	Friends and Family Test – Inpatients	TBC
	Friends and Family Test – Outpatients	TBC

Provide patient-centred services	A&E four-hour wait	95%
	>twelve-hour trolley waits in A&E	0
	Eighteen week waits referral to treatment time – admitted	90%
	Eighteen week waits referral to treatment time – non-admitted	95%
	Eighteen week waits referral to treatment time – incomplete pathways	92%
	Diagnostic waits within six weeks	99%
	Cancelled operations on the day	Seventy-seven or fewer per month
	% outpatient appointments cancelled by hospital	10%
	% outpatient appointments cancelled by patients	12.50%
	% DNA for new outpatient appointments	7%
	% DNA for follow-up outpatient appointments	6.50%
	Cancer 2 week referral to date seen	93%
	Cancer 2 week wait breast referrals	93%
	Thrity-one day diagnosis to treatment	96%
	Thrity-one day second or subsequent treatment – Radiotherapy	98%
	Thrity-one day second or subsequent treatment – Drugs	94
	Thrity-one day second or subsequent treatment – Surgery	94%
	Sixty-two day urgent referral to treatment	85%
	% appointments booked through C&B	95% by December 2014
	Response to complaints within twenty-one days	90%
	Theatre utilization	95%
	Day case percentage	78%
	Emergency re-admissions within thirty days	0%
	Delayed transfers of care	71%
Employing caring and cared for staff	Sickness absence	4%
	Appraisals	95%
	% staff who would recommend STH as a place to work at	TBC
	Staff turnover (rolling twelve months)	7%
	% staff completed mandatory training	90%

See Sheffield Teaching Hospitals NHS Foundation Trust (2014).

Learning activity 21.1: Performance reporting at board level

- In your own organization, is a similar set of performance indicators used at board level to measure and monitor performance?
- Access and review the board papers and minutes of board meetings over the last year to see what performance indicators are being reported to the board, how often they are reported and how the board has used that information in its decision-making.
- Consider whether there are important areas of performance in your organization that are NOT being reported to the board, as far as you can tell from your review of board papers.

Any system of performance implies that there is some form of action following 'poor' performance and some rewards for success. Very often these consequences of performance measurement are mediated through hierarchical managerial relationships – whether in the form of a 'pat on the back' or something more substantial for the organization. Good performance may help deliver personal rewards in career terms for senior managers. In some healthcare systems, successful performance may confer some privileges, such as increased organizational autonomy, lighter touch regulation and oversight or access to some additional resource stream.

Learning activity 21.2

- First, choose an area of acute care that you have some familiarity with (either through work experience or as a patient or user of services). It could be a service such as maternity care, acute medicine, accident and emergency or whatever.
- Imagine you are the newly appointed service manager for the acute care service within a hospital. Research what metrics of performance are available in that area and how they are used. Find out what performance targets are set by regulators or governments. See whether there are performance indicators or data sets collected by other bodies (such as professional associations or hospital associations). Explore how some other hospitals measure and assess performance in that service area. Look at examples of their performance reports.
- Write a short report for your clinical director, summarizing the key dimensions of performance measurement in this clinical service area and listing the performance indicators or metrics you think the two of you would need to know how the clinical service area is performing.

Clinical professionals

For clinical professionals, there is often a natural attraction in developing approaches to measurement in ways that can inform practice. In many healthcare settings, there are examples of clinically led programmes of quality health improvement that exploit basic measurement and assessment cycles as part of a wider programme (Institute for Healthcare Improvement, n.d.; Jones and Woodhead, 2015). In addition, approaches such as clinical audit have become essential activities for many healthcare professionals. Audits can take many forms, including both qualitative and quantitative analyses with a focus on assessing whether care achieved a desired standard. Although using audit cycles is rather different to organizational performance management, in many ways the underlying processes are similar. For example, audits revolve around a familiar cycle. Clinical audit should be seen as a continuous cycle of: (1) deciding which topics to audit; (2) measuring care delivered against standards; (3) acting on the findings – making improvements and changes; and (4) sustaining improvements, including re-audit where necessary (Bullivant and Corbett-Nolan, 2010). Clinical audit can take a variety of forms but in a number of cases these have evolved into systematic and continuous collections of comparative data sets that can be used to guide local practice (Healthcare Quality Improvement Partnership, n.d.).

Service users and the public

There currently exist a variety of ways in which information about health service performance can be released to the public, including in the form of reports, report cards, dashboards and dedicated websites (Shekelle, 2009). The rationale for public reporting of healthcare performance usually fits one of three reasons:

- empowering patients to make choices between healthcare providers – or prompt further participation in healthcare;
- allowing healthcare professionals to identify areas for improvement and providing them with the motivation to do so;
- as a means of accountability leading to improvement through external 'political' influence on the providers or purchasers of healthcare.

The idea of using information about health service performance, including quality, to inform patient choices has been a recurrent theme across many health systems – both private and public sector. In reality, however, the extent to which public reporting fosters a community of informed patient choosing between providers is limited (Marshall et al., 2003; Totten et al., 2012). The ways that patients make choices about healthcare are complex and the reported performance of a given provider may not be significant. However, there is little evidence of a significant impact of public reporting on patient choice.

It has been argued that this may be a reflection of the limitations of the information available or of limited awareness of what is available. A lot depends on the situation. As the Nuffield Review reported, in many cases choices about care providers are often made at times of stress. For example, an elderly relative being discharged from hospital but who would not be able to cope alone at home may need to find a place in a care home fairly quickly – a decision that may have an impact for the rest of their lives. In such circumstances, it has been suggested that widely available performance scores for some choices (for instance about care homes) are really important (Nuffield Trust, 2013).

Although the evidence on patient choice is limited, there is evidence that publication of provider performance measures leads to improvement (Hibbard et al, 2005; Ferris and Torchiana, 2010) – which relies on a different route for change, as healthcare providers respond to areas of underperformance to stimulate improvement – after all, no provider wants to be seen to be bad (Berwick et al., 2003). In one early study of the use of report cards in the USA, Marshall et al. noted:

> Hospitals respond with internal changes, to the publication of comparative performance data, especially in a competitive environment. Currently available report cards are rarely read by individual consumers or purchasers of care and, even if accessed, have little influence on purchasing decisions. (Marshall et al., 2000: 16)

A more recent study of patient choice in the UK noted that:

> The model of choice as a driver for quality improvement assumes that providers receive clear signals from the choices patients make, analyse these and then use the analysis to improve the service provided. Our research suggests that choice did not act as a lever to improve quality in this way; providers were driven more by pressure from a range of other external factors such as the waiting time targets. (Dixon et al., 2010)

Developing a performance framework

Establishing a performance assessment system will typically proceed through a cycle of stages:

- Clarify aims and underlying framework
- Identify suitable measures and thresholds
- Data collection and analysis
- Measurement and reporting
- Application, action and reflection.

The starting point for any approach to performance measurement is usually some overarching framework that places specific measures in context and aligns them to longer term strategic objectives. If the end point is a series of indicators or measures, then the starting point must be to have some understanding of what you are trying to measure and how the pieces fit together.

There are many different ways in which complex ideas such as quality of care or organizational performance can be split into more manageable themes or domains. For example, when seeking to identify the elements of good quality of care, Leatherman and Sutherland (2008) used six distinct domains, as shown in Table 21.2. Variants of these definitions abound.

It is important to emphasize that measuring healthcare performance is usually complex and success is seldom captured by a single measure but is usually multi-dimensional. Thus basic frameworks like this are typically used as a way of organizing a series of much more specific indicators, often in the form of hierarchies (see Box 21.3).

Table 21.2 Six domains of healthcare quality

Quality domain	Principle	Examples of measures
Effectiveness	Healthcare services should be based, as far as possible, on relevant rigorous science and research evidence	• Mortality rates • Compliance with evidence-based guidelines
Access and timeliness	Healthcare services should be timely and provided within the appropriate setting with access to necessary skills, expertise and technology	• Waiting times • Provision of emergency care • Availability of specialist services
Capacity	Healthcare systems should be sufficiently well resourced and with adequate distribution to enable delivery of appropriate services	• Staffing levels • Number and distribution of scanners • Specialized stroke units
Safety	Patients should not be harmed by the care that they receive or exposed to unnecessary risk	• Nosocomial infections • Medication errors • Falls
Patient centredness	Healthcare should be: 1. Based on a partnership between practitioners and patients (and where appropriate, their families) 2. Delivered with compassion, empathy and responsiveness to the needs, values and preferences of the individual patient	• Patient-reported outcomes • Patient survey data on experience of care
Equity	Healthcare should be provided: 1. On the basis of clinical need, regardless of personal characteristics such as age, gender, race, ethnicity, language, socioeconomic status or geographical location 2. In such a way as to reduce differences in health status and outcomes across various sub-groups	• Comparisons of care provided across different sub-populations (for example, older people versus entire population) • Mortality rates by socioeconomic status • Variation in access

Source: Adapted from Leatherman and Sutherland (2008).

Box 21.3 Case study – the three domains of national performance targets for the NHS in Scotland

The table below shows the three domains containing the national performance targets for the NHS in Scotland – reproduced as an example of one way healthcare indicators are organized. The following text is a description from the NHS National Services Scotland Information Services Division website:

Each year, the Scottish Government agrees a suite of national NHS performance targets known as HEAT targets. In return the NHS Boards state how they will commit to meet their targets as outlined in their annual Local Delivery Plans. NHS Scotland performance against the HEAT targets and standards contributes towards the delivery of the Scottish Government's Purpose and National Outcomes; and NHS Scotland's Quality Ambitions. The HEAT system is a web-based information tool supported and maintained by ISD Scotland on behalf of the Scottish Government. The system allows NHS Boards and the Scottish Government to monitor Boards' performance against national HEAT targets and progress is published on the Scottish Government's 'Scotland Performs' website. Data for many of the performance measures used to monitor targets are sourced directly from ISD and, where this is the case, ISD aims to publish timely and useful data on these performance indicators on our website.

Health improvement	Access to service	Standards
• Smoking cessation, most deprived • Detect cancer early • Early access to antenatal services • Efficiency and governance • Financial performance • Reduce CO_2 emissions • Reduce energy consumption	• Faster access to mental health services • Faster access to psychological therapies • IVF treatment waiting times • A&E waiting times • Treatment appropriate to individual • MRSA/MSSA bacteraemias • *Clostridium difficile* infections in ages fifteen plus • Reduction in emergency bed-days for patients aged seventy five plus • Fourteen days delayed discharge • Dementia post-diagnostic support	• Twelve weeks first outpatient appointment • Eighteen weeks referral to treatment • A&E waiting times • Alcohol brief interventions • Ambulance response times • Cancer waiting times • Drug and alcohol treatment waiting times • GP access • Sickness absence rate

Devising indicators

Within any one domain of performance, much more specific statements of what success might look like are required – moreover, these may often need to be measurable. For example, success in delivering safe care may cover indicators related to things like the number of incidences of severe avoidable harm, the presence of incident reporting systems, the operation of reporting systems including training and awareness and specific processes of care that enhance safe care (such as surgery checklists, safety meetings).

The task of turning broad concepts into a series of specific measurable indicators can be challenging and usually involves some compromises. For example, when identifying indicators, there may be issues such as the following:

* Clashes between aspects of performance. Different dimensions of performance may be in conflict; for example, there are often trade-offs between costs and quality. A measure of patient views of the quality of nursing care may be strongly related to the amount of nursing time and number of nurses available. This will tend to be inversely related to measures of economy – and in extremes of efficiency.

- Whose views on performance matter most? As in most things, different stakeholders will have a view of which aspects of performance are most important. A manager may be focused on efficiency, a clinician on clinical quality, and the patient on success in terms of interpersonal care and communication. In most settings, there will be no simple 'fixes' that can get around these issues; rather, it is necessary to be explicit about whose views have been considered in defining the indicator.
- An indicator may capture important aspects of performance but the effects may not be immediately visible – patient outcomes resulting from good-or bad-quality care may take years to accumulate.
- There are occasions when simple quantitative indicators will not capture what is important and assessment has to be based on skilled judgement. For example, how to balance the protection of a 'confused' and frail care user with a respect for a person's basic rights and freedoms.

There's no simple answer to these challenges. The reality is that all systems of performance measurement will involve some degree of compromise. Table 21.3 shows some of the most important criteria that can be used to help think about the strengths and weaknesses of indicator systems.

Table 21.3 Criteria for choosing performance indicators

Relevant	One way of helping to ensure the relevance is to relate the performance indicators to the strategic goals and objectives of the organization or of a specific service area
Clearly defined	A performance indicator should have a clear and intelligible definition in order to ensure consistent collection and fair comparison. Vague descriptions can lead to misinterpretation and confusion
Easy to understand and use	It is important that indicators are described in terms that the user of the information will understand, even if the definition itself has to use technical terminology
Cost effective	Balance the cost of collecting information with its usefulness
Unambiguous	It should be clear whether an increase in an indicator value represents an improvement or deterioration in service
Attributable	Service managers should be able to influence the performance measured by the indicator (that is, it should either be totally within their control or at least open to significant influence)
Responsive	A performance indicator should be responsive to change. An indicator where changes in performance are likely to be too small to register will be of limited use. This can be the case particularly with qualitative (yes/no) indicators, as progress towards achieving a 'yes' is not captured
Avoid perverse incentives	Important to consider what behaviour an indicator ought to encourage. Indicators that might encourage counter-productive activity should be avoided if possible
Statistically valid	Performance indicators based on a small number of cases are likely to show substantial annual fluctuations

Source: Adapted from Audit Commission (2000).

Structure, process or outcome?

One of the most widely used ways of categorizing measures is to distinguish between measures of structure, process and outcome (Donabedian, 1980). Indicators describing the structures of care can include measures such as the number of hospital beds, primary care clinics, operating theatres, specific staff groups or diagnostic imaging equipment. Indicators using these are normally associated with either tracking capital investment or testing the accessibility of services.

Process measures relate to the activities to deliver care and are usually more readily available and more easily influenced. These include measures such as bed days, lengths of stay, treatments given and observations made. Such measures are usually more straightforward to understand and generally easier to collect. Process measures can often be linked to professional standards of care, which can make them more accessible to clinicians and helps in defining what constitutes good/bad performance. Perhaps the biggest advantage of process measures is that they are often 'actionable' – that is, the measure itself prescribes the action that the clinician, institution or health plan needs to take to improve performance.

Outcome measures are concerned with end results (Table 21.4). A health outcome has been defined as 'a change in a patient's current and future health status that can be attributed to antecedent health care' (Donabedian, 1980: 82–3). As such, outcome measures aspire to measure the real impact of care on the health of an individual or population. It is often argued that outcomes measures are preferable to measures of structure or process. In conceptual terms, measurement by outcomes has two advantages: first, it measures a meaningful objective of the system and one that can be fairly well recognized

Table 21.4 Examples of commonly used outcome measures or proxies

Life/death	Measured in terms of survival rates, mortality rates for a population or case fatality for particular patient types
Levels of functional ability	Ability to undertake activities of daily living captured in tools such as the Barthel Index
Clinical measures	These can take the form of standardized scoring instrument such as a Hip score or proxy measures, such as levels of HbA1c in people with diabetes
Patient-reported outcomes	Quality of life or health status questionnaires that typically capture aspects of physical function, social or psychological well-being
Counts of adverse events	Cancer incidence rates; prevalence of infectious disease
Proxy measures based on healthcare events	Emergency admission to hospital – used as an indication of some form of acute crisis of which a subset will be avoidable Immunization and vaccination rate are often used as a proxy for effectiveness

by all actors; second, it also serves in a system where managerial hierarchies seek to allow freedom for lower levels to manage as they see appropriate. That is, to combine structures and process to achieve the best results and not have these dictated from above, as in micro management. This philosophy is common and in England is typified by the system of outcomes frameworks in which the health system is held to account (Department of Health, 2014).

In practice, outcome measures can take a variety of forms. Despite the appeal of outcome measures, and the often vociferous clamour for greater use of outcomes, they do suffer some major drawbacks:

* *Causality.* The relationships between healthcare and subsequent outcomes can be spread over many years and be quite complex. For example, have improvements in mortality rates from cardiovascular disease resulted from better acute care or longer term changes in health-related behaviour and living conditions?
* *Information.* There is less routinely collected and collated information available that directly captures health status – and it is often done at only one or two points in time, which does not permit measurement before and after a given intervention.
* *Multiple confounding.* Many health outcomes may be the result of or be affected by different factors, and it is not always possible to unpick one specific effect, or to separate out other confounding factors. Smoking has been falling – but how much of that can be ascribed to specific 'stop smoking' services or to changes in education and income, or other factors?

Information about patient satisfaction with care (i.e. a judgement on whether patients were happy with what they received) or patient experience (reporting what happened to them) can also play an important part in assessing performance. Assessment from the patient themselves is seen as increasingly important and there are a range of quantitative and qualitative tools to capture patients' view of the care they received. In the English NHS, national surveys of patients have been conducted for over ten years. These are questionnaires distributed to samples of patients in different care settings, such as inpatient, general practice, etc. (Picker Institute Europe, n.d.). In addition, local surveys may be conducted to look at specific services. These have been widely used as performance measures of hospitals at national and local level – although in practice they are limited in the extent to which they can discriminate between the quality of care offered by different providers.

Although debates about the relative merits of these measures persist – especially the debate about process versus outcome measures – most performance monitoring uses a combination of measures of structure, process and outcome. And as Donabedian himself noted in 1988:

> This three-part approach to quality assessment is possible only because good structure increases the likelihood of good process, and good process increases the likelihood of a good outcome. It is necessary, therefore, to have established such a relationship before any particular component of structure, process, or outcome can be used to assess quality. (Donabedian, 1988: 1745)

Learning activity 21.3: Measures of structure, process and outcome

- Consider the service area in which you work, and the performance measures that are commonly used in your organization to report on performance. Split them into the three categories discussed above – structure, process and outcome.
- What is the balance of indicators across these three domains, and is any one domain particularly under-represented – and if so, why?

Sourcing information

One of the critical constraints on any system of performance measurement is the question of how to access the information that is needed. As noted above, notions of performance in healthcare are often complex and multidimensional. Accessing information that captures this is not always easy.

Two strategies can be adopted. The first is to request the information be collected. This approach, typical of many organizational hierarchies, demands that the lower levels of an organization collect the information necessary for their own monitoring. Very often it is argued that the information should have been collected anyway, as they are so important to understanding the delivery of a service – by default, if you do not collect this vital monitoring information anyway, you are probably failing in some respects. In practice, these mandated collection strategies can run into problems, such as these:

- They are a burden on those being assessed and incur a cost that is not always welcome. There is a phrase 'feeding the beast', which refers to the effort required in upward flow of information necessary to pacify the performance managers. When data collection is seen as a burden and of benefit only to someone else, there is a danger that the quality and completeness of data becomes a problem.
- There is a need to ensure consistency of data collection across areas – which can lead to long and protracted debates about definitions of inclusion and exclusion. Even the simplest of ideas, a hospital bed (see Box 21.4), has to be defined with myriad clauses. Although it is quite possible to develop such definitions, ensuring that they are used in a consistent way is not easy. Any uncertainties over definitions may also mean that in the event of observed failures in performance, the immediate defence is to question the data and the definitions.
- Making such bespoke information requests feasible means that you often have to report only on aggregated data – adding a number of events across services or over time. This may mean that the measures that are used are therefore relatively crude and there is not the opportunity to apply exclusions of adjustments after data collection.

Table 21.5 Range of routine data sources used for health performance indicators

Information sources	Examples
Computerized administrative records from hospital	Hospital admissions for effective procedures, e.g. cataracts % procures carried out as day cases
Populations registers of births and deaths	Condition-specific mortality Peri-natal mortality
Clinical data sets	Achievement of clinical targets such as measure of HbA1c in people with diabetes
Specific care registers/databases	Hospital-acquired infections, e.g. *Clostridium difficile* surveillance scheme Specialized registries for specific disease Clinical audit data sets, e.g. Myocardial Ischaemia National Audit Project, National Audit of Dementia.
Adverse events/incidents reporting	Reporting of serious untoward incident (SUI) Numbers and type of complaints
Aggregate returns to government	Numbers of hospital beds; patients staying on mixed-sex wards; delayed transfers of care; staffing levels Uptake of preventive health, e.g. immunization coverage statistics; cancer screening
Patient surveys	Inpatient surveys, primary care surveys
Staff surveys	GMC surveys of trainee doctors and trainers Survey of NHS staff
Other regulatory findings, peer reviews/inspection or accreditation results	Inspection findings from regulators. Specialist training reports and peer review schemes Notifications for lapses in health and safety

Source: Adapted from Audit Commission (2000).

An alternative approach is to use existing information, and Table 21.5 sets out the wide range of routine sources of data used in health performance indicators. This philosophy states that before demanding a new data collection, you should make sure you are using all the data that are already collected. As noted above, the growth of computerized information systems makes this approach much more practicable. The disadvantage with relying on existing information is that sometimes the information you need just hasn't been collected. This can be especially true with the introduction of new services or technologies. The second problem is that although information may appear superficially to be consistent, there are actually subtle or hidden differences in the way terms have been defined and information collected. This is nicely illustrated in Box 21.4, where the simple task of defining what is meant by a hospital bed is shown to be rather more complicated than it at first appears.

Box 21.4   The challenges of data definitions – example of how to define a bed from NHS data model

A Hospital Bed includes any device that may be used to permit a PATIENT to lie down when the need to do so is as a consequence of the PATIENT's condition rather than the need for active intervention such as examination, diagnostic investigation, manipulation/treatment, or transport. Cots should be included in statistics about Hospital Beds where appropriate. It should be noted that:

- A couch or trolley should be considered as a Hospital Bed provided it is used regularly to permit a PATIENT to lie down rather than for merely examination or transport. An example of such an arrangement is a day surgery ward furnished with trolleys
- A PATIENT may need to use a Hospital Bed, couch or trolley whilst attending for a specific short procedure taking an hour or less, such as an endoscopy. If such devices are being used only because of the active intervention and not because of the PATIENT's condition, they should NOT be counted as Hospital Beds for statistical purposes
- A PATIENT needing a lengthy procedure such as renal dialysis may use a Hospital Bed or other means of support such as a couch or special chair. Whatever the device used it should be counted as a Hospital Bed if used regularly for this purpose
- Some procedures require narcosis. If this necessitates the PATIENT to lie down, the Hospital Bed, couch or trolley can be counted as a Hospital Bed if used regularly for this purpose
- A device specifically and solely for the purpose of delivery should not be counted as a Hospital Bed if another device is normally reserved for Antenatal and Postnatal care. Details of the facilities available for delivery in a maternity ward should be included in a WARD inventory.

Source: Health and Social Care Information Centre (n.d.).

Scoring and judging

Performance measures can take a number of guises, from very simple counts to much more complex statistical treatments. Yet for each measure, an understanding is required of what constitutes good or bad performance. This idea can be challenging and there is often a tendency to seek additional explanatory indicators that say something about the context. But if the purpose of the system is to ultimately come to some conclusion about whether performance is good/bad, better or worse than expected, an assessment that is ambiguous or context dependent does not always help. There is certainly a place to acknowledge ambiguity and uncertainty in measures but this is best left to the interpretation. In theory, all indicators have to be calibrated such that they provide a simple verdict on good or bad without caveats and additional clauses.

For many indicators there may a range of values – to ensure capturing good or bad performance is based on an explicit threshold. For example, waiting times in an emergency department must be less than four hours for 95 per cent of patients. In this case, the aim is to see all patients within four hours – but there is an acknowledgement that this may not be possible in all cases – so the expectation is set at 95 per cent.

In some cases, it can be very difficult to identify 'good' or 'bad' from a seemingly simple indicator. For example, a measure based on the number of complaints received is difficult to interpret; a high value may mean poor-quality care or could mean it is easier to complain – a sign of good practice in transparency and patient involvement in the organization. His- torically, judgements of what constitutes good/bad performance were often not based on an absolute statement or value but on a relative performance level compared with other similar organizations – effectively a form of ranking. This is usually easy to do, superficially attrac- tive and easy to communicate – however, there are major statistical problems with using and interpreting rankings and it is not considered good practice.

One of the challenges for many indicators is how to interpret differences between what is observed and what might be expected. In many cases, the measurement process brings with it a certain degree of error that needs be taken account of. For example, patient experience surveys are typically based on a survey of a random sample of patients. It may be that the results would have been slightly different had a different set of patients been selected. If your hospital appears to be scoring slightly worse than the average on patient experience, is that difference real or is it within the normal bounds of random variation? Statistical methods have been developed that seek to quantify the degree of uncertainty about a measure (Spie- gelhalter et al., 2012), and it has been suggested that these be included within performance assessment systems (Bird et al., 2005). When used correctly, these make the systems better at doing what they were intended to do (see Box 21.5).

Box 21.5   Case study – comparative international indicators on quality of care

The OECD Health Care Quality Indicators project, initiated in 2002, aims to measure and compare the quality of health service provision in different countries and forms just one part of the armoury of information from OECD countries. An expert group developed a set of quality indicators at the health systems level, which allows the impact of particu- lar factors on the quality of health services to be assessed. The intention is that com- parative analyses will offer policy-makers a better understanding of their own health systems and identify opportunities for further learning and offer other stakeholders a toolkit to stimulate cross-national learning.

One product – 'Health at a Glance 2013' – compares OECD countries on each component of this framework. It is structured around eight chapters: Health status; Non-medical determinants of health; Health workforce; Healthcare activities; Quality of care; Access to care; Health expenditure and financing; and Ageing and long-term care. Within each section are a range of indicators – typically showing national values on common indicators across a number of years. The selection of indicators used is a combination of the theoretical relevance of the indicator to health balanced by more pragmatic considerations of the availability of the data at country level and the comparability of data collection systems.

Unlike some other reporting structures, OECD information has no formal role. Rather, the information is presented as a resource and in practice is used often selectively in arguments about the merits or otherwise of different healthcare systems. However, such international comparisons have an enduring appeal. The use of international comparisons is common throughout health systems.

Presenting information

In almost all systems of performance measurement, the results of the process need to be presented to a wide audience – with a varying propensity to embrace and understand the underlying detail. The complexity of the elements within a rating and its scoring is intimately linked with the ways in which information is presented – and for whom. The presentation of information to the public, providers and commissioners of care is clearly important and an area where there are no simple answers.

Increasingly sophisticated tools are available for organizing and presenting information and the internet offers a wide range of graphical methods and infographics (see, for example, the Quality Watch website at http://www.qualitywatch.org.uk/). For many people, the simpler the presentation, the better. This often means that different indicators and dimensions of performance are aggregated in some form into a summary rating – at its most simplistic, a 'Red, Amber or Green (RAG)' rating or a scale from 'Poor to Excellent'. The gains are that such simple ratings are easy to interpret and communicate to wider audiences. The disadvantage of summary ratings is that important detail is lost in the aggregation. An organization will typically be good at some things and not at others – yet these distinctions are lost in a summary rating. The ideal is therefore to develop ways that organize information in hierarchies to show both a summary statement and the underlying constituent detail is not lost.

Common criticisms of performance measurement systems

The application of rigid systems of performance assessment and measurement seldom occur without some controversy (Bevan and Hood, 2006). Some of the most common criticisms are discussed below.

Measuring what matters

One of the more fundamental challenges arises where not all people accept some of the priorities and values that are embedded in the performance assessment systems (Mannion et al., 2005). For example, when a target is achieved to the detriment of the services, this is presented as 'hitting the target and missing the point' (Bevan and Hamblin, 2009). In the UK, this is most often quoted in relation to waiting times targets where the need to achieve shorter waits for emergency treatments of inpatient admissions were claimed to be at odds with clinical priorities. There is a real clash between the desires of the system to see reduced waiting times for patient benefits (and probably also some political returns) with the views of a frontline clinician having to make very real choices between the patients they see in front of them. There is the danger that an attractive target may generate unintended consequences for the service. One example from primary care in England was the forty-eight hour target for appointments to see a GP. This led to booking systems that perversely made it more difficult for patients to make an appointment, especially with a doctor of their choice.

There have been examples in England where major failings within an organization were in part ascribed to a management culture that prioritizes achievement of key targets at the expense of wider consideration of care (such as the well-known case of Mid-Staffordshire Hospitals NHS Trust). In the case of hospital ratings systems, one of the unintended consequences of being declared a failing hospital is a wider impact on the organization – described as institutional stigma: 'The resulting risk of stigmatising an entire institution injects huge tensions into health-care organisations and can divert attention from genuine improvement towards superficial improvement or even gaming behaviour (i.e. manipulating the system)' (Lilford et al., 2004: 1147).

Selective measurement

One of the most persistent criticisms is that such systems of performance assessment typically rely on deriving a set of selected measures that are indicative of performance across the board – where the latter is acknowledged to be complex and multifaceted. For example, it is common that in order to construct a measureable and reliable indicator, you have to focus on a very specific case type where the data are available. For example, clinical effectiveness in acute sector hospitals may place a heavy reliance on the outcomes of certain forms of cardiac surgery – just because they are the best data available.

This extends beyond questions of data access to broader issues of what is measureable. For example, in the field of quality of care and safety, there is a view that high-performing organizations are those where there is a different culture – something that is very difficult to measure. The concern is that 'performance indicators are selected on the basis of what is available and practical rather than what is meaningful' (Lilford et al., 2004).

The other side to this is that it is argued that areas that are not measured are ignored. This is even more pronounced where these areas are themselves inherently difficult to measure. For example, failings in interpersonal care, or the failure to treat patients with dignity and respect do not lend themselves to simple performance measurement systems – and yet they have been at the heart of major concerns for the quality of care in England (Francis, 2013). There is also some evidence from QOF that although there may have been improvements in some specific health conditions that the scheme focused on, non-incentivised conditions got worse (Doran et al., 2011).

Methodology

In developing unambiguous performance indicators, disagreement can arise as to which approach to take when devising indicators and adjusting for risks that are beyond the control of those being assessed. The danger is, that without risk adjustment, successful performance can be achieved by selecting low-risk patients and referring high-risk patients elsewhere. The process of aggregating indicators to make them simpler to interpret or comprehensive may bring its own problems. The first is that the aggregation may carry some form of weighting that is not always visible to the untrained eye. Second, it may make the process of calculating the rating opaque, with tables so complex that it is difficult for an organization to understand why its rating has changed.

Gaming

When developing performance measurement, there is a challenge of balance. To get a measure to be taken seriously, the implications of failure need to be clear and significant for those being rated. Yet the more important a performance measure becomes, the chance that people will find opportunities for gaming increases (Smith, 1995). One consequences is captured in Goodhart's law: 'When a measure becomes a target, it ceases to be a good measure.'

For some, the response to the rate of poor performance may be gaming. This does not have to take the form of direct fabrication of data, but may involve more subtle issues of definition. For example, a study of ambulance response times for Category A calls found they had been 'corrected' to under eight minutes in ways that could not be readily explained (Bevan and Hamblin, 2009). As the authors noted, this was 'mainly because targets created a culture in which staff felt under pressure to record the "right" answer'.

Conclusion

Although the use of performance measurement can often prompt heated debate, such indicators have become a fact of life in healthcare management. Structured quantitative performance assessment does offer some significant advantages but it is not a technical fix that will magically clarify all ambiguities and disputes. Performance assessment systems are laden with values, choices and compromises.

On the positive side, these tools allow a much more transparent assessment of performance – and one that can be shared and monitored within health services and beyond. In fact, the process of identifying performance measures can help to clarify the most important goals of the service (NHS Institute for Improvement and Innovation, 2008). And there are examples where failure to achieve a given level of performance can act as a spur to positive change and improvement. As Bevan and Hood (2006) noted: 'Nobody would want to return to the NHS performance before the introduction of targets, with over 20% of patients spending more than four hours in accident and emergency and patients waiting more than 18 months for elective admission.'

However, the creation of a system of performance measures will not of itself prompt change (Mannion and Goddard, 2001). The measurement system has to exist within some form of management system, or set of relationships, that leads to change as a consequence of what the performance measures are saying. Developing the performance assessment system is not a purely technical process – but one that involves collaboration and agreement. As David Pencheon (2008: 20) described: 'Good communication bridges the gaps between measurement, understanding, and improvement.'

Those designing and using systems for performance measurement and management need to think through their options very carefully. It is important that key stakeholders have ownership of and faith in the indicators themselves, often by being involved in their design. Measures need to be explicit and easy to understand, and to leave some space for managerial discretion and 'wriggle room'. The costs of measurement must always be considered, especially if new data collections are involved. The potential for perverse or unintended consequences of measurement always needs to be borne in mind, especially if strong incentives are attached to the results of measurement. The use of the performance measures needs to be reflective, thoughtful and insightful – not a summative rush to judgement. Finally, nothing stands still, and the value and utility of performance measures usually diminish over time, as people and organizations respond to them and as the healthcare system changes.

Learning resources

Dartmouth Atlas: The team from Dartmouth College in the USA have been very influential in thinking about variations in healthcare effectiveness and efficiency and over the past twenty years have established a significant academic reputation. The information they have amassed on key areas of healthcare quality and delivery are organized to show profiles of individual geographic areas and the differences across the USA [http://www.dartmouthatlas.org/].

NHS Choices consultant outcome data: An example of how a wide range of public facing information about performance can be organized and presented. This government-funded website draws on information from across the health sectors and can present information about providers local to the individual. The site also includes a way for members of the public to comment on specific health services [https://www.nhs.uk/service-search/performance/Consultants].

Health Resources and Services Administration (HRSA): Part of the US Department of Health and Human Services, the HRSA website provides a North American perspective on performance management systems with an emphasis on prompting local improvement. There are some good examples of how clinical indicators can be constructed and some description of issues of implementation [http://www.hrsa.gov/quality/toolbox/methodology/performancemanagement/index.html].

Smith, P., Mossialos, E., Papanicolas, I. and Leatherman, S. (eds.) (2009) *Performance Measurement for Health System Improvement: Experiences, Challenges and Prospects*. Cambridge: Cambridge University Press. An excellent overview of performance measurement systems published on behalf of the European Observatory on Health Systems and Policies [http://www.euro.who.int/en/about-us/partners/observatory/publications/studies/performance-measurement-for-health-system-improvement-experiences,-challenges-and-prospects; accessed 10 December 2015].

Nuffield Trust (2013) *Rating Providers for Quality: A Policy Worth Pursuing?*, especially Chapter 6: 'Designing a rating'. London: Nuffield. Report commissioned by the UK government to look at the case for reintroducing a single summary hospital rating in England. The report looks at the history of performance rating in England and discusses some of the challenges in their application [http://www.nuffieldtrust.org.uk/publications/rating-providers-quality].

Pencheon, D. (2008) *The Good Indicators Guide: Understanding How to Use and Choose Indicators*. London: APHO. Short guide aimed at non-executive directors to help people understand and use performance measurement systems. Includes wise advice on the development and interpretation of indicators [http://www.apho.org.uk/resource/item.aspx?RID=44584].

Pollitt, C., Harrison, S., Dowswell, G., Bal, R. and Jerak-Zuiderent, S., *Performance Indicators in Health Care: A Comparative Anglo-Dutch Study*. A series of papers linked to the ESRC looking at the implementation of performance measurement in different countries. The authors look at whether these national systems deliver the types of change that are expected of them, especially with regard to accountability and openness. They also explore the common features of how these systems emerge and evolve in different countries [http://www.esrc.ac.uk/my-esrc/grants/RES-166-25-0051/read].

Picker Institute Europe. The Picker Institute is one of the key international leaders in developing methods to promote patient- and family-centred care. It has been prominent in particular methods to capture the experiences and views of the patients and the public. In England, it has been responsible for running several large national patient surveys as well other work through the NHS. Its website includes examples of different methodological approaches [http://www.pickereurope.org/].

Other useful websites include:

CWF country comparisons: http://www.commonwealthfund.org/interactives-and-data/us-compare-interactive#?ind=1?

University Hospital Birmingham Quality Account: http://www.uhb.nhs.uk/quality-reports.htm.

NHS Choices – CCG outcomes: http://www.nhs.uk/NHSEngland/thenhs/about/Pages/ccg-outcomes.aspx.

Examples of CCG balanced scorecards: http://www.eastridingofyorkshireccg.nhs.uk/about-us/ccg-assurance-framework-201314/.

NZ Atlas of Healthcare Variation: http://www.hqsc.govt.nz/our-programmes/health-quality-evaluation/projects/atlas-of-healthcare-variation/.

Papworth surgeon level outcomes: http://www.papworthhospital.nhs.uk/content.php?/clinical_quality/healthcare_professionals/clinical_outcomes/what_are_our_results.

References

Audit Commission (2000) *On Target: The Practice of Performance Indicators.* London: Audit Commission.

Berwick, D.M., James, B. and Coye, M.J. (2003) Connections between quality measurement and improvement, *Medical Care*, 41 (S1): 130–8.

Bevan, G. and Hamblin, R. (2009) Hitting and missing targets by ambulance services for emergency calls: effects of different systems of performance measurement within the UK, *Journal of the Royal Statistical Society A*, 172 (1): 161–90.

Bevan, G. and Hood, C. (2006) Have targets improved performance in the English NHS?, *British Medical Journal*, 332 (7538): 419–22.

Bird, S.M., Cox, D., Farewell, V.T., Goldstein, H., Holt, T. (2005) Performance indicators: good, bad, and ugly, *Journal of the Royal Statistical Society A*, 168 (1): 1–27.

Black, D. (1982) Data for management: The Körner Report, *British Medical Journal*, 285 (6350): 1227–8.

Bullivant, J. and Corbett-Nolan, A. (2010) *Clinical Audit: A Simple Guide for NHS Boards and Partners.* London: Good Governance Institute [https://web.archive.org/web/20150528211035/http://www.hqip.org.uk/assets/Guidance/HQIP-Clinical-Audit-Simple-Guide-online1.pdf; accessed 10 December 2015].

Care Quality Commission (2015) *Ratings* [http://www.cqc.org.uk/content/ratings; accessed 10 December 2015].

Department of Health (2014) *The NHS Outcome Framework 2015/16* [https://www.gov.uk/government/uploads/system/uploads/attachment_data/file/385749/NHS_Outcomes_Framework.pdf; accessed 10 December 2015].

Dixon, A., Appleby, J., Robertson, R., Burge, P., Devlin, N., Magee, H. et al. (2010) *Patient Choice: How Patients Choose and How Providers Respond* [http://www.kingsfund.org.uk/projects/patient-choice-how-patients-choose-and-how-providers-respond; accessed 10 December 2015].

Donabedian, A. (1980) *The Definition of Quality and Approaches to its Assessment.* Ann Arbor, MI: Health Administration Press.

Donabedian, A. (1988) The quality of care: how can it be assessed?, *Journal of the American Medical Association*, 260 (12): 1743–8.

Doran, T., Kontopantelis, E., Valderas, J., Campbell, S., Roland, M., Salisbury, C. et al. (2011) The effect of financial incentives on incentivised and non-incentivised clinical activities: evidence from the UK's Quality and Outcomes Framework, *British Medical Journal*, 342 (3590): 1–12.

Ferris, R.G. and Torchiana, D.F. (2010) Public release of clinical outcomes data – online CABG report cards, *New England Journal of Medicine*, 363 (17): 1593–5.

Francis, R. (2013) *Report of the Mid Staffordshire NHS Foundation Trust Public Inquiry* [http://webarchive.nationalarchives.gov.uk/20150407084003/http://www.midstaffspublicinquiry.com/report; accessed 10 December 2015].

Health and Social Care Information Centre (n.d.) *NHS Business Definitions: Hospital Beds* [http://www.datadictionary.nhs.uk/data_dictionary/nhs_business_definitions/h/hospital_bed_de.asp?shownav=1; accessed 10 December 2015].

Healthcare Quality Improvement Partnership (n.d.) *National Clinical Audit Registries* [https://web.archive.org/web/20150607070353/http://hqip.org.uk/national-clinical-audit-registries/; accessed 10 December 2015].

Hibbard, J.H., Stockard, J. and Tusler, M. (2005) Hospital performance reports: impact on quality, market share, and reputation, *Health Affairs*, 24 (4): 1150–60.

Institute for Healthcare Improvement (n.d.) Website [http://www.ihi.org/Pages/default.aspx; accessed 10 December 2015].

Jones, B. and Woodhead, T. (2015) *Building the Foundations for Improvement: How Five UK Trusts Built Quality Improvement Capability at Scale Within Their Organisations* [http://www.health.org.uk/publication/building-foundations-improvement; accessed 10 December 2015].

Leatherman, S. and Sutherland, K. (2008) *Quest for Quality: Refining the NHS reforms. A Policy Analysis and Chartbook*. London: Nuffield Trust [http://www.nuffieldtrust.org.uk/publications/quest-quality-nhs-refining-nhs-reforms; accessed 10 December 2015].

Lilford, R., Mohammed, M.A., Spiegelhalter, D. and Thomson, R. (2004) Use and misuse of process and outcome data in managing performance of acute medical care: avoiding institutional stigma, *Lancet*, 363 (9415): 1147–54.

Mannion, R. and Goddard, M. (2001) Impact of published clinical outcomes data: case study in NHS hospital trusts, *British Medical Journal*, 323 (7307): 260–3.

Mannion, R., Davies, H. and Marshall, M. (2005) Impact of star performance ratings in English acute hospital trusts, *Journal of Health Services Research and Policy*, 10 (1): 18–24.

Marshall, M., Shekelle, P., Brook, R. and Leatherman, S. (2000) *Dying to Know: Public Release of Information about Quality of Health Care*. London: Nuffield Trust [http://www.nuffieldtrust.org.uk/sites/files/nuffield/publication/dying-to-know-oct2000.pdf].

Marshall, M., Shekelle, P., Davies, H. and Smith, P. (2003) Public reporting on quality: lessons from the United States and the United Kingdom, *Health Affairs*, 22 (3): 134–48.

National Institute for Health Research (n.d.) *NIHR 'Big Data'* [http://www.nihr.ac.uk/policy-and-standards/nihr-big-data.htm; accessed 8 December 2015].

NHS Benchmarking Network (n.d.) Website [http://www.nhsbenchmarking.nhs.uk/index.php; accessed 10 December 2015].

NHS Institute for Innovation and Improvement (2008) *Balanced Scorecard* [http://www.institute.nhs.uk/quality_and_service_improvement_tools/quality_and_service_improvement_tools/balanced_scorecard.html#B; accessed 10 December 2015].

NHS National Services Scotland (2010) *Heat targets. Quality indicators.* Information Services Division [http://www.isdscotland.org/Health-Topics/Quality-Indicators/HEAT/; accessed 10 December 2015].

Nuffield Trust (2013) *Rating Providers for Quality: A Policy Worth Pursuing?* [http://www.nuffieldtrust.org.uk/publications/rating-providers-quality; accessed 10 December 2015].

OECD (2012) *OECD Mental Health Questionnaire.* Unpublished Health Policy Questionnaire.

Pagliari, C., Detmer, D. and Singleton, P. (2007) *Electronic Personal Health Records* [http://www.nuffieldtrust.org.uk/sites/files/nuffield/publication/elec-personal-health-records-web-final-mar07.pdf; accessed 8 December 2015].

Palmer, D. (2015) *Care.data and Big Data will Fill 'Dangerous Gaps' in NHS and Futureproof it with Genomics, argues Tim Kelsey* [http://www.computing.co.uk/ctg/news/2390081/caredata-and-big-data-will-fill-dangerous-gaps-in-nhs-and-futureproof-it-with-genomics-argues-tim-kelsey; accessed 8 December 2015].

Pencheon, D. (2008) *The Good Indicators Guide: Understanding How to Use and Choose Indicators* [http://www.apho.org.uk/resource/item.aspx?RID=44584; accessed 10 December 2015].

Picker Institute Europe (n.d.) *NHS Surveys* [http://www.nhssurveys.org/; accessed 10 December 2015].

Pollitt, C. (2006) Performance management in practice: a comparative study of executive agencies, *Journal of Public Administration Research and Theory*, 16 (1): 25–44.

Prime Minister's Office (n.d.) *Transparency (Number10) Website* [http://discovery.nationalarchives.gov.uk/details/r/C18816; accessed 10 December 2015].

Propper, C., Sutton, M., Whitnall, C. and Windmeijer, F. (2008) Did 'targets and terror' reduce waiting times in England for hospital care?, *B.E. Journal of Economic Analysis and Policy*, 8 (2) [http://www.degruyter.com/view/j/bejeap.2008.8.2/bejeap.2008.8.2.1863/bejeap.2008.8.2.1863.xml?format=INT; accessed 8 December 2015].

Research Councils UK (n.d.) *Big Data* [http://www.rcuk.ac.uk/research/infrastructure/big-data/; accessed 8 December 2015].

Sheffield Teaching Hospitals NHS Foundation Trust (2014) *Performance Management Framework Review* [http://www.sth.nhs.uk/clientfiles/File/G%20-%20STH%20Performance%20Management%20Framework%20-%20Board%202014_16_04Final.pdf; accessed 10 December 2015].

Shekelle, P. (2009) Public performance reporting on quality information, in P.C. Smith, E. Mossialis, I. Papanicolas and S. Leatherman (eds.) *Performance Measurement for Health Improvement: Experiences, Challenges and Prospects.* Cambridge: Cambridge University Press [http://www.euro.who.int/en/about-us/partners/observatory/publications/studies/performance-measurement-for-health-system-improvement-experiences,-challenges-and-prospects; accessed 10 December 2015].

Smith P. (1995) On the unintended consequences of publishing performance data in the public sector, *International Journal of Public Administration*, 18 (2): 277–310.

Smith, P., Mossialos, E., Papanicolas, I. and Leatherman, S. (eds.) (2009) *Performance Measurement for Health System Improvement: Experiences, Challenges and Prospects.* Cambridge: Cambridge University Press [http://www.euro.who.int/en/about-us/partners/observatory/publications/studies/performance-measurement-for-health-system-improvement-experiences,-challenges-and-prospects; accessed 10 December 2015].

Spiegelhalter, D., Sherlaw-Johnson, C., Bardsley, M., Blunt, I., Wood, C. and Grigg, O. (2012) Statistical methods for healthcare regulation: rating, screening and surveillance, *Journal of the Royal Statistical Society A*, 175 (1): 1–47.

Totten, A.M., Wagner, J., Tiwari, A. (2012) *Public Reporting as a Quality Improvement Strategy*. Rockville, MD: Agency for Healthcare Research and Quality [http://www.ahrq.gov/research/findings/evidence-based-reports/gapqistp.html; accessed 10 December 2015].

White House (n.d.) *Open Government Initiative* [https://www.whitehouse.gov/open; accessed 8 December 2015].

World Health Organization (WHO) *Mental Health Atlas 2011*. Geneva: WHO [http://www.who.int/mental_health/publications/mental_health_atlas_2011/en/].

Index

**Evaluating Improvement and Implementation
for Health**

Ovretveit

*ISBN: 9780335242771 (Paperback)
eISBN: 9780335242788*

2014

Evaluating Improvement and Implementation for Health describes modern
evaluation methods in healthcare and policy making, and challenges some
of the assumptions of the evidence-based healthcare movement:

- Are innovations always an improvement?
- Are they always worth it?
- Can they be implemented?
- More importantly, should they be implemented?

These are questions with practical consequences and questions which
evaluation can answer – if we choose the right methods. This book will help
you do just that – match the right evaluation method to the questions being
asked.

www.mheducation.co.uk

Clinical Governance
Improving the quality of healthcare for patients
and service users

Gottwald and Lansdown

ISBN: 9780335262809 (Paperback)
eISBN: 9780335262816

2014

This new text is an accessible and practical guide to clinical governance in
healthcare, designed to help practitioners and students deliver quality care to
patients and improve the patient experience at every level. Grounded in the
application of clinical governance, it explains in detail what it looks like in
practice. Using common examples of clinical governance challenges, this book
gives real and practical insights into how individuals can contribute to clinical
governance in a range of healthcare settings.

Each chapter includes case studies, reflective activities, tips and real
experiences to help readers apply the theory to practice, and identify areas in
which they can improve the patient experience. This is key reading for all
healthcare practitioners.

www.mheducation.co.uk

Coaching and Mentoring at Work
Developing Effective Practice
Second Edition

Connor & Pokora

ISBN: 9780335243853 (Paperback)
eISBN: 9780335243860

2012

The new edition of this practical, authoritative and popular book has been revised and updated throughout, with two new chapters. It features:

- Nine key principles of effective coaching and mentoring, showing how to apply them
- Broader and deeper discussion of approaches to coaching and mentoring
- Answers to frequently asked questions
- A new chapter on reflective practice, supervision and accreditation
- Ideas about how to be an effective coach or mentor and how to be an effective client
- Self development checklists and prompts, and a wealth of interactive case material
- The Skilled Helper model and how to apply it to coaching and mentoring
- A range of tried and tested tools and techniques
- The hot topics of ethical practice, training and developing a coaching culture

Coaching and Mentoring at Work, 2nd edition is aimed not only at coaches and mentors but also at the other half of the partnership, clients.

education.co.uk

OPEN UNIVERSITY PRESS
McGraw - Hill Education